The HOLY SEE, SOCIAL JUSTICE, *and* INTERNATIONAL TRADE LAW

Assessing the Social Mission of the Catholic Church in the GATT-WTO System

Rev. Dr. Alphonsus Ihuoma

authorHOUSE®

AuthorHouse™
1663 Liberty Drive
Bloomington, IN 47403
www.authorhouse.com
Phone: 1 (800) 839-8640

Published by AuthorHouse 06/29/2018

ISBN: 978-1-5462-4446-2 (sc)
ISBN: 978-1-5462-4445-5 (e)

Print information available on the last page.

This book is printed on acid-free paper.

CONTENTS

ABSTRACT

Man, as a person, is superior to the state, and consequently the good of the person transcends the good of the state. The philosopher Jacques Maritain developed his political philosophy thoroughly informed by his deep Catholic faith. His philosophy places the human person at the center of every action. In developing his political thought, he enumerates two principal tasks of the state as (1) to establish and preserve order, and as such, guarantee justice, and (2) to promote the common good. The state has such duties to the people because it receives its authority from the people. The people possess natural, God-given right of self-government, the exercise of which they voluntarily invest in the state. One cannot agree any less with Maritain.

Since her many years of theological reflection and writing on modern economic issues, the Catholic Church has confirmed that the constitutive purpose of the economy is to serve the common good. The Catholic Church teaches that the economy is legitimate only if it meets the material needs of every member of the human family and the moral demands of justice and solidarity. In other words, the economy should work to serve the needs of the people and not the other way around. One can understand the rationale behind this teaching especially as enunciated in the papal encyclicals and exhortations, the Catholic Social Doctrine, and other teachings of the Magisterium. The whole essence of the Catholic Social Teaching is to safeguard and promote recognition of, and respect for, human dignity.

The Catholic Church does not just teach. A huge chunk of the Church's universal mission is to announce the Gospel message to promote and defend the dignity of the human person. God created the world for the common good and development of all human beings. So, the dignity of the human person is a central issue in the Church's universal mission. The Church reaches out to all the nooks and crannies of the earth for that purpose. She engages in dialogue with governments all over the world, with individuals, organizations, and institutions to proclaim the Good News to all. The Holy See raises its moral voice on issues that concern the human person. This mission takes the Holy See to the United Nations and to other international and regional organizations. For this book, the focus here is the General Agreement on Tariffs and Trade (GATT) and the World Trade Organization (WTO), hereinafter referred to as "GATT-WTO system."

Through its presence at the World Trade Organization, the Holy See serves notably as advocate of the dignity of the human person on economic, social, and political issues. This book addresses issues as to whether the Holy See, the representative body for the Catholic Church, is as effective as it should be in serving as a watchdog on issues within the GATT-WTO system that militate against human dignity. Obviously, the Holy See has a notable influence, but whether its influence is effective enough is another question.

DEDICATION

This book is dedicated to my late parents,
Matilda and Kerian Ihuoma and my late sister
Laeticia Oluchi Otuosorochi Oscar Jatua
and to all who make sacrifices to promote
the dignity of the human person
all over the world.

ACKNOWLEDGEMENTS

In his Encyclical Letter *Peace on Earth,* Pope Saint John XXIII teaches as follows: "Any human society, if it is to be well-ordered and productive, must lay down as a foundation this principle: that every human being is a person; his nature is endowed with intelligence and free will. By this, he has rights and duties of his own, flowing directly and simultaneously from his very nature, which are therefore universal, inviolable, and inalienable. If we look upon the dignity of the human person in the light of divinely revealed truth, we cannot help but esteem it far more highly..." [Pope John XXIII, *Peace on Earth* (1963) 9-10.] At the center of the Catholic Social Teaching are the transcendence of God and the dignity of the human person. The human person is the clearest reflection of God's presence in the world. All the Church's work in pursuit of both justice and peace is designed to protect and promote the dignity of every person.

In 1986, the Catholic bishops of the United States, contributing to Catholic social teaching, wrote, "Catholic social teaching, like much philosophical reflection, distinguishes three dimensions of basic justice: commutative justice, distributive justice, and social justice. Commutative justice calls for fundamental fairness in all agreements and exchanges between individuals or private social groups. Distributive justice requires that the allocation of income, wealth, and power in society be evaluated in light of its effects on persons whose basic material needs are unmet... Social justice implies that persons have an obligation to be active and productive participants in the life of society and that society has a duty to enable them to participate in this way." [U.S. Bishops, *Economic Justice for All* (1986) 68-71.]

The teaching of the Magisterium of the Catholic Church is informative and thought-provoking. In Catholic thought, social justice is not merely a secular or humanitarian matter. Social justice reflects God's essential respect and concern for each person and an effort to protect the essential human freedom necessary for each person to achieve his or her destiny as a child of God. I am a human person and my dignity is priceless, and so is every other human being anywhere in the world.

The Catholic social teaching which is the hub of the Church's social mission is so invaluable as to attract any inquisitive mind and inspire people to explore more into its contents and make contributions on how the Church can do more. My inquisitive mind started with my immediate family vision, particularly my parents Matilda and Kerian, thanks be to God for their lives, though now in heaven. I was exposed early in life to appreciate the dignity of every human being as a Catholic Christian. I thank every member of my family. I thank my diocesan bishop, late bishop Victor Chikwe, who gave me the opportunity for further studies. May his soul rest in peace!

My unalloyed respect and gratitude go to Professor Raj Bhala, Rice Distinguished Professor of Law, and his family. In the first place, without Prof Bhala, I wouldn't have been admitted into the S.J.D program at the Kansas University School of Law. A faculty member told me about his graciousness and readiness to help anybody in need. And so, I contacted him for help. Without seeing me in person, he volunteered to supervise my work - a precondition for admission into the S.J.D program. Throughout the period of my S.J.D program, his family was a great inspiration to me. Through Professor Bhala's inspiration, magnanimous support, and encouragement, my S.J.D research was a huge success. I benefited tremendously from his International Trade Law classes, his library and Authorship - he gave me access to his books; he mentored me vigorously, and supervised me with tremendous commitment. Professor Bhala is a renowned authority in the field of International Trade Law. I am indebted to him and his family.

I am thankful to Professor Virginia Harper Ho and Professor Uma Outka, for the support they gave me during this period. I owe a great deal of my gratitude to Richard Coll, the Policy Advisor for Latin America and Global Trade, Office of International Justice and Peace, United States Conference of Catholic Bishops in Washington D.C. who was my external Examiner during my doctoral program.

The story of my academic progress cannot be complete without a spot for Professor Don Smith, the Director of the Graduate program at the Denver University Sturm College of Law. He was instrumental to the success of my LL.M program in Natural Resources and Environmental Law and Policy at the Sturm College of Law. He also introduced me to the S.J.D program of The University of Kansas School of Law. I owe him a lot of gratitude for his great inspiration, his magnanimity and kindness. I am thankful to Robert Bassett, Adjunct Professor at the Sturm College of Law and Manager of the Minerals Practice Group at Holland & Hart, LLP in Denver, Colorado. I am also indebted to Professor Steve Bain, of Welborn Sullivan Meck & Tooley, P.C.

I am highly indebted to my mother, Alejandra Aldred Adams, who stood behind me in all travails. When she came into my life and my priestly ministry, her life reaffirmed my belief that no matter how wicked the world may seem to be, there are still people out there who are honest, disciplined, gracious, God-fearing, loving and lovable. She has been a great inspiration in my priestly life and in all my academic pursuits since I came to the United States. I am proud to be her son. God will always bless and reward her abundantly.

FOREWORD

In Paragraph 7 of his encyclical Letter, *Caritatis in Veritate*, Pope Benedict XVI writes that the more we strive to secure a common good corresponding to the real needs of our neighbors, the more effectively we love them. Everyone is called to practice this charity, in a manner corresponding to his or her vocation and according to the degree of influence he or she wields in the world. When animated by charity, commitment to the common good has greater worth than a merely secular and political stand would have. Like all commitment to justice, it has a place within the testimony of Divine charity that paves the way for eternity through temporal action. When each person's earthly activity is inspired and sustained by charity, it contributes to the building of the universal city of God, which is the goal of the history of the human family. In an increasingly globalized society, the common good, and the effort to obtain it, cannot fail to assume the dimensions of the whole human family. What that means, in brief, is that the community of peoples and nations must act in such a way as to shape the world in unity and peace.

Globalization is the trend toward a unified, worldwide economy that ought to provide a chance for broad-based, equitable development in the world, more especially creating unique opportunities to the poorest countries. The emerging global market could – and, indeed, should – be a place where developing states export goods in which they have a comparative advantage in exchange for a fair profit that can be invested in the world's poorest and most vulnerable people. But centuries of experience have shown that rich countries are focused, sometimes obsessed, with tilting, sometimes stacking, the terms of international trade, and the rules that underlie those terms, unfairly against developing and least developed countries. Unfortunately, this unbalance negates the founding objectives of the GATT-WTO system. Globalization is warped from a potential blessing into a curse. Through myriad high tariff and non-tariff barriers (including tariff peaks and escalation on products of keen export interest to developing countries), export and export-like subsidies, domestic support that is ostensibly not-trade distorting, a dizzying array of technical and sanitary and phytosanitary measures, and a no less dizzying array of trade remedies, the "haves" effectively deny the "have nots" access to the global market opportunities, and undercut their capability to become global entrepreneurs. To be sure, there are corruptions and self-inflicted wounds among the "have nots," which they can – and indeed, must – take responsibility for rectifying themselves. Still, patterns in the long arch of international trade history have obvious adverse consequences on the poor across the world.

To a noteworthy degree, the multilateral trading system is structured in a way to favor industrialized and post-industrialized WTO Members. The UN, and its allied bodies such as the ILO, have laid down principles, policies, and regulations for equitable, sustainable development. Unfortunately, social justice, properly defined, still eludes international organizations, rendering egalitarian practices somewhat impracticable, even quixotic.

The Catholic Church remains the great light, and perhaps the only reliable hope, available to the whole world, especially to developing and least developed countries. That is because the Catholic Church has no economic trade interests of its own; rather, its position in international affairs is as a pure, moral voice. That is because the Catholic Church places the common good at the center of her missionary mandate. That is because the Catholic Church is the oldest institution in the world that addresses issues affecting humanity. Thus, the social teaching of the Catholic Church on development provides a framework for reorienting international trade around the service of humanity, especially emphasizing egalitarian principles of equality, fairness and social justice. Only these principles, proposed, elaborated, and proclaimed by a veritable, credible 2,000 year-old international organization – the Catholic Church – can break the walls of growing inequality that mounts untold pressures on poor nations and their people. The Church therefore, offers her ethical guidance to the WTO, and to the world, on issues that most challenge our human consciences.

The GATT-WTO system will continue not to realize its full potential unless its Member countries turn around, and explore the moral theology offered to it by the Catholic Church in the context of cross-border import, export, FDI, and IP transactions. Likewise, the Catholic Church will fall short of its full potential if she relents in her watchdog status in world affairs, especially at the WTO. The Catholic Church has achieved a considerable amount, and learned from considerable experience, in international affairs for two millennia. However, considering the growing level of inequality and injustice in the world (which may never change if not robustly confronted), the Church can – and indeed, ought – to do more, because again, what better neutral hope is available to humanity?

Professor Raj Bhala
Leo S. Brenneisen Distinguished Professor of Law
University of Kansas School of Law,
Lawrence Kansas

MAIN ABBREVIATIONS

AD	Anno Domini (In the Year of the Lord)
ACP	African Caribbean and Pacific Countries
ADA	Anti-dumping Agreement
AD	Anti-dumping
AGOA	African Growth and Opportunity Act
AoA	Agreement on Agriculture
ASIL	American Society of International Law
ATC	Agreement on Textile and Clothing
BC	Before Christ
CBD	United Nations Convention on Biological Diversity
CBP	Customs and Border Protection
COP	Common Agricultural Policy
CARICOM	Convocation on the CARICOM Single Market and Economy
CST	Catholic Social Teaching
CVD	Countervailing Duty
DDA	Doha Development Agenda
DDR	Doha Development Round
DFQF	Duty Free Quota Free
DFQFMA	Duty Free Quota Free Market Access
DSB	Dispute Settlement Body
DSU	Dispute Settlement Understanding
EC	European Community
EU	European Union

ECOSOC	United Nations Economic and Social Council
FAO	Food and Agricultural Organization
FLO	Fairtrade Labeling Organizations
FTAs	Free Trade Agreements
G-8	Group of 8 Largest Industrialized Democracies
G20	The Group pf Twenty Finance Ministers and Central Bank Governors
GATS	General Agreement on Trade in Services
GATT	General Agreement on Tariffs and Trade
GDP	Gross Domestic Product
GMOs	Genetically Modified Organisms
GNI	Gross National Income
GSP	Generalized System of Preferences
ICJ	International Court of Justice
ICCPR	International Convention on Civil and Political Rights
ICESCR	International Convention on Economics, Social, and Cultural Rights
ICOs	International Catholic Organizations
ICTSD	International Center for Trade and Sustainable Development
ILO	International Labor Organization
IMF	International Monetary Fund
IPPC	International Plant Protection Convention
ITC	International Trade Center
ITO	International Trade Organization
IPR	Intellectual Property Rights
LDCs	Least Developed Countries
MFA	Multi-Fiber Agreement
MFN	Most-Favored Nation
NAFTA	North American Free Trade Agreement
MIF	Multilateral Investment Fund
NAMA	Non-agricultural Market Access

NFIDCs	Net-Food-Importing Countries
NGOs	Non-governmental Organizations
NTBs	Non-tariff Barriers
OECD	Organization for Economic Cooperation and Development
OIE	Office of International Epizootics
PEA	Pontifical Ecclesiastical Academy
RTAs	Regional Trade Agreements
S & D	Special and Differential Treatment
SID	Small Island Developing Countries
SPS	Sanitary and Phytosanitary
TBT	Technical Barriers to Trade
TRIMS	Trade-Related Investment Measures
TPRB	Trade Policy Review Body
TRIPS	Trade Related Aspects of Intellectual Property Rights
TTIP	Transatlantic Trade and Investment
TTP	Trans-Pacific Partnership
UDHR	United Nations Universal Declaration of Human Rights
UN	United Nations
UNCED	United Nations Conference on Environment and Development
UNCITRAL	United Nations Commission on International Trade Law
UNCTAD	United Nations Conference on Trade and Development
UNDP	United Nations Development Program
UPOV	International Convention on the Protection of New Varieties of Plants
U.S.	United States
WIPO	World Intellectual Property Organization
WTO	World Trade Organization
WWII	Second World War

INTRODUCTION

Laying the Foundation

Globalization in modern times has its blessings and woes: blessings in the sense of trade liberalization and woes in the sense of expanding inequalities. Every day scholars and great thinkers voice their respective perceptions about world events in respect of distant corners of the earth enjoying closer interactions. Is contemporary globalization achieving its desired goals? Christians all over the world, especially Catholics and other proponents of social justice theories, have taken the proverbial "bull by the horns." At the heart of Catholic Social Doctrine on globalization are the concepts of the *dignity of the human person* and the *common good*. Every aspect of human life is judged by how it develops or undermines the life and dignity of the human person.

The value of human activities at all levels must pass the test of if they contribute to the common good of all or not. Choices and institutions created in furtherance of any aspect of human life have meaning only when they satisfy the purpose of the common good or at least, when they are directed toward the achievement of that purpose. All domestic and international structures or arrangements would be more meaningful if they are structured naturally to align with this objective. The voice of the supreme authority of the Catholic Church, the Holy See, on this issue sounds loudest in its execution of its social mission on earth. The Holy See executes this in absolute neutrality, and that enables it to offer orientation and spiritual inspiration which animate the life of nations and mutual relationships.

Ever since the founding of the Church, it has never relented in promoting and supporting the dignity of the human person having been created in the image and likeness of God. The Church positions herself, and is so recognized, as a veritable *moral voice* all over the world. Any laws, institutions, or structures that militate against the full realization of the dignity of the human person are not favored by the Church in any manner. To do this effectively, the Holy See projects its international presence as advocate of the dignity and development of the human person.

In this book, the presence of the Holy See in the global state, particularly at the GATT-WTO, comes into focus as the Church exercises her social mission. With her presence in international affairs, its watchdog status on local, national, and international spheres becomes indispensable. This book posits as its core thesis that the GATT-WTO principles do not emphasize the common good of all since the concept of equality as it concerns the human person is only in writing and never practiced as it should be. Furthermore, this book argues that the Holy See has invested a great deal of its missionary zeal in serving as the moral voice for the whole world, especially in its Permanent Observer status in the GATT-WTO system. However, despite this achievement, more efforts are needed.

In developing and elaborating on the core thesis stated above, this book is divided into seven chapters, starting with Chapter 1, which is a *Preliminary Discourse.* This Chapter states the theses which this book sets out to substantiate, summarizes the significance, structure, and approach, as well as an explication of the major terminology which are very important for a better understanding of the aim of this book.

Chapter 2, the *Literature Review*, is made up of two parts. Part one of this chapter is comprised of the exposé of relevant academic, professional, and official literature regarding a range of issues that are pertinent to the goal of this book. These include implications of the presence of the Holy See in international politics in general, social mission of the Church, the issue of free trade agreements (FTAs), the general nature and structure of the WTO, Observer Status of the Holy See at the WTO, strategies pursued in international trade negotiations, Social justice, developing countries, and the problem of inequality in international trade.

The second segment of this chapter reviews the main findings of the pertinent literature. This review is analytical in nature and serves as the foundation and point of departure for further research as reflected in the entire discourse. The findings of the literature review culminate in the formulation of three hypotheses. (1) Though GATT-WTO objectives have been realized to some extent, much needs to be done; (2) the failure of the WTO over the years warrants the need for a strong moral voice, this time, the Catholic Church; and (3) though the Church has made remarkable interventions in international law in general, and international trade, she needs to flex its missionary muscles more.

The analysis of the above hypotheses starts with a critical synthesis of readings in literature, and unfolds into Chapter 3 with an account of the *Legal and Political Nature of the Holy See.* This account is divided into two parts. The first part provides a historical background of the evolution of the papacy's sovereignty and the Holy See's participation in international affairs and diplomatic relations, zeroing in on international trade. Part II examines the general principles of international law that define the concepts of international personality, sovereignty, and special circumstances of the Holy See. Part II concludes with how state practice, state custom, and treaty law have made the Holy See a unique subject of International law able to function as a neutral sovereign organization. In her unique international status, the Church can establish a ganglion of international relations. Her Permanent Observer Status at the WTO puts her in a stable position to defend human dignity at all levels.

Chapter 4, *Catholic Social Justice Theory*, highlights the moral principles the Holy See brings to international law. The Holy See's main concern in the exercise of its universal mission is propagation of the deposit of faith and not secular or territorial power. This chapter expounds the principles of Judeo-Christian Social Thought as applied in International Law. This chapter is divided into three important parts. Part I portrays the justification for Catholic Social Justice. Part II analyzes the five principles of the Judeo-Christian Social Doctrine, while Part III makes a comparative study of the Church's teaching on the common good and some secular social justice theories as propounded by some philosophers. The aim of this comparative analysis is to confirm the Judeo-Christian social principles as a better option. In all, this chapter streamlines how all international laws, existing or proposed, are evaluated through the lens of the Social

Justice principles articulated by the Catholic Church. It is based on those principles that the Catholic Church favors free trade.

A thorough examination of the five principles of the Catholic Social Doctrine and their justification ushers in Chapter 5, *The Holy See, International Law, and International Trade Law.* The aim of this chapter is to enumerate the tools the Holy See uses to execute her social mission in international law such as the use of concordats, treaties, establishment of *nunciatures*, and its activities as Permanent Observer in international organizations, particularly the United Nations. The chapter advances the argument by reviewing the debates over free trade and the position of the Church.

Chapter 6, *Critique of the Holy See in International Trade*, highlights key international trade law issues which the Holy See has addressed through its social doctrine. The chapter discusses other matters that border on international trade to which the Holy See has been either silent or said little. The chapter takes its reader through Holy See's endorsement of global trade and how it has made its moral voice heard on prevailing issues. The GATT-WTO system deserves recognition for its laudable achievements, but there are certain practices that make the system a *whited sepulcher.*[1] The GATT-WTO has highly commendable aims and objectives, but what happens behind closed doors raises some concerns. This chapter tries to assess whether the Holy See has lived up to expectations on all issues of international concern, especially considering the widening gap between the rich Members of the World Trade Organization (WTO) and the poor ones.

Chapter 7, which is the evaluation and conclusion, is a reflection on the presence of the Holy See in the GATT-WTO system. It examines the course contents of the diplomatic school in Rome. That school is where diplomats who represent and speak for the Church are trained. This exercise examines

[1] The term "whited sepulcher" is a Jewish simile. It is commonly used among the Jews. For example, Jesus Christ used the term in Mt 23:27 to signify the irony of the grave. On the outside, it is painted and designed beautifully but on the inside its stinks of dead bodies. The Merriam-Webster's Collegiate Dictionary, (11th edition) defines the phrase "whited sepulcher" as "a person inwardly corrupt or wicked but outwardly or professedly virtuous or holy." This literary expression symbolizes hypocrisy.

the strengths and weaknesses of the program and makes suggestions for a way forward. Some areas where the Church needs to improve to better perform her unique role in the world, especially at the WTO, will be enunciated. This book concludes with some recommendations for the Holy See in a bid to enhance its universal mission.

CHAPTER ONE

Preliminary Discourse

This chapter is essential as it defines the preliminary clarification of the entire discussion and its central questions as well as streamlines its goal. It is helpful to know why the Holy See is enormously involved in international affairs and why it needs to get even more involved. For a start, clarification of certain terms will make a smooth takeoff. When terms are clarified, a reader understands more the logic of a discourse.

1.1 Opening Remarks

> *"...The Holy See is the oldest established institution in the world. It was the only institution to flourish during the Middle Ages, a leading actor in the Renaissance, and a protagonist in the battles of the Reformation, the Counter-Reformation, the French Revolution, the Industrial era, and the rise and fall of Communism. For centuries, making full use of their famous "infallibility," Popes brought their centralized power to bear on the social outcomes of unfolding historical events...." Throughout history, the papacy has always displayed two facts: that of the world-wide leadership of the Catholic Church and that of one of the planet's best political organizations. While the Popes were blessing their faithful on the one hand, on the other, they were receiving*

> *foreign ambassadors and heads of states and dispatching legates and nuncios on special mission.* [2]

The above statement represents the position of the Church in the world when it is analyzed from the perspective of the tortuous route the Catholic Church has followed in her universal mission. However, the reality of the Church being "one of the planet's best political organizations" does not imply that the Church has selfish secular political interest. On the contrary, when the Catholic Church gets involved in any human question, it is always for protecting and promoting the dignity of the human person. It is always a barometer for the proclamation of the Gospel of Jesus Christ for the common good. From time immemorial, the Catholic Church, hereinafter symbolized as the *Holy See*, has distinguished herself as the moral voice of the whole world.

Similarly, Gerry Adams, Leader of Sinn Féin in Ireland in 1992 said, *"to be a Catholic is still a political thing.... The Church is part of the peoples' struggle."*[3] This observation of Gerry Adams is absolutely correct. It may sound mind-boggling when one analyzes the phrase, "to be a Catholic is still a political thing." Nevertheless, there should be no confusion about this phrase. Gerry Adams made his observation from his historical and political bias. Human beings are by nature political and the Church identifies with them and enlightens their involvement in all aspects of life. By its very nature, the Catholic Church reaches out to all her daughters and sons scattered all over the world. The Church participates in all aspects of humanity's problems irrespective of what it is, be it politics, culture, business, or name it. For this reason, the Catholic Church establishes diplomatic ties with the whole world in pursuit of her universal mission. The Catholic Church speaks human language but guided by the spirit of the Gospel Message she is established to proclaim to the whole world.

---

[2] Frattini Eric, *The Entity: Five Centuries of Secret Vatican Espionage,* St. Martin's Press, 2008, p.1.

[3] See Paul Arthur, "Sinn Féin," in *Encyclopedia Britannica* online available at http://www.britannica.com/EBchecked/topic/546134/Sinn-Féin ("Sinn Féin" means "We Ourselves" or "Ourselves Alone;" a political wing of the Provisional Irish Republican Army (IRA). Sinn Féin, organized in both Northern and the Republic of Ireland, is a nationalist party in Northern Ireland, representing Roman Catholics who want to achieve a united Ireland through whatever means are necessary). *See id.*

The saying is true that

> What gives the Vatican its tremendous power is not its diplomacy as such, but the fact that behind its diplomacy, with all its manifold world-embracing activities… the Vatican diplomacy is so influential and can exert such great power in the diplomatic-political field because it has at its disposal the tremendous machinery of a spiritual organization with ramifications from every country of the world.[4]

Central to the strong ties between the United States of America and the Holy See is the recognition of the latter as "one of the world's most important (*if not the most important*) moral voices."[5] The Catholic Church is not only aware of this recognition but also, to the highest limit possible, depicts this responsibility as an intrinsic feature in its entire mission on earth. Being a religious institution, she exhibits conspicuously the social schema that throws light on the life of the human person, giving individuals a purpose and reason for existence in every age with no geographical boundaries. The basis for this unique role is the central place that is accorded the human person in the world having been created in the image and likeness of God. The image and likeness of God in the human person endows the human person with a unique dignity. The reason for all the activities of the Church is the respect for, and promotion of, this God-given dignity. Because of this, the Catholic Church permeates every aspect of life and appeals to the human mode of decisions and activities, particularly as it concerns socio-economic involvements.

For the above reason, the Catholic Church has several criteria that provide a framework for evaluating areas of socio-economic policies. This strategy synchronizes with the mission of the Church, which is, to

---

[4] Manhattan Avro, The Vatican in World Politics, C.A. Watts & Co., 1949, pp.28-29.

[5] See generally Raymond L. Flinn, *Letter From The Vatican: Common Objectives For Peace,* SAIS REVIEW, Vol. 16, Number 2, Summer-Fall 1996; *See* Monsignor Ettore Balestrore, Vatican Under-Secretary for Relations with States in his briefing to journalists concerning the publication of the first Mutual Evaluation Report on the Holy See and the Vatican City-State (Moral commitments must be accompanied by Compliance), available at http://www.zenit.org/article-35218?

develop a normative socio-economic theory capable of integrating both theology and socio-economic issues. The body of literature that addresses the Church's socio-economic principles is known as the Catholic Social Teaching, which hereinafter will be referred to as CST. The CST is the doorway to the Church's social mission in the world mostly found in detail in the social encyclicals and related Magisterium documents. CST is Catholic Social Justice Theory in practice.

Pope Francis of our time utilizes the instrumentality of CST when he describes the *Year of Faith*[6] as one that motivates the entire Church toward a renewed awareness of her presence in the contemporary world and her mission among peoples and nations. For him, the missionary spirit of the Church is not only about geographical territories but also about peoples, cultures, and individuals. For this reason, the "boundaries" of faith do not only cross places with human traditions but the heart of each man and each woman.[7] Accordingly, a central goal of this book is to examine the social mission of the Church with its *raison d'etre* as the dignity of the human person. Related to the primary objective of the Church's mission is the question: Granted that the Church has a mission to defend human dignity, why is the world incapable of carrying out this same mission?

Since the inception of human civilization, society has been characterized by worldviews, *i.e.*, the manner of understanding the world and humanity's role in it. Worldviews are subjective in nature. They differ from individual to individual and from culture to culture. Often, a dominant worldview may emerge within a society and take on a hegemonic status. Religion emerged to be a source of worldviews, incidentally taking the center stage. Religion positions itself as a barometer for measuring every other worldview in the society. As history proceeded, societies metamorphosed into more complex structures projecting a dominant social ideology that sought to challenge religion. A considerable part of this development was the emergence of a new method of trade that encumbers the whole world.

---

[6] The Catholic Church marked the year 2013 as the *Year of Faith* (from October 11, 2012 to November 24, 2013), remarkably because it is the anniversary of two important events in the life of the Catholic Church: (a) October 11, 2012 was the 50th anniversary of the Second Vatican Council (October 11, 1962 – December 8, 1965) and (b) October 11, 2012 is the 20th anniversary of the publication of the Catechism of the Catholic Church by Pope John Paul II).

[7] *See* Pope Francis I, Address on World Mission Day 2013, available at CatholicCulture.org http://www.catholicculture.org/culture/library/view.recnum?=10306

Trade was structured in a way that helped nations and individuals to amass wealth at the expense of others. To situate the reasonableness of such unfair quest for wealth, society developed theories to buttress the route that is taken for gaining wealth. This terrain accounts for the origin of the philosophy called economics and its concomitant term, capitalism. The mad quest for wealth gave rise to consumerism and materialism, which came to control societal life. With this development, capitalism became the order of the day as the most successful economic system that dominates the society. The overriding impression has been that capitalism is best capable of producing the goods and services individuals want. This position is highly controversial.

To be sure, capitalism is by the way, not the only economic system that relates to the human person. There are other socio-economic systems that affect the dignity of the human person, such as totalitarian and atheistic ideologies (communism and socialism), nationalism, and individualism.[8] All these are overarching worldviews that have affected the way individuals perceive both the world and their fellow human beings. As an economic system, capitalism, like other socio-economic systems, has never had a free ride. Religion extends its lens to any system that relates to the behavior and decision-making of human beings in any way. Humans have at the heart of their socio-economic lives models, such as *homo economicus* and *ens socialis,* meaning that human beings are naturally characterized by economics and *sociableness.* Human beings act either as individuals alone or in groups. In the same vein, human beings are by nature and vocation religious beings.[9]

Economic, social, and religious characteristics of humans are natural tendencies. However, the religiousness of human beings considers ethical principles while formulating theories and models with decisions that emanate from these human characteristics. In examining one of the demerits of capitalism, namely, inequalities of income and wealth, the question that religion asks is whether such a system ensures social justice which entails "providing the conditions that allow associations or

---

[8] *See* CATECHISM OF THE CATHOLIC CHURCH(1994), # 2425 (stating that the Catholic Church rejects all these ideologies because they emphasize primacy of the law of the marketplace over human labor and dignity and thereby perverting the basis of social bonds); *see also* JOHN PAUL II, ENCYCLICAL LETTER CENTISIMUS ANNUS (HUNDRETH YEAR), 1991, nos. 10, 13, 44

[9] *See* CATECHISM OF THE CATHOLIC CHURCH (1994), # 44.

individuals to obtain what is their due, according to their nature and their vocation."[10] Certainly, it is not only religion that has attempted to tackle inequality as it relates to the socio-economic aspect of the human person. There have been a series of attempts from other quarters, such as from the secular quarters.

International organizations and institutions have struggled in different capacities to solve the problem of inequality at different levels. For instance, the 1920s and 1930s were replete with protectionist trade policies and trade barriers, which became increasingly restrictive following World War I. The situation worsened when the United States enacted the *Smoot-Hawley Tariff Act* in 1930, which provided for an increase in tariffs from 38% to 52%.[11] America's trade partners retaliated, and the burden grew heavy for most developing countries.

Governments were then challenged to find some means by which to implement a more cooperative trade-policy relationship, since the 1927 World Economic Conference that aimed at devising a cooperative trade-policy relationship was unsuccessful. The United States did not relent. It enacted the *U.S. Reciprocal Trade Agreement Act of* 1934 through the U.S. Secretary of State, Cordell Hull. His efforts metamorphosed and formed the seedbed of a multilateral institution. This onerous effort by the U.S., which created the International Trade Organization (ITO), was thought to be the much-needed instrument of universal cooperation and peace but the ITO did not realize that dream as originally conceived. This background created a ripe environment for the birth of the General Agreements on Tariffs and Trade (GATT) and, consequently, the World Trade Organization (WTO) negotiations, which occurred between 1946 and 1995.

---

[10] *See* CATECHISM OF THE CATHOLIC CHURCH (1994), #1928.

[11] *See* Eichengreen Barry, "The Political Economy of the Smoot-Hawley" *Research in Economic History* (1989); Irwin Douglas A., "From Smoot-Hawley to Reciprocal Trade Agreements: Changing the Course of U.S. Trade Policy in the 1930s," in Michael D. Bordo, *et al*, (eds), *The Defining Moment: The Great Depression and the American Economy in the Twentieth Century*, University of Chicago Press, 1998; Kindleberger Charlae P., *The World in Depression, 1929-1939*, University of California Press, 1973; Temin Peter, *Lessons from the Depression: The Lionel Robbins Lectures for 1989*, MIT Press, Cambridge Massachusetts, 1989 (The Smoot-Hawley tariff represents the high-water mark of U.S. protectionism in the 20th century)

GATT and its modern incarnation, the WTO, are often characterized as free-trade instruments. The GATT-WTO objective is for "reciprocal and mutually advantageous arrangements[12] directed to the substantial reduction in tariffs and other barriers to trade and to elimination of discriminatory treatment in international commerce."[13] Because of the different categories of membership of the WTO, namely, developed countries, developing countries, and least developed countries, the issue of a common but differentiated agenda was adopted for engendering equality. Therefore, the pertinent question became, and remains, whether equality of membership and purpose has been achieved through reciprocal and mutually advantageous arrangements, non-discrimination, and transparency.

In answering the above question, this book takes cognizance of the huge achievements of the WTO, but emphasizes that what happens in the WTO is part of a broader pattern of neocolonialism in the global economy. This problem has two strands. The first is the selfish interest of the major powers that use their political and economic strength to achieve their ends without minding the effects of such strategies on other countries, groups, or individuals.[14] The second strand concerns what some thinkers refer to as "combination of ideology, paternalism, and missionary zeal." Proponents of a globalized economy adopt all the necessary tactics to impose these pro-globalization concepts on anti-globalization groups without listening to the latter's concerns. In what stands as a new kind of imperialism, the major powers, along with a handful of mostly upper middle-income nations, stick to these globalization tactics because they serve their selfish purposes.[15] Addressing this mentality, this book postulates that equality and non-discrimination are, therefore, not realizable in the operations of GATT-WTO principles without a

---

[12] *See* GATT Article XXVIII, 1994.

[13] *See* World Trade Organization (WTO) – "The GATT Years: From Havana to Marrakesh" available at http://www.wto.org/english/thewto_e/whatis_e/tif_e/fact4_e.htm; *See* also GATT Documents available at http://www.wto.org/english/docs_e/gattdocs_e.htm

[14] Jawara Fatoumata & Kwa Aileen, Behind the Scenes at the WTO: The Real World of International Trade Negotiations – The Lessons of Cancun, Updated ed., Zed Books Ltd, London 2004, p. 269.

[15] *See id.* at 270.

neutral instrument which can influence the application of GATT-WTO principles that can lead to such achievement.

This book also tries to answer a second question that the problem above raises. Is it possible to prevent the developed countries from abusing their political, diplomatic, economic, and commercial strength to subvert an ostensibly democratic system to serve their own interests? If the answer is in the affirmative, how can this be achieved? Through its involvement in the affairs of the human person in the world, the Holy See automatically answers "yes" to this question. This book analyzes the degree of effectiveness of the Holy See in monitoring the issues that militate against the achievement of the GATT-WTO set objectives.

This book further examines the implications of the Observer status of the Holy See at the WTO with suggestions as to which routes it could follow to better realize its social principles in international trade. This book calls for a rededication of the Church's efforts to apply social justice theory to the problems of inequality associated with international trade. The discussion here does not take a "yes" or "no" view as to if the Catholic Church lives up to its Social Justice principles as a WTO permanent Observer. Rather, it gives a more nuanced answer generally: The Church endeavors to do so. However, on certain complex matters, which are embedded in the potential to create greater inequality, the Church could speak with a stronger voice.

1.2 Central Question and Thesis of This Book

The thesis of this book is motivated by multiple inter-related questions, all of which lie at the intersection of Catholic Social Justice Theory, contemporary practical problems in international trade law, and the activities of the Holy See as Permanent Observer at the WTO. These questions are

(1) In general, considering the social mission of the Catholic Church, is the Holy See promoting the common good and dignity of the human person effectively enough to influence the nature, operation, and direction of international trade law?

(2) Is the Holy See, as Permanent Observer to the WTO, effectively influencing the GATT-WTO system in keeping with Catholic Social Justice Theory?
(3) With respect to the present inequalities within the multilateral trading system, which has attracted considerable criticism, should the Holy See do more to influence GATT-WTO rules to foster equity and fairness, and if so, what more should it do?

This book argues "yes" to all three questions, meaning the Church is promoting Catholic Social Justice principles of the common good and dignity of the human person in international trade law through its Permanent Observer function at the WTO, but she needs to do more.

1.3 Goal of this book

What inspired this book is that in all the great body of literature on international trade law and its cognates, few or no research projects have concentrated on the achievements and failures of the Holy See as Permanent Observer in the GATT-WTO system. The volume of literature, research projects, and articles that border on the GATT-WTO system do not provide an exhaustive assessment of the operations of the system. The goal of this discussion, therefore, is to present an assessment of both the workings of the GATT-WTO and that of the Holy See, which serves as a moral voice within the system. Yet the presence of the Holy See supplies the lens that provides this review of the workings of the system. Consequently, this book distinguishes itself as a research project that examines the strengths and weaknesses of the Holy See in the execution of its social mission in the face of the realities of the GATT-WTO-WTO system.

1.4 Conceptual Terminology

A key to useful research is a careful definition of the major concepts in the study. In communication study we have many terms, and many measures. Explication is the procedure that provides linkages between the terms we use in discourse and the measures we use empirically. Without explication, our words are nothing more than words, and our data add nothing to them. Therefore, for a clearer and better understanding of the goal of this book, it is worthwhile to explain some of the technical terms herein. This exercise puts readers on a better path to understanding the point of departure, the focus, and the overall objective of the book. However, explication here is only for the technical terms observable from the topic of discussion. Therefore, explication of the necessary terms in the topic of this book is in order.

1.4.1 Understanding the terms "Holy See" and "the Vatican"

Often, visitors to Lagos in Nigeria get confused over the use of the city as the name of a state, as the name of the city itself, and as the name for the downtown in the same geographical area. Lagos is one of the largest cities, if not the largest, in Nigeria. It is also one of the 36 States that make up the country. When one is in Lagos, one often hears people say they are going to Lagos. It is only when a line is drawn between Lagos (as a state and a city) and the downtown that visitors will understand. These problems also exist with respect to the terms "Holy See" and "the Vatican." These two terms are often used in international law and international relations. But sometimes, they sometimes are used synonymously, one with the other. Such use is mistaken. Though the "Holy See" and "the Vatican" may have the same mandate and vision, though they may commonly interact and belong together, there is a distinction between the two terms. The "Holy See" and "the Vatican" do not mean the same thing even though they work harmoniously together and often have the same purpose.

The term "Holy See"[16] comes from two Latin words *sancta* (meaning "holy") and *sedes* (meaning "chair"). The original Latin term *sancta sedes*

[16] *See* Forshaw B., Holy See, in 7 New Catholic Encyclopedia 44, 2nd ed., 2003; The term "See" refers to the "Chair of Peter": that is, to the symbol of the teaching and governing authority of the first of the Apostles, Simon Peter, whose successor the Pope is: hence, it is qualified as Apostolic or Holy (see President of the Pontifical Commission and the Governorship of Vatican City State, Cardinal Giovanni Lajolo's Lecture on Papal Diplomacy, Nov. 7, 2008 available at

translates as "Holy See." The Latin *sedes* ("See") refers to the office (literally "chair") of Saint Peter.[17] All subsequent popes who are successors of St. Peter have occupied this chair. The occupation of the chair of St. Peter is a characteristic leadership function of the Apostles of Christ. As a result of that apostolic tradition, the "Holy See" is also known as the "Apostolic See." In other words, the "Holy See" is called the "Apostolic See" because access to the chair in question is characterized by apostolic succession.[18] While the "Holy See" refers to the seat of the Pope or Bishop of Rome, the Pope as the Bishop of Rome is also known as the Holy See because of his preeminence and universal responsibility in the Catholic Church.

Generally, the term "Holy See" refers to the composite of the authority, jurisdiction, and sovereignty vested in the Pope and his advisers to direct the worldwide Roman Catholic Church. Moreover, as the "central government" of the Roman Catholic Church, the "Holy See" has the legal personality that allows it to enter into treaties as the juridical equal of a state and to send and receive diplomatic representatives.[19] Though it may sound repetitive, it is important to stress that the "Holy See" is not synonymous with Rome, "the Vatican,"[20] or "the Vatican City State."[21] The "Vatican City" is the physical or territorial base of "the Holy See," almost a pedestal upon which is posed a much larger and unique independent and sovereign authority:

---

http://www.thomasaquinas.edu/news/cardinal-lajolo-lecture-papal-diplomacy

[17] The original Latin term *Sancta Sedes* is therefore translated as "Holy See." *See* D. P.SIMPSON, CASSELL'S LATIN DICTIONARY 533, 543 (5th ed. 1968).

[18] *See* CATECHISM OF THE CATHOLIC CHURCH (1994), # 869 (explaining that St. Peter, the remaining Apostles, and their successors, the popes and bishops, constitute the continuum with regard to the "chair").

[19] *See Vatican City Business Law Handbook, Vol. 1, Strategic Information and Basic Laws*, International Business Publications U.S.A., 2012 edition, available at Ibpus.com – https://play.google.com/books

[20] The *Catholic Encyclopedia* explains the term "Vatican" to mean "the official residence of the Pope at Rome, so named from being built on the lower slopes of the Vatican Hill: figuratively, the name is used to signify the Papal power and influence and, by extension, the whole Church." According to the Office of the Historian of the United States Department of State, the Holy See is the diplomatic representative of the Roman Catholic Church and the Pope with its headquarters in the Vatican City (see U.S. Department of State, Office of the Historian at Holy See http://www.state.gov/p/eur/ci/vt/ or http://history.state.gov/countries/holy-see)

[21] *See generally* C.G. Fenwick, *The New City of the Vatican*, 23 AVE MARIA J. INT'L L. 371 (1929), (distinguishing between the Holy See and the Vatican City State); GORDON IRELAND, "The State of the City of the Vatican," 27 *AVE MARIA J. INT'L L. 271* (1933).

that of the "Holy See."[22] As such, the "Holy See" is the supreme authority and administrative organ of the Catholic Church with the Pope as the supreme head.[23] The "Holy See" refers to the juridical personification of the ministry of the Holy Father (the Pope) through the Dicasteries of the Roman Curia in their service to the Universal Church and humanity.[24]

The Vatican City is a kind of miniscule support-State that guarantees the spiritual freedom of the Pope with minimum territory.[25] In other words, the "Vatican" is the official residence of the Pope in Rome, named as such having been built on the lower slopes of the Vatican Hill; it is figuratively the name used to signify papal power and influence, and by extension, the whole Church.[26] In contrast, the "Holy See" is understood to be the Pope and the Roman Curia, universal and spiritual authority, unique center of communion; a sovereign subject of international law, of a religious and moral character.[27] The 1983 Code of Canon Law, the longest surviving legal system in history, provides that the "Holy See" refers to "... not only the Roman Pontiff but also the Secretariat of State, the Council for the Public Affairs of the Church and other institutions of the Roman Curia."[28]

---

[22] See, The Permanent Observer Mission of the Holy See to the United Nations, New York, "A Short History of the Diplomacy of the Holy See, at http://www.holyseemission.org/about/history-of-diplomacy-of-the-holy-see.aspx last visited September 12, 2013.

[23] James Crawford, The *Creation of States in International Law*, 2nd ed., Oxford, Clarendon Press, 2006, p. 225.

[24] Roman A. Melnyk, *The Vatican Diplomacy at the United Nations: A History of Catholic Global Engagement*, The Edwin Mellen Press, New York, 2009, p. iv.

[25] *See* EDWARD J. GRATSCH, THE HOLY SEE AND THE UNITED NATIONS 1945-1995 (1997), (indicating that the Vatican City provides the Holy See with the political independence necessary for its spiritual mission").

[26] Manhattan Avro, *The Vatican in World Politics*, supra note 5, at p. 11.

[27] *See* Archbishop Jean-Louis Tauran's Lecture on "The Presence of the Holy See in the International Organizations," Catholic University of the Sacred Heart, Milan Italy, April 22, 2002, available at http://www.vatican.va/roman_curia/secretariat_state/documents/rc_seg-st_doc_20020422_tauran_en.html

[28] *See* Canons 360 & 361 of the 1983 Code of Canon Law (The Roman Pontiff usually conducts the affairs of the universal Church through the Roman Curia, which performs its function in his name and by his authority for the good and service of the churches). The Curia is the central administration of the Church. Canon 360 of the 1983 Code provides that the Pope "usually *conducts the business of the universal Church* by means of the Roman Curia" and it performs its function in his name and with his authority, for the benefit and service of the Churches.

1.4.2 The Concept of Social Justice[29]

Widespread poverty and concentrated wealth cannot endure side by side with democracy.

– Thomas Jefferson –

Most philosophers have interpreted the human person as *homo socialis.*[30]As a natural inclination, humans find themselves in a particular time and place and learn who they are directly and self-evidently in the context of family, community, and society.[31] The individual becomes fully human only in the context of relating with other human beings and institutions. It is only through continuous encounters with other persons

---

[29] *See generally* JOHN RAWLS, A THEORY OF JUSTICE (1990); JOHN HUNSAKER & BRENDA HANZL, UNDERSTANDING SOCIAL JUSTICE PHILANTHROPY, National Committee for Responsive Philanthropy (2003); R. DEGAN & M. DISMAN, CULTURAL COMPETENCY HANDBOOK, University of Toronto, (2004)Community Foundations of Canada, THE SOCIAL JUSTICE SPECTRUM (2004); Walker & Walker "Social Inclusion, Anti-racism and Democratic Citizenship," in Anver Saloojee (ed.), *The Laidlaw Foundation* (2003); RAY DEAUX & MARK SNYDER (eds.) THE OXFORD HANDBOOK ON PERSONALITY AND SOCIAL PSYCHOLOGY (2012); THOMAS PATRICK BURKE, THE CONCEPT OF JUSTICE: IS SOCIAL JUSTICE JUST? (2013); LORETTA CAPEHEART & DRAGAN MILOVANOVIC, SOCIAL JUSTICE: THEORIES, ISSUES, AND MOVEMENTS (2007); DAVID MILLER, PRINCIPLES OF SOCIAL JUSTICE (2001); BRIAN BARRY, WHY SOCIAL JUSTICE MATTERS (2005); MAURIANNE ADAMS, *et al* (eds.), TEACHINGS FOR DIVERSITY AND SOCIAL JUSTICE (2010) (Social justice is the distribution of the social and economic resources of society for the benefit of all. Social justice is the process through which society attains a more equitable distribution of power in the political, economic and social realms.

[30] *See for example* RICOEUR PAUL, ONESELF AS ANOTHER TRANSLATED BY KATHLEEN BLAMEY, UNIVERSITY OF CHICAGO PRESS (1992); TILLICH PAUL, THE COURAGE TO BE, NEW HAVEN: YALE UNIVERSITY Press (1952); BELLAH ROBERT *et al*, HABITS OF THE HEART: INDIVIDUALISM AND COMMITMENT IN AMERICAN LIFE. BERKELEY: UNIVERSITY OF CALIFORNIA PRESS, (1996); GADAMER HANS GEORG, TRUTH AND METHOD. SECOND REVISED EDITION (REVISED TRANSLATION BY JOEL WEINSHEIMER AND DONALD G. MARSHALL), NEW YORK, CONTINUUM (1994); BRUNER JEROME, THE CULTURE OF EDUCATION, CAMBRIDGE MASSACHUSSETTS HARVARD UNIVERSITY PRESS (1996); MACINTYRE ALISDAIR, AFTER VIRTUE: A STUDY IN MORAL THEORY, SECOND EDITION. NOTRE DAME, INDIANA, UNIVERSITY OF NOTRE DAME PRESS, (1984).

[31] *Id.*

and institutions that a person becomes and remains an authentically whole person.[32] As a result of this naturally recognized communal structure, issues of justice are taken seriously since issues of rights synchronize with interpersonal relationships. Therefore, human nature has evolved in such a way as to create a natural revulsion to affairs of state that are unfair or unjust.

To be sure, the term "justice" is an age-old topic to which countless great minds have contributed. For present our purposes, suffice it to say the term "justice" refers to more than just the administration of laws. The term "justice" sometimes assumes changeable characteristics; it changes according to time and place. What is considered just in some places may not be so after some time. For instance, there was a time when owning slaves was considered just in ancient Greek and Roman empires, while in modern times, such a practice is considered a crime against humanity. That is not to say "justice" is a morally relative concept. At least from the perspective of the Catholic Church and the Natural Law tradition, there is a distinction between (1) immutable principles of justice and morality, and (2) what a society, in an era, considers as "just" or morally acceptable.

In any event, in modern times, justice has become the foundation of social morality and is concerned with the ordering of society. [33] In this case, "justice" reflects a pattern of social norms and values based on which an individual's conduct is evaluated. In this sense, "justice" becomes the criteria for judging actions of individuals within a society. This idea of "justice" influenced the origin of the concept of "social justice," which is largely a product of modern social and economic developments. Placed side by side, the traditional concept of justice, variously described as conservative or orthodox, focused on the qualities of the "just" (or virtuous) man, while the modern concept of "social justice" postulates a "just society."[34] "Social justice" is based on the idea of a society that gives individuals and groups fair treatment and a just share of the benefits of society.[35]

---

[32] *Id.*

[33] D.D. Rapheal, *Problems of Political Philosophy,* Macmillan, London, 1979, p.105.

[34] O.P. Gauba, *Dimensions of Social Justice*, National Publishing House, New Delhi, 1983, p. 2.

[35] *See* RICOEUR PAUL, ONESELF AS ANOTHER TRANSLATED BY KATHLEEN BLAMEY, UNIVERSITY OF CHICAGO PRESS (1992), *supra* note 29.

The concept of "social justice" is not found in the dictionary. To understand the concept, it is best to dissect it into two constituent terms: "justice" and "social." Generally, the term "justice" connotes rendering to another what is due. The *Black's Law Dictionary* defines the term "jus" as "right;" "justice;" . . . "right."[36] However, the *Merriam-Webster's Collegiate Dictionary* defines the term "justice" as "the maintenance or administration of what is just especially by the impartial adjustment of conflicting claims or the assignment of merited rewards or punishments; the administration of law, especially the establishment or determination of rights according to the rules of law and equity; the quality of being just, impartial or fair; the principle or ideal of just dealing or right action."

From the above lexical definition, the concept of justice is mostly associated with the legal system, with an underlying assumption that justice is tantamount to equal rights, access, and fair treatment. Therefore, the term "social" is prefixed to the term "justice," namely, to ameliorate the hardship occasioned by extreme legality. For purposes of clarity, the *Merriam-Webster's Collegiate Dictionary* defines the term *social* as one that "...relates to human society, the interaction of the individual and the group, or the welfare of human beings as members of society; tending to form cooperative and interdependent relationships with others...."[37]

Based on the above lexicographic definition of the terms "justice" and "social," a relationship is established in such a way that the term "social" goes farther than a mere adherence to the obligations imposed by law.[38] When these two terms are taken together, there is a tendency toward what may be referred to as "inter-individual and inter-group fairness, or societal

---

[36] Henry Campbell Black, M.A., *et al*, *Black's Law Dictionary*, (Centennial ed.) (1891-1991), West Pub. Co., 1992, pp. 598-599 (defining the term "justice" as "proper administration of laws;" in jurisprudence, the constant and perpetual disposition of legal matters or disputes to render every man his due.)

[37] *Merriam-Webster's Collegiate Dictionary*, 11th ed., 2011.

[38] The *Black's Law Dictionary* defines "social justice" as: "justice that conforms to a moral principle, such as, that all people are equal. One or more equitable resolutions sought on behalf of individuals and communities who are disenfranchised, underrepresented, or otherwise excluded from meaningful participation in legal, economic, cultural and social structures, with the ultimate goal of removing barriers to participation and effecting social change." *See* Bryan A. Garner (ed.), *Black's Law Dictionary*, 4th Pocket ed., Thompson Reuters, 2011, p. 426.

impartiality."[39] For instance, in the United States in the first quarter of 2005, the average weekly income for white men was $731.00; for white women, $601.00; for black men, $579.00; and for black women, $506.00.[40] Social justice looks at this scenario with disdain because it lacks fairness. The concept embraces the ethos of distribution to achieve fairness and equality to alleviate any form of discrimination as can be seen from the above example.[41]

From the foregoing, therefore, "social justice" refers to the right ordering of the society. Social justice covers a broader perspective than the more narrowly defined legal aspect of justice. For instance, the legal aspect of justice might stop at the level of punishment of a thief as prescribed by the law; social justice goes further to implement restitution. Social justice denotes conceptions of a just society, whereas justice refers to a practice that is more than just the administration of laws. Therefore, the concept of "social justice" is predicated on the idea that society gives individuals and groups, fair treatment and an equal opportunity to share in benefits and resources.

The Holy See emphasizes social justice philosophy as the best suitable principle in human existence in every society. The Church refers to this sometimes as "social action." Social action is the act of correcting the structures that perpetuate injustice. Through the lens of social justice, the Church examines keenly the problems that militate against human beings in their communities, seeking answers to questions such as "Why is there so much unemployment in our area?" "Why are there so many poor people in our community?" "How will the deforestation of our rain forests affect our global climate?"

Often when social service is performed, there is an inspiration to get involved in solving the problem that created the need in the first place because the two are closely related, often going together. For instance,

---

[39] Boucher Jean Leon, "There Will be Struggle: The Development and Operational Issues of Social Justice Programs at State Universities in the United States of America," in *Journal for Critical Education Policy Studies (JCEPS)*, Vol. 8 Issue 2, 2010, p. 277.

[40] *See* ALLAN K., THE SOCIAL LENS: AN INVITATION TO SOCIAL AND SOCIOLOGICAL THEORY, PINE FORGE PRESS, CA, (2007) (analyzing wealth gaps in society through the structures of race/ethnicity, class, and/or gender); *See also* Bureau of Labor Statistics, 2005.

[41] BOUCHER JEAN LEON, *supra* note 39.

someone comes to a food pantry and tells the food pantry owner she has no food because she lost her job. The owner may know of an employer looking to hire someone right away for a job requiring little or no skills. The owner gives that person food, and then places that person in touch with the employer. The owner has solved both problems for that person, namely (a) the immediate need of food through an act of charity (social service) and (b) the unemployment that created and perpetuated the need. Here, then, is social justice in action.[42]

The Catholic Church does not apply social justice in isolation. In the Catholic Social Teaching, social justice encompasses economic justice.[43] The reason is not far-fetched. All rights, civil, cultural, economic, political, and social, are considered "universal, indivisible, independent and interrelated."[44] Each person born into this world has a right to everything he or she needs, but she is bound up with that of every other creature, and this right gives him or her no license to grab everything he or she can without allowing a share for others. The 1948 United Nations Universal Declaration on Human Rights states that recognition of the inherent dignity and of the equal and inalienable rights of all members of the human family is the foundation of freedom, justice, and peace in the world.[45]

In its social doctrine, the Church teaches that the reason for equal dignity and equal rights of the human person is traceable to the creation of humans in the image and likeness of God, from whom these equal and inalienable rights emanate. For the realization and maintenance of this natural arrangement, the Church calls for the organization of social institutions. When social institutions are justly organized, they provide access to what is good for the person, both individually and in association

[42] E-Catholic 2000, "Social Justice – A Basic Introduction", in *Catholics Online for the Third Millennium* available at http://www.ecatholic2000.com/sj/socjust.shtml

[43] *See* Center for Economic and Social Justice, available at http://www.cesj.org/thirdway/economicjustice-defined.htm (Social and economic rights of peoples are provided for in Articles 16 and 22 through 27 of the 1948 Universal Declaration of Human Rights (UDHR). These rights are also articulated 1966 International Convention on Economic, Social, and Cultural Rights (ICESCR).

[44] *See* the 1993 Vienna Declaration and Program of Action, Part 1, paragraph 5.

[45] *See* Preamble to the United Nations Universal Declaration of Human Rights, 1948 (Article 1 of UDHR states that: *"All human beings are born free and equal in dignity and rights. They are endowed with reason and conscience and should act toward one another in a spirit of brotherhood.")*.

with others.[46] Social justice, as a matter of fact, imposes on each of us a personal responsibility to work with others to design and continually perfect our institutions as tools for personal and social development.[47]

The Church teaches humanity: "charity is the greatest social commandment... requires the practice of justice, and, therefore, calls upon every individual to respect others and their rights."[48] Based on this teaching, society is perceived as promoting social justice when it provides the conditions that accord associations or individuals the opportunity to obtain what is their due, according to their nature and their vocation. The reason for this natural expectation is because social justice is linked to the common good and the exercise of authority.[49] The Church's authority for this teaching stems from the transcendent dignity of the human person.[50] Inequality of any sort, for instance, contradicts equal dignity of human beings naturally endowed. Furthermore, any disparity between individuals and the group contradicts social justice, equity, and human dignity.[51]

1.4.3 Dimensions of Social Justice

Catholic social teaching understands justice more broadly than in simple juridical terms. In a disordered society, as can be seen in some countries of the world, most especially in less developed countries, laws can be structured in such a way as to benefit the powerful to the detriment of the weak members of the society.[52] In that case, unjust laws can be legalized with little or no resistance. In view of the tendency for unjust laws to be legalized in undemocratic societies, Catholic social teaching makes certain

---

46 *Id.*

47 *Id.*

48 CATECHISM OF THE CATHOLIC CHURCH (1994), # 1889.

49 CATECHISM OF THE CATHOLIC CHURCH (1994), # 1928.

50 CATECHISM OF THE CATHOLIC CHURCH (1994), # 1929; *See also* POPE JOHN PAUL II, *SOLLICITUDO REI SOCIALIS* (THE CONCERN OF THE CHURCH FOR THE SOCIAL ORDER), 1987, # 47.

51 CATECHISM OF THE CATHOLIC CHURCH (1994), # 1938.

52 DANIEL G. GROODY, GLOBALIZATION, SPIRITUALITY, AND JUSTICE, Maryknoll, New York, 2008, p. 99.

distinctions when speaking about social justice.[53] It distinguishes between three primary dimensions of social justice, namely, commutative justice, contributive justice, and distributive justice.[54]

Commutative Justice also called contractual justice, concerns obligations arising from relationships between and among individuals, groups, and classes. *Commutative justice* is concerned with what individuals owe to each other. Such relationships involve respect for the rights of the other person, including respect for the property of that person. Commutative justice "binds individual to individual in the sphere of private transactions."[55] An example of commutative justice is a contractual relationship between two parties in which rights and obligations are established; the subject matter can be goods, services, or property.[56] In his *Summa Theologica*, St. Thomas Aquinas explains the concern of commutative justice.

> Commutative justice is concerned with the mutual dealings between two people.... In commutations something is paid to an individual chiefly in buying and selling. Hence it is necessary to equalize thing with thing – equality in *arithmetic* proportion.[57]

Commutative justice, as a matter of fact, demands "economic justice in exchange of goods by barter or selling." What this means is that "there must be exact equivalence between what is agreed and what is paid."[58] Therefore, this type of justice "commands that exchange be of equal value... [and because it] operates by the standard of strict equality," it

---

[53] For details on "legalized injustice," see Harold V. Bennett, Injustice Made Legal: Deuteronomic Law and the Plight of Widows, Strangers, and Orphans in Ancient Israel, Eerdmans, Grand Rapids, (2002).

[54] *See* THOMAS AQUINAS, SUMMA THEOLOGICA, II-II, 61, 5.

[55] DAVID BOHR, CATHOLIC MORAL TRADITION, Our Sunday Visitor (1999), p. 337.

[56] RAJ BHALA, TRADE, DEVELOPMENT, AND SOCIAL JUSTICE, Carolina Academic Press, 2003, p. 384.

[57] SAINT THOMAS AQUINAS, SUMMA THEOLOGICA, IIa IIae Q. 61 Art. 1, Art. 2, *quoted in* CHARLES RODGERS, AN INTRODUCTION TO CATHOLIC SOCIAL TEACHING, Ignatius Press, (2000), p. 28 (emphasis original).

[58] CHARLES RODGERS, AN INTRODUCTION TO CATHOLIC SOCIAL TEACHING, *supra* note 57, at 27.

is "violated by theft, fraud, and unjust damage."[59] For example, in law of Contract, commutative justice entails a right of restitution for funds already paid in the event of non-performance of a duty for which payment is made.[60] It is based on this reciprocity that one can rightly infer that "without commutative justice, no other form of justice is possible."[61]

Distributive Justice concerns obligations of a community or government to the individual members of the community or citizens of the polity, particularly about the allocation of public social goods.[62] In other words, *distributive justice* is concerned with what a community owes to an individual. Concerning this type of justice, Saint Thomas Aquinas says

> Distributive justice distributes common goods proportionately. . .. In distributive justice, we find equality in *geometric* proportion; a person's station is considered.[63]

The above citation implies that the governing authority of that community or country regulates the benefits and burdens of membership in a community or of citizens in a country. Distributive justice is concerned with how authorities distribute benefits and burdens accruing from the incidence of societal membership. Hence,

> Distributive justice deals with the society's duty to the individual. It pertains to the relationship of the whole to

---

[59] DAVID BOHR, CATHOLIC MORAL TRADITION, *supra* note 16, at 337-338.

[60] RAJ BHALA, TARDE, DEVELOPMENT, AND SOCIAL JUSTICE, *supra* note 56, at 384. Commutative justice seeks to ensure that human dignity and social responsibility are the basis of all economic transactions, contracts and promises, recognizing that employers have an obligation to their workers to provide humane working conditions and to pay fair wages, and workers owe employers conscientious and diligent work in exchange for these fair wages. *See* U.S. NATIONAL CONFERENCE OF CATHOLIC BISHOPS, *Economic Justice for All: Pastoral Letter on Catholic Social Teaching and the U. S. Economy,* 1986, # 69.

[61] *See* CATECHISM OF THE CATHOLIC CHURCH (1994), # 2411 (stating that contracts are subject to commutative justice which regulates exchanges between persons in accordance with a strict respect for their rights. Commutative justice obliges strictly; it requires safeguarding property rights, paying debts, and fulfilling obligations freely contracted).

[62] RAJ BHALA, *supra* note 56, at 384.

[63] SAINT THOMAS AQUINAS, SUMMA THEOLOGICA, IIa IIae Q. 61 Art. 1, Art. 2, *quoted in* CHARLES RODGERS, AN INTRODUCTION TO CATHOLIC SOCIAL TEACHING, *supra* not 57, at 28 (emphasis original).

> the parts, and seeks to provide the minimum material resources that are necessary for individuals to have a humane and dignified life. As members of a human community, individuals have a right to have their basic needs met unless absolute scarcity makes this impossible. Distributive justice seeks the well-being of all members of the community, which means one's basic rights must be safeguarded and protected. It also puts *special emphasis on protecting society's weaker members, advocating a greater solidarity* with the poor *members.*[64]

Legal Justice (also called contributive justice) is concerned with what an individual owes to community. It pertains to obligations of a person to a community or of a citizen to a government. Whereas commutative and distributive justices are considered as types of "particular" justice, "legal" justice is called "general" justice. The term "general" plays the function of defining coverage. Therefore, legal or general justice pertains both to the bearers and subjects of authority who practice it by making and implementing legislation that favors the common welfare.[65]

---

[64] DANIEL G. GROODY, GLOBALIZATION, SPIRITUALITY, AND JUSTICE, *supra* note 52, at 100 (emphasis added). Distributive justice pertains to "the distribution of the goods and honors of the State among its citizens according to their contribution to the commonweal." *See* CHARLES RODGERS, AN INTRODUCTION TO CATHOLIC SOCIAL TEACHING, *supra* note 57, at 27. As a general criterion for distributive justice, the allocation of goods and honors ought to be in some relation to the needs and contributions of the members of community or polity. A classic example is a progressive tax system, implying payment based on ability to pay, coupled with the expenditure of tax revenues on the housing, food, education, and health needs of the poor. *See* RAJ BHALA, *supra* note 56, at 384-85. "Perversions of distributive justice include all kinds of corruption, favoritism toward individuals or groups, all kinds of oppression, and all unrelieved poverty." *See* DAVID BOHR, *supra* note 55, at 338. The example of unrelieved poverty as a perversion of distributive justice clearly suggests the question of the "just-ness" of special and differential treatment rules could be analyzed in terms of this type of justice (*i.e.*, not only in terms of social justice). For such an approach, *see* Frank J. Garcia, *Trade and Inequality: Economic Justice and the Developing World, 21 MICHIGAN JOURNAL OF INTERNATIONAL LAW 975 (2000). See also* Frank J. Garcia, *Building a Just Trade Order for a New Millennium, 33 THE GEORGE WASHINGTON INTERNATIONAL LAW REVIEW 1015 (2001)* (discussing international trade law from the perspective of distributive justice).

[65] DAVID BOHR, CATHOLIC MORAL TRADITION, *supra* note 55, at 338.

Contributive justice recognizes the responsibility of individuals to the common good. What this means is that people have a duty to look out not only for their own welfare but also for the welfare of others. Part of this obligation is fulfilled through the participation of individuals (whether an ordinary individual or one who is a leader in the political society) in the civic life of a community, including paying taxes and voting in elections.[66]

One thing that is of great importance is for the society to acknowledge that though these three dimensions of social justice are conceptually distinct, they complement one another. Taxes can be used to show this complementarity. A citizen owes the duty to pay taxes to the government (this is a matter of legal justice). The duty to determine tax liability based on a criterion of fairness, like the ability to pay, is a duty that the government owes its citizens (and this is a matter of distributive justice).[67]

One of the problems that anti-globalization critics have against the WTO is the global trade body's inability to celebrate the distinctness and enhancement of these dimensions of justice, especially its indifference to social justice as a brand of justice. This weakness extends to the WTO's inability to define social justice as effective as it should have in connection with the Third World Members. This brings the uniqueness of the Catholic social justice to the limelight.[68] Generally, social justice, as stated above, is justice in society in general. In other words, social justice pertains to the common good.[69] Social justice concerns rights and duties at a societal level. Individuals and groups interact in the society economically, politically, socially, and otherwise. For that reason, they have duties to perform to bring about harmony.

From the theological point of view, social justice is a dimension of justice distinct from the other types of justice. Social justice's distinctness is seen in its use of moral reasoning to take into consideration the fact that relationships between individuals have an *institutional or structural*

---

[66] DANIEL G. GROODY, *supra* note 52, at 100.

[67] RAJ BHALA, *supra* note 56, at 385.

[68] *See* DAVID BOHR, CATHOLIC MORAL TRADITION, *supra* note 55, at 337 (stating that in the Encyclical Letter *Quadragesimo Anno*, Pope Pius XI used the term "social justice" eight times. The *Quadragesimo Anno* is one of the first instances in which the term appears, at least in Catholic social teaching).

[69] CHARLES RODGERS, AN INTRODUCTION TO CATHOLIC SOCIAL TEACHING, *supra* note 57, at 27.

dimension.70 From the Catholic perspective, social justice is "the obligation of all parties to apply the Gospel to the structures, systems, and institutions of society which are the framework in which all human relationships take place."[71] And for social justice to empower individuals and groups to create and implement these frameworks, they must exhibit an active interest in necessary social and economic reforms. This is service to God, and that is why Saint Thomas Aquinas says,

> Justice is a habit whereby a man renders to each one his due by constant and perpetual will. *Just as love of God includes love of neighbor, - so too the service of God includes rendering to each one his due.72*

The goal of this book is centered on social justice as propagated by the Catholic Church in her universal mission. It is social justice that operates predominantly from the perspective of the common good. It is not determined by a court of law. It is a principle that respects the human person.

> Respect for the human person proceeds by way of respect for the principle that "everyone should look upon his neighbor (without any exception) as 'another self,' above all bearing in mind his life and the means necessary for living it with dignity." No legislation could by itself do away with the fears, prejudices, and attitudes of pride and selfishness which obstruct the establishment of truly fraternal societies. *Such behaviors will cease only through the charity that finds in every man a "neighbor," a brother.*[73]

---

[70] DAVID BOHR, CATHOLIC MORAL TRADITION, *supra* note 55, at 337 (emphasis added).

[71] RICHARD P. MCBRIEN, CATHOLICISM, (new ed.), HarperOne, 1994, p. 946.

[72] THOMAS AQUINAS, SUMMA THEOLOGICA, IIa IIae Q. 58 Art. 1 and 6, quoted in CHARLES RODGERS, AN INTRODUCTION TO CATHOLIC SOCIAL TEACHING, *supra* note 57, at 26 (emphasis added).

[73] SECOND VATICAN ECUMENICAL COUNCIL, GAUDIUM ET SPES (The Pastoral Constitution on the Church in the Modern World), December 7, 1965, # 27 § 1 (emphasis added). *See also* CATECHISM OF THE CATHOLIC CHURCH (1994), # 1931. The duty of making oneself a neighbor to others and actively serving them becomes even more

At the core of social justice is respect for each person's human dignity and an overall commitment to the common good. When the common good and respect for the dignity of the human person are placed at the center of every activity, whether at the community, national, or international level, the issues of inequality, injustice, exploitation, and marginalization will be brought under control. This is the point of departure of this book.

1.4.4 The Social Mission of the Church

In understanding Catholic Social Justice Theory and the application of it by the Catholic Church to contemporary problems in international trade law, it is helpful to explain the social mission of the Catholic Church with what the indefatigable Pope John Paul II said in Chile in 1987. Latin America, the demographic hub of Catholicism, was during long-delayed transitions to democratic politics and market-oriented economics throughout the 1980s. Because of this, Pope John Paul II visited the continent many times. One of the hideouts of social injustice was within Chile under General Augusto Pinochet, who remarked, concerning appeals for change from Chilean bishops, that the bishops should not be acting as a political party but should rather "spend ninety percent of their time praying."[74] In his reaction to Pinochet's misguided conception of the mission of the Church, Pope John Paul II taught that the Church's defense of basic human rights can never be divorced from the central mission of

---

urgent when it involves the disadvantaged, in whatever area this may be. *"As you did it to one of the least of these my brethren, you did it to me." See* CATECHISM OF THE CATHOLIC CHURCH (1994), # 1932. *See also* Mt. 25: 40. The Catholic Church teaches that good neighborly principle is in tandem with the concept of Charity when she reveals that:

> The duty of making oneself a neighbor is the path of Charity ..., the love of God and of neighbor. Charity is the greatest social commandment. It respects others and their rights. It requires the practice of justice, and it alone makes us capable of it. Charity inspires a life self-giving.

See id. at # 1889.

[74] George Weigel, *The Witness to Hope: The Biography of Pope John Paul II (1920-2005),* 1st ed., Harper Perennial, 1999, p. 531

the Church; the Church leaders cannot not merely "stay in the sacristy and do nothing," abandoning the cause of human rights.[75]

On another trip to Latin America, Pope John Paul II had an overnight stop in Montevideo, Uruguay, where he held one of his impromptu airborne press conferences. While walking up and down the aisle of his Alitalia jet, he responded to a question from a reporter as to whether he would help restore democratic politics in Chile, saying: "Yes, yes, I am not the evangelizer of democracy; I am the evangelizer of the Gospel. To the Gospel message belong, of course, all the problems of human rights, and if democracy means human rights, then it also belongs to the message of the Church."[76] Continuing this understanding, the present Pope Francis explains that the Pontifical diplomatic service, which is at the center of the Church's social mission, must open up understanding for a diplomat, working in charity to understand the need for sensitivity to differing cultures and to interact with people in worlds far from home.[77]

Pope John Paul II was right. The Catholic Church is inspired by the full revelation of the truth about the human person as contained in the Gospel. Therefore, in fulfilling her mission of proclaiming the Gospel, the Church bears witness to human person, to his dignity and his vocation in the communion of persons. The Church teaches humans the demands of justice and peace in conformity with divine wisdom.[78] The Church makes a moral judgment about economic and social matters, "when the fundamental rights of the person or the salvation of souls requires it."[79] The social mission of the Church focuses on a new world order centered on the rights and freedoms of every individual rooted in the moral laws of human behavior revealed by God through the teachings of Christ, as proposed by Christ's Church.[80] Based on this authority, the Church is missionary by her

---

[75] *Id.*

[76] Soru Roberto, "Pope on Latin Trip, Attacks Pinochet Regime," in *New York Times*, April 1, 1987, pp. AI, A10.

[77] *See* Pope Francis I Address to the Pontifical Ecclesiastical Academy, Vatican City June 6, 2013, available at http://www.zenit.org/en/articles/pope-s-address-to-the-pontical-ecclesiastical-academy

[78] *See* CATECHISM OF THE CATHOLIC CHURCH (1994), # 2419.

[79] *See SECOND* VATICAN ECUMENICAL COUNCIL, The Pastoral Constitution on the Church in the Modern World (*GAUDIUM ET SPES*), supra note75, at 76.

[80] Martin Malachi, *The Keys of this Blood: Pope John Paul II Versus Russia and the West for Control of the New World Order*, Touchstone, New York, 1990, p. 19.

very nature,[81] and her mission is *ad gentes* (*i.e.*, to the nations). The mission of the Church is a universal call to holiness, which includes a universal call to evangelize the whole world.[82]

The focus on moral order in her mission makes the authority of the Church distinct from that of political authorities. The Church is concerned with the temporal aspects of the common good because they are ordered to the transcendental reality, our ultimate end. Therefore, the Church strives to inspire right attitudes with respect to earthly goods and in socio-economic relationships,[83] spreading grace beyond the formal boundaries of the Church. Being a mission by its very nature, it sticks to the missionary imperative for people to love one another in fulfillment of our duties to others; the salvation that Christ offers us "must be made concretely available to all." [84] This point clearly distinguishes the Church in its behavior within international organizations such as the Permanent Observer in the WTO, from nations represented by political authorities in them, such as WTO Members.

Pope Paul VI presented a grand synthesis of the social mission of the Church and her moral emphasis as a concrete picture of the unity of all creation, which gives credence to the mandate to reach out to all. He described four concentric circles that hold all humankind. For this Pontiff, mankind was not to be seen polarized, but together in one large circle as one race, already united by God as one species. The circle of humankind includes everyone: atheists, other religions, and other Christians. The next, smaller circle is that of all religions, united because they all seek God. The third inner circle is that of Christians, united because they believe in and love Christ. The fourth innermost, smallest circle is that of

---

[81] POPE JOHN PAUL II, *REDEMPTORIS MISSIO* (THE MISSION OF THE REDEEMER), December 7, 1990, no. 62.

[82] Weigel George, The Witness to Hope, *supra* note 74, at p. 634.

[83] *See* CATECHISM OF THE CATHOLIC CHURCH (1994), # 2420.

[84] Weigel George, The Witness to Hope, *supra*, note 74, at p. 635. [The focus of Pope John Paul II's encyclical letter, "*The Mission of the Redeemer*" (*Redemptoris Missio*), is establishment of the impelling nature of the Church's mandate to spread the message of salvation to all the corners of the earth. . . ."].

Catholics. Catholics reach out and draw others in to embrace the truth and salvation.[85]

What Pope Paul VI taught was that the Church is impelled to spread the Gospel of unity, the Gospel of love and peace to the whole world, since her sons and daughters are scattered in all the countries of the world. From the foregoing, the mission of the Church is "religious and moral in character"[86] and cuts across all cultures, peoples, groups or institutions. In its social mission, the Church can rightly assume the government of the world because it is not limited by territorial or cultural boundaries. The Church is characterized by the existence of spiritual values that guide behaviors. In her participation in international affairs, the Church serves as an instrument for moderating behaviors of individuals, groups and nations in consonance with spiritual values and morality. International law or treaties alone are not enough to regulate international cooperation. The Catholic Church supplies the neutral barometer for influencing the application of equitable principles that guarantee peace and harmony.

1.4.5 International Trade Law – GATT-WTO System

Without fussing over the meaning of the terms "international," "trade," or "law," it is useful to explain the concept of "international trade law" and show the link between "international trade" and "international trade law." International trade (also called world trade) is the exchange of goods and services across national boundaries,[87] while international trade law is public law that orders such activity.[88] International trade law regulates the global exchange of goods, services, and intellectual property.

Traditionally, most international trade agreements have been bilateral (trade between two nations). However, globalization has made

---

[85] POPE PAUL VI, ENCYCLICAL LETTER *ECCLESIAM SUAM* (ON THE PATHS OF THE CHURCH), 1964, nos. 96-115.

[86] United Nations, "Selected Legal Opinions of the Secretariat of the United Nations and Related Inter-Government Organizations," *UN.Doc.ST/LEG/8* (1962), at 236.

[87] Drubbel Bart, ed., The 21st Century Webster's International Encyclopedia, 1st ed., Trident Press International, Florida, 2003, p. 573.

[88] *See generally* GARCIA FRANK J., TRADE, INEQUALITY, AND JUSTICE: TOWARD A LIBERAL THEORY OF JUST TRADE, Transnational Publishers Inc., (2003).

international trade increasingly multilateral, such as when countries within a region sign trade treaties or when the nations of the world get together for that purpose. World trade, which is facilitated by electronic payments transactions, takes place between a wide range of businesses, consumers, and governments and involves an immense variety of products, services, and intellectual property. For instance, logs are exported from the United States to countries such as Japan, Mexico, and Germany to be processed and shipped back to the United States to be sold.

A distinction between international and domestic trade can also throw more light on the meaning of the term. The motivation and behavior of parties within international trade is not strictly different from domestic trade. The main difference is that international trade is typically costlier and more complex than domestic trade. The reason is distance and border issues, which impose costs such as tariffs, time, and costs due to border delays. Other costs associated with country differences include language, culture, legal systems, etc.

Another distinction is that international trade fosters mobility of labor more than domestic trade does. International trade also is structured to enhance broader participation. This fact places international trade law as a strong weapon recognizing the term "internationalism," which is "the policy or principle of cooperation among nations especially in politics and economics."[89] For order, international trade law regulates "community interests or actions between different nations,"[90] especially issues that relate to socio-economic activities.

Some agencies, commissions, and organizations have tried to describe international trade law. According to the American Society of International Law (ASIL), international trade law focuses on how countries conduct trade in goods and services across national borders.[91] The function of "how" in the above description of international trade law may appear confusing. The "how" above is to be understood from the perspective of

[89] *See* READER'S DIGEST ILLUSTRATED ENCYCLOPEDIC DICTIONARY, Vol. A-K, Rider's Digest Association Inc., New York, 1987.

[90] *See* THE OXFORD ENGLISH DICTIONARY, 2nd ed., Oxford University Press, New York, 2001

[91] *See* THE AMERICAN SOCIETY OF INTERNATIONAL LAW (ASIL), especially, ASIL Guide to Electronic Resources for International Law, available at http://www.asil.org/iell.cffm last visited August 21, 2013.

the operation of law. Law as a concept is characterized by the terms "rule," "order," "regulation," and "binding" in most cases.[92] Thus, international trade law regulates export and import issues that arise in international trade in goods and services.[93]

The United Nations General Assembly defines the concept of the "law of international trade" as "the body of rules governing commercial relationships of a private law nature involving different countries."[94] Activities that are involved in achieving peace through trade are to be ordered in such a way as to achieve the purpose for which international trade originated. It is for this purpose that there exist the General Agreement on Tariffs and Trade (GATT), the General Agreement on Trade in Services (GATS), and the other agreements that are annexed to the Agreement Establishing the World Trade Organization (WTO Agreement).[95]

---

[92] The Merriam-Webster's Collegiate Dictionary defines law among other things, as *"a binding custom or practice...; a rule of conduct or action prescribed or formally recognized as binding or enforced by a controlling authority; the whole body of such customs, practices or rules...."*

[93] *Id.*

[94] *See* Resolution 2102(XX), adopted by the United Nations Assembly on December 20, 1965 (a special report on a preliminary study on the progressive development of the law of international trade in anticipation of the creation of the United Nations Commission on International Trade Law (UNCITRAL). The establishment of the UNCITRAL was informed by obvious considerations, namely, that international trade cooperation among states promotes friendly relations and maintenance of peace and security; international trade promotes the interests of all peoples, particularly developing countries; it harmonizes the divergent issues arising from the laws of different states in matters relating to international trade; secures broader participation of states (both industrialized and developing nations);(see UN –GENERAL ASSEMBLY RESOLUTION 2205 (XXI) of December 17, 1966, establishing the United Nations Commission on International Trade Law).

[95] *See generally* BHALA RAJ, MODERN GATT LAW Vol. 1, 2nd ed., Sweet & Maxwell, UK, 2013; BHALA RAJ, INTERNATIONAL TRADE LAW: INTERDISCIPLINARY THEORY AND PRACTICE, 3rd ed., Mathew Bender & Co., 2008; BHALA RAJ, TRADE, DEVELOPMENT, AND SOCIAL JUSTICE, supra note 56; Irwin Douglas A., *et al,* THE GENESIS OF THE GATT (2008); Hoekman Bernard M. & Petros Mavroidis, WORLD TRADE ORGANIZATION:LAW, ECONOMICS, AND POLITICS (2007); Jackson John H., SOVEREIGNTY: THE WTO AND CHANGING FUNDAMENTALS OF INTERNATIONAL LAW, (2006); Joerges Christian & Ernst-Ulrich Petersmann eds., CONSTITUTIONALISM, MULTILEVEL TRADE GOVERNANCE AND SOCIAL REGULATION (2006); Gethring Markus W., et al, WORLD TRADE LAW IN PRACTICE (2006); Barton John H. et al, THE EVOLUTION OF THE TRADE REGIME – POLITICS, LAW, AND ECONOMICS OF THE GATT AND THE WTO (2006); Cass Deborah Z., CONSTITUTIONALIZATION OF THE WORLD TRADE ORGANIZATION: LEGITIMACY, DEMOCRACY, AND COMMUNITY IN THE INTERNATIONAL

Though GATT sometimes has been described as overly controversial, it is the "Constitution"[96]of international trade law. Controversy is characteristic of every Constitution, and so it is with GATT, especially when the term "Constitution" is not restricted to a document defined by national boundaries. There are many "examples of international and non-governmental organizations and private sector bodies that have constitutive documents."[97] GATT is the document that contains "the fundamental legal principles on which the modern multilateral trading system is organized and operates."[98] An examination of the historical account of GATT throws more light on its operations and significance.

With the economic dislocations caused by the First and Second World Wars (particularly the Second World War), the need arose for countries of the world to design means for appropriate reconstruction. Being the world's most powerful economy, the United States was favored to exert considerable political pressure in gaining foreign acceptance for economic policies.[99] GATT was originally conceived and proposed by the United States Department of State as a design for a post-Second World War international economic order, which included a multilateral trade body.[100]

In designing this project, the U.S. worked harmoniously with its ally, the United Kingdom. This understanding between the U.S. and the United Kingdom culminated in August 1941 with what is known as the *Atlantic Charter,*[101] in which,

---

TRADING SYSTEM (2005); Jackson John H., THE JURISPRUDENCE OF GATT AND THE WTO: INSIGHTS ON TREATY LAW AND ECONOMIC RELATIONS (2000); WTO Secretariat: FROM GATT TO THE WTO: THE MULTILATERAL TRADING SYSTEM IN THE NEW MILLENIUM (2000).

[96] Bhala Raj, Modern GATT Law: A Treatise on the Law and Political Economy of the General Agreement on Tariffs and Trade and Other World Trade Organization Agreements, Vol. 1, 2nd ed., Sweet & Maxwell, UK, 2013, pp. 3-7.

[97] *Id.*

[98] *Id.*

[99] Peet Richard, Unholy Trinity: The IMF, World Bank and WTO, SIRD, Kuala Lumpur, 2003, p. 148.

[100] *See* "Suggested Charter for an International Trade Organization," 93 COMMERCIAL POLICY SERIES (U.S. Department of State 1946) especially *U.S. Proposals* in DEPARTMENT OF STATE PUBLICATION No. 2411 (1945); "*U.S.* Suggested Charter" in DEPARTMENT OF STATE PUBLICATION No. 2598 (1946).

[101] The Atlantic Charter was a joint declaration released by U.S. President Franklin D. Roosevelt and British Prime Minister Winston Churchill on August 14, 1941, following a

> the U.S. and the United Kingdom have "'common principles . . .' to seek territorial expansion; to seek the liberalization of international trade; to establish freedom of the seas, and international labor, economic, and welfare standards.... With the commitment to support the restoration of self-governments for all countries that had been occupied during the war and allowing all peoples to choose their own form of government."[102]

The *Atlantic Charter* was a significant initiative that paved the way for wider negotiations involving other countries of the world in a bid to establish a world economic order that would tackle the economic maladies of post-World War II. A one-time U.S. official explains the situation as follows:

> Nations have often undertaken economic discriminations and raised up trade barriers with complete disregard for the damaging effects on trade and livelihoods of other peoples, and, ironically enough, with similar disregard for the harmful resultant effects upon their own export trade.... The resultant misery, bewilderment, and resentment, together with other equally pernicious causes, paved the way for the rise of those very dictatorships which have plunged almost the entire world into war.[103]

In search of the solution to the above problem, many more countries participated in negotiations broader than the Atlantic Charter, because of which the GATT was drafted following the untiring efforts of two Preparatory Committees of the United Nations, namely, the *London*

---

meeting of the two heads of state in Newfoundland. The Atlantic Charter provided a broad statement of U.S. and British war aims. Churchill and Roosevelt met on August 9 and 10, 1941, aboard the U.S. Augusta in Placentia Bay, Newfoundland, to discuss their respective war aims for the Second World War and to outline a postwar international system. (For more details, see U.S. DEPARTMENT OF STATE – OFFICE OF THE HISTORIAN available at http://history.state.gov/milestones/1937-1945/AtlanticConf)

102 *Id.*

103 *See* Speech by Under Secretary of State Wells, U.S. Department of State COMMERCIAL POLICY SERIES No. 71, Pub. No. 1660, (1941).

Preparatory Committee (October 15 – November 20, 1946), and the *Geneva Preparatory Committee* (April 10 – October 30, 1947).

On October 30, 1947, delegates from 23 countries signed the GATT[104] as a document and an institution that would make the world safe for free trade.[105] In the same year, 1947, a United Nations Conference on Trade and Employment was held in Havana, Cuba, with the aim of establishing the International Trade Organization (ITO) to complete the construction of a post-war multilateral economic regime initiated several years earlier. The broader negotiation in issue aimed to establish the International Trade Organization (ITO).[106] As part of the ITO negotiations, various countries streamlined the process of lowering trade barriers, mainly tariffs, among themselves.

The GATT was intended to implement and protect the results of tariff reduction commitments agreed upon during the ITO negotiations. Many politicians were vehemently opposed to the ratification of the ITO Charter through domestic legislations in the contracting countries, notably in the U.S.[107] Therefore, no major trading country ratified the ITO Charter and it never came into existence. Because of this problem, the GATT assumed the form of an interim accord.[108] That is, GATT, though a provisional, skeletal framework, became the central artifice for tariff-cutting negotiations.

After efforts to establish an international trade organization failed in 1948, the GATT served as a provisional forum for contracting parties to address international trade matters. Over the years, GATT contracting

---

104 The official citation to the original publication of GATT is *Final Act,* Geneva, 55 U.N.T.S. 194 (1947).

105 Bhala Raj, MODERN GATT LAW, MODERN GATT LAW, Vol. 1, *supra* note 96, at 7.

106 *See* William Davey, A VERY BRIEF HISTORY OF THE GATT/WTO SYSTEM in Guzman Andrew T. & Pauwelyn Joost H.B., eds., International Trade Law (2003) (The International Trade Organization, ITO, was to be the third wing of an international economic triad consisting of the International Bank for Reconstruction and Development (World Bank), and the International Monetary Fund (IMF) to promote economic development, the reconstruction of Europe, and the expansion of global trade).

107 There were many reasons for which the politicians feared the ITO Charter: They were suspicious about the creation of yet another international organization, the ITO in addition to the Bretton Woods institutions, the IMF, and the International Bank for Reconstruction and Development (IBRD), or World Bank. They were concerned about surrendering American sovereignty to such institutions. See Bhala Raj, *supra* note 96 at 7.

108 *Id.*

parties conducted a series of multilateral negotiations known as "Rounds" to lower trade barriers among them. The first five GATT trade Rounds after 1947 focused on lowering tariffs. The Kennedy Round in the 1960s expanded discussions from tariff cuts to more general trade rules, leading to the negotiation of the GATT anti-dumping code. In the 1970s, contracting parties in the Tokyo Round of talks lowered tariffs further and concluded with various codes. Those codes were plurilateral, meaning only some contracting parties joined. The Tokyo Round concentrated on issues concerning non-tariff trade barriers, such as voluntary restraint agreements and technical standards.

The following Round, launched in 1986, built upon the progress made in the Tokyo round and in previous negotiations. Known as the Uruguay Round, it was, up to that time, the largest and most comprehensive trade Round. In the Uruguay Round, GATT members agreed to lower tariffs, reduce non-tariff barriers, discipline trade remedies, and extend trade rules into several new areas, including trade in services and intellectual property. At the conclusion of the Uruguay Round, representatives from most of the 123 participating countries signed a declaration in Marrakesh, Morocco, creating the World Trade Organization (WTO), which included bringing the agreements and commitments concluded during the Round under the new WTO.[109] On January 1, 1995, the WTO officially replaced the GATT along with the informal forum it had provided for more than four decades.[110] Since its establishment, the WTO has been the governing body of international trade, setting and enforcing rules of trade between nations.[111]

---

[109] By this development, WTO provisions are meant to supersede GATT provisions in the event of any conflicts between the two (see WTO Article XVI: 4 which states that in the event of any conflict between a provision of WTO Agreement and a provision of any of the Multilateral Trade Agreements, the provision of the WTO Agreement will prevail to the extent of that inconsistency).

[110] *See* OFFICE OF THE UNITED STATES TRADE REPRESENTATIVE, HISTORY OF THE WTO PART ONE, November 25, 2009, available at http://www.ustr.gov/about-us/press-office/blog/2009/november/history-wto-part-one

[111] Bhala Raj, *Dictionary of International Trade Law*, 2nd ed., Mathew Bender & Co., 2012, p. 913.

Manifestly, the WTO is largely built on the edifice of GATT and has evolved considerably since the era of the original 23 contracting parties.[112] Presently, there are approximately 160 Members of the WTO. Roughly 80 percent of the Membership consists of developing or least developed countries.

1.4.6 The Concept of "Family of Nations"

Setting aside a complex discussion of the term "family," which is not central to the discussion herein, the term "family" is born of "intimate community of life and love."[113] According to the *Merriam-Webster online Dictionary*, the term "family of nations" is defined as a "group of nations recognized as having equal status under international law," *having right and access to everything held in common.*[114] The family is the natural community in which human social nature is experienced; it is born from a communion of persons.[115] Here the term "communion" connotes the personal relationship between the "I" and the "thou," while the term "community" transcends this personal framework and moves toward a "society," a "we."[116]

A society built on a family scale is the best guarantee against drifting off course into individualism or collectivism, because within the family the human person is always at the center of attention as an end and never as a means. The concept of family therefore carries with it the natural features of social responsibility and solidarity.[117] The family does not exist for the society or state, but society and the State exist for the family.[118] The family

---

[112] Stoll Peter-Tobias, World Trade Organization, in Rudolf Bernhardt (ed.), "*Encyclopedia of Public International Law,*" Vol. 4, Q-Z, Amsterdam, 2000, p. 1530.

[113] Pope John Paul II, Post-Synodal Apostolic Exhortation *Christifideles Laici* 40, AAS 81, 1989, at 468

[114] *See* the definition of "family of nations, " Merriam-Webster online Dictionary available at http://www.merriam-webster.com/dictionary/family%20of%20nations (emphasis is mine)

[115] John Paul II, Letter to Families, *Gratissimam Sane, 7 AAS 86, 1994,* at 875; *see also* CATECHISM OF THE CATHOLIC CHURCH (1994) # 2206.

[116] *Id.*

[117] CATECHISM OF THE CATHOLIC CHURCH (1994) # 2224.

[118] See Article 16 (3) of the Universal Declaration of Human Rights (UDHR) of the United Nations (defining the family as the natural and fundamental group unit of society and is entitled to protection by society and the State).

possesses inviolable rights and finds its legitimization in human nature and not in being recognized by the State.[119]

Central to these inviolable rights is the issue of human dignity, which each member of a family possesses naturally and on equal terms. For that reason, all humans are born free and equal in dignity.[120] Every human person possesses inherent dignity and worth, as well as equal and inalienable rights. This common dignity possessed by every person accounts for the equality of every member of a family and, therefore, all members of the human family. The concept of equality is a significant feature of the family. Members of every family possess equal dignity. No matter the appellative stance, any notion of the term "family" must have this characteristic feature of equality, and this throws light on the parallel between the traditional concept of "family" as a union of a man and a woman and the extended conception of "family of nations" relating to the United Nations' concept of it.

In the "family of nations," like the family defined by marriage, the language of duty is used to convey a universal responsibility to a communal good. However, unlike in the context of marriage, the family of nations is described in an aspirational manner in terms of "equality" among the various members. In the family of nations, while all members have duties to this family, each member of the family is nominally equal, and all members have a responsibility to ensure that equality.

In marriage, both women and men ought to have duties that streamline an equal dignity instead of dichotomizing their different roles. Husband and wife should complement each other's role in other to enhance equality. In the same way, it is wrong to suggest that the "family of nations" is characterized by an equal dignity in the face of dichotomy or exploitation. For example, just as women's equal role should not remain on the status of "helpmate" as part of the common heritage of humankind, the developing world is not seen as playing an analogous role as the "servant" to the industrialized world. To suggest, for example, that the "family of nations,"

[119] *See* Holy See, CHARTER OF THE RIGHTS OF THE FAMILY, PREAMBLE, D-E, Vatican Polyglot Press, Vatican City, 1983, p. 6.

[120] PONTIFICAL COUNCIL FOR JUSTICE AND PEACE, COMPENDIUM OF THE CATHOLIC SOCIAL DOCTRINE, 2004, nos. 144-148 on the 'Equal Dignity of all People' available at http://www.vatican.va/roman_curia/pontifical_councils/justpeace/documents/rc_pc_justpeace_doc_20060526_compendio-dott-soc_en.html

is where one party provides "service" to the other, would result in a very inhumane, unequal world order.[121]

An understanding of the phrase "family of nations" throws more light on the social mission of the Catholic Church in her vision of an international world order. The United Nations, in its Proclamation of the International Year of the Family in 1994, describes the term "family" as follows: "Families assume diverse forms and functions from one country to another, and within each national society. These express the diversity of individual preferences and societal conditions."[122] The United Nations also explained that family policies must be formulated to bring families into conformity with the Convention on the Elimination of all Forms of Discrimination against Women and the Convention on the Rights of the Child, which protect the rights of individuals against family claims and intrusions. This document labels family traditions and inherited cultural values, including religion, as obstacles[123] "perpetrating attitudes that have, at times, worked to the detriment of society and some family members, notably women."[124]

It was in respect of the concept of "social justice" that the United Nations describes the term "family" as having no fixed definition. Based on the growing influence of the concept of "social justice" in the society, the United Nations teaches that there is no relatively fixed definition of "family." The Church teaches that the family is a natural, universal, and irreplaceable community, rooted in human nature.[125] The "family," in all ages and in all corners of the globe can be defined as a man and woman

---

[121] Traditional conception of marriage tended to create role differentiation between and women, but events have given rise to a shift whereby, women are no longer perceived as "helpmate mates" to men in traditional marriage. This is a development in the right direction; otherwise, traditional conception of marriage would have flawed the concept of social justice. Commitment to equality is central to the mission of "social justice." The Church should explore new ways of addressing non-traditional conception of marriage as Pope Francis I has taught.

[122] See United Nations Proclamation on the International Year of Families, 1994 (I.3.b).

[123] See United Nations Proclamation on the International Year of Families, 1994, (I.3.a and III. B. 25).

[124] *See* Proclamation on the International Year of Families at (III. B. 15).

[125] *See generally* PONTIFICAL COUNCIL FOR JUSTICE AND PEACE, THE COMPENDIUM OF THE SOCIAL DOCTRINE OF THE CHURCH, 2004, available at http://www.vatican.va/roman_curia/pontifical_councils/justpeace/documents/rc_pc_justpeace_doc_20060526_compendio-dott-soc_en.html

bonded together through a socially-approved covenant of marriage to regulate sexuality, to bear, raise, and protect children, to provide mutual care and protection, to create a small home economy, and to maintain continuity between the generations, those going before and those coming after. It is out of the reciprocal, naturally recreating relations of the family that broader communities grow, such as tribes, villages, peoples, and nations.[126] However, it will be wrong for Christians to stick to the old-fashioned understanding of marriage as an institution where women are not equal to men. Likewise, it will be wrong for industrialized nations to understand global trade as an avenue for perpetrating inequality. As an expression of the concept of "family of nations," international trade is characterized by equality of participating parties, *i.e.,* WTO Members.

The Church teaches that people are the true members of the "family of nations"; the States are only instruments. In that light, Pope John Paul II taught that the United Nations must be a place where nations recognize one another as members of a "family," inspired by mutual solidarity and by a concern for the common good of all humanity.[127] In the light of this vision, Pope Benedict XVI emphasized that the concept of family is associated with the "responsibility to protect," as a concrete expression of concern for the weakest members of the society.[128] The responsibility to protect projects the image of the family in reference to the United Nations as a community founded on interdependence, on mutual trust, on reciprocal aid, and on sincere respect.[129]

The family of nations has the responsibility to look after the weakest members,[130] and not to engage them in competition in unfair circumstances.

---

[126] *See generally,* Murdock G. P., SOCIAL STRUCTURES, New York, Macmillan, (1949) and William N. Stephens, THE FAMILY IN CROSS-CULTURE PERSPECTIVE, New York, Holt, Reinhart and Winston, (1963).

[127] *See* Lombardi Editorial, The Family of Nations on the Vatican Radio, The Voice of the Pope and the Church in Dialogue with the World, September 30, 2011 available at http://en.radiovaticana.va/news/2011/10/08; see also Archbishop Dominique Mamberti, Holy See on Main Challenges Facing the Family of Nations, An Address Given on Tuesday October 8, 2011, at the 66th Session of the U.N. General Assembly, available at http://www.zenith.org/en/articles

[128] *Id.*

[129] *Id.*

[130] *See* Archbishop Dominique Mamberti, the Secretary for Relations with States in the Vatican Secretariat of States, at the 66th Session of the United Nations General Assembly,

It may be good to elaborate a little more on the duty to protect regarding the concept of "family of nations" from the Church's perspective. The Catholic Church teaches that,

> The responsibility to protect must be understood not only in terms of military intervention, which should always be the last recourse, but above all, as an imperative for the international community to be united before the crisis and to create agencies for correct and sincere negotiations, to support the moral force of law, to seek the common good, and to incite governments, civil society and public opinion to identify the causes and to offer solutions to crises of all kinds, acting in close collaboration and solidarity with the affected populations and placing above all, the integrity and security of all the citizens. Hence it is important that the responsibility to protect is the criterion and motivation that underlies all the work of the States and of the United Nations Organization to restore peace, security and the rights of man.[131]

The Church proffers its abundant saving resources in its eloquent expression of its solidarity and respectful affection for the whole human family to which it belongs. Because the Church identifies every aspect of the society as belonging to the human family, it always calls for dialogue between them in finding a common solution to the different problems that may confront them in any way.[132]

1.4.7 Concepts of "Free Trade" and "Fair Trade"

In the struggle for commercial co-existence and ecological sustenance, several trade policies have been formulated in view of globalization. To make concrete the goal of globalization, the General Agreements on Tariffs and Trade (GATT) was signed at the UN Conference for Trade and Employment in 1947, subsequently culminating in the birth of the

---

September 30, 2011.

131 *Id.*

132 SECOND VATICAN ECUMENICAL COUNCIL, GAUDIUM ET SPES (Pastoral Constitution on the Church in the Modern World), *supra* note 75, at 3.

WTO in 1995. The main objective of the GATT-WTO system was to promote "free trade" among Members by the reduction of tariff burdens on importers. When the ethical values of "free trade" were questioned, "fair trade" came into being. However, these two concepts of commerce between countries are often confused with each other, and there are many misconceptions surrounding both ideas.

Though the bid to increase industrialization has great benefits, it also has its negative impacts: environmental destruction, labor exploitation, increasing inequalities, and so on. This is a result of free trade which is widely practiced all around the world. For example, sometimes we find ourselves paying a lower price for a product because the cost of production was brought down to a minimum by paying minimum wages to the workers employed. This scenario occurs in our world. But we have to bear in mind, too, that not every low-priced product is a result of free trade, and not every high-priced product is an output of fair trade.

Free trade is understood as liberalization of trade with no government interference in the form of regulations, tariffs, quotas, or taxes, which allow producers to yield, manufacture, or sell their products within, as well as outside, domestic frontiers. By this, producers can price their products at lower rates, which further stimulate competition. On the downside, benefits like tax holidays and subsidies to domestic producers are also withdrawn. Free trade is also characterized by unrestricted flow of labor, materials, goods, and funds. Because of these features of "free trade," countries tend to endorse free trade agreements.

Moreover, consumers applaud "free trade" because increased competitiveness, due to the presence of international producers, compels domestic producers to deliver high quality products at reasonable prices which are at par with the competition. The consumer, therefore, has a wide variety of the same product from which to choose. Without free trade, consumers would have limited choices in the market. With its feature of "no government intervention" policy, free trade can lead to monopoly in the international markets, especially when corporations from developed countries take advantage of such trade frolicking to unleash unfair practices. Experience shows that free trade negatively impacts the environment, which accumulates overtime. When this happens, as we can see from the ongoing debates on climate change, the consumer ultimately pays a heavy price in the long run. This price far outweighs the benefits of low-cost, widely varied products.

The main objective for "free trade" markets is to bridge the gap between the poor and the rich, to stimulate economic growth, and to raise the quality of life. Unfortunately, multinational corporations from industrialized nations engage in "free trade" to knowingly or unknowingly exploit farmers, especially farmers in poorer countries. Activities of extractive industries not only degrade the environment but also impoverish farmers as a result. The concept of "free trade" may sound very lucrative, and it may come across as a viable trade mechanism that brings all the market forces to perfect balance. However, this very idea is contradicted by the fact that not everyone involved in this process is given equal opportunity by means of fair access to resources.

The concept of "fair trade"[133] was developed to focus on promoting, inter alia, poverty alleviation and sustainable development, gender equality, fair working conditions, transparency and accountability in the global trading system, and sound environmental practices.[134] Thus, fair trade is concerned with exchanges that follow the demands of justice. Fair trade seeks to promote equitable labor practices and environmental and social

---

[133] Fair trade has been defined as,

A trading partnership based on dialogue, transparency, and respect that seeks greater equity in international trade. It contributes to sustainable development by offering better trading conditions to, and securing the rights of, marginalized producers and workers – especially in the south.

See FAIR TRADE RESOURCE NETWORK (FTRN) www.FTRN.org ; *see also* the definition of "Fair Trade" by the INTERNATIONAL FAIR-TRADE ASSOCIATION, NETWORK OF EUROPEAN WORLD SHOPS AND EUROPEAN FAIR TRADE ASSOCIATION, *quoted in* Cephas Lumina, "Free Trade or Just Trade? The World Trade Organization, Human Rights and Development" (part 1), 14 LAW DEMOCRACY, & DEVELPOMENT, (2010), p. 26, available at www.ajol.info/index.php/ldd/article/viewFile/68289/56371 last visited September 23, 2013.

[Advocates of Fair Trade argue its focus is to help developing countries overcome lingering effects of centuries of colonialism, which created an export oriented economy and a commercial infrastructure that promotes exports. Fair Trade is to help re-engineer the value chain of production so that more value stays in a poor country, and is distributed across the society of the producers as a whole.] *See* John Sweeney, "Why Fair Trade Does not Mean an End to Free Trade," FINANCIAL TIMES, 29November 2006, p. 15; *see also* RAJ BHALA, DICTIONARY OF INTERNATIONAL TRADE LAW, *supra* note 111, p. 297.

[134] *Id.*

standards in the production of goods and services that are exported from poor countries to developed countries.

Fair trade advocates focus on the wages and working conditions of labor in developing markets. For example, a fair-trade advocate will fight to increase the wage rates of workers and improve their working conditions, especially when a large multinational corporation chooses to pay pennies per hour for labor in one country instead of dozens of dollars per hour elsewhere. Proponents of fair trade suggest that companies and governments should regulate trade to ensure that workers receive a just level of compensation and a safe working environment.

Countries practicing fair trade aim at protecting domestic producers. Women and the disabled are greatly benefited by the fair-trade policy as they are paid fair wages for their work. The government provides support to producers by providing them with credit, training, and advanced technological equipment. Fair trade truly seeks to bring a balance between producers belonging to developed, developing, and under-developed countries.

The market approaches for goods produced under free trade and fair trade are distinct from each other. While free trade aims at attracting more consumers to increase sales turnover and generate more profits, fair trade aims at educating the consumers about the benefits of producing goods without the exploitation of labor or the environment. Thus, fair trade mainly thrives on the demand created by the consumers for such products. Often, fair trade products may not be labeled so because labeling has not been made mandatory by most governments. However, free trade products may be labeled as being "recycled" or "sustainably cultivated," but it does not mean that these products were produced with fair means. In 2009, the Fairtrade Labeling Organizations International (FLO) reported that the sales turnover of fair trade products was €3.4 billion, showing an upward trend. The practice of fair trade has helped 1.2 million farmers so far by providing adequate infrastructure to improve living conditions and garner sufficient funds to harvest crops over the past 40 years.

Trade is deemed ineffective in fulfilling the objectives for which it was formed if it fails to solve certain economic problems of developed and developing nations alike, as well as for the producers and consumers. Some economists have criticized fair trade, interpreting it as being a means to cover up an inefficient market system. The case of Nestle, which is deemed as the world's largest food and Nutrition Company, is informative here. In 2005, Nestle was criticized as the globally "least responsible company" for its role in provoking the coffee crisis, which left millions of coffee producers cash-strapped. To improve its public image, in 2007, the company ran a fair-trade campaign for its coffee called "Coffee with conscience." The heavily promoted advertisements stated that Nestle was trying to enhance the living condition of farmers affected by low coffee prices (the fate brought about by the company itself).

Internationally recognized consumer brands like Sainsbury, Cadbury, and Starbucks have already initiated a fair-trade conversion process for their products. The government's efforts to effectuate a prosperous economy can be achieved by the co-existence of "free trade" and "fair trade." The latter can help bring poor farmers and producers up to par with their affluent counterparts, so they can participate in free trade with equal opportunity. This can only be effective on the condition that producers do not resort to unethical practices to bring down costs. When "free trade" and "fair trade" co-exist harmoniously, a globally effective trading system is realizable.

CHAPTER TWO

Review of Scholarly Literature on the Holy See, Catholic Social Justice Theory, and the GATT-WTO System

The exploration of understanding the social mission of the Church in the GATT-WTO system is extremely difficult without some available literature on the GATT-WTO system, social justice, and on the Holy See. This book owes its successful completion to the scholarly literary works of renowned authors and analysts.

This Chapter concentrates on the major scholarly works that are related to the influence of the Holy See in the GATT-WTO system with special attention to the social mission of the Church and social justice in international trade law. This chapter is divided into two sections. They are the *Survey of Major* Sources and an *Analysis of Major Sources*. The *Survey of Major Sources* focuses on key literary works directly related to, and relevant to, an understanding of the Church as an institution, the social mission of the Church, social justice, and international trade. The literature review aims to reveal the principal contributions of the main books relating to the topic of this book. The second section, an *Analysis of the Major Sources*, examines the relevant substantive findings and conclusions drawn from the literary works. These have provided the foundations for this book and have also paved the way for the need for further research on the subject.

2.1 Survey of the Major Sources

These sources examine topics such as (1) The Legal and Political Nature of the Holy See, (2) The Catholic Social Doctrine and the Social Mission of the Church, and (3) The GATT-WTO System. Analyzing these sources this this segment of chapter Two highlights the uniqueness of the Church's social mission in the GATT-WTO system as it relates to social justice, especially against the backdrop of concepts of injustice, inequality, and exploitation. The sub-sections are treated systematically from an analytical standpoint.

2.2 Legal and Political Nature of the Holy See

The literature reviewed critically in this sub-section provides the overall background of the historical event that characterizes the role of the Holy See as the "moral voice" of the world. This historical analysis focuses specifically on circumstances and controversies that surround the recognition of the Holy See in international law and politics.

The sources that fall under this category are:

1. Hyginus Eugene Cardinale, THE HOLY SEE AND THE INTERNATIONAL ORDER (1976)
2. James Crawford, THE CREATION OF STATES IN INTERNATIONAL LAW (2006)
3. Roman A. Melnyk, VATICAN DIPLOMACY AT THE UNITED NATIONS: A HISTORY OF CATHOLIC GLOBAL ENGAGEMENT (2009)
4. Robert F. Illing, AMERICA AND THE VATICAN: TRADING INFORMATION ATER WWII (2011)
5. Cyrus Shahrad, SECRETS OF THE VATICAN (2007)
6. Daniel L. Bethlehem ed., THE OXFORD HANDBOOK OF INTERNATIONAL TRADE LAW (2009)
7. Robert John Araujo & John A. Lucal, PAPAL DIPLOMACY AND THE QUEST FOR PEACE: THE VATICAN AND

INTERNATIONAL ORGANIZATIONS FROM THE EARLY YEARS TO THE LEAGUE OF NATIONS (2004)

8. Bernad J. O'Connor, PAPAL DIPLOMACY: JOHN PAUL II AND THE CULTURE OF PEACE (2005)
9. Jorri C. Duursma, FRAGMENTATION AND THE INTERNATIONAL RELATIONS OF MICRO-STATES: SELF-DETERMINATION AND STATEHOOD (1996)
10. Michael Collins, THE VATICAN (2011)
11. Bart McDowell, INSIDE THE VATICAN (2005)
12. Reese J. Thomas, INSIDE THE VATICAN: THE POLITICS AND ORGANIZATION OF THE CATHOLIC CHURCH (1998)
13. Francis X. Blouin Jr., ed., VATICAN ARCHIVES: AN INVENTORY AND GUIDE TO HISTORICAL DOCUMENTS OF THE HOLY SEE (1998)
14. Vincent Viaene ed., THE PAPACY AND THE NEW WORLD ORDER: VATICAN DIPLOMACY, CATHOLIC OPINION AND INTERNATIONAL POLITICS AT THE TIME OF LEO XIII (2005)
15. Robert Calderisi, EARTHLY MISSION: THE CATHOLIC CHURCH AND WORLD DEVELOPMENT (2013)
16. Avro Manhattan, THE VATICAN IN WORLD POLITICS (1949)

For a long period of time, and even to the present, there has been a heated debate among scholars and observers about what the mission of the Catholic Church in the world is all about. Some scholars reason that the mission of the Church in the world is to evangelize while others opine that the Church's mission is to civilize. Those who propose evangelization as her primary mission argue that even if the Church is to civilize, it should be a strictly religious, supernatural goal.[135] Their argument is that Christ

[135] *See generally,* Michael Fahye, "The Mission of the Church: To Divinize or to Humanize?" *Proceedings CTSA* (1976); Dean M. Kelley, WHY CONSERVATIVE CHURCHES ARE GROWING (1977); Jeffrey K. Hadden, THE GATHERING STORM IN THE CHURCHES (1969); Lothar Rütti, ZUR THEOLOGIE DER MISSION (1977); Thomas Kramm, ANALYSR UND BEWÄHRUNG THEOLOGISCHER MODELLE ZUR BEGRÜNDUNG DER MISSION (1979); Roger D. Haight, "Mission: The Symbol for

gave the Church "no proper mission in the political, economic, or social order."[136] They reason that the Church will have surrendered her original calling to the world if she redirects her energy pursuing social mission as precondition for her evangelization.[137] Proponents of social justice issues as the preoccupation of the Church in her mission reason strongly that the Church will fail in her mission if she is oblivious of the political, cultural and socio-economic problems facing humanity.

These two positions, which originated in the United States, made an unnecessary attempt at dividing the Church's many tasks without exploring how these two positions are interrelated. Such efforts only dichotomize between the dual roles on the Church in the world, and such is unnecessary because such an exercise runs the risk of prioritizing one task as much more specifically related to the Church's mission than the other. In fact, we must make it crystal clear that both responsibilities are central to the Church's mission. Any attempt at drawing a dividing line causes more problems than it may solve.

The proclamation of God's reign has legal, political, and socio-economic implications. The literary works lined up under the key sources show that all activities of the Church as interconnected. These sources, *inter alia*, address questions regarding the history of the gradual involvement of the Holy See in the world along with the corresponding development of its legal status in international law. They also examine, on a more practical level, the evolution of the relationship between international intergovernmental organizations and the Holy See, especially in the light of the right and duty of the Church to proclaim, always and everywhere, the

---

Understanding the Church Today," *TS 37* (1976); Roger L. Shinn, "Political Theology in the Crossffire," Journal of Current Social Issues 10 (1972); Jacques Ellul, THE POLITICAL ILLUSION, (1967), FALSE PRSENCE OF THE KINGDOM (1972), THE POLITICS OF GOD AND THE POLITICS OF MAN (1972); Richard S. Wheeler, PAGANS IN THE PULPIT 9174).

[136] *See* Flannery Austin ed., Vatican II - *Guadium et Spes* (*The Pastoral Constitution On The Church In The Modern World),* December 7, 1965, no. 42 ; Pope Pius XII, Allocution to Historians and Artists, *AAS 48 (1956*), P. 212.

[137] *See generally,* John A. Coleman, "American Catholicism and Strategic Social Theology," in *The Catholic Church: The United States Experience*, Irene Woodward ed., (1978); John A. Coleman, "The Mission of the Church and Action on Behalf of Justice," *Jurist* 39 (1979); James M. Gustafson, The Church as Moral Decision Maker (1962); This is based on American and Latin American emphasis on cultural pluralism and voluntarism.

moral principles in relation to the fundamental rights of the human person, who is naturally endowed with dignity.[138]In the entirety of its activities, the Church does not deemphasize any of its spiritual, moral, or socio-political principles for any reason. The body of literature listed under this category is characterized by its account of the involvement of the Church in all the events that involve the human person from time immemorial. An analysis of some of the books listed lays credence to this assertion.

For example, in *Fragmentation and the International Relations of Micro-States* (1996), Jorri Duursma provides a thorough international legal account of the European micro-states, the Vatican being one of them. This book examines the notions of self-determination and statehood in the context of international law and provides solutions for problems of secession. It explains that the Lateran Agreements between Italy and the Holy See in 1929 established the Vatican City and gave the State its present territory. The book states the Vatican City, seat of the Holy See, comprises the smallest entity to claim statehood. Characterized by the Vatican's lack of a permanent population, lack of territorial entity status, and being subordinate to the Holy See, this book raises concern over the Vatican's claim to statehood under the traditional criteria.

Jorri Duursma, however, posits "constitutive" and "reparative" theories as solutions to the deficiencies of the Vatican in statehood attributes. What her theories imply, ordinarily, is that the recognition and admission of the micro-states in international organizations, including the Vatican, not only makes up for the lack of conventional statehood attributes but also repairs and constitutes the legal status of the entities as States. In fact,

[138] *See generally,* Melnyk Roman A., VATICAN DIPLOMACY AT THE UNITED NATIONS: A HISTORY OF CATHOLIC GLOBAL ENGAGEMENT, (2009); Canon 747 §2 of THE CODE OF CANON LAW, 1983; Illing Robert E., AMERICA AND THE VATICAN: TRADING INFRMATION AFTER WORLD WAR II (2011); Manhattan Avro, THE VATICAN IN WORLD POLITICS (1949); Robert John Araujo & John A Lucal, PAPAL DIPLOMACY AND THE QUEST FOR PEACE: THE VATICAN AND INTERNATIONAL ORGANIZATIONS FROM THE EARLY YEARS TO THE LEAGUE OF NATIONS (2004); Bernard J. O'Connor, PAPAL DIPLOMACY: JOHN PAUL II AND THE CULTURE OF PEACE (2005); Michael Collins, THE VATICAN (2011);Reese J. Thomas, INSIDE THE VATICAN: THE POLITICS AND ORGANIZATION OF THE CATHOLIC CHURCH (1998); Vincent Viaene ed., THE PAPACY AND THE NEW WORLD ORDER: VATICAN DIPLOMACY, CATHOLIC OPINION AND INTERNATIONAL POLITICS AT THE TIME OF LEO XIII (2005).

what Duursma reasons that notwithstanding the deficiency of statehood criteria, a micro-state becomes a state by and through recognition and admission into international organizations. Through this process, the United Nations not only offers recognition of their sovereign equality but also enhances that sovereignty by providing more juridical certainty and political protection against external interference in their internal affairs.[139]

Much credit should be given to Duursma for her innovative thoughts on this issue. Still, it is worth noting that today, the classic doctrines of recognition and declaratory and constitutive theories are no longer self-contained, nor are they mutually exclusive. They are now understood as steps that assist observers in focusing their analysis of incidents of recognition. They are used in tandem to describe different aspects of recognition and describe the distinguishing features, not so much of the institution of state recognition generally, but rather of incidents of recognition.

Instead of looking for new theories to prove Vatican statehood, it is more informative to know that though it may be debatable, the Vatican City appears to meet the capacity requirement for statehood. The unique status of the Holy See has developed over many centuries, during which it was accepted by other states as possessing international authority. The international personality of the Holy See cannot be said to be created by the Lateran Treaty, which merely created the State of the Vatican City.[140] The Holy See bases its international status on its religious and spiritual authority, not on the territory of the Vatican City.[141]

---

139 Duursma Jorri C., Fragmentation and the International Relations of Micro-States: Self-Determination and Statehood, (Cambridge Studies in International and Comparative Law), Cambridge University Press, 1996, p. 142 (emphasis added).

140 See generally Grant Richard W., THE HOLY SEE IN INTERNATIONAL RELATIONS (1986); Gratsch Edward J., THE HOLY SEE AND THE UNITED NATIONS 1945-1995 (1997); Hyginus Eugene Cardinale, THE HOLY SEE AND THE INTERNATIONAL ORDER (1976) (showing that the Holy See has three different meanings. It can be used to indicate the Pope; it can refer to the other departments of Church government; it is also used to describe the Pope as the visible head of the Church. "Holy See" is also sometimes used to denote the spiritual organization of Papal government).

141 *See* RESTATEMENT (THIRD) OF THE FOREIGN RELATIONS LAW OF THE UNITED STATES [sections] 201 (1986), in Louis Henkin *et al.*, INTERNATIONAL LAW CASES AND MATERIALS 24 (3rd ed. 1993), at 300.

James Crawford, in his 2006 book *The Creation of States in International Law*, acknowledges that "the legal status of the Vatican City has been the subject of much study and some controversy," but admits that "the position of the Vatican City State is peculiar and criterion for statehood in its case only marginally (if at all) complied with."[142] Following the traditional requirements of statehood, some have rightly concluded that "the Vatican does not meet the criteria for statehood" because it has no accredited diplomats, for a start, and only serves as a territorial prop for the Holy See, which ratifies most of the treaties.[143] However, concerning this criticism, Crawford reasons that the relationship between Vatican City and the Holy See "is a matter for some perplexity."

Furthermore, Crawford argues that the best modern characterization of this issue is that "the Holy See is not a state in international law, but has an international legal personality of its own which permits it to take international actions such as the conclusion of treaties and maintenance of diplomatic relations."[144] This conclusion has led others to opine that the Vatican City claim to statehood is doubtful, and the personality of the Holy See, as a politico-religious hybrid, is "even more difficult to solve" and can only be characterized by the way individual states relate to it.[145] Not surprisingly, this conclusion, intentionally or not, potentially marginalizes the voice of the Holy See in international legal, economic, and political affairs.

Notwithstanding the above legal reasoning, other sources examine the issue of statehood as it relates to the Vatican City State and Holy See from

---

[142] James Crawford, *supra* note 23, at 221-5.

[143] *See* Article 1 of the Montevideo Convention on the Rights and Duties of States, Montevideo, Uruguay, December 26, 1933 which came into force on December 26, 1934, available at http://www.cfr.org/sovereignty/montevideo-convention-rights-duties-states/p15897 This treaty was signed at the International Conference of American States in Montevideo, at the Seventh International Conference of American States. *See also* TRIGGS GILLIAN D., INTERNATIONAL LAW: CONTEMPORARY PRINCIPLES AND PRACTICES (2006).

[144] JAMES CRAWFORD, *citing* Jorri Duursma, Fragmentation and International Relations of Micro-States: Self-Determination and Statehood, p. 225.

[145] *See for example*, BROWNLIE IAN, PRINCIPLES OF PUBLIC INTERNATIONAL LAW (2003); Crawford James, BROWNLIE'S PRINCIPLES OF PUBLIC INTERNATIONAL LAW (2013); ROBERT F. ILLING, AMERICA AND THE VATICAN: TRADING INFORMATION AFTER WORLD WAR II (2011).

a different perspective. They assert that the Vatican diplomatic experience is tremendously strategic in the international personality of the Holy See, which indirectly incorporates the Vatican City State. Bernard J. O'Connor, in his 2005 book, *Papal Diplomacy: John Paul II and the Culture of Peace,* writes that Pope John Paul II was among the most experienced diplomats on the international scene, thereby unifying the issues of authority and statehood of the Holy See with that of the Vatical City State (or Vatican simply put).

Bernard O'Connor reasons that during his 25-year pontificate, John Paul II gave over 2,000 speeches to representatives of the United Nations, to 172 ambassadors accredited to the Holy See, to non-governmental entities, and to inter-governmental organizations. He writes that this staggering number of major speeches – roughly 80 every year, or one about every 4 or 5 days – is organized around diverse themes: international collaboration, human rights awareness, diplomatic negotiation, the dignity of the human person, sovereignty, freedom, and promoting the culture of peace, to mention but a few. The themes bespeak the wealth of the diplomatic experience of the Holy See on the international arena in execution of its mission to the whole world.

Explaining the reason for the Holy See's wealth of expertise on diplomatic issues, Michael Collins in his 2011 book, *The Vatican,* traces the 2000-year long history of the Church and Papal influence characterized by priceless treasures. Similarly, in *Inside the Vatican*, McDowell Bart examines centuries of Vatican history, describing the days of the Roman Empire, the glorious years of the Renaissance, and the power struggle between the Church and State which endured from the late 7th century until 1929. These long years of its dogged existence explains the uniqueness of the Vatican and Holy See in the world in terms of its extraordinary power, influence, and endurance on international issues affecting human beings and society.

Inside the Vatican: The Politics and Organization of the Catholic Church, authored by Reese J. Thomas in 1998, is worthy of mention. Reese describes the Vatican as a unique international institution, again in terms of extraordinary power and influence. The Catholic Church is not known as the Vatican, and so when Reese refers to the Vatican as an "institution" or "organization," it sounds like he is using incorrectly the Vatican synonymously with the Holy See or Catholic Church. However, Reese is entirely correct in appreciating the structuring of the Vatican and showing how the bureaucracy of congregations, agencies, secretariats, tribunals, nunciatures, and offices harmoniously serve the universal Church. This arrangement functions powerfully well in a changing world to be able to face the challenges of the new millennium. Even more fascinating is Reese's account of the period of the 2,000 years in which the Church has been effectively structured. Long centuries of endurance account for the Church's international uniqueness, while realizing its universal mission of promoting and defending the dignity of the human person in all its ramifications.

Francis X. Blouin Jr., in his 1998 *Vatican Archives: An Inventory and Guide to Historical Documents of the Holy See,* examines the wisdom of the Holy See and Vatican preserving official records produced by the Vatican administrative agency. This account is a resource of incomparable richness for the history of the papacy and the governments, organizations, and agencies as well as the countries with which the papacy has been in contact. The account explains the historical prowess of the Holy See and thereby outlines the systematic way the Church has approached the world in its universal mission. The result is a research tool that enhances and expedites access to a broad range of disciplines. This tool, coupled with other works mentioned, demonstrates that the Holy See has "grown grey hairs," as Africans say, in its involvement in international affairs.

The implication of the many years of the Holy See's presence in international affairs is that the Catholic Church is one of the most experienced, if not the most experienced, entity in influencing world affairs. In her mission on earth, especially her social mission, the Church shares the message of hope from her unique wealth of experience. Whether the Holy See, strictly speaking, satisfies the Montevideo Convention requirements for statehood or not, as so many writers like Gillian Triggs, and Ian Brownlie[146] and a host of others have doubted, is not the issue. The crux of the matter is the international recognition over many years

---

[146] *See generally* Ian Brownlie, "Boundary Problems and Formation of New States" in D. Freestone, *et al* (eds.), *Contemporary Issues in International Law: A Collection of the Josephine Onoh Memorial Lectures* (1974); "Rebirth of the State" in M.D. Evans (ed.), *Aspects of Statehood and Institutionalism in Contemporary Europe* (1997).

by many governments around the world and the endurance and resilience of the Holy See, which is longer and stronger than all governments. Not surprisingly, therefore, "nearly every country maintains diplomatic ties with the Holy See, and for which it has long secured Permanent Observer status at the United Nations."[147]

Roman Melnyk takes the above argument to another level. His 2009 book, *Vatican Diplomacy at the United Nations: A History of Catholic Global Engagement* commemorates the 45th year of the Holy See's mission at the United Nations. *Vatican Diplomacy at the United Nations* is a critical review of the history of the Holy See's human rights diplomacy by moral exhortation from its inception in the family of the United Nations to the present period. The book, in broad terms, gives an account of the developmental ecclesial history, diplomatic ecclesiology, ecclesiastical laws and operational policies, practices and procedures that regulate the ecclesiastical administration and practice of the professional pontifical ecclesiastical Foreign Service ministry and diplomatic mission apostolate of the universal Church. Roman Melnyk's goal is to situate Vatican diplomacy as it relates to international diplomacy in the United Nations.

In all these activities, the Holy See applies its *sui generis* ecclesiastical moral rights of diplomacy of conscience. In doing so, the interest of the Holy See in the international arena is defined as one to promote the common good and the dignity of each human person on earth. That interest, simply put, is the social mission of the Holy See on the world

---

[147] *See* "Consequences of the Catholic Church's claim of Statehood," in *Los Angeles Times*, April 11, 2010; Ian Brownlie, "Rebirth of Statehood" in ASPECTS OF STATEHOOD AND INSTITUTIONALISM IN CONTEMPORARY EUROPE 5(Malcolm D. Evans ed., 1996); Hugh M. Kindred et al. eds., INTERNATIONAL LAW CHIEFLY AS INTERPRETED AND APPLIED IN CANADA (1987); O'Connell D.P., INTERNATIONAL LAW (1970); Oppenheim Lassa F.L., INTERNATIONAL LAW: A TREATISE (1955); Hentin Louis, INTERNATIONAL LAW: POLITICS AND VALUES (1995); Barry E. Carter & Philip R. Trimble, INTERNATIONAL LAW 411 (1991); . (States, international organizations, individuals, corporations, and other entities have varying status under international law); *see also* Roalyn Higgins, PROBLEMS AND PROCESS: INTERNATIONAL LAW AND HOW WE USE IT 39(1994)("The classic view has been that international applies only to stats."); Ignazseidl-Hohenveldern, CORPORATIONS UNDER INTERNATIONAL LAW 5 (1987) ("The idea that public international law addressed itself only to states and that therefore only states could be persons and subjects under public international law was not abandoned until the end of the 19th century.").

stage. This unique mission sets the Holy See apart from every other nation or institution in the world.

Melnyk examines the impact of the Holy See's diplomatic engagement in international law and politics as one that has developed since the 19th century. The Catholic Church was present at the signing of the United Nations Charter and has been influential as a Permanent Observer at the United Nations. So, *Vatican Diplomacy* points out that though the Church's professional pontifical ecclesiastical diplomatic apostolate of women and the laity is yet to be fully realized, the Holy See has effectively engaged on international issues in the 21st century, including issues such as environmental/human ecological and biotechnological diplomacy.

The Holy See's diplomatic practice and procedure have been influenced since 2004 by the dynamism and upgrade occasioned by the publication of the *Compendium of the Social Doctrine of the Church* by the Pontifical Council for Justice and Peace. That is why Dr. Melnyk goes on to trace how the moral, legal, and diplomatic obligation of the Holy See is periodically reviewed to be upgraded and to redefine the diplomatic permanent observer stature and operational status of the Holy See. The Catholic Church reiterates this point stating: "The immediate aim for the Vatican Council was to let some fresh air into the Church and to promote within her an *aggiornamento*."[148] The Church guards and teaches her sacred deposit of Christian doctrine more effectively and is determined never to depart from the sacred treasure of truth. She must ever look to the present, to the new conditions and the new forms of life introduced into the modern world.[149]

Vatican Diplomacy highlights the great presence of the Holy See at the United Nations within the context of current world events and its important contribution to the work of the United Nations in the service of humanity. This book is superb, unearthing the uniqueness of the

[148] Bishop Butler Dom B.C., *The Theology of Vatican II,* Darton, Longman & Todd, 1967 & 1981, p.6. (The term *aggiornamento* is an Italian word usually translated as "bringing up to date," updating or renewal. In his opening speech at the opening of the Vatican II Council on October 11, 1962, Pope John XXIII said, "In the present development of human events, through which mankind appears to be entering a new order, one must, rather, discern a hidden plan of Divine Providence." He also said that the purpose of the Vatican II is to "let in some fresh air into the Church.").

[149] *See* Pope John Paul II's opening speech to the Second Vatican Council, October 11, 1962.

international presence of the Holy See in promoting social justice from the United Nations' perspective. This is especially true in the diplomatic mission of the universal Church for the cause of preserving the international diplomatic civil and moral order and for the cause of achieving the moral diplomatic excellence of human rights, justice, and peace.

Accordingly, this book takes the holistic view of the Holy See's mission in the world. Therefore, the work edited by Vincent Viaene and published in 2005 is relevant. The book, *The Papacy and the New World Order: Vatican Diplomacy, Catholic Opinion and International Politics at the Time of Leo XIII,* depicts the Holy See as "Director-general of the Humanitarian forces of the world." That status of the Holy See is much needed in the world, where nations and institutions have become more than ever the motors of globalization as against the interest of the human person, whose dignity ought to be more important in every life event.

The presence of the Holy See in international affairs has been a long and intricate story that spans centuries with its enormous influence.[150] The 2004 book, *Papal Diplomacy and the Quest for Peace,* gives an account of the Holy See and its long relationship with the international order. Authors Robert Araujo and John Lucal explore the institutional framework within which the Holy See has engaged temporal sovereigns through active involvement in international organizations. The authors also analyze the similarities and differences as to how the spiritual and temporal sovereigns conduct themselves in these organizations. The objective of this venture, according to *Papal Diplomacy and the Quest for Peace,* is that the Holy See wants to exert its influence in the venue of these international organizations to ensure that the voices of all, not just some, but all human beings are adequately heard.

2.2.1 Critical Analysis

The foregoing literary works give credence to the central thesis of this book - that in its international presence, the Holy See has no selfish

[150] *See* Lucal A. John & Araujo Robert John, Papal Diplomacy and the Quest for Peace: The Vatican and International Organizations from the Early Years to the League of Nations (2004).

secular agenda but rather, advocates social justice for all. It is significant to recount the history of the Holy See and Vatican diplomacy because such history provides a valuable perspective on the role of the Church in international affairs. From early times, the Holy See has been an expression of the Church's focus for a more just and humane world as expressed in international law and relations between states.

The Church employs membership - that is, her Permanent Observer status in international organizations and institutions to project her mission in multilateral relation, to raise freely her moral voice in favor of peace, the dignity of the person, religious liberty, and other issues the Church upholds for the good of all humanity.[151] The literature reviewed in this sub-section reveals the evolution of the relationship between international intergovernmental organizations and the Holy See, particularly the link with other international bodies, in the light of the right and duty of the Church to proclaim everywhere the moral principles in relation to the fundamental rights of the human person.[152]

This book does not preoccupy itself with proving the authenticity of Vatican statehood because the exercise has been controversial and, in any event, is not directly pertinent to the social justice theory and international trade law. The books that concentrate on proving or disproving the validity of Vatican statehood do not offer much for this book. Moreover, when the real implications of the position of the Vatican in the life of the Catholic Church are understood, such proof becomes unnecessary. The proof of statehood of the Vatican is not as crucial to the thesis of this book as is the recognition of the Holy See as an international person and recognition of the juridical personification of the ministry of the Pope.

The Church does not join international organizations based on the grounds of her statehood but as a sign of her esteem for these organizations; her recognition of international organizations as instruments of unity between States as well as instruments of service to the entire human family; and above all, her willingness to offer her unique contributions to building international relations, which is important to the promotion of

---

[151] *See* Roman A. Melnyk, Vatican Diplomacy, *supra* note 24.

[152] *See* Canon 747 § 2 of the 1983 Code of Canon Law.

human dignity.[153] That is why the Holy See's Permanent Observer status is appropriate from its neutral stance.

Thus, most of the sources above are relevant to this book in terms of their concentration on the many years of the Holy See's engagement in world affairs through utilization of the resources available in international organizations, agencies, and institutions. For book to prove successfully the thesis it sets out prove, and which centers on the Holy See's advocacy in support of human rights and dignity in the context of the GATT-WTO system, it must show the Holy See is well positioned in the world for this purpose. The diplomatic expertise of the Church is historically resilient and well-structured so much so that the Church has successfully ventured into venues in which issues that affect the dignity of the human person are discussed.

The GATT and its successor, the WTO, are such institutions, and indeed are the leading ones in international trade law at the multilateral level. For this reason, the Church has established healthy relations with most countries of the world, including most WTO Members (China being a notable exception). In business parlance, if you do not say, "Here I am," nobody will say, "There you are." The Church does not embark on its mission for any selfish business purposes rather her involvement is for the common good of all humanity. To do so, it needs to say, "Here I am" as a Permanent Observer at the WTO, and WTO Members need to say, "There you are."

2.3 Secular Philosophy and Social Justice Theory

This sub-section has no direct relevance to the topic of this discussion, but some contributors have analyzed some secular principles of social justice in such a way as to apply concrete human experiences that are relevant to Catholic Social Justice Theory. Because some of these concrete human experiences are relevant to Catholic social justice, this section of literature review analyzes a few of them that may be relevant and readily available as a way of advancing the whole argument herein. They include:

[153] *See* Address of His Holiness Pope Benedict XVI to the General Assembly of the United Nations Organization, New York, April 18, 2008; also available at *UN/GA 58/314* (2008).

1. John Stuart Mill, *Utilitarianism and Other Writings,* ed. Mary Warnock (1962)
2. Brian Barry, WHY SOCIAL JUSTICE MATTERS (2005)
3. Thomas Patrick Burke, THE CONCEPT OF JUSTICE: IS SOCIAL JUSTICE JUST? (2013)
4. Sayyid Qutb, SOCIAL JUSTICE IN ISLAM (2000)
5. Rose George, NINETY PERCENT OF EVERYTHING: INSIDE SHIPPING, THE INVISIBLE INDUSTRY THAT PUTS CLOTHES ON YOUR BACK, GAS IN YOUR CAR, AND FOOD ON YOUR TABLE (2013)

The book *Economic Justice: Philosophical and Legal Perspectives,* edited by Helen Stacey, contains a good number of papers that examine the economic impact of the U. S. financial market meltdown of 2008 and its devastating impact both in the U. S. and worldwide. One consequence of this crisis is the widening of the gap between rich and poor. With little end in sight to global economic woes, it has never been more urgent to examine and re-examine the values and ideals that animate policy about the market and the workplace, along with formal and informal economic institutions at the level of the nation, state, and internationally.

Helen Stacey's *Economic Justice* does not emphasize it, but the problems that take their cue from a widening gap between the rich and the poor are enormous. Experience teaches us that a widening gap between the rich and the poor is fraught with a vicious socio-economic climate, which can cause deterioration in national competitiveness, high crime rates, social unrest, and political instability. Re-entering existing debates and provoking new ones about economic justice, this book makes a timely contribution to a normative assessment of the economic values and the institutions that activate those norms.

Rose George's Ninety *Percent of Everything,* describes as appalling how officers, shipping companies, or their employment agencies have shafted sailors out of their wages and treated them shabbily even though they work tirelessly to achieve the purpose of the maritime transportation of international foods and products. She writes that under the flag of convenience rule, ships register with countries that have relatively lax regulations that are detrimental to the human person. She interprets this situation as "human waste" from production to terminal disposal. *Ninety Percent of Everything* enumerates the hardships and injustice meted to seamen on board, long working hours (illegal in most countries), poor pay, cramped quarters, unhygienic environment, and crimes, from petty theft to rapes and even murder, all adjudicated by the unquestioned authority of the ship's captain. The book judges this treatment as unfair and the principles unjust.

Sayyid Qutb's book, *Social Justice in Islam,* addresses social justice from the Islamic perspective. The book examines the persistence of gross socio-economic inequality in Muslim societies. It is a significant study that assesses cultural chauvinism, filled with denigration of cultures and religions. This book contains a sharp critique of sexual harassment and the commodification of women. Of the five pillars of the Quran, namely, daily statement, daily prayer, Hajj, Ramadan, and charity, Qutb singles out the practice of *zakat* (charity) and explores its political implications. The practice of *zakat* is ordinarily viewed as a form of charity, a type of alms for the poor.

By and large, *Social Justice in Islam* argues that *zakat* properly understood, provides a means for rectifying the imbalances and monetary instabilities of the market while preserving private property and commerce. This practice enables the protection and just distribution of common goods and provides both principles and practices that secure social welfare without breeding dependency or diminishing human dignity. The high point of this book is its recognition of the significance of human dignity to economic justice and political order.

Theories of social justice may have similar or divergent currents of argument, but one thing is clear: they converge on the extra juridical concept of fairness that is focused on denouncing injustice and socio-economic inequalities. They promote an understanding of how discriminatory concepts such as race, gender, status in life, class, culture, history, and nationality can help people understand and combat some injustice and hinder them from recognizing and combating others. Likewise, these concepts are congruent with Catholic Social Justice Theory.

However, one point that needs to be explored more is that these writers appear not to emphasize the importance of the dignity of the human person. Respect for the dignity of the human person, which is not discriminatory, comes first. This is what distinguishes the Catholic Social Doctrine from these other theories. While one can argue that some secular philosophical theories must have served as a springboard for Catholic social thought in some way, the uniqueness of Catholic Social Justice Theory centers on the dignity of the human person as the bedrock. It does not propound philosophical theories in the abstract. Though the social justice philosophy of the Catholic Church is highly pragmatic and gives incentive of her mission in the whole world, one cannot afford to ignore the influence of secular philosophy on Catholic Social Justice Theory. An account of literature on Catholic Social Thought will clarify this point.

2.4 Literature on Catholic Social Justice

Catholic Social Teaching or Catholic Social Doctrine is a body of social principles and moral teaching articulated in papal, conciliar, and other official documents dealing with the economic, political, and social order. This teaching is rooted in the Hebrew and Christian Scriptures, as well as in traditional philosophical and theological teachings of the Church. The characteristic features of Catholic Social Teaching position the Church as one of the major global actors capable of serving as peacemaker and an "ethical reservoir."

The sources under this Sub-section present the social teachings of the Catholic Church dealing with normative issues and capable of having tremendous impact on world politics. The Catholic Social Doctrine is treated in such a way as to showcase the Church as the strongest moral voice and liberation force pushing against political, economic, social, and legal issues that are detrimental to the dignity of the human person all over the world. The aim of the Catholic Social Doctrine is to help purify reason and to contribute to the acknowledgement and attainment of what is just.[154] The key sources under this section are as follows:

1. ENCYCLICALS AND DOCUMENTS ON SOCIAL JUSTICE

[154] Pope Benedict XVI, ENCYCLICAL LETTER *Deus Caritas Est* ("God is Love"), Liberia Editrice Vaticana, 2006, no. 28.

(a) Pope Leo XIII, RERUM NOVARUM (On the Condition of Labor) (1891)
(b) Pope Pius XI, QUADRAGESIMO ANNO (After Forty Years) (1931)
(c) Pope John XXIII, MATER ET MAGISTRA (Christianity and Social Progress) (1961)
(d) Pope John XXIII, PACEM IN TERRIS (Peace on Earth) (1963)
(e) Vatican II Council, GAUDIUM ET SPES (The Pastoral Constitution on the Church in the Modern World) (1965)
(f) Pope Paul VI, POPULORUM PROGRESSIO (On the Development of Peoples) (1967)
(g) Pope Paul VI, OCTOGESSIMA ADVENIENS (A Call to Action) (1971)
(h) Synod of Bishops, JUSTICIA IN MUNDO (Justice in the World) (1971)
(i) Pope John Paul II, LABOREM EXERCENS (On Human Work) (1981)
(j) Pope John Paul II, SOLICITUDO REI SOCIALIS (On Social Concerns) (1987)
(k) Pope John Paul II, CENTESIMUS ANNUS (The Hundredth Year) (1991)
(l) Pope Benedict VI, DEUS CARITAS EST (God is Love) (2005)
(m) Pope Benedict VI, CARITAS IN VERITATE (Love in Truth) (2009)
(n) Pope Francis I, EVANGELII GAUDIUM (Proclamation of the Gospel in Today's World) (2013)

2. COMPENDIUM OF THE SOCIAL DOCTRINE OF THE CHURCH (2004)
3. CATECHISM OF THE CATHOLIC CHURCH (2003)
4. VATICAN II COUNCIL DOCUMENTS (1965)

5. Charles Rodgers, AN INTRODUCTION TO CATHOLIC SOCIAL TEACHING (2000)
6. Charles Curran, CATHOLIC SOCIAL TEACHING 1891-PRESENT: A HISTORICAL, THEOLOGICAL, AND ETHICAL ANALYSIS (2002)
7. Kenneth R. Himes ed., MODERN CATHOLIC SOCIAL TEACHING: COMMENTARIES AND INTERPRETATIONS (2005)
8. Kenneth R. Himes, CHRISTIANITY AND THE POLITICAL ORDER: CONFLICT, COOPTATION, AND COOPERATION (2013)
9. Kenneth Himes, RESPONSES TO 101 QUESTIONS ON CATHOLIC SOCIAL TEACHING (2002)
10. Edward P. Deberri, et al, CATHOLIC SOCIAL TEACHING: OUR BEST KEPT SECRET (2003)
11. Michael Pennock, CATHOLIC SOCIAL TEACHING: LEARNING AND LIVING JUSTICE (2007)
12. Thomas Massaro, LIVING JUSTICE: CATHOLIC SOCIAL TEACHING IN ACTION (2011)
13. Thomas Massaro, CATHOLIC TEACHING AND UNITED STATES WELFARE REFORM (1998)
14. Philip Land, CATHOLIC SOCIAL TEACHING AS I HAVE LIVED, LOATHED AND LOVED IT (1995)
15. Marvin L. Kier, CATHOLIC SOCIAL TEACHINGS AND MOVEMENTS (2001)
16. Perry Roets, CATHOLIC SOCIAL TEACHINGS: A BRIEF SOCIAL CATECHISM (1999)
17. Mary Jo Bane & Lawrence M. Mead, LIFTING UP THE POOR: A DIALOGUE ON RELIGION, POVERTY & WELFARE REFORM (2003)
18. Jerry Windley-Daoust, LIVING JUSTICE AND PEACE: CATHOLIC SOCIAL TEACHING IN PRACTICE (2008)
19. David O'Brien & Thomas Shannon, CATHOLIC SOCIAL THOUGHT: THE DOCUMENTARY HERITAGE (2010)

20. Daniel K. Finn, THE MORAL ECONOMY OF MARKETS: ASSESSING CLAIMS ABOUT MARKET AND JUSTICE (2006)
21. Daniel K. Finn, THE MORAL DYNAMICS OF ECONOMIC LIFE (2012)
22. Daniel Finn ed., THE TRUE WEALTH OF NATIONS: CATHOLIC SOCIAL THOUGHT AND ECONOMIC LIFE (2010)
23. Rupert J. Ederer, ECONOMICS AS IF GOD MATTERS: MORE THAN A CENTURY OF PAPAL TEACHING (2011)
24. Thomas E. Woods, THE CHRCH AND THE MARKET: A CATHOLIC DEFENSE OF THE FREE ECONOMY (2005)
25. Daniel G. Groody, GLOBALIZATION, SPIRITUALITY, AND JUSTICE (2008)

The Church teachings regarding Catholic Social Justice are culled from scripture, the Catechism of the Catholic Church, encyclicals, and other Church magisterium documents. While many Church documents touch on the social mission of the Church, there is no definitive list of Catholic Social Teaching documents. The sources above are some of the major sources that are available. These sources reflect on the central philosophy of the Church's social mission: The followers of Jesus Christ fundamentally share the joys and hopes, the sorrows and anxieties, of the women and men of this age, especially those who are poor or in any way oppressed in any part of the world.[155] This conception of the human person stems from his being created in the image and likeness of God and in his natural inclination as a social being who can only flourish in the society as an individual and in community.[156]This is the point of departure of the Popes who have written their social encyclicals to promote the dignity of the human person.

---

[155] *See generally* Vatican II, *Gaudium et Spes (The Pastoral Constitution on the Church in the Modern World)* especially # 1 (The Church (and therefore Christians) cherishes a feeling of deep solidarity with the human race and its history. She addresses the whole of humanity and understands its presence and function in the world as such).

[156] PONTICAL COUNCIL FOR JUSTICE AND PEACE, *supra* note 120, at 94.

In his encyclical, *Caritas in Veritate* (Charity in Truth), Pope Benedict XVI taught that charity demands justice in recognition of and respect for legitimate rights of individuals and peoples. Though Pope Benedict XVI supported earthly (human) city according to law and justice, he went beyond that position by projecting that charity outstrips justice and completing it with the logic of giving and receiving. Christianity is not just about alms giving, rather Christian charity is intimately connected with personal love and personal encounters with the grace of Christ.[157] According to Pope Benedict XVI, because it is human, all human activity, including economic activity, must be ethically structured and governed.[158]

We must return to the centrality of the human being, to a more ethical vision of activities and of human relationships without the fear of losing something, and this is the point that distinguishes Catholic Social justice from secular forms of humanitarian aid.[159] Reiterating this position, Pope Francis I teaches that over and above business, logic, and the parameters of the market is the human being; men and women are human beings by virtue of their profound dignity: they should be offered the possibility of living a dignified life and of actively participating in the common good.[160]

Like other popes, the thoughts of Pope Benedict XVI are reflective of the fact that the popes use the message of the Gospel to shed light on societal issues. Moreover, for the purpose of this book social justice issues, because "evangelization would not be complete if it does not take account of the unceasing interplay of the Gospel and of man's concrete life, both personal and social."[161] For instance in his encyclical Letter R*erum Novarum* (*On the Condition of labor*), the first social encyclical to be published and considered by later Popes as the foundational social justice-teaching document of the modern era, Pope Leo XIII addressed the plight of the workers in the Industrial Revolution. *Rerum Novarum* calls for the protection of the weak and the poor through the pursuit of

---

[157] Roland Tracey, *Benedict XVI: A Guide for the Perplexed*, T & T Clark, 2010, p. 91.

[158] POPE BENEDICT XVI, ENCYCLICAL LETTER, *Caritas in Veritate* (Charity in Truth) 2009, # 36.

[159] Roland Tracey, *supra* note 157.

[160] Pope Francis I, Address to the *Centesimus Annus Pro Pontifice* Foundation, May 25, 2013.

[161] POPE PAUL VI, APOSTOLIC EXHORTATION *Evangelii Nuntiandi* (Evangelization in the Modern World), 1975, # 29 (Evangelization is most effective when the Gospel is presented with issues that border on social justice).

justice while excluding socialism and class struggle as legitimate principles of change. It endorses the dignity of labor, the right to private property, and the right to form and join professional associations. In *Pacem in Terris* (Peace on Earth), Pope John XXIII addressed the entire spectrum of relations between individuals, between individuals and the community, and between nations of the world. For him, peace can only be established through inviolable respect for human rights based on mutual trust and unity.

In his encyclical Letter, *Quadragessimo Anno* (On the Reconstruction of the Social Order) in 1931, which marked the fortieth anniversary of the issuance of Leo XIII's seminal encyclical Letter, *Rerum Novarum (On the Condition of Workers),* Pope Pius XI taught that the economic and moral orders are not distinct from each other, but the former depends in no way on the other. Pope Pius XI emphasized that the living wage paid to workers should be just. Economic life must be considered and treated as together free from total domination by public authority. Workers should be given a stake in the ownership of their business against socialism, communism, and even capitalism as well as individualism, which are economic extremes.

Both Pope Leo XIII and Pope Pius XI favored the understanding that labor is not a commodity and that the contract between employers and their employees should not impinge upon the recognition and respect for human dignity, which is the hub of the Catholic social mission. In consideration of human dignity, workers should be paid a living wage and employers of labor should neither take advantage of market conditions nor defraud them or treat them unfairly. They both discourage excessive taxation on workers, considering their obligations to their families. Both encyclicals are against the "downsizing" of social security systems but support combating hunger and poverty.

In the *Gaudium et Spes (Pastoral Constitution on the Church in the Modern World)*, a document of Vatican II, the Church addresses the human family in the context of everything that envelops it. The Church views the world as the theatre of human history, bearing the marks of its travail, its triumphs, and failures. Though the world is a globalized society, it is still a family where love ought to be identified as God's greatest gift to humanity; everything is shaped by love and everything is directed toward it. In charity we see love as a vocation because it gives real substance to the personal relationship with God and with one's neighbor; it is the principle not only of micro-relationships (with friends, with family members or within small groups) but also of macro-relationships (social, economic, and political ones).[162] Love is therefore the service that the Church carries out in order to attend constantly to the sufferings and needs, including material needs, of the human person.[163] Love respects the inherent dignity of the human person.

In *Populorum Progressio (On the Development of Peoples), and Octogessimo Adveniens (A Call to Action)*, on the 80th anniversary of *Rerum Novarum,* Pope Paul VI highlighted and deplored the gap between the rich and poor nations and the worsening marginalization of the poor, reminding all that the goods of the earth are intended by God for equal benefit of everyone. For him, the new name of peace is development, and which should be directed toward integral human development and necessary conditions for growth in the solidarity of peoples. In *Octogessimo Adveniens,* Pope Paul VI urged Christians to live up to the duty of participation in social and political reform because of the need for genuine renewal in domestic and international societal structures. This is interesting as this point is at the heart of this book.

The CST aims at addressing issues of inequality and injustice, which militate against the dignity of the human person in the society. These two encyclicals raised fundamental issues that promote human dignity in such a way as to prompt Pope Benedict XVI in his encyclical Letter, *Caritas in Veritate* to repeatedly refer to *Populorum Progressio* and *Rerum Novarum* as the now-classic encyclicals from which all subsequent social encyclicals have taken their own measure.[164]

In *Laboren Exercens* (On Human Work), *Sollicitudo Rei Socialis (On Social Concern*), and *Centesimus Annus* (*One Hundred Years After*), Pope John Paul II reiterated the practical concerns of his predecessors: the necessity of just wages, decent working conditions, the importance of trade unions, and so on. Like other Popes, he asserted the priority of labor over capital and does not see any conflict between the two. He somehow

---

162 POPE BENEDICT VI, ENCYCLICAL LETTER, *Caritas in Veritate* (2009) # 2.

163 POPE BENEDICT XVI, ENCYCLICAL LETTER, *Deus Caritas Est* (God is Love) 2005, # 19.

164 POPE BENEDICT XVI, ENCYCLICAL LETTER, *Caritas in Veritate (2009),* # 8.

differed from his predecessors over the issue of private property. He placed very much less emphasis on the natural right to own property. He was more concerned to underline that it is subordinate to the requirement that property be used for the common good of all.

Pope John Paul II took the issue to another level when he taught that states have the duty to provide welfare benefits to the unemployed, envisaging that states make grants to mothers and families and guarantee availability of affordable healthcare and pensions. Another departure from his predecessors are his thoughts on disabled members of the workforce and migrant workers. He criticized multinational corporations for offering poor wages and working conditions to workers in developing countries.

Faced with new situations and issues, Catholic social teaching thus gradually developed and has now found a comprehensive presentation in the *Compendium of the Social Doctrine of the Church*, published in 2004. The reason for the *Compendium*, as Pope John Paul II put it in 1996, was for the social teaching of the Church to be better known. The *Compendium of the Social Doctrine of the Church* was embarked upon for knitting together important statements, conferences, speeches, and writings on great contemporary social issues into a consistent and readable text. This text proposes an integral and solidary humanism capable of creating a new social, economic, and political order, with a basis on the dignity and freedom of every human person to be brought into peace, justice, and solidarity.[165]

In its structure, the Compendium is organized into three sections. The first section deals with the overarching context of God in Christ calling the Church to a social mission for the whole of humanity based on reverence for the inherent dignity of the human person and support for inalienable human rights. The second section follows, to a large extent, the structure of Vatican II's Pastoral Constitution on the Church in the Modern World (*Gaudium et Spes*), considering specifically, various areas of social life, human work, economic life, political community, international issues, the environment, and the issue of peace. The third section is a summary of the essence of the Church's social doctrine concluding with the ultimatum for people to commit themselves to the task of building a civilization of love.

---

[165] PONTIFICAL COUNCIL FOR JUSTICE AND PEACE, *supra* note 120, at 19.

The preamble to the *Compendium* makes it clear that the citations of magisterial texts are drawn from documents of differing authority, because of which the Compendium is prone to debate, and constant adaptation or updating. What the Compendium contains are the fundamental elements of the Church's social doctrine and because of this, Episcopal Conferences are permitted to make appropriate applications to suit their local situations.[166] The foundation of the Church's teaching against social injustice is based on the Ten Commandments of God, especially as it concerns the right of the poor to sustenance and justice. Historically, this discipline was embodied in the practice of the sabbatical and jubilee years to redistribute land, free indentured labor, and remit debts.[167] It was not just to remind Israel of its founding principle but also to be continually invoked to eliminate discrimination and economic inequalities.[168]

The *Compendium* adopts the Jewish jubilee as a cornerstone in its pillars of bringing freedom to the poor, the oppressed, the blind, and those in prison. With this the Church teaches that the salvation of humans can never ignore their social and public life. In the inner dimension of humans is rooted the commitment to justice and solidarity to build up their social, economic, and political life.[169] Therefore the Church's social doctrine is itself a valid instrument of evangelization.[170] The *Compendium* teaches that anything that concerns humans, including situations and problems

---

[166] *Id.* par. 8.

[167] *See generally,* R. De Vaux, ANCIENT ISRAEL (1961); Max Weber, ANCIENT JUDAISM (Translated from German) (1952) The Talmud conjectures an actuality of observance beginning with fourteen years after Joshua's entrance into the Promised Land and until Sennacherib's conquest. Therefore, there was no observance or counting till renewal was made by Jeremiah; this continued (for 36 years) till the First Destruction. The only historic records of liberty and release, however, are in Jer. 34:14 and Nehemiah 10:32. Perhaps here "the social crisis demanded an immediate solution." Many maintain that the law of Jubilee appears to set out an ideal of justice and social equality which was never realized. Also, it is highly probable that the Sabbatical year was an interpolation from priestly law into the Book of the Covenant in the face of the improbability of the actual execution of the prescriptions among the pre-exilic husbandmen. Nevertheless, it could be based upon an institution connected with the intermittent husbandry of itinerant shepherds or a stipulation concerning the itinerant shepherd-rights as to fallow pasturage on the land of settled sibs.

[168] PONTIFICAL COUNCIL FOR JUSTICE AND PEACE, *supra* note 120 ¶ 23-24.

[169] PONTIFICAL COUNCIL FOR JUSTICE AND PEACE, *supra* note 120, ¶ 40.

[170] POPE JOHN PAUL II, *CENTESIMUS ANNUS* (One Hundredth Anniversary of *Rerum Novarum*), May 1, 1991, # 54.

regarding justice, freedom, development, relations between peoples, and peace, is not foreign to evangelization.[171]

The *Compendium* dedicates Chapter Three to the issue of the dignity of the human person, and the issue of human dignity is the crux of the matter. In the *Compendium*, the Church teaches that the dignity of the human person is fundamental to the construction of a just society. This is tantamount to an understanding of the mission of the Church as one that includes the recognition and promotion of human rights. Chapter Four examines the principles of the Church's Social Doctrine and this situates the hub of the Church's teaching in the principle of the common good, the universal destination goods, and the principles of subsidiarity, participation, and solidarity.[172] Under this section, the *Compendium* projects the concept of social justice.

It is, however, surprising to see that social justice is given a sketchy and underdeveloped treatment considering that it is a key concept. The reason for this lukewarm treatment is not stated and, as a matter of fact, calls for further research. Therefore, this book undertakes in-depth research into this concept from the philosophical and secular perspectives and brings to bear the outcome on the Church's entire social justice principle.

Concerning the role of the State in social justice, the *Compendium* recognizes that the State must intervene to supply certain functions, but such intervention must not be longer than necessary. The reason for this is based on the stand of the Church on personal responsibility. If the scope of the welfare State is over-extended, the reality of personal responsibility, in the instance of the concept of private property, will be lost. A critical examination of this position appears to see the Church as underestimating the necessary role of the State in providing a secure and equitable environment for business. In other words, the Church's view of the welfare State is highly abstract.

The *Compendium* only prescribes that the State's intervention in economic activities must be commensurate with society's real needs. In other words, the State must favor the free exercise of economic activity as well as establish limits for the autonomy of the parties in order to

---

171 PONTIFICAL COUNCIL OF JUSTICE AND PEACE, *supra* note *120*, ¶ 66.

172 PONTIFICAL COUNCIL FOR JUSTICE AND PEACE, *supra* note 120, ¶ 166.

defend those who are weaker.[173] This teaching does not go without some difficulties which arise from questions about who decides, how, and on what basis?

The *Compendium* also reflects the Magisterial documents like Papal encyclicals in its teachings about human work and economic and political life as well as international issues such as peace, the environment, and the free market. For example, their reflection on human work portrays the Church as deeply involved with the rights of workers in capitalism and its historic debate with forms of socialism and communism. The *Compendium* teaches that the Church defends the inalienable dignity of workers and the self-realization of the person in such a way that, work is for humans, and not humans for work.[174] Also, the teaching encourages formation of unions as a mouthpiece for class struggle, which governs social life, organizing, for example, peaceful strike actions to obtain necessary benefits. The text supports the participation of workers in ownership, management, and profits of industries in which they work, insisting on the recognition of equal rights and the dignity of women and children.[175]

Concerning international market issues, the *Compendium* recognizes that it may seem that underdevelopment is impossible to eliminate, but this is only a difficulty which can be confronted with strong and resolute determination because development is not only an aspiration but also a right that, like every right, implies a corresponding duty.[176] It therefore requires an equitable distribution of goods on a world scale.[177] As a result of this, the *Compendium* laments protectionism and trade discrimination against developing countries that hinder development, along with deteriorating terms of trade, resulting in a widening gap between rich and poor countries.[178] This document reiterates that free trade is fair only when it is in consonance with the demands of justice.[179] Because of the

---

[173] PONTIFICAL COUNCIL FOR JUSTICE AND PEACE, *supra* note 120, ¶ 351.

[174] PONTIFICAL COUNCIL FOR JUSTICE AND PEACE, *supra* note 120, at 268 & 272 (a recall of Pope Leo XIII's Rerum Novarum).

[175] PONTIFICAL COUNCIL FOR JUSTICE AND PEACE, *supra* 120, nos. 281, 295 and 296.

[176] PONTIFICAL COUNCIL FOR JUSTICE AND PEACE, *supra* note 120, at 446.

[177] PONTIFICAL COUNCIL FOR JUSTICE AND PEACE, *supra* note 120, at 448.

[178] PONTIFICAL COUNCIL FOR JUSTICE AND PEACE, *supra* note 120, at 364.

[179] *See id.* at 366.

foregoing, this book undertakes to explore the issue of Catholic social justice with particular emphasis on the Church's social mission in the face of the GATT-WTO system.

Books on Catholic social justice that were written before the advent of the *Compendium of the Social Doctrine* drew their lead from the scriptures, the Vatican II documents, papal encyclicals, the Catechism of the Catholic Church, or Church history. Since the advent of the *Compendium,* it is odd to see any contemporary literature on this topic that does not explore the *Compendium* as the main source. An example here is Jerry Windley-Daoust's *Living Justice and Peace: Catholic Social Teaching in Practice,* which has been variously criticized for its inclination towards militant leftist/Marxist ideology, its praise of socialism/communism, for being historically wrong, and above all, for not using the principles enunciated in the *Compendium of the Catholic Social Doctrine.* In contrast, most books on Catholic Social Thought are faithful to the Magisterium of the Church, and therefore applied most materials present in the *Compendium.*

In his book *An Introduction to Catholic Social Teaching,* for instance, Charles Rodgers extensively cites Catholic authorities emphasizing that political and socio-economic issue must be centered on the inherent freedom and dignity of the human person. Charles Curran in his *Catholic Social Teaching 1891-Present: A Historical, and Ethical Analysis,* offers a comprehensive analysis and criticism of Catholic Social Teaching from the perspective of theology, ethics and Church history. *Catholic Social Teaching 1891-Present,* reviewed the methodology and content of the documents of Catholic Social Teaching, generally understood as comprising twelve papal letters beginning with Pope Leo XIII's encyclical *Rerum Novarum,* some Vatican II documents, and some pastoral letters of United States bishops.

Charles Curran asserts that the fundamental basis for this body of teaching comes from an anthropological perspective that recognizes both the inherent dignity and the social nature of the human person. This is in line with the Church's teachings on political and economic matters, which chart a middle course between the two extremes of individualism and collectivism. One of the interesting points in *Catholic Social Teaching 1891-Present,* is its emphasis on the historical continuity of Catholic Social Doctrine, exhibiting therefore its resilient qualities.

2.4.1 Critical Analysis

Some authoritative documents of the Church have been criticized for not taking cognizance of other subjects that are not theology or philosophy, such as science, technology, economics, and others. For instance, some papal encyclicals like Pope Pius XI's *Quadragesimo Anno* (On Social Reconstruction of the Social Order) and Pope Leo XIII's *Rerum Novarum* (On the Condition of Workers) have been attacked for prescribing reliable living wage for workers.[180] This attack is based on the position that economic and moral orders are distinct; economics is a bona fide science possessing an internal coherence of its own.

The argument goes on to assert that the teaching of the Church on fair living wages is inextricably bound to certain economic preconditions, and when these economic preconditions are incorrect, the moral analysis upon which the Church bases its conclusions becomes unacceptable. For instance, the critics assert that an increase in the material well-being of workers may increase unemployment. However, a closer analysis of this criticism shows that it is somewhat plausible.

The Church has never ignored the place of reason in her teachings. Faith and reason are fundamentally complementary in the Church's teachings. They are "two wings on which the human spirit rises to the contemplation of truth."[181] The Church employs the contributions of experts in different subjects, though the extent of the involvement of these experts is what needs additional research. But the Church takes cognizance of different subjects associated with its doctrines. Moreover, the Church does not attempt to structure or organize society but only tries to appeal to, guide, and form consciences.[182] It is not for the Church's teaching to specify any one form of government that countries must adopt to execute social justice so long as the common good, public wellbeing and private property are being promoted.

From available records, the most powerful authority in Catholic social teaching is Papal encyclicals, for which the situation has been described as

---

[180] *See* Thomas Woods Jr., *Morality and Economic Law: Toward A Reconciliation* available at http://www.mises.org or http://archive.lewrockwell.com/woods/woods8.html

[181] POPE JOHN PAUL II, ENCYCLICAL LETTER *Fides et Ratio* (Faith and Reason), 1998, no. 1.

[182] PONTIFICAL COUNCIL FOR JUSTICE AND PEACE, *supra* note 120, ¶ 81.

the "Papalization of Catholicism."[183] This refers to the growing development of the centrality given to the Papacy in recent times and may be interpreted as a diminishment of the role of the other segments of the universal Church. There needs to be decentralization of teaching responsibilities in such a way as to involve the wider participation of most classes of Catholics, for instance, academics, students, congregations, and so on. Catholic social teaching should also consider cultural inclinations of people as another incentive to decentralize the teaching of the social principles.

Decentralizing the teaching authority of the Catholic Church will open the door for more lay participation in formulating responses to social questions instead of concentrating all the teaching arrangements on the Roman hierarchy. This is what *Catholic Social Teaching 1891-Present* expounds when it encourages opening CST to a broader range of voices in the name of greater responsiveness. David O'Brian and Thomas Shannon, in their book, *Catholic Social Thought: The Documentary Heritage* (2010) looks forward for the day when CST anthologies would expand beyond the set of encyclicals and bishop statements. The laity has a major role to play in the living witness of CST.

A growing criticism of the documents that constitute Catholic Social Thought is the issue of sexism. In *101 Questions on Catholic Social Teaching*, Kenneth Himes addresses sexism by re-examining the "complementarity model of gender roles" and calls on CST to address the issue more. The *Compendium of the Social Doctrine of the Catholic Church* regrettably did not use inclusive language. Inclusive language is now widely regarded as part of the normal courtesies of discourse.

To use non-inclusive language as has been the practice of the Catholic Church is needlessly counter-productive and may result in some people who would otherwise be keenly interested in the *Compendium,* now refusing to look at it. Non-English-speaking groups may not realize how sensitive this issue is in English-speaking countries, particularly in the United States. Part of what this book addresses is any form of discrimination in international trade against which the Church preaches its social mission. Though it may be addressed as gender or linguistic discrimination, it is still a form of discrimination

---

183 *See* Thomas A. Shannon, "Roman Catholic Social Thought: Historical, Methodological, and Analytic Perspectives," A Paper presented at the *Collegium Colloquy on Faith and Intellectual Life* at the Saint John's University, Collegeville, Minnesota, June 2, 2000.

unacceptable to the Church.[184] This book sets out to research reasons why the issue of "gender discrimination" as proposed by critics of the Church's social mission is flawed. This will be discussed in in detail in chapter 7.

2.5 Literature on the GATT-WTO System

The topic of this book revolves around social justice as propagated by the Holy See in the international arena, particularly in international trade law. The key sources under this section trace the issue of social justice in the GATT-WTO system as a powerful weapon with which, though still on the Permanent Observer status, the Holy See influences the operations of the system. Has the GATT-WTO system achieved economic wellbeing for all countries? Historically, and based on available resources, the GATT-WTO system has done a lot to prepare the ground for regulated free trade, but the issue of justice and fairness requires further research. These key sources support this assertion.

In the 1930s, the world witnessed terrible trade barriers which caused economic depression and consequent military aggression. The need arose for an open trading system that would engender economic stability and peace. The post-World War II goal of establishing an open and nondiscriminatory trading system with the goal of raising the economic wellbeing of all countries became obvious. Therefore, the key sources here explore to what extent social justice works in the operations of the GATT-WTO system. These sources are:

1. THE WORLD TRADE ORGANIZATION: UNDER STANDING THE WTO available at http://www.wto.org
2. Raj Bhala, MODERN GATT LAW: A TREATISE ON THE LAW AND POLITICAL ECONOMY OF THE GENERAL AGREEMENT ON TARIFFS AND TRADE AND OTHER WORLD TRADE ORGANIZATION AGREEMENTS (Vols. 1 & 2) (2013)

[184] POPE JOHN PAUL II, ENCYCLICAL LETTER *Laborem Exercens* (On Human Work), 1981, # 19.

3. Raj Bhala, TRADE, DEVELOPMENT, AND SOCIAL JUSTICE (2003)
4. Raj Bhala, INTERNATIONAL TRADE LAW: INTER DISCIPLINARY THEORY AND PRACTICE (2008)
5. Raj Bhala, INTERNATIONAL TRADE LAW (DOCUMENTS SUPPLEMENT (2008)
6. Eric A. Posner & Alan O. Sykes, ECONOMIC FOUNDATIONS OF INTERNATIONAL LAW (2013)
7. Kelsey Timmerman, WHERE AM I WEARING: A GLOBAL TOUR TO THE COUNTRIES, FACTORIES, AND PEOPLE THAT MAKE OUR CLOTHES (2012)
8. Andrew T. Guzman & Joost H.B. Pauwelyn, INTERNATIONAL TRADE LAW (2009)
9. Sue Arrowsmith & Robert D. Anderson, THE WTO REGIME ON GOVERNMENT PROCUREMENT: CHALLENGE AND REFORM (2011)
10. Rorden Wilkinson & James Scott, TRADE, POVERTY, DEVELOPMENT: GETTING BEYOND THE WTO's DOHA DEADLOCK (2013)
11. Ernst-Ulrich Petersmann, INTERNATIONAL ECONOMIC LAW IN THE 21ST CENTEURY (2012)
12. Frank J. Garcia, TRADE, INEQUALITY, AND JUSTICE: TOWARD A LIBERAL THEORY OF JUST TRADE (2003)
13. Frank J. Garcia, et al (eds.) GLOBAL JUSTICE AND INTERNATIONAL ECONOMIC LAW: OPPORTUNITIES AND PROSPECTS (2012)
14. Frank J. Garcia, GLOBAL JUSTICE AND INTERNATIONAL ECONOMIC LAW: THREE TAKES (2013)
15. Richard Peet, UNHOLY TRINITY: THE IMF, WORLD BANK AND WTO (2003)
16. James Harrison, THE HUMAN RIGHTS IMPACT OF THE WORLD TRADE ORGANISATION (2007)
17. Donatella Alessandrini, DEVELOPING COUNTRIES AND THE MULTILATERAL TRADE REGIME: THE FAILURE AND PROMISE OF THE WTO'S DEVELOPMENT MISSION (2010)

18. A.K Koul, GUIDE TO THE WTO AND GATT: ECONOMICS, LAW AND POLITICS (2006)
19. David A. Gantz, LIBERALIZING INTERNATIONAL TRADE AFTER DOHA: MULTILATERAL, PLURILATERAL, REGIONAL, AND UNILATERAL INITIATIVES (2013)
20. Federico Ortino & Ernst-Ulrich Petersmann (eds.), THE WTO DISPUTE SETTLEMENT SYSTEM 1995-2003 (Vol. 18) (2004)
21. Gregory C. Shaffer & Ricardo Melendez-Ortiz (eds.), DISPUTE SETTLEMENT AT THE WTO: THE DEVELOPING COUNTRY EXPERIENCE (2010)
22. Ross Becroft, THE STANDARD OF REVIEW IN WTO DISPUTE SETTLEMENT: CRITIQUE AND DEVELOPMENT (2012)
23. Kamal Malhotra, MAKING GLOBAL TRADE WORK FOR PEOPLE (2003)
24. Melaku Geboye Desta, THE LAW OF INTERNATIONAL TRADE IN AGRICULTURAL PRODUCTS: FROM GATT 1947 TO THE WTO AGREEMENT ON AGRICULTURE (2002)

For centuries, international trade has been essential to the wealth and power of nations and defended a system through which all could benefit. This culminated in the establishment of the GATT-WTO system to achieve furthering the goal of global trade. The GATT-WTO system has made remarkable achievements through the instrumentality of negotiations of trade agreements among members. However, for some time now, emphasis has shifted to the role of fair trade as an engine of distributive justice and has been a sensitive topic in globalization and global justice debates. The problem that scholars and experts have sought to solve is how to structure international trade to benefit all. The key sources under this section acknowledge the many achievements of the GATT-WTO system, but still, they emphasis the need for a structure that is more pragmatic and more transparent than what is presently on the ground.

According to *Understanding the WTO*,[185] the GATT was provisionally made to promote and secure the liberalization of world trade. Its main achievement centered on continual reductions in tariffs which, to a large extent, helped consistent trade growth and strengthened membership because of the recognition of multilateral trade as an anchor of development and an instrument of economic and trade reform. However, during the Tokyo Round in the 1970s, member governments discovered that GATT's success in reducing tariffs was low, coupled with a series of economic recessions during this period and the early 1980s. There was need to protect sectors that were facing increased foreign competition which undermined the credibility and effectiveness of GATT. Also, because world trade became far more complex than it was in the 1940s, it became difficult for GATT arrangements to effectively handle issues of globalization, trade in services, expansion in international investment, and other issues. GATT members resorted to reinforcing and expanding the multilateral system, an exercise that eventually led to the creation of the WTO.

As to whether the GATT-WTO system is adequately solving the problems associated with international trade, the key sources under this section make some obvious responses. The answers in these sources appear to be "yes" and "no," while considering even though there are the many achievements of the system, the issues of equality, transparency, and fairness are far from realized. These sources pay attention to social clauses that ought to be incorporated into the GATT-WTO system as a solution to these intractable problems. In *Modern GATT Law*, Professor Raj Bhala analyzes the relevant rules and nuances, historical background, policy justifications and practical implications, as well as the interpretations of the 39 Articles of GATT.

While acknowledging the achievements of the GATT-WTO system, he writes that trade transactions embody cultural, moral, and religious values and, therefore, have implications for human, animal, and plant life and health. Because of the capitalist ideology of world trade, *Modern GATT Law* is to be understood in the context of the economic development of poor countries, which include special and differential treatment provisions. Therefore, Professor Raj Bhala in his 2003 book *Trade, Development,*

---

185 *See* World Trade Organization especially "Understanding the WTO" available at http://www.wto.org

and Social Justice, also projects a similar fairness argument. He uses five arguments, including Catholic and Islamic concepts and principles of social justice, to proffer solutions to the problem of the large and growing divide between the "First and Third world" schism, which threatens the GATT-WTO system. Striking a balance between the critics of the GATT-WTO claim and its defenders, he proposes specific improvements to make international trade law more socially just for all.

Looking at the same issue from another perspective, Kamal Malhotra, in his book *Making Global Trade Work for People,* published in 2003, examines the GATT-WTO system and sees international trade as the best way to lift the poor out of poverty and achieve sustainable development. This book contributes to the major debates surrounding globalization and the impact of trade on the poor, on social stability, and on the environment. A key message of this book is that an evaluation of the multilateral trade regime should be based on whether it maximizes possibilities for human development, especially in developing countries.

Any arrangement that does not benefit the developing and least developed countries contradicts the vision of international trade. A body of literature of international trade law advances that argument further. Melaku Desta's 2002 book, *The Law of International Trade in Agricultural Products: From GATT 1947 to the WTO Agreement on Agriculture* is a good example. This book argues that, though it has been customary to treat agriculture as the general exception to trade rule, and despite the decline in tariffs in recent times, the level of effective protection against the flow of agricultural trade has been steadily rising. Such obnoxious practices are almost entirely at the behest of developed countries and to the detriment of developing countries.

In their 1996 book, *Political Economy of the World Trading System: From GATT to WTO,* Bernard Hoekman and Michel Kostecki stressed the need to integrate the developing economies more tightly into the world trading system.[186] The authors discuss the shortcomings of the special, differential treatment principle of the GATT-WTO system, decrying the rising use of procedurally protectionist barriers mounted by major developed countries against developing- country exports and calling for

[186] *See also,* Bernard M. Hoekman & Michel M. Kostecki, *The Political Economy of the World Trading System,* Oxford University Press (2008).

serious modifications. In *Where Am I Wearing*, published in 2012, Kelsey Timmerman, a journalist and traveler, introduces the world to the human side of globalization. When he concluded a journey that took him from Honduras to Bangladesh to Cambodia to China and back, Kelsey discusses the issue of "sweatshops."[187] The people who work in these factories all live in poverty while their employers enjoy the bounteous wealth which accrues from the businesses. This book rhetorically reflects on the solution.

Other books were straightforward in their prescription of justice for all as the best solution to hardline injustice. For instance, in *Justice at Work: Globalization and Human Rights of Workers*, Robert Senser discusses how 21st century globalization can and must be transformed to serve not only the rights of business and business people but also the rights of labor and workers. Senser must have been greatly influenced by his Catholic background, but in all, his viewpoint gives credence to the thesis of this book especially as he exposes the issues of sweatshops and child labor as socially unfair.

In *Fair Trade from the Ground Up: New Markets for Social Justice*, published in 2012, April Linton raises concern about the role of middlemen in the chain of supply of goods and services and proffers economic justice and social change as a viable and sustainable alternative to charity. This book makes a case that fair trade as it is presently structured is not able to implement the promises of raising living standards in developing countries. In his books *Trade, Inequality and Justice: Toward a Liberal Theory of Just Trade,* published in 2003, *Global Justice and International Economic Law: Three Takes,188* and another one he edited with others, *Global Justice and International Economic Law: Opportunities and Prospects,189* Frank Garcia

[187] *See generally* KELSY TIMMERMAN, WHERE AM I WEARING: A GLOBAL TOUR TO THE COUNTRIES, FACTORIES, AND PEOPLE THAT MAKE OUR CLOTHES (2012) (indicating that the concept of "sweatshop" is used because employees who make our clothes in Honduras, Bangladesh, Cambodia, China, and in most countries work in shops and factories for long hours at very low wages and under unhealthy conditions. If this is not addressed, international trade will degenerate from an engine of development for all to a system that benefits few people at the expense of many).

[188] FRANK J. GARCIA, *GLOBAL JUSTICE AND INTERNATIONAL ECONOMIC LAW: THREE TAKES,* Cambridge University Press, (2013).

[189] CHI CARMODY, FRANK J. GARCIA & JOHN LINARELLI, *GLOBAL JUSTICE AND INTERNATIONAL ECONOMIC LAW: OPPORTUNITIES AND PROSPECTS,* ASIL Studies in International Legal Theory, (2012).

argues that recent crises in world trade policy are seedbeds of economic inequality and injustice. Drawing on political and moral theory and legal philosophy, these books develop a Rawlsian model for justice as fairness in international trade law. *Trade, Inequality and Justice spotlights* the normative role of the principle of special and differential treatment in making the wealthy markets of developed nations benefit developing economies but also proposes modification of existing special and differential treatment to meet modern developments.

The book *Global Justice and International Economic Law: Opportunities and Prospects* acknowledges efforts of the GATT-WTO system in developing institutions and infrastructure to promote global interdependence in a way that not only liberalizes international trade but also becomes a dense web of treaty commitments at the multilateral, regional, and bilateral levels. This book discusses how international lawyers tend to uncritically accept comparative advantage as the principal normative yardstick for justifying these institutions. On the other hand, moral and political philosophers have developed the concept of global justice, which is like a custard pie that never hits hard. What is needed according to this book, *Global Justice*, is a multidisciplinary approach which hinges on distributive justice.

In *Global Justice and International Economic Law: Three Takes*, Frank Garcia uses John Rawls's liberalism, communitarianism, and consent theory, which he describes as" three takes" to conceptualize the problem of global justice. The book emphasizes that thefts, coercion, and exploitation are vices that should not have links with international trade. This book, from all indications, is Frank Garcia's after-thought following the publication of *Global Justice and International Economic Law: Opportunities and Prospects*, which he co-edited.

Some of the key sources in this section provide an in-depth commentary on the debate over some controversial innovations in the GATT-WTO system. A.K. Koul's 2006 book, *Guide to the WTO and GATT: Economics, Law, and Politics*, for instance, discusses the debate over the GATT-WTO issues that have remained unsettled, such as the WTO dispute settlement mechanism; the General Agreement on Trade in Services (GATS); the Agreement on Trade-Related Investment Measures (TRIMS); the Agreement on Trade-Related Aspects of Intellectual Property Rights (TRIPS); areas still covered by the General Agreement on Tariffs and

Trade (GATT) 1947; the Most Favored Nation (MFN) concept; special provisions relating to agriculture and textiles; sanitary and phytosanitary measures; technical barriers to trade; pre-shipment inspection; and import licensing procedures.

Arguments within the WTO and among scholars over such controversial matters as regulation of competition, setting of labor standards, and environmental controls, as well as thorny concerns raised by the enforcement of intellectual property rights and limitation on investments, are held up to scrutiny for their legal merits. The author describes all the major precedent-setting cases in WTO jurisprudence and analyzes their effect to date and the trends they have set in motion. These WTO cases relate to perceived discrimination against developing nations which must balance their WTO commitments with the structural adjustments demanded by the World Bank and International Monetary Fund (IMF) regimes.

In his book, *Liberalizing International Trade after Doha: Multilateral, Plurilateral, Regional, and Unilateral Initiatives,* David Gantz regrets the frivolous attitude toward post-Uruguay and Doha Rounds. This is true because it was during these broadly comprehensive Rounds that important innovations which should have helped control the controversies in the GATT-WTO system were negotiated. The book suggests that developed countries, which are not comfortable with these laudable innovations, will have too much to lose if they elect the option of abandoning the WTO.

The book further discloses that if there is reason for cautious optimism post-Doha, it is because there are alternatives to a comprehensive package of new or amended multilateral agreements. And in addition to a likely consensus on a few noncontroversial multilateral elements of Doha, the alternatives include existing and future "plurilateral" trade agreements, new or revised regional trade agreements covering both goods and services, and liberalized national trade laws and regulations in the WTO member nations. However, a close study of these alternatives may streamline their inadequacies without the entire arrangement in the GATT-WTO system.

Concerning WTO dispute settlement culture, the book, *The WTO Dispute Settlement System 1995-2003*, authored by Federico Ortino and Ernst-Ulrich Petersmann, discusses the 10th anniversary of the WTO settlement mechanism. It states that in its ten years of existence, the

WTO dispute settlement system has continued to differentiate itself in many ways from more conventional international judicial proceedings such as those before the International Court of Justice (ICJ) or regional integration courts. The regular participation of third parties, the emphasis at all levels of the ordinary meaning of the text of WTO rules, and the raft of proposed amendments to the Dispute Settlement Understanding (DSU) all characterize WTO jurisprudence.

The essays in this book center on rules which emphasize proposed improvements and clarifications in areas such as special and differential treatment of less-developed countries, surveillance of implementation, compensation, and suspension of concessions. Other contributions discuss jurisprudential and practical issues such as discrimination, trade-related environmental measures, subsidies and countervailing measures, and trade-related intellectual property rights.

On the other side of the divide, the book *Dispute Settlement at the WTO: The Developing Country Experience* by Gregory C. Shaffer and Ricardo Meléndez-Ortiz, and published in 2014, critiques the dispute settlement arrangement of the GATT-WTO system from the perspective of developing countries. This book provides a much-needed understanding of how the WTO dispute settlement system operates behind the scenes for developing countries. Providing a bottom-up assessment of the challenges, experiences, and strategies of individual developing countries, it assesses what these countries have done and can do to build the capacity to deploy and shape the WTO legal system, as well as the daunting challenges that they face. Given the serious domestic governance shortcomings in most of the countries examined, which certainly exist in other countries, and given the extreme political difficulties of changing retaliation rules, the focus on domestic governance and improved operation within the existing system is not only a sound one but also the only realistic one.

In his book *The Standard of Review in WTO Dispute Settlement: Critique and Development,* Ross Becroft critiques how the WTO scrutinizes domestic measures to determine compliance with the WTO agreements. This scrutiny, known as the standard of review, is particularly relevant when WTO panels are examining measures involving controversial domestic policy issues. The author argues that the current WTO standard of review is inadequate. He would prefer a flexible standard based on the responsibilities retained by WTO members under the WTO Agreements. This new standard of review would better reflect the autonomy contemplated for members under the WTO rules and reduce the scope for the contention that the WTO is overreaching its mandate.

2.5.1 Critical Analysis

The body of literature under this section vehemently lauds the tremendous achievements of the GATT-WTO system since its establishment. At least it is obvious that trade has become the single most important part of the expansion of economies since the advent of globalization. Global institutions governing the conditions of trading relations among countries have acquired great political-economic power. However, some super powers have exploited the global governance of international trade in such a way as to employ it as an avenue for exerting significant control over national economies, and this has generated a lot of apprehensions, especially for poor countries.

The operation of international trade, experience has taught us, has only been intermittently regulated through rounds of bilateral and multilateral negotiations. Powerful Members have unilaterally abrogated agreements and initiated retaliatory actions because the mechanism on the ground tilts in their favor. Poor countries are handicapped in that respect and there is not much they can do in enforcement mechanisms.

The foregoing is not a yardstick for writing off the GATT-WTO system. The sources under this section make a critique of the present structure of the GATT-WTO as one that requires an incentive that will generate justice and fairness, which is presently not readily available to the developing and least developed Members. The Uruguay and Doha Rounds have fantastic agreements and negotiating instruments, but the implementation of the issues negotiated at those rounds is the problem. This book sets out to explore Catholic Social Justice Theory as a neutral instrument that can help the GATT-WTO system achieve the stated objectives. In doing this, this book measures to what extent the Holy See has exerted the much-needed influence in its social mission as a Permanent Observer.

CHAPTER THREE

Legal and Political Nature of the Holy See

In the whole wide world, the Catholic Church is known to be the only religious institution that has diplomatic relations with other states, along with much concern with international law and affairs. At the center of this uniqueness is the Holy See, which is the supreme organ of the government of the Catholic Church the world over. The Holy See is to the Church what the government is to the State, with a characteristic difference in the monarchical constitution of the Church, which is of divine origin. Therefore, it is not easily subject to change unlike the constant flux philosophy of the Pre-Socratic Hiraclitus, but rather like the spots of the leopard.[190]

Ever since the Lateran Treaty of 1929, which defined the sovereignty and independence of the Holy See and gave it the Vatican City State as its territory, there have been controversies and heated discussions in the international community over its international and juridical status. There is not much blame for interested parties in the controversy because of the atypical status of the Holy See in the international realm.

To examine the nature of the Holy See in international law, this chapter explores the international status of the Holy See. Furthermore, this chapter would trace the significance of the international status of the Holy See in

---

[190] HYGINUS EUGENE CARDINALE, THE HOLY SEE AND THE INTERNATIONAL ORDER, Smythe, Gerrards Cross, Toronto, 1976, p. 85; (The term Holy See has three different but related meanings. Sometimes the term *Holy See* denotes the Pope together with the central offices of the Roman Curia; sometimes it designates the Pope in his role as the visible head of the Church possessing the *Apostolic primacy* as successor of St. Peter; sometimes it indicates the spiritual organization of Papal government).

the light of the social mission of the Church. The nature and functions of the Vatican City State are also brought into focus to clarify its relationship with the Holy See. An examination of the historical origins and legitimacy of the role of the Holy See in international law will throw more light on its international personality and sovereignty. This leads to another related discussion on the Nature of the Holy See's diplomacy in Chapter Four.

3.1 Historical Background of the Holy See

The Holy See's diplomatic history began in the fourth century, but the boundaries of the Papacy's temporal power have shifted over the centuries. During the struggle for Italian unification from 1860 to 1870, most of this area became part of Italy. By an Italian law of May 13, 1871, the temporal power of the Pope was abrogated, and the territory of the papacy was confined to the Vatican and Lateran palaces and the villa of Castel Gandolfo. The popes consistently refused to recognize this arrangement. The Lateran Treaty of February 11, 1929, between the Vatican and the kingdom of Italy, recognized the sovereignty of the Holy See.

3.2 The Papal States[191] and the "Roman Question"[192]

Popes in their secular role ruled portions of the Italian peninsula for more than a thousand years until the middle of the 19th century,

---

191 *See* Encyclopedia Britannica Online available at http://www.britannica.com/EBchecked/topic/441848/Papal-States [Papal States, also called Republic of Saint Peter or Church States,(Italian *Stati Pontifici* or *Stati della Chiesa)*, are territories of central Italy over which the Pope had sovereignty from 756 -1870. Included were the modern Italian regions of Lazio (Latium), Umbria, and Marche and part of Emilia-Romagna, the extent of the territory, along with the degree of papal control]; See Schnürer, G., States of the Church, in *The Catholic Encyclopedia*, Robert Appleton Company, 1912 Retrieved October 30, 2013 from New Advent available at http://www.newadvent.org/cathen/14257a.htm

192 *See generally* ENCYCLOPAEDIA BRITANNICA Online at http://www.britannica.com/EBchecked/topic/462365/Pius-IX/5759/The-Roman-Question; As early as the 4th century, the popes had acquired considerable property around Rome (called the Patrimony of St. Peter). From the 5th century, with the breakdown of Roman imperial authority in the West, the popes' influence in central Italy increased as the people of the area relied on them for protection against barbarian invasions.

when the Kingdom of Italy seized many of the Papal States. In 1870, the pope's holdings were further circumscribed when Rome itself was annexed. Disputes between the popes and Italy were resolved in 1929 by three Lateran Treaties, which established the independent state of Vatican City and granted Roman Catholicism special status in Italy. In 1984, a concordat between the Holy See and Italy modified some earlier treaty provisions, including the primacy of Roman Catholicism as the Italian state religion.[193]

The "Roman Question" had its origins in an ideological conflict. The conflict here is between the secularizing and modernizing tendencies of Liberalism and the resistance to this development on the part of the Catholic Church.[194] The Roman Question was a political dispute between the Italian Kingdom and the Roman Catholic Church (the papacy), which lingered between 1861 (the year the papacy lost its Papal States) and 1929 (the year it signed the Lateran Pacts with the Italian kingdom).[195]

From the 8th century through the middle of the 19th century, the popes held sway over the Papal States.[196] The temporal power of the papacy dates from the 9th century, when Pepin-le-Bref and his son Charlemagne created the Papal States.[197] The Papal States existed as the territorial base for the central government of the Catholic Church.[198] In 1860, after prolonged civil and regional unrest, King Vittorio Emmanuele II's army seized the Papal States, leaving only Rome and the surrounding coastal regions under papal control. In 1870, King Vittorio Emmanuele II captured Rome itself and declared it the new capital of Italy, ending papal claims to temporal power. Pope Pius IX and his successors disputed the legitimacy of these acts and proclaimed themselves to be "prisoners" in the Vatican.[199]

---

193 *See* CIA, The World Factbook, *The Holy See (Vatican City)* available at https://www.cia.gov/library/publications/the-world-factbook/geos/vt.html

194 *See* Pollard John F., THE VATICAN AND ITALIAN FASCISM 1929-1932: A STUDY IN CONFLICT, Cambridge University Press, (2005).

195 *See* "The Roman Question: Eighty Years of Deadlock," in *The Times,* February 10, 1929 available at http://webspace.webring.com/people/qs/sabathage/times1.html

196 *See* Agency C & Department U., "Vatican City" (2012) available at http://www.eoearth.org/view/article/172990

197 Crawford James, *supra* note 23 ¶ 221.

198 *Id.*

199 *Id.*

3.2.1 The Period of Persecution and the Christianization of Rome[200]

For the first 280 years of Christianity's history, Christianity was almost banned by the Roman Empire. During the early years of the Catholic Church in Rome, the Roman Empire viewed the Church as dissident in nature. This gave birth to the period of persecution of the Church in Rome, more especially the Valerian persecution. As a result of this development, it was difficult for the Church to establish relations with the outside world. This made it practically impossible for other sovereign powers to recognize the Holy See or the Vatican as an international personality.

The difficulty of the Church changed with the conversion of the Roman Emperor Constantine and the legalization of Christianity with the Edict of Milan in 313 AD.[201] Emperor Constantine envisioned Christianity as a religion that could unify the Roman Empire, which at that time was beginning to fragment and divide.[202] For this reason, Constantine summoned the Council of Nicaea in an attempt to unify first the Church, and consequently, the Empire.[203] Emperor Constantine allowed and even promoted the Christianization of pagan beliefs and practices. He permitted pagan and non-biblical beliefs to get new Christian identities.[204]

Though the Council of Nicaea could not achieve the ulterior motive for which Emperor Constantine summoned it, the Church summoned a wide variety of important councils which were result-oriented. The preoccupations of these important councils were not simply spiritual and ecclesial issues; they addressed issues about which the universal Church

---

200 *See generally* Araujo Robert J., "The Holy See: International Person and Sovereign," in *Ave Maria International Law Journal,* Inaugural Issue, Vol. 1, 2011

201 See Francis Murphy X., *Vatican Politics: The Metapolitique of the Papacy,* 19 CASE W. RES. J. INT'L L., 375 (1987) (which reviews the history of international politics and relations of the Catholic Church); see also Joseph Lecler, S.J., THE TWO SOVEREIGNTIES: A STUDY OF THE RELATIONSHIP BETWEEN THE CHURCH AND STATE (1952) (Examining in detail the historical perspective about the transformation of the Catholic Church).

202 *Id.*

203 CARDINALE HYGINUS E., THE HOLY SEE AND THE INTERNATIONAL ORDER, *supra* note 190 (showing that the results of the Nicene Council were anything but positive at least in that regard).

204 *Id.*

expressed concern.[205] Pope Leo responded to this wider concern by sending emissaries to both Church-related councils and to the courts of temporal sovereigns.[206] These early legations represented not only the spiritual sovereignty of the Holy See but also a temporal sovereignty, an avenue to make their voice heard in other political settings.[207]

The Church's selfless interest in secular politics helped to reinstate the Church's natural position in its mission to the world.[208] It was based on this development that the Church had authority to acquire territories which it administered.[209] At this early stage, the Holy See was preoccupied with protecting these territories and the rest of Christendom from the invasions of non-Christians from the North and East.[210]

---

205 *See generally* THE CATHOLIC ENCYCLOPEDIA, General Councils available at http://newadvent.org/cathen/04423f.htm (last visited October 31, 2013) (showing that the Church Councils concentrated on issues wider than ones that are simply spiritual and ecclesial; they also considered the Church's relationship with individuals and entities that exercise temporal sovereign powers).

206 See *Id.*; *See also* J.N.D. KELLY, OXFORD DICTIONARY OF POPES 44 (1986). Pope Leo the Great sent an emissary to the Council of Chalcedon in 453. He also sent Julian of Cos as his legate to Emperor in Constantinople to serve as the Pope's representative at the court there in Constantinople. See *Id.*

207 *See* CARDINALE, *supra* note 190, at 34-35 (showing the Holy See as continuing with a more renewed vigor to participate in international politics through Papal diplomacy, serving as arbitrator or mediator in international and domestic disputes, entering into treaties, concordats, and other international agreements; and participating in the activities of organizations.

208 *See* ARAUJO, *supra* note 200, at 5. The secular authority of the Roman Empire reinforced the position of the Catholic Church in Rome and beyond, including the position of the Papacy and the Holy See, enabling the Church to acquire territories with the aim of resembling other temporal powers, though with some interruptions from the 8th century when King Vittorio Emmanuele's army attacked and seized the Papal States in 1870.

209 *See* L. DUCHESNE, THE BEGINNINGS OF THE TEMPORAL SOVEREIGNTY OF THE POPES: AD 754-1073 (1908).

210 *See* THOMAS F. X. NOBLE, THE REPUBLIC OF ST. PETER: THE BIRTH OF THE PAPAL STATE 680-825 (1984). The Church became a power to reckon with in Italy. The Church did not stop at that. It expanded its secular powers to establish purposeful relations with other sovereigns and political entities.

3.2.2 The Church in the Medieval Era[211]

From the 9th century to 1520, the Church combined both spiritual and temporal life. There was no clear line between them that divided the spiritual and temporal involvement of the Church, as was the predominant practice in Western Europe.[212] Before the intermingling of these two aspects of life, the Church was for centuries free from serious interference by civil rulers. It was only Charlemagne who interfered with the power of the Church for reasons of his marital problems and the title he inherited from his late father Pepin.[213] A remarkable feature of the chaotic 9th and 10th centuries were that the Church, including the Papacy, became the prey of the powerful.

During the 11th century, the Church made great political reforms regarding its relationship with the State, particularly during the Papacy of Pope Gregory VII and Urban II. This political transformation concerned the exercise of papal power and the authority of the Holy See. The goal was to exclude civil rulers from meddling in Church matters.[214] This was a political strategy that made the position of temporal sovereigns diminish while the power of the Pope grew stronger, though not without some

---

[211] *See generally* ARAUJO, THE HOLY SEE, *supra* note 200; CARDINALE, THE HOLY SEE AND INTERNATIONAL ORDER, *supra*, note 190; JOSEPH BERNHART, THE VATICAN AS A WORLD POWER (George N. Shuster, trans.) 1939; CHARLES PICHON, THE VATICAN AND ITS ROLE IN WORLD AFFAIRS (Jean Misrahi, trans.) (1950); ROBERT A. GRAHAM, S.J., VATICAN DIPLOMACY: A STUDY OF CHURCH AND STATE ON THE INTERNATIONAL PALNE (1959).

[212] *See* generally THE COLUMBIA ELECTRONIC ENCYCLOPEDIA, (2012).

[213] *See* THE CATHOLIC ENCYCLOPEDIA, Charlemagne, available at http://newadvent.org/cathen/03610c.htm (last visited October 31, 2013). Charlemagne inherited the title "Patricius Romanus" which carried with it a special obligation to protect the temporal rights of the Holy See. He also married the daughter of Desiderius, to which the Pope objected even though Charlemagne remained adamant. The dominions of the Holy See bore the first brunt of his wrath, though his influence was benignant. See also ENCYCLOPEDIA BRITANNICA, Charlemagne, available at http://www.britannica.com/EBchecked/topic/106546/Charlemagne (last visited October 31, 2013).

[214] *See* CHURCH AND STATE THROUGH THE CENTURIES: A COLLECTION OF HISTORIC DOCUMENTS WITH COMMENTARIES (1954) (Sydney Z. Ehler, LL.D. & John B. Morrali Ph.D. trans. and eds.) [hereinafter cited as CHURCH AND STATE] a work containing an anthology of documents and commentary that are generally relevant to this book.

hiccups.[215] One could understand the reason because from that time on, Europe functioned as a Christian realm united under the Pope.[216]

The influence of the Holy See continued to be felt tremendously throughout this period with the Pope's joint use of both spiritual and temporal authority[217] For instance, in 1155, Pope Adrian IV issued a Papal Bull in which he empowered King Henry II to attack and conquer Ireland.[218] The influential position of the Holy See in the medieval era continued until the 15th century when the Popes were reduced to being Renaissance princes.[219] Starting from the middle of the 15th century, temporal powers resisted the great influence wielded by the Holy See.[220]

---

215 *See* I.S. Robinson, THE PAPACY 1073-1198: CONTINUITY AND INNOVATION (1990) (examining the details of the growth of Papal influence in the west during the Middle Ages).

216 *See id.*

217 Although he would ultimately prevail over Pope Gregory VII, King Henry IV succumbed to and dealt with Papal authority for some years. For example, in October 1076, Emperor Henry declared his obedience to the Holy See before God, the Pope, and the empire. While civil authorities expected him to bend to the wishes of temporal authorities, Pope Boniface VIII advanced the formidable papal European presence and papal primacy against King Philip the Fair of France in 1302. See Brian Tierney, THE CRISIS OF CHURCH AND STATE, *infra*, note 190; *Papal Bull Unam Sanctam*, promulgated on Nov. 18, 1302, available at http://www.newadvent.org/docs/bo08us.htm (last visited November 1, 2013) (showing assertion of papal primacy over temporal power. Pope Benedict stated, "We are informed by the texts of the gospels that in its power are two swords, namely the spiritual and the temporal." Certainly, the one who denies that the temporal sword is in the power of Peter has not listened well to the Word of the Lord…." *Id.* Continuing, Pope Boniface added "Both swords, therefore, are in the power of the Church, that is to say, the spiritual and the material sword but the former is to be administered for the Church the latter by the Church; the former in the hands of the priest; the latter by the hands of kings and soldiers, but at the will and sufferance of the priest. Id.; See also CHURCH AND STATE, infra note 214 ¶ 3-37 (expatiating on the historical context of the "two swords"); OTTO GIERKE, POLITICAL THEORIES OF THE MIDDLE AGES (1959) (examining the relationship between the spiritual and temporal powers); *See also* Pope Leo XIII, *Immortale Dei, (Encyclical Letter on the Christian Constitution of States)* ¶ 11-13 (1885) (addressing the Church's powers and sovereignties).

218 *See* Pope Adrian IV, The Bull of Pope Adrian IV Empower Henry II to Conquer Ireland, AD 1155.

219 *See* Brian Tierney, THE CRISIS OF CHURCH AND STATE 53-73 (1980) (narrating the dispute between civil and Church authorities, particularly between Pope Gregory VII and King Henry IV, in which the latter prevailed).

220 Philip Hughes, The International Action of the Papacy – Introductory: Before the Reformation, *THE TABLET*, November 2, 1940 ¶ 346; *see also* Walter Ullman, "The Development of the Medieval Idea of Sovereignty," *ENG. HIST. REV., Jan. 1, 1949, no. CCL.*

The Holy See used the opportunity of resistance by civil authorities to strengthen its international mission with the understanding that this venture is not to be determined by territorial holdings. The Church based its mission on having its moral voice heard in international realms.

One feature of this début into international affairs was centered on the mission of the promotion of the dignity of the human person so that human rights may be mutually shared regardless of race, color, ethnicity, or religion. A case in point was when anti-Semitism became prevalent in Western Europe during this period in review. Pope Gregory X in 1272 exhorted Christians all over the world, especially in Europe, to acknowledge and respect the rights to the self-determination and existence of the Jewish people.[221] The Holy See has made serious efforts to make its voice heard on human rights issues in such a way as to protect the Jews from persecution and forced conversion. The Holy See had even started raising its moral voice concerning human rights before 1948.[222] Another remarkable achievement of this period was the Holy See's inspiration to mediate in conflicts among rival temporal powers.[223]

[221] Pope Gregory X, *Papal Protection of the Jews* promulgated on October 7, 1272, available at http://www.us-israel.org/jsource/antisemitis/Papal_Protection_of_the_Jews.html (last visited November 2, 2013); *See also A Quo Primum* available at http://www.newadvent.org/docs/be14aq.htm (last visited October 30, 2013)(discussing the mistreatment of the Jews by members of the Church and therefore stating the Church's resolve for atonement and forgiveness. This featured prominently at the Vatican II Council. A Declaration on the Relationship of the Church and the non-Christian Religions (*Nostra Aetate)* was made on October 28, 1965, repudiating actions and attitudes against the Jewish people.

[222] The Universal Declaration of Human Rights was proclaimed by the United Nations General Assembly in Paris, France on December 10, 1948 (General Assembly Resolution 217 A (III); (A *Magna Carta* for all humanity highlighting the universality, the indivisibility, and the interrelationship of all human rights).

[223] *See* John Keating Cartwright, Contributions of the Papacy to International Peace, *8 CATH. HIST. REV.* 160 (1928); F. Matthews-Giba, O.F.M, Religious Dimensions of Mediation, *27 FORDHAM URB. L.J 1695* (2000) (showing the momentous influence of the Holy See on human affairs, prevailing over belligerents to avoid war or at least delay wars in some instances); Edward G. Bourne, The Demarcation Line of Alexander VI: An Episode of the Period of Discoveries, *1 YALE REVIEW 35,* 55 (1892) (discussing how Pope Alexander VI created a Line of Demarcation that separated the zones of colonial exploration between the then great powers, Portugal and Spain)

3.2.3 The Period of European Exploration and Colonization

The period of the European exploration and colonization adventure succeeded in the medieval era for purposes of strengthening the national, economic, temporal sovereignty of the European Empire. The "Holy See no longer considering itself as a flat disk surrounded by an immense void"[224] exerted a unique influence commensurate to the characteristics of the new era. The period of European exploration and colonization was a ripe opportunity for the Holy See to spread its tentacles by bringing the message of Christ to the colonies. The Holy See either supported the European exploitative colonization or acted as a silent bystander.[225] Eventually this undisturbed exploitation of the natives changed, with the Holy See' preaching in support of human dignity and human rights.[226]

---

[224] *See* ARAUJO, *supra* note 200, at 8.

[225] *Id.*

[226] Bartolomé de las Casas, a 16th century Spanish historian, social reformer, and Dominican friar who also became a bishop, spent 50 years actively fighting slavery and the violent and exploitative colonial abuse of indigenous peoples, especially by trying to convince the Spanish court to adopt a more humane policy of colonization. His dogged efforts resulted in several improvements in the legal status of the natives, and in an increased colonial focus on the ethics of colonialism. Considered as one of the first advocates of universal human rights, he influenced the Holy See's strong advocacy for human rights, starting with Pope Paul III's Bull in 1537. See KENNETH PENNINGTON, BARTOLOMÉ DE LAS CASAS AND THE Tradition of the Medieval Law, 1993, available at http://faculty.cua.edu/pennington/Law508/LasCasas2.html See especially, Pope Paul III, *Sublimus Dei* (trans. "From God on High," on the enslavement and evangelization of Indians) May 29, 1537; by the early sixteenth century, European nations, including Spain and Portugal, had established empires in North America, South America, and the islands of the Caribbean. Throughout the process of empire building, they had attempted to enslave the native population. The Bull *Sublimus Dei* is an official proclamation from the pope, usually setting forth a decision to which all Roman Catholics must adhere. *Sublimus dei* forbade the enslavement of the native peoples of the Western Hemisphere. The key reason given by Pope Paul III was that native peoples are as much human beings as Europeans. As such, they have souls in need of the church's salvation and also possess the ability to accept that salvation. To treat these native peoples as less than humans ("dumb brutes created for our service") would prohibit their salvation available at http://www.papalencyclicals.net/Paul03/p3subli.htm (an early example of papal admonitions about how to deal with foreign peoples and social justice; the Roman Pontiff, Pope Paul III, issued the following Bull "To all faithful Christians" with regard to the treatment of the American Indians demanding that the native folk be respected, that their freedom be honored, and their right to possession of their property. He clearly demanded that the Indians not be enslaved, "should the contrary happen, it shall be null and have no effect." See also John Eppstein, THE CATHOLIC TRADITION OF THE LAW OF NATIONS 418-26 (1935).

This marked the inception of the extension of the moral voice of the Catholic Church in the international community.

While the temporal powers were vying for new lands, natural resources, material wealth, and power, the Holy See concentrated on spreading the Word of God, which also included monitoring inhuman activities of the colonists. Civil powers saw the position of the Holy See at this period in history as a serious challenge and reacted in defense of their worldly agenda. This came in the form of questioning the authority of the Pope. This challenge was not only fiercely organized but it was heightened by the Protestant Reformation, which gave a new role to the Holy See, as well as altered the latter's international presence.

The temporal sovereigns enacted laws that added vitality to their powers and which conflicted with the influential moral voice of the Holy See.[227] The challenge mounted by these temporal sovereigns against Papal

---

[227] *See* CHURCH AND STATE, supra note 214, at 163-164; *Also see generally*, CANNON JOHN ASHTON, THE OXFORD COMPANION TO BRITISH HISTORY (1997); JULIET GARDINER & NEIL WENBORN, THE COLUMBIA COMPANION TO BRITISH HISTORY (1997); CHRISTOPHER HAIGH, ENGLISH REFORMATIONS: RELIGION, POLITICS, AND SOCIETY UNDER THE TUDORS (1993); DAVID LOADES, HENRY VIII COURT, CHURCH AND CONFLICT, National Archives, (2007); JASPER GODWIN RIDLEY, HENRY VIII, (1985) (discussing anti-Papal powers of Parliament in England aimed at legally declaring some children as bastards and others as free born. For instance, The First Succession Act of Henry VIII's reign was passed by the Parliament of England in March 1534. The Act was formally titled the Succession to the Crown Act 1533 or the Act of Succession 1533 often dated as 1534.The Act made then yet unborn Princess Elizabeth, daughter of King Henry VIII by Anne Boleyn, the true successor to the Crown by declaring Princess Mary, daughter of the King by Catherine of Aragon, a bastard. The Act also required all subjects, if commanded, to swear an oath to recognize this Act as well as the King's supremacy. Under the Treasons Act 1534, anyone who refused to take the oath was subject to a charge of treason. This happened to Sir Thomas More, who refused to swear the oath because it acknowledged the anti-Papal powers of Parliament in matters of religion. The Act was later altered by the Second Succession Act, which made Elizabeth illegitimate, and the Third Succession Act, which returned both sisters to the line of succession); other moves by temporal leaders to exert more authority included The Peace of Ausburg in the 16th century available at http://www.britannica.com/EBchecked/topic/42767/Peace-of-Augsburg where Emperors mediated between Catholics and the Lutherans over ownership of Ecclesiastical lands; The Edict of Nantes 1598 available at http://www.britannica.com/EBchecked/topic/402718/Edict-of-Nantes (Emperor Henry IV of France granted the Calvinist Protestants of France (also known as Huguenots) substantial rights in a nation still considered essentially Catholic); The Peace of Westphalia 1648 available at http://www.britannica.com/EBchecked/topic/641170/Peace-of-Westphalia (where Emperor

authority militated against the establishment of the *Respublica Christiana.* Therefore, the 17th century period, which was characterized by the Protestant Reformation, eroded the unified Christian religion that was tied to Rome and the Holy See. This rivalry and opposition of the Holy See's influence only decreased the enormous influence of the Church in international law and politics; it never was eliminated entirely. For instance, while the American and French Revolutions decreased the temporal power of the Holy See in the 19th century, the European powers and the Vienna Congress recognized the sovereignty of the Holy See.[228]

3.2.4 The Period of Italian Unification and the Confiscation of the Papal States

The 19th century ushered in serious challenges to the Holy See, which undermined its influence.[229] The campaign for the unification of the Italian States was the most detrimental blow, which impacted heavily on the temporal sovereignty of the Holy See at this period.[230] On September 20, 1870, Italian troops occupied Rome and invaded the Papal States as the final step of the *Risorgimento.*[231] Rome, which used to be the capital

---

Ferdinand III of France between May and October in Osnabrück and Münster, among other things, resolved a thirty-year conflict of mono-denominational and bi-denominational issues that existed between Catholics, Calvinists and Lutherans).

228 *See* ARAUJO, *supra* note 200, at 10.

229 *See generally,* LASSA FRANCIS LAWRENCE OPPENHEIM, INTERNATIONAL LAW: A TREATISE (1955) (discussing some of the challenges the Holy See contended with concerning its influence in international politics. For instance, Napoleon Bonaparte quarantined the Pope, though briefly, and the Papal States were made to be under the French control for about five years, 1809 to 1814. *See also* Georges Guyau, "Napoleon Bonapart I," in *The Catholic Encyclopedia*, available at http://www.newadvent.org/cathen/10687a.htm (last visited October 13, 2013).

230 ARAUJO, *supra* note 200, at 10.

231 This is an Italian political expedition that aimed at unifying Italy as a Kingdom, otherwise referred to as *Risorgimento. Risorgimento,* (an Italian word meaning "Rising Again"), was a 19th-century movement for Italian unification that culminated in the establishment of the Kingdom of Italy in 1861. The *Risorgimento* was an ideological and literary movement that helped to arouse the national consciousness of the Italian people, and it led to a series of political events that freed the Italian states from foreign domination and united them politically. See for details ENCYCLOPEDIA BRITANNICA, available at http://www.britannica.com/EBchecked/topic/504489/Risorgimento (last visited September 23, 2013)

of the supreme government of the Catholic Church, was made the capital of the Italian kingdom under King Emmanuelle II.[232] The intrusion of temporal authorities in the affairs of the Holy See gave rise to secularism in Italy. For this reason, Pope Pius IX issued the encyclical *Notis et Nobiscum* regarding the attack on the Papal States and, therefore, on the temporal authority of the Holy See.[233] Still on the issue of the confiscation of the Pontifical States, Pope Pius IX issued a more direct encyclical, *Respicientes,* in which the Pope protested vehemently against the loss of the Papal States and condemned the action without giving any weight to the reason for such confiscation.[234]

The loss of the Papal States affected neither the influence of the Holy See in international law nor its international personality.[235] Instead, the influence of the Holy See increased in the outside world.[236]Araujo

---

232 CARDINALE, *supra* note 190.

233 Pope Pius IX, *Notis et Nobiscum* (*On the Church in the Pontifical States*) December 8, 1849, available at http://www.papalencyclicals.net/Pius09/p9nostis.htm (denouncing socialism and communism for attempting to confuse the faithful with new doctrines, and speaking against plots and conspiracies created by revolutionaries and rationalists in order to overthrow the temporal power of the Catholic Church; deploring the problem of indifferentism in matters of religion; urging Italians to obey their legitimate political authorities, but adding that Christianity protects true liberty and equality, and declaring such revolutions are therefore useless).

234 Pope Pius IX, *Respicientes* (Protesting the Taking of the Pontifical States) November 1, 1870, available at http://www.papalencyclicals.net/Pius09/p9respic.htm (last visited November 4, 2013), (dealing with the excommunication of the King of Italy and those who cooperated with him from the Catholic Church for confiscating the Papal States); see also, Daniela Fernanda & Stefano Solari (eds.), "Humanism and Religion in the History of Economic Thought (Selected Papers from the 10th Aispe Conference) in *Collana di Studi e ricerche dell'Associazione Italiana per la Storia del Pensiero Economica,* Vol. VI, Milano, Italia, 2010; Roberto de Mattei, PIUS IX, (trans. By John Laughland) (2004) (examining the Papal encyclical *Respicientes* and the protestation and condemnation of the confiscation of the Pontifical States).

235 *See generally* S. WILLIAM HALPERIN, ITALY AND THE VATICAN AT WAR: A STUDY OF THEIR RELATIONS FROM THE OUTBREAK OF THE FRANCO-PRUSSIAN WAR TO THE DEATH OF PIUS IX (1939); See also LILIAN PARKER WALLACE, THE PAPACY AND EUROPEAN DIPLOMACY – 1869-1878 (1948)

236 *See* ROBERT A. GRAHAM, THE RISE OF THE DOUBLE DIPLOMATIC CORPS IN ROME: A STUDY IN INTERNATIONAL PRACTICE 1870-1875 (1952) (examining how foreign nations would normally establish relations with the Holy See different from the one with Italy); *See also* Josef Kunz, The Status of the Holy See in International Law, *46 Ave Maria J. INT'L L. 308,* 311 (1952) (discussing the continued increase of interest of States in the Vatican as an observation point); *See also* ARAUJO, *supra* note 200, at 11.

quotes an observer of this period as noting that "Governments which had no relations with the Holy See established them; Governments that had broken off relations have restored them. Governments which had second-class relations raised them to first class."[237]

More importantly, irrespective of the absence of territorial sovereignty,[238] the Holy See was enormously involved in international mediation and arbitration courtesy of invitations from other states for that purpose.[239] In other words, the absence of territory under their authority did not deter the Popes from maintaining international relations with other countries, independent of the Kingdom of Italy. For instance, in resolving their dispute over the Caroline Islands in 1885, Germany and Spain invited the Holy See to mediate between them.[240] There were many other countries that requested the Holy See to mediate their disputes even though they were not, traditionally speaking, Catholic countries.[241] They relied upon the neutrality and the uniqueness of the Holy See's moral voice for an amicable resolution of their international disputes.[242]

3.3 The Historical Origins of the Vatican[243]

---

237 ARAUJO, *supra* note 200, at 11; *see also* L.J.S Wood, Vatican Politics and Policies, *128 ATLANTIC MONTHLY 398,* 404 (1921).

238 Robert F. Illing, America And the Vatican: Trading Information After WWII, History Publishing Co., NY, 2011 P. 56 (confirming that from 1870 to 1929, the Popes had no territory under their authority, but they nonetheless managed to maintain their administrative and diplomatic independence from the Kingdom of Italy, all under the rubric of the Holy See).

239 ARAUJO, *supra* note 200, at 12.

240 *See* JAMES BROWN SCOTT, SOVEREIGN STATES AND SUITS BEFORE ARBITRAL TRIBUNALS AND COURTS OF JUSTICE 95 (1925) (discussing the Pope's invitation by Germany and Spain to mediate and how the Pope responded).

241 For example, countries like Great Britain, the United States of America, Germany, and others are not traditionally Catholic countries. See John Eppstein, *supra* note 198 ¶ 470-74 (listing about 30 instances in which the Holy See either mediated or arbitrated disputes between rival states); *See* ARAUJO, *supra* note 200, at 12; CARDINALE, *supra* note 190, at 89.

242 *See id.* At 88-89.

243 *See generally,* CARDINALE HYGINUS E., THE HOLY SEE AND THE INTERNATIONAL ORDER (1976); Broderick Robert C. (ed.), CATHOLIC ENCYCLOPEDIA (1990); Knight Kevin, NEW ADVENT: THE CATHOLIC ENCYCLOPEDIA (2009); ENCYCLOPEDIA OF CATHOLIC HISTORY (1995).

The name "Vatican" predates Christianity and comes from the Latin *Mons Vaticanus*, meaning Vatican Mount. The "Vatican" as a territory was already in use in the time of the Roman Republic for a marshy area on the west bank of the Tiber River across from the city of Rome. Under the Roman Empire, many villas were constructed there, after Agrippina the Elder (14 BC – 18 October AD 33) drained the area and built her gardens in the early 1st century AD.

Before the arrival of Christianity, it is supposed that this originally uninhabited part of Rome (the *ager vaticanus*) had long been considered sacred, or at least not available for habitation. This area became the site of the martyrdom of many Christians after the Great Fire of Rome in AD 64. Ancient tradition holds that it was in this circus that Saint Peter was crucified upside-down. In 326 AD, the first Church, St. Peter's Basilica, was built on the tomb of St. Peter. From then on, the area became more populated because of activities related to St. Peter's Basilica. The Vatican City State, sovereign and independent, is the survivor of the Papal States, which in 1859 comprised an area of some 17,000 sq. miles (44,030 sq. km).

As early as the 5th century during the pontificate of Pope Symmachus (9498-514), a palace was constructed near the site of St. Peter's Basilica. Popes in their secular role gradually came to govern neighboring regions, popularly called Papal States. These Papal States involved a large portion of the Italian peninsula. In 1870, the Roman troops under Emperor Vittorio Emmanuele invaded and seized the Papal States, including the Vatican, which was made the capital of the then newly created Kingdom of Italy.[244] The confiscation of the Vatican came to an end following the Lateran

[244] There were a series of attacks on the Papal States before this last blow. Pope Pius IX, the youngest Pope in memory, was elected in 1846. He started great reforms which stopped because of politically motivated violence which broke out in Rome at that time. This violence led to his overthrow and the establishment of a short-lived Second Roman Republic. Austrian and French troops put a *finis* to this febrile attempt at reform. This sorry state was given a *coup-de-grace* in 1870 when the victorious troops of the new Kingdom of Italy under Emperor Vittorio Emmanuelle entered Rome, defeated the resistance of the Catholic Church, and confiscated the Papal States. From 1870 to 1929, the Popes were reduced to the status of being only the heads of the Catholic Church, with no opportunity to freely administer the Papal States as they had before. However, this did not prevent the Holy See from continuing its international relations with other States independent of the Italian Kingdom. See ROBERT A. ILLING, *supra* note 209 at p. 54.

Treaty in 1929. One of the agreements of the Lateran Treaty was the creation of the State of the Vatican City.

3.3.1 Issue of Vatican Statehood[245]

During the period from 1870-1929, the Church-State relationship which existed between the Holy See and the Italian State underwent several stages of development in the context of changes in the Italian political landscape.[246] The collapse of the Papal States and subsequent occupation of Rome in the year 1870 by King Vittorio Emmanuelle II's forces created a difficult situation for the Italian State and the reigning Pope Pius IX. The confiscation and occupation of the Papal States created a situation whereby two sovereigns operated within the same territory.[247] From 1870 until the conclusion of the negotiations of the Lateran Treaties, the Holy See could not be regarded as a foreign State different from the Kingdom of Italy.[248] The Italian Parliament and Senate exerted much-desired energy in addressing the Church-State issues which arose at that time. The legislature unilaterally passed a legislation known as *"La Legge della Guarentigie"* (The Law of the Guarantees) in 1871.[249]

---

[245] *See generally,* ROMAN A. MELNYK, VATICAN DIPLOMACY AT THE UNITED NATIONS: A HISTORY OF CATHOLIC GLOBAL ENGAGEMENT (2009); JOSEPH BERNHART, THE VATICAN AS A WORLD POWER (George N. Shuster, trans.) (1939); CHARLES PICHON, THE VATICAN AND ITS ROLE IN WORLD AFFAIRS (Jean Misrahi, trans.) (1950); ROBERT A. GRAHAM, VATICAN DIPLOMACY: A STUDY OF CHURCH AND STATE ON THE INTERNATIONAL PLANE (1959); HYGINUS EUGENE CARDINALE, THE HOLY SEE AND THE INTERNATIONAL ORDER (1976); SIDNEY Z. EHLER & JOHN B. MORRALI (trans. & eds.), CHURCH AND STATE THROUGH THE CENTURIES: A COLLECTION OF HISTORIC DOCUMENTS WITH COMMENTARIES (1954).

[246] MELNYK, *supra* note 24, at 8.

[247] *Id.*

[248] JAMES CRAWFORD, *supra* note 23, at 221.

[249] *See* "La Legge della Guarentigie," in *Gazzetta Ufficiale del Regno D'Italia*, no. 134, May 15, 1871; For English trans., *see* S.Z. EHLER & J.B MORRALL (eds.), Church and State Through the Centuries, Westminster, The Newman Press, 1954, pp. 287-291. The Law of Guarantees was divided into two sections, namely, (a) The Prerogatives of the Supreme Pontiff and of the Holy See, and (b) Relations of the State with the Church. Articles 1 & 4 of this section 1 describe the Roman Pontiff as "sovereign," "sacred," and "inviolable," with a range of privileges and an annual endowment from the State to pay for the Church's expenses

The Law of Guarantees did not effectively ensure a clear-cut separation of Church and State, which was its original goal. Rather, the Law of Guarantees curtailed the freedom of actions of the Holy See in temporal matters.[250] Its implementation was left to the discretion of the Italian State and was not in conformity with the principles of international law regarding agreements between sovereign states.[251] Because of the foregoing, Pope Pius IX had no other option except to formally reject the Law of Guarantees and to pass a decree known as *Non expedit* in 1874, forbidding Catholic participation in Italian parliamentary activities.[252]

However, the Italian government did not rest on its oars. The Italian government continued to address its relations with the Holy See within the framework of the Law of Guarantees.[253] The present state of affairs did not deter the Holy See from conducting foreign relations within the context of

---

and building maintenance. Article 5 of section 1 provides grants access to the Vatican, the Lateran, and Castel Gandolfo residences. Article 9 assures freedom of the Roman Pontiff to perform his spiritual ministry. Another important provision is Article 11 which provides that the reception of envoys and sending of legates would follow the process of international law stipulations. Article 12 assures freedom of communication between the "Episcopate and the whole Catholic world;" *see id.* at 289. Section II deals with "Relations of the State with the Church" provided for in Articles 13-19. Although the Bishops were not required to take oaths to the King (article 15), the disposal of ecclesiastical goods and the conferring of benefices outside the city of Rome was subject to the authority of the State 9article 16).

250 In establishing a State fund for the Church, article 4 provides as follows: "The endowment of an annual income of 3,225,000 lire is reserved for the benefit of the Holy See. With this sum, equal to that which figures in the Roman Budget under the headings: 'Apostolic Palaces, Sacred College, Ecclesiastical Congregations, Secretariat of State and Diplomatic Representation Abroad,' provision shall be made for the personal income of the Sovereign Pontiff and the various ecclesiastical needs of the Holy See, the usual maintenance and upkeep of the Apostolic Palaces and their dependencies, the salaries, gratuities and pensions of the attendants mentioned in the preceding Articles and those attached to the Pontifical Court and for the accidental expenses, such as the maintenance and upkeep of museums and libraries pertaining to the Court and salaries, wages and pensions of those employed there [...]" *See id.* at 288. Article 16 restricts the authority of the Church in temporal affairs, subjecting some areas to royal assent: "However, until otherwise provided by special law spoken of in article 18, the acts of those authorities which have as their object the disposal of ecclesiastical goods and the provision to major or minor benefices, except those of the city of Rome and the Suburban Sees, shall remain subject to the 'exequatur' and the royal 'placet'" *see id* at 290. Article 17 of the Law of Guarantees provides for spiritual and disciplinary Pontifical acts to be in conformity with the Italian State Law and public order.

251 MELNYK, *supra* note 24, at 9.

252 *Id.*

253 *Id.*

the existing diplomatic practices and legal parameters.[254] The absence of agreement between the Holy See and the Italian government lingered till the 20th century – a problem that has come to be known as the "Roman Question." The Holy See's strong aversion to the Law of Guarantees never changed anything, and all the efforts mounted to find a lasting resolution to the "Roman Question" proved abortive up until the mid-1920s, when more reliable efforts emerged.

The advent of Pope Pius XI (1922-1939) and Benito Mussolini (Prime Minister of Italy) renewed the momentum for the resolution of the impasse between the Holy See and the Italian Kingdom.[255] Cardinal Pietro Gasparri and Prime Minister Benito Mussolini, representing the Holy See and the Italian State, respectively, embarked on thirty months of intensive negotiations to resolve the strained relationship between the two institutions.[256] The product of their negotiations was the 1929 Lateran Treaty Agreements, which were signed at the Lateran Palace. The Lateran Agreements were three in number, namely,

- The Conciliation Treaty – A treaty recognizing the independence and sovereignty of the Holy See and creating the State of the Vatican City;[257]

---

[254] In consonance with Articles 11 and 12 of the Law of Guarantees which provided for issues concerning international relations and communication, the Law ensured the Holy See's ability to function in international affairs. For instance, Article 11 states that "envoys of foreign governments, accredited to His Holiness, shall enjoy in the Kingdom all the prerogatives and immunities accorded to diplomatic agents of international law. Offences against them shall be punished with the penalties liable for offences against envoys of foreign powers accredited to the Italian government. Envoys of His Holiness accredited to foreign Governments are assured, in the territory of the Kingdom, of prerogatives and immunities customary according to the aforesaid International Law to facilitate their departure to the place of their mission and their return from it." Article 12 provides that that, "The Sovereign Pontiff may correspond freely with the Episcopate and with the whole Catholic world, without any interference by the Italian Government. For this purpose, he is to have the right of establishing, in the Vatican or in his other residences, postal and telegraph offices staffed by his chosen employees [...]" *see id* at 289

[255] MELNYK, *supra* note 24, at 10.

[256] *Id.*

[257] *See Trattato Fra La Santa Sede e L'Italia,* February 11, 1929, in *AAS, 21 (1929),* pp. 209-279, *see* WILLIAMSON (trans.), Conciliation Treaty, in *AAS, pp. 42-50.* The Conciliation Treaty consists of 27 Articles replacing Section 1 of the abrogated Law of Guarantees 91871). The Conciliation Treaty recognizes the sovereignty of the Holy See in international matters and

- The Financial Convention – defining the relations between the government and the Church within Italy;[258] and
- The Concordat – A financial convention providing the Holy See with compensation for its losses during the 1870 unrest and confiscation of the Papal States

The articles of the Conciliation Treaty address *inter alia* the issues of sovereignty, jurisdiction, and international relations. For example, article 2 of the Conciliation Treaty stipulates as follows: "Italy recognizes the sovereignty of the Holy See in the international sphere, with the attributes inherent in its nature and in conformity with the requirements of its mission in the world. Italy recognizes the full propriety and the absolute power and sovereign jurisdiction of the Holy See over the Vatican as actually constituted with all the appurtenances and endowments, creating in such mode *la citta del Vaticano* for that special end by the modality of the present Treaty."[259]

---

sovereign jurisdiction over the Vatican City State as provided for in Articles 2 &3. This Treaty recognizes the person of the Supreme Pontiff as sacred and inviolable in the whole of Italy, with penalties for public libel or offences (see art. 8). Article 9 stipulates that in consonance with international law, persons permanently domiciled within the Vatican City State are subject to the sovereignty of the Holy See. By Articles 12 & 19, the Italian State recognizes that the Holy See has the right to passive and active legation, with accredited representatives to the Holy See accorded diplomatic immunity, privileges, freedom of movement, etc., in line with international law. Articles 13-16 recognizes that the four Basilicas, the residence at Castel Gandolfo, specific universities, seminaries, and other major properties and churches are owned by the Catholic Church. Article 21 assures the access to and safe passage for purposes of visiting the Pope, his legates, cardinals, and other dignitaries for conclaves or councils. Articles 22 & 23 provide for international law enforcement issues, while art. 24 states that the Holy See will not accept temporal political rivalry with the State of Italy.

[258] *See Convenzione Finanziaria,* February 11, 1929, in *AAS, 21 (1929*), PP. 273 -274 (English translation is on pp. 50-51). The Financial Convention is made up of three articles, though considered an integral part of the Lateran Treaty. Article 1 provides for Indemnity payments by the Italian State to the Holy See which consists of both cash and consolidated stock equal to a cash sum of 750 million Italian lire and 5% Italian Bearer Bonds with a nominal value of 1 billion Italian lire. Article 2 provides the above payments are applicable on the condition that the Holy See accepts them as final settlement arising from the events of 1870 (the confiscation of the Papal States). Article three provides for stamp duty and tax exemption regarding these transactions.

[259] *See* Article 2, Conciliation Treaty, 1929.

Article 4 of the Conciliation Treaty contains tremendous implications. It provides for the exclusive sovereignty of the Holy See over the Vatican City State giving the Italian State no right of interference. The provisions of the Financial Convention are stipulated for payments by the Italian State to the Holy See as settlement for wrongs inherent in the confiscation of the Papal States in 1870. The Concordat contains 45 articles, which give more details of the Lateran Treaty.[260] However, in 2001, Pope John Paul II replaced the 1929 Treaty with *La Nuova Legge Fondamentale dello Stato della Cita del Vaticano.261*

3.4 Overview of the Independence and Sovereignty of the Holy See

The preceding section discussed the historical account of the Vatican rise to statehood. The Italian government and the Holy See signed three agreements (Lateran Treaties) in 1929, resolving a dispute that had estranged a cordial Church-State relationship. The first agreement was a treaty that recognizes and defines the independence and sovereignty of the Holy See, creating and giving the Holy See its territory as the Vatican City State. The second agreement was a Concordat defining the relations between the government of Italy and the Church within Italy and granting

---

[260] *See* Concordato Fra La Santa Sede e L'Italia February 11, 1929, in *AAS, 21 (1929),* PP. 275-294; *see* English translation in WILLIAMSON, PP. 52-66. The 45 articles of the Concordat, among other things, replaced Section II of the abrogated Law of Guarantees (1871). The Concordat provisions address the freedom of the Catholic Church to exercise its spiritual mission with jurisdiction in ecclesiastical matters.

[261] Pope John Paul II, *motu proprio La Nuova Legge Fondamentale Dello Stato della Citta del Vaticano,* in AAS *suppl.,* 71 (2000), pp. 75-83. Earlier in 1984, a concordat between the Holy See and the Italian State modified certain provisions of the 1929 Treaty, including the primacy of Roman Catholicism as the Italian state religion. This new fundamental law of the Vatican gives the Supreme Pontiff power to be the Head of State of the Vatican and the Catholic Church all over the world. As a Head of State, the new Law invests the Pope with executive, legislative, and judicial powers, and to govern the Vatican State through the Pontifical Commission for the Vatican City State. Judicial power is exercised in the name of the Supreme Pontiff by the Magistrate, Court of First Instance, Court of Cessation, and Court of Appeal. Executive power is exercised through the *Governatorate,* while legislative power is exercised through the Commission made up of appointed cardinals. *See* MELNYK, supra note 24, for details.

Roman Catholicism a special status in Italy. The third agreement was a Financial Convention providing the Holy See with compensation for its losses in 1870 following Italy's attack and confiscation of Rome. This discussion proceeds from this point to examine how the Italian recognition of the independence and sovereignty of the Holy See strengthened the latter's existing relations with foreign States as it is today.

The international personality of the Holy See stems from the internal legal order of the Church is not derived from any State or other subject of international law, and therefore the Holy See is sovereign.[262] It is in the originality of the Holy See's legal order *vis-à-vis* international law that resides the stark difference between the nature of the Holy See's international personality and the personality of other non-States.[263]

Originally, States were the only entities conceived as subjects of international law.[264] The issue of the international personality of the Holy See and the Vatican City State has brought a different perspective in international law. The Holy See, as personified in the Pope of the Catholic Church, has acquired significant international status over the centuries. The Holy See appears to have acquired such international recognition and authority primarily based on its long-standing involvement and achievement in world affairs over a period of many centuries. Some writers have viewed the Holy See's unique international status as an exception to the general rule that only States are subjects of international law. And as a matter of fact, debates have been heated on many occasions as to whether

---

262 H.F. KOCK, "Holy See," in R. Bernhardt (ed.), ENCYCLOPEDIA OF PUBLIC INTERNATIONAL LAW, vol. 10, 1987, pp. 230-233 (stressing that the internal legal order of the Holy See does not derive from international law or any institution or arrangement in the world other than the Holy See itself). "Sovereignty" is defined as "the self-sufficient source of political power, from which all specific political powers are derived: the international independence of a State, combined with the right and power of regulating its internal affairs without foreign dictation," *see* BLACK'S LAW DICTIONARY 1396 (6TH ed.) (1990).

263 *See* GORDON IRELAND, "The State of the City of the Vatican," *27 AM. J. INT'L L. 271*, 272 (1933) (stating that the relations between the Church and the various States have existed from time immemorial).

264 *See* OPPENHEIM L., INTERNATIONAL LAW (2nd ed. 192), *reprinted in* REBECCA WALLACE, INTERNATIONAL LAW 59 (2ND ed. 1992); only States can bring cases before the International Court of Justice (ICJ), See Art. 34.1, ICJ, June 26, 1945 (stating that only States may be parties to a case before the ICJ).

the international status arises from the Holy See's status as head of the Church or as ruler of the Vatican City State.

The United Nations' status of the Holy See has also generated discussions at different levels. When the Holy See first enquired about becoming a member of the UNO, the speculation was that the Holy See "would not be capable of fulfilling all of the responsibilities of membership."[265] Nonetheless, the Holy See was accorded a non-member State observer status following Pope Paul VI's appointment of the Holy See's first envoy to the United Nations.[266] The status of non-Member State observer gives the Holy See an edge over other organizations[267] and makes the Holy See participate in the United Nations on the same level as if it were a full-fledged Member.[268]

---

[265] *See* JAMES CRAWFORD, *supra* note 23, at 224-225; on this matter, United States Secretary of State Cordell Hull added that "the protection of the integrity of the Vatican as an independent State would not be increased by its membership (of the United Nations") ¶ *USFR 1944/I, 960-3, 962.*

[266] Bell Charles W., "Taking Aim at the Holy See: Group Wants UN to Limit its Credentials," in N.Y. Daily News, September4, 1999, available at http://www.seechange.org/media/NY%20Daily%20News%209499.htm (last visited November 14, 2013); prior to its acceptance of non-member State status, the Holy See was "active as an ad-hoc and at times formal observer to various UN bodies . . . usually at its own request." See CATHOLICS FOR CHANGE, THE CATHOLIC CHURCH AT THE UNITED NATIONS: CHURCH OR STATE? available at http://www.seechange.org/PDF/See%20Change%20Briefing%20Paper.pfd (last visited November 14, 2013).

[267] *See* R.G. SYMBESMA-KNOL, THE STATUS OF OBSERVER IN THE UNITED NATIONS 63 (1981) (indicating that the Holy See's benefits to being an observer are "fundamentally different from those of other observers who, though non-member observers like the Holy See, but can never qualify for participation on an equal footing with the Member States.").

[268] *Id. See also U.N. Jurid. Y.B. 164, 167, U.N. Doc. ST/LEG/SER.C/13 1975;* YASMIN ABDULLAH, THE HOLY SEE AT THE UNITED NATIONS CONFERENCES: STATE OR CHURCH? *96 COLUM. L. REV., 1835, 1843* (1996), at p. 71(the Holy See's non-membership status is exalted to a large degree as to participate in the work of the United Nations on the same level as other members) UN membership would directly involve the Holy See in political, economic, and commercial conflicts arising between the states, particularly CARDINALE, *supra* note 200, at 259).

3.4.1 The Concept of Respublica Christianorum[269]

The concept of the *Respublica Christianorum* needs a little attention here in order to understand the international personality of the Holy See a little better. *Respublica Christianorum* depicts a legal-political order in which the Roman Pontiff occupied a position of religious supremacy not just within the Catholic Church's parameter but also within the legal fabric of the "universal medieval" state. Obviously, the Holy See is a non-territorial body with a long history in international affairs.[270]

Based on this historical reality, Arangio-Ruiz believes that the Holy See must have participated in the process of making the first rules of international law, which would govern relations among potentates who were escaping from this universal *Respublica*. The Holy See must have equally participated in the application of these first rules on international law to the egalitarian relations they came to cover.[271] With this egalitarian arrangement, the Holy See was stopped from being in the position of legal authority, which it occupied in the "universal medieval" legal order. The egalitarian structure put the Holy See in a position of juxtaposition to, and equality with, the coexisting sovereign potentates.[272]

Before the year 1870, the involvement of the Holy See in international affairs was associated with the government of the Papal States. For this reason,

---

[269] The etymological definition of the Latin term "*respublica*" derives from two Latin words "res" meaning "thing" and "*publica*" meaning "public," altogether meaning "the public thing." As a noun, the term "respublica" is synonymous with (Government, politics and diplomacy) "the State," "republic" or "commonwealth." *See* THE AMERICAN HERITAGE OF THE ENGLISH LANGAUGE, (4th ed. 2000). Respublica is used to mean "the state as a unit making foreign commitments, and certainly he can and does use words like *urbs, oppidum, civitas, natio, patria, populus, regnum* and *imperium*." See WILLIAM R. EVERDELL, THE END OF KINGS: A HISTORY OF REPUBLICS AND REPUBLICANS, University of Chicago Press (2000); THE FIRST MODERNS: PROFILES IN THE ORIGIN OF TWENTIETH-CENTURY THOUGHT, University of Chicago Press, (1997). William Everdell's work is available at www.cscs.lsa.umich.edu/~crshalizi/reviews/first-moderns/ last visited May 11, 2014. Excerpts of William Everdell's article that explains the Latin term "republica" can be found his article Wikipedia free encyclopedia.

[270] Gaetano Arangio-Ruiz, "The Nature of the International Personality of the Holy See," *REVUE BELGE DE DROIT INTERNATIONAL*, 1996, P. 359.

[271] *Id.*

[272] KOCK, *supra* note 262; *See also* CADINALE, *supra* note 190, at 76 (showing that the international personality of the Holy See that started with the relations between the Church and the various Papal states has existed from time immemorial.

the controversy over its separate legal status did not arise.[273] It is difficult to say at precisely what time the Holy See claim to long-standing supremacy has lost objective vitality in its external relations.[274] It is reasonable to assume that when the *Resplubica Christiana's* legal order ceased to exist and the claim of the Holy See to "supranationality" lost its weight, the egalitarian system of international law took center stage for good. At this stage, the Holy See found itself in a position of *par inter pares* within the international legal order.[275]

3.4.2 International Personality of the Holy See[276]

Some writers have argued that the Holy See had no international standing at all after 1870.[277] But the true position is that the Holy See

---

[273] CRAWFORD, *supra* note 23, at 226.

[274] *See* Josef L. Kunz, THE STATUS OF THE HOLY SEE IN INTERNATIONAL LAW, 46 *AM. J. INT'L L.* 308, 309 (1952) (indicating that the relationship between the Holy See and the Christian states formed the original international community showing the supremacy of the Holy See also); see also JORRI C. DUURSMA, FRAGMENTATION AND INTERNATIONAL RELATIONS OF MICRO-STATES: SELF-DETERMINATION AND STATEHOOD 377 (1996) (stating that the Papal states consisted of the present Italian regions of Romagna, Marche, Umbria, and the Patrimony of St. Peter, including Rome; see also CARDINALE, *supra* note 190, ¶ 99 (indicating that in 1859 the territory of the Papal State covered 17,218 square miles in central Italy and had a population of well over three million people).

[275] ARANGIO-RUIZ, *supra* note 270, at 360. *See also* ILLING, supra note 145; ARAUJO, *supra* note 200 (indicating the atypical nature of the international personality of the Holy See and examining the tremendous influence it has exerted in international law and politics to the effect that it is treated as a fully-fledged member of international organizations such as the UNO though its status is still as an Observer)

[276] *See* ROBERT A. GRAHAM, VATICAN DILOMACY: A STUDY OF CHURCH AND STATE ON THE INTERNATIONAL PLANE (1959) (indicating that though the central mission of the Church is religious, the Holy See is a subject of international law and is capable of international rights and obligations).

[277] *See* CRAWFORD, *supra* note 23, at 226; ARAUJO, *supra* note 200 (showing the peculiar nature of the international personality of the Holy See over which have been heated debates). Also, many, especially those working for internationally focused nongovernmental organizations that have seen first-hand the impact of the Holy See at the UN and other international organization, have questioned the rationale behind such wide recognition. But it is not just NGOs that have questioned the nature of the Holy See's statehood. To similar question from Vladimir Putin in 2003, Pope John Paul II answered, "Look out the window. What kind of state do I have here? You can see my whole state right from this window." *See* Daniel Williams, "For Ailing Pope, Many Projects Remain Unfinished," WASHINGTON

retained what it had always had after the confiscation of the Papal States in 1870.[278] Considering the extent of its use of existing legal rights and duties, together with its capacity to conclude treaties and accredit envoys, it is reasonable to support the view that the Holy See maintained its international personality.[279] Therefore, it does not sound right to assert that the events of 1870 nullified the international personality of the Holy See.[280]

As *a fortiori,* the international personality of the Holy See did not encounter any significant change following the Lateran Agreement and the creation of the State of the Vatican City in 1870.[281] The essence of the Lateran Treaty is seen in conferring new international respects, rights, and obligations territorially, legally, and politically on the Holy

---

POST, October 7, 2003. The Pope acknowledged that it requires some efforts to square the current reality of the Holy See, the government of a territorial holding known as Vatican City, with the common understanding of what a state is. See also *Editorial,* CATHOLIC FOR CHOICE (2013) www.catholicforchoice.org

[278] *See* R.A. GRAHAM, THE RISE OF THE DOUBLE DIPLOMATIC CORPS IN ROME: A STUDY IN INTERNATIONAL PRACTICE (1952)(explaining the reason for this position as dependent on the Holy See's continued exercise of its legal rights and duties including accrediting envoys; the Holy See continued to accredit envoys to and to receive Legates from the Holy See, continuing concordats with foreign states); see also A. P. SERENI, the Italian conception of international law (1943); S. Z. EHLER, "The Recent Concordats," *104 H.R. 5* (1961); See also ROBERT F. ILLING, AMERICAN AND THE VATICAN (2011), *supra* note 145 (indicating that though the Holy See was deprived of territory, the situation did not eliminate its sovereignty and independence as manifested in its continued international relations with other States independent of the Kingdom of Italy from 1870 to 1929).

[279] ARANGIO-RUIZ, *supra* note 270, at 360.

[280] *See generally Ponce v Roman Catholic Apostolic Church, 210 US 296, 318 (1907)* ('The Holy See still [*sic* after 1870] occupies a recognized position in international law, of which the courts must take juridical notice'); Also, ARANGIO adds "There was no interruption in the international personality of the Holy See following the taking of Rome and the so- called *debellatio* of the 'Papal State' by the Italian Kingdom in 1870. Once the population and the territory of that State were annexed by Italy, the Church simply found itself deprived of the elements over which it had previously exercised both the governmental authority under its own internal law and international legal rights identical to those of any other sovereign, such as a State, endowed with a territory and a population. . .. The Italian legislation the Law of Guarantees was just the internal legal instrument by which the Italian State ensured compliance, by its organs and subjects, with Italy's international obligation to respect the independent status of the Holy See: an obligation with which the Italian Government had clearly committed itself to comply at the 1870 annexation." *See* ARANGIO-RUIZ, *supra* note 270, at 361.

[281] *Id.*

See.[282] These new developments should rather be seen from the perspective of invigorating the pre-1870 structure of the Holy See's international personality.

This foregoing proof of the Holy See's international personality and sovereignty has more weight than any exercise aimed at proving statehood as it concerns the Holy See.[283] The Holy See contends that the secular domain of the Vatican City State is meant to assure, but is not required for, its full autonomy and statehood in the exercise of foreign affairs.[284] Articles 2 and 4 of the 1929 Lateran Treaty provide that the Holy See's sovereignty is an inherent attribute of its nature in accordance with the traditions and demands of its mission in the world.[285] It is based on that sovereignty that the Holy See, together with Italy, created the Vatican City State, on which the Holy See has exclusive sovereignty and jurisdiction.[286]

The Holy See does not fulfill the Montevideo Convention's constructive elements of statehood namely, (1) a permanent population; (2) a defined territory; (3) a government; and (4) the capacity to enter relations with other states.[287] However, an over-emphasized reliance on the Montevideo Convention's definition of statehood will not adequately explain why the Holy See enjoys the type of international status it presently possesses. The Holy See exists and operates independent of all others. It executes its ministerial functions through its officials as it deems proper for reasons found in its natural mission in the world.[288]

---

282 *Id.*

283 ILLING, *supra* note 145, at 55 (showing the baffling and controversial conception of the concept of the Holy See, for which it has been described as "an anomaly," an "atypical entity," or an "entity *sui generis*").

284 *See* Maria L. Hecker, "Constitutional Issues Raised by Diplomatic Relations between the United States and the Holy See," *15 HASTINGS CONST. L. Q. 101, 103* (1987)

285 DI GIOVANNI LAJOLO, "DIPLOMAZIA VATICANA: Uno Strumento docile e fedele al Papa," in *30 GIORNI* March 2006, available at http://www.30giorni.it/aticoli_id_10264_l1.htm?id=10264 last visited January 25, 2014.

286 *Id.*

287 *See* Art. 1 of the Montevideo Convention on the Rights and Duties of States, December 26, 1933, *reprinted in* 49 Stat. 3097, 3100; MONTEVIDEO CONVENTION (1933), *supra* note 116; *see also* RESTATEMENT (THIRD) OF FOREIGN RELATIONS LAW § 201 (1987).

288 ARAUJO, *supra* note 200, at 29 (showing that the natural mission of the Catholic Church, that is the Holy See, is to exercise its religious functions and to pursue its spiritual ends in the world. And I add that, in the exercise of its religious activities and in its pursuit of its

The religious activities carried out and the spiritual ends pursued by the Catholic Church constitute the foundation of the international legal status of the Holy See.[289] These worldwide activities and purposes of the Catholic Church, together with its size, which is unequaled among other churches, account for the unique position of prestige the Holy See occupies in the world. The Holy See's historical condition of independence and sovereignty rests upon the above factors for which it commands respect from all governments. The Holy See's independence and sovereignty is in turn the basis of its international legal personality. However, one should be careful not to interpret this understanding as a way international law qualifies the Catholic Church as an international person specialized in religious or spiritual functions.[290]

Recognizing that the international status of the Holy See is founded on its religious activities and spiritual objectives is not tantamount to adoption of an international religion.[291] Though the Holy See's mission

---

spiritual ends, the Holy See strikes agreements with the individual governments of the world for purposes of rights and obligations that may be involved. This also brings the Holy See into the international arena where most rights and obligations are legal structures for inter-State cooperation).

289 *See* RESTATEMENT (THIRD) OF THE FOREIGN RELATIONS LAW OF THE UNITED STATES, (1986) Section 201, in LOUIS HENKIN *et al.,* INTERNATIONAL LAW CASES AND MATERIALS 242 (3rd ed.) (1993) (stressing that the Holy See does not participate in international relations on the authority of having nominally satisfied the objective criteria for statehood put forward by the Montevideo Convention; neither does it base its international status on the Lateran Treaty. It bases its international personality on its religious and spiritual authority from time immemorial).

290 *See* ARANGIO-RUIZ, *supra* note 270, at 363-64 (indicating that "although the nature of the Catholic Church's interests and activities is, especially nowadays, the main factor of the Holy See's title to participate in international relations as an equal member of the "society of States," and although the title's very nature gives the Holy See's international personality despite the not minor criticisms that some periods or aspects of its multisecular tradition undoubtedly deserve, a degree of solidity probably higher than that of the personality of many existing States, it is not *qua* religious organization that the Holy See enjoys and international personality....The truth is that the Holy See has become a power among the powers: where, by power is meant any entity factually existing as a sovereign and independent unit and participating as such in international relations. This concept has nothing to do with any major or superior military, economic and/or political power....") *See id.*

291 *See LOUIS* HENKIN *et al, supra* note 289, at 300 (implying, in my own opinion, that there will be international confusion if other religious groups are allowed to interpret it as such; by that, international politics and law will be besieged with a ganglion of religious and spiritual principles).

may relate most frequently to religious and spiritual matters, this does not have any adverse effect on the legal/temporal nature of its international rights and obligations.[292] This logic follows from the understanding that the nature of a regional or international treaty is not altered by the treaty's subject matter.[293]

Professor Arangio-Ruiz makes the above point clearer when he explores a comparative analysis arguing that,

> Just as States, the Holy See also takes part in diplomatic relations. Just as any other sovereign body, in other words, the Catholic Church is endowed with the rights and is subject to the obligations deriving from the rules of customary or conventional international law applicable to the Church's diplomatic relations with any States or other international persons. The fact that the Holy See's diplomacy deals principally with matters of cult or religious interest does not make the legal regime of those relations any different from the international legal regime of diplomatic relations between States.[294]

From the wealth of his diplomatic experience as an erudite American diplomat who served the United States in different countries including the Vatican, Robert Illing confirms the above position when he wrote,

> The concept of the Holy See as a perfect sovereign entity grew up centuries ago and is recognized explicitly by all Catholic states and in practice by any state that maintains diplomatic relations with the Pope as head of the universal Catholic Church..., all Catholics are the people of the Holy See, the territory is made up of all those lands over which the Pope exercises "spiritual sovereignty...."[295]

---

[292] *Id.* at 365.

[293] *Id.*

[294] *Id.* at 365.

[295] ILLING, *supra* note 145, at 55.

In addition, the long history of the Catholic Church involvement in international matters is undeniably significant in assessing her international personality. People should be interested in tracing how the Holy See, the government of the Catholic Church came to enjoy such unique international recognition – a position which no other religion has ever held. The Catholic Church invokes the authenticity of history in clarifying such important issue as to why she has a unique position in international affairs. For instance, a meeting was held at the United Nations in 1947, and part of the issues that featured an exchange between Ivan Rand of Canada and Brother Simon Bonaventure, a representative from the Holy See *Custos* of the Holy Land. (*Custos* is the Holy See's designated custodian that maintains the Holy Land's Catholic shrines and monuments.) Ivan Rand was inquiring about the Holy See's legal claim to these shrines, to which Brother Bonaventure replied, "Throughout six hundred years it has been legally recognized since we are here."[296]

It might be advisable for those who may ask similar questions to reflect of Brother Bonaventure's assertion. The Catholic Church is an entity with religious and temporal presence stretching back centuries, and interacts with the norms of modern statecraft.[297] Suffice the foregoing assertion to imply that the Holy See could have acquired its international status at the United Nations and other international organizations through a process of custom following its long history of international presence.

Suffice this to mean that debates over the veracity of the Holy See's sovereignty and international personality appear to be an exercise in futility. It will be like a furious horseman who jumped on his horse and went out in search of the same horse on which he is riding. The reason for this is not far-fetched. The Holy See possesses the capacity to engage other States in international relations. Therefore, obviously, most of the countries of the world maintain diplomatic relations with it.[298]

---

[296] *See* UN Special Committee of Palestine, United Nations General Assembly, August 6, 1947. See also CATHOLICS FOR CHOICE, *supra* note 277, at 3.

[297] *See* CATHOLICS FOR CHOICE *supra* note 277, at 3.

[298] The Holy See maintains diplomatic relations with 188 countries of the world.

3.4.3 The International Status of the Vatican City State

As already disclosed above, the State of the Vatican was created in 1929 as part of the Lateran Treaty. The Vatican City State is the smallest area in the world that is elevated to the status of a State.[299] Though non-permanent,[300] the official population of the Vatican City State is 839.[301]

> The Vatican City State has a feature that distinguishes it from other States, and concerning this Crawford writes that: "unlike other States the Vatican City exists not to support its inhabitants but to provide a base for the central administration of a non-State entity, the Catholic Church: it is not a distinct society but an annex or appendage of the Papacy.[302]

Another special feature of the Vatican City State is that, though having internationally acclaimed statehood status, it still depends on the Italian government for the provision of certain services. The Italian government still executes certain governmental functions on behalf of the Vatican City State. For example, the Italian police patrol the Piazza San Pietro. The Italian railway transportation, other forms of transit systems,

---

[299] *See* CRAWFORD, *supra* note 23, at 222; see also CENTRAL INTELLIGECE AGENCY, CIA, THE WORLD FACTBOOK: HOLY SEE (VATICAN CITY), https://www.cia.gov/library/publications/the-world-factbook/geos/vt.html (last visited November 17, 2013) (indicating that the Vatican city State is a landlocked enclave in Rome, Italy, the world's smallest state; beyond the territorial boundary of Vatican City, the Lateran Treaty of 1929 grants the Holy See extraterritorial authority over 23 sites in Rome and five outside of Rome, including the Pontifical Palace at Castel Gandolfo, that is, the Pope's summer residence).

[300] See CRAWFORD, *supra* note 23, at 223 (stating that the Law respecting Citizenship and Residence in the Vatican City of June 7, 1929: 130 BFSP 1018, has a provision whereby male children who reach the age of 25 normally lose Vatican nationality automatically; female children lose their nationality on marriage circumstances. Cessation of residence or of official employment in the Vatican City also determines nationality.

[301] See CIA, *supra* note 193

[302] *See* CRAWFORD, *supra* note 23, at 223(showing that the position of the Vatican City is peculiar and therefore the criteria for statehood in its case are only marginally complied with. Other factors that support statehood exist).

communications, sanitation systems, and water supply are all services which Italy performs for the Vatican.[303]

The Vatican City State possesses its own currency, but Italy mints this currency for the Vatican.[304] Both States freely accept the currency of the other.[305] The Vatican City State has few or no industrial activities within the Vatican City.[306] It therefore depends upon Italy for the food and physical goods consumed in the City State.[307] The Italian government also agreed to provide punishment for crimes committed in the Vatican City State.[308]

The Vatican is closely tied to Italy only by necessity and consent. However, the arrangement whereby the Vatican receives necessary services from Italy does not limit its independence.[309] The Vatican City State possesses a personality under international law. For this reason, it enters into international agreements.[310] It is noteworthy that it is the Holy See that internationally represents the Vatican City State.[311] Therefore, when the Holy See enters into agreements for the Vatican City State, it uses this formula: "acting on behalf and in the interest of the Vatican City State."[312] This does not, however, limit the international personality of the Vatican.[313]

---

303 *See* Articles 3, 6, & 7 of the 1929 Lateran Treaty

304 CARDINALE, *supra* note 190, at 277.

305 *Id.*

306 DUURSMA, *supra* note 139, at 375 (commercial activities within the Vatican City are limited to "the sale of souvenirs and stamps and collection of revenues from the Vatican museums;" and I add, the Bank of the Holy Spirit).

307 YASMIN ABDULLAH, *supra* note 268, at 1867.

308 CARDINALE, *supra* note 190, at 120.

309 DUURSMA, *supra* note 139, at 415 (in practice Italy does not exercise any substantial control over the Vatican City; at least the Lateran Treaty did not just pretend to create an independent State within the city of Rome).

310 See "A Short History of the Diplomacy of the Holy See," on the PERMANENT OBSERVER MISSION OF THE HOLY SEE TO THE UNITED NATIONS, New York, http://www.holyseemission.org/about/hisory-of-diplomacy-of-the-Holy-See (last visited November 12, 2013).

311 *Id.*

312 *Id.*

313 *See* U.S. DEP'T OF STATE, Background Note: Holy See, http://www.state.gov/r/pa/ei/bgn/3819.htm (last visited November 21, 2013) (implicit classification of the Holy See and the Vatican City State separately, representing the Vatican City State as a "sovereign,

The term "Vatican City State" instead of the "Holy See" appears in a couple of international agreements involving the Catholic Church.[314] The Vatican City State's membership of such bodies is a proof that it possesses international status. The United Nations recognizes this uniqueness:

> In the Listing of country names, published annually by the United Nations, a note is added to the Holy See's entry, stating that – in United Nations documents, the term "Holy See" is to be used except in texts concerning the International Telecommunications Union and the Universal Postal Union, where the term "Vatican City State" is to be used.[315]

For the above reason, the list of the Observer members of the World Trade Organization (WTO) contains the name of the Holy See with the Vatican City State in brackets.[316] It is for this reason that Crawford quotes an analyst on the purposes of Draft ILO's[317] Convention on the Law of Treaties as saying that the Vatican is one of the "entities recognized as being States on special grounds."[318] To make this point clearer, this book will now examine the relationship between the Holy See and the Vatican City State.

---

independent territory," and representing the Holy See as "a sovereign judicial entity under international law").

314 PERMANENT OBSERVER MISSION OF THE HOLY SEE, *supra* note 307.

315 *Id.*

316 *See* "Understanding the WTO: MEMBERS ABD OBSERVERS," available at http://www.wto.org/english/thewto_e/whatis_e/tif_e/org6_e.htm (last visited November 21, 2013).

317 ILO stands for International Labor Organization (In the post–World War I euphoria, the idea of a "makeable society" was an important catalyst behind the social engineering of the ILO architects. As a new discipline, international labor law became a useful instrument for putting social reforms into practice. The utopian ideals of the founding members—social justice and the right to decent work—were changed by diplomatic and political compromises made at the Paris Peace Conference of 1919, showing the ILO's balance between idealism and pragmatism. Therefore, the ILO was established with the idea of reconstructing and protecting the objectives of labor unions with the aim of enhancing social justice as it relates to labor standards); *see ILC Yearbook, 1956/II, 107 & 108* (examining the unique nature of some signatories to the ILO's Law of Treaties).

318 JAMES CRAWFORD, *supra* note 23, at 223 (indicating that the international status of the Holy See itself contributed to the acknowledgement of the statehood of the Vatican).

3.4.4 The Relationship between the Holy See and the Vatican City State

As mentioned above, the Vatican exists to provide a base for the central administration of a non-State entity, the Catholic Church. As a matter of fact, the Vatican is not a distinct society but an appendage to the Holy See.[319] There is a unique relationship that exists between the Vatican and its government, the Holy See. In some States such as Somalia, the existence of territory and population compensate for the virtual absence of a central government required for statehood, whereas in the case of the Vatican City State, the strength and influence of the Holy See compensate for its tiny territory and lack of permanent population.[320]

It has been widely accepted that the Holy See and the Vatican City State are two distinct legal persons.[321] The reason for this argument is

---

[319] *Id.*

[320] *Id.*

[321] Christian Nwachukwu Okeke, *Controversial Subjects Of International Law*, Rotterdam University Press 1974, pp. 65-78; Art. III (1) of the Spanish Concordat, Vatican City, August 27, 1953, 1 PERMANENT OBSERVER MISSION OF THE HOLY SEE, *supra* note 275

Id.

See "Understanding the WTO: MEMBERS ABD OBSERVERS," available at http://www.wto.org/english/thewto_e/whatis_e/tif_e/org6_e.htm (last visited November 21, 2013).

ILO stands for International Labor Organization (In the post–World War I euphoria, the idea of a "makeable society" was an important catalyst behind the social engineering of the ILO architects. As a new discipline, international labor law became a useful instrument for putting social reforms into practice. The utopian ideals of the founding members—social justice and the right to decent work—were changed by diplomatic and political compromises made at the Paris Peace Conference of 1919, showing the ILO's balance between idealism and pragmatism. Therefore, the ILO was established with the idea of reconstructing and protecting the objectives of labor unions with the aim of enhancing social justice as it relates to labor standards); *see ILC Yearbook, 1956/II, 107 & 108* (examining the unique nature of some signatories to the ILO's Law of Treaties).

CRAWFORD, *supra* note 23, at 223 (indicating that the international status of the Holy See itself contributed to the acknowledgement of the statehood of the Vatican).

Id.

obvious. As has been discussed above, both the Holy See and the Vatican City are parties to many multilateral treaties. Examples include the Universal Postal Union (UPU) and the International Telecommunications Union (ITU) already mentioned above, but there are more.[322] Altogether, it is correct to say that while the Holy See has concluded some bilateral treaties, the Vatican City State has ratified others.[323] One can infer a kind of division of labor in ratifying treaties. It appears that while the Vatican City State enters into agreements that are of a strictly functional nature, the Holy See concludes agreements that are related to the special mission of the Catholic Church.[324]

Though the Vatican City State and the Holy See exist as two distinct legal persons, they also have a legal relationship, which some writers have described as a "real union,"[325] or as a form of vassalage.[326] However, a closer look at the relationship that exists between the Holy See and the Vatican City State shows that to use terms such as "real union" or "vassal," is inappropriate because the Holy See is not a foreigner to the Vatican City State.[327] It appears better to understand the relationship between the Vatican and the Holy See as one of State and government. In this arrangement, even though the Holy See is the supreme government of the

---

*Id.*60 BFSP 698 (showing that the Holy See and the Vatican City State are two distinct legal persons notwithstanding the harmonious co-existence between them).

322 See *United Nations Treaty Series Online Collection (UNTS)*, available at http://treaties.un.org/Pages/UNTSOnline.aspx?id=1 (last visited November 21, 2013) (showing the discrepancy between where the Vatican City State is listed as having ratified the Brussels Postal Convention (September 23, 1953) and (where the Holy See is listed as having ratified the 2964 Vienna Postal Convention (April 22, 1968); The Secretariat of State clears this discrepancy with respect to the UPU and ITU, indicating that the Holy See is a 'Member also in the name and on behalf of Vatican City State.' The same formula was adopted regarding membership of the International Telecommunications Satellite Organization and the International Institute for the Unification of Private Law; originally, the Statute of the International Atomic Energy Agency (IAEA) was ratified by the term 'Vatican City' (August 20, 1957), but when amended in 1961, it was accepted by the Holy See on January 11, 1962; See CRAWFORD, *supra* note 23 at 227-9 for more details.

323 *Id.*

324 CRAWFORD, *supra* note 23, at 229.

325 *See* A.P SERENI, THE ITALIAN CONCEPTION OF INTERNATIONAL LAW (1943); Ehler S.Z., "The Recent Concordats," 104 *Historical Review* (1961).

326 KUNZ, *supra* note 274; H.F. Cumbo, "The Holy See and International Law," *2 ILQ 603*, (1948).

327 CRAWFORD, *supra* note 23, at 230.

Vatican, it also possesses a non-territorial status in addition.[328] The Holy See combines functions associated with its mission in the world with its role as the independent government of a populated territory.[329] The Holy See is both an international person and the government of an independent State.[330] Its diplomatic history reflects this unique character.

3.5 Overview of Holy See's Diplomacy

This section explores Vatican diplomacy.[331] It goes further to examine how the Holy See engages in diplomatic ties with other nations, institutions, organizations, or agencies with the aim of promoting "social justice."[332]

---

[328] *Id.*

[329] *Id.*

[330] *Id.*

[331] This book uses the terms "Vatican Diplomacy" and "Holy See Diplomacy" interchangeably for the single reason that they exist for each other and an understanding of the relationship between the Vatican City State and the Holy See dispels any confusion over the use of the two terms.

[332] *See* CIA World Factbook, https://www.cia.gov/library/publications/the-world-factbook/ (The Holy See conducts active diplomacy. It maintains formal diplomatic relations with 176 nations that are members of the United Nations. The Vatican also has relations with Taiwan, the Cook Islands, and the Sovereign Order of Malta. It has a "special" relationship with the European Union. Seventy-eight of these maintain permanent diplomatic missions accredited to the Holy See and resident in Rome. The rest have missions located outside Italy with dual accreditation. The Holy See maintains 106 permanent diplomatic missions to nation-states. Further, the Holy See has a separate permanent diplomatic mission to the European Union in Brussels. The Holy See also maintains relations of a special nature with the Palestine Liberation Organization and has a delegate to the Arab League in Cairo). The Holy See is especially active in international organizations. The Holy See is a permanent observer in the following international organizations: United Nations (UN), Organization of American States (OAS) in Washington, African Union (AU), World Tourist Organization (WTO), World Trade Organization (WTO), World Health Organization (WHO), World Food Program (WFP), United Nations Educational, Scientific and Cultural Organization (UNESCO), United Nations Environment Program (UNEP), United Nations International Drug Control Program (UNDCP), United Nations Center for Human Settlements (UNCHS), Latin Union (LU), International Organization for Migration (IOM), International Labor Organization (ILO), International Fund for Agricultural Development (IFAD), and the United Nations Food and Agriculture Organization (FAO). The Holy See is a member of the Organization for the Prohibition of Chemical Weapons (OPCW), Organization for Security and Cooperation in Europe (OSCE), International Telecommunication Satellite Organization (ITSO), World Intellectual Property Organization (WIPO), International Institute for the Unification of

Social justice is central to the assessment of the extent to which the Church has exerted its influence in the world, particularly in the GATT/WTO system. And as such, the Holy See's diplomatic efforts play a major role in the exercise of her universal mission of serving and consolidating the human community according to Christ's mandate. Though the Church's primary role is the preaching of the Gospel message to all, she effectuates this by embracing the temporal wellbeing of believers and non-believers alike.[333] This is consistent with Christ's mandate for the Church to go into the whole world and preach the Gospel to every creature.[334]

The mission of the Holy See is, however, not limited to purely diplomatic efforts, since it indicates certain juridical relations between nations. The Holy See has a universal mission that distinguishes it from every other earthly society, and it seeks to continue through the centuries

---

Private Law (UNIDROIT), United Nations High Commissioner for Refugees (UNHCR), United Nations Conference on Trade and Development (UNCTAD), International Grains Council (IGC), International Committee for Military Medicine (ICMM), International Atomic Energy Agency (IAEA), and the Preparatory Commission for the Comprehensive Nuclear Test Ban Treaty Organization (CTBTO).

The Holy See is also an observer on an informal basis of the World Meteorological Organization in Geneva (WMO), United Nations Committee of Peaceful Use of Outer Space (UNCOPUOS), International Strategy for Disaster Reduction (ISDR), International Maritime Organization (IMO), African Asian Legal Consultative Committee (AALCC) and the International Civil Aviation Organization (ICAO).

In 1971, the Holy See announced the decision to adhere to the nuclear Non-Proliferation Treaty (NPT) in order to "give its moral support to the principles that form the base of the treaty itself." The Holy See is also a participating state in the OSCE and a guest of honor to the Parliamentary Assembly of the OSCE.

[333] *See* Vatican II Document, *Gaudium et Spes (The Pastoral Constitution on the Church in the Modern World),* December 7, 1965, No. 42; the Church addresses itself to every aspect of human life in exercising its mission to proclaim the gospel to all, to communicate to society Christian values, and to safeguard the rights of the Christian faithful as well as the transcendent quality and the fundamental rights of all human persons. Therefore, the Church attempts to engage in constructive dialogue with political authorities and with the international community of nations and supranational organizations. In this secular aspect of their mission, the pontifical legates exercise a role which is rooted in a fundamentally ecclesial reality. See Charles D. Balvo, "Legates of the Roman Pontiff," in John P. Beal et al., (ed.), *New Commentary on the Code of Canon Law* (2000).

[334] *See* Mk 16:15 expounded in Vatican II Document, *Ad Gentes Divinitus (Decree on the Church's Missionary Activity),* December 7, 1965, No. 5 (indicating that the Church is to seek out the lost in the whole world; the Church is missionary in character and orientation).

the salvific work of its Founder, Christ.[335] Archbishop Valerio Valeri, a one-time Nuncio to Vichy, France, said concerning the connection between the mission of the Church and her diplomacy

> The development in time and according to circumstances of this mission can also be called diplomacy, if one wishes, but only in an elevated sense, above the purely natural and political order. From this point of view, the supreme law of the Church, and indeed of the Holy See, is the salvation of souls. All its activity is always directed to this end...even when the Church, because of historical circumstances had to concern itself with its temporal interests.[336]

Examining the mandate of Christ to his Church, the Church should concentrate on sharing the divine Presence of her Founder, Jesus Christ, and should have no need of diplomacy. However, the Holy See assumes some more dynamism because (a) the Church is universal in character; and (b) her members are scattered in different countries of the world. These two realities are the motivating factors. They make the Holy See's use of diplomacy not only legitimate but also an effective means of fulfilling her mission on earth.[337]

---

[335] *See* Archbishop Valerio Valeri, *Le Relazioni Internazionali della Sancta Sede dope il Secundo Conflitto Mondiale (International Relations of the Holy See after the Second World War, Rome,* Centro Italiano di Studi per la Reconciliaziona Internacionale, 1956, (Speech given in Rome on February 23, 1956 under the auspices of the Italian Study Center for International Reconciliation, Rome, Banco di Roma), pp. 23-24

[336] *Id.*

[337] Msgr. Igino Cardinale, Le *Saint-Siege et la Diplomatie: Apercu Historigue et Practique de la Diplomatie Pontificale (The Holy See and Diplomacy: An Historical, Juridical and Practical Survey of Pontifical Diplomacy),* Paris, Desclee & Cie, Editeurs, 1962, p. 18; see also PIERRE See is also a participating state in the OSCE and a guest of honor to the Parliamentary Assembly of the OSCE.

See Vatican II Document, *Gaudium et Spes (The Pastoral Constitution on the Church in the Modern World),* December 7, 1965, No. 42; the Church addresses itself to every aspect of human life in exercising its mission to proclaim the gospel to all, to communicate to society Christian values, and to safeguard the rights of the Christian faithful as well as the transcendent quality and the fundamental rights of all human persons. Therefore, the Church attempts to engage in constructive dialogue with political authorities and with the international community of nations and supranational organizations. In this secular aspect of their mission, the pontifical legates exercise a role which is rooted in a fundamentally

Without delving into the history of the Holy See's diplomacy, it is, however, important to note that it started around the 4th century and has some peculiarities as follows:

> Since the fourth century the Catholic pontifical ecclesiastical Foreign Service of the Universal Church of Rome has been the world's one and only all-male religious professional diplomatic service advocating a human rights conscious diplomacy on the international plane for the cause of the moral excellence of peace. Thus, the professional global diplomatic service apostolate of the Roman Catholic Church, under the authority of the Holy See's Office of the Papal Secretariat of State, is the world's only Christ-centered, faith-based, ecclesiastical human rights centric foreign service ministry of a sovereign state promoting *irenology*— the study of peace and the practice of peace building — through the ecclesiastical diplomatic art and science of moral exhortation in the 21st century.[338]

---

ecclesial reality. See Charles D. Balvo, "Legates of the Roman Pontiff," in John P. Beal et al., (ed.), *New Commentary on the Code of Canon Law* (2000). *See* Mk 16:15 expounded in Vatican II Document, *Ad Gentes Divinitus (Decree on the Church's Missionary Activity),* December 7, 1965, No. 5 (indicating that the Church is to seek out the lost in the whole world; the Church is missionary in character and orientation). *See* Archbishop Valerio Valeri, *Le Relazioni Internazionali della Sancta Sede dope il Secundo Conflitto Mondiale (International Relations of the Holy See after the Second World War, Rome,* Centro Italiano di Studi per la Reconciliaziona Internacionale, 1956, (Speech given in Rome on February 23, 1956 under the auspices of the Italian Study Center for International Reconciliation, Rome, Banco di Roma), pp. 23-24. *Id.* D'AUTERMONT, *LE SAINT-SIEGE EN DROIT INTERNACIONAL (THE HOLY SEE IN INTERNATIONAL LAW),* Paris, Jonve & Cie, Editeurs, (1910); JOHN FRANCIS MORLEY, *THE VATICAN DIPLOMACY AND THE JEWS DURING THE HOLOCAUST, 1939-1943*, unpublished Ph.D. book New York University (1979) (stressing that that in her diplomatic relations with States, the Holy See sends representatives who are willing to help the nations, the needy, and the Churches to find that peace which must guide humankind to the achievement of its supreme destinies).

[338] *See* "Vatican Diplomacy, the UN & World Peace: 2009 in Review," *Ecclesiastica Diplomatica: The Royal Ecclesiastical Institute On Vatican State/ Holy See Pontifical Ecclesiastical Law & Diplomacy,* available at http://www.vaticandiplomacy.org/ (last visited November 22, 2013) (The Roman Pontiff sends his legates in virtue of his spiritual and moral authority, rather than as the supreme temporal ruler of the State of Vatican City. To illustrate this point, during the nearly sixty-year period when the Roman Pontiff did not possess a territory, the

It is obvious then that the origins of the Holy See's diplomatic service are traceable to the very first centuries of the Catholic Church. It is therefore considered the oldest in the world. At its inception, the diplomatic service of the Holy See took off with the Popes dispatching legates or envoys to represent them at important Church councils or for other matters. This continued until the 16th century when the pontifical legates became officially known as "apostolic nuncios" (Papal ambassadors). From this period onwards, "nunciatures" were established for exchanging diplomatic representatives between the Holy See and other states.[339]

3.5.1 Meaning and Definition of Vatican Diplomacy

In discussing the meaning of Vatican diplomacy, the focus is on the interest and achievements of the Catholic Church in the areas of international order, namely, political, socio-economic, and religious matters. These aspects of international life are the three main ways that lead to the attainment and maintenance of world peace. Holy See diplomacy draws its meaning from these areas of international concerns above, which are represented respectively by the terms "diplomacy," "development," and "ecumenism."[340] For this reason, Archbishop Cardinale says

> Diplomacy aims at persuading nations to live together and to collaborate for their own good and that of all mankind; for development purposes to convince those who must assist those who have not, in reaching a stage of reasonable prosperity; ecumenism strives to induce the Churches to

---

international community, in accord with a long-accepted practice, continued to recognize his right to send legates and receive ambassadors. See Robert Graham, VATICAN DIPLOMACY (1959)

339 *Id.*

340 *See* Archbishop Hyginus Cardinale, "The Contributions of the Holy See to World Peace," (Adapted from an address given by the Apostolic Delegate to the United Kingdom, Archbishop H.E. Cardinale, at Boston College, March 27, 1968; reprinted in the Congressional Record, Washington D.C.) and available at http://www.ewtn.com/library/HUMANITY/HOSEWOPE.HTM (last visited November 22, 2013).

> overcome their differences in a spirit of charity and truth so as to fulfill God's will of unity of faith and order.[341]

The Holy See exerts herself to the best of her ability to improve the state of world peace through tireless efforts in the three areas mentioned above.[342] This is why the Church has been described as "a sovereign moral voice, the expression of the Papacy on the international scene."[343] The Holy See has also been referred to as "a moral superpower in international affairs."[344] It is called a "moral superpower" and rightly so because its diplomatic service is a product of an ancient and proven practice. The Holy See's diplomatic service not only works for the freedom of the Church (*libertas Ecclesiae*) but also for the defense and promotion of human dignity as well as social order based on justice, truth, freedom, and love.[345]

From the above explanation, diplomacy generally is "the art of creating humane and reasonable relations among peoples animated by a high ideal, aimed at establishing the rule of law, justice and peace in the international community."[346] As a matter of fact, Vatican diplomacy may be defined as a system by which, through accredited pontifical representatives, the Holy See strives to secure the reconciliation and unification of the world through

---

341 *Id.*

342 *Id.*

343 *See* Archbishop Jean-Louis Tauran, "The Presence of the Holy See in the International Organizations," Catholic University of the Sacred Heart, Milan, Italy, April 22, 2002, available at http://www.vatican.va/roman_curia/secretariat_state/documents/rc_segst_doc_20020422_tauran_en.html (last visited November 22, 2013).

344 *See* THOMAS J. REESE, INSIDE THE VATICAN: THE POLITICS AND ORGANIZATION OF THE CATHOLIC CHURCH, (1998).

345 PONTICICAL COUNCIL FOR JUSTICE AND PEACE, COMPENDIUM OF THE SOCIAL DOCTRINE OF THE CHURCH (2004), # 445; the international activity of the Holy See is manifested objectively under different aspects: the right to active and passive legation; the exercise of *ius contrahendi* in stipulating treaties; participation in intergovernmental organizations, such as those under the auspices of the United Nations; and mediation initiatives in situations of conflict. In doing so, the Holy See offers non-partisan service to the international community because it does not seek advantage for itself but only the good of the entire human family. In this context, the Holy See particularly avails itself of its own diplomatic personnel. *See id. at 444*

346 Sweeney Francis (ed.), *The Vatican and World Peace,* London, Colin Smythe, 1970, p. 96.

the prosperous growth of individuals and the entire world in a harmonious concert of nations.[347]

3.5.2 Legal Foundations of Pontifical Legations

Right from the inception of the Church, the Popes have always sent legates to represent them. For example, the Popes sent legates to the major ecumenical councils.[348] Later, pontifical legates were also sent to civil authorities. The reason for this is that the Church has the right to send both passive and active delegates:

> The Roman Pontiff, in exercising his responsibilities as the visible head and the principal spiritual leader of the Catholic Church, makes use of representatives or legates to act as liaisons both to the particular churches and to the states and public authorities throughout the world.[349]

Toward the end of the 15th century, papal representation became a permanent practice.[350] Following a necessary reform of the program regarding preparation, designation, and functions of pontifical legates and its subsequent consolidation, legates were commissioned in a permanent and stable fashion.[351] This practice, however, did not work without some controversies. The major problem was the role of the pontifical legates

---

347 CARDINALE, *supra* note 334; Tom Farer, "Diplomacy," in Mary Hawkesworth & Maurice Kogan (ed.), *Encyclopedia of Government and Politics*, London & New York, Routledge, 1992, Vol. 2, pp. 1025-38; Robert Graham, *The Vatican Diplomacy: A Study of Church and State on the International Plane,* Princeton, Princeton University Press, 1959, pp. 11-12; *see also* Ecclesiastica Diplomatica, *supra* note 297. Collaboration in the development of the whole person and every human being is in fact a duty of all towards all and must be shared by the four parts of the world: East and West, North and South. See POPE JOHN PAUL II, ENCYCLICAL LETTER SOLLICITUDO REI SOCIALIS (On Social Concerns) (December 30, 1987), # 32

348 *See* CHARLES D. BALVO, *supra* note 333, p. 490.

349 *Id.*

350 *Id.*

351 *Id.*

in relation to the pastoral ministry of the bishops of the local dioceses.[352] There was a need to clarify the role of the pontifical legates in relation to the proper pastoral ministry of the bishops of the local dioceses in the countries where legates are sent to represent the Popes.[353]

To address the above clash of responsibilities, the canons of a 1969 document known as *motu proprio Sollicitudo omnium ecclesiarum* were utilized. The *motu proprio Sollicitudo omnium ecclesiarum* is the principal source of canons 362-367 of the 1983 Code of Canon Law, which defines the legal nature of papal legation. These canons are very important as they were made to streamline and clarify the role of the legates. This cleared the controversy that emanated in the pontifical legates' exercise of their official duties in relation to the bishop of the local dioceses.[354]

The Pope has the independent authority to appoint, send, transfer, and recall legates either to particular churches in various nations or regions or to states and public authorities.[355] At this point, it is pertinent to state that there are two types of legates under pontifical right of legation. First, there are legates appointed to particular churches or to the states and public authorities to which they are sent.[356] Second, there are legates who are designated as delegates or observers in a pontifical mission at international councils, or conferences and meetings, to represent the Apostolic See.[357]

---

[352] *See* A. Talamanca, "I Rappresentanti Pontifici nella Nuova Normativa Canonica," in W. Schulz & G. Feliciani (ed.), *Vitam Impendere Vero: Scritti in Onore di Pio Ciprotti, Libreria Editrice Vaticana*, 1986, pp. 276-288 (examining the conflict of the extent of duties of pontifical legates in relation to the proper pastoral ministry of bishops).

[353] *See* CHARLES D. BALVO, *supra* note 333

[354] *See id*; (These canons 331 and 362-367 reflect the theological reality that, as the successor of St. Peter, the Roman Pontiff is "a permanent and visible source and foundation of unity of faith and fellowship" and has the mission to confirm his brother bishops and the people of God in the faith, in the *communio* which is the Church. The bishops, as pastors to the particular churches spread throughout the world, exercise their office collegially, in communion with and under the authority of the Roman Pontiff. In this context, with due regard for the external, social, and juridical dimensions of the Church, the pontifical legates are recognized as an effective, though certainly not exclusive, means of maintaining the bonds which link the Roman Pontiff with the bishops of the world, as well as with all the members of the Christian faithful); see also the Vatican II, *Lumen Gentium (The Dogmatic Constitution on the Church)*, November 21, 1964, # 18.

[355] *See* canon 363 of the 1983 Code of Canon Law

[356] *See* canon 363 § 1 of the 1983 Code of Canon Law

[357] *See* canon 363 § 2 of the 1983 Code of Canon Law

This power is innate, that is, proper to the office of the Roman Pontiff.[358] Nevertheless, in the exercise of his legal duty as it pertains to the mission and recall of legates appointed to states, the Pope must observe the norms of international law.[359]

3.5.3 The Duties of Pontifical Legates (Nuncios)[360]

Pope Paul VI describes the Holy See's diplomacy as a way of representing the claims of conscience and morality in a world where power politics tends to prevail.[361] When the Pope sent the first emissaries to represent him at the court of the Emperor of Constantinople, they were simply known as papal representatives. However, by the 11th century, these Papal envoys were called "Nuncios," meaning "messengers."[362] Then, in the 16th century, Papal Nuncio came to mean a Papal representative with a permanent

---

[358] *See* canon 331 of the 1983 Code of Canon Law (which confers on the Pope a free exercise of supreme, full, immediate, and universal ordinary power in the Church).

[359] *See* canon 362 of the 1983 Code of Canon Law; see also UNITED NATIONS, *Treaty Series* UN Publications, New York, 1964, 95-126 (This concerns the Vienna Convention, which was organized by the United Nations; the final document was signed on April 18, 1961, by representatives of the nations of the world and of the Holy See. The Vienna Convention contains 54 articles. The purpose of the Vienna Convention is the codification of diplomatic law in the form of an international convention on diplomatic intercourse, privileges, and immunities. March 4 to April 22, 1963, the United Nations Conference on Consular Relations was held at Neue Hofburg in Vienna. This 1963 Convention on Consular Relations, consisting of 79 articles which codified the rules governing consular relations in general, facilities, privileges and immunities relating to the consular posts, career consular officers, and other members of a consular post. *See id. at* 510-513.

[360] *See* canon 364 of the 1983 Code of Canon Law for details of ecclesial responsibilities of Papal legates (stating that functions of papal legates include promoting and fostering relations between the Holy See and governments; dealing with questions pertaining to relations between Church and State; drafting and implementing of concordats or similar agreements; and seeking the opinion and counsel of local bishops in executing these functions).

[361] *See* Peter Hebblethwaite, The *Year of Three Popes*, Collins, Glasgow, 1978, p.30

[362] *See id*, ¶ 32 (indicating that when Pope Paul VI addressed his envoys to the Far East at Manila, the Philippines in 1970, he said, "The nuncio's role is also evolving. Until now the nuncio was a little more than the Pope's representative to governments and churches. Above all, his activity was of a hierarchical and administrative nature; in a certain sense he remained a stranger to the local Church.")

diplomatic status.[363] The 1815 Protocol of Vienna[364] and its codification in the early 1960s raised Papal nuncios to the rank of ambassadors under international law.[365]

As ambassadors, they have the responsibility of promoting both the spiritual and civil rights of people. Thus, the envoys of the Holy See are sent to various countries not just to defend the rights of the Church but also to defend and serve the rights and needs of the people there. Put another way, the Holy See's diplomatic relationship with states is a form of love and service because

> The ecclesiastical diplomat brings words of understanding; he is the advocate of the just causes of the population; he collaborates with the government and with the nation in which he is a guest.[366]

The goal of Holy See diplomatic relations with other states and organizations is a dedication to the principles of justice and charity.[367] The Vatican diplomat is depicted as representing Christ and His Church, as bearing Christ in his heart.[368] Normally, the concern of the Nuncio should be for the Church in the country to which he is assigned in addition to what Cardinale describes as

---

[363] *See* PIERRE D'AUTERMONT, LE SAINT-SIEGE EN DROIT INTERNATIONAL (THE HOLY SEE IN INTERNATIONAL LAW (1910); MSGR. IGINO CARDINALE, LE SAINT-SIEGE ET LA DIPLOMATIE: APERCU HISTORIGUE, JURIDIGUE ET PRATIQUE DE LA DIPLOMATIE (THE HOLY SEE AND DIPLOMACY: AN HISTORICAL, JURIDICAL AND PRACTICAL SURVEY OF PONTIFICAL DIPLOMACY) (1962).

[364] *See* Archbishop Jean-Louis Tauran, Lecture on "The Presence Of The Holy See in the International Organizations," Catholic University of the Sacred Heart, Milan, Italy, April 22, 2002, available at http://www.vatican.va/roman curia/secretariat state/documents/rc seg-st doc 20020422 tauran en.html (last visited September 23, 2013) (stating that after the Treaty of Westphalia and especially in the course of the 18th century, pontifical diplomacy had a lower profile because of the recurrent invasions of the Papal States. However, the Congress of Vienna of 1815 restored all its prestige).
See MSGN. IGINO CARDINALE, *supra* note 334.

[365] *Id.*

[366] *See* MONTINI IGINO CARDINALE, *supra* note 334, at 194.

[367] *See* VALERIO VALERI, *supra* note 332, at 23.

[368] *See* MONTINI IGINO CARDINALE, *supra* note 334, at 197.

> The moral, cultural, and social problems which belong to the major interests of mankind such as the respect for human rights, the promotion of international order, the development of friendly ties among all nations through peaceful coexistence, through respect for justice, and the promotion of human progress.[369]

With time, the role of the Vatican diplomat metamorphosed into activities that went beyond the narrow juridical confines of Canon Law to embrace humanitarian responsibilities. In other words, the Nuncio's activities extended to concerns for the needs of all those living in the Nuncio's host country. Therefore, Pope Paul VI taught that the Nuncio ". . . must confer himself zealously with the probe of peace, of progress and of the collaboration of people in view of the spiritual, moral and material good of the entire human family."[370]

Because of the uniqueness of the Holy See's diplomacy and the dual nature of the duties of pontifical legates, the Vatican diplomat has traditionally been acknowledged as the dean of the diplomatic corps in the various states to which he is sent. In 1961, the United Nations Conference on Diplomatic Relations and Immunities recognized and confirmed the precedence of Papal Nuncio when the Conference said

> This precedence has always been granted to the Papal Nuncio in homage to the Holy See, which he represents. For among the members of the international community, the Holy See alone is distinguished by its special nature and by the peculiar characteristics of its methods and aims. These are directly inspired by spiritual and moral values and ideals, and constitute all that is most sublime, most precious, and most worthy of respect in the eyes of all nations.[371]

---

369 *See id*; at p. 38

370 *See* Pope Paul VI, Apostolic Letter, *Sollicitudo Omnium Ecclesiarum (The Care of all the Churches),* on the DUTIES OF PAPAL REPRESENTATIVES, June 24, 1969 in CARDINALE, *supra* note 326 ¶ 314

371 *See* MONTINI IGINO CARDINALE, *supra* note 334, at p. 157

3.5.4 Mechanisms of Vatican Diplomacy: The Concordat

In a bid to promote and foster relations between the Apostolic See and the states, the pontifical legates seek to promote the common good and the resolution of conflicts in a peaceful manner, by negotiation and dialogue.[372] To maintain good relations, the papal legates get involved in such fields as education, health care, and other social programs in which the particular churches and public authorities are involved.[373] To guarantee the free exercise of its mission, the papal legates sometimes engage in written agreements which are of two types, namely, concordats and other treaties.[374]

Concordats, otherwise known as *modus vivendi*, are unique to the Holy See.[375] Concordats consist of agreements concluded between the Holy See and the government of a state concerning ecclesiastical matters.[376] Agreements of this kind usually deal with issues such as access to places of worship, establishment of religious schools, the teaching of religion in state or public schools, and the provision of religious services to prisoners and military personnel. To do this, the pontifical legates engage the state in negotiations and in the end, draft and sign the agreement on behalf of the Holy See.[377]

To continue to act in defense of the cause of peace,[378] the Holy See's diplomatic service extends to international organizations, agencies, and

---

372 *See* CHARLES D. BALVO, *supra* note 333, at 496; *see also* ARCHBISHOP JEAN-LOUIS TAURAN, *supra* note 328 confirming the origin of this right of precedence as coming from the recognition of the papacy as a moral power *sui generis*. This is confirmed by the events that followed; between 1870 and 1929 (the year of the creation of Vatican City State), when the Popes were to be stripped of all temporal power, they continued to exercise the active and passive rights of legation).

373 *Id.*

374 *See* James R. Fox, *Dictionary of International and Comparative Law*, New York, 1992, p. 83; Clive Parry, John P. Grant, *et al.*, Encyclopedic Dictionary of International Law, New York, 1986, p. 71.

375 *See* ARCHBISHOP JEAN-LOUIS TAURAN, *supra* note 27 (stating that concordats are treaties that are in solemn form or accords on specific subjects).

376 *See* Melquiades J. Gamboa, Elements of Diplomatic and Consular Practice: A Glossary, Central Law Book Pub., Philippines, 1966, p. 62.

377 CHARLES D. BALVO, *supra* note 345.

378 *See* Pope Benedict XVI, "Address on Vatican Diplomacy," *reported by* CATHOLIC WORLD NEWS, May 12, 2013 http://www.vaticandiplomacy.org/specialarticles.htm (last

conferences. This is implemented by means of treaties and bilateral and multilateral agreements. In these international organizations, agencies, or conferences, the Holy See is either a fully-fledged member or an observer. As an observer, the Holy See is admitted to negotiations on resolutions, declarations, conventions, and plans of action. This is an important facet of the Holy See's activity because conventions and treaties, once adopted, form international law. The Holy See's presence is to promote ethical issues.

The representatives of the Holy See make contributions to the international debate on current issues: development, peace, security, eradication of poverty, access to education and health, rights of the children, women's issues, right to life, and religious rights. The international debates are opportunities for the Holy See to shed the light of Catholic Social Thought on issues being debated. At this juncture, therefore, it becomes pertinent to discuss Catholic Social Justice Theory.

---

visited October 12, 2013) (emphasizing that the Church never ceases to proclaim and defend fundamental human rights, including the right of every person to life, food, housing, work, health care, the protection of the family, and the promotion of development. The Catholic Church does not seek any special status from secular governments. Rather, the Church asks only "the legitimate conditions of freedom for her mission," and promises cooperation with all civil authorities in promoting the common good.).

CHAPTER FOUR

Catholic Social Justice Theory

The term "social justice," was coined and introduced into Catholic social ethics in the mid-1800s by an Italian theologian and Jesuit priest, Luigi Taparelli D'Azeglio.[379] Father Luigi's thoughts on social justice came ostensibly to replace Thomas Aquinas's terms "legal justice" and "general justice," which were in danger of being misconstrued in the modern context.[380] For Taparelli, social justice is not a metaphor, nor the extension of virtue language to "anthropomorphized collectives."[381] Taparelli held that social justice is distinct from both commutative justice and distributive justice.[382] Thomas Behr takes a cue from this and defines social justice as

---

[379] *See* BRIAN J. BENESTAD, CHURCH, STATE, AND SOCIETY: AN INTRODUCTION TO CATHOLIC SOCIAL DOCTRINE (2011) (indicating that a Jesuit philosopher by the name of Luigi Taparelli D'Azeglio was the first to use the concept of social justice in his major work, Saggio teoretico di diritto"). *See also* J.J Ziegler, "The teachings of Vatican II, Paul VI, John Paul II, and the Catechism of the Catholic Church" The Catholic World Report (CWR), available at http://www.catholicworldreport.com/Item/2257/what_is_social_justice_part_two.aspx#.UpTrBI2A3ug (last visited August 23, 2013).

[380] Marvin L. Mich, *Catholic Social Teaching and Movements,* Mystic, Conn. 2000, pp. 80-81, 423-25, no. 58 (examining details of Thomas Aquinas's terms "legal justice" and "general justice" and associated modern misinterpretation.).

[381] *See* THOMAS C. BEHR of the University of Houston in a paper delivered in 2003 at the annual conference of the Pontifical Academy of St. Thomas Aquinas, cited on *the Catholic World Report, supra* note 343.

[382] *See id.* (in which John Hardon defines commutative justice as "the virtue that regulates those actions which involve the rights between one individual and another individual" and distributive justice as "the virtue that regulates those actions which involve the rights that an individual may claim from society.")

> A legal order and normative ideal within a society by which individuals and their various associations are given the maximum range of liberty in pursuit of their proper ends, with a minimum of interference from superior authorities, *i.e.*, only to the extent necessary to orient general activity towards the common good, and governed by the principles of conflicting rights, prudence, and, ultimately, of charity. This is not the only way that Taparelli uses the term, but it is arguably the most important of his uses.[383]

Luigi's "social justice" appeared in an 1894 curial document and a 1904 encyclical. Later, Pope Pius XI (1922-39) made it part and parcel of Catholic social doctrine.[384] The earliest appearance of the term "social justice" in a curial document was in 1894, when the Sacred Congregation of the Council for the Propagation of Faith, ruling on a canonical question, stated "a new practice of social justice was born from that principle 'the despoiled before all things ought to be restored.'"[385] The term appeared again in the 1904 encyclical *Iucunda Sane,* when Pope Pius X wrote that Pope St. Gregory the Great acted as a "public defender of social justice" [*publicus iustitiae socialis adsertor*] during his years as a legate in Byzantium."[386]

Pope Pius XI also used the term "social justice" in his 1923 encyclical, *Studiorum Ducem*, when he wrote

> Thomas refutes the theories propounded by Modernists in every sphere...in sociology and law, by laying down sound principles of legal and social, commutative and

---

[383] *Id.*

[384] *See* John F. Cronin, "Forty Years Later: Reflections and Reminiscences, 1971," in C. Curran & R. McCormick (ed.), *Readings*, pp. 73-74 (stating that social justice apparently entered the vocabulary of official Papal teaching by way of students of German solidarist Heinrich Pesch, especially Gustav Gundlach and Oswald von Nell-Breuning, drafter of Pope John XXIII's encyclical *Quadragesimo Anno*).

[385] *See* Acta Sanctae Sedis, 1894-95, p. 131, in *Documenta Catholica Omnia (Acts and Documents of the Holy See)*. http://www.documentacatholicaomnia.eu/04z/z_18941895__Sancta_Sedes__Acta_Sanctae_Sedis_27__LT.pdf.html (last visited October 23, 2013).

[386] *See* J. J. ZIEGLER, THE CATHOLIC WORLD REPORT, *supra* note 378.

> distributive, justice and explaining the relations between justice and charity.[387]

Pope Pius XI referred to St. Thomas Aquinas teaching on justice as "sound principles of social justice." The principles, which Pope Pius was referring to here, are specifically those which are denied by the most prominent modern political philosophers, from Hobbes and Locke to Hegel and Marx.[388] In another encyclical, Pope Pius XI threw more light on social justice as it concerns workers' wages when he wrote

> Every effort must therefore be made that fathers of families receive a wage large enough to meet ordinary family needs adequately. But if this cannot always be done under existing circumstances, social justice demands that changes be introduced as soon as possible whereby such a wage will be assured to every adult workingman.... It is contrary to social justice when, for the sake of personal gain and without regard for the common good, wages and salaries are excessively lowered or raised; and this same social justice demands that wages and salaries be so managed, through agreement of plans and wills, in so far as can be done, as to offer to the greatest possible number the opportunity of getting work and obtaining suitable means of livelihood.[389]

---

[387] *See* POPE PIUS XI, "*Studiorum Ducem* (*On St. Thomas Aquinas*)," cited in *The Catholic World Report, supra* note 343; *See also* Pope Pius XI, *Studiorum Decem (On St. Thomas Aquinas)* EWTN.com, http://www.ewtn.com/library/encyc/p11studi.htm (last visited November 27, 2013).

[388] *See* J. J. ZIEGLER, *supra* note 378 (rebutting the misinterpretations and attacks of modern philosophers Hobbes, Locke, Hegel, Marx, and others on St. Thomas Aquinas's thoughts on "legal justice" and "general justice," and thereby reading the social justice thoughts of Luigi Taparelli D'Azeglio into the earlier thoughts of St. Thomas Aquinas.)

[389] POPE PIUS XI, *QUADRAGESIMO ANNO* (On Reconstruction of the Social Order), #s 71 & 74[many writers have judged social justice as the keynote of the encyclical *Quadragesimo Anno* stressing that social justice specifies the directive principle of social institutions: not competition but the common good; see David O'Brien, "A Century of Social Teaching: Context and Comments," in John A. Coleman (ed.), *One Hundred Years of Catholic Social Teaching* (1991)]; for both Pope Leo XIII and Pope Pius XI, the paradigmatic "worker" was the "working man," laboring to support his family. And I add that, with the dynamic nature

Following this development, Pope Pius XII and Pope John XXIII adopted the teachings of Pope Pius XI on social justice, whole and entire. As a result of the adoption of Pope Pius XI's teaching on social justice, Pope Pius XII in 1952 taught that society "ought to be renewed according to principles of charity and social justice."[390] Pope John XXIII also prayed in 1960 that Christians might "offer to their fellow citizens examples of all virtues, in the first-place social justice and charity."[391]

Social justice taking the center stage in all Church documents followed the foregoing. The Catholic doctrine on social justice was set forth with tremendous authority. All thoughts on the Church's social mission came to use social justice as the paradigm. For example, all the Papal social encyclicals, Vatican II documents, the Catechism of the Catholic Church, including Papal Exhortations, letters, and addresses, employ the principles of social justice.[392] With this amount of authority vested in the term "social

---

of the Church's social teaching, and following inclusive language, this paradigm also includes the "working woman" laboring to support her family; *see* QUADRAGESIMO ANNO, no. 3

[390] *See* J. J. ZIEGLER, *supra* note 378.

[391] *Id.*

[392] See *for e.g.* Second Vatican Ecumenical Council, *Nostra Aetate (*Declaration on the Relation of the Church with Non-Christian Religions), 28 October 1965, *no.* 3 (the Council Fathers exhorted Christians and Muslims to "preserve as well as to promote together for the benefit of all mankind social justice and moral welfare, as well as peace and freedom"); in *the Pastoral Constitution on the Church in the Modern World (Gaudium et Spes),* the Council Fathers observed that "excessive economic and social differences between the members of the one human family or population groups cause scandal and militate against social justice, equity, the dignity of the human person, as well as social and international peace," see no. 29 (The Council Fathers called for the creation of an "organism of the universal Church" whose role would be "to stimulate the Catholic community to promote progress in needy regions and international social justice"—in the original Latin, "social justice among nations"). Imprecise translations of papal documents can make the study of the Magisterium's teaching on social justice more challenging. At times, the words "social justice" appear in English translations where it does not appear in the Latin – for example, in *Paenitemini,* Pope Paul VI's 1966 apostolic constitution on fast and abstinence, where *condicionem socialem aequiorem* [a fairer social condition] is rendered as "social justice," or in paragraph 61 of *Populorum Progressio,* Pope Paul's 1967 encyclical on the development of peoples, where *iustitiae* [of justice] is rendered as "social justice." In 1923, Pope Pius XI wrote that St. Thomas Aquinas established "sound principles" of social justice. In his 1967 apostolic letter *Roma Altera,* Pope Paul VI wrote that St. Robert Bellarmine (1542-1621), the Jesuit doctor of the Church, set forth "the beginnings of the doctrine on social justice." Pope Paul VI's Apostolic Letter *Roma Altera* "refers to the years in which Bellarmine was archbishop of Capua, and in that capacity Bellarmine did take some steps to protect the poor and the socially disadvantaged, but within a context of what

today we would call philanthropy rather than properly social justice. In other words, during his time in Capua Bellarmine helped the poor, but he never theoretically and systematically reflected on social justice as part of his doctrinal views." By explicitly mentioning Bellarmine, one of the greatest theologians of the Church, in this context, Pope Paul VI wanted to give a strong signal of the importance of the issue of social justice within the history of Catholic doctrine, *see* STEFANIA TUTINO, EMPIRE OF SOULS: ROBERT BELLARMINE AND THE CHRISTIAN COMMONWEALTH (2010). The term "social justice" also appeared again in Pope Paul VI's famed 1968 encyclical on the regulation of births, *Humanae Vitae,* in which he urged governments not to adopt population policies that violate natural law. Pope Paul VI wrote, "No one can, without being grossly unfair, make divine Providence responsible for what clearly seems to be the result of misguided governmental policies, of an insufficient sense of social justice, of a selfish accumulation of material goods, and finally of a culpable failure to undertake those initiatives and responsibilities which would raise the standard of living of peoples and their children," *see* POPE PAUL VI, ENCYCLICAL LETTER *Humanae Vitae (*On the Regulation Birth*),* 1968, no 23; In *Sancti Stephani Ortum,* his 1970 Apostolic Letter to Hungarian Catholics, Pope Paul VI wrote that the Christian is called to foster a "respect for the human life just conceived, whose sole and highest Lord is God Himself; due reverence for human dignity; liberty of conscience; the advance of social justice; the will for serving the common good; a true and just peace." In a January 1971 address to the Council of the General Secretariat of the Synod of Bishops, Pope Paul VI said "More in these days, the Catholic Church should unite for social justice, which should be established in today's world, and certainly in so difficult a time in its history." Four months later, Pope Paul issued his apostolic letter *Octogesima Adveniens,* on the eightieth anniversary of Pope Leo XIII's landmark social encyclical *Rerum Novarum.* Although the term "social justice" did not appear in *Rerum Novarum,* the encyclical's message, said Pope Paul, "continues to inspire action for social justice. Since the period in which the encyclical *Rerum Novarum* denounced in a forceful and imperative manner the scandal of the condition of the workers in the nascent industrial society, historical evolution has led to an awareness of other dimensions and other applications of social justice." Pope Paul added, as he called upon Christians to "perceive an original application of social justice" in addressing urban problems; *see* POPE PAUL VI, *Octogesima Adveniens* (On the Occasion of the Eightieth Anniversary of the Encyclical "*Rerum Novarum*"), 1971, nos. 1, 5 & 12. In June 1971, Pope Paul spoke briefly about social justice in *Evangelica Testificatio,* his Apostolic Exhortation on the Renewal of Religious Life according to the Teaching of the Second Vatican Council. "It is certainly true that religious institutes have an important role to fulfill in the sphere of works of mercy, assistance and social justice; it is clear that in carrying out this service they must be always attentive to the demands of the Gospel;" see Pope Paul VI, Evangelica Testificatio (On the Renewal of Religious Life according to the Teaching of the Second Vatican Council, 1971, no. 16.

The term "social justice" did not appear again in a major papal document until 1979, when Blessed John Paul II wrote his first encyclical. In *Sollicitudo Rei Socialis,* his 1987 encyclical on the 20th anniversary of Populorum Progressio, Pope John Paul II taught that "peace, so desired by everyone, will certainly be achieved through the putting into effect of social and international justice;" see POPE JOHN PAUL II, *Sollicitudo Rei Socialis, (*On the twentieth anniversary of *Populorum Progressio*), 1987, no. 39; Three years later Pope John Paul II in his apostolic *Constitution on Catholic Universities, Ex Corde Ecclesiae,* wrote, "The Christian spirit

justice," it becomes worthwhile at this juncture to explore what justifies social justice. Put another way, the next section, taking cognizance of the huge interest, the Catholic Church has in the concept of social justice, will try to explore what justification there is for social justice generally. The discussion of the justification for social justice will zero in on what unique circumstances motivate the Holy See to exert its authority in promoting social justice. This point will help in the assessment of the Holy See's use of this mechanism in her involvement in international affairs, particularly, in its Observer status at the WTO.

4.1 Justification for Social Justice

It has been suggested that system-justifying attitudes reflect a "moral motivation" to protect society, and "the benefits of justifying the system are not just palliative, they are meaning-providing and can often be important for human flourishing."[393] System justification can indeed inspire people to celebrate and vindicate truly just institutions and practices. Nevertheless, the same motivation can lead us—as it may have led Aristotle—to venerate those features of the social system (*e.g.*, customs, traditions, and practices) that deserve to be changed.[394]

---

of service to others for the promotion of social justice is of particular importance for each Catholic university, to be shared by its teachers and developed in its students;" in 1990, Pope John Paul II promulgated the *Code of Canons of the Eastern Churches,* which affirmed that the Christian faithful are "obliged to promote social justice" (25 §2) and stated that it is "desirable that the Catholic faithful undertake any project in which they could cooperate with other Christians, not alone but together, such as works for charity and social justice;" see Code of Canons of the Eastern Churches, 25 § 2; under the leadership of Cardinal Joseph Ratzinger, the Congregation for the Doctrine of the Faith affirmed the international dimensions of the question of social justice while criticizing a Marxist interpretation of class struggle. In 1987, at a meeting in Detroit, Pope John Paul II exhorted his listeners to be attentive to the common good and the demands of social justice. He said, "Do not let this hour pass without renewing your commitment to action for social justice and peace. Turn to the Gospel of Jesus Christ to strengthen your resolve to become instruments for the common good!"

393 *See* J. HAIDT & J. GRAHAM, "Planet of the Durkheimians, "Where Community, Authority, and Sacredness are Foundations of Morality," in J. Jost, A. C. Kay, & H. Thorisdottir (eds.), *Social and Psychological Bases of Ideology and System Justification*, (2009).

394 *See* GEORAGE A. MILLER, PSYCHOLOGY: THE SCIENCE OF MENTAL LIFE (1991); RICHARD KRAUT, FOUNDERS OF MODERN POLITICAL AND SOCIAL THOUGHT (2002). It would be difficult to find a more astute justice theorist or a greater

Research by social psychologists establishes the grounds of concern for the welfare of other persons or groups and how these are related to the concern individuals feel for their own welfare.[395] From research in social psychology, there are two grounds for system justification. They are "self-interest" and "justice motive." Social psychology not only studies reasons for the perpetration of injustice, but also the vectors that make it possible for persons to think and care and work for others.[396] Studies in social psychology concerning the justification for justice presage inquiries into "altruism," "pro-social behaviors," and above all, "justice motive," that is, the extent to which people are motivated to promote fair treatment of others. In other words, social psychology does not concentrate merely on considerations of self-interest.[397]

The point is not that justice and self-interest are always opposed. Plainly, they are not. In fact, a sense of justice may originate in humans and other primates in the self-protective desire to insure that they receive what

---

authority on ethical behavior in the entire history of Western civilization than Aristotle. And yet there are aspects of his belief system that strike contemporary audiences as anomalous and obviously wrong-headed, possibly even immoral. Probably the most obvious example is his spirited defense of the institution of slavery as practiced by so many of his fellow Athenian citizens. It is not the case that no one in ancient Greece had ever raised moral objections about slavery; several philosophers of Aristotle's era had criticized the practice, but Aristotle apparently rejected those criticisms. How could such a brilliant ethical mind possibly find itself arguing that such a brutal, exploitative institution as slavery was not only necessary but also just? The answer, it seems, must do with system justification, defined as the conscious or unconscious motivation to defend, bolster, and justify existing social, economic, and political institution, and arrangements. One way in which people engage in system justification is using stereotypes (such as Aristotle's stereotypes of slaves and masters) that ascribe to individuals and groups characteristics that render them especially well-suited to occupy the status or positions that they do in the current social order. It is important to point out that members of disadvantaged groups sometimes internalize system-justifying stereotypes and evaluations of themselves, and this almost surely has the consequence of decreasing their likelihood of rebelling against the status quo or participating in collective action aimed to change it. *See id.*

[395] *See* SOLOMON E. ASCH, "Effects of Group Pressure upon the Modification and Distortion of Judgment," in H. Guetzkow (ed.), *Groups, leadership and Men,* (1951). Studies of independence and conformity: A minority of one against a unanimous majority, Psychological Monographs, *70 (Whole no. 416*) (1956); "Opinions and Social Pressure," in A. P. Hare, E. F. Borgatta and R. F. Bales (eds.), *Small groups: Studies in Social Interaction, (1966), pp. 318-324*

[396] *Id.*

[397] *Id.*

they deserve.[398] When members of disadvantaged groups band together to push for civil rights or other improvements in their quality of life, they are fighting on behalf of social justice as well as personal and collective self-interest.[399] Nevertheless, the purest evidence of a justice motive in human beings comes from cases in which people are willing to risk or sacrifice their own welfare to insure that others are treated fairly.[400]

Bringing this discussion to our world in the light of the disparities between individuals, between individuals and groups, and between rich and poor countries, it stands to reason to ask: what is the justification for the clamor for social justice? Most people are deeply offended by the growing inequalities among countries of the world. Such people express their disgust by whining all the time about the expanding grey areas of globalization. The situation is still the same with WTO's special and differential package. Experience has taught us that whining about inequalities and the fact that globalization and special and differential

---

[398] *See* Sarah F. Brosnan, "At a crossroads of disciplines," *Journal of Social Justice,* 19 (2006) pp. 218-227; Frans B. M.de Waal & Sarah F. Brosnan, "Review of "What it Means to be 98% Chimpanzee" by Jonathan Marks and "In Defense of the Soul: What it means to be human" by Ric Machuga," in *Science and Spirit, 41* (Jan/Feb 2003)

[399] *See for example,* FRANCES FOX PIVEN & RICHARD A. CLOWARD, POOR PEOPLES' MOVEMENTS: WHY THEY SUCCEED, HOW THEY FAIL, New York, Vintage Books, (1979); Robert B. Albritton, "Social Amelioration through Mass Insurgency? A Reexamination of the Piven and Cloward Thesis," in *The American Political Science Review,* Vol. 73, No. 4 (1979), pp. 1003-1011 (showing an example of research that combines both social theory and social praxis in its methodology. By analyzing historic movements of social policy shifts, they suggest not only causal explanations of social policy shifts but also implications for strategies by which the poor can achieve economic and political gains from governments and members of the elite ordinarily inured to their demands.)

[400] *See, for instance,* Gene H. Lerner, "Selecting Next Speaker: The Context-sensitive Operation of a Context-free Organization," in *Language in Society,* 32(2) (2003), pp.177-201, http://www.soc.ucsb.edu/faculty/lerner/pub/publications.htm (last visited November 29, 2013).

treatment are like "whited sepulchers"[401] might be a waste of time and energy.[402]

Instead of this fruitless exercise that falls on the deaf ears of the major trading powers, our preoccupation should be to find answers to the question as to why trade officials of world super powers should accept a plea to break the wall of nequalities.[403] There is no other way to put it better than when Professor Raj Bhala writes

> The plea for handouts, for more special and differential treatment, almost necessarily falls on deaf ears in the capital cities of the major trading super powers. Why should senior trade officials in Washington, D.C., Brussels, Tokyo, or Ottawa listen if the theoretical underpinnings for that plea are not well thought out or put forth systematically? It is not that these officials are immune from feeling pity or doing charity. It is that they are not paid in their official capacity, to act on feelings of pity or to be generous unless, that is, they can be shown a reason for charity. Simply saying to them "because we are poor and you are rich" ought to be compelling enough. But, in the hardheaded world in which these officials must operate, typically it is not. They need to hear more than the mantra of inequality if they are to renovate their trade programs and aid budgets for the Third world. Put bluntly, whining leads nowhere.[404]

[401] Expression with origin from the Scriptures, pointing out the hypocritical attitude of the Pharisees, who Jesus described as living like "whitewashed tombs that look handsome on the outside but full of the bones of the dead and every kind of corruption inside" Matthew 23:27; (the state of pretending to have virtues, moral or religious beliefs, principles, etc., that one does not actually have. Hypocrisy involves the deception of others and is thus a kind of lie. Hypocrisy is not simply failing to practice those virtues.)

[402] BHALA RAJ, TRADE, DEVELOPMENT, AND SOCIAL JUSTICE, *supra* note 56, at 373 (indicating that whining about an "unjust" global trading system, or pleading for more hand-outs from rich countries, is not effective advocacy strategy.)

[403] *Id.*

[404] *Id.*

The need for convincing strategies may be worsened by the type of attitude that pleaders such as the poor countries portray. We normally say, "He who goes to equity must go with clean hands." It becomes worrisome to look at the governments of poor countries who, though on the begging side, come with hands besmirched with unclear conscience, inept, undemocratic and possessing corrupt administrative principles. Of course, governments of the poor countries "are very much to blame for sluggish economic growth and skewed income distribution."[405] With a situation like that, a credible case for better special and differential treatment made on behalf of developing countries become unattractive and therefore not persuasive enough. The problem is no longer "unjust" global trading system, but corrupt and deceptive governments of poor countries.

To keep the ball rolling toward a lasting solution to inequalities in international trade, there is a need for a better conception of effective advocacy strategy. The concept of special and differential treatment, which is needed, is one that not only concentrates on persuading rich countries to assist poor countries. It is strategies that will also help poor countries establish a fair and equitable distribution mantra. It is in search of this more suitable strategy that this book projects social justice, especially as utilized by the Holy See in her universal mission. This book sets out to make this case.

There are two grounds of justification for more charitable trade preferences for poor countries in the GATT/WTO system. These two justifications are what have been referred to as "our" self-interest, and "their" social justice.[406] This book extends the social justice justification to the level of Catholic social justice, a theory which has no territorial or class limitations.

The first justification is self-interest. Self-interest is associated with utilitarianism, but it is not the same as utilitarianism. The industrialized countries, with the United States as the number one example, fall under this category. The reasoning behind self-interest justification is based on

---

[405] *See id.* at 374

[406] *Id.*

the thrust that helping poor countries would benefit the rich countries, which are helping. The way this works is that,

> The First World can choose to offer better Almsgiving Rules because it suits the interests of the First World. Selfishness, or self-love, in a collective national sense, is the dominant impulse here. That is, on balance, better special and differential treatment, particularly in the sense of more generously Almsgiving Rules – helps the rich countries, in terms of a net benefit-cost calculation of other self-interest.[407]

Almsgiving in the context of international trade relations means any gratis transfer of help (in the form of finance, human capital, or technology) from a rich country to a developing country either directly or indirectly. This gesture is normally meant to assist the developing country in question to implement the rules of international trade law in order to compete more successfully in world markets.[408] Almsgiving rules benefit the rich countries in that better special and differential treatment of poor countries would not only help the latter grow into robust trading partners of the former but also help rich countries grow into more stable societies. The self-interest goal here is that a better special and differential strategy enhances the peace and security of rich countries even though such a device is projected as an obvious way to help poor countries rise.[409]

Comments made in different quarters after the September 11, 2001, terrorist attacks on the United States lay credence to self-interest as justification for fair treatment of developing countries. One such comment came from the National Conference of American Bishops as published in its 1986 Pastoral Letter

---

[407] *See id.* (defining Almsgiving Rule as a rule that calls for an unconditional transfer (direct and indirect) of financial capital, human capital, or technology from a developed country to a developing country, (1) where the developing country has no ownership or possessory claim to the thing transferred, other than pursuant to the rule itself, and (2) which yields a tangible economic gain to the developing country). See RAJ BHALA, *supra* note 56 ¶ 135.

[408] *See id.*at 138

[409] *Id.* at 375

> Unless conscious steps are taken toward protecting human dignity and fostering human solidarity in these relationships [between the United States and developing poor countries], we can look forward to increased conflict and inequity, threatening the fragile economies of these relatively poor nations far more than our own relatively strong one.[410]

An analysis of the above statement made by American bishops shows that increased conflict and inequity do not go without a corresponding threat from within and without. Wealthy nations in general and America, cannot claim any immunity to the negative effects of deprivations of human dignity and gaps in human solidarity. Another example is worth examining, this time from a market strategist:

> To constrain [the terrorists'] reach further, and continue to work for a new world balance, the industrialized world should strive to fight against its own protectionism. The way to share our bounty – *in a manner that would also benefit us, incidentally* – is to make our rich world a home for the talented in the developing world, Islamic or not, and for their wares and products. If we want to seize the moment, then we would follow the victory against terrorism by lowering trade tariffs and immigration requirements.... Capitalism has a clean set of rules. Obey them and you create wealth. Don't and you won't. What should be ensured is that if nations stay poor, they do so through the fault of their rulers and not because of the actions of those outside their borders.[411]

---

[410] National Conference of Catholic Bishops, *Economic Justice for All: A Pastoral Letter on Catholic Social Teaching and the U.S. Economy* ¶ 252 (1986), in CATHOLIC SOCIAL THOUGHT – THE DOCUMENTARY HERITAGE 572 (David J. O'Brien & Thomas A. Shannon eds. 1992); *see also* RAJ BHALA, *supra* note 56, at 375.

[411] DAVID ROCHE, *THERE IS NO CLASH OF CIVILIZATIONS,* WALL STREET JOURNAL EUROPE, November 29, 2001, at 6 with emphasis added in RAJ BHALA, *supra* note 56, at 376.

Apparently, the above quotations from the American Catholic bishops and the London market strategist are nothing new. Similar ideas have been expressed in the past showing self-interest as a justification for assistance to poor countries. In 1817, David Ricardo propounded his "Comparative Advantage" theory in support of free trade, an extension of Adam Smith's theory of "Absolute Advantage."[412] The Secretary of State during the tenure of President Franklin Roosevelt, Cordell Hull, extended David Ricardo's theory of Comparative Advantage under the Reciprocal Trade Agreements Act of 1934.[413] Hull's reason for doing so was because free trade is closely linked to international peace and stability.[414]

Hull's projection of self-interest in this case was a form of national security. National security concerns can be brought into the calculations, (not to support protection for a domestic industry, which is the usual way they are used), but to support market-opening initiatives for developing country exports.[415] This makes sense in so many ways:

---

[412] *See* ADAM SMITH, THE WEALTH OF NATIONS, London, 1776; DAVID RICARDO, THE PRINCIPLES OF POLITICAL ECONOMY AND TAXATION, 1817 [The theory of absolute advantage was advanced to buttress Smith's argument that if there was no government involvement in trade, and if each individual was left to do what in his or her own best interest, then there would be more goods and services available, prices would be reduced, and the wealth of each nation, measured as the welfare of the citizens, would increase. Smith's theory was offered to replace mercantilism. (Mercantilism encourages exports and discourages imports). The theory of comparative advantage advances and refines Smith's theory of absolute advantage. Ricardo agreed with Smith's view that if there was no government involvement in trade and if everyone was left to do what is in his or her own best interest, then there would be more goods and services available, prices would be reduced, and the wealth of each nation would increase. Ricardo's comparative advantage theory extends Smith's view to the case where one of the two countries has an absolute advantage in both commodities, and shows that even here trade is good for both countries.]

[413] *See* RAJ BHALA, *supra*, note 56, at 376 (stating that Secretary of State, Cordell Hull extended Ricardo's theory by promulgating that trade is in the self-interest of the United States (and other developed countries) for more reasons than just the net welfare benefits specialization of production and increased consumption that result from the exercise of comparative advantage). With his Reciprocal Trade Agreements Act of 1934, Hull dismantled the Smooth-Hawley tariffs enacted under the Tariff Act of 1930, (see *9 USC Chapter 4 - TARIFF ACT OF 1930).*

[414] RAJ BHALA, *supra*, note 56.

[415] *Id.*

> Granting special dispensations may help these countries (poor countries) grow to a position of wealth in which they can be better customers *(i.e.,* buy more goods and services from the First World) and better suppliers (*i.e.,* sell more goods and services needed by the First World). To the extent that position is a stable one, then the First World would be better off not only because of its vibrant economic relationships, but also because of its greater security. The fast-growing countries of the Third World may be less likely to sponsor, or acquiesce to, terrorism, war, narcotics trafficking, (hijacking of ships in Somali and Ethiopia coasts), or other forms of behavior unacceptable to the First World[416]

Put another way, the common saying "prevention is better than cure" is *ad rem* in this discussion. The Somali and Ethiopian pirates that have ravaged the Indian Ocean for many years now is a case in point. Though hundreds of the young men (Somali pirates) have been jailed, it has not stopped the insurgency.[417] Would it be sound reasoning for wealthy and fast-growing economies to think that their counter attacks would bring the activities of the pirates in the Horn of Africa to an end?

The answer to the above question is not supposed to be in the affirmative. Contracting local gendarmes or use of Delta Force commando raids, cruise missiles, and smart bombs as strategy to counter the attacks

---

[416] *See id.* (Emphasis added).

[417] Thomas Mountain, *The Pirates of Puntland: A Tale of Somali Pirates, Ethiopia and the U.S.A.*, in COUNTERPUNCH, August 27-29, 2010, available at http://www.counterpunch.org/2010/08/27/a-tale-of-somali-pirates-ethiopia-and-the-u-s-a/ (last visited December 2, 2013) (indicating that many reasons are given for what drives these pirates but the question not being asked is how they have managed to get away with extorting over a quarter of a billion dollars from the international community. The fact remains that despite the assembled flotillas from much of the world's navies, with unmanned drones flying overhead and satellites in space watching their every move, the Somali pirates of Puntland have been almost unimpeded in collecting their loot and returning to their lairs.... Ethiopia has about 80 million people and with its abundance of water, rich agricultural land, minerals and now even oil, should be a rich country, at the very least able to feed its own people). Somali and Ethiopia are dependent on debt forgiveness which taken alone does not help project human dignity. Attacks on the ships carrying consignments for the international community affect the rich countries more.

of Ethiopian and Somali pirates has not, and cannot, solve this problem. In only two weeks, Somali pirates held hostage over two hundred sailors seventeen ships and three vessels, namely, a Greek bulk carrier, a Thai fishing boat, and an Iranian bulk freighter and also a huge tanker, the *Sirius Star,* carrying up to 2 million barrels of Saudi oil.[418] The adverse effect of this piracy was so much and so disastrous that it affected trade and contributed to a humanitarian crisis.[419]

Let's look at this scenario: suppose wealthy members of the WTO negotiate for a better special and differential treatment for Ethiopia, Somalia, and the like; they are assisted to engender responsible government; the young men ravaging the Indian Ocean become gainfully employed; would the situation not change for the better? It would not only bring about healthy economic development, it would also bring with it stability and peace for the rich nations. A structure like this has self-interest as its motive, but is projected as Almsgiving to the poor countries. How can a right-thinking person expect least developed countries (LDCs) like Somalia and Ethiopia to merely watch the wealth from rich countries being shipped across from their coast and not do anything? Yes, they receive debt forgiveness and aids from time to time, but it is obvious that when one is taught how to fish instead of getting the gift of fish all the time, the person is preoccupied.

The first justification for Almsgiving is one of selfishness and is palatable to policy makers of rich countries since its goal is "for their own good." It does not matter that out of it comes charity to poor countries. Though the primary aim is national security, but the question is, is it not possible for a country to establish its national security and yet experience

---

[418] *See* Global Research Online, Piracy Payback: UN Plans Blitz on Somali Bases, November 20, 2008, available at http://www.globalresearch.ca/piracy-payback-un-plans-blitz-on-somali-bases/11064 (last visited December 2, 2013). The Center for Global Research (CRG) is an independent research and media organization based in Montreal. CRG is a registered non-profit organization in the province of Quebec, Canada. It was established on the 9th of September 2001. In addition to the Global Research websites, the Center is involved in book publishing, support to humanitarian projects as well as educational outreach activities including the organization of public conferences and lectures. The Center also acts as a think tank on crucial economic and geopolitical issues. The Global Research website at www.globalresearch.ca publishes news articles, commentary, background research, and analysis on a broad range of issues, focusing on social, economic, strategic, and environmental processes.

[419] *Id.*

tension from other countries that lack national security? In answering this question, Nigerian oil production is called to mind. Because of Dutch disease, which is prevalent in Nigeria, and the fact that the youth felt that multinational oil corporations were in complicity with the corrupt government in Nigeria, kidnapping of expatriates for ransom became a lucrative business.[420]

Developed countries may have security within their national borders, but that is nothing compared to the menaces coming from poor countries without stability. However, instability in poor countries may generate international threats such as are prevalent in the Middle East, particularly Iran, Iraq, Yemen, and North Korea. Such international threats might be so mind-boggling as to hinder developed countries enjoyment of the wealth and freedom. What is a better approach apart from justification almsgiving with self-interest as its motive? The second argument in favor of an altruistic special and differential treatment may be to solve the problem that almsgiving with self-interest as motive cannot solve.

A more generous special and differential treatment in favor of poor countries is otherwise explained by the principles of social justice. This argument may sound unpersuasive or irrelevant to hard liners.[421] While the first justification above is self-love, this second justification is love of another. Social justice takes into consideration "concern for the poor and

---

420 *See* Philip Catherine, *British Hostages Moved by Niger Rebels after Botched Rescue, THE TIMES*, London, January 19, 2009; since 2006, militant groups in Nigeria's Niger Delta, especially the Movement for the Emancipation of the Niger Delta (MEND), have resorted to taking hostage foreign employees of oil companies as part of the conflict in the Niger Delta. More than 200 foreigners have been kidnapped since 2006, though most were released unharmed; *see also Nigerian Telegraph Newspaper*, May 27, 2010, reporting with confirmation of the State Department that "more than 110 U.S expatriates had been kidnapped in Nigeria since January 2009." For this reason, most developed countries advised their citizens to desist from travelling to Nigeria because of "the very high risk of kidnapping, armed robbery and other armed attacks in these areas." The paper also reports that militant groups in the Niger Delta area of Nigeria use this strategy to put pressure on both the Nigerian government and oil companies to distribute the country's oil wealth more fairly. The Benghazi incident is not good news either. With all the security in the U.S., her four nationals, including Ambassador Christopher Stevens, were killed in a bomb attack at the U.S. Consulate in Libya' *see* Samira Said, Jomana Karadsheh & Laura Smith-Spark, *Benghazi hit by blast on anniversary of U.S. Consulate attack,* CNN REPORT, September 11, 2013, available at http://www.cnn.com/2013/09/11/world/africa/libya-benghazi-blast/ (last visited December 2, 2013).

421 RAJ BHALA, *supra* note 56, at 377.

a vision of right order in trade relations with poor countries."[422] In other words, more generous Almsgiving Rules than what presently exist will help the poor countries more. This book is not interested in weighing which of the two justifications is better. The two justifications are necessary. Self-interest and social justice complement each other better than what now exists in special and differential treatment. However, a more generous special and differential treatment of poor countries in international trade law will help them more and enhance international peace and security.

The justification of social justice generates hope from developed countries. It offers a uniquely compassionate vision for international trade law.[423] Every day we see people who need our help in one way or the other: victims of natural disasters, victims of fire outbreaks, or even victims of injustice.[424] For instance, when *shari'a code* was applied to the case of Safiya Husaini and Amina Lawal and a sentence of death by stoning was handed down to them, the international community rallied round them. They were supported legally and materially.[425]

---

[422] *Id.*

[423] *Id.*

[424] See for instance the type of solidarity and support given to Safiya Husaini, a Nigerian Muslim woman who was sentenced to death by stoning for committing adultery and conceiving a child out of wedlock; see *Interights on behalf of Safia Yakubu Husaini et al. v. Nigeria, African Commission on Human and Peoples' Rights, Comm. No. 269/2003* (2005); INTERIGHTS works to ensure that human rights standards are protected and promoted effectively in domestic courts and before regional and international bodies, contributing to the development of a cumulative and progressive interpretation of international human rights law. It provides expertise and advice on human rights litigation regarding issues of particular international, regional, or national importance. In cases where important principles are at stake, INTERIGHTS may act as co-representative, a "friend of the court" (*amicus curiae*) or advisor to counsel. During the ugly cases of sentencing Muslim women to death by stoning in Nigeria and other parts of the world, INTERIGHTS stood its ground with donations from all over the world; (adopted by the African Commission on Human and Peoples' Rights at its 37th Ordinary Session held in Banjul, The Gambia from 27 April to 11 May 2005). The case was the same during the case of Amina Lawal.

[425] *See Nigeria: Debunking Misconceptions on Stoning Case*, MONTHLY UPDATE (Human Rights Watch), New York, September 2003, available at http://hrw.org/update/2003/09#4 (last visited August 12, 2013); *see also Editorial, Saved from Stoning*, N.Y. TIMES, September 17, 2003, at A14 (describing potential motivation behind the reversal of Ms. Amina Lawal's conviction and outlining the history and recent growth of sharia in Nigeria); Somini Sengupta, *Lawal Defies Death by St*oning, AFR NEWS, September 30, 2003, LEXIS, News Library, Middle East & Africa File; *Saving Amina Lawl: Human Rights Symbolism and the Dangers of Colonialism*, HARVARD LAW REVIEW, Vol. 117, No. 7, May 2004, pp. 2365-2386.

Other examples include disasters like the Haitian earthquake, the typhoon disaster in the Philippines, and so on. In all these circumstances, people did not search for justifications to give charity to these poor people in far-off lands. The international community supported the victims with aid like food, clothing, money, water supply, medicine, etc. Now looking at this generosity though induced by tragedy, one can ask why people were that generous. Obviously, most people will say it is out of human sympathy. That's a perfect answer. What happens when millions of people in the poor countries are seen suffering because their countries are poor? This is what this second justification, social justice, sets out to address.

The Holy See projects social justice as a veritable instrument in its mission in the world. Therefore, the Holy See bolsters social justice in such a way as to draw the definition and elaboration of this concept from the Catholic theology. The justification of social justice is traceable to the time of Jesus Christ. Therefore, social justice aspires to be substantive in its nature, specific in its recommendations, and theological in its foundation.[426] As a matter of fact, for a better understanding of the theological bearing of social justice, this book will examine its roots in the theological virtues. In tracing the theological basis of social justice, I intend to deviate from conventional wisdom.[427] Too much emphasis on conventional wisdom in this regard has been counter-productive. This book therefore, resorts to theological argument in exploring the relationship between developed countries and less developed countries in the GATT-WTO system.

4.1.1 Theological Virtues of Faith, Hope, and Charity

The special and differential treatment provisions of the GATT-WTO system are aimed at helping the underprivileged Members of the WTO. Unfortunately, drafters of the GATT-WTO articles must have taken their

[426] RAJ BHALLA, *supra* note 56, at 380.

[427] When we talk about conventional wisdom, we refer to the rhetoric of pro-Third World philosophy as it concerns international economic policies, especially as it relates to international trade. By conventional wisdom here then, we refer to bickering about how uncharitable developed countries are in their policies on international economic activities and how uncharitable the GATT-WTO law is to developing countries; *see* RAJ BHALA, *supra* note 56, at 132.

cue from certain branches of the law, international relations theory, and international conventions. This is not proper. When we are considering principles that can help poor people or countries, we should consider theological concepts relating to helping the poor and not legal principles.

Generally, virtue can be defined as a benefit flowing from a certain behavior. This sounds teleological or even implies utilitarianism.[428] According to the *Oxford Dictionary*, the term "virtue" is defined as "moral excellence, uprightness, goodness…a good quality."[429] In Catholic theology, "virtue" is "a good quality of the mind, by which we live rightly, of which no one can make bad use …."[430] Virtue is a "habit or permanent disposition which inclines a person to do good and to avoid evil."[431] It is "[a] good habit that enables a person to act according to right reason enlightened by faith and to do so with relative ease and with perseverance despite obstacles."[432] The Catechism of the Catholic Church defines it as "[a] habitual and firm disposition to do good."[433] Raj Bhala interprets this as meaning "to do justice and avoid injustice."[434] His interpretation is in line with the conception of social justice in international trade negotiations.

Virtue allows the person not only to perform good acts but also to give the best of him/her. The virtuous person invests himself in what is good with no reservations. A virtuous person pursues whatever is good and chooses whatever is good in concrete actions.[435] Catholic theology categorizes virtues into human virtues, moral virtues, cardinal virtues and theological virtues.[436] Under the category of cardinal virtues, we

---

428 RAJ BHALA, *supra* note 56, at 391.

429 *The Oxford Dictionary and Thesaurus* 1718-19 (American ed.1996)

430 Brian J. Benestad, *Church, State, and Society: An Introduction to Catholic Social Doctrine*, Washington D.C., The Catholic University of America Press, 2011, p.117.

431 Leo J. Trese, "The Faith Explained," (1991) *quoted in* RAJ BHALA, *supra* note 56, at 392.

432 John O'Connor, *The Essential Catholic Handbook: A Summary of Beliefs, Practices, and Prayers*, Liguori Books, 1997, p. 261 (with emphasis added).

433 *See* CATECHISM OF THE CATHOLIC CHURCH (1994), # 1804.

434 RAJ BHALA, *supra* note 56, at 392.

435 *See* CATECHISM OF THE CATHOLIC CHURCH (1994), # 1804.

436 *Human virtues* are firm attitudes, stable dispositions, habitual perfections of intellect and will that govern human actions, order human passions, and guide human conduct according to reason and faith. They make possible ease, self-mastery, and joy in leading a morally good life. The virtuous man is one who practices the good freely. The *moral virtues* are acquired by human effort. They are the fruit and seed of morally good acts; they dispose all the powers of the human being for communion with divine love, *See id. Cardinal virtues* are four in number,

have four virtues, one of which is "justice." Under theological virtues, we have faith, hope, and charity. Human virtues are rooted in theological virtues. Theological virtues adapt man's faculties to participate in the divine nature.

When we talk about the theological virtues, we think about what we must do as a matter of moral obligation. In the same vein, when we talk about why international trade law should be more just, we are talking about what Members ought to do as a moral imperative. Therefore, implementation of a more charitable special and differential treatment becomes a moral obligation for developed Members of the WTO. A moral obligation does not need to be lawful. In fact, it goes beyond what is lawful. It is "whatever that is true, whatever that is honorable, whatever that is just, and whatever that is gracious…."[437]

Theological virtues are the foundation of Christian moral activity. Theological virtues animate a person's moral activity and give such activity a special character.[438] Thomas Aquinas teaches that theological virtues are principles that order human beings to supernatural happiness, *i.e.*, to God. These principles are habits which are designated theological because (1) they have God as their object – being ordered to God; (2) they are infused into the souls of human beings making it possible for them to live up to the expectation of what is spiritual in them;[439] and (3) they are made known to us only by divine revelation in the Sacred Scripture.[440] The theological virtues are faith, hope, and charity.

The *Concise Oxford American Dictionary* defines "faith" as "complete trust or confidence in someone or something."[441] This would mean that faith in a person or institution is characterized by readiness to make

---

namely, prudence, justice, fortitude, and temperance, *see id.* Justice disposes to respect the rights of each and to establish in human relationships the harmony that promotes equity regarding persons and to the common good; *see* CATAECHISM OF THE CATHOLIC CHURCH (1994), No. 1807.

437 *See* CATECHISM OF THE CATHOLIC CHURCH (1994), # 1803.

438 For this reason, Raj Bhala adds emphasis to the definition of a "virtue" as:

The facility, disposition, or attitude that moves one to accomplish moral good and to do it joyfully and perseveringly even against obstacles and at the cost of sacrifice; *see* RAJ BHALA, *supra* 56, at 392.

439 *See* CATECHISM OF THE CATHOLIC CHURCH (1994), # 1813.

440 Thomas Aquinas, *Summa Theologica,* I-II, qu. 52, a. 1

441 The *Concise Oxford American Dictionary* 2006, p. 321.

sacrifices with no mixed feelings with no reservations. In Catholic theology, Thomas Aquinas explains faith as a habit of the intellect whose act is to believe truths, which are not seen, at the command of the will and under the influence of grace.[442] For faith to be effective, a person must possess the virtue of charity, the effect of which is always to direct the soul toward a good end. For this reason, faith is essentially linked with love and good deeds.[443] When we look at commitments made by WTO Members, it is hard not to believe that they made such commitments for nothing. The WTO Members made such commitments because of the great faith they have in the GATT/WTO system. It is unthinkable to claim to have faith in something without a corresponding readiness to make sacrifices.

The GATT-WTO system is structured to liberalize trade, especially in such a way as to help developing countries benefit fully from the global trading system. The GATT/WTO system liberalizes trade in such a way as to create an atmosphere that helps to increase opportunities for trade-related consultation and cooperation among members.[444] Faith in the GATT/WTO system should make members pursue tenaciously the objectives of the system with love and thirst for good deeds. It is good logic to argue that a show of a lack of faith in the system projects itself in picking and choosing the objectives of the system for instance, in observing the objectives for selfish gains. When members have faith in the GATT/WTO system, then there is hope for the poor countries. For this reason, hope is a virtue to be reflected upon.

The Concise Oxford American Dictionary defines "hope" as "a feeling of expectation and desire for a certain thing to happen;" "a person or thing that may help or save someone;" "grounds for believing that something good may happen."[445] Some of the synonyms of the term "hope" are "goal," "aim," "design," "plan," "expectation," etc. If these synonyms are interpreted well in line with the GATT/WTO system, then hope has a prime place in the system. International trade is therefore designed for

---

[442] BRIAN J. BENESTAD, *supra* note 379, at 118-9 (indicating that faith is a virtue because it inclines the intellect infallibly to seek its object "which is the truth," and living faith also directs the will to its last end "on account of which it assents to what is true").

[443] THE NEW JERUSALEM BIBLE, Galatians 5:6 (Faith works only through love); James 2:17 (Faith that does not go with good deeds is quite dead).

[444] *See* GATT Article 1; see also GATT Preamble (Paragraph 1).

[445] *See The Concise Oxford American Dictionary* 430 (2006).

sustainable economic development in a way that contributes to a balanced world economy, in a way that fosters and assists industrial and general economic development particularly for countries still in the early stages of industrial development.[446] For the reason of helping poor countries stand on their feet, Catholic theology emphasizes the virtue of hope.

According to Catholic theology, the virtue of hope responds to the aspiration of happiness, which God has placed in the heart of every person.[447] The virtue of hope inspires the activities of human beings and keeps them away from discouragement.[448] Buoyed up by hope, human beings are preserved from selfishness and led to the happiness that flows from charity.[449] The Catholic Church projects hope for all, using the implications of the incarnation of Jesus Christ as a case in point. The Holy See presents to the world humanism enriched by the human encounter with Christ, an encounter in which Christ did not alienate humanity but revealed the full truth of its dignity and glorious destiny.[450]

The Catholic Church teaches Members of the WTO to imitate Christ, whose faith in the human condition was shown not by self-assertion but by self-immolation. In the case of international trade, Members of the WTO should invest interest in working toward getting poor countries out of the quagmires of economic and social poverty. The reason for this is traceable to the faith members have in the GATT/WTO system which is buoyed up by charity, which is also one of the theological virtues.

The term "charity" is defined as "the voluntary giving of help …to others in need;" "kindness and tolerance in judging others;" "love of humankind, typically in a Christian context."[451] This is a very interesting

---

[446] *See* GATT Article 1.

[447] *See* CATECHISM OF THE CATHOLIC CHURCH (1994) # 1818.

[448] *Id.*

[449] *Id.*

[450] *SECOND* VATICAN ECUMENICAL COUNCIL, *Gaudium Et Spes supra* note 75, # 22; *see also* GEORGE WEIGEL, WITNESS TO HOPE: THE BIOGRAPHY OF JOHN PAUL II, 1920-2005, *supra* note 74, at 169, (indicating that in his encounter with humanity, Jesus did not alienate humanity but rather lived in that drama and thereby created the path to human fulfillment; the Catholic Church teaches Members of the WTO to imitate Jesus Christ, who made a unique sacrifice which restored hope to human beings. Such hope is comparable to the hope that the GATT-WTO system is out to establish, and with faith in the system, poor countries can be removed from the quagmires of economic and social poverty).

[451] *See* THE CONCISE OXFORD AMERICAN DICTIONARY 149 (2006).

definition. The reason is that without charity the membership of poor countries in the GATT/WTO system is a waste of time. Without charity, the set objectives of the GATT/WTO system, especially as it concerns the less-privileged Members, can no longer be achievable. When families go to a restaurant with minors, a special seating arrangement and special menu are prepared for them; they are not treated the same as adults. This arrangement is aimed at making them comfortable as they sit with the adult members of their families. Compare this scenario with membership of the WTO. The aims and objectives of the GATT/WTO system can only be realized through the application of the special and differential treatment, which must be respected by all members.

In Catholic theology, the term "charity" is given the same meaning as the term "love." To strengthen that reasoning, the Catechism of the Catholic Church teaches

> The Apostle Paul has given an incomparable depiction of charity: charity is patient and kind; charity is not jealous or boastful; it is not arrogant or rude. Charity does not insist on its own way; it is not irritable or resentful; it does not rejoice at wrong, but rejoices in the right. Charity bears all things, hopes all things, and endures all things.[452]

Because of the above citation, the Church also teaches that the fruits of the virtue of charity include joy, peace, and mercy. It is clear then that charity demands beneficence and fraternal correction. And by this teaching, charity is to be understood as benevolence. Charity also fosters reciprocity; otherwise charity would remain disinterested and generous. Charity is understood as friendship and communion. The Church cannot give a better explanation of the virtue of charity than she has already given. The virtue of charity should be applicable in the operations the GATT/WTO system in such a way that rich members will express the faith thcy have in the system by being freely charitable to poor members.

> If we turn away from evil out of fear of punishment, we are in the position of slaves. If we pursue the enticement

[452] CATECHISM OF THE CATHOLIC CHURCH (1994) # 1825; *see also* 1 Cor. 13: 4-7.

> of wages...we resemble mercenaries. Finally, if we obey *(if we cooperate or have a change of heart)* for the sake of the good itself and out of love...we are in the position *(of people who exercise their freedom).*[453]

It is only when a person does not do things voluntarily that resistance and mixed feelings will set in. If we have the virtues of faith (which is a weapon for commitment), charity (which animates and inspires all the virtues), and hope (which inspires trust), then cats and rats can live together in harmony. If poor members of the WTO trust the developed Members because they exhibit faith in the system by treating the former with charity, then controversy will vanish or at least diminish.

In evaluating how theological virtues apply to social justice and therefore to the GATT-WTO system, I am going to examine four theological metaphors that fall under Catholic and Islamic theological frameworks. The aim of this line of argument is to depart from traditional argument as justification for charity meant for the less privileged countries, that is, that the developed nations and the GATT-WTO law are uncharitable to the less developed countries. In doing this, I intend to analyze four theological metaphors under a theological framework. This analysis will also show that different types of special and differential treatment offered to underprivileged WTO Members can be captured in one of these four categories.[454] This analysis takes the form of homilies, calling for mortification, mercy, forgiveness, and almsgiving.[455] These concepts are derived from the Bible and the Qur'an.

4.1.2 Connections between Theological Virtues and Mortification

Those who use conventional wisdom, particularly pro-Third World proponents, are always heard saying developed countries are uncharitable in their importation policies and that GATT-WTO law is unfair to less

---

[453] St. Basil, *Reg. fus. tract., prol.* 3: PG 31, 896 B.

[454] RAJ BHALA, *supra* note 56, at 136.

[455] *Id.*

developed countries. Professor Bhala refers to this conventional wisdom as a kind of "whining," disclosing that this line of thinking is informed by Marx's critique of capitalism and western economic policies.[456] In tracing the connection between the theological virtues and mortification, this book sets out to switch gears from the conventional wisdom. It intends to rely on some metaphors drawn from Catholic theology to prove the indispensability of social justice as it concerns the GATT/WTO system, especially as it relates to poor countries. In exploring the theological justification of social justice, this book takes for granted a continuum of special and differential treatment rules. This book also recognizes the GATT-WTO law as still applicable to the theological framework upon which this unique argument rests.

The lexicographic meaning of the term "mortification" is "subduing (the body or its needs and desires) by self-denial or discipline."[457] This lexicon definition is important in this discussion because of the closeness to the theological understanding. In Catholic theology, mortification means renunciation or denying oneself of something which otherwise would bring self-satisfaction. For instance, a person may abstain from food, alcohol, or purchasing of perfumes and jewelry, for some obvious reasons.

The relationship between mortification and the cardinal virtues is instructive here, too. The practice of mortification demands the application of two cardinal virtues, namely, temperance toward what that which is pleasant and fortitude (or courage) to manage instinctual aversion from difficulties or pain.[458] An act of forbearance amounts to self-sacrifice for a

---

[456] *See id.* at 132.

[457] *See Concise Oxford American Dictionary, supra,* at 576.

[458] JOHN A. HARDON. S.J., THE CATHOLIC CATECHISM 198 (The cardinal virtues are the four principal moral virtues. The English word "cardinal" comes from the Latin word *cardo,* which means, "hinge." All other virtues hinge on the four cardinal virtues of prudence, justice, fortitude, and temperance. While fortitude as a virtue is commonly called courage, it is different from much of what we think of as courage today. Fortitude allows us to overcome fear and to remain steady in our will in the face of obstacles, but it is always reasoned and reasonable; the person exercising fortitude does not seek danger for danger's sake. While prudence and justice are the virtues through which we decide what needs to be done, fortitude gives us the strength to do it. While fortitude is concerned with the restraint of fear so that we can act, temperance is the restraint of our desires or passions. Food, drink, and sex are all necessary for our survival, individually and as a species; yet a disordered desire for any of

more noble purpose than the enjoyment of a certain pleasure. In this vein, mortification comes from

> The Latin word which means "death;" the Christian ideal (Luke 9:23 and Galatians 5:24) of "dying to self" through the deliberate restraint of unruly passions and appetites; the struggle against one's evil inclinations so as to bring them in conformity with the will of God.[459]

To establish the connection between the theological virtues and mortification, it is necessary to depart from the rigorous theory of the concept of justice. Otherwise, this book can never avoid the status quo, which is boring. Catholic theology suggests a different meaning of justice that blends with the virtue of mortification. It is possible to use the theological paradigms to measure the justness of the legal pillars upon which the multilateral trading system rests. Justice and mortification, as conceived by Catholic theology, are some of these paradigms.

From the perspective of Catholic theology, social justice concerns the application of the Gospel to social frameworks. A good example here is when the Gospel is applied to a legal or economic system. The significance of the Gospel message is found in two important Commandments of Christ, namely, love of God and love of one's neighbor.[460] These two Commandments portray charity according the teaching of the *Catechism of the Catholic Church:*

> This is the path of charity, that is, of the love of God and of neighbor. Charity is the greatest social commandment. It respects others and their rights. It requires the practice

---

these goods can have disastrous consequences, physical and moral. Temperance is the virtue that attempts to keep us from excess, and, as such, requires the balancing of legitimate goods against our inordinate desire for them).

459 *See* JOHN O'CONNOR, THE ESSENTIAL CATHOLIC HANDBOOK, *supra* note 432, at 214 (with emphasis added, *in* RAJ BHALA, *supra* note 56, at 143).

460 CATECHISM OF THE CATHOLIC CHURCH (1994) (teaching that the greatest commandments as loving the Lord your God with your whole heart, with all your soul, and with all your mind, and with all your strength; and the second is love of your neighbor as yourself; love does no wrong to a neighbor; love is therefore the fulfilling of the law); *see id* # 2196; *see also* Luke 2:51.

> of justice, and it alone makes us capable of it. Charity inspires a life of self-giving…"[461]

Social justice demands charity for it to be practical. Charity, as can be read from the above citation, is not only one of the virtues but also the greatest of all the virtues. In the above citation also, charity is taught to be the "greatest social commandment." In other words, charity promotes social justice. Raj Bhala interprets this so well in writing that

> To behave in a socially just manner is to build charity into societal frameworks, and *vice versa.* Rules within those frameworks can be judged as "socially just" if they have the virtues attendant to them, in the Catholic sense of a disposition toward good (righteousness), and a disposition away from evil.[462]

Charity is one of the theological virtues, and as mentioned above, the theological virtues relate directly to God. The human virtues are rooted in the theological virtues, which we understand are the foundation of every Christian moral activity. Mortification itself is a human virtue. And for purposes of applying the virtue of mortification in international trade, we talk about "external" and "internal" mortification. In a theological point of view, "external" mortification refers to the denial of sensual pleasure, while "internal" mortification refers to discipline over emotions.[463]

In the international trade law context, external mortification concerns the surrender of a right to impose tariff or non-tariff in the normal course of trade relations. Examples are granting duty-free treatment to certain products of a developing Member country, or in eliminating quotas on that product. In a case like this, a developed country gives up the pleasure of gaining tariff revenue or quota rents. Internal mortification is when a developed Member country unilaterally gives up a trade remedy case, which it would otherwise have initiated concerning a hostile action of a

---

[461] *See* CATECHISM OF THE CATHOLIC CHURCH (1994) # 1889.

[462] RAJ BHALA, *supra* note 56, at 518.

[463] *See id.* at 144.

poor country. For instance, a developed country exercises self-restraint in the sense of foregoing the imposition of a trade remedy, such as anti-dumping, or countervailing duty, or a safeguard action.[464] Both external and internal mortification are ways developed countries can, through self-restraint, forego an economic benefit that would have been gained through imposition of a tariff or quota.[465]

In all the above examples about self-restraint by developed countries, the underprivileged countries stand to gain some financial or other advantage. For example, if a developed country does not impose a trade barrier on imports from the poor country, then the exporters in the less privileged country may gain through increased sales and thereby make more profits from the developed country concerned. Also, if a developed country foregoes pursuing a trade remedy against a poor country, then the exporters in this poor county will benefit from more market access to the developed country.[466] These are obviously different ways of being charitable to the less developed countries without resorting to legal principles.

Drawing a parallel between mortification from the theological perspective and its legal version is necessary. In international trade law, "mortification" means the giving up of a legal right. Mortification is an act of self-denial by developed WTO Members. In the practice of self-denial, developed countries do not press a legal claim, which they are otherwise entitled to do, against the less privileged WTO Members.[467] When the developed countries endorsed the special and differential treatment during the Uruguay Round, "they, of their own volition, gave up their right; they accepted not to press a legal claim" against any poor Members of the WTO.[468] You cannot eat your cake and still claim to have it.

---

[464] *Id.*

[465] *See id.* at 144-145

[466] *Id.*

[467] *See* RAJ BHALA, *supra 56*, at 143-144.

[468] *Id.*

4.1.3 Connections between Theological Virtues and Mercifulness and Forgiveness

In suggesting international charity to less privileged countries, the best strategy regarding the debt burden borne by Third World countries is debt forgiveness of all or a part of it. In the context of the special and differential treatment, the expectation would be to forgive the less privileged countries their transgression in international trade law. Forgiveness as a strategy for charity is also closely linked with the virtue "mercy."

The Merriam-Webster's Collegiate Dictionary defines the term "mercy" as "compassion or forbearance shown especially to an offender or to one subject to one's power."[469] The term "mercy" is almost equivalent to the term "forgiveness," which is defined as "to give up resentment of or claim to requital for; to grant relief from payment of; to cease to feel resentment against."[470] The need for the virtue of mercy is stressed in a document, the *Decree on Justification*, as issued by the Council of Trent in 1525 where it reads, "the only remedy for great evils, the only way of plucking them out, is to forgive and to give;"[471] adding that

> When persons come for help, no matter what their problems may be, two things they always need and that the counselor should offer by word and example are forgiveness of injuries (real or imagined) and great generosity, both covered by the concept of mercy.[472]

From the above analysis, there is no clear-cut distinction between the two terms "mercy" and "forgiveness." These two terms go together in the context of the theological framework under review. Considering the connection between the two terms, the term mercy, as it relates to special and differential treatment, is a virtue with a discipline that empowers and requires forgiveness. Developed countries are to forgive unilaterally a past or expected future violation by developing countries of any international

---

[469] *See The Merriam-Webster Collegiate Dictionary* (11th ed., 2010), at 777.

[470] *See* The Merriam-Webster's Collegiate Dictionary (11th ed., 2010), at 491.

[471] *Quoted in* HARDON, THE CATHOLIC CATECHISM *supra* note 432, at 203.

[472] HARDON, supra 458, at 203 (with emphasis added in RAJ BHALA, TRADE, DEVELOPMENT, AND SOCIAL JUSTICE, *supra* note 56, at 146).

trade law obligation otherwise owed by the less developed countries to the developed countries.[473]

For the rule of mercy to apply, there must be certain presumptions. First, there must be an underlying rule of international trade law in place and applicable to all trade nations, in this case the WTO Members. Second, there must be a legal obligation violated already, or at least impending. Third, the victim of the legal obligation transgressed must possess the power and mandate to pardon the transgressor, as may be conferred by the GATT-WTO system. Fourth, the victim must proclaim unilaterally a pardon of the past or anticipated violation,[474] in imitation of the nature of God, who forgives out of his love and goodness.[475]

Catholic theology expounds *inter alia* the virtues of mercy and forgiveness in its teaching on the corporal and spiritual works of mercy as follows:

> The corporal works of mercy (following from the Gospel, especially Matthew 25:31-46) are to feed the hungry, give drink to the thirsty, cloth the naked, visit the imprisoned, shelter the homeless, visit the sick, and bury the dead. The spiritual works of mercy, also rooted in the Scriptures, are to counsel the doubtful, instruct the ignorant, admonish sinners, comfort the afflicted, forgive offenses, bear wrongs patiently, and pray for the living and the dead.[476]

When we apply the seven corporal works of mercy and the seven spiritual works of mercy to special and differential treatment of the GATT-WTO system, we see them reflect the material needs of developing countries and what ought to be the disposition of developed countries toward the developing countries.[477] Manifestations of mercy look much

---

[473] *See* RAJ BHALA, *supra* 56, at 146.

[474] *Id.*

[475] *See* JOHN O'CONNOR, THE ESSENTIAL CATHOLIC HANDBOOK, *supra*, at 432.

[476] *See* JOHN O'CONNOR, THE ESSENTIAL CATHOLIC HANDBOOK 209-210 (1997); *see also* LEO J. TRESE, THE FAITH EXPLAINED 164-169 (1997) (for detailed discussion of the seven corporal and seven spiritual works of mercy).

[477] The seven corporal works of mercy are dubbed as such because they pertain to the body, or in Latin corpus. *See LEO J.* TRESE, *supra* note 431, at 164; *see also* the CATECHISM OF

like almsgiving.[478] A closer examination of the seven corporal works of mercy shows that three of them, namely, feeding the hungry, giving drink to the thirsty, and clothing the naked, are parallel to works of charity. Acts of charity are designed to help less developed countries adjust to be able to perform without any obvious limitations in the global trading system.

An analysis of the spiritual works of mercy is worthwhile also. When an act of mercy applies to the global trading system, the sixth spiritual work of mercy, namely, to bear wrongs patiently, comes into play. To bear wrongs patiently indicates forgiving injuries, not without bounds. Things that can limit mercy include frequency, subject matter, and nature of the violation.[479]

We can delineate rules of special and differential treatment that are merciful in nature. First, an act of mercy to a developing country can take the form of permanent or temporary forgiveness. An example of permanent forgiveness is when a developing country is exempted from adhering to a legal obligation for a period lasting if the country involved remains a less developed country. By way of contrast, a developing country is said to be forgiven temporarily when the exemption lasts for a prescribed period. This temporary forgiveness is understood in trade law language to be delayed implementation of a legal obligation.[480]

For a clearer understanding of the discipline of mercy in relation to the special and differential treatment, it is good to use practical examples of what Raj Bhala calls "pillars of GATT." [481] Examples of mercy in this regard can be in the form of exempting a less privileged Member country from the most-favored nation ("MFN") or national treatment obligations of GATT Articles I:I and III:1-2 & 4, respectively. It can also take the form of exempting a developing country from the tariff-binding commitments made by that developing country under GATT Article II:I, or from the general prohibition concerning restrictions concerning quantity provided

THE CCATHOLIC CHURCH (1994), # 2447.

[478] THE ESSENTIAL CATHOLIC HANDBOOK refers to "almsgiving" in its entry on mercy. *See* ESSENTIAL CATHOLIC HANDBOOK, *supra* note 432, at 210.

[479] RAJ BHALA, *supra note 56*, at 148.

[480] *See id.* at 149.

[481] *See* RAJ BHALA, INTERNATIONAL TRADE LAW: THEORY AND PRACTICE (chapters 11-14) (3rd ed. 2007) (examining the pillars of GATT and exceptions thereto).

for in GATT Article XI:I. In all these scenarios, merciful treatment can be permanent or temporary.[482]

Lastly, mercy or forgiveness, as they concern help to less privileged countries, take their bearing from the theological virtues. Because a developed Member country has faith in the GATT-WTO system, it takes all the objectives stipulated seriously. By this disposition, a level playing ground is made possible for the poor Members to emerge from their developmental difficulties. This can only be possible if developed countries are charitable to poor countries in the form of mercifulness and forgiveness.

4.1.4 Connection between Theological Virtues and Almsgiving

Almsgiving consists of special and differential treatment measures that require developed countries to assist developing countries, especially where the former is offering charity to the latter. Normally, unconditional *gratis* transfer of assistance characterizes almsgiving, such as financial capital, human capital, or technology from developed countries to less privileged countries.[483] In a situation like this, the recipients have no possessory claim to the thing(s) transferred to them by the donor developed countries except as may be stated in the rules guiding such obligation. There are three potential kinds of alms involved in special and differential treatment, namely, money, services, and technological know-how, all measured in financial or economic gains.[484]

The theological virtue of charity motivates the act of almsgiving. Therefore, charity is the virtue associated with almsgiving. This understanding is clear, considering the conception of charity as a virtue,

---

[482] RAJ BHALA, *supra note 56.* at 149.

[483] This book does not go into the lexicographic definition of the term almsgiving. The reason for this omission is obvious. There is no great difference between the secular connotation of "almsgiving" and its theological definition. *The Concise Oxford American Dictionary* defines "giving alms" as "giving of money or food to the poor," *see* THE CONCISE OXFORD AMERICAN DICTIONARY, *supra,* at 23 (2006). Similarly, *The Essential Catholic Handbook* defines "Almsgiving" as an act of giving material or financial assistance to a needy person, and this act is motivated by Christian charity." *See* JOHN O'CONNOR, THE ESSENTIAL CATHOLIC HANDBOOK, *supra* note 432, at 125.

[484] *See id.* at 150.

which shows love of God and neighbor. It is not surprising then that special and differential treatment calls for self-denial in the industrialized counties to bring help with industrialization in poor countries. In this sense, the virtue of mercy and almsgiving go together. The corporal works of mercy examined above are also examples of almsgiving.[485] Obviously, the virtue of mercy might lead to, and in fact does become, an act of almsgiving.[486]

Almsgiving is also indicative of conversion. This is almsgiving understood in a religious sense. In the Catechism of the Catholic Church, almsgiving, together with fasting and prayer, express conversion in relation to oneself, to God, and to others.[487] Interior penance is

> A radical reorientation of our whole life, a return, a conversion to God with all our heart, an end of sin, a turning away from evil, with repugnance toward the evil actions we have committed.[488]

The above teaching presents the virtue of almsgiving as an external manifestation of an interior conversion.[489]This external manifestation of interior conversion involves almsgiving to another.[490] Interior conversion is the basis for giving alms, a product of charity. In international trade law, conversion refers to legal obligation and legal policy, and almsgiving, which as a product of it, is also an economic one. When developed countries give alms (as explained above), it is an internal conversion manifested in a show of charity to developing WTO Members.[491] The way it works is that because of interior conversion, developed countries are motivated by

---

485 *See* JOHN O'CONNOR, THE ESSENTIAL CATHOLIC HANDBOOK, *supra* note 432, at 125, 209-210; *see also* LEO J. TRESE, THE FAITH EXPLAINED, *supra* note 431, at 164-169 (1997) (for detailed analysis of the corporal and spiritual works of mercy); see also THE CONCISE OXFORD AMERICAN DICTIONARY, p. 23 (2006) (defining the term "alms" as originating from the Latin word *eleos* which means "mercy").

486 *See* CATECHISM OF THE CATHOLIC CHURCH (1994), *supra,* at # 1829 (teaching that one of the fruits of the theological virtue of charity is "mercy").

487 *See* CATECHISM OF THE CATHOLIC CHURCH (1994), # 1434.

488 *See* CATECHISM OF THE CATHOLIC CHURCH (1994), # 1431.

Id.

489 *Id.*

490 *See* RAJ BAHLA, *supra* note 56, at 152.

491 *See id.* at 153.

charity to acknowledge the need for economic and social development in the poor countries. For this reason, industrialized countries assist poor countries in a form of "almsgiving."[492]

The above examination of the theological virtues from the perspective of the Catholic teaching is relevant, as they are presented as the motivation for the implementation of the virtues of Mortification, Mercifulness (forgiveness), and Almsgiving. The projection of the theological justification of the special and differential treatment is unique in the sense that such a teaching not only departs from conventional wisdom but also provides food for thought for a doubting Thomas. Instead of whining about the *status quo*, which has been counterproductive because of resistance from different angles, theological justification of the special and differential treatment dovetails with the principles of Catholic social teaching, which is next in this discussion.

4.2 Overview of Five Principles of Judeo-Christian Social Doctrine

According to the *Merriam-Webster's Collegiate Dictionary,* the term "Judeo-Christian" describes any teaching or practice of moral values "having historical roots in both Judaism and Christianity."[493] Put another way, the term "Judeo-Christian" refers to the common ethical standards of Christianity and Judaism such as the Ten Commandments. Judeo-Christian principles embody Jewish monotheistic and Christian theological systems containing trans-historical normative thoughts intended for application to contemporary socio-economic life. The Judeo-Christian principles are associated with biblical, God-based moral values.[494] Therefore, Judeo-Christian values, right and wrong, good and evil, are derived from God, not from reason alone, nor from the human heart, the state, or majority

---

[492] *Id.*

[493] *Merriam-Webster's Collegiate Dictionary* 676 (11th ed., 2010).

[494] See DENNIS PRAGER, THE CASE FOR JUDEO-CHRISTIAN VALUES: PART IV, January 11, 2005, available at http://www.theroadtoemmaus.org/RdLb/31JdXn/Jd/PragerJdXnValus.htm (last visited December 8, 2013) (Dennis Prager is a Conservative columnist who inaugurated a periodic series of columns devoted to explaining and making the case for Judeo-Christian values in 2005).

rule. The Judeo-Christian source of morality contains objective realities. Judeo-Christian religions believe that because human beings are created in the image and likeness of God, their moral value system is God-based.[495]

The *New York Times* reported that President Ronald Reagan once compared the foundation of American morality with that of Europe. In comparing the two societies, President Reagan emphasized that Americans are widely regarded as "more comfortable with notions of good and evil, right and wrong than the Europeans."[496] The reason is as President Reagan said, "America is a Judeo-Christian society."[497] The Judeo-Christian system differs from secular principles:

> One of the most obvious and significant differences between secular and Judeo-Christian values concerns human worth. One of the great ironies of secular humanism is that it devalues the worth of human beings. As ironic as it may sound, the God-based Judeo-Christian value system renders man infinitely more valuable and significant than any humanistic value system. The reason is simple: Only if there is a God who created man is man worth anything beyond the chemicals of which he is composed. Judeo-Christian religions hold that human beings are created in the image of God. If we are not, we are created in the image of carbon dioxide. Which has a higher value is not difficult to determine. Contemporary secular society has rendered human beings less significant than at any time in Western history.[498]
>
> First, the secular denial that human beings are created in God's image has led to humans increasingly being equated with animals. That is why over the course of

---

495 *Id.*

496 *See* DENNIS PRAGER, THE CASE FOR JUDEO-CHRISTIAN VALUES: PART II, January 11, 2005, available at http://www.theroadtoemmaus.org/RdLb/31JdXn/Jd/PragerJdXnValus.htm last visited June 12, 2013).

497 *Id.*

498 *See* DENNIS PRAGER, THE CASE FOR JUDEO-CHRISTIAN VALUES: PART IV, February 8, 2005.

> 30 years of asking high school seniors if they would first try to save their dog or a stranger, two-thirds have voted against the person. They either don't know what they would do or actually vote for their dog. Many adults now vote similarly.[499]

American religious historians have taught that the present meaning of "Judeo-Christian" regarding ethics first appeared in print in the *New English Weekly* on July 27, 1939, with the phrase, "the Judeo-Christian scheme of morals." The historians also pointed out that the term gained much currency in the 1940s, promoted by groups which evolved into the National Conference of Christians and Jews, to fight anti-Semitism by expressing a more inclusive idea of American values rather than just Christian or Protestant.[500] Prominent champions of the Judeo-Christian morality also identify it with the historic American religious traditions. For this reason, the Jewish Conservative columnist Dennis Prager writes:

> The concept of Judeo-Christian values does not rest on a claim that the two religions are identical. It promotes the concept that there is a shared intersection of values based on the Hebrew Bible ("Torah"), brought into our culture by the founding generations of biblically oriented Protestants, that is fundamental to American history, cultural identity, and institutions.[501]

---

[499] *Id.*

[500] *See* Mark Silk, "Notes on the Judeo-Christian Tradition in America," *American Quarterly,* 36(1), 1984, pp. 65-85; *see also* Jonathan Sarna, *American Judaism: A History,* Yale University Press, 2004, p. 266.

[501] Prager Dennis, "The Case for Judeo-Christian Values," part 5, *Worldnetdaily.com,* February 15, 2005; *see also* BERNARD BAILYN, THE IDEOLOGICAL ORIGINS OF THE AMERICAN REVOLUTION, Harvard University Press (1992); MICHAEL NOVAK, ON TWO WINS: HUMBLE FAITH AND COMMON SENSE AT THE AMERICAN FOUNDING, Encounter Books, (2002) especially Chapter One; [This concept of America's unique Bible-driven historical and cultural identity was developed by historians as they studied the first centuries of America's history, from the Pilgrims through Abraham Lincoln. The statements and institutions of the founding generation that have been preserved are numerous, and they explicitly describe many of their biblical motivations and goals, their interest in Hebrew [48] and the Hebrew Bible, their use of Jewish and Christian images and ideas. In the words of patriot Benjamin Rush, "The Old Testament is the best refutation that

Commenting on the Founding Fathers of the United States in 1952, President Dwight Eisenhower said, "All men are endowed by their Creator…our form of government has no sense unless it is founded in a deeply felt religious faith, and I don't care what it is. With us of course it is the Judeo-Christian concept, but it must be a religion with all men created equal."[502] President Eisenhower's assertion later got some legal analytical support, though indirectly.[503]

It is interesting how a superpower like the United States can recognize the Judeo-Christian values in both political and legal corners. It does not appear that other Presidents of the United States saw any toehold to continue Eisenhower's example. One wonders if the terrain is continuous at all levels in history. There have been scanty efforts toward promotion of social justice from the civil society.

> Clinton initiated a high-profile national conversation on race in 1997, but took little action to assist "impoverished people, disproportionately colored, who are locked away

---

can be given to the divine right of kings, and the strongest argument that can be used in favor of the original and natural equality of all mankind." James Witherspoon, president of Princeton, teacher of James Madison and later a member of the Continental Congress, and one of the most influential thinkers in the Colonies, joined the cause of the Revolution with a widely publicized sermon based on Psalm 76, identifying the American colonists with the people of Israel. Of fifty-five printed texts from the Revolutionary period, thirty-three took texts from the Hebrew Bible. Thomas Jefferson, in the Declaration of Independence, referred to God twice in Hebrew terms, and Congress added two more: Lawgiver, Creator, Judge, and Providence. These Judeo-Christian values were especially important at the key foundational moments of the settling of America, the War for Independence and the Civil War]. *Id.*

502 *See quoted* in Patrick Henry, "'And I Don't Care What it is:' The Tradition-History of Civil Religious Proof-Text," *Journal of the American Academy of Religion,* 49 (1), March 1981, pp. 35-47.

503 In the legal case of *Marsh v. Chambers, 463 U.S. 783 (1983)*, the Supreme Court of the United States held that a state legislature could constitutionally have a paid chaplain to conduct legislative prayers "in the Judeo-Christian tradition; "*see for details Marsh, Nebraska State Treasurer, et al v. Chambers, 463 U.S. 783 (1983).* In *Simpson v. Chesterfield County Board of Supervisors,* the Fourth Circuit Court of Appeals held that the Supreme Court's holding in the Marsh case meant that the "Chesterfield County could constitutionally exclude Cynthia Simpson, a Wiccan priestess, from leading its legislative prayers, because her faith was not 'in the Judeo-Christian tradition.'" Chesterfield County's board included Jewish, Christian, and Muslim clergy in its invited list; *see Simpson v. Chesterfield County Board of Supervisors, 404 F.3d 276 (4th Cir. 2005).*

> in pestilent and crime-ridden inner cities or forgotten rural or small-town wastelands, people who are bereft of the money, training, skills, or education needed to escape their plight."[504]

In late 2011, Germany-based *Bertelsmann Stiftung* compared 31 OECD nations on their fostering of six factors that contribute to social justice: poverty prevention, access to education, labor-market inclusion, social cohesion and non-discrimination, health, and intergenerational justice. The United States ranked poorly, coming in 27th out of 31.[505] This is surprising, especially considering the position of the United States in the world and the fact that most countries look up to it as a pacesetter. A sense of inequality is as American as apple pie. Americans accept this as part of their social system, but they decry a "lack of fairness in public policy".[506] If social justice is an issue in the United States, how will the U.S and other superpowers address social justice matters in international discussions and negotiations? Would one take such development as an index that the World Day of Social Justice as declared by the United Nations General Assembly on February 20, 2007, did not achieve the desired goal?

The World Day of Social Justice was chosen as a date to remind and encourage all Member States of the United Nations to promote national activities and enhance social justice. In 2011, U.N Secretary General said, "Equal opportunity, solidarity and respect for human rights are essential

---

504 Daniel Denvir, "America needs Social Justice, not another dumb 'Conversation about Race,'" in *the Guardian* online, March 29, 2013 available at http://www.theguardian.com/commentisfree/2013/mar/29/america-social-justice-not-dumb-conversation-race (last visited December 15, 2013).

505 *See* BERTELSMANN FOUNDATION, "Too Little of a Good Thing: Social Justice in the USA," in *Social Justice in the OECD – How Do the Member States Compare?*, March 2, 2012, available at http://www.bfna.org/article/too-little-of-a-good-thing-social-justice-in-the-usa (last visited December 15, 2013).

506 *See id.* In the Bertelsmann Foundation Report, the U.S. was third to last in poverty prevention, trailed only by Chile and Mexico, due to its "alarming" poverty levels. Whereas in Denmark, only 1 in 27 children lives in poverty, for instance, in the United States that rate is above 1 in 5. And as the report puts it: "Under conditions of poverty, social participation and a self-determined life are possible only with great difficulty." *See* Dan Froomkin, "New Social Justice Index Places U.S. Near Bottom" in *The Huffington Post* available at http://www.huffingtonpost.com/2011/10/27/social-justice_n_1035363.html (last visited November 12, 2013).

to unlocking the full productive potential of nations and peoples."[507] In 2013, the United Nations enjoined that we can only build the world we want if we intensify our efforts to achieve a more inclusive, equitable, and sustainable development path built on dialogue, transparency, and social justice.[508]

When the goal of the United Nations is understood well about social justice, then,

> The World Day of Social Justice should support efforts of the international community in poverty eradication, the promotion of full employment and decent work, gender equity, access to social well-being and justice for all. It is a call for all countries to take concrete actions, which give meaning to the universal values of human dignity and opportunity for all. This day underpins the UN General Assembly's recognition that social development and social justice are indispensable for the achievement and maintenance of peace and security within and among nations. Above all, economic growth should promote equality and social justice based on social justice and respect for all human rights and fundamental freedoms.[509]

The Judeo-Christian perspective of social justice is older than the initiative of the United Nations, as it concerns social justice. It will not be odd to state that the United Nations has been influenced by the traits of Judeo-Christian morality, especially when it declared on February 20, 2013, the World Day of Social Justice, that

---

[507] *See* Ban Ki-moon (UN Secretary General), *Message for the World Day of Social Justice February 20, 2011,* available at http://www.cost.eu/media/newsroom/social-justice (last visited October 23, 2013).

[508] *See* Secretary-General Ban Ki-moon Message for the 2013 World Day of Social Justice, available at http://www.un.org/en/events/socialjusticeday/index.shtml (last visited December 15, 2013)

[509] EUROPEAN COOPERATION IN SCIENCE AND TECHNOLOGY (COST), *World Day of Social Justice,* February 19, 2012; COST is an intergovernmental framework for European Cooperation in Science and Technology, allowing the coordination of nationally-funded research on a European level.

> Social justice is an underlying principle for peaceful and prosperous coexistence within and among nations. We uphold the principles of social justice when we promote gender equality or the rights of indigenous peoples and migrants. We advance social justice when we remove barriers that people face because of gender, age, race, ethnicity, religion, culture or disability. [510]

It raises serious concerns for the United Nations to declare the World Day of Social Justice on a yearly basis without a corresponding initiative to incorporate the goal of the United Nations into national and international policies and debates. The world is in a state of chaos as there have been agitations from different quarters concerning inequalities, exploitation, and discrimination, often leading to unrest. The Catholic Church's indispensability and neutrality, as well as her unrelenting push at all levels for social justice that is inclusive, calls for more attention. To avoid relativism that may downplay the indispensable nature of social justice, it is important to retrace the principles of Judeo-Christian social justice as taught by the Catholic Church.

For centuries, the Catholic Church used the term *doctrina civilis* (teachings about political order) in its teaching about interpersonal relationships. In doing this, the Church made *iustitia legalis* (legal or general justice) the chief virtue of justice, holding sway over all other species of justice. The Catholic Church taught that general justice is the most characteristic of the polity. However, after the Pontificate of Leo XIII (1878-1903), the Catholic changed her *doctrina civilis* to *doctrina socialis* and *iustitia legalis* to *iustitia socialis*. Though it was Fr. Luigi Taparelli D'Azeglio who propounded social justice in such a way as to provoke the engagement of the entire Church, the Popes gave the topic wider authority and publicity.

The content of the Catholic Social Teaching is defined in Pope John Paul II's post-synodal apostolic exhortations devoted to the life of the Church in various regions. In Ecclesia in America, Pope John Paul II taught that,

---

[510] *See* U.N. SECRETARY-GENERAL BAN KI-MOON, *supra* note 507.

> By her social doctrine the Church makes an effective contribution to the issues presented by the current globalized economy. Her moral vision in this area rests on the threefold cornerstone of human dignity, solidarity, and subsidiarity. The globalized economy must be analyzed in the light of the principles of social justice, respecting the preferential option for the poor who must be allowed to take their place in such an economy, and the requirements of the international common good.[511]

The principles of the Catholic Social Teaching are the principle of the dignity of the human person; the principle of the common good; the principle of subsidiarity; the principle of solidarity; and the preferential option for the poor. This book will now explore these principles one by one.

4.3 First: Dignity of the Human Person

The Catholic Church invests herself in human affairs in the whole world and works hard to provide answer to moral problems which may arise. In the exercise of her indispensable mission in the world, there are moral questions that come into play. First, what should be the relationship of the individual to the society? Second, what are the principles that should guide public behavior, particularly the official acts of the leaders in the society? Third, what should a society do about a distinct sub-group, namely, individuals who, by some measure relative to a societal average or standard, are less-privileged? The Catholic social theory distinguishes itself in providing answers to the above questions using the CST principles mentioned above.

The principles of social doctrine derive from human nature as a source of inspiration. The social teaching of the Catholic Church projects the society as ordered not according to maximization of profit, the needs of a nation, or the greed of the disordered human heart. Rather, a society is said to be well ordered when it is channeled to the intrinsic worth,

[511] Pope John Paul II, Post-Synodal Apostolic Exhortation *Ecclesia in America (The Church in America),* Mexico City, January 22, 1999, the twenty-first of Pontificate of Pope John Paul II.

freedom, and dignity of every human person.[512] The dignity of the human person is a consequence of being made in the image and likeness of God. Thus, human dignity is a gracious gift from God.[513] The dignity or sacredness of the human person in the larger Catholic tradition rests on the understanding from the book of Genesis that the human person is created in the image of God. St. Thomas Aquinas proves that the human person is created in the image and likeness of God because the human being possesses divine attributes such as intellect, free will, love, and the power of self-determination.[514]

The unique nature of the human beings is highly appreciated in the sense that God made them master of all earthly creatures to subdue them and use them for the glory of the creator.[515] This is a kind of personal elevation of the human person which does not give enough importance to the other created realities. Other created realities are only instrumental about the human person.[516] To explain the circumstance of this exalted position further, *Gaudium et Spes* cites *Psalm 8: 5-6* to show that God made the human person a little less than the angels, crowned the human person with honor and glory, and subjected all things to the human person.[517]

A point that must not be forgotten is the fact of the universality of Catholic social teaching even as it concerns the dignity of the human

---

[512] SECOND VATICAN ECUMENICAL COUNCIL, *Gaudium Et Spes (The Pastoral Constitution on the Church in the Modern World), supra* note 75, #26.

[513] RAJ BHALA, *supra,* note 56, at 421.

[514] Charles E. Curran, *Catholic Social Teaching 1891 – Present: A Historical, Theological, and Ethical Analysis,* Georgetown University Press, 2002, p. 132 [Catholic social teaching believes that human beings are created in the image and likeness of God (Gen. 1:26-27). The focal point of CST is the human person, made in the image of God, and so having fundamental freedom and dignity, the basis for human rights]. Creation by God is what gives the human person this dignity; *see* POPE LEO XIII, ENCYCLICAL LETTER, *Rerum Novarum (On the Condition of the Working Classes),* May 15, 1891, #18; POPE JOHN XXIII, *MATER ET MAGISTRA (On Christianity and Social Progress),* May 15, 1961, #s 214 & 249); He is made in God's image; rooted in his own nature, which is physical and spiritual; is responsibility for his actions; possesses capacity for self-mastery and intrinsic moral and religious requirements, *see* LEO XIII, RERUM NOVARUM, #s 4 & 5; JOHN XXIII, MATER ET MAGISTRA, #s 55 & 208.

[515] *See* CHARLES CURRAN, CATHOLIC SOCIAL TEACHING 1891- PRESENT (2002), *supra* note 4514, at 132.

[516] Daniel M. Cowdin, "John Paul II and Environmental Concern: Problems and Possibilities," in *Living Light* 28 (1991), 44-52.

[517] *See* VATICAN II, GAUDIUM ET SPES, *supra* note 75, # 12.

person. The Catholic Church teaches that "All things hold true not only for Christians, but for all people of good will in whose hearts grace works in an unseen way.[518] This explains the signification of Jesus' advent into the riddles of the human situation. This universal character of the mission of the Catholic Church in the world endorses her authority to reach every nook and cranny of the whole world. Therefore, when the Catholic social teaching emphasizes the God-given dignity of the human person and makes it the focal point, we understand why. By the fundamental dignity of the human person, each human person is unique, unrepeatable, and priceless (of inestimable value).

All the social encyclicals base their teaching on the dignity of the human person. For instance, Pope John Paul II captioned an entire chapter of his *Centesimus Annus* on "The Person as the Way of the Church" and insisted on the fundamental importance of human dignity.[519] Human dignity does not depend on human effort, work, or accomplishments:

> All human beings have a fundamental, equal dignity because all share the general gift of creation and redemption from God. Such an approach runs counter to what people often think in our capitalistic and competitive society. Many people believe that human dignity is something we earn on our own and create for ourselves, but that is not the case. Consequently, all human beings have the same fundamental dignity, whether they are brown, black, red, or white; rich or poor; young or old; male or female; healthy or sick. In practice, we often tend to act as if certain more prestigious or influential or wealthy people have more dignity than poor people and others. That is

---

[518] *See id.* at # 22.

[519] Pope John Paul II, *Centesimus Annus (*Encyclical Letter on the Hundredth Anniversary of *Rerum Novarum*), 1991, Nos. 53-62 [*Centesimus Annus* celebrates Pope Leo XIII's encyclical Letter, *Rerum Novarum,* which based the fundamental right of the worker on the God-given dignity. It is worthwhile to remember that the first social encyclical, *Rerum Novarum* sparked off a ganglion of interests with human dignity as a focal point in the Catholic Church, especially from the perspective of the teachings of the Magisterium]

> not true because God's gift is the basic source of human dignity for all.[520]

The understanding of the above quotation is of essence to the goal of this book. This is because a practical appreciation and application of equality based on the fundamental dignity of the human person will solve all the problems of inequality at every level in the world. It will make the world appreciate the universal mission of the Catholic Church; it will also make the Holy See more committed to this mission; and lastly, it will reaffirm human dignity and its appurtenances. This book will now proceed by exploring the appurtenant characteristics of human dignity.

4.3.1 Equal Human Dignity

The phrase "equal human dignity" appears in public international law and in most international agreements. For instance, the Preamble of the United Nations Charter declares the resolution of the United Nations:

> [T]o reaffirm faith in fundamental human rights, in the dignity and worth of the human person, in the equal rights of men and women and of nations large and small.[521]

---

[520] CHARLES CURRAN, CATHOLIC SOCIAL TEACHING, 1891- PRESENT (2002), *supra* note 514, at 132

[521] The Preamble of the United Nations Charter in full is as follows: WE, THE PEOPLES OF THE UNITED NATIONS, DETERMINED

- to save succeeding generations from the scourge of war, which twice in our lifetime has brought untold sorrow to mankind, and
- to reaffirm faith in fundamental human rights, in the dignity and worth of the human person, in the equal rights of men and women and of nations large and small, and
- to establish conditions under which justice and respect for the obligations arising from treaties and other sources of international law can be maintained, and
- to promote social progress and better standards of life in larger freedom, AND FOR THESE ENDS
- to practice tolerance and live together in peace with one another as good neighbors, and
- to unite our strength to maintain international peace and security, and
- to ensure, by the acceptance of principles and the institution of methods, that armed force shall not be used, save in the common interest, and
- to employ international machinery for the promotion of the economic and social advancement of all peoples,

Generally, the phrase "equal human dignity" can be described as follows: it is the "human" person who has "dignity," and "equality" pertains to the rights of men and women of large and small countries. The term "human" includes children (children's rights, *e.g.*, with respect to minimum working age), the unborn (rights of the fetus, *e.g.*, in respect of right to life at any stage in life), men and women (at or past the age of maturity, *i.e.*, adults). Concerning nations, it includes nations large and small, rich or poor[522] No matter in which category any person belongs, all human beings are equal. It is in respect of human beings who are citizens of countries that all countries are deemed equal. Reference to "equal rights" in the *Universal Declaration of Human Rights, the International Covenant on Civil and Political Rights* and the *Helsinki Accords*,[523] is by implication, tantamount to equal human dignity.

The philosophical origin of the concept of equal human dignity is traceable to the period when philosophers and theologians embarked on enquiries into how human beings (individually and collectively, including governments) ought to treat one another. The period of these enquiries began in the 18th century and lasted through the Napoleonic Wars of 1804-1815, and particularly of the late Enlightenment German philosopher, Immanuel Kant (1724-1804).[524]

HAVE RESOLVED TO COMBINE OUR EFFORTS TO ACCOMPLISH THESE AIMS Accordingly, our respective Governments, through representatives assembled in the city of San Francisco, who have exhibited their full powers found to be in good and due form, have agreed to the present Charter of the United Nations and do hereby establish an international organization to be known as the United Nations.
See Preamble of the U.N. Charter at http://www.un.org/en/documents/charter/preamble.shtml

[522] Raj Bhala, "Philosophical, Religious, and Legalistic Perspectives on Equal Human Dignity and U.S. Free Trade Agreements," in Baldo Kresalja Rosselló (ed.), *Anuario Andino de Derechos Intelectuales*, Año VIII-N.° 8, Lima, 2012, p. 99.

[523] *See* Oscar Schachter, Human Dignity as a Normative Concept, *77 AM.J. INT'L L. 848, 848 (1983) (*for a detailed discussion on equal human dignity in international public law); for a discussion of equal human dignity in relation to the 1948 Universal Declaration of Human Rights, and in particular whether that Declaration is coherent and rests on a genuinely universal approach to dignity, or is essentially an instrument of western cultural imperialism, see Mary Ann Glendon, "International Law: Foundations of Human Rights – The Unfinished Business," in Michael A. Scaperlanda & Teresa Stanton Collett (eds.), *Rediscovering Self-Evident Truths – Catholic Perspectives on American Law,* 319-320 (2007)

[524] See RAJ BHALA, "Philosophical, Religious, and Legalistic Perspectives on Equal Human Dignity," in Baldo Kresalja Rosselló (ed.), *Anuario Andino de Derechos Intelectuales,* Año

A summary of Kantian thought on equal human dignity is that "international justice is not merely a function of how nation-states behave toward each other, but also of how they behave toward their citizens."[525] Thus, the international legal order cannot be deemed just if the nation-states that constitute this order abuse individual rights. International law must penetrate the level of the nation-states and mean something for the individuals who comprise those states.[526] Kant proceeded to proffer how individuals should be treated: "Whenever human dignity is at stake, we are obliged to fight for its recognition and protection."[527] However, the Kantian Categorical Imperative contains details and the source of his concept of "equal human dignity." In his Categorical Imperative, Immanuel Kant beckoned all "to treat every human being as an end, not as a means."[528]

While Immanuel Kant deserves special mention for his thoughts on equal human dignity, the Catholic social doctrine is revered for its stance on the concept. The Catholic Church promotes the worth of the human person from natural conception to natural birth.

> The dignity of each human being is not a gift from the society of which he or she is a part. It is not a legal right or customary privilege flowing from the society to the individual. Respect for human dignity is not justified by sentimentality *(i.e.*, that it is "nice" to do so) or by secular democratic theory (which champions individual rights). Thus, that dignity is not rightly available for a society to withdraw or curtail by law (including an international

VIII-N.° 8, Lima, 2012, p. 100.

[525] *See generally* James Bohman & Matthias Lutz-Bachmann (eds.), *Perpetual peace: The Essays on Immanuel Kant's Cosmopolitan Ideal,* The MIT Press (1997); Fernando R. Tesón, *The Kantian Theory of International Law*, 92 COLUM. L. REV. 53 (1992) *quoted in* RAJ BHALA, Philosophical, Religious, and Legalistic Perspectives on Equal Human Dignity, *supra* note, at 100-101

[526] *Id.*

[527] Heiner Bielefefeldt, Autonomy and Republicanism: Immanuel Kant's Philosophy of Freedom, *25 POL. THEORY* 524, 525 (1997) quoted in RAJ BHALA, Philosophical, Religious, and Legalistic Perspectives on Equal Human Dignity, supra note, at 100

[528] *See* Oscar Schachter, Human Dignity as a Normative Concept, 77 AM. J. INT'L L. 848, 849 (1983).

> agreement like an FTA), extra-legal means (*e.g.*, the use of force) or any other measures.[529]

Also, all human beings share a common Creator who shows no partiality.[530] Pope Leo XIII expressed this natural equality due to the circumstance of the origin of human beings.

> Each and all are redeemed and made sons of God, by Jesus Christ, "the first-born among many brethren"; that the blessings of nature and the gifts of grace belong to the whole human race in common, and that from none except the unworthy, is withheld the inheritance of the kingdom of Heaven. "If sons, heirs also; heirs indeed of God, and co-heirs with Christ." Such is the scheme of duties and of rights, which is shown forth to the world by the Gospel. [531]

The glory of God shines on the face of every person. This glory of God that everyone possesses is the basis for equal dignity of every human person.[532] It is the ultimate foundation of the radical equality and brotherhood among all people, regardless of their race, nation, sex, origin, culture, or class.[533] Pope John XXIII taught, with tremendous authority, that all human beings are equal in natural dignity.[534]

---

[529] RAJ BHALA, Philosophical, Religious, and Legalistic Perspectives on Equal Human Dignity, *supra* note 522, at 101

[530] CATECHISM OF THE CATHOLIC CHURCH (1994), # 1934 [indicating that God shows no partiality (Acts 10:34; cf. Rom 2:11; Gal 2:6; Eph 6:9), since all people have the same dignity as creatures made in his image and likeness. The Incarnation of the Son of God shows the equality of all people with regard to dignity: "There is neither Jew nor Greek, there is neither slave nor free, there is neither male nor female; for you are all one in Christ Jesus" (Gal 3:28; cf. Rom 10:12; 1Cor 12:13, Col 3:11)].

[531] POEP LEO XIII, ENCYCLICAL LETTER, RERUM NOVARUM ("On the Conditions of the Working Classes"), May 15, 1891, # 25.

[532] SECOND VATICAN ECUMENICAL COUNCIL, GAUDIUM ET SPES, *29 AAS 58 (1966),* 1048-1049.

[533] PONTIFICAL COUNCIL FOR JUSTICE AND PEACE, COMPENDIUM OF CATHOLIC SOCIAL DOCTRINE, supra note 120, # 144.

[534] POPE JOHN XXIII, ENCYCLICAL LETTER, Pacem In Terris ("Peace on Earth"), April 11, 1963, # 44

The Catholic Church teaches that the common good and personal growth of individuals and society is only realized when all human beings and institutions recognize the equal dignity of human beings. Likewise, in international relations, especially in international trade agreements, authentic progress of the international community is only possible through pragmatic recognition and application of conditions of equality among peoples and nations.[535] In all, to safeguard and promote human dignity, the whole human family must adopt the equal dignity of human beings and nations as the only way to celebrate universal brotherhood.[536]

4.3.2 Respect for Human Dignity

While the sources of the Catholic social doctrine are the scriptures, the teaching of the ancient and great theologians of the Church, and the Magisterium, its foundation and primary object are

> The dignity of the human person with its inalienable rights, which form the nucleus of the truth about the human person[537]

Every person, from the moment of conception to natural death, has inherent dignity and a right to life consistent with that dignity. Human life at every stage of development and decline is precious and, therefore, worthy of protection and respect. It is always wrong to attack innocent human life. The Catholic tradition sees the sacredness of human life as

[535] POPE JOHN XXIII, ENCYCLICAL LETTER PACEM IN TERRIS, *47-48 AAS 55 (1963),* 279- 281; Pope Paul VI, Address to the General Assembly of the United Nations (4 October 1965), *5 AAS 57 (1965),* 881; John Paul II, Address to the Fiftieth General Assembly of the United Nations (5 October 1995), *13 L'Osservatore Romano,* English edition, 11 October 1995, p. 9-10.

[536] Paul VI, Address to the General Assembly of the United Nations, *5 AAS 57 (1965)*, 881; PAUL VI, ENCYCLICAL LETTER POPULORUM PROGRESSIO, *43-44 AAS 59 (1967)*, 278-279.

[537] Vatican Congregation for Catholic Education, "Guidelines for the Study and Teaching of the Church's Social Doctrine in the Formation of Priests," No. 4, December 30, 1988, released on June 27, 1989, in *Origins*, Vol. 19, No. 11, August 3, 1989.

part of any moral vision for a just and good society.[538] Every human being is created in the image of God and redeemed by Jesus Christ, and therefore is invaluable and worthy of respect as a member of the human family.[539]

Pope Leo XIII, in launching the *Rerum Novarum*, which heralded modern Catholic Social Justice Theory, taught concerning the rationale for respect for the human person:

> All human beings have the same Father who is God the Creator, the same benefits of nature and gifts of divine grace belong in common to the whole human race: "we are children, we are heirs as well; heirs of God and co-heirs with Christ."[540]

The above citation is significant since the understanding of the close link between God the Creator and the human person will help us to understand the inviolability of the respect for the human person. Therefore, the arrow of causation starts with God, who created us in a way. By respecting that way, we respect God. Therefore, respect for human dignity is an inalienable right. The failure of a society to respect this dignity is an index that the society has become oppressive. Political and economic societies are particularly susceptible to this vice.[541] In turn, oppression is a legitimate reason for individuals to turn their back on the

---

[538] William J. Byron (ed.), *Ten Building Blocks of Catholic Social Teaching*, available at http://www.holynameofmaryparish.com/documents/10Catholic_Social_teachings.pdf (last visited December 16, 2013) [indicating that principles, once internalized, lead to something. They prompt activity, impel motion, and direct choices. Unfortunately, many Catholics do not adequately understand that the social teaching of the Church is an essential part of Catholic faith. This is a list of ten principles that guide Catholic social teaching. The first eight of these principles were culled from the relatively brief "Reflections of the U.S. Catholic Bishops," as the second subtitle of Sharing Catholic Social Teaching describes this published product of the (U.S.) National Conference of Catholic Bishops. The two last principles are culled from additional texts].

[539] *See id; see also* Vatican II, GAUDIUM ET SPES, *supra*, Nos. 26-27 (asserting that all human beings must see within every person both a reflection of God and a mirror of themselves, and must honor and respect human dignity as a divine gift).

[540] LEO XIII, ENCYCLICAL LETTER, RERUM NOVARUM, (May 15, 1891), ¶ 24, *quoted* in CHARLES RODGERS, AN INTRODUCTION TO CATHOLIC SOCIAL TEACHING, Ignatius Press, (2000) p. 34.

[541] RAJ BHALA, *supra* note 481, at 421

society; to rescind their fidelity to that society; and in so many instances, revolt against the society.[542]

The respect we have for God reaches the human person by extension since we have a sound logic that the arrow of causation starts with God, who created human beings. The uniqueness of human beings is seen in each person having been created unique, unrepeatable, and of inestimable value. And so, by respecting the true origin of all persons and these three attributes of each person, we respect God. As a matter of fact, it is good to emphasize that respect for human dignity is an inalienable right conferred by God on each human being in a special, one-time, and priceless manner.[543] Respect for human rights means respect for the dignity and worth of every human being[544]. This implies that, in addressing every activity that concerns the human person, respect for his God-given dignity must be put into consideration.

Respecting the dignity of the human person would not be complete without the common good principle. Human beings have the natural propensity to live in society. So, it is divinely ordained that human beings should live with their fellow human beings. People are endowed with a social nature. Indeed, God destined human beings for civil society.[545] In her promotion of the common good, the Catholic Church emphasizes, human beings should embrace the human family principle, and avoid all forms of domination and exploitation of others. Considering GATT-WTO principles of non-discrimination, freer trade, transparency, fair competition, development and economic reforms, the common good of human beings should be top on the list. Unfortunately, these principles have not been implemented accordingly. The intervention of the Holy See is therefore necessary.

---

542 *See* CHARLES RODGERS, S.J., *supra* note 57, at 14

543 Raj Bhala, "Philosophical, Religious, and Linguistic Perspectives on Equal Human Dignity and U.S. Free Trade Agreements," *in* Baldo Kresalja Rosselló (ed.), *Anuario Andino de Derechos Intelectuales*, Aňo VIII – N.° 8, Lima, 2012, p. 106.

544 *See* GEORGE WEIGEL, WITNESS TO HOPE, *supra,* note 74, at 348

545 *See* POPE LEO XIII, ENCYCLICAL LETTER *Rerum Novarum* (On the Condition of Labor) 1891, # 38; ENCYCLICAL LETTER *Immortale Dei* (On the Christian Constitution of States) 1885, #3: POPE PIUS XI, ENCYCLICAL LETTER *Quadragesimo Anno* (On the Fortieth Anniversary of *Rerum Novarum*) 1931, # 118, ENCYCLICAL LETTER *Divini Redemptoris* (On Atheistic Communism) # 29.

4.3.3 Freedom of the Human Person and its Limits

In his homily to a Cuban congregation in1998, Pope John Paul II enjoined all to choose the way of freedom and justice as the foundation of the people's dignity.[546] The chief characteristic feature of the dignity of the human person should be freedom. There is more to the rationale that individuals must be free to associate than a social contract-type bargain between individuals and society.[547] Catholic Social Justice Theory places much emphasis on the eternal destiny of every human being in the society. If an individual is unduly constrained by, for example, international trade agreements, then he cannot exercise his free will to choose whether to embark on a path in contemplation of the after-life, or which path to choose. Why not? Because he is not free to choose right from wrong, a man cannot work toward a spiritual end.[548]

Human dignity demands that a person act according to a free choice which is personally motivated and prompted from within. The dignity of the human person is realized when he uses his free initiative.[549] It also confirms his power to make choices and be responsible for his actions.[550]Human

[546] *See* GEORGE WEIGEL, *supra* note 74, at 811; (adding that by defending religious freedom "the Church defends their freedom of each individual, of families, of different social units, which are living realities with a right to their own sphere of autonomy and sovereignty").

[547] RAJ BHALA, *supra* note 56, at 421.

[548] *Id.*

[549] PONTIFICAL COUNCIL FOR JUSTICE AND PEACE, COMPENDIUM OF CATHOLIC SOCIAL DOCTRINE, (2004), *supra* note 95, # 136; [The proper exercise of personal freedom requires specific conditions of an economic, social, juridic, political and cultural order that "are too often disregarded or violated. Such situations of blindness and injustice injure the moral life and involve the strong as well as the weak in the temptation to sin against charity. By deviating from the moral law man violates his own freedom, becomes imprisoned within himself, disrupts neighborly fellowship and rebels against divine truth". Removing injustices promotes human freedom and dignity; nonetheless, "the first thing to be done is to appeal to the spiritual and moral capacities of the individual and to the permanent need for inner conversion, if one is to achieve the economic and social changes that will truly be at the service of man"]; *see id,* at 237; *see also* CATECHISM OF THE CATHOLIC CHURCH (1994), # 1740; Congregation for the Doctrine of the Faith, Instruction Libertatis Conscientia, *75 AAS 79 (1987),* 587.

[550] *See* PONTIFICAL COUNCIL FOR JUSTICE AND PEACE, *supra* note 120, # 135; *See also* John Paul II, Encyclical Letter *Veritatis Splendor, 34, AAS 85* (1993), 1160- 1161; SECOND VATICAN ECUMENICAL COUNCIL, *Pastoral Constitution on the Church in the Modern World, GAUDIUM ET SPES, 17, AAS 58* (1966), 1038; CATECHISM OF THE

freedom is guided by a person's dependence on God as his Creator.[551] The power to decipher good from evil does not belong to humans but to God alone (see Gen. 2:16-17). Human freedom is determined by a person's ability to understand and accept God's commands.

Human freedom is, nevertheless, not unlimited because it is moderated by moral law given by God. Therefore, human freedom finds its authentic and complete fulfillment precisely in the acceptance of God-given moral law.[552] A person's right and freedom stop where another person's right and freedom begin. This is understood from the perspective of equality of human beings since they have the same dignity and rights flowing from the same source.[553]

For self-fulfillment, the human person must be free. There can be no morality without freedom. It is only in freedom that the human person can turn to what is good.[554] Freedom is a basic feature of human dignity. The question is: what type of freedom is the Church talking about? In the contemporary world, freedom is highly regarded and assiduously pursued; unfortunately, the world often cultivates freedom in wrong ways as a license to do anything it pleases, even evil.[555] When the Catholic Church advocates for the freedom of the human person, it is not just any type of freedom. What the Catholic Church emphasizes is "genuine freedom." Genuine freedom is an outstanding manifestation of the divine image of the human person, for God willed to leave man in the power of his own counsel. The reason for this liberty is for the person to seek his Creator of his own accord and to freely arrive at full and blessed perfection by cleaving to God.[556]

CATHOLIC CHURCH (1994), at 1733; Gregory of Nyssa, *De Vita Moysis, II, 2-3 PG 44*, 327B-328B, (*unde fit, ut nos ipsi patres quodammodo simus nostri ... vitii ac virtutis ratione fingentes*); JOHN PAUL II, ENCYCLICAL LETTER CENTESIMUS ANNUS, *13, AAS 83* (1991), 809-810.

[551] *See* CATECHISM OF THE CATHOLIC CHURCH, (1994), # 1706.

[552] John Paul II, Encyclical Letter Veritatis Splendor, *35 AAS 85* (1993), 1161-1162.

[553] *See* CATECHISM OF TH CATHOLIC CHURCH (1994), # 1935.

[554] *See* SECOND VATICAN ECUMENICAL COUNCIL, GAUDIUM ET SPES, # 11.

[555] *See* Robert A. Sirico & Maciej Ẓięba, O.P (ed.), *The Social Agenda: A Collection of Magisterial Texts*, Pontifical Council for Justice and Peace, Libreria Editrice Vaticana, 2000, # 48.

[556] *See* SECOND VATICAN ECUMENICAL COUNCIL, GAUDIUM ET SPES, *supra* note 75, at # 17; *see also* Sirach 15:14

The Catholic Church emphasizes the liberty of the human person in its entire mission. Addressing the World Council of Churches in Switzerland in 1984, Pope John Paul II said the vision of the Church's action in the world is built on "the defense of the human person, of his dignity, of his liberty, of his rights, of the full meaning of his life."[557] Defense of the freedom of the human person is a basic moral responsibility of all Christians.[558] The reason for this is not far-fetched.

> Man is born into freedom and for freedom. Made in God's image and likeness, he must be able to obey God's law in freedom. In this way he can be happy in this life and, when life is over, receive the reward of eternal life. He must therefore have political and economic freedom, because only through them can he make the free choices in his life which will enable him to serve God worthily.[559]

To make moral decisions, that is, to opt for good over evil, presumes that each person enjoys the requisite political and economic freedom to exercise this choice.

Put another way, freedom is understood as connatural to the human person and as the distinctive sign of man's nature. The freedom of the individual finds its basis in man's transcendent dignity. It is on this basis that Pope John Paul II said that man is inseparable from freedom, a freedom which no external force can take away, a freedom which constitutes the fundamental right of the human person both as an individual and as a member of society.[560] Man is free because he possesses the faculty of self-determination about what is true and what is good.[561]

Although everyone possesses a right to be respected in his journey in search of the truth, there exists a prior and grave moral obligation to

---

557 Pope John Paul II, Address to the World Council of Churches, June 25, 1984, pp. 6-8.

558 *See* March 1986 *Instruction on Christian Freedom and Liberation, quoted in* GEORGE WEIGEL, WITNESS TO HOPE, *supra* note 74, at 458.

559 *See* CHARLES RODGERS, *supra* note 57, at 16.

560 *See* Pope John Paul II, World Day of Peace Message, 1981, # 5.

561 *Id.*

seek the truth and to adhere to it once it is known.[562] This truth is seen, for example, in the mission of the Catholic Church in the world. In her mission in the world, the Catholic Church proclaims the fundamental requirement of freedom as a precondition for an honest relationship about truth. The Church also carries with her in her mission the warning for the world to avoid every kind of illusory freedom, every kind of superficial unilateral freedom, every freedom that fails to enter the truth about the human person and the whole world.[563]

Freedom is not merely a right that one claims for oneself. It is also a duty that one undertakes about others. If it is really to serve the freedom of each human individual, each community must respect the freedoms and rights of other individuals and communities. This respect sets a limit to freedom. This same respect also gives freedom its logic and dignity since human beings are by nature social beings.[564] The implications of an individual as a social being will be discussed subsequently, but it is worthwhile to understand that in line with freedom, the social nature of the human person limits the exercise of freedom.

It is also important to emphasize at this point that the exercise of freedom does not imply a right to say or to do anything at any time. It would be wrong, for instance, to maintain that the human person, "the subject of this freedom," is "an individual who is fully self-sufficient and whose finality is the satisfaction of his own interests in the enjoyment of earthly goods."[565] Freedom demands conditions of

---

562 POPE JOHN PAUL II, ENCYCLICAL *LETTER Veritatis Splendor ("On the Splendor of Truth"),* August 6, 1993, # 34, (stating also that the splendor of truth shines forth in all the works of the Creator and, *in a special way, in man, created in the image and likeness of God (cf. Gen 1:26). Truth enlightens man's intelligence and shapes his freedom, leading him to know and love the Lord*).

563 POPE JOHN PAUL II, ENCYCLICAL LETTER *REDEMPTOR HOMINIS ("On the Redeemer of Man"),* March 4, 1979, # 12, (teaching also that is in a divine mission, the *Church in statu missionis,* for the sake of upholding the God-given dignity of the human person, particularly for the salvation of human beings); *see Redemptor Hominis,* # 21.

564 *See* POPE JOHN PAUL II, WORLD DAY OF PEACE MESSAGE, 1981, at # 7.

565 *See* Congregation for the Doctrine of the Faith, *Libertatis Conscientia (Instruction on Christian Freedom and Liberation),* March 22, 1986, # 13 [The individualistic ideology inspired by this concept of man favored the unequal distribution of wealth at the beginning of the industrial era to the point that workers found themselves excluded from access to the essential goods which they had helped to produce and to which they had a right. This has

an economic, social, political, and cultural kind, which make possible its full exercise. These conditions have often been either disregarded or violated due to concomitant abuse of the dignity of human beings and their inalienable rights.[566] When the gap between the rich Members and the developing and Least Developed Countries (LDCs) of the WTO keeps widening instead of diminishing, the exercise of freedom becomes extremely difficult.

4.3.4 Social Nature of Human Beings

Human beings are social animals and, more precisely, created to associate with others. They have a need for intimacy and to be with others.[567] The social nature of the human person makes him fit to be a political animal with the innate propensity to develop more complex communities.[568] God created human beings to constitute one family and treat one another in a spirit of brotherhood. For this reason, human beings are called to love God and their neighbor as the first and greatest

---

given birth to powerful liberation movements from the poverty caused by industrial society. Certain Christians, both lay persons and pastors, have not failed to fight for a just recognition of the legitimate rights of workers. On many occasions the Magisterium of the Church has raised its voice in support of this cause. But more often than not the just demands of the worker movement have led to new forms of servitude, being inspired by concepts which ignored the transcendental vocation of the human person and attributed to man a purely earthly destiny. These demands have sometimes been directed towards collectivist goals, which have then given rise to injustices just as grave as the ones which they were meant to eliminate]; *see id.*

566 *See id.* at # 1.

567 *See* SECOND VATICAN ECUMENICAL COUNCIL, GAUDIUM ET SPES, *supra* note 75, # 24 (teaching that the twofold commandment of love of God and neighbor illustrates social nature of humans is characteristic of, and therefore unity calling for moral obligations toward one another).

568 *See* ARISTOTLE, NICHOMACHEAN ETHICS, Book VIII; *See also* ARISTOTLE, POLITICS, 1252 b; *See also* CHARLES CURRAN, CATHOLIC SOCIAL TEACHING, *supra note 514,* at 133 (confirming that Catholic social teaching alludes to the Catholic philosophical tradition's insistence on the social nature of human beings as originating from Thomas Aquinas, who was shaped by the Christian tradition and by Aristotelian philosophy – insisting also that the human being is social and political by nature. For this reason, the state is natural and necessary for human beings); *see also* POPE LEO XIII, RERUM NOVARUM, # 37

commandment. The human person cannot fully find himself except through the sincere gift of himself.[569]

The social nature of the human person makes it evident that the progress of the human person and the advance of society itself hinge on one another.[570] For this reason, the Catholic Church insists on the communitarian and social nature of human beings. The social aspect of human existence is not something added to the person but an essential part of the human reality. Because of his inherent social nature, human beings need the social ties of family, associations, and political community for their proper development.

> Life in the society is not something accessible to the human person himself alone; through his dealings with others, through mutual service, and through fraternal dialogue, the individual develops all his talents and becomes able to rise to his destiny.[571]

In testifying that the human person is essentially a social being, the Catholic Church makes us understand that because of his social nature, the need for the human person to live in the society is indispensable.[572] Because of his social nature, the human person lives in relationship with all other

[569] *See* ROBERT A. SIRICO & MACIEJ ZIĘBA, O.P, (ed.), THE SOCIAL AGENDA, *supra* note 550, # 60.

[570] The natural social disposition of men and women also makes it evident that the origin of society is not found in a "contract" or "agreement," but in human nature itself, and from this arises the possibility of freely creating different agreements of association. It must not be forgotten that the ideologies of the social contract are based on a false anthropology; consequently, their results cannot be — and in fact they have not been — profitable for society or for people. The Magisterium has declared such opinions as openly absurd and entirely disastrous; see Pope Leo XIII, Encyclical Letter *Libertas Praestantissimum: Acta Leonis XIII,* 8 (1889), 226-227.

[571] SECOND VATICAN ECUMENICAL COUNCIL, GAUDIUM ET SPES *(THE PASTORAL CONSTITUTION ON THE CHURCH IN THE MODERN WORLD)*, *supra* note 75, # 25.

[572] See CATECHISM OF THE CATHOLIC CHURCH, (1994), # 1879 (stating that society for the human person is not an extraneous addition but a requirement of his nature. Through the exchange with others, mutual service and dialogue with his brothers and sisters, the human person develops his potential).

human beings and with everything God has made.[573] The social nature of human beings is made by God, who created humanity and willed it so.[574] Human nature, in fact, reveals itself as the nature of a being that responds to its own needs. This is based on a relational subjectivity, that is, in the manner of a free and responsible being who recognizes the necessity of integrating himself in cooperation with his fellow human beings and who is capable of communion with them on the level of knowledge and love.[575]

Community of life is a relational characteristic of human beings. It originates from their natural characteristic, which distinguishes them from the rest of earthly creatures.[576] Social activity carries in itself a particular sign of man and of humanity that of a person at work within a community of persons.[577] This is the sign that determines man's interior traits and in a sense, constitutes his very nature.[578] The human person is for this reason called from the very beginning to life in society. "God did not create man as a 'solitary being' but wished him to be a 'social being.' Social life, therefore, is not exterior to man: he can only grow and realize his vocation in relation with others."[579]

Social ties bring many advantages to the human person for the strengthening and betterment of human qualities and for the protection of human rights.[580] While social ties can help the human person to find

---

[573] *See* CHARLES CURRAN, CATHOLIC SOCIAL TEACHING, *supra* note 510, at 133.

[574] Pope John XXIII, Encyclical Letter *Pacem in Terris (On Establishing Universal Peace in Truth, Justice, Charity, and Liberty),* April 11, 1963, # 9.

[575] SECOND VATICAN ECUMENICAL COUNCIL, *GAUDIUM ET SPES*, *supra* note 75, # 25 [The social nature of man shows that there is interdependence between personal betterment and the improvement of the society. Insofar as man by his very nature stands completely in need of life in society, he is and he ought to be the beginning, the subject and object of every social organization].

[576] *See* SECOND VATICAN ECUMENICAL COUNCIL, *GAUDIUM ET SPES*, 12: *AAS 58* (1966), 1034; *See also* CATECHISM OF THE CATHOLIC CHURCH (1994), # 1879

[577] *See generally* PONTIFICAL COUNCIL FOR JUSTICE AND PEACE, *COMPENDIUM OF THE SOCIAL DOCTRINE OF THE CHURCH, supra* note 120.

[578] *See* POPE LEO XIII, ENCYCLICAL LETTER *Libertas Praestantissimum (*On the Nature of Human Liberty) 1888, nos. 226-227.

[579] *Id.*

[580] This is also referred to as "socialization," which connotes mutual relationships and interdependence, which in turn give rise to a variety of associations and organizations, both public and private. Socialization brings with it advantages that make for the strengthening and betterment of the qualities of human life and for the protection of its concomitant inalienable rights; socialization expresses the natural tendency for human beings to associate with one

fulfillment in his vocation in the society, the social environment, if unfairly directed, can lead to evil ends. For instance, frequent upheavals have been recorded in the social order stemming from economic, political, and social tensions, especially because of selfishness and pride.[581] A case in point is the tension that rages between the rich and developing Members of the WTO, which is a central preoccupation of this book. The structures on the ground do not appear to adequately help poor countries rise from poverty.

Summarily, the social doctrine of the Church teaches that the social nature of the human person is not completely fulfilled in the State alone. The social nature of the human person is realized in various intermediary groups, such as the family, including economic, social, political, and cultural groups, which all originate from human nature and are directed toward the common good.[582] It will be hopeless and unacceptable for poor countries to work side by side with the developed countries of the world in international trade if the structures on the ground do not help to eliminate inequality.

Human nature in fact, reveals itself as a nature of a being that

> responds to his own needs. This is based on a relational subjectivity, that is, in the manner of a free and responsible being who recognizes the necessity of integrating himself in cooperation with his fellow human beings, and who is capable of communion with them on the level of knowledge and love. A society is a group of persons

---

another for the sake of attaining objectives that exceed individual capacities; *see id.* at # 25; *see* CATECHISM OF THE CATHOLIC CHURCH (1994), # 1882; POPE JOHN PAUL II, ENCYCLICAL LETTER *CENTESIMUS ANNUS*, # 12; socialization also develops the qualities of the person, especially the sense of initiative and responsibility, and helps guarantee human rights; *see* POPE JOHN XXIII, ENCCLICAL LETTER *Mater Et Magistra*, # 60.

581 SECOND VATICAN ECUMENICAL COUNCIL, GAUDIUM ET SPES, # 25.

582 POPE JOHN PAUL II, ENCYCLICAL LETTER *SOLLICITUDO REI SOCIALIS* (On the Social Concern of the Church), December 30, 1987, #s 15 & 28; [Pope John Paul referred to this system as "subjectivity" of society which goes together with "subjectivity" of the individual]; *see* POPE JOHN PAUL II, ENCYCLICAL LETTER *Centesimus Annus*, at 13. *See also* CATECHISM OF THE CATHOLIC CHURCH (1994) # 1881 (stating that each community is defined by its purpose which it obeys, but the human person is and ought to be the principle, the subject and end of all social institutions).

> bound together organically by a principle of unity that goes beyond each one of them.[583]

The social nature of the human person suggests a self-giving that creates an atmosphere of mutual understanding and common good, which can help in the self-fulfillment of the human person in the society. An individual in isolation cannot realize himself in the society. The social nature of the human person involves communities, organizations, and associations at the local, regional, national and international levels.[584] Asocial behavior breeds pride, selfishness, and other negative impulses, which make a person self-centered in his cocoon, with penchant dominating his neighbor. For the sake of the realization of human nature, every individual, association, organization, or country ought to search for what is good and pursue it for his/its own good and the good of others, for the purpose of the common good.[585]

The human person is the purpose and end of every society, and the state, including any social organization, exists to serve the human person. The human person does not exist to serve the state or any social organization.[586] The human person is the end and purpose of every state and social organization. Therefore, in international trade, any country that advances agreements that are not favorable to other Members will be running afoul of the course of the social nature of the human person. Projecting the image of a country against the principle of equality, which characterizes the dignity of the human person, promotes inequalities in international trade. When applied to the WTO, international trade should operate to liberate the human person, at least for the sake of his inalienable

[583] PONTICAL COUNCIL FOR JUSTICE AND PEACE, *supra* note 120, at 149.

[584] *See* JOHN PAUL II, ENCYCLICAL LETTER *SOLLICITUDO REI SOCIALIS,* 26: *AAS 80* (1988), 544-547; SECOND VATICAN ECUMENICAL COUNCIL, *PASTORAL CONSTITUTION ON THE CHURCH IN THE MODERN WORLD, GAUDIUM ET SPES, 76: AAS 58* (1966), 1099-1100.

[585] *See id.* at # 150.

[586] CHARLES RODGERS, *supra* note 57, at 13; (stating that this is also "a principle which a healthy civil society must foster," first, that "the citizen has rights which the State cannot take away from him, and [second] that man is the end and purpose of every social organization"); *see id,* at 35.

dignity, from any arrangement that militates against the spiritual quest for each person toward the afterlife.[587]

4.3.5 Rights of Peoples and Nations

The Catholic Church identifies and proclaims human rights as one of the most significant attempts to respond effectively to the inescapable demands of human dignity.[588] In affirming these rights, the Church makes it an extraordinary opportunity in modern times to more effectively recognize and universally promote human dignity as a characteristic inscribed by God the Creator in humans.[589] The Magisterium of the Catholic Church takes serious cognizance of the positive value of the Universal Declaration of Human Rights, adopted by the United Nations on December 10, 1948. Pope John Paul II defines these human rights as "a true milestone on the path of humanity's moral progress."[590] It is noteworthy that the roots of human rights are to be found in the dignity

---

587 *See* RAJ BHALA, *supra* note 56, at 107.

588 *See* Second Vatican Ecumenical Council, Declaration *Dignitatis Humanae, 1 AAS 58* (1966), 929- 930.

589 *See* Second Vatican Ecumenical Council, *Pastoral Constitution on the Church in the Modern World, Gaudium et Spes, 41 AAS 58* (1966), 1059-1060; Congregation for Catholic Education, *Guidelines for the Study and Teaching of the Church's Social Doctrine in the Formation of Priests,* 32, Vatican Polyglot Press, Rome, 1988, pp. 36-37 [Respect for human dignity necessarily means the promotion of human rights because they derive from that dignity, which in turn is divine in origin and nature. And these rights are founded on the axiom of respect for human dignity itself]; see CHARLES RODGERS, *supra* note 488, at 29; THOMAS MASSARO, S.J., LIVING JUSTICE – CATHOLIC SOCIAL TEACHING IN ACTION, Sheed & Ward (2000) [Stating that

The Catholic view of human rights is distinctive because it is grounded on a complete theological framework, in which God is the ultimate source of our rights . . .. In comparison, purely secular doctrines of rights have no similar foundation in a compelling portrayal of human nature and its origin. In a sense, they are doctrines without a solid theory behind them. They are exposed to the weighty charge that rights just seem to "float around," sticking to people without any justification behind their passing claims. See THOMAS MASSARO, LIVING JUSTICE, *supra,* at 118.

590 *See* Pope John Paul II, Address to the 34th General Assembly of the United Nations (October 2, 1979), *7 AAS 71* (1979), 1147-1148; [for John Paul II, this Declaration "remains one of the highest expressions of the human conscience of our time;" *see* Address to the Fiftieth General Assembly of the United Nations (October 5, 1995), 2 *L'Osservatore Romano,* English edition, October 11, 1995, p. 8.

that belongs to each human being.[591] This dignity, inherent in human life and equal in every person, is perceived and understood first by reason.

The ultimate source of human rights is not found in the will of human beings, neither are they found in the reality of the State, nor in public powers. Rather, these human rights are found in man himself and in God his Creator.[592] Human rights are fundamental because they are "universal, inviolable, and inalienable."[593] Human rights are said to be "universal" because they are present in all human beings, without exception of time, place, or subject. They are "inviolable" because "they are inherent in the human person and in human dignity"[594] and because "it would be useless to proclaim human rights, if they are not protected against violation by all people, everywhere, and for all peoples.[595] Lastly, human rights are "inalienable" because "no one can legitimately deprive another person, whoever they may be, of these rights, since this would do violence to the dignity in human nature."[596]

The Church Magisterium is vehement in teaching that the society is made for the human person and not vice versa. Pope Pius XI taught that the society is made for the human person and not vice versa, because of which, society is a natural means man must use to reach his destined end. The human person must exercise his rights with others in the society by mutual collaboration for the attainment of earthly happiness. The human

---

591 Second Vatican Ecumenical Council, *Pastoral Constitution on the Church in the Modern World, Gaudium et Spes, 27 AAS 58* (1966), 1047-1048; See also CATECHISM OF THE CATHOLIC CHURCH, *supra*, at 1930.

592 Pope John XXIII, Encyclical Letter *Pacem in Terris, supra, at AAS 55,* (1963), 278-279.

593 Pope John XXIII, Encyclical Letter *Pacem in Terris, AAS 55* (1963), 259.

594 *See* Pope John Paul II, Message for the 1999 World Day of Peace, *3 AAS 91* (1999), 379.

595 Pope Paul VI, Message to the International Conference on Human Rights, Teheran, (April 15, 1968) *L'Osservatore Romano*, English edition, May 2, 1968, p. 4; [Respect for the human person entails respect for the rights that flow from his dignity as a creature. These rights are prior to the society and must be recognized by it. They are the basis of the moral legitimacy of every authority; by flouting them, or refusing to recognize them in its positive legislation, a society undermines its moral legitimacy; see Pope John XXIII, *Pacem in Terris (On establishing Universal Peace in Truth, Justice, Charity, and Liberty),* April 11, 1963, at 65; if it does not respect them, authority can rely on force or violence to obtain obedience from subjects; it is the Church's duty to remind men of good will of these rights and to distinguish them from unwarranted or false claims; *see* CATECHISM OF THE CATHOLIC CHURCH (1994), # 1930].

596 *See* Pope John Paul II, Message for the 1999 World Day of Peace, *3 AAS 91 (1999)*, 379.

person should be allowed a reasoned exercise of his rights in line with the natural and social gifts available in the society as an opportunity to develop himself with others. This is only possible when he is allowed the use of his naturally endowed reason and free will.[597]

Professor Raj Bhala, in saying that respect for human dignity is an inviolable human right, meant there is a connection between respect for human dignity, on the one hand, and human rights, on the other hand.[598] Theologians agree that there is such a connection:

> Law, morality, justice, the common good, and human rights are inter-linked in the Christian understanding of things. The purpose of the law is to give justice, to see that each gets what is his due; we know what is just because the moral law of God instructs us. The common good [*which will be discussed in detail below*] means the good of each and the good of all. And we can see that the good is being achieved when all have their human rights. These two are founded in God's law; being made in God's image and likeness; all men must be treated according to their dignity.[599]

Because human rights are ordained by God and endorsed by the United Nations as fundamental to human nature, the Catholic Church

---

[597] POPE PIUS XI, ENCYCLICAL LETTER, *Divini Redemptoris* (On Atheistic Communism), March 19, 1937, # 29.

[598] RAJ BHALA, *supra* note 56, at 422; Raj Bhala, Philosophical, Religious, and Legalistic Perspectives on Equal Human Dignity and U.S. Free Trade Agreements, *supra* note 522, at 119.

[599] CHARLES RODGERS, *supra* note 57, at 46. *See also* DAVID BOHR, CATHOLIC MORAL TRADITION, supra note 55, at 324 (observing that "Pope Leo XIII rooted his social ethics in *the supreme value of the human person,"* and "all political and social structures need to respect and respond to *this primary moral claim of human dignity,*") (emphasis added by Raj Bhala).

has promoted and protected these rights in different forms and at different levels.[600] In summary, there are ten such human rights, as follows:[601]

1st. *The Right to Life and Development, from conception to its natural end*[602]

The human person has a right to live; to bodily integrity and the means necessary for proper development; to adequate food, clothing, housing, medical care, rest; to choose his state of life and to set up a family, [and] necessary social services . . . (which include care during) unemployment, illness or permanent disability or when through no fault of the person, is deprived of the means of livelihood.[603] President Thomas Jefferson of the

---

[600] The inalienable human rights available to the human person are not without corresponding duties. Hence, Pope John XXIII teaches:

The natural rights of which we have so far been speaking are inextricably bound up with as many duties, all applying to one and the same person. These rights and duties derive their origin, their sustenance, and their indestructibility from the natural law, which in conferring the one imposes the other. Thus, for example, the right to live involves the duty to preserve one's life; the right to a decent standard of living, the duty to live in a becoming fashion; the right to be free to seek out the truth, the duty to devote oneself to an ever deeper and wider search for it. Once this is admitted, it follows that in human society one man's natural right gives rise to a corresponding duty in other men; the duty, that is, of recognizing and respecting that right. Every basic human right draws its authoritative force from the natural law, which confers it and attaches to it its respective duty. Hence, to claim one's rights and ignore one's duties, or only half fulfill them, is like building a house with one hand and tearing it down with the other. *See* POPE JOHN XXIII, ENCYCLICAL LETTER PACEM IN TERRIS (Peace on Earth), April 11, 1963, Nos. 28-30.

[601] *See* POPE JOHN XXIII, ENCYCLICAL LETTER, PACEM IN TERRIS ("On Peace on Earth") ¶¶ 23-24 (April 11, 1963), *quoted in* CHARLES RODGERS, *supra* note 57, at 24.

[602] *See* POPE JOHN PAUL II, ENCYCLICAL LETTER EVANGELIUM VITAE (On the Gospel of Life), *2 AAS 87 (1995),* 402 (indicating that "Man is called to a fullness of life which far exceeds the dimensions of his earthly existence, because it consists in sharing the very life of God. The loftiness of this supernatural vocation reveals the greatness and the inestimable value of human life even in its temporal phase. Life in time, in fact, is the fundamental condition, the initial stage and an integral part of the entire unified process of human existence")

[603] David Hollenbach, *Claims in Conflict*, Woodstock Studies 4, Paulist, New York, (1979), *cited in* Daniel G. Groody, *Globalization, Spirituality, and Justice: Navigating the Path to Peace,* Maryknoll, New York, 2008, p. 111; Raj Bhala, Philosophical, Religious, and Legalistic Perspective son Equal Human Dignity and U.S. Trade Agreements, *supra,* note 491, at 120; CHARLES RODGERS, *supra* note 488, at 30; See also POPE JOHN PAUL II, ENCYCLICAL LETTER EVANGELIUM VITAE (On the Gospel of Life), March 25, 1995;

United States buttressed this right when he said that "the care of human life and happiness, and not their destruction, is the just and only legitimate object of good government.[604]

2nd. *The Right to be respected*

The human person has a right to be respected, that is, "to a good name, to freedom in investigating the truth, and (within the limits of the moral order and the common good) to freedom of speech and publication, to pursue whatever profession he may choose," and to be accurately informed about public affairs.[605]

3rd. *The Right to Education on Moral and Cultural Values*

The human person has the right to a good general education, technical or professional training consistent with the degree of educational development in his own country, to engage in advanced studies, to (as far as possible) positions of responsibility proportionate with his talent and skill.[606] If a person is involved in any international affair directly or

---

(with Pope John Paul II asking: "And how can we fail to consider the violence against life done to millions of human beings, especially children, who are forced into poverty, malnutrition and hunger because of an unjust distribution of resources between peoples and between social classes? And what of the violence inherent not only in wars as such but in the scandalous arms trade, which spawns the many armed conflicts which stain our world with blood? What of the spreading of death caused by reckless tampering with the world's ecological balance, by the criminal spread of drugs, or by the promotion of certain kinds of sexual activity which, besides being morally unacceptable, also involve grave risks to life?"), *Evangelium Vitae*, # 10

604 *See* GEORGE WEIGEL, WITNESS TO HOPE, *supra* note 74, at 354 (indicating that Pope John Paul II insisted that "Nothing surpasses the greatness or dignity of a human person," and that life is the centerpiece of human dignity).

605 *See* CHARLES RODGERS, *supra* note 57, at 30; *See also* MATTHEW F. KOHMESCHER, CATHOLICISM TODAY: A SURVEY OF CATHOLIC BELIEF AND PRACTICE 156 (Paulist press, 3rd ed., 1999) ("We all have the duty not only to respect the basic rights of others but to work with them in order that these rights be respected, cherished and promoted by all. We should do this not to gain our own selfish ends but because it is right and just to treat others as we would want to be treated."); POPE JOHN XXIII, ENCYCLICAL LETTER PACEM IN TERRIS ("Peace on Earth") #s 63-65 (declaring that "[t]he influence of the State must never be exerted to the extent of depriving the individual citizen of his freedom," and that "[i]t must augment his freedom while guaranteeing protection of everyone's rights.")

606 CHARLES RODGERS, *supra* note 57, at 30; RAJ BHALA, *supra* note 56, at 423.

indirectly, the person should have the right to a quality education that is commensurate with international expectation. This right goes with the concomitant right in investigating the truth within the limits of moral order and the common good. It goes with the right to freedom of speech and publication and freedom to pursue whatever profession a person chooses. It is also within the parameters of this right that a person has a right to share in the benefits of his culture.[607]

4th. *The Right to Worship According to One's Conscience608*

The human person has an inalienable right to worship God according to his conscience and to profess his religion privately or publicly, provided the rights of others are respected at the same time.[609] The Catholic Church has always defended and promoted human rights, of which religious freedom is the centerpiece.[610]

5th. *The Right to Choose a Lifestyle*

The human person has the right to choose any lifestyle which appeals to him. The human person can elect to start a family, in which case he marries and enjoys equal rights and duties with his spouse, or he may choose not to marry. Whatever choice a person makes, the interests of the family, the primary cell of the society, must take into consideration social and economic affairs, as well as in the spheres of faith and morals.

---

[607] POPE JOHN XXIII, ENCYCLICAL LETTER, PACEM IN TERRIS, # 12.

[608] *See id.* a 14 (indicating that right to worship is one of being able to worship God in accordance with the right dictates of his own conscience, and to profess his religion both in private and in public . . . "this is the very condition of our birth, that we render to the God who made us that just homage which is His due; that we acknowledge Him alone as God, and follow Him. It is from this ligature of piety, which binds us and joins us to God, that religion derives its name.).

[609] *See id,* at 30. See also POPE JOHN PAUL II, RESPECT FOR HUMAN RIGHTS: THE SECRET OF TRUE PEACE (Message of His Holiness Pope John Paul II on the World Day of Peace 1999, n. 5 (stating that "religious freedom constitutes the very heart of human rights" because "religion expresses the deepest aspirations of the human person . . . and basically it offers the answer to the question of the true meaning of life," and adding that "no one can be compelled to accept a particular religion whatever the circumstance or motive.").

[610] GEORGE WEIGEL, *supra* note 74, at 350.

The choice must aim at strengthening the family and assisting it in the fulfillment of its mission.[611]

6th. The Right to Work – Economic rights

The human person has an inherent right to be given an opportunity to work and to exercise his personal initiative in the work he does. His freedom to work must be under such conditions that do not tend to weaken his physical or moral fiber. In his freedom to work, he is entitled to wages that are consistent with the precepts of justice, enough to allow him and his family a standard of living consistent with human dignity.[612] "Nature imposes work upon man as a duty, and man has the corresponding natural

---

[611] *See* POPE JOHN XXIII, ENCYCLICAL LETTER PACEM IN TERRIS, nos. 15-16; *See generally* THOMAS MASSARO, S.J., LIVING JUSTICE, *supra,* note 584, at 124 (discussing family life).

[612] CHARLES RODGERS, *supra* note 57, at 31. Pope Leo XIII states that: [T]he first [task]... is to save workers from the brutality of those who make use of human beings as mere instruments in the creation of wealth, impose a burden of labor which stupefies minds and exhausts bodies. Let workers and employers make bargains freely about wages but there underlies a requirement of natural justice, higher and older than any bargain: a wage ought not to be insufficient for needs. See POPE LEO, RERUM NOVARUM, # 45, quoted in CHARLES RODGERS, *supra* note 57, at 34 (and emphasis added by RAJ BHALA, "Philosophical, Religious, and Linguistic Perspectives on Equal Human Dignity," *supra,* note 518, at 121; See also Pope JOHN PAUL II, ENCYCLICAL LETTER LABOREM EXERCENS ("On Human Work") nos. 25-27 (stating the task involved in the human person's right to work as the means to fulfill human dignity; it is a person who works who "ought to imitate God, his Creator in working," and who "by means of work . . . participates in the activity of God himself...as given particular prominence by Jesus Christ," and "the Christian finds in human work a small part of the Cross of Christ"). *See also* LABOREM EXERCENS nos. 16-19 (discussing the right and duty to work, and identifying no more important way of securing a just relationship between the worker and the employer" than payment of "just remuneration" because it is "a practical means whereby the vast majority of people can have access to those goods which are intended for common use: both the goods of nature and manufactured goods," and "is the concrete means of verifying the justice of the whole socioeconomic system"). See also CHARLES RODGERS, *supra* note 57, at 61 (stating "it is the task of the state to ensure economic freedom and to see that that freedom is not abused, but that, through it, all may have access to the means of a decent livelihood") and # 63 (1) discussing the spiritual significance of work, in that man, having been created in God's image, shares in the creative activity of God through work, and can liken vicissitudes at work to the hardships endured by Jesus; (2) arguing that Jesus gave work a new dignity because he spent most of his earthly life working with his hands; and (3) affirming that "the subject of work is more important than the work done or the object achieved by it.").

right to demand that the work he does shall provide him with the means of livelihood for himself and his children. Such is nature's categorical imperative for the preservation of man."[613] The right to work is a right that constitutes efficacious means of asserting one's personality and exercising responsibility in every field, and an element of solidity and security for family life, and of greater peace and prosperity in the State.[614]

7th. The Right to Participate in Meetings and Associations

Because they are social in nature, human beings have the right to meet together and form associations with their fellow human beings. Human beings have the right to organize associations in a manner that, using their sense of initiative and duties, aims at achieving their objectives in life. These associations are essential for safe guarding human freedom and dignity, especially when they are not debarred from using their sense of responsibility.[615] In forming and joining these associations, the human person participates in economic activities suited to a degree of responsibility; he secures a wage in accordance with justice; he owns private property, including productive goods.[616]

---

[613] See POPE JOHN XXIII, ENCYCLICAL LETTER PACEM IN TERRIS, # 20.

[614] *See id.* at # 21.

[615] *Id.* at #s 23-24.

[616] CHARLES RODGERS, *supra* note 57, at 31. Pope John XXIII teaches: The dignity of the human person also requires that every man enjoy the right to act freely and responsibly. For this reason, therefore, in social relations, man should exercise his rights, fulfill his obligations and, in the countless forms of collaboration with others, act chiefly on his own responsibility and initiative. This is to be done in such a way that each one acts on his own decision, of set purpose and from a consciousness of his obligation, without being moved by force or pressure brought to bear on him externally. For any human society that is established on relations of force must be regarded as inhuman, inasmuch as the personality of its members is repressed or restricted, when in fact they should be provided with appropriate incentives and means for developing and perfecting themselves. See POPE JOHN XXIII, PACEM IN TERRIS (Peace on Earth), # 34 (emphasis added in RAJ BHALA, *supra* note 56, at 424). See also POPE JOHN PAUL II, RESPECT FOR HUMAN RIGHTS, *supra* note 604, no. 20 (teaching that by protecting workers' rights and enhancing workers' solidarity in a conservative manner within the framework of common good, and by eschewing class egoism, conflict and political power battles, trade unions play an indispensable role in advancing social justice). *See also* POPE JOHN PAUL II, ENCYCLICAL LETTER LABOREM EXERCENS ("On Human Work") September 20, 1981, # 20.

8th. The Right to Private Property

The human person has a natural right to ownership of private property, including that of productive goods. This natural right is one that the State cannot suppress. It, however, entails a social obligation as well. It is a right which must be exercised not only for one's own personal benefit but also for the benefit of others. Freedom and the right to ownership of private property is an opportunity to celebrate the social nature of the human person, especially in enabling a person to enter relations with others.[617]

9th. The Right to Migrate

Every human being has the right to freedom of movement and of residence within and without the confines of his own State. When just reasons are available, a person must be permitted to emigrate to other countries and secure residence there if he so wishes.[618] "The fact that he is a citizen of a State does not deprive him of membership in the human family, nor of citizenship in that universal society, the common, world-wide fellowship of men."[619]

---

617 See POPE JOHN XXIII, ENCYCLICAL LETTER MATER ET MAGISTRA (On the Church as Mother and Teacher), May 15, 1961, # 19 (asserting that the right to ownership of private property "is a right which constitutes so efficacious a means of asserting one's personality and exercising responsibility in every field, and an element of solidity and security for family life, and of greater peace and prosperity in the State.") See POPE JOHN XXIII, PACEM IN TERRIS, # 21. *See also,* CHARLES RODGERS, *supra* note 57, at 31 & 61 (stating that man "must have freedom to choose his work, to prosper at it and to own property," and "unless he has these freedoms, all other freedoms are at risk from his economic masters") (emphasis added in RAJ BHALA, *supra* note 56, at 424). Interestingly, Church Fathers such as Saint Ambrose viewed private property as an illusion because property belongs to God. Private ownership, and more specifically inequality of distribution, was unknown before the Fall of Adam and Eve, and was said by them to be a consequence of sin. Consequently, St. Ambrose characterized almsgiving by an avaricious person as the restitution of goods stolen from the poor. See generally THOMAS MASSARO, supra note 584, at 132-138 (discussing the rights and responsibilities of private property ownership).

618 See POPE PIUS XII'S CHRISTMAS RADIO BROADCAST MESSAGE, (1952), *AAS 45 (1953)* 36-46.

619 See POPE JOHN XXIII, ENCYCLICAL LETTER PACEM IN TERRIS (On Peace on Earth), April 11, 1963, # 25. See also CHARLES RODGERS, supra note 57, at 31. See for example POPE PAUL II, supra note 604, ¶ 23 (teaching that "man has the right to leave his native land for various motives – and also the right to return – in order to seek better

10th. The Right to Political and Legal Protection

The human person is not an object or an inert element in a society. The human person is rather the subject, the basis, and the purpose of every society. As result of this, he must be esteemed.[620] Every human being has the right to actively participate in public life and contribute to the common welfare of his fellow citizens. For this right to be available to human beings in a society, they also have the inalienable right to juridical security. Human beings are entitled to legal protection that is effective, unbiased, and above all, just, making them immune from any arbitrary treatment. As a matter of fact, human beings have the right to have the human rights enshrined in the political and legal systems of their countries.[621]

---

conditions of life in another country," and that "the most important thing is that the person working away from his native land, whether as a permanent emigrant or as a seasonal worker, should not be placed at a disadvantage in comparison with the other workers in that society in the matter of working rights") (emphasis added) see RAJ BHALA, *supra* note 56, at 424-425).

[620] *See* POPE PIUS XII'S CHRISTMAS RADIO BROADCAST MESSAGE, (1944), *AAS 37* (1945) 12.

[621] POPE JOHN XXIII, ENCYLCLICAL LETTER PACEM IN TERRIS (Peace on Earth), April 11, 1963, #s 26-27. See also CHARLES RODGERS, *supra* note 57, at 31. The government authority in a political or economic society is responsible for providing this protection. That responsibility is especially important with respect to poor members in the society. This importance derives from more than just the preference for the poor (one of the principles of Catholic social doctrine to be discussed below). Pope Leo XII puts this bluntly as follows: "Rich people can protect themselves; the poor have to depend above all upon the State." POPE LEO XIII, ENCYCLICAL LETTER RERUM NOVARUM (On the Condition of Working Classes) nos. 37-38, *quoted in* CHARLES RODGERS, *supra* note 488, at 35. See also RAJ BHALA, *supra* note 518, at 123. This responsibility does not inexorably compel the conclusion that democracy is the best form of government, and Catholic Social Justice Theory does not say that either. Saint Thomas Aquinas urged a mixed form of government, combining monarchy, aristocracy, and democracy, thereby providing the respective advantages of an authoritative figure, involvement of qualified persons, and choice by the people. See SAINT THOMAS AQUINAS, SUMMA THEOLOGICA *Ia & IIae Q. 105 Art. I* (Richard J. Regan (ed.), University of Scranton 1999) quoted in CHARLES RODGERS, *supra* note 57, at 40.

More generally, for a discussion of Galesian theory (named after Pope Galesius, whose Pontificate was in the 5th century, from 492-496 A.D.), see DAVID BOHR, *supra* note 55, at 309. Briefly, the Galesian theory holds that the Church and State are powers established by God on earth to operate autonomously in different spheres, the ecclesiological and secular, respectively, and that Church authorities are to respect and support each other. This theory dominated most of the medieval era, though the reign of Charlemagne was marked by a "theocratic character," and starting in the 11th century A.D., conflict between popes and

When we talk about human rights, we do not limit it to individuals alone. Also, there are rights of peoples and nations.[622]

> What is true for the individual is also true for peoples. The Magisterium teaches that international law rests upon the principle of equal respect for States, for each people's right to self-determination and for their free cooperation in view of the higher common good of humanity.[623]

Experience has shown that peace rests not only on respect for human rights but also on respect for the rights of peoples, and particularly, the right to independence of nations.[624] The rights of nations are still seen as human rights, but they are fostered at the level of community life.[625] A nation has fundamental rights just like individuals.

> A nation has a fundamental right to existence, to its own language and culture, through which a people expresses and promotes ... its fundamental spiritual 'sovereignty,' to shape its life according to its own traditions, excluding, of course, every abuse of basic human rights and the

---

Emperors were "the norm of the next several centuries." *See Id. at 309.* The opposite of the Galesian theory is "hierocratic" theory, articulated by Pope Boniface VIII in *Unam Sanctam* (1302), whereby the Church is viewed as superior to the State. Hence, a Pontiff was authorized to intervene in political matters to save souls. *See Id. at 311. See* CHARLES RODGERS, *supra* note 57, at 50-54, for details of political theories on this topic.

The responsibility for providing legal protection of human rights also does not inexorably mean that the government must regulate the ownership and use of private property. Regulation entails the risk of undermining the institution of private property. Hence, the key principle that ought to constrain the government from excessive intervention is promotion of the common good. *See id,* at 61. See also RAJ BHALA, *supra* note 56, at 425

622 POPE JOHN PAUL II, ENCYCLICAL LETTER SOLLICITUDO REI SOCIALIS, 33: *AAS 80 (1988),* 557-559; JOHN PAUL II, ENCYCLICAL LETTER CENTESIMUS ANNUS, 21: *AAS 83 (1991),* 818-819.

623 John Paul II, Letter on the occasion of the fiftieth anniversary of the outbreak of the Second World War, *8 L'Osservatore Romano,* English edition, September 4, 1989, p. 2.

624 *Id.*

625 John Paul II, Address to the Fiftieth General Assembly of the United Nations (5 October 1995), *8 L'Osservatore Romano,* English edition, October 11, 1995, p. 9.

> oppression of minorities, to build its future by providing an appropriate education for the younger generation.[626]

The fundamental rights of nations are inalienable, especially in international law and politics. This upholds the sovereignty of nations and enables each nation to in turn, protect the rights of its citizens. International order requires a balance between particularity and universality whereby each nation has it as a primary duty to live in peace, respect, and solidarity with other nations.[627] Pope John XXIII authoritatively teaches

> Nations are the subjects of reciprocal rights and duties. Their relationships, therefore, must likewise be harmonized in accordance with the dictates of truth, justice, willing cooperation, and freedom. The same law of nature that governs the life and conduct of individuals must also regulate the relations of political communities with one another.[628]

What concerns do human rights have with international trade? There is an established commitment of the Catholic Church to promote human rights as the only way to peace and the common good. It is important to point out here that establishing a reliable connection between human rights and international trade or the operations of the WTO will enhance the latter's credibility. Once international trade is structured in such a way as to always contemplate the inalienable rights of human beings, and Members of the WTO reciprocate accordingly, then the mission of the Catholic Church is achieved fully. However, the complexities of human life and political aberrations in the world can militate against the full accomplishment of the mission of the Catholic Church to that regard. The concentration of this book therefore, is assessment of the degree of effectiveness, or ineffectiveness of the Holy See as it concerns influencing the operations of the WTO in her social mission.

---

[626] *Id.*

[627] PONTIFICAL COUNCIL FOR JUSTICE AND PEACE, supra note 120, # 157.

[628] POPE JOHN XXIII, ENCYCLICAL LETTER, PACEM IN TERRIS (Peace on Earth), April 11, 1963, # 80.

4.4 Second: Common Good

The secret to understanding the principle of the common good is to think of "common" as applying to every and therefore to each person without exception, and "good" as that which contributes to human flourishing. Therefore, it is reasonable to understand the principle of the common good as the foundation of human rights.[629] The common good consists of three essential elements, namely, (1) respect for and promotion of the fundamental rights and prosperity of the person; (2) the development of the spiritual and temporal goods of society; and (3) the peace and security of the group and of its members.[630]

One of the earliest references in Christian literature to the concept of the common good is found in the *Epistle of Barnabas.* This Epistle decries living entirely isolated since such solitary existence does not justify a person. Alternatively, a consistent and a collective search for the common good is a lifestyle that justifies human life.[631] The concept of the common good was a topical issue in the *City of God* where Saint Augustine of Hippo

---

[629] SECOND VATICAN ECUMENICAL COUNCIL, GAUDIUM ET SPES, *26 AAS 58* (1966), 1046; CATECHISM OF THE CATHOLIC CHURCH (1994), #s 1905-1912; POPE JOHN XXIII, ENCYCLICAL LETTER MATER ET MAGISTRA *AAS 53* (1961), 417-421; POPE JOHN XXIII, ENCYCLICAL LETTER PACEM IN TERRIS, *AAS 55 (1963)*, 272-273; POPE PAUL VI, APOSTOLIC LETTER OCTOGESIMA ADVENIENS, *46 AAS 63 (1971), 433-435.*

[630] *See* CATECHISM OF THE CATHOLIC CHURCH (1994), #s 1907-1912[stating that the common good presupposes respect for the human person and resides in the conditions for the exercise of the natural freedoms indispensable for the development of the human vocation, such as "the right to act according to a sound norm of conscience and to safeguard… privacy, and rightful freedom also in matters of religion." Secondly, that the common good requires the social wellbeing and development of the group itself. Development is the epitome of all social duties. Certainly, it is the proper function of authority to arbitrate, in the name of the common good, between various interests, but it should make accessible to each what is needed to lead a truly human life: food, health, work, education and culture, suitable information, the right to establish a family, and so on. Thirdly, the common good requires peace, that is, the stability and security of a just order. It presupposes that authority should ensure by morally acceptable means the security of society and its members. It is the basis of the right to legitimate personal and collective defense.].

[631] *See* PETER KIRBY, "Historical Jesus Theories," in *Early Christian Writings,* 2001, 4: 10, available online at http://www.earlychristianwritings.com/text/barnabas-lightfoot.html (last visited March 12, 2013).

argues that the wellbeing of a human person is found in the common good of the entire society.[632]

Augustine's understanding was taken up and, under the influence of Aristotle, developed by Thomas Aquinas. Aquinas's conception of the common good became standard in Roman Catholic moral theology. Against that background, the common good became a central concept in the modern tradition of Catholic social teaching, beginning with the foundational encyclical, *Rerum Novarum,* a papal encyclical by Pope Leo XIII issued in 1891. This addressed the crisis of the conditions of industrial workers in Europe and argued for a position different from both laissez-faire capitalism and socialism.

The importance of the principle of the common good is seen in the teaching that the cause of social justice is advanced through consistent commitment toward the common good. Social justice refers to justice in the society in general. What this implies is that social justice is principally concerned with the common good.

> It is the essence of social justice to demand from everyone all that is necessary for the common good. But, just as in the living organism, it is impossible to provide for the good of the whole unless each single part and each individual member is given what it needs for the exercise of its proper functions. So too, it is impossible to care for the social organism and the good of society as a unit unless each single part and each individual member . . . is supplied with all that is necessary for the exercise of his social functions.[633]

4.4.1 Meaning of Common Good

The common good comprises the sum of social conditions which allow people, either as groups or as individuals, to reach their fulfillment

---

[632] See SAINT AUGUSTINE, THE CITY OF GOD (trans. By Marcus Dods), Modern Library Giant (1st ed., 1950), Book XIX, chaps. 5-17.

[633] POPE PIS XI, ENCYCLICAL LETTER, DIVINI REDEMPTORIS (1937), quoted in DAVID BOHR, CATHOLIC MORAL TRADITION, *supra* note 544, at 338.

more fully and more easily.[634] In other words, the common good concerns the life and wellbeing of all human beings. Though public authorities are expected to work for the common good, they are equally bound to respect the fundamental and inalienable rights of the human person.

> The common good does not consist in the simple sum of the particular goods of each subject of a social entity. Belonging to everyone and to each person, it is and remains "common," because it is indivisible, and because only together is it possible to attain it, increase it and safeguard its effectiveness, with regard also to the future. Just as the moral actions of an individual are accomplished in doing what is good, so too the actions of a society attain their full stature when they bring about the common good. The common good, in fact, can be understood as the social and community dimension of the moral good.[635]

The human person should practically and always seek the common good at all levels of social life. The human person cannot find fulfillment in himself, that is, apart from the fact that he exists "with" others and "for" others.[636]

> A society that wishes and intends to remain at the service of the human being at every level is a society that has the common good — the good of all people and of the whole person— as its primary goal.[637]

---

634 SECOND VATICAN ECUMENICAN COUNCIL, GAUDIUM ET SPES, supra note 75, # 26. The rights and obligations that are involved in reaching the fulfillment of the goal of human dignity should be the concern of the whole human race. Every group must take into account the needs and aspirations of every other group as members of the human family.

635 PONTIFICAL COUNCIL FOR JUSTICE AND PEACE, COMPENDIUM *supra* note 120, at 164.

636 *See id.* at 165.

637 *See* CATECHISM OF THE CATHOLIC CHURCH (1994), # 1912.

Common good means "the good of the whole people, and of each person, under just law."[638] Pope Leo XIII identifies the common good with elements of good governance when he taught:

> Statesmanship consists in making the structure and administrative functioning of the State conduce to public and private property: sound morals, family life, regard for religion and justice, moderate taxes equitably levied, growing industry and trade, a flourishing agriculture, the greater well-being and happiness of the citizens.[639]

The term "common" encompasses the good of everyone, and of the association of which he is a part. The political society is established for the very purpose of securing the common good, "the good of each and the good of all."[640] As an incentive to pursue the common good, leaders of society must bear in mind respect for human dignity, which in the practical sense means ensuring for everyone the maximum freedom consistent with the good of all individuals.[641]

The principle of the common good is a very constitutive element of the significance and authentic reason for the existence of the family and other social groups. Social groups such as associations, enterprises of an economic nature, cities, regions, States, and the international community will be worthless if the central issue of their existence is not the common

---

[638] CHARLES RODGERS, AN INTRODUCT TO CATHOLIC SOCIAL TEACHING, *supra* note 57, at 15; *see also* POPE JOHN XXIII, ENCYCLICAL LETTER, MATER ET MAGISTRA, # s 65-67 (explaining that privately established associations like corporate enterprises "collaborate in the pursuit of their own specific interests and those of the common good."

POPE LEO XIII, ENCYCLICAL LETTER RERUM NOVARUM, *supra* note 357, at 33 (emphasis added).

[639] POPE LEO XIII, ENCYCLICAL LETTER RERUM NOVARUM, # 33.

[640] CHARLES RODGERS, AN INTRODUCTION TO CATHOLIC SOCIAL TEACHING, *supra* note 57, at 42 (emphasis added); see also THOMAS MASSARO, LIVING JUSTICE, *supra* note 584, at 121 (stating that "to speak of the common good is to recognize that there are numerous rightful goals in life beyond our own private benefits.")

[641] CHARLES RODGERS, AN INTRODUCTION TO CATHOLIC SOCIAL TEACHING, *supra* note 57, at 42

good.[642] Therefore, the WTO and, therefore, international trade will be found hugely wanting if its primary goal is not to promote the common good effectively.

4.4.2 Responsibility of Everyone for Common Good

A pertinent question here is who oversees pursuing the common good? This is another way of asking the question, who should promote the common good? St. Thomas Aquinas provides the answer in his *Summa Theologica*. He puts the onus on leaders ("the sovereign") as the figures principally responsible for pursuit of the common good.[643] He taught that leaders of a political society ought to be devoted to the common good. In the same vein, leaders of an economic society ought to share this responsibility as their primary objective. Leaders of the society at all levels should hold up ownership of private property as one that has a social character, thereby promoting use of property not only for individual interests but also for the common good.[644]

Though leaders have the onus to pursue the common good, it involves everybody in the society. Every individual in the society must cooperate and invest his potentials toward developing and attaining the common

---

642 *See* POPE JOHN XXIII, ENCYCLICAL LETTER PACEM IN TERRIS *AAS 55 (1963)*, 272. [Human interdependence is increasingly and gradually spreading throughout the world. The unity of the human family, embracing people who enjoy equal natural dignity, implies a universal common good. This good call for an organization of the community of nations able to "provide for the different needs of men; this will involve the sphere of social life to which belong questions of food, hygiene, education, . . . and certain situations arising here and there, as for example . . . alleviating the miseries of refugees dispersed throughout the world, and assisting migrants and their families." The common good is always oriented towards the progress of persons: "The order of things must be subordinate to the order of persons, and not the other way around. This order is founded on truth, built up in justice, and animated by love. *See also* CATECHISM OF THE CATHOLIC CHURCH (1994), #s 1911& 1912; *see* GAUDIUM ET SPES, #s 28 & 84.

643 SAINT THOMAS AQUINAS, SUMMA THEOLOGICA IIa IIae Q. 58 Art. 6, *quoted* in CHARLES RODGERS, AN INTRODUCTION TO CATHOLIC SOCIAL TEACHING, *supra* note 57, at 27.

644 POPE PIUS XI, ENCYCLICAL LETTER, QUADRAGESIMO ANNO, (May 15, 1931) # 49 (property here includes profits from import-export transactions, as well as real estate or personal assets).

weal.[645] Every human activity must have the common good, also a superior goal. It is difficult to attain the common good, but it is achievable if all the human instincts are involved in its pursuit.[646] For this reason, the common good requires the untiring ability and effort of every human being to seek the good of others as though it were one's own good.[647]

Certain factors influence the need for the principle of the common good. These factors include the social conditions of each historical period, respect for the fundamental rights of the human person and respect for and the integral promotion of the person.[648] This notwithstanding, the main reasons the Catholic Church canvasses for the common good is none other than for the commitment to peace; for the purpose of the organization of the State's powers; for a sound juridical system; for the protection of the environment; and for the provision of essential services to all. Provision

---

645 POPE John XXIII, ENCYCLICAL LETTER MATER ET MAGISTRA, AAS *53 (1961)*, 417; POPE PAUL VI, APOSTOLIC.
LETTER OCTOGESIMA ADVENIENS, *46 AAS 63 (1971*), 433-435; CATECHISM OF THE CATHOLIC CHURCH (1994), 191; *See particularly*, CATECHISM OF THE CATHOLIC CHURCH (1994, # 1913 (indicating that "participation in the pursuit of the common good is the voluntary and generous engagement of a person in social interchange. It is necessary that all participate, each according to his position and role, in promoting the common good. This obligation is inherent in the dignity of the human person.").

646 CATECHISM OF THE CATHOLIC CHURCH (1994), # 1914 (stating that to achieve the common good through the active participation of everybody, each person must take charge of the areas for which one assumes personal responsibility, such as taking care of the education of family, conscientious work, *advocating for justice and the common good at every level irrespective of the person or institution involved.* Every individual should participate in, and advocate for, the good of others and of the society in general); See also POPE JOHN PAUL II, ENCYCLICAL LETTER CENTESIMUS ANNUS ("On the Hundredth Anniversary of *Rerum Novarum*"), (May 1, 1991), # 43.

647 Saint Thomas Aquinas places "knowledge of the truth about God" and "life in society" at the highest and most specific level of man's *"inclinationes naturales" (Summa Theologiae, I-II, q. 94, a. 2: Ed. Leon. 7, 170* (*"Secundum igitur ordinem inclinationum naturalium est ordo praeceptorum legis naturae ... Tertio modo inest homini inclinatio ad bonum secundum naturam rationis, quae est sibi propria; sicut homo habet naturalem inclinationem ad hoc quod veritatem cognoscat de Deo, et ad hoc quod in societate vivat").*

648 CATECHISM OF THE CATHOLIC CHURCH (1994), # 1907 (stating that the common good resides in the conditions for the exercise of the natural freedoms indispensable for the development of the human vocation, such as "the right to act according to a sound norm of conscience and to safeguard . . . privacy, and rightful freedom also in matters of religion"). See SECOND VATICAN ECUMENICAL COUNCIL, GAUDIUM ET SPES, *supra* note 75, # 26 § 2.

of essential services accrue from respect of human rights such as provision of food, housing, work, education, and access to culture, transportation, basic health care, the freedom of communication and expression, and the protection of religious freedom.[649] For the principle of the common good to operate on the international level, the Catholic Church enjoins every nation to work vehemently towards the common good of the whole of humanity worldwide.[650]

The Catholic Church continues her relentless effort in promoting the common good at all levels worldwide. In line with this mission of the Catholic Church, Pope Pius XI wrote:

> The distribution of created goods, which, as every discerning person knows, is laboring today under the gravest evils due to the huge disparity between the few exceedingly rich and the unnumbered propertyless, must be effectively called back to, and brought into conformity with, the norms of the common good, that is, social justice.[651]

When individuals gather in the community, national, regional, or international arena, they should place the highest emphasis on the common

---

[649] SECOND VATICAN ECUMENICAL COUNCIL, GAUDIUM ET SPES (PASTORAL CONSTITUTION ON THE CHURCH IN THE MODERN WORLD), *26, AAS 58 (1966), 1046-1047 (*indicating for the common good to be achievable, the social order must undergo constant improvement, be founded on the truth, built on justice, and enlivened by love; it should grow in freedom towards a more humane equilibrium. For this objective to be attained there must be a renewal of attitudes and far-reaching social changes); see id. *See also* POPE JOHN XXIII, ENCYCLICAL LETTER PACEM IN TERRIS (Peace on Earth), April 11, 1963, # 53.

[650] POPE JOHN XXIII, ENCYCLICAL LETTER MATER ET MAGISTRA, *AAS 53 (1961), 421.*

[651] POPE PIUS XI, ENCYCLICAL LETTER QUADRAGESIMO ANNO ("On Reconstruction of the Social Order"), May 15, 1931, # 58 (pointing out that the need for unreserved promotion of the common good is *ad rem* in a period where a "new kind of economic life that had arisen and the new developments of industry had gone to the point in most countries that human society was clearly becoming divided more and more into two classes. One class, very small in number, was enjoying almost all the advantages which modern inventions so abundantly provided; the other, embracing the huge multitude of working people, oppressed by wretched poverty, was vainly seeking escape from the straits wherein it stood."); *see id*, at 3.

good of all in their deliberations. Special and differential treatment of developing countries at the WTO should not have any hidden agenda. It should be for helping poor countries emerge from their poverty levels and to develop. The principle at stake is the pursuit of the good. Leaders of every society ought to pursue the common good.

4.4.3 Universal Destination of Goods

To better appreciate the principle of the common good, we must explore the significance of the principle of the universal destination of goods. The Catholic Church teaches that "God destined the earth and all it contains for all men and all peoples so that all created things would be shared fairly by all mankind under the guidance of justice tempered by charity."[652] The original source of the principle of the universal destination of goods is traceable to God the Creator, who created both the earth and man, and who gave the earth to human beings so that they might have dominion over it by their work and enjoy its fruits (Gen 1:28-29).

God gave the earth to the whole human race for the sustenance of all its members, without excluding or favoring anyone.[653]

> God destined man for civil society according to the dictates of his very nature. In the plan of the Creator, society is a natural means which man can and must use to reach his destined end. Society is for man and not vice versa. This must not be understood in the sense of liberalistic individualism, which subordinates society to

[652] CONGREGATION FOR THE DOCTRINE OF THE FAITH, INSTRUCTION LIBERTATIS CONSCIENTIA, *75, AAS 79 (1987),* 587.

[653] PONTIFICAL COUNCIL FOR JUSTICE AND PEACE, *supra* note 120, at 171 (stating further that this is the foundation of the universal destination of the earth's goods. The earth, because of its fruitfulness and its capacity to satisfy human needs, is God's first gift for the sustenance of human life. The human person cannot do without the material goods that correspond to his primary needs and constitute the basic conditions for his existence; these goods are indispensable if he is to feed himself, grow, communicate, associate with others, and attain the highest purposes to which he is called [362]. *See* POPE JOHN PAUL II, ENCYCLICAL LETTER CENTESIMUS ANNUS, *31, AAS 83 (1991), 831; POPE PIUS XII, Radio Message for the Fiftieth Anniversary of Rerum Novarum AAS 33 (1941), 199-200.*

> the selfish use of the individual, but only in the sense that by means of an organic union with society and by mutual collaboration the attainment of earthly happiness is placed within the reach of all. In a further sense, it is society that affords the opportunities for the development of all the individual and social gifts bestowed on human nature. These natural gifts have a value surpassing the immediate interests of the moment, for in society they reflect the divine perfection, which would not be true were man to live alone.[654]

The Catholic Church propagates the principle universal destination of goods with great vigor. Every human person has the natural and universal right to use the goods of the earth because God ordained it to be so. God gave the earth and its wealth to humans for their sustenance.[655] For this reason, the right to the common use of the goods of the earth is the "first principle of the whole ethical and social order" and "the characteristic principle of Christian social doctrine."[656] It is based on this perception that the Catholic Church feels bound in duty to specify the nature and characteristics of this principle and to make them such a huge part of its social mission.[657]

The universal destination of goods is a social justice principle that emphasizes a natural right inscribed in human nature.[658] It is an inalienable

---

654 POPE PIUS XI, ENCYCLICAL LETTER DIVINI REDEMPTOR, # 544.

655 PONTIFICAL COUNCIL FOR JUSTICE AND PEACE, *supra* note 120, at 171.

656 POPE JOHN PAUL II, ENCYCLICAL LETTER LABOREM EXERCENS, *19 AAS 73 (1981),* 525; POPE JOHN PAUL II, ENCYCLICAL LETTER SOLLICITUDO REI SOCIALIS, *42 AAS 80 (1988),* 573.

657 *See* PONTIFICAL COUNCIL FOR JUSTICE AND PEACE, *supra* note 120, at 173 (stating that universal destination and utilization of goods do not mean that everything is at the disposal of each person or of all people, or that the same object may be useful or belong to each person or all people. If it is true that everyone is born with the right to use the goods of the earth, it is likewise true that, to ensure that this right is exercised in an equitable and orderly fashion, regulated interventions are necessary, interventions that are the result of national and international agreements, and a juridical order that adjudicates and specifies the exercise of this right.)

658 PONTIFICAL COUNCIL FOR JUSTICE AND PEACE, *supra* note 120, at 171; *See also* SECOND VATICAN ECUMENICAL COUNCIL, GAUDIUM ET SPES *supra* note 75, # 69 (stating that God destined the earth and all it contains for all men and all peoples so that

right because it is inherent the human person.[659] The Catholic Church affirms this teaching further when Pope Paul VI reiterates that

> It is innate in individual persons, in every person, and has priority about any human intervention concerning goods, to any legal system concerning the same, to any economic or social system or method: "All other rights, whatever they are, including property rights and the right of free trade must be subordinated to this norm [the universal destination of goods]; they must not hinder it, but must rather expedite its application. It must be considered a serious and urgent social obligation to refer these rights to their original purpose."[660]

However, accessibility to the goods of the earth is not without some order. Each person must have access only to the level of wellbeing necessary for his full development.[661] Earthly goods are not at the disposal of each person or of all people without some order. Access to the goods of the earth is exercised in an equitable and orderly fashion. Because every person has equal access to earthly goods, certain institutions, particularly governments, intervene to harmonize the exercise of the right to these earthly goods. Governments use the methods of national, regional, and international agreements for this purpose. The governments also employ a juridical system that adjudicates and specifies the exercise of the right to the use of earthly goods.[662]

---

all created things would be shared fairly and by all humankind under the guidance of justice tempered by charity); POPE PIUS XII, ENCYCLICAL LETTER SERTUM LAETITIAE ("On the Hundred and Fiftieth Anniversary of the Establishment of the Hierarchy in the United States), *AAS 31, (1939)*, P. 642.

[659] POPE PIUS XII, Radio Message for the Fiftieth Anniversary of *Rerum Novarum,* AAS *33 (1941),* 199.

[660] POPE PAUL VI, ENCYCLICAL LETTER POPULORUM PROGRESSIO, *22, AAS 59 (1967),* 268; POPE PIUS XI, POPULORUM PROGRESSION ("On the Development of Peoples"), March 26, 1967, # 22

[661] PONTIFICAL COUNCIL OF JUSTICE AND PEACE, *supra* note 95, at 172

[662] *See id.* at # 173; *see generally* POPE PAUL VI, ENCYCLICAL LETTER POPULORUM PROGRESSIO.

By the principle of the universal destination of goods, the Catholic Church beckons to all peoples, nations, regional, and international organizations to make the origin and purpose of earthly goods as the basis for all economic vision.[663] Because of the Church's teaching authority, she invites all to employ moral values, particularly, fairness and solidarity in all economic systems in the world. Any effort aimed at harnessing earthly goods must eschew exclusion and exploitation but in the alternative, promote the wellbeing of all peoples.[664] In the exploitation and distribution of earthly goods, whoever is involved should always do so with certain moral values and common good as the foundation:

> The universal destination of goods requires a common effort to obtain for every person and for all peoples the conditions necessary for integral development, so that everyone can contribute to making a more humane world, "in which each individual can give and receive, and in which the progress of some will no longer be an obstacle to the development of others, nor a pretext for their enslavement."[665]

When the WTO's objective, *inter alia*, includes special and differential treatment of poor Members to rise to the level of developed Members, it is an encouraging development. But experience has shown that the special and differential treatment is structured in such a way that it is difficult to achieve its stated purpose. Part of what this book sets out to do is to formulate a way forward from the perspective of the theological principle of universal destination of earthly goods.

---

[663] POPE JOHN XXIII, ENCYCLICAL LETTER MATER ET MAGISTRA (On the Church as Mother and Teacher), May 15, 1961, # 43 (indicating that the right of every man to use these for his own sustenance is prior to every other economic right, even that of private property. The right to the private possession of material goods is admittedly a natural one; nevertheless, in the objective order established by God, the right to property cannot stand in the way of the axiomatic principle that "the goods which were created by God for all men should flow to all alike, according to the principles of justice and charity.").

[664] *See id.* at 174.

[665] See CONGREGATION FOR THE DOCTRINE OF THE FAITH, LIBERTATIS CONSCIENTIA, *90, AAS 79 (1987), 594*; See also PONTIFICAL COUNCIL FOR JUSTICE AND PEACE, *supra* note 120, at 175.

4.4.4 The Issue of Private Property

Human beings are enjoined to be fruitful, to multiply, and to subdue the earth.[666] In the execution of this divine assignment, human beings engage in labor and use their intelligence and industry. Through industry, that is, human work, an individual acquires a portion of the earth for his own possession. This is the origin of private property.[667] By virtue of ownership of private property or other forms of private ownership, an individual is able to express his personality; he is able to exercise his role in the society and in the economy.[668] Private property enhances an individual's exercise of his personal and family freedom. Private ownership of property is an opportunity for a person to exercise his individual responsibility, and "this constitutes one of the conditions for civil liberty."[669]

Notwithstanding the social security, the rights and services that the society provides for people, private ownership, and other forms of ownership constitute a source of security also. This applies to both ownership of earthly goods and the possession of professional skills necessary for the provision

---

[666] See Genesis 1:28.

[667] POPE JOHN PAUL II, ENCYCLICAL LETTER CENTESIMUS ANNUS, *31, AAS 83 (1991),* 832 (The original source of all that is good is the very act of God, who created both the earth and man, and who gave the earth to man so that he might have dominion over it by his work and enjoy its fruits (Gen 1:28). God gave the earth to the whole human race for the sustenance of all its members, without excluding or favoring anyone. *This is the foundation of the universal destination of the earth's goods.* The earth, because of its fruitfulness and its capacity to satisfy human needs, is God's first gift for the sustenance of human life. But the earth does not yield its fruits without a human response to God's gift without work. It is through work that man, using his intelligence and exercising his freedom, succeeds in dominating the earth and making it a fitting home. In this way, he makes part of the earth his own, precisely, the part which he has acquired through work; this is the origin of individual property. Obviously, he also has the responsibility not to hinder others from having their own part of God's gift; indeed, he must cooperate with others so that together all can dominate the earth.)

[668] SECOD VATICAN ECUMENICAL COUNCIL, GAUDIUM ET SPES, # 71.

[669] POPE LEO XIII, ENCYCLICAL LETTER RERUM NOVARUM, *AAS 23 (1890-1891),* PP. 643-646; POPE PIUS XI, ENCYCLICAL LETTER QUADRAGESIMO ANNOS, *AAS 23 (1931),* P. 191; Pope Pius XII, Radio Message for the Fiftieth Anniversary of *Rerum Novarum*, June 1, 1941, *ASS 33 (1941),* P. 199; Pope Pius XII, Christmas Message, (1942), *ASS 35, (1943),* p. 17; Pope Pius XII, Radio Message, September 1, 1944, *AAS 36, (1944*), p. 253; POPE JOHN XXIII, ENCYCLICAL LETTER MATER ET MAGISTRA, *AAS 53, (1961),* pp. 428ff.

of services. What this means is that private ownership of property is lawful since it does not hinder any form of public ownership.[670] A competent authority can even transfer private property to public ownership, but this must be within the parameters of the common good, and provided adequate compensation follows.[671] Private ownership is not to hinder the principle of the common good; otherwise, it loses its authenticity.[672]

The Catholic Church also brings knowledge of new economic systems and technological advancement to bear on the principle of the universal destination of goods. New economic systems and technological progress constitute a form of ownership. Ownership of knowledge, technology and know-how is decisive on issues concerning exploitation of earthly goods because the wealth of the industrialized nations is based much more on this kind of ownership than on natural resources.[673]

Social justice demands that technology and science ought to serve the primary needs of the human person. It ought not to be an opportunity

---

670 POPE PAUL II, ENCYCLICAL LETTER LABOREM EXERCENS, *14, AAS 73 (1981),* 613 [Christian tradition has never recognized the right to private property as absolute and untouchable. On the contrary, it has always understood this right within the broader context of the right common to all to use the goods of the whole of creation; the right to private property is subordinated to the right to common use, to the fact that goods are meant for everyone]; *See also* POPE LEO XIII, ENCYCLICAL LETTER RERUM NOVARUM, ACTA LEONIS XIII, 11 (1892), 102 (indicating that private property is not a property; what matters is a just regulation of it).

671 POPE PAUL VI, ENCYCLICAL LETTER POPULORUM PROGRESSIO, *22-23 AAS 59 (1967),* 268-269 (stating that private property, in fact, regardless of the concrete forms of the regulations and juridical norms relative to it, is in its essence only an instrument for respecting the principle of the universal destination of goods; in the final analysis, therefore, it is not an end but a means).

672 SECOND VATICAN ECUMENICAL COUNCIL, GAUDIUM ET SPES, *69, AAS 58 (1966),*1090 (stating that the human person "should regard the external things that he legitimately possesses not only as his own but also as common in the sense that they should be able to benefit not only him but also others." The universal destination of goods entails obligations on how goods are to be used by their legitimate owners. Individual persons may not use their resources without considering the effects that this use will have; rather, they must act in a way that benefits not only themselves and their family but also the common good. From this there arises the duty on the part of owners not to let the goods in their possession go idle and to channel them to productive activity, even entrusting them to others who are desirous and capable of putting them to use in production); See PONTIFICAL COUNCIL FOR JUSTICE AND PEACE, *supra* note 120, at 178.

673 POPE JOHN PAUL II, ENCYCLICAL LETTER CENTESIMUS ANNUS, *32, AAS 83 (1991), 83.2.*

for industrialized countries, which have ownership of scientific and technological progress, to exploit the poor countries that haven't such knowledge.

> New technological and scientific knowledge must be placed at the service of mankind's primary needs, gradually increasing humanity's common patrimony. Putting the principle of the universal destination of goods into full effect therefore, requires action at the international level and planned programs on the part of all countries. It is necessary to break down the barriers and monopolies, which leave so many countries on the margins of development, and to provide all individuals and nations with the basic conditions which will enable them to share in development.[674]

The Catholic Church supports ownership of private property as an aspect of the dignity of the human person insofar as such ownership respects the common good principle. The right to ownership of private property is not realizable, if there are no fair labor standards. Also, private property would be a fairy tale if WTO agreements are not directed in a way that recognizes the peculiar circumstances of workers in poor countries. Sermonizing about ownership of private property would tantamount to preaching to the choir, if international trade agreements are not made in respect of the dignity of the human person. In that case, the GATT-WTO system should make respect for equality of human dignity a fundamental issue in such a way as to know that a peasant farmer in Nigeria has the same dignity as a business executive at the Wall Street in New York.

4.4.5 Task of the Political Community

The Catholic Church teaches that the reason political authority exists is for society to achieve the common good. Therefore, Pope John XXIII

---

[674] PONTIFICAL COUNCIL FOR JUSTICE AND PEACE, supra note 120, at 179; *see also* POPE JOHN PAUL II, ENCYCLICAL LETTER CENTESIMUS ANNUS (On The Hundredth Anniversary Of *Rerum Novarum*), May 1, 1991, # 35.

taught "the attainment of the common good is the sole reason for the existence of civil authorities."[675] Without the political authority taking the lead in attaining the common good, individual persons cannot achieve it.[676] The state guarantees coherency, unity, and order in the civil society for the society to attain the common good. Political institutions are indispensable because, under normal circumstances, they guarantee material, cultural, moral, and spiritual goods in the society.[677] These goods are necessary for the full development of persons, families, or intermediate groups in the society.[678] Life in the society draws its meaning from the attainment of the common good.[679]

To attain the common good, the State should establish democratic structures. In doing this, decisions are not just to be made by most representatives elected by the people. Those responsible for government should interpret the common good of their country and not merely by guidelines streamlined by the majority. Decisions should also take into consideration the effective good of all the members of the community, including the minority.[680] This requirement is important because the principal tasks of the state are to establish and preserve order, guarantee justice, and promote the common good.[681]

---

675 POPE JOHN XXIII, ENCYCLICAL LETTER, PAEM IN TERRIS (April 11, 1963), # 54.

676 CATECHISM OF THE CATHOLIC CHURCH (1994), # 1910 (stating that each human community possesses a common good which permits it to be recognized as such; it is in the political community that its most complete realization is found. It is the role of the State to defend and promote the common good of civil society, its citizens, and intermediate bodies). See also id, at 1920 (indicating that every human community needs an authority in order to endure and develop).

677 SECOND VATICAN ECUMENICAL COUNCIL, GAUDIUM ET SPES, *74, AAS58 (1966),* 1095-1097; POPE JOHN PAUL II, ENCYCLICAL LETTER REDEMPTOR HOMINIS, *17, AAS 71 (1979),* 295-300.

678 CATECHISM OF THE CATHOLIC CHURCH (1994), # 1923 (indicating that political authority must be exercised within the limits of the moral order and must guarantee the conditions for the exercise of freedom).

679 POPE LEO XIII, ENCYCLICAL LETTER RERUM NOVARUM, *ACTA LEONIS XIII, 11 (1892),* 133-135; POPE PIUS XII, RADIO MESSAGE FOR THE FIFTIETH ANNIVERSARY OF RERUM NOVARUM, *AAS 33 (1941),* 200.

680 PONTIFICAL COUNCIL FOR JUSTICE AND PEACE, *supra* note 120, at 169; *See also* CATECHISM OF THE CATHOLIC CHURCH (1994), # 1908.

681 D.Q. McInerny, "The Social Thought of Jacques Maritain," *The Catholic Social Science Review* 12 (2007), p. 157.

For the state to serve its purpose naturally, legislators must, in constantly changing conditions, resort to the norms of morality, constitutional provisions, and the common good.[682] The executive branch should coordinate societal activities with discretion, in the spirit of the rule of law with a just consideration of circumstances which may arise. The courts must administer justice impartially without being influenced by favoritism or pressure. The good order of the society demands that individual citizens and intermediate bodies be effectively protected by the law in the exercise of their rights of fulfillment of their obligations.[683]

Discussing liberation theology in a conference in 1968 in Medellín, Colombia, the Latin American bishops emphasized that leaders ought to make decisions "on the basis of the common good rather than on the good of privileged persons."[684] This manner of making decisions is of great importance to international trade issues. Therefore, Professor Thompson observes that

> An inegalitarian power structure can turn either an export oriented policy or an import substitution strategy toward more inequality. It is not only trade policy that is important, but whose interests the policy is intended to serve.[685]

Concerning relations between states, the Church lays weight to the teaching that nations are the subjects of reciprocal rights and duties.

---

[682] POPE JOHN XXIII, ENCYCLICAL LETTER, PACEM IN TERRIS, # 65 (teaching that the inalienable rights of the human person are the basis of the moral legitimacy of every authority; by flouting them, or refusing to recognize them in its positive legislation, a society undermines its own moral legitimacy).

[683] POPE JOHN XXIII, ENCYCLICAL LETTER PACEM IN TERRIS, May 11, 1963, # 69.

[684] DAVID BOHR, CATHOLIC MORAL TRADITION, *supra* note 55, at 355. The Latin American Episcopal Conference had two meetings in 1968 at Medellín, Colombia, and in 1979 at Pueblo, Mexico, with themes centered on liberation theology. These two meetings produced two seminal documents in liberation theology. For a summary of these two documents, *see* Peter J. Henriot, S.J. *et al.*, (eds.), *Catholic Social Teaching: Our Best Kept Secret*, 134-143 (3rd ed. 1992).

[685] J. MILBURN THOMPSON, JUSTICE AND PEACE: A CHRISTIAN PRIMER 48 (1997), quoted in RAJ BHALA, *supra* note 56, at 426.

Their relationships between states must be harmonized in accordance with the dictates of truth, justice, willing cooperation, and freedom. The same law of nature that governs the life and conduct of individuals must also regulate the relations of political communities with one another. International relations must follow the dictates of the natural law, that is, the moral order that places human dignity and the common good above every other philosophy.[686]This book analyzes whether the WTO follows the precepts of natural law and whether the Holy See has done enough to remind the WTO to do so.

4.5 Third: The Principle of Subsidiarity

The Latin root of the term subsidiarity is the noun *subsidium*, which means *help, aid, support, promotion,* or *development687.* The principle of subsidiarity means the degree of aid or assistance needed to accomplish a task or meet an obligation.[688] The principle of subsidiarity promotes the dignity of the human person in his relations with the family, groups, associations, and other local territorial realities. These institutions are very necessary because they correspond to the very nature of the human person. Through participation in institutions or associations relating to economic, social, cultural, sports-oriented, recreational, professional, and political expressions, the human person achieves effective social growth.[689]

686 *Id.* at 80-84 [One of the principal imperatives of the common good is the recognition of the moral order and the unfailing observance of its precepts. "A firmly established order between political communities must be founded on the unshakable and unmoving rock of the moral law, that law which is revealed in the order of nature by the Creator Himself, and engraved indelibly on men's hearts.... Its principles are beacon lights to guide the policies of men and nations. They are also warning lights—providential signs—which men must heed if their laborious efforts to establish a new order are not to encounter perilous storms and shipwreck."] *See id.* at 85.

687 PONTIFICAL COUNCIL FOR JUSTICE AND PEACE, *supra* note 120, at (stating that based on this principle, all societies of a superior order must adopt attitudes of help [*subsidium*], that is, of support, promotion, and development with respect to lower-order societies, *i.e.*, communities. Excessive intervention by the state can threaten personal freedom and initiative. The principle of subsidiarity sets limits for state intervention). *See* CATECHISM OF THE CATHOLIC CHURCH (1994), #1885.

688 PONTIFICAL COUNCIL FOR JUSTICE AND PEACE, *supra* note 120, at 186.

689 *See* CATECHISM OF THE CATHOLIC CHURCH (1994), # 1882.

Human relationship is made possible by the creative subjectivity of the individual.[690] For this reason, *civil society* is understood as the sum of the relationships between individuals and intermediate social groupings.[691] "This network of relationships strengthens the social fabric and constitutes the basis of a true community of persons, making possible the recognition of higher forms of social activity."[692]

Individualism has no place in Catholic Social teaching. In the same vein, the principle of subsidiarity is opposed to all forms of collectivism.[693] The human person establishes relations that are characterized by mutual understanding and love with others. In their mutual co-existence, human beings ought to respect each person's dignity through identifying each person as a neighbor.[694] The duty of making oneself a good neighbor becomes more imperative with the presence of the less privileged.[695] With relations established in intermediate associations and institutions, the universal and inviolable rights and duties of the human person stand out.[696]

---

690 POPE JOHN PAUL II, ENCYCLICAL LETTER SOLLICITUDO REI SOCIALIS, *15 AAS 80 (1988), 529*; POPE PIUS XI, ENCYCLICAL LETTER QUADRAGESIMO ANNO *AAS 23 (1931), 203*; POPE JOHN XXIII, ENCYCLICAL LETTER MATER ET MAGISTRA *AAS 53 (1961), 439*; SECOND VATICAN ECUMENICAL COUNCIL, GAUDIUM ET SPES, 65, *AAS 58 (1966)*, 1086-1087; CONGREGATION FOR THE DOCTRINE OF THE FAITH, INSTRUCTION LIBERTATIS CONSCIENTIA, *73, 85-86 AAS 79 (1987),* 586, 592-593; POPE JOHN PAUL II, ENCYCLICAL LETTER CENTESIMUS ANNUS, *48 AAS 83 (1991),* 852-854; CATECHISM OF THE CATHOLIC CHURCH (1994), #s 1883-1885.

691 POPE PIUS XI, ENCYCLICAL LETTER QUADRAGESIMO ANNO AAS 23 (1931), 203; POPE JOHN PAUL II, ENCYCLICAL LETTER CENTESIMUS ANNUS, *48 AAS 83 (1991), 852-854*; CATECHISM OF THE CATHOLIC CHURCH (1994), # 1883.

692 POPE JOHN PAUL II, ENCYCLICAL LETTER CENTESIMUS ANNUS, *49 AAS 83 (1991), 854-856*; POPE JOHN PAUL II, ENCYCLICAL LETTER SOLLICITUDO REI SOCIALIS, *15 AAS 80 (1988),* 528-530.

693 *See* CATECHISM OF THE CATHOLIC CHURCH (1994), # 1885.

694 SECOND VATICAN ECUMENICAL COUNCIL, GAUDIUM ET SPES, *supra* note 75, # 1 & 27; *see also* CATECHISM OF THE CATHOLIC CHURCH (1994), # 1931 (indicating that everyone should look upon his neighbor, without any exception, as "another self," above all bearing in mind his life and the means necessary for living it with dignity).

695 *See* CATECHISM OF THE CATHOLIC CHURCH (1994), # 1932 (stating that serving oneself and being a neighbor to others and actively serving them becomes more urgent when it involves the disadvantaged, in whatever area this may be).

696 SECOND VATICAN ECUMENICAL COUNCIL, GAUDIUM ET SPES, *supra* note 75, # 27.

The family and the state correspond more directly to the nature of the human person.[697] They are necessary for his growth and development. The creation of voluntary associations and institutions at all levels, including national and international levels are therefore indispensable in societal life.[698] Participation in these associations and institutions is tantamount to socialization, which shows the natural tendency for human beings to associate with one another to attain goals that exceed individual capacities. The principle of subsidiarity helps develop the quality of a person, particularly his sense of initiative and responsibility, as well as guarantees his inalienable rights.[699]

On the level of international relations, the principle of subsidiarity that is inevitable in a situation where inequalities exist includes such a case as in the GATT/WTO system. Though the special and differential treatment is aimed at assisting poor countries to reach desired development in consonance with the objectives of the WTO, the discipline of subsidiarity must apply. When economic, institutional, and juridical assistance is rendered to developing countries, it should not be an avenue to restrict the existing space of the latter. Their initiative, freedom, and responsibility should not be compromised.[700] The principle of subsidiarity should apply in such a way as to primarily support poor Members of the WTO, and at the same time encourage their sense of initiative and responsibility.

4.6 Fourth: The Principle of Solidarity

---

[697] *See* CATECHISM OF THE CATHOLIC CHURCH (1994), # 1882.

[698] POPE JOHN XXIII, ENCYCLICAL LETTER MATER ET MAGISTRA, May 15, 1961, # 60 (indicating that the principle of subsidiarity is the expression of a natural, well-nigh irresistible urge in man to combine with his fellows for the attainment of aims and objectives which are beyond the means or the capabilities of single individuals. In recent times, this tendency has given rise to the formation everywhere of both national and international movements, associations, and institutions with economic, cultural, social, sporting, recreational, professional, and political ends).

[699] SECOND VATICAN ECUMENICAL COUNCIL, GAUDIUM ET SPES, supra note 75, # 25 § 2; POPE JOHN PAUL II, ENCYCLICAL LETTER CENTESIMUS ANNUS, # 12.

[700] PONTIFICAL COUNCIL FOR JUSTICE AND PEACE, *supra* note 120, at 186.

Ordinarily, the term solidarity means interdependence, but the principle of solidarity, as understood and propagated by the Catholic social teaching, takes the term "interdependence" to a higher level. The principle of solidarity is understood in terms of "friendship."[701] Solidarity invokes in all peoples the inspiration to build the bonds of common life. Solidarity creates the awareness of the bond of interdependence between individuals and peoples and among nations of the world. Solidarity highlights in a way the intrinsic social nature of the human person, the equality of all in dignity and rights, and the common path of individuals and peoples towards an ever more committed unity.[702]

Governments and their citizens have no excuse in any situation where solidarity is lacking. Advances in information and computer technologies have given rise to increased volumes of commerce and information exchange. Furthermore, technology advances have broken the barriers that used to impede relationships between people and nations who are separated by great distances and are unknown to each other.[703] But despite this achievement that technology has recorded, there continue to be huge inequalities between rich and poor countries.[704] Inequalities of this nature are "stoked also by various forms of exploitation, oppression and corruption that have a negative influence on the internal and international life of

---

[701] POPE JOHN PAUL II, ENCYCLICAL LETTER, SOLLICITUDO REI SOCIALIS (For the Twentieth Anniversary of *Populorum Progressio),* December 30, 1987, #s 38-40 [stating that Solidarity helps us to see the "other"-whether a person, people, or nation - not just as some kind of instrument with a work capacity and physical strength to be exploited at low cost and then discarded when no longer useful, but as our "neighbor," a "helper" (cf. Gen 2:18-20), to be made a sharer on a par with ourselves, in the banquet of life to which all are equally invited by God. This explains the importance of reawakening the religious awareness of individuals and peoples. Thus, the exploitation, oppression, and annihilation of others are excluded].

[702] The concept of *solidarity or interdependence* can be likened to the classical theme of socialization, repeatedly examined by the Church's social doctrine; See POPE JOHN XXIII, ENCYCLICAL LETTER MATER ET MAGISTRA, *AAS 53 (1961), 415-417;* SECOND VATICAN ECUMENICAL COUNCIL, GAUDIUM ET SPES, *42 AAS 58 (1966),* 1060-1061; POPE JOHN PAUL II, ENCYCLICAL LETTER LABOREM EXERCENS, *14-15 AAS 73 (1981),* 612-618.

[703] PONTIFICAL COUNCIL FOR JUSTICE AND PEACE, *supra* note 120, at 192.

[704] *See id* (stressing that the acceleration of interdependence between persons and peoples needs to be accompanied by equally intense efforts on the ethical-social plane, to avoid the dangerous consequences of perpetrating injustice on a global scale. This would have very negative repercussions even in the very countries that are presently more advantaged)

many States."[705] The GATT-WTO system has wonderful objectives, but in practice, injustice on a global scale continues to frustrate the realization of such objectives.[706]

4.6.1 Solidarity as a Social and Moral Principle of Humankind

The principle of solidarity, also articulated in terms of "social charity," is a demand of human and Christian brotherhood.[707] An arrangement that derogates from this natural order is inhuman.

> An error, today abundantly widespread, is disregard for the law of human solidarity and charity, dictated and imposed both by our common origin and by the equality in rational nature all men, whatever nation they belong to. This law is sealed by the sacrifice of redemption offered by Jesus Christ on the altar of the Cross to his heavenly Father, on behalf of sinful humanity.[708]

The principle of solidarity is both a social principle and a moral principle.[709] As a social principle, solidarity ought to dominate relationships between individuals and peoples, as well as nations. Relationships that

---

705 POPE JOHN PAUL II, ENCYCLICAL LETTER SOLLICITUDO REI SOCIALIS, *11-22 AAS 80 (1988),* 525-540.

706 Different institutions and organizations have applied different strategies with little or no solution. Therefore, this book endorses the ethical-social paradigm, though approaching it from the perspective of assessment of the Holy See's application of such on the international plane.

707 POPE JOHN PAUL II, ENCYCLICAL LETTER, SOLLICITUDO REI SOCIALIS, nos. 38-40; POPE JOHN PAUL II, CENTESIMUS ANNUS, no. 10.

708 POPE PIUS XII, ENCYCLICAL LETTER, SUMMI PONTIFICATUS (On the Unity of Human Society), October 20, 1939, AAS 31 (1939), # 423.

709 CATECHISM OF THE CATHOLIC CHURCH (1994), #s 1939-1942 (teaching that socio-economic problems can be resolved only with the help of all the forms of solidarity: solidarity of the poor among themselves, between rich and poor, of workers among themselves, between employers and employees in a business, and solidarity among nations and peoples. International solidarity is a requirement of the moral order; world peace depends in part upon this.); see *also* CATECHISM OF THE CATHOLIC CHURCH (1994), # 1941.

have followed patterns that are bereft of solidarity must be purified and transformed into structures of solidarity through the creation or appropriate modification of laws, market regulations, and juridical systems.[710]

Pope John Paul II teaches that awareness of interdependence among individuals and nations ought to create a moral attitude of solidarity with one another. He further observed that this awareness that arises out of international trade and many other cross-border events which occur daily,

> is not a feeling of vague compassion or shallow distress at the misfortunes of so many people, both near and far. On the contrary, it is a *firm and persevering determination* to commit oneself to the *common good* that is to say, the good of all and of each individual, because we are all really responsible for all. This determination is based on the solid conviction that what is hindering full development is that desire for profit and that thirst for power already mentioned. These attitudes and "structures of sin" are only conquered - presupposing the help of divine grace - by a *diametrically opposed attitude:* a commitment to the good of one's neighbor with the readiness, in the gospel sense, to "lose oneself" for the sake of the other instead of exploiting him, and to "serve him" instead of oppressing him for one's own advantage (cf. Mt 10:40-42; 20:25; Mk 10:42-45; Lk 22:25-27).[711]

On certain occasions, tensions arise between the individual and the society in determining the good of the individual and the good of all. It is often a challenge to the society to resolve such tension, and the reason for this difficulty is that the basis for human solidarity is forgotten. The basis for human solidarity in a political or economic society comes from a shared political or economic ideology. Professor Bhala observes that often, peoples' response wrongly assumes solidarity to be a human product, of

---

[710] JOHN PAUL II, ENCYCLICAL LETTER SOLLICITUDO REI SOCIALIS, 36, 37 *AAS 80 (1988)*, 561-564; John Paul II, Apostolic Exhortation *Reconciliatio et Paenitentia, 16 AAS 77 (1985)*, 213-217.

[711] POPE JOHN PAUL II, ENCYCLICAL LETTER, SOLLICITUDO REI SOCIALIS, # 38.

the intellect, of experience, or of both, whereas it is none of these. This misdirection also believes that political and economic leaders can create solidarity.[712]

> States and political philosophies and parties have the duty to encourage solidarity, but they cannot of themselves create it. It must be the product of a vision of life, which transcends that important sphere of secular life with which the state is concerned. It must be the product of a culture, of a philosophy or a theology, which the state cannot control.[713]

Such a resort to a common divine link among interested parties is the best strategy in resolving tension that arises because of selfishness. In the pursuit of a selfish interest, the most persuasive rationale for restraint is appreciating the love of others as oneself.[714] It is an acceptance of a shared origin in God and shared interest in God as "the measure of human purpose and happiness."[715] Pope Pius XII wrote in his *Summi Pontificatus* concerning this teaching:

> Scripture tells us how God made us in his own image and likeness. This is a marvelous vision that enables us to see the human race in the one common origin in God. Christ commanded us to love one another as he has loved us. In this perspective individuals are not isolated like grains and sand, but united by their very nature and eternal destiny.[716]

---

[712] RAJ BHALA, TRADE, DEVELOPMENT, AND SOCIAL JUSTICE, *supra* note 56, at 428.

[713] CHARLES RODGERS, AN INTRODUCTION TO CATHOLIC SOCIAL TEACHING, *supra* note 57, at 41.

[714] RAJ BHALA, TRADE, DEVELOPMENT, AND SOCIAL JUSTICE, *supra* note 56, at 430.

[715] See CHARLES RODGERS, AN INTRODUCTION TO CATHOLIC TEACHING, *supra* note 57, at 25.

[716] POPE PIUS XII, ENCYCLICAL LETTER, SUMMI PONTIFICATUS (1939) ¶¶ 36-42, *quoted in* CHARLES RODGERS, AN INTRODUCTION TO CATHOLIC SOCIAL TEACHING, *supra* 57 (emphasis added). The soundest basis for such solidarity is the truth that the whole human race is made in God's image and likeness, and that all men and women

When it is impossible for political and economic ideologies to produce a lasting solidarity, we resort to metaphysics to engender a transcendent vision as taught in the 1965 Second Vatican Ecumenical Council, *Gaudium et Spes*,

> Men, families and the various groups that make up the civil community are aware that they cannot achieve a truly human life by their own unaided efforts. They see the need for a wider community, with which each one makes his specific contribution every day toward an ever-broader realization of the common good. For this purpose, they set up a political community according to various forms. The political community exists, consequently, for the sake of the *common good*, in which it finds its full justification and significance, and the source of its inherent legitimacy. Indeed, the common good embraces the *sum of those conditions of the social life whereby men, families and associations more adequately and readily attain their own perfections.717*

Put another way, through solidarity, "we recognize human interdependence not only as a necessary fact but also as a positive value in our lives."[718] The full potential and dignity of the human person is realized through a life that he shares with others. Mutual benefit comes through just cooperation with others in society.[719] The consequence is a transformation from an inner attitude about solidarity, not manifested in action, to the engagement in external activities "that demonstrate our commitment to the well-being of others."[720]

---

are therefore entitled to be treated accordingly, to be given their rights and be expected to accept their responsibilities as sons and daughters of God. *Id.*

717 SECOND VATICAN ECUMENICAL COUNCIL, GAUDIUM ET SPES (1965), *quoted in* RAJ BHALA, TRADE, DEVELOPMENT, AND SOCIAL JUSTICE, *supra* note 56, at 429.

718 THOMAS MASSARO, LIVING JUSTICE, *supra* note 589, at 120.

719 *Id.*

720 *See id.* at 121. *See also* POPE JOHN XXIII, ENCYCLICAL LETTER *Pacem in Terris* (Peace on Earth) 1963, # 36 stating that human society must primarily be considered as something pertaining to the spiritual through which humans share their knowledge, and pass

Until the principle of solidarity is employed in the negotiations that go on in the GATT-WTO system, inequalities, exploitation, and injustice will continue to be the order of the day. Multilateralism as it is presently organized has not solved the problem of inequality between individuals and between nations. Rather, imbalance is on the increase. The imbalance in question involves the scandal of glaring inequalities not merely in the enjoyment of possessions, but in the exercise of power. The state of inequality between individuals and between nations does not only exist, but it is increasing.[721] Human interdependence is a human value that should guide every aspect of life in the society. The GATT-WTO system will be more goal-oriented and fairer if human interdependence is the guiding principle in all multilateral negotiations. When that principle is considered in every multilateral transaction, stalemates in international trade negotiations would reduce tremendously.

4.6.2 Solidarity and Common Growth of Humankind

The Catholic Church teaches that there is an intimate connection between solidarity and the common good, between solidarity and the universal destination of goods, between solidarity and equality among human beings and peoples, and between solidarity and peace in the world.[722] This is the reason why the Catholic Church supports ties that

---

on to others the best of their own cultural heritage expressed in mutual exchange of economic, social, and political values bereft of inequalities. This is explained by the marriage between the concepts of good neighbor and Charity. *See* foot note 73 above.

[721] *See* POPE JOHN XXIII, ENCYCLICAL LETTER *Mater et Magistra* (The Church as Mother and Teacher – Christianity and Social Progress) 1961, # 69, ENCYCLICAL LETTER *Pacem in Terris* (Peace on Earth) 1963, # 63; SECOND VATICAN ECUMENICAL COUNCIL, *Gaudium et Spes, supra* note 75, at 63, 71 & 88; POPE PAUL VI, ENCYCLICAL LETTER *Populorum Progressio* (On the Development of Peoples) 1967, # 8 & 9; POPE JOHN PAUL II, ENCYCLICAL LETTER *Dives in Misericordia* (Rich in Mercy) 1980, #11, ENCYCLICAL LETTER *Sollicitudo Rei Socialis* (On Social Concern on the Twentieth Anniversary of *Populorum Progressio)* 1980, nos. 9, 12-16, 28, 39, 42 & 44-45.

[722] POPE JOHN PAUL II, ENCYCLICAL LETTER SOLLICITUDO REI SOCIALIS, 17, 39, 45 *AAS 80 (1988),* 532-533, 566-568, 577-578. International solidarity too is required by the moral order; peace in the world depends in large part on this - SECOND VATICAN ECUMENICAL COUNCIL, GAUDIUM ET SPES, *83- 86 AAS 58 (1966),* 1107- 1110; POPE PAUL VI, ENCYCLICAL LETTER, POPULORUM PROGRESSIO, *48 AAS 59*

unite individuals and social groups in which they participate and share their natural gifts and exercise human freedom for common growth. It is an opportunity for men and women to engage in beneficial sharing with their neighbors beyond individual and interests as opposed to separation and fragmentation.[723] The principle of solidarity has the character of inspiring willingness in a person to give himself for the good of his neighbor. It makes a person live a life that goes beyond any selfish interest.[724]

Furthermore, the principle understanding of solidarity requires that women and men recognize and have an awareness of the fact that they are debtors to the society in which they live. The reason they are debtors is because of the conditions of everyday life, made by a legacy of our culture and of all the components that society has produced, such as knowledge, technology, and material and immaterial goods. Also, they must recognize the social interaction of humanity so that present and future generations

---

(1967), 281; Pontifical Commission IUSTITIA ET PAX, At the Service of the Human Community: an Ethical Approach to the International Debt Question (27 December 1986), I, 1, Vatican Polyglot Press, Vatican City, 1986, p. 11; CATECHISM OF THE CATHOLIC CHURCH (1994), #s 1941 & 2438.

[723] Solidarity is one of the basic principles of *Rerum Novarum* (See POPE JOHN XXIII, ENCYCLICAL LETTER MATER ET MAGISTRA, *AAS 53 [1961], 407*). "What we nowadays call the principle of solidarity ... is frequently stated by Pope Leo XIII, who uses the term 'friendship', a concept already found in Greek philosophy. Pope Pius XI refers to it with the equally meaningful term 'social charity'. Pope Paul VI, expanding the concept to cover the many modern aspects of the social question, speaks of a 'civilization of love.'" (POPE JOHN PAUL II, ENCYCLICAL LETTER CENTESIMUS ANNUS, *10 AAS 83 [1991], 805*); Solidarity is one of the basic principles of the entire social teaching of the Church (CONGREGATION FOR THE DOCTRINE OF THE FAITH, INSTRUCTION LIBERTATIS CONSCIENTIA, 73 AAS 79 [1987], 586). Starting with Pius XII (ENCYCLICAL LETTER SUMMI PONTIFICATUS, *AAS 31 [1939], 426-427*), the term solidarity is used ever more frequently and with ever broader meaning: from that of "law" in the same encyclical to that of "principle" (POPE JOHN XXIII, ENCYCLICAL LETTER MATER ET MAGISTRA, *AAS 53 [1961], 407*), that of "duty" (POPE PAUL VI, ENCYCLICAL LETTER POPULORUM PROGRESSIO, *17, 48: AAS 59 [1967]*, 265-266, 281) and that of "value" (POPE JOHN PAUL II, ENCYCLICAL LETTER SOLLICITUDO REI SOCIALIS, *38 AAS 80 [1988]*, 564-566), and finally that of "virtue" (POPE JOHN PAUL II, ENCYCLICAL LETTER SOLLICITUDO REI SOCIALIS, 38, *40 AAS 80 [1988]*, 564-566, 568-569).

[724] CONGREGATION FOR CATHOLIC EDUCATION, GUIDELINES FOR THE STUDY AND TEACHING OF THE CHURCH'S SOCIAL DOCTRINE IN THE FORMATION OF PRIESTS, 38, Vatican Polyglot Press, Rome 1988, pp. 40-41.

can "share the same gift in solidarity."[725] In other words, sharing of the gifts of the principle of solidarity is intergenerational in nature. Wherever a person finds oneself, sharing one's gifts in social interaction and moderated by respect for human dignity is the soundest way to make the human person grow.

As Members of the WTO, what promotes common growth is the readiness of the Members to imbibe the principles of cooperation and create fairer and more humane conditions of interaction in international trade. The principle of solidarity can only promote common growth of humankind when industrialized countries see themselves practically as indebted to the poor Members of the WTO in such a way as to enable them, through trade negotiations, to rise from their hopeless situations. Where this does not happen, we can conclude that growth is not realizable within the parameters of the GATT-WTO system.

4.7 Fifth: Preferential Option for the Poor

The Catholic Church emphasizes concern for those falling below some generally agreed-upon standard. The phrase "option for the poor" has its roots in the Medellin Conference of Latin American bishops in 1968.[726] This phrase, "option for the poor," generated a lot of controversies.[727] One

---

[725] PONTIFICAL COUNCIL FOR JUSTICE AND PEACE, *supra* note 120, at 195.

[726] Though a clear-cut expression of this phrase is not found in the documents of the 1968 Medellin Conference in Colombia, it was at that Conference that the discussion started. It was at Pueblo, Mexico, in 1979 (10 years later) that the Latin American bishops adopted a clear and prophetic option expressing preference for and solidarity with the poor. See Henry Volken, S.J., "Preferential Option for the Poor," in *Promotio Justitiae,* No. 29, January 1984, pp. 11-26, at 15. However, "the notion of the preferential option for those who are weak and vulnerable has been present within the Christian tradition from the very start," because "the ministry of Jesus, in both words and deeds, was deeply wrapped up with this commitment to the wellbeing of the least fortunate." See THOMAS MASSARO, LIVING JUSTICE: CATHOLIC SOCIAL TEACHING IN ACTION, *supra* note 584, at 158

[727] Some people saw the phrase as "summary and symbol of the Catholic Church's new approach to the social question; others saw it as a way the Catholic Church took sides in a class struggle as opposed to Marxist's class option; still others interpret the term "option" as suggesting the English word "optional," which is indicative of fundamental scriptural commitment. *See* DONAL DORR, OPTION FOR THE POOR: A HUNDRED YEARS OF VATICAN SOCIAL TEACHING, Orbis Books, Maryknoll, New York, 1983, p. 209 (stating that those who favor the phrase "option for the poor" see it as a way that the Catholic

month before the Second Vatican Council, Pope John XXIII stressed that the Church's concern for the underdeveloped world is because the Catholic Church is "the Church of all, and especially the Church of the poor."[728] Pope John Paul II was emphatic on the issue of preference for the poor though with more tilt toward a better definition of the phrase originally used.[729] Pope John Paul II did not depart from identifying the Church as "the Church of the poor," but he made important clarifications concerning the meaning of the phrase, "option for the poor," which was variously misinterpreted.

In *Ecclesia in Asia*, Pope John Paul II affirmed the preference for the poor explaining that

> In seeking to promote human dignity, the Church shows a preferential love of the poor and the voiceless, because

---

Church commits itself more in promoting social justice). It is obvious that no one would ignore the authentic demands to take the poor more seriously than any other segment of the society, to unite with their needs and their demands . . .. We see the neighbor whom we must love as ourselves pre-eminently in the poor. God has more than a preferential option for the poor. . . What is beyond debate is the straightforward law that obligates us to reduce inequalities at our own expense, to do nothing that widens the gap between the rich and the poor. This is no mere "preferential option for the poor;" it is a plain identification with them. See Arnold Jacob, "The Bishops and the Poor: A Jewish Critique," in *Strain*, quoted in FRED KAMMER, S.J., DOING FAITHJUSTICE: AN INTRODUCTION TO CATHOLIC SOCIAL THOUGHT, Paulist Press, New York, 2004, p. 268.

[728] *See* GUSTAVO GUTIÉRREZ, "The Church of the Poor," in *The Month,* July 1989, p. 264. Other Popes that later emphasized this point include Pope Paul VI who used the phrase "a preferential love of the poor," Pope John Paul II restated the phrase as, "preferential yet not exclusive love of the poor," obviously to correct whatever misinterpretations people have about the phrase. See FRED KAMMER, DOING FAITHJUSTICE, *supra* note 727, at 145-146.

[729] See Jean-Yves Calvez, S.J., "The Preferential Option for the Poor: Where Does it Come for Us?" in *Studies in the Spirituality of Jesuits*, Vol. 21, No. 2, March 1989, p. 23. Here, Jean-Yves states, *inter alia* that, "... the Pope, in a whole series of addresses in 1984-1985 was rather chagrined that he could have given the impression of not believing in the preferential option for the poor, or of not believing in it very strongly. To a group of cardinals in Rome, December 21, 1984, the Pope emphasized: "This option which is emphasized today with particular force by the episcopacy of Latin America, I have confirmed repeatedly.... I gladly seize this occasion to repeat that engagement with the poor constitutes a dominant motif of my pastoral activity, a concern that is daily and ceaselessly part of my service of the people of God. I have made and I do make this option. I identify myself with it. I feel it could not be otherwise, since it is the eternal message of the Gospel. This is the option Christ made, the option made by the apostles, the option of the Church throughout its two thousand years of history."

> the Lord has identified himself with them in a special way (cf. Mt. 25:40). This love excludes no one, but simply embodies a priority of service to which the whole Christian tradition bears witness.[730]

Though the class of the "poor" is dominated by the materially deprived, there are other "poor" people for whom a preference is to be given.

> The special option for the poor, far from being a sign of particularism or sectarianism, manifests the universality of the Church's being and mission. *This option excludes no one.* This is why the Church cannot express this option by the means of reductive categories, which would make this preference a partisan choice and a source of conflict.[731]

The above citation makes a lot of sense since a general definition of the term "poor" can include those who may not be materially deprived, but suffer injustice. It is understandable why the term "poor" can be given a general definition to include those who may not be suffering any form of material deprivation, but are rather suffering injustice. It will be important to add also that "option for the poor" includes those who are materially affluent, but are ignorant of Christian principles of social justice. This important lack in their lives is a sign of spiritual and social poverty. The significance of such an inclusive definition of the term "poor" is for a deeper understanding of why the poor need a preference.

In the first place, the Church describes the class of poor people as the "innumerable multitude of people - children, adults, and the elderly suffering under the intolerable burden of poverty; many millions of people who are deprived of hope in many parts of the world."[732] The Church's

---

[730] Pope John Paul II, "Ecclesia in Asia," November 6, 1999, # 34 in *Origins*, Vol. 29, No. 23, November 18, 1999, p. 376.

[731] CONGREGATION FOR THE DOCTRINE OF THE FAITH, LIBERTATIS CONSCIENTIA supra note 560, # 68 *quoted in* CHARLES RODGERS, AN INTRODUCTION TO CATHOLIC SOCIAL TEACHING, *supra* 57, at 35 (emphasis added).

[732] POPE JOHN PAUL II, ENCYCLICAL LETTER, SOLLICITUDO REI SOCIALIS (On Social Concern), (December 30, 1987), # 13.

assessment is based on the various sectors of the society, such as production and distribution of foodstuffs, hygiene, health and housing, availability of drinking water, working conditions (especially for women), life expectancy, and other economic and social indicators.[733]

Other forms of poverty consist of deprivations. The Church finds the general picture very disappointing, considering the huge gap between the developed nations and poor nations.[734] A perfect example is the denial or abuse of human rights, such as the right to religious freedom, the right to share in the building of society, the freedom to organize and to form unions, or to take initiative in economic matters.[735] Also in economic issues, the dignity of the individual has been relegated to the background due to exploitation and marginalization of workers in the productive systems and other similar scenarios. This is mostly the plight of Third World countries.[736]

Pope John Paul II also stated that those involved in this poverty include agricultural and industrial workers who are materially deprived in comparison with some agreed-upon minimum standard. And Pope Leo XIII had earlier declared that "wage earners are numbered among the multitude of the poor," and because of this, they need special attention of governmental authorities responsible for acting on behalf of the common good.[737]

Getting down to brass tacks, and calling the minds of those in authority to the ugly situation faced by many farmers, Pope John Paul II spoke about farm workers whose toils involve

> Considerable difficulties, including unremitting and sometimes exhausting physical effort and a lack of appreciation on the part of society, to the point of making agricultural people feel that they are social outcasts and of

---

[733] *See id.* at 14.

[734] *Id.*

[735] *See id.* at 15

[736] POPE JOHN PAUL II, ENCYCLICAL LETTER, CENTESIMUS ANNUS (On the Hundredth Anniversary of Rerum Novarum), at 33 (May 1, 1991).

[737] POPE LEO XIII, ENCYCLICAL LETTER, RERUM NOVARUM (On the Condition of Working Classes), May 15, 1891, ¶¶ 37-38, *quoted in* CHARLES RODGERS, AN INTRODUCTION TO CATHOLIC SOCIAL TEACHING, supra note 57, at 35.

> speeding up the phenomenon of their mass exodus from the countryside to the cities and unfortunately to still more dehumanizing living conditions. Added to this are the lack of adequate professional training and of proper equipment, the spread of a certain individualism, and also *objectively unjust situations.* In certain developing countries, millions of people are forced to cultivate the land belonging to others and are exploited by the big landowners, without any hope of ever being able to gain possession of even a small piece of land of their own. There is a lack of forms of legal protection for the agricultural workers themselves and for their families in case of old age, sickness or unemployment. Long days of hard physical work are paid miserably. Land, which could be cultivated, is left abandoned by the owners. Legal titles to possession of a small portion of land that someone has personally cultivated for years are disregarded or left defenseless against the "land hunger" of more powerful individuals or groups.[738]

The Social Justice Theory of the Catholic Church teaches that the primary moral principle is human dignity. This being the case, she frowns at any degradation of that dignity. Pope John Paul II taught "poverty and deprivation are unworthy of the human person."[739] To fight this type of abuse of the dignity of the human person, the Church teaches the use of preferences enshrined in law. The second moral principle identifies human solidarity as a basis for pursuit of the common good. Pope John Paul II traces the connection between human solidarity, on the one hand, and assistance for the poor, on the other hand:

> The exercise of solidarity within each society is valid when its members recognize one another as persons. Those who

---

[738] POPE JOHN PAUL II, ENCYCLICAL LETTER, LABOREM EXERCENS (On Human Work), September 14, 1981, # 21 (emphasis original); See also RAJ BHALA, *supra* note 56, at 435.

[739] *See id.* at 48

> are more influential because they have a greater share of goods and common services should feel responsible for the weaker and be ready to share with them all they possess. The same criterion is applied, by analogy, in international relationships. Interdependence must be transformed into solidarity, based upon the principle that the goods of creation are meant for all. That which human industry produces through the processing of raw materials, with the contribution of work, must serve equally for the good of all.[740]

The analogy to preferences in international trade law is obvious: they are a product of solidarity. Rules on special and differential treatment constitute a legalized preference borne of solidarity among WTO Members, and, in particular, of rich Members with poor Members.[741] In addition to appeal to human dignity and to the responsibility of the rich as a rationale for the preferential option for the poor, the Old Testament legal codes can buttress those points. Examples include legal codes such as the Decalogue (*Exodus* 20:1-17) and the Book of the Covenant (*Exodus* 20:22-23:33). They articulate a form of social justice that embraces consideration of the poor.[742]

In his Encyclical Letter, *Sollicitudo Rei Socialis,* Pope John Paul II highlights the preferences for the poor with famous scriptural stories.

---

[740] POPE JOHN PAUL II, ENCYCLICAL LETTER, SOLLICITUDO REI SOCIALIS (On Social Concern), December 30, 1987, # 39.

[741] RAJ BHALA, TRADE, DEVELOPMENT, AND SOCIAL JUSTICE, *supra* note 56, at 433.

[742] *Id.* In line with the Old Testament endorsement of the preferential option for the poor, the New Testament provides its own rationale. Jesus gave a compelling example of the way to take care of the needs of the poor. Practical instances of Jesus' preferences for the poor are found in his teachings such as the Beatitudes (Mt. 5:3-11; Luke 6:20-26, the parable of the rich man and Lazarus (Luke 16:19-31, the parable of the Good Samaritan (Luke 10:29-37), and Jesus' teaching on inviting the poor as guests for lunch or dinner (Luke 14:12-14). However, Jesus' "paschal mystery [i.e., the Easter Mystery, which is the mystery of the Passion, Resurrection, and ascension of Christ] is the ultimate ground and source of Catholic social teaching." See DAVID BOHR, CATHOLIC MORAL TRADITION, *supra* note 55, at 355-356. Expressions of the preferences are also recorded in Jesus' lifestyle of charity. That lifestyle is obvious in the scriptural accounts of his healing miracles. These healing stories include the cleansing of a leper (Mark 1:40-42), the healing of the paralytic (Mark 2:3-12), and so on.

> [G]iven the worldwide dimension which the social question has assumed, this love of preference for the poor, and the decisions which it inspires in us, cannot but embrace the immense multitudes of the hungry, the needy, the homeless, those without medical care and, above all, those without hope of a better future. It is impossible not to take account of the existence of these realities. To ignore them would mean becoming like the "rich man" who pretended not to know the beggar Lazarus lying at his gate (cf. Lk 16:19-31).[743]

Placing more emphasis on this preferential option for the poor, Pope John Paul II wrote in the same encyclical *Sollicitudo Rei Socialis* that, *the love of preference for the poor* is a *special form* of primacy in the exercise of Christian charity" that "affects the life of each Christian inasmuch as he or she seeks to imitate the life of Christ."[744] The preferential option for the poor also applies to our *social responsibilities* and hence our manner of living, and to the logical decisions to be made concerning the ownership and use of goods."[745] Those decisions must be informed not only by a sense of the validity and necessity of private property, but also by the characteristic principle of Christian social doctrine," namely, that "the goods of this world are *originally meant for all*."[746] In performing our social responsibilities in an economic society, we are to keep in mind that "private property . . . is under a '*social mortgage*,' which means that it has an intrinsically social function, based upon and justified precisely by the principle of the universal destination of goods."[747]

---

[743] POPE JOHN PAUL II, ENCYCLICAL LETTER, SOLLICITUDO REI SOCIALIS ("On Social Concern"), December 30, 1987, # 42

[744] POPE JOHN PAUL II, ENCYCLICAL LETTER, SOLLICITUDO REI SOCIALIS ("On Social Concern"), December 30, 1987, # 42 (emphasis Original)

[745] POPE JOHN PAUL II, ENCYCLICAL LETTER, SOLLICITUDO REI SOCIALIS ("On Social Concern"), December 30, 1987, # 42 (emphasis Original)

[746] POPE JOHN PAUL II, ENCYCLICAL LETTER, SOLLICITUDO REI SOCIALIS ("On Social Concern"), December 30, 1987, # 42 (emphasis Original)

[747] POPE JOHN PAUL II, ENCYCLICAL LETTER, SOLLICITUDO REI SOCIALIS ("On Social Concern"), December 30, 1987, # 42 (emphasis added); See also RAJ BHALA, supra note 56, at 435.

The United States Catholic bishops highlight the significance of the preferential option for the poor in teaching that

> Far from being an arbitrary restriction on the life of the people, these codes made life in community possible. The specific laws of the covenant protect human life and property, demand respect for parents and the spouses and children of one's neighbor, and manifest a special concern for the vulnerable members of the community: widows, orphans, the poor, and strangers in the land. . .. The codes of Israel reflect the norms of the covenant: reciprocal responsibility, mercy, and truthfulness. They embody a life in freedom from oppression: worship of the One God, rejection of idolatry, mutual respect among people, *care and protection for every member of the social body*. Being *free and being a co-responsible community* is God's intentions for us.[748]

From the foregoing, one can rightly infer that preference for the poor not only makes life in the community possible, but it also promotes the dignity of the human person, as well as inspires people to conduct their social responsibilities pragmatically. The question at this juncture is how it applies in the context of the GATT-WTO system. An available record shows that roughly 80 percent of the WTO Members are underdeveloped countries. Most of the rich WTO Members are (officially or not) predominantly Christian, at least historically or traditionally. Therefore, by their sufferings (presently or in the past), their traditional religious backgrounds, or (for some countries) both, virtually every WTO Member is able to grasp the importance of the preferential option for the poor. It is almost impossible for the GATT-WTO system to realize its objectives without some sort of manifest preference for the poor.[749]

---

[748] National Conference of U.S. Bishops, Economic Justice for All: A Pastoral Letter on Catholic Social Teaching and the U.S. Economy, 1986, # 36, available at http://www.usccb.org/upload/economic_justice_for_all.pdf

[749] RAJ BHALA, TRADE, DEVELOPMENT, AND SOCIAL JUSTICE *supra,* note 56, at 434.

4.8 Dialectic between the Common Good and Utilitarianism

The term "utilitarianism" is derived from the Latin verb *uti* ("to use," "to take advantage of"), and the adjective *utilis* (meaning "useful"). True to its etymology, utilitarianism as an ethical concept and theory emphasizes "the usefulness (or otherwise) of any or every human activity." What is useful is that it gives pleasure and excludes its opposite; pleasure is the essential ingredient of human happiness.[750]

The original leader of the Utilitarians was an English philosopher Jeremy Bentham (1748-1832). John Stuart Mill (1806-1873) came later to refine Bentham's utilitarian thought. For Jeremy Bentham, society must be made more rational, and the first step in this direction is to recognize that people act out of self-interest. Moreover, everyone has an interest in experiencing pleasure and avoiding pain.[751] "Nature has placed mankind under the governance of two sovereign masters, pain and pleasure. It is for them alone to point out what we ought to do, as well as to determine what we shall do."[752] Jeremy Bentham thought that this is simply a fact of human nature, and there is nothing we can do to change it. However, once we understand that all people seek pleasure and avoid pain in everything they do, we can take steps to be better pleasure-seekers and pain-avoiders.[753]

It is helpful, at this point, to analyze Jeremy Bentham's socio-economic thought in which he inferred that the business of government is to promote the greatest happiness of the greatest number of people in society.

> Bentham did not mean that we should seek pleasure in immediate gratification – in getting drunk, for example – because the pain we or others suffer later will probably outweigh the short-term pleasure. He meant, rather,

---

[750] KAROL WOJTYLA, LOVE AND RESPONSIBILITY (trans. by H.T. WILLETTS), Ignatius Press, 1993, p. 35.

[751] Terence Ball & Richard Dagger, *Political Ideologies and the Democratic Ideal* (6th ed.), Pearson Education Inc., 2006, pp. 65-66.

[752] JEREMY BENTHAM, INTRODUCTION TO THE PRINCIPLES OF MORALS AND LEGISLATION, Hafner, New York, 1948, p. 1.

[753] TERENCE BALL & RICHARD DAGGER, POLITICAL IDEOLOGIES, *supra* note 751, at 66.

> that we should seek utility. Something has utility – a hammer for a carpenter, for instance, or money for almost everyone – if it helps someone to do what he or she wants. Because people want to be happy, utility promotes happiness.[754]

John Stuart Mill refined Jeremy Bentham's thought from a plain hedonistic version. For J.S. Mill,

> "Utility" or the "greatest happiness principle" holds that actions are right in proportion as they tend to promote happiness; wrong as they tend to produce the reverse. By happiness is intended pleasure and the absence of pain….[755]

Thus, utilitarianism proposes two ethical principles. First, the end goal of life is happiness. The reason for this is that human beings universally desire happiness. The quest for happiness is natural in human beings, and this is the reason they desire it. Second, the rightness of acts is determined by their contributions to happiness.[756] This makes utilitarianism a form of teleology, that is, *teleos* (the end) determines what is right. The right is determined by calculating the amount of good to be produced. Thus the "good" is prior to the "right" and the right is dependent upon it.[757] When utilitarianism is put in the perspective of international trade, developed Members of the WTO can do anything to achieve happiness for themselves at the expense of poor Members. This will make the special and differential treatment objective sterile.

Utilitarianism sounds plausible, but it has several loopholes. The basic idea of utilitarianism that actions are determined to be right or wrong depending on if they promote happiness has obvious implications when the question of justice comes into play. Traditional notions of

---

[754] *Id.*

[755] John Stuart Mill, *Utilitarianism,* New York, Bobbs-Merrill, 1966, p. 10.

[756] Karen Lebacqz, *Six Theories of Justice: Perspectives from Philosophical and Theological Ethics,* Augsburg Pub. House, 1986, p. 16.

[757] *Id. See also* FRANK LOVETT, RAWLS'S A THEORY OF JUSTICE, Continuum Int'l Pub. Group, 2011, pp. 30-37.

justice appear to be flouted by a theory that claims the "right" act is whatever maximizes happiness for a greater number of persons. This is discriminatory. Consideration of happiness overrides individual rights or claims. For instance, if the bloodshed of a threatened race riot could be averted by the framing and lynching of an innocent person, the utilitarian would say it is right to do so.[758] Thus, so long as the "greater good" requires it, all individual rights and claims will be ignored. John Rawls argues that this is unjust.[759]

Other objections to the utilitarian ethics abound. First, it is not always clear what the outcome of an action will be, nor is it always possible to determine who will be affected by it. Judging an action by the outcome is therefore hard to do beforehand. Second, the calculations required to determine the right action may be both complicated and time consuming. Many occasions will not permit the time, and many individuals may not even be capable of the calculations. Since the greatest good for the greatest number is described in aggregate terms, good may be achieved under conditions that are harmful to some, so long as that harm is balanced by a greater good. The theory fails to acknowledge any individual rights that could not be violated for the sake of the greatest good. Indeed, even the murder of an innocent person would seem to be condoned if it served the greater number. This is opposed to social justice and, therefore, unacceptable in interpersonal relationships.

Utilitarianism, like other forms of philosophical reasoning, is interested in conceptual and analytic categories. Unfortunately, utilitarianism has obvious logical lapses as can be seen in the foregoing. The uniqueness of the Catholic social teaching is seen in its broad understanding of justice, which goes beyond commutative exchange into distributive and social justice, discussed above. Catholic social doctrine supplies the deficiencies of utilitarian ethics by focusing more directly on social problems and

---

[758] KAREN LEBACQZ, SIX THEORIES OF JUSTICE, *supra* note 756, at 17-18.

[759] JOHN RAWLS, A THEORY OF JUSTICE, Cambridge, Harvard University Press, 1971, pp. 15 & 27 (indicating that utilitarianism violates the demands of justice by permitting losses to some to be compensated by gains to others. It may be expedient, but it is not just that some should have less in order that others may prosper. Utilitarianism appears not to respect differences between persons).

concrete issues of justice, which tend toward the realization of the common good.[760] This makes it a better and more acceptable approach.

The Catholic social teaching is rooted in the following principles: (1) the dignity of the human person based on equality and respect of such; (2) the social nature of human beings; and (3) the universal destination of goods.[761] The dignity of the human person stems from the basic fact that he is created in the image of God. The transcendental worth of every individual is the foundation on which social teaching ought to be based. People are prior to institutions and institutions exist for the people, not the other way around. Human beings have inalienable rights which neither the state nor any institution has authority to abuse.

The principle of the common good is such that individualism has no place in the Catholic social teaching.[762] The dignity of the human person is only realizable in the community with others.[763] Also, the dignity of the human person, which has the feature of equality, requires the pursuit of the common good. The common good comprises "the total of social conditions which allow people, either as a group or as individuals, to reach their fulfillment more fully and more easily.[764] Every socio-economic and

---

760 *See* J. Brya Hehir, "John Paul II: Continuity and Change in the Social Teaching of the Church," in John W. Houch & Oliver F. Williams (ed.), *Co-Creation and Capitalism: John Paul's Laborem Exercens,* Lanham, Md. University Press, 1983, p. 124 (stating that modern tradition on Catholic social teaching which began in 1891 with Pope Leo XIII's encyclical *Rerum Novarum* and later on, other Papal encyclicals, conciliar documents, and other efforts, provides a systematic, normative theory relating to concrete social conditions of human beings).

761 The principle of common good is explained from the perspective of the universal destination of goods. At the moment of creation, God destined the earth and all it contains for the good of all peoples to be shared fairly by all humankind under the principles of justice and charity. *See* SECOND VATICAN ECUMENICAL COUNCIL, GAUDIUM ET SPES supra note 75, at # 69. God gave the earth to the whole human family for the sustenance of all its members, without excluding anyone. This is why Catholic social doctrine makes the common use of the goods of the earth "the first principle of the whole ethical and social order." This is also "the characteristic principle of the Christian social order." See PONTIFICAL COUNCIL FOR JUSTICE AND PEACE, supra note120, at 171; POPE JOHN PAUL II, ENCYCLICAL LETTER, LABOREM EXERCENS (On Human Work), September 14, 1981, # 19; POPE JOHN PAUL II, ENCYCLICAL LETTER, SOLLICITUDO REI SOCIALIS (On Social Concern), December 30, 1987, # 42.

762 *See* CATECHISM OF THE CATHOLIC CHURCH (1994), #1928.

763 *See* CATECHISM OF THE CATHOLIC CHURCH (1994), # 1926.

764 *See* CATECHISM OF THE CATHOLIC CHURCH (1994), # 1906.

political decision must respect the principle of the common good. Thus, the fundamental moral criterion for all economic, social, and political decisions is to be at the service of all people, especially the poor.[765] For this reason, the state has the duty to defend and promote the common good of the society, not just for some segments of the society, as utilitarianism would normally propose.

[765] *See* the 5th Principle of CST "Preferential Option for the Poor" above for details on the rationale for the Catholic Church's defense of the poor. *See especially* note 740. *See also* POPE JOHN XXIII, PACEM IN TERRIS, *supra* note 73.

CHAPTER FIVE

The Holy See, International Law, and International Trade Law

The Latin text of Matthew's Gospel reads: "D*ocete omnes gentes,"* meaning "Go make disciples of all nations . . . teaching them to observe all that I have commanded you" (Mt. 28:19). This command expresses the universal missionary mandate, which Christ entrusted to his Apostles after his earthly mission. It is a command that the Church cannot afford to ignore. The Apostles and their successors have this duty with both individuals and all peoples wherever they live in the world. This answers the query as to why in "unimpeded and beckoning, sensitive and complex" circumstances, as well as in occasions that are "hostile and impervious to friendly dialogue,"[766] the Catholic Church never relents in carrying out this great mandate.[767]

Pope Pius XII, in his 1951 encyclical letter, *Evangelii Praecones,* recognized the upheavals and dangers in the world because of people being divided by conflicting interests. He situated the universal mission of the

[766] POPE PAUL VI, ENCYCLICAL LETTER *Ecclesiam Suam* (On the Paths of the Church), August 6, 1964), # 13 (stating *inter alia,* the duty that is incumbent on the Catholic Church as that of correcting the defects of its own members and of leading them to greater perfection; to find the way to achieve wisely a sweeping global renewal that not only recognizes but also promotes the dignity of the human person at all levels). *See id.* at # 11 [teaching that the Church has an assiduous and efficacious concern (divorced from temporal interest) toward educating humankind to foster a rational and civilized method of agreements for peaceful relations between nations] *See id.* at 16.

[767] *See* POPE PAUL VI, ENCYCLICAL LETTER, ECCLESIAM SUAM (On the Paths of the Church), August 6, 1964, #13.

Catholic Church as that of establishing the Kingdom of God throughout the whole world. To establish the Kingdom on earth, the Catholic Church's mission in the world has the goal of preaching to all women and men to practice natural and Christian virtues. The Church also works for all to embrace brotherly and common fellowship, which transcends racial conflicts and national frontiers. The Catholic Church "rejects discords, flees division, and abhors disputes." The Christian faith and universal Christian charity transcend all opposing camps and national boundaries, and therefore, reach out to the ends of the earth for that same purpose.[768]

In the preceding chapter, this book discussed the rationale behind the principles of the social justice theory of the Catholic Church. The foundation of Catholic social doctrine is based on the natural dignity of the human person, which stems from being created in the image and likeness of God. Possession of human dignity is a gift that God gave to every individual equally. Human dignity goes with concomitant inalienable rights of the human person. Respect for human rights means respect for the dignity and worth of every human being. For this reason, Pope John Paul II teaches:

> The cause of peace could only advance "through the definition and recognition of, and respect for, the inalienable rights of individuals and of the communities of peoples."[769]

The Catholic Church has, down through the centuries, based her teachings upon the philosophical and theological reflections of many Christian thinkers. Based on that, the Catholic Church has made significant contributions in directing international law to synchronize with the common good of the whole human family.[770] International law is inseparable from Catholic tradition and its underlying Judeo-Christian

---

[768] *See* POPE PIUS XII, ENCYCLICAL LETTER *Evangelii Praecones* (On Promotion of Catholic Missions), June 2, 1951, nos. 2 & 3.

[769] Pope John Paul II, Address to the 34th General Assembly of the United Nations Organization, quoted in George Weigel, Witness to Hope, *supra* note 74, at 348.

[770] Eugene R. Milhizer President, Dean and Professor of Law, "Dean's Introduction" in *Ave Maria International Law Journal*, available at http://legacy.avemarialaw.edu/ILJ/index.cfm last visited October 12, 2013.

viewpoint. Moreover, natural law is the foundational source of all law, including international law. Notable examples of the profound influence of Catholic thought in international realm include the Augustinian origins of the just war theory and the development of modern diplomacy.[771]

Looking to the future, Catholic thinking has much to contribute to the wide array of contemporary global issues, such as nuclear proliferation, state-sponsored terrorism, the protection of women and children, immigration and freedom to travel, racial and religious hostility and discrimination, political self-determination movements, and widespread financial crises. These and other international concerns hinge on the concepts of human dignity and the common good, which are discussed above. In a post-modern age, the slogan "might is right" has become the order of the day; moral relativism and conscious rejection of religious tradition hold sway. This is highly regrettable. Attention to the authentic Catholic perspective is indispensable with respect to directing the course of debates that concern the dignity of the human person and in influencing decisions and policy that concern the same concepts.[772]

The above reason accounts for why

> Christ gave his Church no proper mission in the political, economic or social order. The purpose that he set before her is a religious one. But out of this religious mission came a function, a light, and an energy, which can serve to construct and consolidate the human community according to the divine law. Moreover, in virtue of her mission and nature, she is bound to no particular form of human culture, nor to any political, economic, and social system. Hence, the Church by her very universality can be a very close bond between diverse human communities and nations. For this reason, the Church admonishes her own sons and daughters, but also humanity as a whole, to overcome all strife between nations and races in this family spirit of God's children. The mission of the Church

[771] *Id.*

[772] *Id.*

> encourages social dynamism, progress toward indissoluble unity, healthy socialization, and civil and economic cooperation. In other words, the Church is an instrument of communion.[773]

Globalization has created a new landscape with its obvious consequences. Communications, financial investments, open markets, and technological advances have all changed the planet into a "global village." For instance, globalization now makes it possible for actions taken in one country of the world to have an impact on other countries. A decision made in the New York or Tokyo stock market has immediate consequences in Nigeria, Amsterdam, or Paris. Multinational corporations and their extractive operations have influenced mobility of labor for socio-economic and political reasons. As a response to this development, international and regional arrangements and mechanisms have been put in place for purposes of collaboration and corresponding agreements.

Considering the implications of globalization, the Holy See strives to contribute to the governance of international relations by offering a specific ethical and values-oriented perspective. Salvation is not only available to those who believe in Christ; it is also equally offered concretely to all peoples.[774] This perspective has the potential for a realistic impact on such issues as the relationships between rich and poor, developed and developing countries, on reconciliation, on the maintenance of peace, and on concerns related to disarmament.

Following the vision of this book it is noteworthy that the Catholic Church gets seriously involved in international affairs to influence decisions that accrue as they may affect the dignity of human beings. She participates generally in international law by either making her voice heard in international negotiations for international law or by critiquing international law already in place in her bid to promote respect for

[773] SECOND VATICAN ECUMENICAL COUNCIL, GAUDIUM ET SPES, December supra note 75, # 42; *See also* Pope Pius XII, "Allocutions to Historians and Artist," March 9, 1956, in *AAS 57 (1956)*, P. 212; SECOND VATICAN ECUMENICAL COUNCIL, LUMEN GENTIUM (Dogmatic Constitution on the Church), November 24, 1964, # 1.

[774] POPE JOHN PAUL II, ENCYCLICAL LETTER, *Redemptoris Missio* (On the Permanent Validity of the Church's Missionary Mandate) December 7, 1990, # 10; Jesus Christ carries out his salvific enterprise through the instrumentality of the Church; *see id,* at # 9

human dignity. The Holy See tries to make its voice heard in the WTO-GATT system, especially in the negotiations of agreements or in their implementations, or both.

5.1 Mission of the Holy See in International Law Generally

In her missionary mandate, the Church can bring the Gospel, by witness and word, to all people and nations.[775] The missionary mandate of the Church is not limited to mere ecclesial preaching of the Gospel. It is very extensive. Lay people are also present and active as missionaries. Lay people participate in the missionary mandate by applying the Gospel message to the vast and complicated world of politics, society, and economics on the local, national, and international levels.[776] The Holy See engages in direct and wide-ranging relations in the intergovernmental arena. By participating in international life in that fashion, the role of the Holy See articulates and supports the activity of the whole Church, which it represents. This role of the Holy See adds, moreover, as mentioned, a spiritual and ethical dimension to the debates regarding the tough problems confronting the human family.[777]

---

[775] *See id.* at # 92. In his Address to an audience at Seton Hall University in the year 2000, Angelo Cardinal Sodano, Secretary of State of the Vatican, quoted Pope John Paul II as appealing that "world leaders should respect the primacy of spiritual values in the lives of individuals and peoples," stressing that the Catholic Church's mission is cooperative in the transformation and ennobling of humanity in the light of the saving message of Christ. *See* Angelo Cardinal Sodano, "Addressing the Future: The Holy See's Presence in International Affairs," September 5, 2000, *Seton Hall Journal of Diplomacy and International Relations*, Winter/Spring 2001, p. 87.

[776] *See id.* # 72. *See also* POPE PAUL VI, APOSTOLIC EXHORTATION, *Evangelii Nuntiandi* (On Evangelization in the World), December 8, 1975, # 70 [indicating that this includes other realities which are open to evangelization, such as human love, the family, the education of children and adolescents, professional work, and suffering. The more Gospel-inspired lay people there are engaged in these realities, clearly involved in them, competent to promote them and conscious that they must exercise to the full their Christian powers which are often buried and suffocated, the more these realities will be at the service of the kingdom of God and therefore of salvation in Jesus Christ, without in any way losing or sacrificing their human content but rather pointing to a transcendent dimension which is often disregarded].

[777] ARCHBISHOP JEAN-LOUIS TAURAN, THE PRESENCE OF THE HOLY SEE IN INTERNATIONAL ORGANIZATIONS, *supra* note 27.

The Holy See is a player in international law.[778] It is the only religious institution in the world that has access to diplomatic relations in international law.[779] The Holy See has more diplomatic relations (188 countries) than any other country of the world, including the United States, which is second, having diplomatic relations with 177 countries. For this reason and others stated above, it is held as an international legal person by most countries.[780] The reason for this is historical and lies in the universal power and supra-national character of the Catholic Church in Western history since the medieval era, from which the international community of today derives.[781] The international character of the Papacy contributes to this, too. Once elected a Pope in the conclave, the head of the Catholic Church assumes international character in realization of the universal mission entrusted to it.[782]

The reasons that prompt the Holy See to actively participate in the daily struggles of the human family are neither selfish economic nor related to the military nor political. Pope John Paul II succinctly stated the reason the Holy See is involved in international affairs when he noted that:

> There can be neither true human progress nor durable peace without the courageous, loyal, disinterested search of a growing cooperation and unity among the peoples. For this reason, the Church encourages every initiative that can be undertaken, every step that can be realized, both on a bilateral and multilateral level. He added that respect for the fundamental demands of the human person is required. "Christians are more attentive to this vocation of men and women to cooperation and to unity

---

[778] CARLO FOCARELLI, INTERNATONAL LAW AS A SOCIAL CONSTRUCT: THE STRUGGLE FOR GLOBAL JUSTICE, Oxford University Press, 2012, p. 216.

[779] *See* ARCHBISHOP JEAN-LOUIS TAURAN, The Presence of the Holy See in International Organizations, Catholic University of the Sacred Heart, Milan, April 22, 2002, available at http://www.vatican.va/roman_curia/secretariat_state/documents/rc_segs_doc20020422_tauran_en.html (last visited January 17, 2014).

[780] *See* CARLO FOCARELLI, INTERNATIONAL LAW AS A SOCIAL CONSTRUCT, *supra* note 778, at 44.

[781] *Id.*

[782] ARCHBISHOP JEAN-LOUIS TAURAN, THE PRESENCE OF THE HOLY SEE IN INTERNATIONAL ORGANIZATIONS, *supra* note 27.

> because, in the plan of salvation, the Gospel message reveals to them that Jesus of Nazareth died 'to gather into one the dispersed children of God' (John 11, 52) .... The Church...in the same way is convinced to be able to contribute effectively to this work of reconstruction of the human family and of its history, thanks to evangelical love. It is for this reason also, that the Holy See establishes relations with each of your Governments and takes part in the activity of international organizations."[783]

From discussions in Chapter 3 above, it is generally understood that the Holy See's international personality does not stem from its claim over purely temporal matters. Rather, the international personality of the Holy See materializes from its religious and spiritual authority and mission in the world.[784] Archbishop Cardinale expanded this understanding perfectly well when he wrote

> [A]s a subject of international law, the Catholic Church is an atypical organism. That is to say, considering her particular purpose, the social means she employs to further this purpose and her peculiar nature and social

[783] POPE JOHN PAUL II, Discorso ai Capi di Stato e ai Rappresentanti delle Missioni straordinarie, (Address at the Installation of Diplomatic Missions), October 23, 1978; *See also* SECOND VATICAL ECUMENICAL COUNCIL, GAUDIUM ET SPES, *supra* note 75, # 40.

[784] *See Address of Pope Paul VI to the United Nations* (Oct. 4, 1965) where the Pontiff stated: "We have been on the way for a long time and We bear with Us a long history; here We celebrate the end of a laborious pilgrimage in search of a colloquy with the whole world, a pilgrimage which began when We were given the command: 'Go and bring the good news to all nations.' And it is you who represent all nations."
Pope Paul VI also noted that the Holy See's position as an *expert in humanity* provided the foundation for the *"moral and solemn ratification"* of the UN. *Id.* The Pope's UN address reflected the Pastoral Constitution on the Church in the Modern World (*Gaudium et Spes*), which was to be promulgated at the end of the Second Vatican Council on December 7, 1965. While noting that *Christ did not give the Church a proper mission in the political, economic or social order,* the Pastoral Constitution also acknowledged that *the Church functioned as a light and energy which can serve to structure and consolidate the human community.* As a matter of fact, when circumstances of time and place create the need, she can, and indeed should initiate activities on behalf of all men." *See* SECON VATICAN ECUMENICAL COUNCIL, GAUDIUM ET SPES, *supra* note 75, # 42 (emphasis added).

> structure, the Church cannot be put on exactly the same level as a State, or any other subject of international law. Hence, her position is analogous to, but not identical with, that of a national State.[785]

Some commentators have explained that the status of the Holy See that makes it enjoy an international personality is an "anomaly,"[786] the Holy See is an "atypical organism,"[787] an entity *sui generis.*[788] Whatever the argument may be, the statehood-like status of the Holy See is undeniable.[789] From the perspective of diplomatic exchange, the Holy See has diplomatic relations with one hundred and eighty-eight countries.[790] This obviously makes the point clearer.[791]

It is a principle of law that wherever there are rights, there is a person or a subject of such rights. Due to the fact that positive international law recognizes in the Holy See one or more international rights, there is no need to bicker over whether the Holy See has international personality

[785] HYGINUS EUGENE CARDINALE, THE HOLY SEE AND THE INTERNATIONAL ORDER, *supra* note 190, at 80-81.

[786] *See* REBECCA WALLACE, INTERNATIONAL LAW (3rd ed., 1997) *supra* note 264, at 76.

[787] *See* HYGINUS EUGENE CARDINALE, supra note 190, at 80-81.

[788] *See* IAN BROWNLIE, PRINCIPLES OF PUBLIC INTERNATIONAL LAW (5th ed., 1995), at 64; *See* also MALCOLM SHAW, LAW 172, (Cambridge, 4th ed., 1997); some commentators have equally questioned the status and international personality of the Holy See especially during the period from 1870 to 1929 when it held no territorial sovereignty; *see* L. See OPPENHEIM, 1 INTERNATIONAL LAW §§ 106, 107 (Lauterpacht ed., 8th ed. 1955) (noting that "[a] state without a territory is not possible, although the necessary territory may be very small, as in the case of the Vatican City, the Principality of Monaco, the Republic of San Marino, or the Principality of Leichtenstein."); See ROBERT JOHN ARAUJO, supra note 200, at 33 (particularly footnote 159); *See Id.* at 108; Oppenheim however concedes that, [its] international personality is here recognized [sic] to be vested in an entity pursuing objects essentially different from those inherent in national States.... A way is thus opened for direct representation in the sphere of International Law of spiritual, economic, and other interests lying on a plane different from the political interests of States. *See id.* at 107.
See Robert John Araujo *International Personality of Intergovernmental Organizations: Do Their Capacities Really Depend Upon Their Constitutions, 4 INDIAN J. INT'L L. 1, 42, 61* (1964).

[789] *See* ROBERT JOHN ARAUJO, *supra* note 200, at 32.

[790] *See* Bilateral and Multilateral Relations of the Holy See, available at http://www.vatican.va/roman_curia/...0010123_holy-see-relations_en.html last visited January 17, 2014

[791] *See* ROBERT JOHN ARAUJO, supra note 200, at 33

in international law.[792] The Holy See possesses active and passive rights of legation and rights of concluding concordats.[793] In line with this argument from the perspective of the capacity to have rights and duties, Prof. Tiyanjana Maluwa[794] establishes that the international personality of the Holy See is based on social need. Social need here is as it concerns the community, rather than a conventional application of personality as accorded to states.[795]

What the above assertions boil down to be that the Holy See may, strictly speaking, not be a state or an international organization, but it derives its international personality by the special functions it executes "recognized as significant for the international community."[796] The Holy See participates in and influences negotiations of international agreements and similar legal instruments. The Holy See engages in diplomatic exchange with about 188 countries. The Holy See is also involved in and contributes immensely to the decision-making of various international organizations.[797] The social needs that inspire the Holy See in its universal mission have its bearing in the dignity of the human person, which it promotes without territorial boundaries. This mission has roots in the recognition, safeguarding, and promotion of the dignity of the human person.

---

[792] *See generally*, MARIO FALCO, THE LEGAL POSITION OF THE HOLY SEE BEFORE AND AFTER THE LATERAN AGREEMENTS: TWO LECTURES DELIVERED AT THE UNIVERSITY OF OXFORD (1935)

[793] *Id.* at 15 Here Falco adds that:

In reality the attitude of states in general towards the Holy See proves that they have recognized in the person of the Pope the supreme head of the Catholic religion, who as such possesses not only the highest moral authority but also exceedingly great political influence; hence they have recognized in the Pope one who has the capacity of willing and acting not only in the spiritual sphere but also in the sphere of temporal interests and inter-state relations—an international person. *See id.* at 16

[794] *See* Tiyanjana Maluwa, The Holy See and the Concept of International Legal Personality: Some Reflections, 19 *COMP. & INT'L L. J. OF S. AFR. 1* (1986).

[795] *Id. at 11.*

[796] *See Id. at 12.* Here the definition of international personality is determined by the answer to the question: Does the entity as the Holy See engage in activities that serve the interests of the international community?

[797] *See Id.* at 23-24, 26.

Professor Arangio-Ruiz[798] emphasizes that the Holy See's unique, or *sui generis*, personality is not limited to purely spiritual or religious matters.[799] The Holy See does not preoccupy itself with roles that are incident to the sovereignty it exercises over others. Nevertheless, it possesses a character that makes it more powerful in international relations.[800] What Arangio-Ruiz tries to put across is that the nature of the Holy See's mission in international law is such that its moral voice is necessary in any international matters that may affect the human person in any way. The mission of the Holy See is not restricted to the activities of other sovereign nations. Therefore, in her mission in the world, the Catholic Church has no territorial limitations.[801] Therefore, the sovereignty of the Holy See is "supra-national."[802]

In the final analysis, the Holy See is known to possess an exceptional nature within the family of nations. As a sovereign subject of international law, its mission is one of essentially religious and moral order. And its mission is universal in scope with territorial dimensions and autonomy for the pastoral ministry of the Pope.[803] In all these engagements, the Holy

---

[798] Gaetano Arangio-Ruiz, "On the Nature of the International Personality of the Holy See," *29 REVUE BELGE DE DROIT INTERNACIONAL (R.B.D.I.)* 354 (1996).

[799] *See Id.* at 362-363.

[800] Id. at 364-365. Arangio-Ruiz adds:

It is hardly necessary to add that, just as there is no real foundation for the alleged "specialty" of the Holy See's personality, there is no foundation for the alleged limitations of the Holy See's legal capacity mentioned by some scholars. If the Holy See has ceased, for example, to participate in military operations, it is because of its lofty inspiration, its own constitution, and legal order and its choices, not because of any international legal incapacity. *See id.*

[801] IAN BROWNLIE, PRINCIPLES OF PUBLIC INTERNATIONAL LAW, supra note 145, at 98-117.

[802] HYGINUS EUGENE CARDINALE, THE HOLY SEE AND THE INTERNATIONAL ORDER, supra note 190, at 93-94, where Archbishop Cardinale explains as follows:

In recent years one finds the term supra-national often used as an attribute of the Church and the Holy See. This is to be understood in an entirely different sense from the meaning of the word used in a political context, where it is perfectly homogeneous. For this reason, such an attribute should be applied sparingly and cautiously to religious bodies . . .. [They] are often referred to as supra-national rather than international entities in the sense that by their very nature they are not tied to any particular people, nation or form of political government but carry out a spiritual mission that is universal, i.e., directed to all mankind without distinction. *See Id*

[803] See MALCOLM SHAW, INTERNATIONAL LAW, *supra* note 788, at 782 (quoting the joint 11th and 12th Reports to the United Nations Committee on the Elimination of Racial

See plays a role in international order concerned with issues of peace, the common good, and the overall welfare of the human person.[804] Ties to any political system do not bind the Holy See, because of its role and competence. The political community and the Church are autonomous and independent of each other in their own fields. However, both are devoted to the vocation of the human person, though under different perspectives.

> The Church...founded in the love of the Redeemer, contributes towards the spread of justice and charity among nations and within the borders of the nations themselves. By preaching the truths of the Gospel and clarifying all sectors of human activity through its teaching and the witness of its members, the Church respects and encourages the political freedom and responsibility of the citizens.[805]

Today, three main areas of concern appear to dominate and guide the involvement of the Holy See in the international organizations, namely, human rights, peace, and solidarity. The Holy See is consistent in making human rights a "global language." Following its age-old goal, the Holy See does not just want to see the Preamble to the 1948 U.N. Charter on paper,

---

Discrimination, UN Doc. CERD/C/226/Add.6, (1993); *See also* Summary Record of the 991st Meeting of the Committee on the Elimination of Racial Discrimination, U.N. Doc. CERD/C/SR.991 (1993) [stating that: "As the supreme governing body of the Catholic Church, the Holy See was recognized as a sovereign subject of international law. Its territory, the Vatican City State, was very small, its only function being to guarantee its independence and the free exercise of its religious, moral and pastoral mission. Its participation in international organizations, most notably the United Nations, and its accession to international conventions such as the Convention on the Elimination of All Forms of Racial Discrimination differed profoundly from those of States which were communities in the political and temporal sense."]. *Id.* at # 2

[804] *See* JOSEF KUNZ, The Status of the Holy See in International Law, *46 AM. J. INT'L Law. (1952),* at 310. Here, Kunz noted that:

The Holy See is . . . a permanent subject of general customary international law vis-à-vis all states, Catholic or not. That does not mean that the Holy See has the same international status as a sovereign state. But the Holy See has, under general international law, the capacity to conclude agreements with states . . . [be they concordats or general international treaties].

[805] SECOND VATICAN ECUMENICAL COUNCIL, GAUDIUM ET SPES, # 76.

but more especially wants to see to its implementation. The Preamble to the U.N. Charter, among other things as stated above, seeks to promote and safeguard the dignity and worth of the human person and all issues incidental to it.[806] Issues that are incidental to the dignity of the human person include human rights, justice, social progress, better standards of life, religious freedom, economic and social advancement of all peoples, and so on.[807]

> Authentic peace is only possible if the dignity of the human person is promoted at every level of society, and every individual is given the chance to live in accordance with this dignity. Any human society, if it is to be well-ordered and productive, must lay down as a foundation this principle, namely, that every human being is a person, that is, his nature is endowed with intelligence and free will. Indeed, precisely because he is a person, he has rights and obligations which flow directly and immediately from his very nature. And these rights and obligations are universal, inviolable and inalienable. The truth about man is the keystone in the resolution of all the problems involved in promoting peace. To teach people this truth is one of the most fruitful and lasting ways to affirm the value of peace.[808]

In its involvement in the international order, the Holy See does not make its voice heard in a vacuum. It participates in national and international discussions and negotiations and tries to make issues at stake pass through the crucible of ethical principles. The Holy See uses strategies

---

[806] *See* Preamble of the 1948 United Nations Charter.

[807] *Id.* The speeches delivered in New York before the General Assembly of the United Nations by Pope Paul VI in 1965 and Pope John Paul II in 1979 and 1995 provide an eloquent illustration of the lofty religious aim that inspires the Holy See's involvement in the international community, namely, that *world affairs be imbued with the Gospel of the dignity of the person and the family, the Gospel of harmony and peace, and, moreover, the Gospel of truth, justice, and love. See* ANGELO CARDINAL SODANO, *infra* note 844, at 90 [emphasis added].

[808] Pope John Paul II, Message for the XXVIII World Day of Peace, 1995, n.1.

such as its status as Permanent Observer in regional and international organizations and Specialized Agencies; the establishment of nunciatures in countries with which it has diplomatic relations; it also uses treaty-making strategies, particularly concordats.

5.1.1 The Holy See and Treaty Law[809]

The Holy See has a long history of negotiating international agreements. These international agreements are categorized into two parts, namely (1) treaties, and (2) concordats. Prior to 1870, during the period between 1870 through 1929, and the period after 1929, the Holy See has participated in negotiating, signing, and ratifying many international agreements. There have been many international negotiations between the Holy See and temporal sovereigns with respect to formulating treaties and other agreements, including consular matters.[810] In the Lateran Treaty, the Holy

[809] See Tiyanjana Maluwa, The treaty-making capacity of the Holy See in theory and practice: A study of the *jus tractum* of a non-state entity, *COMP. & INT'L L. J. of S. AFR. Vol. 20, No. 2 (JULY 1987), pp. 155-174.*

[810] For example, the Concordat of Worms between Pope Calixtus II and King Henry V, concluded in 1122, was between sovereigns and involved more than simply church relations. In addition, it dealt with issues of temporal sovereignties and became something more. See HYGINUS CARDINALE, *supra* note 190, at 275-294; See also ARAUJO, *supra* note 200, at 46.

See became involved with international agreements on both bilateral[811] and multilateral[812] levels.[813]

The international personality of the Holy See can also be examined in the context of treaty law. Though States are the principal parties in relations governed by international law, there are also "international actors" that have the capacity to validly participate. For a party to have capacity in this respect to make valid international treaties and agreements, that party must, among other requirements, possess international legal

[811] On a bilateral level, the Holy See and Spain entered a variety of treaties involving common interests in the Holy Land (December 21, 1994), economic issues (October 10, 1980 and January 3, 1979), religious assistance to the Spanish armed forces (August 5, 1980)], and education and cultural matters (January 3, 1979). The Holy See also has agreements with Sweden and Israel. Each of these three State sovereigns registered their respective agreements with the Holy See with the United Nations. The act of registration suggests that the instrument has legal implications and provides "tangible evidence that the agreement is to be regarded as a treaty and that that is the intention of the parties concerned." *See* ARAUJO, *supra* note 200, at 47-48.

[812] On the multilateral level, the Holy See participated in negotiations leading to some of the principal twentieth century international legal instruments. For example, it signed, ratified, or acceded to such agreements as: The Geneva Conventions of August 12, 1949 (along with the two additional Protocols of 1977); the New York Convention on the Recognition and Enforcement of Foreign Arbitral Awards of June 10, 1958; two of the Law of the Sea Conventions of 1958; the Vienna Convention on Diplomatic Relations of April 18, 1961; the Vienna Convention on Consular Relations of April 24, 1963; the Vienna Convention on the Law of Treaties of May 23, 1969; the Vienna Convention on Succession of States with Respect to Treaties of August 22, 1978; the International Convention on the Elimination of All Forms of Racial Discrimination of December 21, 1965; the Convention on the Rights of the Child of November 20, 1989; the Convention Relating to the Status of Refugees of April 22, 1954; the Convention on Long-Range Transboundary Air Pollution of November 13, 1979; and the Ottawa Convention (Convention on the Prohibition of the Use, Stockpiling, Production, and Transfer of Anti-Personnel Mines and on Their Destruction) of March 1, 1999. In addition, the Holy See has also assisted in drafting and signing the 1975 Final Act (Helsinki Accords) of the Conference on Security and Co-Operation in Europe (now the Organization for Security and Co-Operation in Europe), and it is a member of the Organization. The Holy See is also a signatory to the Vienna Convention on the Representation of States in Their Relations with International Organizations of a Universal Character of March 14, 1975. *See* ARAUJO, *supra* note 200, at 47.

[813] In 1936 an American doctoral candidate at the University of Geneva completed his book on the impact of the Lateran Treaty on the Holy See's treaty and concordat-making power and diplomatic practice. Whilst the author's work contained in his published thesis is somewhat dated, it nonetheless provides an important contemporary insight into the impact of the 1929 Agreement between the Holy See and Italy. *See* Oliver Earl Benson, *Vatican Diplomatic Practice as Affected by the Lateran Agreements*, (1936) (Imprimerie Georges Thone, Liege).

personality. Treaty-making capacity implies that an entity is endowed with international personality.[814] The Holy See is one of the entities that have the capacity to make valid international treaties and agreements.

It is one thing to be an international legal person and another thing to have the capacity to make treaties and agreements of international juridical nature. Hence, it doesn't follow that because an entity possesses international personality, it automatically qualifies to make treaties with other sovereigns. "The ability to enter into treaties only provides evidence that an entity has international personality. The capacity to conclude international agreements is not a qualifying requirement for international personality but one of the possible consequences of such personality."[815]

The term "treaty" can be used as a broad, generic, or restricted term given to a document. Michael Brandon defines the term "treaty" when he writes

> In international jurisprudence, it is generally acknowledged that the term "treaty" is employed in two senses. First,

---

[814] *See Id.* at 155.

[815] *See id. at 156; See also* Oliver James Lissitzyn, "Territorial entities other than independent States in the Law of Treaties," 125 *Hague Recueil 1 ((1965) p.* 15 (stating "If an entity has treaty-making capacity it is an international person, but if we are told that an entity has international personality we cannot conclude that it has treaty-making capacity, since it may only possess some other capacity"); contrasted with I. I. Lukashuk, "Parties to Treaties - The Right of Participation," *135 Hague Recueil* 231 (1972), 237, (arguing that "it is obvious that a subject of international law can only be such an entity that possesses the capacity to be a party to treaties.") Lissitzyn's view represents the correct position on the issue because not every international person necessarily possesses the particular capacity of concluding treaties. A good example is afforded by individuals, who may be regarded as subjects of international law for certain purposes, but it cannot be concluded that they are invested with treaty making capacity. Therefore, even if it is accepted that the Holy See does possess some form of international legal personality, it is still necessary to investigate whether or not the consequential capacity of concluding treaties has been recognized and accepted as accompanying that personality. Lukashuk's view is incorrect. His reasoning is wrong for one fundamental reason: the ability to enter into treaties only provides evidence that an entity has international personality. The capacity to conclude international agreements is not a qualifying requirement for international personality but one of the possible consequences of such personality. Here it is necessary to note the following: to say that an entity is endowed with international personality only denotes that it is endowed with some legal capacities; it does not tell us what these particular capacities are. One such capacity (or one of the several capacities) could be the capacity to conclude treaties. *See* TYANJANA MALUWA, *supra* note 809, at 156.

> it denotes a particular but imprecisely defined kind of international instrument which records the fact of an agreement reached by the mutual consent of the parties thereto and a legal significance attaches to any instrument thus designated. Secondly "treaty" is a generic term of a great variety of international instruments each recording the fact of an [agreement,] and each possessing a different name according to its title or context.[816]

From the above definition, a formal international instrument containing the facts of an international agreement in one, two, or more documents is a treaty. A treaty has been identified with terms such as "convention," "covenant," or "pact."[817] Less formal agreements are variously called "arrangements," "understandings," "accords," "agreements," *modus vivendi* and so on.[818] Whatever the choice of nomenclature is does not matter. What matters is that the international agreement is binding on the parties involved and affects their legal relations in realizing the aims and objectives of such agreement. Article 2 of the 1969 Vienna Convention on the Law of Treaties defines "treaty" as,

> [An] international agreement concluded between States in written form and governed by international law, whether embodied in a single instrument or in two or more related instruments and whatever its particular designation.[819]

---

[816] Michael Brandon "Analysis of the terms 'Treaty' and 'International Agreement,'" *The American Journal of International Law (AJIL)* Vol. 47, No. 1 (Jan. 1953), p. 49.

[817] TIYANJANA MALU WA, *supra* note 809, at 157.

[818] *Id. See also* LORD MCNAIR, LAW OF TREATIES, Oxford, Clarendon Press, (1961). Here Lord McNair indicates that,

[The] word treaty denotes a genus, which includes many differently named instruments in which States or the Heads of State embody international agreement. [There] is no canon, which determines which name is appropriate in each case. *See id. at 3.*

[819] Vienna Convention on the Law of Treaties, May 22, 1969, Official Publication in United Nations, *Treaty Series,* vol. 1155, p.331 available at http://www.worldtradelaw.net/misc/viennaconvention.pdf (last visited January 20, 2014). The Convention was adopted on 22 May 1969, and opened for signature on 23 May 1969, by the United Nations Conference on the Law of Treaties. The Conference was convened pursuant to General Assembly resolutions 2166 (XXI) of 5 December 1966, and 2287 (XXII) of 6 December 1967. The Conference held two sessions, both at the Neue Hofburg in Vienna, the first session from 26 March to 24 May

Prior to 1945, classical theory on international law regarding treaties had posited that the scope of parties to treaties be restricted only to states as the proper subjects of the system of law.[820] After 1945, the scope of parties to treaties was broadened to include entities that are not states. Though States are the primary subjects of international law, possessing the primary capacity to conclude treaties, states do not have a monopoly of that capacity. International organizations can also conclude agreements governed by international law of much the same character as those concluded by states.[821] With this development, treaties came to be viewed as follows: Treaties are the union of wills (meeting of minds) involving obligations between members of the community governed by international law.[822]

Article 3 of the *Vienna Convention on the Law of Treaties* throws more light on this issue because its provisions explain the issue of scope in questions. The fact that the present Convention does not apply to international agreements concluded between States and other subjects of international law or between such other subjects of international law, or to international agreements not in written form, shall not affect,

(a) the legal force of such agreements;
(b) the application to them of any of the rules set forth in the present Convention to which they would be subject under international law independently of the Convention;

1968, and the second session from 9 April to 22 May 1969. In addition to the Convention, the Conference adopted the Final Act and certain declarations and resolutions which are annexed to that Act. Entry into force was on 27 January 1980, in accordance with Article 84(1).

820 *See* CRANDALL SAMUEL B. TREATIES, THEIR MAKING AND ENFORCEMENT (2nd ed.), Washington, John Byrne & Co., (1916), p. 3; FENWICK, CHARLES G., INTERNATIONAL LAW (3rd ed.) New York, Appleton – CenturyCrofts Inc., (1948) P. 318; *See also,* the definition adopted by the *Harvard Research in (1935) 29 AJIL Supp. 653.*

821 T.I.H Detter, "The organs of international organizations exercising their treaty-making power," *38 BYIL (1962), 421; See generaly,* JOHANNES WILHELMUS SCHNEIDER, TREATY-MAKING POWER OF INTERNATIONAL ORGANIZATIONS (1959).

822 Kraus U, "*Systems et Jonetions des traites internationaux*" 50 *Hague Reweil* ((1934), p. 311; *See also* GEORGE GRAFTON WILSON, HANDBOOK OF INTERNATIONAL LAW (3rd ed.), West Publishing Co., St. Paul, (1939) p. 199.

(c) the application of the Convention to the relations of States as between themselves under international agreements to which *other subjects of international law* are also parties.[823]

Though it may be controversial to use this reasoning, the "other subjects of international law" envisaged by the above provision refers to international organizations. The Holy See is characteristically one of them. Therefore, the Holy See's participation in international treaties is a veritable legal instrument in its social mission in the world. Some distinguished legal experts have laid credence to the argument that the phrase "other subjects of international law" refers to entities other than states, such as the Holy See.[824] It is based on this reasoning that the Holy See is capable of negotiating and entering treaties as an equal with States' parties.[825]

---

[823] *See* Article 3 of the 1969 Vienna Convention, *supra* note 796.

[824] *See* Documents of the Eleventh Session including the Report of the Commission to the General Assembly, [1959] *2 Y.B. Int'l L. Comm'n 96, ¶ 7 UN Doc. A/CN.4/SER.A/1959/ Add.1* (commentary to Art. 2 of the Vienna Convention on the Law of Treaties), stating on quote that,

It has always been a principle of international law that entities other than States might possess international personality and treaty-making capacity. An example is afforded by the Papacy particularly in the period immediately preceding the Lateran Treaty of 1929 when the Papacy exercised no territorial sovereignty. The Holy See was nevertheless regarded as possessing international treaty-making capacity. Even now, although there is a Vatican State under the territorial sovereignty of the Holy See, treaties are entered into not by reason of territorial sovereignty over the Vatican State, but on behalf of the Holy See, which exists separately from that state." Also, the Commission commented concerning the term "treaty" as used in the draft article as covering only international agreements made between two or more States or other subjects of international law.

The phrase "other subjects of international law" is designed to provide for treaties concluded by

(a) international organizations

(b) *the Holy See, which enters into treaties on the same basis as states,* and

(c) other international entities such as insurgents which may in some circumstances enter into treaties. (Emphasis added.) *See also* Documents of the Fourteenth Session including the Report of the Commission to the General Assembly, [1962] 2 *Y.B. Int'l L. Comm'n 162*, ¶ 8, UN Doc. A/CN.4/SER.A/1962/Add.1 (commentary to Art. 1 of the Law of Treaties) (emphasis added). On Para 2 of commentary to Art 3 *ILC Yrbk Vol 2 (1959)* 96, the Commission categorically observed as follows: The phrase "other subjects of international law" is primarily intended to cover international organizations, to remove any doubt about the Holy See, and to leave room for more special cases, such as an insurgent community to which a measure of recognition had been accorded.

[825] *See* ARAUJO, *supra* note 190, at 45.

European and American authorities and legal scholars have endorsed the treaty-making capacity of the Holy See.[826] Despite this recognition, other authorities and legal scholars, particularly in Russia, have vehemently stated that the Holy See has no such capacity.[827] The reason for their argument came from the Soviet Union's indisposition towards acknowledging absolute and dominant state sovereignty over any religious organization. In other words, Soviet authorities do not recognize the international personality and treaty-making capacity of the Holy See. For them, the Holy See is characteristically unprecedented and exceptional. Therefore, its specific nature disqualifies it from possessing the treaty-making capacity to participate in international treaties.[828] As part of its universal mission, the Holy See made relentless efforts to dialogue with the Russian Federation, though not in a bid to fight for international recognition. The Holy See is already an established person and subject of international law.[829] The Holy See's untiring effort to establish foreign relations with the Russian Federation is a response to its goal to protect and promote the dignity of the human person without territorial boundaries.[830]

---

[826] See TIYANJANA MALUWA, *supra* note 809, at 161.

[827] *Id.*

[828] *See id.* at 161-163; *see also* LUKASHUK, *supra* note 809, at 279. Lukashuk is the main opponent of the Holy See's international personality and treaty-making capacity in international law. It is illogical to argue that the Holy See has no personality in international law simply because it has a unique or unprecedented nature. It is also bizarre to suggest that because of its spiritual nature, the Holy See is not qualified to take part in treaty-making. The position of the Soviet Union was unpopular because a super majority of temporal sovereigns in the world acknowledges that the Holy See is a subject of international law and possesses international personality so much so that it has the capacity to take part in treaty-making. It is a contradiction for the Soviet Union to watch the Holy See participate in treaty-making at the United Nations and to turn around and bicker over the Holy See's capacity for such international activity. *See for details* MALUWA, *supra* note 809, at 161-163.

[829] *See* generally ARAUJO, *supra* note 200.

[830] Holy See-Soviet Union relations were marked by a long-standing persecution of the Roman Catholic Church by the Soviet Union. After a long period of resistance to atheistic propaganda beginning with Benedict XV and reaching a peak under Pius XII, the Holy See attempted to initiate a pragmatic dialogue with Soviet leaders during the papacies of Pope John XXIII and Paul VI. In the 1990s, Pope John Paul II's diplomatic policies were cited as one of the principal factors that led to the dissolution of the Soviet Union. The end of World War I brought about the revolutionary development, which Benedict XV had foreseen in his first encyclical. With the Russian Revolution, the Vatican was faced with a new ideology and government, which rejected not only the Catholic Church but religion as a whole. "Some

The Russian Federation's denial of the Holy See as a person and subject of international law is now history, following the success of the long-drawn out dialogue between the two entities. This attests to the effectiveness of the strategy of initiating dialogue with any country, no matter how

---

hope developed among the United Orthodox in Ukraine and Armenia, but many of the representatives there disappeared or were jailed in the following years. Several Orthodox bishops from Omsk and Simbirsk wrote an open letter to Pope Benedict XV, as the Father of all Christianity, describing the murder of priests, the destruction of their churches and other persecutions in their areas. Persecution of the adherents of Catholicism continued in the Communist world even with the efforts of Pope Pius XI and Pope Pius XII to initiate meaningful dialogue, which were unsuccessful. Pope John XXIII and Paul VI succeeded to some extent in initiating dialogue with the communist world. At least the situation of the Church in Poland, Hungary, and Romania improved somewhat during the pontificate of Pope Paul VI. John Paul II has been credited with being instrumental in bringing down communism in Eastern Europe, by being the spiritual inspiration behind its downfall, and a catalyst for "a peaceful revolution" in Poland. Lech Wałęsa, the founder of the 'Solidarity' movement, credited John Paul II with giving Poles the courage to rise up. "The pope started this chain of events that led to the end of communism," Wałęsa said. "Before his pontificate, the world was divided into blocs. Nobody knew how to get rid of communism. "He simply said, 'Do not be afraid, change the image of this land....'" In December 1989, John Paul II met with Soviet leader Mikhail Gorbachev at the Vatican, and each expressed his respect and admiration for the other. Gorbachev once said, 'The collapse of the Iron Curtain would have been impossible without John Paul II.' On John Paul's passing, Mikhail Gorbachev said: "Pope John Paul II's devotion to his followers is a remarkable example to all of us." In February 2004, Pope John Paul II was nominated for a Nobel Peace Prize honoring his life's work in opposing Communist oppression and helping to reshape the world. *See* "John Paul II and the Fall of the Berlin Wall," available at http://www.writespirit.net/authors/pope-john-paul-ii/pope-john-paul-fall-berlin-wall%7ctitle=Pope last visited January 11, 2013. *See also* HANSJAKOB STEHLE, DIE OSTPOLITIK DES VATIKANS, Piper, München, 1975, pp. 139-141. During the Pontificate of Pope Benedict XVI, the Soviet Union and Holy See established official relations March 15, 1990. On September 15, 1991 the Holy See recognized Russia as a successor to the USSR. Russia and the Holy See upgraded their diplomatic relations to full ambassadorial relations in 2009. The increased level of relations followed improvements in the working relationship between the Holy See and the Orthodox Patriarchate of Moscow. Now the Holy See has an Apostolic Nunciature in Moscow as its diplomatic mission in the Russian Federation. See INTERFAX, "Vatican names new ambassador to Russia," February 21, 2011, available at http://www.interfax-religion.com/?act=news&div=8217 last visited June 13, 2013. [Interfax Group is a leading provider of critical information on Russia, China, and emerging markets of Eurasia, serving the diverse needs of investors, corporations, financial professionals, and the media. Interfax provides about 100 specialized information services, supplying weekly and daily intelligence reports with industry analysis, business information, real-time news, market data, and ratings and credit reports. The leader in the CIS, the Interfax Group has a global operational network, with over 1000 staff daily turning out over 3000 stories from over 70 bureaus worldwide.]

unreceptive any country or institution may prove itself. The Holy See does not hesitate to utilize a ganglion of possible contacts the world offers it, though some of them are hostile and impervious to friendly dialogue. The Holy See uses each opportunity as an avenue to intervene for fraternal solutions to problems that militate against the enjoyment of human dignity and solidarity.[831]

Considering its missionary commitment, the Holy See has continued to conclude treaties and other international agreements, sometimes on behalf of the Vatican City State and at other times on its own behalf.[832] These other international agreements, apart from international treaties, constitute a category of agreements that do not require the contracting party to be a State or territorial entity for it to be valid. The difference between these two categories can be seen considering the function, nature, and goal of such agreements, and whether or not the parties are territorial entities or States.[833] More than half of the bilateral agreements entered into by the Holy See on its own behalf, not on behalf of the State of the Vatican, are called Concordats.[834]

5.1.2 The Holy See and the Use of Concordats

Concordats are described as one of the earliest legal instruments in international agreements.[835] A Concordat is an agreement concluded between the Holy See and a state for the regulation of various aspects of the affairs of the Catholic Church in that state.[836] Legal scholars agree with this definition, but opinions differ over the juridical nature of Concordats. The International Law Commission is of the view that Concordats fall under the generic meaning of the term "treaty" and not under municipal law.[837]

[831] *See especially* POPE PAUL VI, ENCYCLICAL LETTER, ECCLESIAM SUAM (On the Paths of the Church), August 6, 1964, # 13 & 15.

[832] See MALUWA, *supra* note 794, at 162.

[833] *Id.*

[834] *Id.*

[835] Ehler "The Recent Concordats" (1961) 104 *Hague Recueil1* at 6, quoted in TIYANJANA MALUWA, *supra* note 788, at 163.

[836] *Id.*

[837] *See* Para 5 of commentary to Art 1 *ILC Yrbk Vol 2* (1962) 162.

The International Law Commission, confirmed by *Harvard Research in International Law* taught that

> As to concordats between the Holy See and foreign states, the great majority of writers of international law have adopted the view that they are not to be classified as treaties. Their argument is that in concluding such agreements the Pope acts not in his capacity as a temporal sovereign of a state ... but as the spiritual head of the Roman Catholic Church, and that the matters in which the concordats deal are, in the main, not political in character but religious and ecclesiastical and therefore, not a proper matter for treaty regulation. . .. A number of writers maintain the contrary thesis, although they recognize that a concordat is a type of a treaty *sui generis.* They argue that even if it were true that concordats deal in the main with religious and ecclesiastical matters, it is not less true that they are negotiated by one who is competent and was competent between 1870 and 1929, to enter into agreements with foreign States, and that concordats are in fact concluded in the form of diplomatic agreements or instruments. In fact, also, as they point out, their content has often included matters of a civil and legal character.[838]

What emerges clearly from the above observation is that the writers, who oppose the view that concordats are treaties, even in the broader sense of the term, base their argument on two issues: statehood and the spiritual content of the instruments. To the above points, some writers have added another issue: concordats are internal concessions given by the concerned states to the Holy See.[839]

As discussed above, when the term "treaty" is given a wider definition, it would mean an agreement between two or more subjects of international law to be regulated by international law. The designation given to any

---

[838] *See* Harvard Research on International Law, *AJ (1935) 29 AJIL* 653, *quoted in* TIYANJANA MALUWA, *supra* note 809, at 163.

[839] TIYANJANA, supra note 809, at 163.

of such international agreements does not matter. The question now is whether the term "concordat" fits into the above definition. There is a strong debate about whether concordats qualify as international agreements like treaties. Legal opinion is divided on that issue. For some commentators, concordats do not qualify because they have no binding force and therefore are ineffective.[840] Other commentators argue that concordats cover issues that concern merely the Catholic Church and that of the other contracting State.[841]

The argument that the coverage of concordats is limited to what concerns the Catholic Church and the other contracting entity, is not an acceptable assertion. The reason for this objection is that concordats generally include issues that cover not only internal Church matters. Concordats also address issues of morality, religious observances, education, marriage, and other family issues identified in the Universal Declaration of Human Rights (UDHR), the International Covenant on Civil and Political Rights (ICCPR), and the International Covenant of Economic, Social, and Cultural Rights (ICESCR). Other matters that are covered in concordats are issues of State aid to Church affiliated hospitals, schools,[842] and other related institutions, as well as resolution of property disputes.[843]

Attempting to draw a distinction between Concordats and other treaties is not necessary.[844] This is because both the Holy See and other parties to Concordats intend them to be legally sanctified instruments, binding, enforceable, in accord with the principle of good faith and *pacta sunt servanda.* They both accept Concordats as veritable aspects

---

840 *Id.* at 162.

841 *See* ARAUJO, supra note 200, at 49.

842 *See* JOHN P. BEAL et al., NEW COMMENTARY ON THE CODE OF CANON LAW,1983 CODE, c. 365, Paulist Press, New York, (2000), pp. 496-497.

843 See Roland Minnerath, "The Position of the Catholic Church Regarding Concordats from a Doctrinal and Pragmatic Perspective," Address Before the Symposium at the Catholic University of America, Columbus School of LAW, (April 8, 1997) in *47 CATH. U. L. REV. 467* (1998). Regarding international agreements in international law, Monsignor Minnerath observed:

[T]hese instruments have all the same legal force. They are treaties between two subjects of international law, each one sovereign in its own sphere: spiritual and political. They are negotiated, signed and ratified according to current international practice. Under the regime of the League of Nations, some Concordats were even registered in the Record Book of International Treaties in Geneva.

844 *See* MALUWA, *supra* note 794, at 162-174.

of international relations. If a person gives his dog a name, whatever passers-by say concerning the name is their own problem. This is essential in identifying the international personality of the Holy See and, therefore, its ability to participate in international agreements freely.

However, the Code of Canon Law addresses the uniqueness of some of the topics that Concordats embodies.

> The interests of the Holy See can be of a purely religious or moral nature, such as questions of justice, development of peoples, world peace, etc. They can also be of a material nature, ranging from seeking aid for needy areas and relief for disaster victims, to special support for the Church in its ministry and various apostolates.[845]

It is important at this juncture to discuss the international significance of Concordats in the context of Canon Law. It is a fact that, following the secularization politics of France in 1905, some states severed their diplomatic relations with the Holy See temporarily.[846] Though such diplomatic relations were later restored, while these states in question temporarily walked away from their concordatory responsibilities, the Holy See did not depart from the principle of *pacta sunt servanda.* Because of the Holy See's faithfulness to the dictates of agreements, in making the canons, the Code states that no provision of the Code of Canon Law can "abrogate or derogate from the pacts [concordats, treaties, and other

[845] *See* JOHN P. BEAL, *supra* note 333.

[846] *See* Raymond L. Buell, "France and the Vatican," *36 POL. SCI. Q. 30* (1921); because of the movement toward secularization, Pope Pius X issued the encyclicals *Vehementer Nos* (On the French Law of Separation) promulgated on Feb. 11, 1906, and *Une Fois Encore* (On the Separation of Church and State) promulgated on Jan. 6, 1907. *See also* Abbe Felix Klein, Breaking and Renewing Diplomatic Relations between France and the Holy See, *112 THE CATH. WORLD 577* (1921). For an interesting legal case involving the display of the Vatican Flag in France during this era see Editorial Comment, "The Papacy in International Law," *8 AM. J. INT'L L. 864 (1914*). When Portugal followed France's example a few years later by enacting secularizing legislation that separated the relation between Church and State, Pope Pius X promulgated *Iamdudum* (On the Law of Separation in Portugal) on May 24, 1911.

international agreements] entered upon by the Apostolic See with nations or other political societies."[847]

Since the Holy See has the capacity to participate in international treaties and other agreements, it becomes pertinent to analyze the structures it has put on the ground in the pursuit of its universal mission in the context of international relations. The Holy See establishes nunciatures and diplomatic relations in countries around the world for purposes of participating in international agreements and dialogue. However, whether these nunciatures and diplomatic missions have been as effective as expected in using dialogue and international agreements to apply the Christian principles entrusted to the Church is another question to be addressed.

5.1.3 Establishment of Nunciatures

As mentioned above, the Holy See has no selfish interest in its presence in international arena. Its interest is primarily to promote the dignity of the human person in the community of peoples, as well as other fundamental values.[848] For this reason, the Catholic Church is characterized by notions of communion (*kiononia*) and service (*diakonia*). In pursuit of this dual role, the Church seeks, "to introduce the light which comes from the Gospel and to make available to men and women the saving power which

---

[847] *See* the 1983 CODE OF CANON LAW, c.3. This same canon continues by stating, "[these pacts] therefore continue in force as presently, notwithstanding any prescriptions of this Code to the contrary." Id. The Commentary to this canon states that the Code only regulates the "internal life" of the Church, and

it does not apply to international legal relations. The activities of the Church among the family of nations and its participation in international organizations are subject to the general norms of international law. Since the Holy See is an international juridic person, it has the capacity to conclude agreements with other such persons, i.e., all sovereign states and international associations and organizations formed by them . . .. Should there ever be a conflict between the canons and the pacts, the pacts must stand. *See id.*

Moreso, Canon 365 reminds pontifical legates that they ought to act in accordance with the "norms international law." See *id. See also* Canon 354 of the 1983 CODE OF CANON LAW; *See also* ARAUJO, *supra* note 200, at 50.

[848] ARCHBISHOP NIKOLA ETEROVIC, "Pontifical Ecclesiastical Academy Celebrated 300 Years in 2001," ECCLESIASTICA DIPLOMATICA, available at http://www.vaticandiplomacy.org/pontificalecclacademy.htm last visited June 2, 2013.

the Church, guided by the Holy Spirit, receives from her Founder.[849] The Church is, therefore, not only a community of salvation; she is also a people which redeems. The Church is not only a people redeemed, but also a people which redeems.[850]

Being both a community of those who have been saved and an instrument through which salvation is offered to others; the Catholic Church employs certain institutional means to achieve her goal.[851] These means include papal representation. Roman Pontiffs began to send out personal legates to maintain contacts with the particular Churches in different parts of the world, and to engage in continuous dialogue with the civil authorities responsible for the destiny of nations. To accomplish this diplomatic mission, the Holy See establishes nunciatures in different countries as points of contact of the Pope's legates.[852]

---

[849] SECOND VATICAN ECUMENICAL COUNCIL, GAUDIOM ET SPES, December 7, 1965, # 3.

[850] Angelo Cardinal Sodano, "Addressing the Future: The Holy See's Presence in International Affairs," SETON HALL J. of DIPL. & INT'L RELATIONS, Winter/Spring 2001, p. 89.

[851] *Id.*

[852] An apostolic nunciature is an official diplomatic mission of the Holy See holding the stature of an embassy. A Papal diplomatic representative holding the title "apostolic nuncio" heads it. Currently within the Holy See's pontifical ecclesiastical Foreign Service ministry and diplomatic mission apostolate, the apostolic nuncio is the highest-ranking member of the ecclesiastical diplomatic staff. See "The Apostolic Nunciature and the Head of Mission, the Apostolic Nuncio," available at ECCLESIASTICA DIPLOMATICA http://www.vaticandiplomacy.org/apostolicnunciatures.htm last visited January 24, 2014. This is probably why the *Merriam-Webster's Collegiate Dictionary* (11th ed. 2011) defines "nunciature" as (1) a papal diplomatic mission headed by a nuncio; and (2) the office or period of office of a nuncio. ((Also, THE CONCISE OXFORD AMERICAN DICTIONARY (2006) defines the term "nuncio" as "a papal ambassador (in the Catholic Church) to a foreign court or government." The MERRIAM-WEBSTER'S COLLEGIATE DICTIONARY (11th ed. 2011) defines "nuncio" as "a papal legate of the highest rank permanently accredited to a civil government." The term Papal "Pro-nuncio" is also used. According to the online OXFORD DICTIONARY, "Pro-nuncio" comes from the 1960s Italian *pro-nunzio,* from pro- "before" + nunzio "nuncio," used to designate "a papal ambassador to a country that does not accord the Pope's ambassador automatic precedence over other ambassadors." See OXFORD DICTIONARY online available at http://www.oxforddictionaries.com/us/definition/american_english/pro-nuncio last visited January 24, 2014. On June 24, 1969, Pope Paul VI, who during Vatican Council II had expressed the wish that the functions of papal legates be more clearly defined, issued the Motu Proprio "*Sollicitudo omnium Ecclesiarum*"(The Care of All the Churches), which dealt with precisely such issues as the ones that concern papal representation. This Motu Proprio categorized the papal representatives as follows: *apostolic nuncio,* an archbishop with the rank of ambassador who represents the Holy Father to the local

With origins that can be traced back to the very first centuries of the Catholic Church, the diplomatic service of the Holy See is the oldest in the world.[853] In the early centuries of the Church, this was executed in relation to the Popes sending legates (envoys) to Church councils and synods for their representation.[854] By the fifteenth century, these legates assumed permanency. During the sixteenth century, they became officially known as "apostolic nuncios" (Papal ambassadors).[855] Exchange of representatives began to take place between countries with established "nunciatures" (Papal embassies) and the Holy See.[856] It eventually came to be an expression of ecclesial communion and as a means for promoting the Christian faith.[857]

Catholic Church and to the State or government; *apostolic pro-nuncio,* same functions and rank as a nuncio, though not dean of the diplomatic corps; *apostolic delegate,* an archbishop representing the Pope only to the local Church because the particular country and the Holy See do not have diplomatic relations; *charge d'affaires,* who heads the nunciature in the absence of a nuncio or apostolic delegate. A fifth category, *inter-nuncio,* disappeared with the new Code of Canon Law 1983. Only the title "nuncio" is now used in nominations: the prefix "pro" has been dropped.

853 See Editorial of London's Diplomatic Magazine, A View of Vatican Diplomacy, April 17, 2010, available at http://www.diplomatmagazine.co.uk/index.php?option=com_content&view=article&id=253:vatican-diplomat&catid=3737:features&itemid=100 last visited January 21, 2014. See also *CIN Totus Tuus,* VATICAN DIPLOMACY, *April 11, 1997,* available at http://www.catholic-pages.com/vatican/diplomacy.asp last visited January 25, 2014; indicating that the world's oldest diplomatic service is that of the Holy See, and it origins can be traced to the very first centuries of the Catholic Church when papal legates, "*legati a latere,*" were sent by the Popes to represent them at important councils or for other matters. In fact, a legate was present at the Council of Nicea in 325. "Nuncio" is equivalent to an "Ambassador" according provision of Article 14 § 1 of the Vienna Convention on Diplomatic Relations 1961: The heads of diplomatic missions are the ambassadors, nuncios, envoys, ministers, and internuncios accredited to Heads of States or *Charges d'affaires* accredited Ministers of Foreign Affairs available at http://legal.un.org/ilc/texts/instruments/english/conventions/9_1_1961.pdf last visited January 25, 2014.

854 *Id.*

855 *See id.* In the mid-15th century, permanent papal representation began to appear and by the 16th century, history records the establishment of apostolic nunciatures in different countries, with an exchange of representatives between those countries and the Holy See. The very first apostolic nunciature was established in Venice in 1500. *Id.*

856 *Id.*

857 ANGELO CARDINAL SODANO, *supra* note 850. These missions were used as means of ensuring contact with heads of the various states. The first Apostolic Nunciatures sprang up in Spain, France, the Republic of Venice, and the various states that are now Germany and Austria. *See id.*

The astronomical increase in the numerical strength of Apostolic Nunciatures in the last quarter of a century is worthy of mention. Under the papacy of Paul VI and John Paul II, and then from 1963 to 2005, the number of States that established diplomatic relations with the Holy See increased from 46 to 174.[858] In 1978, after the death of Pope Paul VI, the nunciatures and apostolic delegations in Africa constituted less than half of the total number of Pontifical representatives around the world; the African continent gave a relatively greater number of representatives of the Holy See than other continents, a little less than half the total number (43 to 117).

During the pontificate of John Paul II, there was a sharp expansion of the network of Delegations and Nunciatures across the continents of the world. This numerical growth was strongest in Europe (from 18 to 45 Offices), mainly because of the events of 1989, which affected the former Soviet Union and several countries in Central and Eastern Europe and Central Asia. Under the pontificate of John Paul II also, the number of Papal representations doubled in Asia (from 19 to 38), and in the Americas (from 24 to 36), Oceania (from 5 to 15) and Africa (from 43 to 53).[859]

Vatican diplomacy has sometimes been wrongly understood as an expression of the Vatican City State. It is instead an expression of the supreme authority of the Catholic Church, the Holy See. It was the Holy See that was signatory to the Vienna Convention and not the State of the Vatican City. The Holy See is prior to the Vatican City State, which serves as its base. It is important to mention also that the Holy See has the oldest diplomatic service in the world.[860] As affirmed in the Vienna Diplomatic Convention of April 18, 1961, the Holy See's ambassadors (apostolic nuncios), are considered the deans of the diplomatic corps of the country to which they are accredited.[861] Where such precedence *de iure*

---

[858] As of January 2014, the Holy See has established diplomatic relations with 188 countries around the world.

[859] DI GIOVANNI LAJOLO, "DIPLOMAZIA VATICANA: Uno Strumento docile e fedele al Papa," in *30 GIORNI*, March 2006, available at http://www.30giorni.it/articoli_id_10264_l1.htm last visited October 23 2013.

[860] See CIN *Totus Tuus*, VATICAN DIPLOMACY, April 11, 1997, available at http://www.catholic-pages.com/vatican/diplomacy.asp last visited January 25, 2014.

[861] See UNITED NATIONS CONFERENCE ON DIPLOMATIC INTERCOURSE AND IMMUNITIES, especially Article 16 of the Vienna Convention on Diplomatic Relations and

does not exist, the Holy See, nonetheless, sets up a nunciature, which is headed by a nuncio with the rank of ambassador.

The Holy See's diplomacy has two important facets of law and charity that impel its representatives to work hard for wounded humanity saved by Jesus Christ. Apostolic nuncios (or papal nuncios) play the essential role of strengthening and making ever more effective the bonds of unity which connected the Apostolic See and the particular Churches.[862] For instance, it is the duty of Apostolic Nuncios to nominate and present local bishops of the countries of their assignment. Papal legates also work hard to promote and maintain healthy relations between the Holy See and representatives of the individual states.[863] In all, the international diplomatic efforts of the Holy See are aimed at fighting inhuman ideologies in the world.[864] In all these efforts, the Holy See never relents in proclaiming and defending

Optional Protocol on Disputes April 18, 1961 available at http://www.state.gov/documents/organization/17843.pdf *See also* U.S. Depart of State, DIPLOMACY IN ACTION: Deans of the Diplomatic Corps 1893 to Present, March 1, 2013 available at http://www.state.gov/s/cpr/93591.htm

[862] For details on the responsibilities of the Papal Nuncios and other representatives which have been discussed above, see cc. 364 & 365 of the 1983 CODE OF CANON LAW; Canon 364 defines the duties of a legate: "to send information to the Apostolic See on the conditions of the particular churches ...; to assist the bishops by action and counsel, while leaving intact the exercise of the bishops' legitimate power; to foster close relationships with the conference of bishops ... ; to transmit or propose the names of candidates to the Apostolic See in reference to the naming of bishops ..." Also among those functions: "to strive for the promotion of matters which concern peace, progress and the cooperative efforts of peoples; to cooperate with the bishops to protect what pertains to the mission of the Church and the Apostolic See in relations with the leaders of the state; to exercise the faculties and fulfill the other mandates committed to him by the Apostolic See." "The function of pontifical legate," affirms Canon 367, "does not cease when the Apostolic See becomes vacant unless the contrary is determined in the pontifical letters; it does cease, however, when his mandate has been filled, when he has been informed of his recall, or when his resignation has been accepted by the Roman Pontiff." *See also* SECOND VATICAN ECUMENICAL COUNCIL, DIGNATATIS HUMANAE (Dignity of the Human Person), December 7, 1965, # 1(discussing responsible freedom for the human person as it befits his/her freedom in relation to spiritual values); GAUDIUM ET SPES, # 41 (indicating that the faith that the Church preaches can raise the dignity of human nature above all fluctuating opinions, adding that no human law is powerful enough as to safeguard and promote the dignity and freedom of the human person as the Gospel that the Church preaches to the world in her diplomatic relations and in her entire universal mission); *See also* POPE JOHN XXIII, ENCYCLICAL LETTER, PACEM IN TERRIS, # 75.

[863] ARCHBISHOP NIKOLA ETEROVIC, *supra* note 848.

[864] On October 4, 1965, Pope Paul VI addressed the U.N. General Assembly reminding heads of state that "the UN represents the obligatory path of modern civilization and world peace,"

fundamental human rights.[865] As part of its diplomatic mission, the Holy See proffers "peaceful coexistence" as an alternative to" ideologies of power."[866]

The Holy See is conscious of the basic values of its diplomacy. The specific characteristics of Vatican diplomacy are (1) promoting the moral and ethical aspects of issues that concern the human person and the world in general; (2) universal unity, for reason of which it has no natural boundaries because it is universal and concerns all peoples of the world; and (3) humanitarian and non-territorial; a diplomacy which always sides with people, not with a given parliament or particular administration.[867] The Holy See also engages in international diplomatic relations to act in defense of the cause of peace by getting all nations of the world to overcome the temptations toward clashes between cultures, ethnic groups, and different worlds.[868]

The Holy See is consistent in reaching out to the human person irrespective of the hurdles it may encounter. Therefore, the Holy See

---

adding that "what they should proclaim ceaselessly are the fundamental human rights and duties of men and women, their dignity and freedom and, above all, religious freedom." *See id.*

[865] Address of TARCISIO CARDINAL BERTONE titled "HUMAN RIGHTS IN THE MAGISTERIUM OF POPE BENEDICT XVI," On the Occasion of the Sixtieth Anniversary of the Universal Declaration of Human Rights, Spanish Episcopal Conference, Madrid, Spain, February 4, 2009, quoting Pope Benedict XVI as reminding the U.N. General Assembly on April 18, 2009, that the Universal Declaration "was the outcome of a convergence of different religious and cultural traditions, all of them motivated by the common desire to place the human person at the heart of institutions, laws and the workings of society, and to consider the human person essential for the world of culture, religious and science;" available at "Speeches on Papal Diplomacy" on ECCLESIATICA DIPLOMATICA http://www.vaticandiplomacy.org/speechespapaldiplomacy.htm last visited January 25, 2014.

[866] See CATHOLIC WORLD NEWS, "Pope Benedict XVI Expresses Hope to Expand Vatican Diplomacy," May 12, 2005, available at SPECIAL ARTICLES ON VATICAN DIPLOMACY http://www.vaticandiplomacy.org/special articles.htm last visited January 25, 2014. Here, Pope Benedict XVI indicated also that the Catholic Church does not seek any special status from secular governments; the Church only asks for "the legitimate conditions of freedom for her mission," and promises cooperation with all civil authorities in promoting the common good. *See id.*

[867] ARCHBISHOP CELESTINO MIGLIORE, at an Interview by Director of Thomas Aquinas College Relations, ROME, during the College's Summer 2006 Commencement Ceremonies, AVAILABE AT Special Articles – ECCLESIASTICA DIPLOMATICA http://www.vaticandiplomacy.org/specialarticles.htm last visited November 4, 2013.

[868] *See* CATHOLIC WORLD NEWS, *supra* note 860.

can be said to be involved in a mission of labor with compassion for human beings. For this reason, Vatican diplomacy as practiced by the Holy See occupies a unique place in the world. Therefore, it champions the poor and promotes all initiatives that further the cause of justice, peace and forgiveness. Forgiveness guarantees the efficacy of justice and peace.[869] Because the concerns of the human person are not limited to a country or merely international law, Vatican diplomacy also delves into the affairs of international organizations and NGOs. The deliberations of these institutions also impact the human person, the subject of Holy See's presence in international affairs.

5.1.4 The Holy See as a United Nations Permanent Observer

As stated above, the reasons that prompt the Holy See to participate actively in human affairs are the same reasons that prompt it to get involved with international organizations. The Holy See's presence in international organizations is for purposes of executing its universal mission of courageous, loyal, and impartial search for growth in cooperation and unity among peoples.[870] For this reason, the Church embarks upon and encourages every initiative that can help in realizing this objective, on both bilateral and multilateral levels. In a letter to the Chancellor of Germany on the occasion of the G-8 meeting in June 2007, Pope Benedict XVI enumerated the major themes which prompt the service of the Holy See. These themes include unity of the human family, its common destiny, the

[869] See ARCHBISHOP NIKOLA ETEROVIC, *supra* note 842.

[870] SECOND VATICAN ECUMENICAL COUNCIL, GAUDIUM ET SPES, #4O; See also ARCHBISHOP SILVANO M. TOMASI, WELCOME TO THE HOLY SEE MISSION TO THE UNITED NATIONS IN GENEVA: A HISTORICAL INTRODUCTION, available at http://holyseemissiongeneva.org/index.php?option=com_content&view=article&id=738&Itemid=64 last visited January 25, 2014 (stating that the Church takes part in the activities of international organizations to effectively contribute to the work of the reconstruction of the human family); see also Discorso di Giovanni Paolo II ai Capi di Stato e ai Rappresentanti delle Missioni straordinarie, 23 ottobre 1978.

inalienable dignity of the human person, and attention to the poor and the least privileged.[871]

Pope Pius XII and Pope John XXIII laid the foundation for the birth of the United Nations, so to speak. However, the Popes' initiative was inspired by the thoughts and pragmatism of some of the Catholic faithful.[872] Prior to the official formation of the U.N., Pope Pius XII had projected a picture of the U.N. as a perfect answer to the yearnings "from the depths calling for justice and spirit of collaboration in a world ruled by a just and compassionate God."[873] Unfortunately, human beings who have ignored social justice, or who are selfish, inhabit this same world. Pope Pius XII therefore stated that to forestall any repeat of the Second World War, which was caused by global imbalance fostered by greed, power struggles, rivalry, and hostility, there is a need for a new international alliance devoid of these vices. He reiterated the need for a new world order and enumerated the principles that would engender peace if universal support were garnered.[874]

The thoughts and documents of Pope Pius XII indirectly exerted a significant influence in the formation of the United Nations.[875] Pope Pius XII's teachings influenced, not only the key players in the formation of

---

[871] For an exhaustive review and reporting of original texts of the Holy See's areas of concern and of the philosophical and theological foundations on which rests such concern, *see* ANDRÉ DUPUY, WORDS THAT MATTER: THE HOLY SEE IN MULTILATERAL DIPLOMACY, Anthology (1970-2000) New York, The Path of Peace Foundation, 2003, pp. 752.

[872] *See generally,* Emeka Xris Obiezu, O.S.A., "The Holy See in the United Nations: An Assessment and Critique," *NTR, Vol. 26 No. 1,* September 2013.

[873] *See* John Courtney Murray, "The Pattern for Peace and the Papal Peace Program," in Joseph Rossi, *Uncharted Territory: The American Catholic Church and the United Nations, 1946-1972,* Washington D.C., The Catholic University of America Press, 2006, p. 37.

[874] *See* John Cornwell, Hitler's Pope: The Secret History of Pius XII, New York, Viking Penguin, 1999, p. 233; *See also* POPE PIUS XII, ENCYCLICLA LETTER, SUMMI PONTIFICATUS (" On the Supreme Pontiff," or "Darkness over the Earth" as it was known in English Language) (calling on all nations to have recourse to the sovereignty of Christ).

[875] *See* Catholic League for Religious and Civil Rights, "The Christmas Editorial," December 2, 2008, available at http://www.catholicleague.org/pius/nyt_editorials.htm. The leadership impact of Pope Pius XII at that time was not recognized only by religious sources. *The New York Times* editorials of Christmas Day 1941 and 1942 recognized the singular contribution of Pope Pius XII toward ensuring a "real new order" based on "liberty, justice, and peace." See especially Pope Pius XII's Christmas Eve messages of 1941 and 1942. *The New York Times* editorials in question acknowledged Pope Pius XII as "a lonely voice in the silence and darkness enveloping Europe," describing his peace program as richer than the Atlantic Charter

the United Nations but also others. For instance, the eight-point *Atlantic Charter* reflected on all four of the principles of peace as taught by Pope Pius XII.[876] As if the indirect influence of his works were not enough, Pope Pius XII initiated direct efforts to have the Church registered as a member of the United Nations. Pope Pius XII who approached the United States Secretary of State, Cordell Hull, for what it would take to have the Vatican as a member of the UN. Even though Secretary Hull answered that the Vatican would be unable to fulfill the requirements for membership,[877] it is recorded that Pope Pius XII was out to translate his leadership ideas into more concrete reality than what would have been the case as a full member.

The inspiration emanating from the works of Pope Pius XII must have also attracted a number of other Catholic Christians who attended the initial UN conferences as delegates from the Catholic Church.[878]

---

in advocating an end to all national monopolies of economic wealth. In its Christmas Day editorial in 1941, the *New York Times* wrote,

> As we realize that he is the only ruler left on the Continent of Europe who dares to raise his voice at all. The last tiny islands of neutrality are so hemmed in and overshadowed by war and fear that no one but the Pope is still able to speak aloud in the name of the Prince of Peace.

See Margherita Marchione, "The Truth about Pope Pius XII," *The Catholic League for Religious and Civil Rights,* March 27, 2000, http://www.catholileague.org/the-truth-about-o=poe-pius-xii/; See also EMEKA XRIS OBIEZU, O.S.A., THE HOLY SEE IN THE UNITED NATIONS, *supra* note 872, at 30-31.

[876] After the Second World War, two world superpowers held a secret maritime meeting between President Franklin Delano Roosevelt of the United States and UK Prime Minister Winston Churchill. That was in August 1941, and the summit produced the short but profoundly influential *Atlantic Charter.* Barely 300 words long, it would shape the course of the twentieth century. In Placentia Bay off the coast of Newfoundland, Winston Church and Franklin D. Roosevelt met to discuss the issues surrounding the British war efforts. While Churchill was unable to persuade Roosevelt to join the war, the pair did lay down the foundation for the Lend-Lease agreement. Additionally, the leaders signed the Atlantic Charter. This document outlined a plan for a postwar world which included the principal of self-governance, free trade, and peace among all nations. All future conferences, including those that included Joseph Stalin, would affirm these basic ideas. See *Atlantic Charter,* August 14, 1941, 55 Stat. 1600, E.A.S. No. 236; See also John Courtney Murray, "The Pattern for Peace and the Papal Peace Program," in Joseph Rossi, *Uncharted Territory: The American Catholic Church and the United Nations, supra* note 857, at 37.

[877] See JAMES CRAWFORD, THE CREATION OF STATES IN INTERNATIONAL LAW, *supra* note 23, at 152-161.

[878] *See* JOSEPH ROSSI, *supra* note 877, at 30-33.

Encouraged by Pope Pius XII's Peace program, increasingly considered to be an indispensable Christian model of peace for the postwar world order, many Catholic faithful participated in the formulation of the UN's foundational documents.[879] The Popes, the pontifical legates, and the other members of the clergy owe it as a primary mission to take the Gospel message to the nooks and crannies of the world. What is at issue is the Church's spiritual mission.

The contribution of the Holy See and the Catholic Christians in general, has been great and has been felt in all corners of the world. Opposition from certain NGOs concerning the presence of the Holy See at the UN has not yielded any negative impact. Even when these antagonizing groups disseminate misleading information to discredit the Holy See, it has not dissuaded nations from acknowledging the Papal right of legations.[880] Their challenge is that the Holy See's presence at the UN should be reduced to that of an international NGO to divest the Holy See of its participatory dialogue status at the UN. Fortunately, their

---

[879] Arthur Jones, "Catholics were there at the Start," *National Catholic Reporter,* October 1, 1999, p. 1. Prominent among committed Catholic Christians is Catherine Schaeffer of the Catholic Association for International Peace, one of the early first Catholic NGOs with specific relations to the United Nations. Schaeffer took part in the drafting of the San Francisco 1945 UN Charter and the drafting of the Universal Declaration of Human Rights ratified in 1968. Schaeffer and her other colleagues, like Alba Zizzamia, also made an enduring contribution in redressing the imbalance caused by disproportionate government influence in the UN. Schaeffer and her colleagues were responsible for the insertion of Article 70 of the UN Charter, which provided for the inclusion of NGOs in the UN structure. They also fought hard to insert issues concerning women on the UN agenda. These Catholic women equally influenced putting women in administrative positions within the UN. That was the beginning of NGOs' presence at the UN. See JOSEPH ROSSI, *supra* note 877, at 189, 193 &194; *See also* Jean Gartlan, At the United Nations: The Story of the NCWC/USCC Office for United Nations Affairs 1946-1972, Baltimore, Gateway Press, 1998, pp. 67-77.

[880] These NGOs include The National Secular Society, Catholics for Free Choice, and the Center for Reproductive Law and Policy, among others. See National Secular Society, "Catholic Church Abuses its Position at the UN," February 4, 2004, http://www.secularism.org.uk/32964.html last visited July 2, 2013; Catholics for Free Choice is an organization based in Washington, DC, USA, actively promoting a pro-choice agenda, publicly challenging the Catholic Magisterium on reproductive issues, with affiliated members in about 40 states, available at http://www.catholicsforchoice.org last visited January 26, 2014; The Center for Reproductive Law and Policy is a law firm located at 120 Wall Street, New York City. It is specialized in constitutional law, health and health care law, and civil rights. With more than 10 attorneys on the staff, more than fifty percent of their practice is devoted to litigation, actively advocating pro-choice issues.

arguments have been peripheral and have not been effective in convincing the UN member states against valuing the contributions of the Holy See at the UN. Instead of eroding the influence of the Holy See, it has rather equipped it the more.[881]

Being a signatory to and having ratified the Vienna Convention on Consular Relations, the Holy See has gone on to join a good number of international organizations.[882] The level of acceptance of the Holy See's mission by the international community of nations has matured into a fruitful relationship of cooperation and attentiveness. The Holy See has made unique contributions to substantive issues of debate, the formulation of international law, interreligious dialogue, and advocacy in defense of human dignity, human rights, and the common good throughout the world.[883]Diplomatic relations between the Holy See and other nations soared after the Second Vatican Council.

It is important to remember that the Holy See had been participating in some international organizations that predate the UN, such as the Universal Postal Union, the International Telecommunication Union, and the International Labor Organization. The Holy See's membership in these earlier organizations helped to pave the way for its present status in the UN. The Holy See began to attend the UN General Assembly's sessions as an observer in 1951 due to its membership in the Universal Postal Union and the International Telecommunication Union.[884]

It was in appreciation of, and high expectation of, the Holy See that inspired UN Secretary General U. Thant in 1964 to invite the Holy See formally to send a Permanent Observer to the United Nations.[885] The Holy See received other invitations continuously to attend and participate in interventions in a wide-range of United Nations meetings, international

---

[881]

[882] *See* footnote 329 above for the number of international organizations and agencies that the Holy See and the Vatican City State belong to.

[883] ROMAN A. MELNYK, VATICAN DIPLOMACY AT THE UNITED NATIONS, *supra* note, at 24.

[884] *See* EMEKA XRIS OBIEZU, *supra* note 872, at 32. UN membership is open to all "peace-loving states which accept the obligations" stipulated in the UN Charter, and "in the judgment of the UN, are able and willing to perform these obligations." See United Nations Charter, Article 4 § 1.

[885] *Id. See also* United Nations General Assembly, 58th Session, *Resolution 58/314*, p. 1.

conferences, and sessions of the General Assembly.[886] To fulfill its universal social and spiritual mission, the Holy See took part in the post-World War II work of international organizations and UN Specialized Agencies.[887] The privilege of Permanent Observer status is not provided for in the UN Charter, but it has become an enduring custom granted to states with some limitations to becoming full members.

To be granted the privilege of Permanent Observer status, the applicant must have fulfilled the requirements stipulated by the UN Office of Legal Affairs. These requirements include full membership in one or more specialized agencies of the UN and recognition as a state by member-states of the UN.[888] Therefore, when the Holy See applied for this status in 1964, it had already become a full member of at least two UN specialized agencies and enjoyed diplomatic relations with at least 14 member-states of the UN, though it has more than that number.[889]

Following the above point, the Holy See's achievements on the international arena, its unique structure, and its long history of advocacy for the dignity of the human person, the UN General Assembly acknowledged the Holy See's Permanent Observer status on April 6, 1964. In 2004, the UN elevated the Permanent Observer status of the Holy See to a height that is almost equal to the status of a member-state.[890]

---

[886] Pope John Paul II remarked,"Pope Paul VI initiated the formal participation of the Holy See in the United Nations Organization, offering the cooperation of the Church's spiritual and humanitarian expertise." *See* EMEKA XRIS OBIEZU, *supra* note 872, at 33.

[887] *See* ROMAN MELNYK, *supra* note 24, at 67-68; H. De Riedmatten, "The Part Played by the Holy See in International Organizations," in *Concilium,* 8 (1970), pp. 74-93; A. de Jong, "Concordats and International Law," in *Concilium,* 8 (1970), pp. 104-11.

[888] *See* United Nations Public Information Office, "The Question of Observer Status in the United Nations: The Case of Non-Member States," February 4, 2000 in *The Catholic Church at the United Nations: Church or State?* September 2009, available at http://www.catholicsforchoice.org/topics/politics/The-catholic-church-at-the-united-nations-church-or-state.asp last visited November 4, 2013.

[889] *See* William Schabas, "Notes on the Legal Status of the Vatican City and Holy See," (1994) in *The Catholic Church at the United Nations: Church or State? Id.*

[890] *See* R.G. Sybesma-Knol, "The Status of Observers in the United Nations," Brussels; Brussels University Press, (1981), in *The Catholic Church at the United Nations. See id.* [Permanent Observer status confers not only the right to participate in the sessions and workshops of the General Assembly and other organs of the UN. It also confers on such states other privileges, such as placing items on the provisional agenda of the UN General Assembly and greater access to the plenary sessions of the UN and its main committees, as well as the Security Council. More importantly, a Permanent Observer has the right to vote in

At its 92nd Plenary Session in New York on July 1, 2004, the UN General Assembly by a Resolution,

> 1. Acknowledges that the Holy See, in its capacity as an Observer State, shall be accorded the rights and privileges of participation in the sessions and work of the General Assembly and the international conferences convened under the auspices of the Assembly or other organs of the United Nations, as well as in United Nations conferences as set out in the annex to the present resolution;
> 2. Requests the Secretary-General to inform the General Assembly during the current session about the implementation of the modalities annexed to the present resolution.[891]

It is important to analyze what the Permanent Observer status of the Holy See entails. Having Permanent Observer status at the United Nations means that the Holy See has the right to speak, to take the floor, and to participate in shaping the consensus through negotiation. As a Permanent Observer, the Holy See has no voting rights neither does it have the right to bring candidates forward for positions. What the Holy See has is the

---

all UN conferences. This accounts for the unshakable position of the Holy See at the United Nations, making it possible for the Holy See to project the Gospel message, which not only safeguards but also promotes the dignity of the human person, respect for the fundamental human rights, the common good, equality of nations with the subsidiarity, and solidarity principles of the Catholic social doctrine.].

[891] *See* UN General Assembly Resolution July 1, 2004 A/RES/58/314, "Participation of the Holy See in the Work of the United Nations. The Resolution also stated per Archbishop Celestino Migliore, in his address to the General Assembly as follows:

In the context of strengthening the role of the United Nations and revitalizing the work of the General Assembly, the adoption of this resolution is an important step forward and reflects the lofty values and collective interests shared by the Holy See and the United Nations. We are committed to the same objectives, which necessitate the protection of fundamental human rights, the preservation of the dignity and worth of the human person and the promotion of the common good. To achieve those goals, the international community must build upon the strong edifice of law – law not of whim and caprice, but of principles stemming from the universality of human nature. With an edifice built on such principles guiding our efforts, we can be assured of success in our common quest for lasting, universal justice and peace.

See UN General Assembly, 58th Session, 92nd Plenary meeting, *A/58/PV.92,* July 16, 2004, in Official Records of the United Nations General Assembly, p. 2.

right to speak. This is very important. Voting rights and full membership would entail participation in questions of a political nature or in military or economic issues.

Embarking on such issues would go beyond the social mission of the Holy See in such a way as to engage the members of the United Nations in unhealthy competition, which is outside the mandate that Jesus Christ, gave his Church. One great thing that happens to the Holy See, as a Permanent Observer, is that of having the right to speak and address the United Nations as an opportunity to apply the principles of Catholic social doctrine. CST principles address issues that militate against the dignity, fundamental rights of the human person, the common good, the unity of the human family, and social justice.[892] It is an opportunity to convey the Gospel message to the world body.[893]

---

[892] *See* Pope John Paul II, "Dignity of the Human Person Founded on Justice and Peace," Address to the 34th Plenary Session of the United Nations General Assembly, October 2, 1979; See also Pope Benedict XVI, Address to the 62nd Session of the United Nations General Assembly 95th Plenary Meeting, New York April 18, 2008. At the 50th UN General Assembly Plenary Session, Pope John II observed:

The United Nations Organization needs to rise more and more above the cold status of an administrative institution and to become a moral center where all nations of the world feel at home and develop a shared awareness of being, as it were, a family of nations.

See Pope John Paul II, Address to the 50th UN General Assembly, October 1995; Messages for the World Day of Prayer for Peace, (1980), at 7; 91998), at 1; (1999), 2; POPE JOHNPAUL II, ENCYCLICAL LETTER *Centesimus Annus* (1999), # 21.

[893] *See* Pope Paul VI, "Appeal for Peace," Address of Pope Paul VI to the 20th Session of the United Nations General Assembly, New York, October 4, 1965. Beginning with Paul VI, the Roman Pontiffs and the Holy See's representatives as Permanent Observers have addressed the General Assembly of the United Nations on a number of occasions. In many of these instances, the various Pontiffs and their representatives have lauded the mission and success of the UN, though not without drawing attention to its deficiencies. In his address to the 20th Session of the United Nations General Assembly, he praised the labor and sacrifice of member-states in pursuing the cause of world peace. Pope Paul VI referred to the UN as a "great school of learning" in which all the participants are students, implying even the Church members. This has terrific ecclesiological significance. It is an expression of the humble recognition by the Second Vatican Ecumenical Council that the Church must not only teach but should also learn from the world. The appreciation that the world has something to offer the Church is a humble affirmation of the basic doctrine that the spirit that inspires and permeates the Church is also at work in the world. This theological principle is the basis for the present role of the Holy See as both pupil and teacher in "this great school of learning" that is the United Nations. See Pope Paul VI, "Appeal for Peace," at 9, where he said, "... the United Nations is the great school... and we are today in the Assembly Hall of the school. Everyone taking his place here becomes a pupil and also a teacher... "; See also The Second Vatican Ecumenical

The activities of the Holy See at the United Nations are categorized into three levels. First, the Holy See makes unique contributions to international debate on current issues. The issues that prompt the Holy See to speak out are development, peace, security, eradication of poverty, access to education, religious freedom, issues of equality, and so on. With the right to speak at the United Nations General Assembly, the Holy See can throw the light of Catholic social doctrine summarized in *Compendium of the Social Doctrine of the Church* to the world.

Second, the Holy See contributes to the building of a consensus. Being a Permanent Observer, the Holy See is admitted to negotiations on resolutions, declarations, conventions, and treaties. This is an important aspect of the Holy See's operations at the United Nations because conventions and treaties, once adopted, form international law. In the same vein, international treaties tend to regulate not only the reciprocal obligations between states but also deal more with rights of the individual (*e.g.*, rights of the child, women's rights, and religious rights to life). If the Holy See is part of the entities that make international law, it is a ripe opportunity to do well in its universal mission. In all, the Holy See promotes the views of the Catholic Church on relevant social, civil, cultural, and development issues through its contribution to the negotiations within the United Nations.

Third, the Holy See is the mouthpiece of the voiceless. This is a very challenging and difficult but interesting and gratifying side of the activities of the Holy See because of its humanitarian nature. Advocating for the voiceless answers the question as to why the Catholic Church engages in international debates, dialogues, and negotiations in finding solutions to social problems. Social problems originate from abuse of human right, and the rights of peoples; questions of justice and peace; and issues of cooperation for the development of peoples. When the Holy See takes the floor at the United Nations General Assembly or any of its Specialized Agencies or at any international organizational gathering, it is for the common good.

Council, GAUDIUM ET SPES, nos. 11 & 22 (teaching that the "Spirit who leads the Church also 'fills the earth,' and the same grace with which the Church is blessed is equally at work in the heart of 'all men of good will.'"

The Holy See has assumed Permanent Observer status in most international Organizations, the United Nations, and its specialized agencies, for obvious reasons. The reason is primarily to provide an eloquent illustration of the religious objective that inspires the Holy See's involvement in the international community. The aim of the Holy See is that world affairs may be imbued with the Gospel of the dignity of the human person, the family, the gospel of harmony and peace, the gospel of truth, justice, and love.[894]

The reason the Holy See shows presence in international organizations is, therefore, not questionable. With its Permanent Observer status in the United Nations and its Specialized Agencies and other international organizations, the Holy See is strategically positioned to execute its social mission. In the GATT-WTO system, the Holy See utilizes its Permanent Observer position to advocate for the less privileged while also promoting the honest efforts of the well-to-do. In sending its legation to the WTO negotiations, for instance, the Holy See is expected to be eloquent in objecting to practices that would ordinarily hamper the dignity of the human person; that would occasion abuse of the rights of a person; or that would be a seedbed for inequalities in trade-related matters.

5.1.5 Catholic NGOs at the UN and Other International Organizations

The Catholic Church is blessed with many non-governmental organizations (NGOs) that form what is known as the International Catholic Organizations (ICOs). The ICOs is a community of Nations that pursues a very important work of confrontation and collaboration to achieve conventions, recommendations, and useful actions to the development of peoples in such fields as Human Rights, Social Justice, Public Health, *etc.* They take their cue from the Church's humanitarian vision of evangelization. In the Catholic organizations that make up the ICO is seen a necessary path of humanity seeking unity. In other words,

[894] ANGELO CARDINAL SODANO, *supra* note 850, at 91.

the Holy See is present through these NGOs in different international organization where they operate on consultative basis.[895]

The Catholic Church has more than 30 NGOs at the UN and other international organizations all over the world.[896] These NGOs enhance the fruitful vitality of the Church with regard to her apostolic and prophetic mission toward contemporary International Community.[897] The ICOs find their essential mission in the source of the Gospel, and as a result, they are characterized by "catholicity."[898] "Catholicity" is the feature that places the ICOs in an organic relationship to the Catholic Church and her Magisterium, enjoying the bond to the Holy See as instruments of mission in the world. The mission of the Catholic NGOs is one that requires a specific engagement, a mediation stage between the Gospel and the society, between the Universal Church and the community of nations. It has been said that these ICOs are indispensable because they often speak on issues that are too technical for the Church.[899]

The presence of the ICOs at the UN and other international organizations came to be through the authority of the United Nations Charter which has a provision for cooperation between the United Nations and the representatives of civil society. Article 71 of the UN Charter gives the Economic and Social Council (ECOSOC) authority to "make suitable arrangements for consultation with non-governmental organizations which are concerned with matters within its competence," i.e., matters related to international economic and social development. Consultative status grants NGOs the privilege to participate in a range of UN meetings and conferences as a well as to publish written, and in some cases, oral statements relating to topics discussed at such fora. These NGOs relate to the UN therefore, through different activities, including lobbying, implementation of projects and monitoring.[900] By these modes of participation, ICOs are precious witnesses of charity and evangelization.

895 THE CARITAS IN VERITATE FOUNDATION WORKING PAPERS, International Catholic Organizations and Catholic Inspired NGOs, Their Contribution to the Building of International Community, Mathias Nebel (2012).

896 *Id.*

897 *Id.*

898 *Id.*

899 *Id.*

900 *Id.*

In his encyclical Letter, *Fides et Ratio*, Pope John Paul II taught that announcing the Gospel of truth is a service to God and humanity. This mission for the truth makes the believing community a partner in humanity's shared struggle to arrive at the truth.[901] Acceptance of the truth will result in the reversal of unfair practices, transformation of exploitative institutions, and a change of unjust laws to engender reciprocal rights and duties. Rejection of truth is the bane of the society that results in a social fracture within the society. It is important that the Church and her organizations join hands in pursuit of and spread of the truth in season and out of season. When this truth is consistently proffered in the GATT-WTO system, it would minimize existing inequalities, if not erase it entirely.

5.2 The Issue of Free Trade

Commercial transactions among peoples and nations of the world have given rise to tremendous growth in economic and social interaction in the world. The earliest form of interaction from the economic and social perspectives was barter trade, which metamorphosed into what is today known as "world trade."[902] Trade among nations of the world is one of the major engines of globalization. It is not out of place to say that world trade is the primary reason for globalization. Globalization refers to the growing interdependence of countries resulting from the increasing integration of trade, finance, people, and ideas in one global marketplace. International trade and cross-border investment flows are the main elements of this integration. Globalization has rapidly brought together markets from incredibly diverse countries and cultures. The obvious implications of this diversity can have unintended and negative consequences, which this book will explore later.

Globalization, which started after World War II, has accelerated considerably since the mid-1980s. Globalization was driven by two

[901] Pope John Paul II, ENCYCLICAL LETTER *Fides et Ratio* (On the Relationship Between Faith and Reason) 1998, # 2.

[902] *See* Adrian E. Tschoegl, "International Barter," Working Paper, Alfred P. Sloan School of Management, Massachusetts Institute of Technology, May 1978 (for detailed discussion on international barter).

important factors, namely, technological advances and trade liberalization. Technological advances have made transportation, communication, and computation hugely available and tremendously affordable. It has become feasible for a firm to locate different phases of production in different countries. Because of increasing liberalization of trade and capital markets, governments have somewhat responded to the demand not to protect their economies from foreign competition or influence through import tariffs and no-tariffs such as import quotas, export restraints, and legal prohibition.[903]

Despite the influence that trade has had on the advent of globalization, debates exist as to whether trade is worthwhile. It is instructional to state that trade has existed from time immemorial even though it might have assumed different forms in different historical epochs. The different stages of trade development have their respective features culminating in the debate over merits and demerits of international trade. Professor Raj Bhala makes this observation clear enough:

> International trade law did not start on 30 October 1947, with the General Agreement on Tariffs and Trade (GATT). Trade economics did not begin with Adam Smith (1723-1790) and Ricardo (1772-1823), and their respective Laws of Absolute and Comparative Advantage. Trade itself did not commence after the Second World War (1939-1945). The roots of the study and praxis of trade are ancient and interdisciplinary. The presumption that trade ought to be free remains highly controversial.[904]

The obvious question that has preoccupied economists for a long-time running is whether free trade ought to be or not. Many legal and economic thinkers have proffered arguments in favor and against free trade. However, the greatest arguments are the ones posited by Adam

---

[903] *See* World Bank, "Globalization and International Trade," available at http://www.worldbank.org/depweb/beyond/beyondco/beg_12.pdf last visited January 30, 2014.

[904] *See* RAJ BHALA, INTERNATIONAL TRADE LAW: INTERDSICIPLINARY THEORY AND PRACTICE (3rd ed. 2008), Mathew Benda & Co., p. 3.

Smith and David Ricardo. Their discussion will throw more light on where we are today in world trade.

5.2.1 Case of Free Trade: Smith and Ricardo

Free trade is one of the most debated topics in economics of the 19th, 20th, and 21st century. Arguments over free trade are centered on economic, moral, and socio-political grounds. However, at the heart of every contention is the integral link between trade and morality. This debate features ancient and medieval commercial thoughts on foreign trade, represented by Plutarch of Delphi (46-127 A.D.) and the Roman lyric poet, Horace (65-8 B.C.). For Plutarch,

> God created the sea to promote interaction and to facilitate commerce between various peoples of the earth. . . . Without the exchanges made possible by the sea . . . man would be "savage and destitute."[905]

On the other side of the divide, Horace, in his Odes, writes,

> [T]he sea brought contact with strangers who could disrupt domestic life by exposing citizens to the bad manners and corrupt morals of barbarians.[906]

Since these two great thinkers initiated their thoughts on the pros and cons of foreign commerce, there have been heated debates on if international trade should be encouraged. A grounded assessment of the weight behind the various camps that participated in this debate will determine why the Holy See has taken up the type of stand it has, concerning globalization in general, and global trade. Should trade be encouraged because it is an opportunity for peaceful interaction that advances prosperity? Or should international trade be discouraged because it is a threat to morality and civic security?

---

905 See DOUGLAS A. IRWIN, AGAINST THE TIDE, 11-12 (1996) *quoted in* RAJ BHALA, *See id.*

906 *See id.* at 12.

Ancient thinkers featured prominently in this debate. Generally, ancient thinkers believed that commercial activities of traders created a lot of problems to the morality of the people. For the ancient philosopher, Plato (428/427-348/347 B.C.), especially in his *Republic*, retail trade was an occupation beneath the dignity of a Greek citizen. Such jobs should be for incompetent aliens in the Greek City-State. In his *Republic* however, Plato conceded to the need for importation of necessary goods which the city-state is unable to produce, but on the condition, that it in turn exports its own surplus products.[907]

Aristotle (384-322 B.C.) is another ancient philosopher worthy of mention here. In his *Politics,* Aristotle did not endorse commerce especially as it concerned dependency on foreign trade. He, however, thought that port facilities should only be established for purposes of necessities that were not accessible within the city-state. For him, such port facilities should be separate from the functioning of the city-state and their functioning monitored by authorities to ensure that vices did not come with merchandise. The position of the ancient Roman, Cicero (106-43 B.C.), in his work, *De Officiis*, was that to buy merchandise at one price and sell it at a higher price to make profit is unacceptable unless such exchange brings great benefits or, in the alternative, enhances the intelligence of Romans. Other Greek and Roman thinkers supported foreign trade in their own way.[908]

Once free trade is accepted, the next important step to follow is to consider why trade takes place to understand how international trade increases the welfare of its citizens. To do this, the principles of absolute and comparative advantage as propounded by two prominent English economists will be considered to bolster this discussion.

It was in the years 1776 and 1826 that a standard theory about international trade was propounded by Adam Smith in his work, *Inquiry into the Nature and Causes of the Wealth of Nations* (1776); and David Ricardo's *The Principles of Political Economy and Taxation (1817)/Principles of Economics (1951).* Adam Smith and David Ricardo were opposed to the dominant mercantilist philosophy of the 17th and 18th centuries, as observed in England. Mercantilism advocated severe restrictions on

[907] *See* RAJ BHALA. INTERNATIONAL TRADE LAW, *supra* note 904, at 4.

[908] *Id.*

import, and aggressive efforts to increase exports thereby projecting a one-sided and unfair foreign trade. The resulting export surplus was supposed to enrich the nation through the inflow of precious metals.[909] Opposed to the mercantilist ideology, Smith and Ricardo both laid out the case for international trade.[910]

Adam Smith, who is regarded as the father of modern economics, countered mercantilist ideas by developing the concept of *absolute advantage.* A country has an absolute advantage economically over another, in a particular good, when it can produce that good at a lower cost. Using the same input of resources, a country with an absolute advantage will have greater output. Smith argued that it was impossible for all nations to become rich simultaneously by following mercantilist prescriptions because the export of one nation is another nation's import. However, all nations would gain simultaneously if they practiced free trade and specialized in accordance with their absolute advantage.

Though Smith successfully established the case for free trade, he did not develop the concept of comparative advantage. Because absolute advantage is determined by a simple comparison of labor productivities, it is possible for a nation to have absolute advantage in nothing. A few major trading countries appear to have an absolute advantage in a large array of goods, and small countries would seem to be helpless.[911] This is a problem that the theory of absolute advantage is not able to tackle. David Ricardo advanced the theory of comparative advantage as a refinement of Smith's absolute advantage principle.[912]

---

[909] See RAJ BHALA, INTERNATIONAL TRADE LAW, *supra* note 904, at 201 (indicating that mercantilism is not an anti-trade doctrine. Rather, it is an anti-free trade doctrine that calls for government intervention to generate a trade surplus. Such surplus can be used to invest in assets in other countries, and such investments can give the surplus country economic and political influence in the other countries. Mercantilists sought to maximize wealth by maximizing exports and minimizing imports. Mercantilists, therefore, favored a trade policy that creates restrictions, such as high tariffs on imports and support for exports, such as subsidies for exports). *Id.* at 201-202.

[910] RAJ BHALA, INTERNATIONAL TRADE LAW, *supra* note 904, at 201. In his An Inquiry into the Wealth of Nations, Adam Smith investigated the benefits of free trade, in response to the prevailing economic orthodoxy of the 17th and 18th centuries, namely, mercantilism.

[911] *Id.*

[912] In his Law of Comparative Advantage, Ricardo argued international trade is mutually beneficial for countries even if one has an absolute advantage in the production of all goods,

The theory of comparative advantage advances and refines Smith's theory of absolute advantage. Ricardo agreed with Smith's view that if there was no government involvement in trade and if everyone was left to do what is in his or her own best interest, then there would be more goods and services available, prices would be reduced, and the wealth of each nation would increase. Ricardo's comparative advantage theory extends Smith's view to the case where one of the two countries has an absolute advantage in both commodities, and it shows that even here trade is good for both countries.[913]

Therefore, in his theory of comparative costs, Ricardo suggested that countries would specialize and trade in goods and services in which they have a comparative advantage. It is easy to see that if countries have an absolute advantage, there are advantages to trade. However, what happens if one country has an absolute advantage over its trading partners in the production of many goods? Specialization and trade can still result in welfare gains made from trade.[914] A country has a comparative advantage in the production of a good or service that it produces at a lower opportunity cost than its trading partners. Some countries have an absolute advantage in the production of many goods relative to their trading partners. Some have an absolute disadvantage. They are inefficient in producing anything, relative to their trading partners. The theory of comparative costs argues that, put simply, it is better for a country that is inefficient at producing

---

under the following terms:
For the country with an absolute advantage in both goods, Ricardo advised specializing in the production of, and exporting, the good in which it has the greatest absolute advantage.

For the country with an absolute disadvantage in both goods, Ricardo suggested specializing in the production of, and exporting, the good in which it has the least absolute disadvantage.

See RAJ BHALA, *supra* note 56, at 207.

[913] *See id.* at 207-208 (showing that the Law of Comparative Advantage is the stated logic for negotiating, drafting, implementing, and enforcing rules to liberalize trade on a multilateral, regional, or bilateral basis. It is true that the Law of Comparative Advantage is not the only rationale for rules oriented toward freer trade; it is not even universally accepted because other supporting rationales exist. However, Comparative Advantage is the major economic paradigm for international trade law).

[914] David Ricardo, *The Principles of Political Economy and Taxation,* London, J. M. Dent & Sons, Ltd., date not listed p. 82.).

a good or service to specialize in the production of that good it is least inefficient at, compared with producing other goods.

A country has a comparative advantage in the production of a good if it can produce that good at a lower opportunity cost relative to another country. The theory of comparative advantage explains why it can be beneficial for two parties (countries, regions, individuals and so on) to trade if one has a lower relative cost of producing some good. What matters is not the absolute cost of production but the opportunity cost, which measures how much production of one product is reduced to produce one more unit of the other good.

Ricardo's theory of comparative advantage creates hope for technologically backward countries by implying that they can be a part of the world trading system even though their labor productivity in every good may be lower than that in the developed countries. In the Ricardian model, trade is a win-win situation, as workers in all trading countries can consume more of all goods. Ricardo was blissfully unaware of the complications that would be created if his model included another factor such as capital and if the producers had responded to changes in factor price ratio in favor of the cheaper factor.

The comparative advantage model has many unrealistic assumptions, which ignore the fact that the real world consists of many countries producing many goods using many factors of production. Each market is assumed to be perfectly competitive, when there are many industries in which firms have market power. Labor productivity is assumed to be fixed and full employment is guaranteed. The model assumes that technology differences are the only differences that exist between the countries. Finally, in a dynamic context, comparative advantage changes as trade in goods and capital alter the trading countries' factor endowments.

A little evaluation of the theories of Smith and Ricardo will help in this discussion. The difference between Smith's principle and Ricardo's principle is seen in the value attached to their respective thoughts. Ricardo specifically states where he differs from Smith on the rate of profits due to international trade. While Ricardo agrees with Smith on the tendency for the profit rate to realize a "general" level based on capitalists seeking the highest returns for their capital, Ricardo's value theory necessitates a difference from Smith. Whereas Smith believes that a country which reforms from mercantilist protectionism to free trade will realize higher profits in general, Ricardo's value theory states that even the profits in the free trade sector(s) will fall to the general rate regulated by the surplus profit on marginal lands.

5.2.2 The Catholic Church's Thoughts on Free Trade

In the thinking of the philosophers of the ancient, medieval, and modern periods, it is all about maximizing profits and subsequent developments which accrue from such economic profits. Little or nothing is said about the worth of the human person. This disregard for the dignity of human beings accounts for economic extremes such as capitalism, communism, socialism, and totalitarianism. If economic gains are prior to the dignity of the human person, human beings are made to be a means to an end, and this is absurd. Every economic or social activity ought to be directed toward the safeguard and promotion of the human person and not vice versa.

In their theories, Smith and Ricardo missed out on the role of demand as an explanation of terms of trade in exchange. The Utilitarians, particularly J.S. Mill, did introduce "reciprocal demand." Alfred Marshall further advanced the role of demand in terms of the "offer curve" which, according to him, cures Ricardian theoretical deficiency. Unfortunately, the utilitarians did not recognize the dignity of the human person. Therefore, Catholic social teaching on trade deserves a discussion here.

First and foremost, Catholic social teaching is present to both free trade and the freedom to trade with respect to the human person involved. Free trade is a secular arrangement, normally political and economic policy, whereby two or more countries agree on non-tariff barriers through negotiation. Freedom to trade, on the other hand, promotes respect for the right of a person to acquire or alienate property or goods without undue interference. Freedom to trade originates from the dignity of the human person. Because of its close link with human dignity and freedom, the Catholic Church safeguards and promotes the right of the human person's freedom to trade.[915] On the other side of the divide, the Catholic Church can only support free trade since it tallies with its social doctrine.

Free international trade is justified by the principles of Catholic social tradition. According to God's design, all human beings form one all-encompassing global family or global community. The contemporary market culture identifies international trade as essential for overcoming poverty and promoting the global common good. In practice in recent times, however, it is not contributing to the well-being of those in poverty in the way social justice demands. The establishment of a level playing field, while important, is not adequate.

International trade is a central component of international economic relations. International trade contributes immensely to the rapid economic growth of many developing countries. The preferential option for the poor calls for international trade. It provides a frame of reference for international trade. The plight of the less privileged is such that the need arises for an equitable trading system that will help the poor and allocate resources with fairness and justice. For this reason, benefits that accrue from trade ought to be fairly distributed in a way that ensures that exports from developing countries receive fair prices reached by negotiated agreement among all trading partners. Developing nations have a right to receive a fair price for their raw materials, which allows for a reasonable degree of profit.[916]

The Catholic social tradition places highest value on the dignity of the human person and the sacredness of all human life regardless of gender, class, ethnicity, nationality, or race. The emphasis is on people over things, being over having. Human work is an expression of human dignity, an acknowledgement of the reasoning that the economy exists to serve people, not vice versa. In human work also, human beings express their social nature in the form of establishment of relationships, what one can today refer to as networking. It is only in relationship to and with others that human beings realize the fulfillment of their dignity and rights.

---

[915] *See* PONTIFICAL COUNCIL FOR JUSTICE AND PEACE, COMPENDIUM OF THE CATHOLIC SOCIAL DOCTRINE OF THE CHURH, supra note 120, # 177.

[916] United States Catholic Bishops, Economic Justice for All: Pastoral Letter on Catholic Social Teaching and the U.S. Economy, 1986, # 267 available at http://www.usccb.org/upload/economic_justice_for_all.pdf

The principle of solidarity reminds people that they constitute one family characterized by interconnection, which in turn demands respect and value. There are mutual obligations to promote the rights and development of all peoples. Therefore, international structures must reflect justice because human beings reach out to one another to enhance development. In an arrangement where people celebrate solidarity, humanity appears much more interactive, transforming the sense of being close to one another into true communion.[917] When the gap that separates and alienates human beings is narrowed to a reasonable extent, the special claim of poor and vulnerable people ought to get the greatest response.[918]

The values of interpersonal relations cannot be over-emphasized. The human creature is defined through interpersonal relations. It is not in isolation that the human person establishes worth, but by placing himself or herself in relation with others.[919] The more authentically the human person expresses himself or herself in interpersonal relations, the more his or her own personal identity matures. According to Pope Benedict XVI,

> Just as a family does not submerge the identities of its individual members...so too the unity of the human

---

[917] *See* POPE BENEDICT XVI, ENCYCLICAL LETTER *Caritas In Veritate* (Charity in Truth), June 29, 2009, # 53. Development is identified with the inclusion-in-relation of all individuals and peoples within the one community of human family, built in solidarity on the basis of fundamental values of justice and peace. *See id.* # 54.

[918] *See* POPE JOHN PAUL II, ENCYCLICAL LETTER *Centesimus Annus*, May 1, 1991, # 41. The concept of alienation needs to be led back to the Christian vision of reality, by recognizing in alienation a reversal of means and ends. When man does not recognize in himself and in others the value and grandeur of the human person, he effectively deprives himself of the possibility of benefitting from his humanity and of entering into that relationship of solidarity and communion with others for which God created him. Indeed, it is through the free gift of self that man truly finds himself. The human person's essential "capacity for transcendence" makes this gift possible. Man cannot give himself to a purely human plan for reality, to an abstract ideal, or to a false utopia. As a person, he can give himself to another person or to other persons, and ultimately to God, who is the author of his being and who alone can fully accept his gift. A man is alienated if he refuses to transcend himself and to live the experience of self-giving, and of the formation of an authentic human community oriented towards his final destiny, which is God. A society is alienated if its forms of social organization, production, and consumption make it more difficult to offer this gift of self and to establish this solidarity between people. See also SECOND VATICAN ECUMENICAL COUNCIL, GAUDIUM ET SPES, # 24.

[919] POPE BENEDICT XVI, ENCYCLICAL LETTER *Caritas in Veritate*, # 53.

> family does not submerge the identities of individuals, peoples and cultures, but makes them more transparent to each other and links them more closely in their legitimate diversity.[920]

Because the dignity of the human person is superior to every other principle, the principle of subsidiarity recognizes in the human person the capacity to give something to others. Reciprocity is at the center of what it is to be human. With this understanding, the principle of subsidiarity is well-suited to manage globalization and direct it towards authentic human development. The principle of subsidiarity is a concrete expression of the principle of solidarity.[921]

It is evident that the principle of free trade by itself is inadequate for regulating international agreements. It can work when the parties involved respect the principle of equality; in such cases, it stimulates progress and rewards efforts. Pope Paul VI teaches "in order for international trade to be human and moral, social justice requires that it restore to the participants a certain equality of opportunity."[922] When all forms of dichotomy between industrially developed nations and poor countries are obliterated through the principle of justice, then such agreements will make sense. However, when the nations involved are far from equal, free trade becomes only a barometer for exploitation.

Therefore, Catholic teaching is that trade relations cannot be based solely on the principle of free unchecked competition, for it very often creates an economic dictatorship. Free trade can only be just when it conforms to the demands of social justice.[923] International trade is indispensable especially when the nations involved ensure that the trading system treats the poorest segments of developing countries' societies fairly, eschewing all forms of human rights violations.[924]

Material creation has been given to human beings to sustain their lives and to help them realize their God-given potentials. God gave the

---

920 *Id.* at 53.

921 *See id.* at 57.

922 POPE PAUL VI, ENCYCLICAL LETTER POPULORUM PROGRESSION (On the Development of Peoples), March 26, 1967, # 61.

923 *See id.* at nos. 58-59.

924 United States Catholic Bishops, Economic Justice for All, *supra* note 60, # 269.

resources of the earth, including human ingenuity for the material needs of every human being, favoring no one and excluding no one.[925] Every person has a right to these resources. These material goods correspond to the primary needs of the human person and constitute the basic conditions for his existence.[926] Without these basic needs met, it becomes impossible for the human person to develop himself fully.

Every economic structures and arrangement must give priority to the basic material needs of the human person. For the human person to feed himself, grow, communicate, associate with others, and attain the highest purposes, for which he is created, these material goods ought to be at his disposal.[927] As stated above, the human person has the universal right to use the goods of the earth based on the principle of the universal destination of goods.[928] The right to use these material goods is not only the whole essence of the ethical and social order but also one of the primary reasons why the Holy See registers its international presence in world affairs, as well as makes its voice heard.

The material resources of the earth are scattered all over the world. However, it is not evenly distributed in nature: only some locations have oil; only some locations have gold; only some locations have forest resources; only some have fish resources; only some have uranium; and so forth. This is like the agricultural industry; some concentrate on livestock; some specialize in hunting; some produce more rice than others; some are richer in vegetables; and others in fruits. People who are not lucky enough to be farmers specialize in arts and crafts, the baking industry, textiles, and other areas. Such specialization, as a matter of fact, necessitates exchange between these different specialists. To realize God's purpose for providing

[925] PONTIFICAL COUNCIL FOR JUSTICE AND PEACE, *supra* note 120, at 171 [indicating that the purpose of the fruitfulness of the earth is for it to satisfy human needs and to sustain human life. See also POPE JOHN PAUL II, ENCYCLICAL LETTER *Centesimus Annus*, # 31.

[926] Pope Pius XII, Radio Message for the Fiftieth Anniversary of *Rerum Novarum, AAS 33* (1941), 199-200.

[927] *Id.*

[928] See PONTIFICAL COUNCIL FOR JUSTICE AND PEACE, *supra* note 120, at 172.

everybody with material resources, exchange, otherwise called "trade," becomes necessary. This is what is referred to as "the universal economy."[929]

5.2.2.1 The Ancient and Patristic Periods

During the Patristic period, early Christian Fathers of the Catholic Church viewed trade as ethically unacceptable, recalling how Jesus Christ overturned the tables of merchants in the Temple and threw them out. They taught that commerce is a breeding exercise for *the Seven Deadly Sins,* namely, anger, covetousness, envy, greed, lust, pride, and sloth. Saint Augustine of Hippo, in his book *Exposition of the Book of Psalms*, taught people to desist from trade activities as a form of repentance.[930]

Most of the ancient philosophers and theologians were not supportive of the importation of non-necessary merchandise; neither did they endorse exportation of necessities. For them, self-sufficiency could better be achieved through autarky.[931] Later, particularly during the Medieval era, and with the introduction of the Doctrine of the Universal Economy, philosophers and theologians began to favor free trade. The Doctrine of the Universal Economy taught that:

> Trade between regions should be accepted as beneficial and even be permitted to run its course free from interference.... Providence deliberately scattered resources and goods around the world unequally to promote commerce between different regions. According to [noted economist] Jacob Viner [who identifies the Doctrine as the oldest, long-lived economic precept, and a forerunner of the factor endowments theory of trade, such as the Hecksher-Ohlin Theorem], [there are] four distinct elements [in

929 Jacob Viner, "Essays on Intellectual History of Economics," in Douglas A. Irwin, Princeton, Princeton University Press, (1991), p. 42; *See also* Jacob Viner, *The Role of Providence in the Social Order,* Princeton University Press, (1972); particularly chap. 2, "Providential Elements in the Commerce of Nations," pp. 32-54.

930 *See* Saint Augustine of Hippo, "Exposition of the Book of Psalms," *quoted in* RAJ BHALA, INTERNATIONAL TRADE LAW: INTERDISCIPLINARY THEORY AND PRACTICE, *supra* note 890, at 4.

931 *Id.*

> the Doctrine]. First, it embraces the stoic-cosmopolitan belief in the universal brotherhood of man. Second, it describes the benefits to mankind arising from the trade and exchange of goods. Third, it embodies the notion that economic resources are distributed unequally around the world. Finally, it attributes this entire arrangement to the divine intervention of a God who acted with the deliberate intention of promoting commerce and peaceful cooperation among men.[932]

Saint Thomas Aquinas discussed the issue of trade in his treatise, *De Regno,* where he rejects widespread trade. For him, a city should be self-sufficient in food. Self-sufficiency portrays greater perfection, provides greater safety, avoids dangers of foreign influence, and avoids avarice. Though opposed to complete free trade, Saint Thomas Aquinas agreed that some form of trade is needed for the provision of certain necessities of life. The reason for his concession to some form of trade is because no one location has all it needs, and different locations have resources in such abundance that they would be wasted if not traded to places they are needed.

> Still trade must not be entirely kept out of a city, since one cannot easily find any place so overflowing with the necessities of life as not to need some commodities from other parts. Also, when there is an overabundance of some commodities in one place, these goods would serve no purpose if they could not be carried elsewhere by professional traders. Consequently, the perfect city will make a moderate use of merchants.[933]

---

[932] *See* DOUGLAS A. IRWIN, *supra* note 904, at 15.

[933] Thomas Aquinas, *On Kingship, to the King of Cyprus*, trans. by G.B. Phelan, revised with an introduced and notes by I. T. Eschmann, Toronto, Pontifical Institute of Medieval Studies, (1982), 75-78. See also *Summa Theologiae* 2-2, q. 77, a. 4 where Saint Thomas Aquinas defends profits made by traders because of the beneficial services such traders render in the society. Still in his *Summa Theologiae*, Saint Thomas delineates three kinds of useful economic activities, namely, storing goods, importing necessity goods, and transporting goods to regions of scarcity. He teaches that it is not sinful to make pecuniary gains from

Subsequently, theologians and philosophers that came after Saint Thomas Aquinas discussed free trade from the perspective of the Doctrine of the Universal Economy, synthesizing the Doctrine with moral precepts.[934] One remarkable point worthy of note is the ecumenical tradition that different religious groups and organizations established about free trade. For instance, the *Qur'an* contains many verses (*ayat*) that address interaction among peoples, streamlining the upright conduct that merchants are to exhibit in commercial activities.

5.2.2.2 Period between Post-World War II and the Mid-1960s

An interesting issue that has been discussed above is the *Universal Destination of Goods.* The "Universal Destination of Goods" is a principle that the Catholic Church uses to teach about God's benevolence in making the resources of the earth available to every human being in such a way as to show that all human beings have an equal right to these goods.[935] God gave material resources to the world for providing for the material needs of everyone. The Church shows the connection between the principle of the universal destination of goods and trade when she taught that

> It would be well if the various nations in unity of purpose, common counsel and concerted endeavor, would strive to promote a healthy international economic cooperation by prudent pacts and institutions since in economic matters,

---

these activities. However, Saint Thomas taught that it is more dignified to engage in domestic production than trade. Trade, for him, is morally virtuous if conducted with proper motives. For more details on Saint Thomas Aquinas' thoughts on free trade, see Douglas Irwin, *Against the Tide: An Intellectual History of Free Trade*, Princeton, Princeton University Press, (1996), pp. 18-19.

[934] See RAJ BHALA, INTERNATIONAL TRADE LAW, *supra* note 904, at 5.

[935] See POPE JOHN PAUL II, ENCYCLICAL LETTER *Centesimus Annus* (On the Hundredth Anniversary of *Rerum Novarum*), May 1, 1991, Chapter 4, "Private Property and the Universal Destination of Material Goods," nos. 30-43. See also PONTIFICAL COUNCIL FOR JUSTICE AND PEACE, COMPENDIUM OF THE SOCIAL DOCTRINE OF THE CHURCH, supra note 120, at 171-180.

> they are largely dependent upon the other and need one another's help.[936]

For many years running, the Catholic Church has never relented in her efforts at spreading principles of just commerce around the world. The period between the First and Second World Wars and the Great Depression of the 1930s is a case in point. International trade was drastically affected because this period was characterized by unemployment, blocking of importation of goods, outflow of capital, and devaluation of currencies, which supported exports of goods but discouraged importation. Retaliation on the part of disadvantaged nations became a merry-go- round. The U.S. was a prime offender in this perspective following the Smoot-Hawley Tariff, which Congress enacted in 1930. All these culminated in the outbreak of World War II.

After the Second World War, there was need for reconstruction and restoration. As a follow up to the Versailles Treaty, which had put an end to the grievances of the First World War, there was a need to forestall a repeat of such a war. The world established the United Nations Organization, particularly its Security Council, to deter further military aggression. There were also institutional arrangements to beef up this scheme by promoting trade through reduction of tariffs and other trade barriers and by helping poorer nations' economic development. For these reasons, three institutions, called "Bretton Woods institutions," were established. They are the International Bank for Reconstruction and Development (the World Bank), the International Monetary Fund (IMF), and the General Agreement on Tariffs and Trade (GATT).[937]

With this development, the world went all out to show the connection between free trade and peace. In search of such a link, the United States Secretary of State under President Benjamin Franklin's administration painted a picture of the need to find peace through trade. He observed that the 1930s was a period characterized by "unhampered free trade

---

[936] POPE PUIS XI, ENCYCLICAL LETTER QUADRAGESIMO ANNO ("On the Reconstruction of the Social order, Forty Years After the *Rerum Novarum*), May 15, 1931, # 89; *See generally also* Stephen Rowntree (SJ), "The Ethics of Trade Policy in Catholic Political Economy," in *Theological Studies, 65* (2004).

[937] See DOUGLAS IRWIN, FREE TRADE UNDER FIRE, Princeton, Princeton University Press, (2002), 158-164.

that dovetailed with peace, high tariffs, trade barriers, and economic competition with war."[938] The Catholic Church came out boldly in defense of human dignity, though in search of this new world order. The Church emphasized the need for a freer trade that is moderated by moral principles referred to as the "new postwar moral order" indicating that hoarding of the resources of the earth is selfish:

> Within the limits of a new order founded on moral principles, there is no place for the cold and calculating egoism which tends to hoard the economic resources and materials destined for the use of all to such an extent that nations less favored by nature are not permitted access to them.[939]

Continuing in his economic thoughts reflecting the situation of things during post-World War II, Pope Pius XII regretted that war-torn nations only received aid because of their inability to take part in free trade. He further observed that countries of the world should follow God's providential design for free trade when he taught that

> None is in a better position than you to appreciate the contrast between the disorders in the field of economic relations, which has reigned in many countries for some time past - and the law, order, and harmony that God has imprinted on all creation. The goods of the earth, whose exchange ought to stabilize and maintain economic equilibrium among nations, has become the object of political speculation.[940]

---

[938] Cordell Hull, "Memoirs", 2 vols., New York, Macmillan, (1948) *quoted in* DOUGLAS IRWIN, *Free Trade Under Fire*, supra note 923, at 159; *See also* Jacob Viner, The Role of Providence in the Social order, *supra* note 900, at 32-54.; See also DOUGLAS IRWIN, AGAINST THE TIDE, supra note 904, at 15-25.

[939] See Pope Pius XII, "Christianity and the World Crisis," in Vincent A. Yzermans (ed.), *The Major Addresses of Pope Pius XII, Christian Addresses*, vol. 2, St. Paul Minneapolis, North Central, (1965), p. 45.

[940] Vincent A. Yzermans (ed.), The Unwearied Advocate: Public Addresses of Pope Pius XII, St. Cloud Minnesota, St. Cloud Bookshop, (1956), pp. 241-242.

The Catholic Church taught at that period that it was not fair for nations devastated by war to have to rely on aid. The normal relation between nations ought to be one of mutually beneficial commercial exchange (trade). For this reason, the Church insisted that:

> What remains of economic relations between nations is, strictly speaking no longer an exchange, the mutual action and reaction of which could do good everywhere. . .. Despite noble efforts, we are still far from a normal state of things, wherein exchange of goods between nations is, at one and the same time, the necessary compliment to their respective national economies and a tangible sign of their flourishing condition.[941]

The Catholic Church encourages trade as long as it is guided by moral principles, especially as directed by Catholic social doctrine. It is, however, opposed to the 19th century trade regime practiced under mercantilism. The Church taught that it is a contradiction for a country to promote its own exports and at the same time hinder importation from other countries. Pope Pius XII indicated that "We preferred not to speak of the fatal inconsistency of those who, in proposing free world traffic for their own goods, deny to others this natural liberty."[942]

---

[941] Id. *See also* STEPHEN ROWNTREE, *supra* note 936, at 600-601.

[942] *See* DOUGLAS IRWIN, FREE TRADE UNDER FIRE, *supra* note 937, at 174-178 [also indicating that the ability to export (dependent on the absence of trade barriers) is referred as a "natural liberty" in commercial parlance.] The phrase "natural liberty" is a reference to the 17th century natural law philosophers' thoughts. Suárez, who was Catholic, and Grotius, a Protestant philosopher, observed that international trade should be free, not so much because of natural law precepts, but those of the *jus gentium,* which specify how natural law precepts have come to govern the relations among nations:

> A state might conceivably exist in isolation and refuse to enter into commercial relations with another state even if there were no unfriendly feeling involved, but it has been established by the *jus gentium* that commercial intercourse shall be free, and it would be a violation of the system of law if such intercourse were prohibited without reasonable cause.

See DOUGLAS IRWIN, AGAINST THE TIDE, *supra* note 904, at 22-23. *See also* De Legibus, ac Deo Legislatore (1612) quoted in Francisco Suárez (S.J.), *Selections from Three Works of Francisco Suárez*, vol. 2, Oxford, Clarendon, (1934), at 347.

Because of the universal character of the social mission of the Catholic Church that embraces every individual or institution, the Church was also concerned about the level of poverty in the former colonies of some super powers in the world. How could the world overcome this poverty and get these former colonies that eventually gained independence to achieve prosperity through meaningful development? The Church was uncomfortable with the prevalent situation. Because of this unfair scenario, the Church called for

> Relationship between economically advanced commonwealths and those that are in the process of development, the most pressing question of the day, [observing with disappointment that] . . .. The economically developed countries enjoy a high standard of living while all the others "experience dire poverty."[943]

Based on this inequality, the Church advocated for monetary and technical assistance to poor countries though she taught that such outside aid is not the ultimate solution to the poverty in question. What poor countries need, the Catholic Church teaches, is rather expertise and investment capital to develop their economies which are groping in the woods in their primitive states.[944] The human family should always embrace the principle of solidarity in such a way that industrialized countries help poor nations through movements of goods, capital, and people, especially moderated by principles of fairness and justice.[945] In a situation such as this, poor countries should be made to study the paths that rich countries followed so as to embrace more efficient policies and fair distributive regimes.[946]

---

943 POPE JOHN XXIII, ENCYCLICAL LETTER *Mater Et Magistra*, # 157.

944 *See id.* at 163.

945 See POPE JOHN XXIII, ENCYCLICAL LETTER *Mater Et Magistra*, # 155. It is therefore obvious that the solidarity of the human race and Christian brotherhood demand the elimination as far as possible of these discrepancies. With this object in view, people all over the world must co-operate actively with one another in all sorts of ways, so as to facilitate the movement of goods, capital, and men from one country to another. *Id.*

946 *See* POPE JOHN XXIII, ENCYCLICAL LETTER MATER ET MAGISTRA, nos. 167-168.

The teaching of the Second Vatican Council is uniquely centered on the growing relations of economic interdependence between nations. In this authentic document, the Catholic Church teaches investment decisions should not only take cognizance of the huge gap between the rich countries and the poor ones but should work toward solving the problems of such poverty.[947] Technological advancement resulting in enhanced trade ought to meet the ever-expanding needs of the whole human family.

> Progress in the methods of production and in the exchange of goods and services has made the economy an instrument capable of better meeting the intensified needs of the human family.... It was for this reason that the Church in the course of the centuries has worked out, in the light of the Gospel, principles of justice and equity demanded by right reason for individual and social life and also for international relations.[948]

The foregoing analysis shows that the Catholic Church teaches that during the post-Second War period, freer trade was necessary for the economies of war-torn countries to recover and for the development of the economies of economically backward nations. The Church discovered that unbalance trade relations between rich nations and poor countries hampered the beneficial nature of free trade. The Church lauded the honesty of some colonizers who provided their former territories with skills and technical know-how to enable them to explore and exploit the benefits of many untamed lands. The structural machinery they introduced to their former colonies, though not modern, helped to reduce ignorance and disease, to promote communication, and to improve living conditions. However, some colonial masters exploited their former colonies by making them cheap sources of primary mineral and agricultural products with obvious negative impacts.[949]

---

[947] SECOND VATICAN ECUMENICAL COUNCIL, GAUDIUM ET SPES, # 70.

[948] Id. at 63.

[949] See POPE PAUL VI, ENCYCLICAL LETTER POPULORUM PROGRESSIO (On the Development of Peoples) March 26, 1967, # 7. *See also* STEPHEN ROWNTREE, *supra* note 936, at 605.

Pope Paul VI rejected what is referred to as "dependency theory" whereby economic underdevelopment is traceable to unequal and dependent relations between rich countries and poor countries. In this ugly arrangement, industrialized countries exploit poor countries by engaging them in a commercial exchange in which manufactured goods are traded for primary products and minerals.[950] The unfairness is seen in the exchange of manufactured goods whose prices are increasingly higher with primary commodities (such as crude minerals and raw agricultural products) whose prices are low and have remained low. With this structure on the ground, the rich countries will ever grow richer at the expense of the poor countries. This is unfair to the poor countries, whose economies can never develop if the situation remains the way it was.[951] One understands

[950] Jon Hendricks, "Dependency Theory," in *Encyclopedia of Sociology*, (2nd ed. 2000). In his article, Jon Hendricks quotes Andrew Gunder Frank as having formulated "the premise for dependency theory," namely, "contemporary underdevelopment is a result of an international division of labor exploited by capitalistic interests." See Andre Gunder Frank, "Capitalism and Underdevelopment in Latin America" (1967), and "Latin America: Underdevelopment or Revolution (1969) *quoted by* Jon Hendricks. *See id.*

[951] *See* POPE PAUL VI, ENCYCLICAL LETTER POPULORUM PROGRESSIO, # 57. Because of these unbalanced trade relations between rich and poor countries, Pope Paul VI viewed international trade as exploitative and therefore didn't give endorsement. It sounds reasonable that if free trade, which should help poor countries to develop their economies, turns around to hurt them, then free trade occasions such damaging effects and should therefore be discouraged. So, Pope Paul VI's rejection of free trade is based on the opinion that free trade has overall good results, that free trade is the sole norm that governs international economic relations. Pope Paul VI reasoned,

> It is evident that the principle of free trade, by itself, is no longer adequate for regulating international agreements. It certainly can work when both parties are about equal economically; in such cases it stimulates progress and rewards effort. That is why industrially developed nations see an element of justice in this principle. But the case is quite different when the nations involved are far from equal. Market prices that are freely agreed upon can turn out to be most unfair. It must be avowed openly that, in this case, the fundamental tenet of liberalism (as it is called), as the norm for market dealings, is open to serious question. . .. The highly developed nations have already come to realize this. At times they take appropriate measures to restore balance to their own economy, a balance that is frequently upset by competition when left to itself. Thus, it happens that these nations often support their agriculture at the price of sacrifices imposed on economically more favored sectors. Similarly, to maintain the commercial relations which are developing among them, especially within a common market, the financial, fiscal and social policy of these nations tries to restore comparable opportunities to competing industries that are not equally prospering.

why Pope Paul VI did not look at international trade with any positive support, since free trade was harmful to poor countries and only favored the rich ones.

The Church was right under Pope Paul VI in rejecting free trade at this period because of the level of unfairness that was in vogue. There ought to have been some reorganization of the workings of free trade to establish equal opportunity between rich and poor countries. Pope Paul VI found the solution to this plaguing problem in a situation whereby international agreement were negotiated with equal participation of rich and poor countries alike.[952] Therefore, Pope Paul VI reasoned that competitive markets should be kept in check by being constantly scrutinized with just and moral principles.[953]

Also, important in the Church's thoughts on free trade is the case of multinational corporations with enormous size and financial resources

---

See Pope Paul VI, ENCYCLICAL LETTER Populorum *Progressio*, nos. 58 & 60.

[952] *Id.* at 60.

[953] *See id.* at 61. The stand of Pope Paul VI about modifying the unbalanced relations between rich and poor countries under competitive market also constitutes his thoughts in his Apostolic Letter *Octogesima Adveniens* (On the 80th Anniversary of *Rerum Novarum*), May 14, 1971. He still objected to an international arrangement in which rich countries exploit the poor ones, calling instead for mutual dependence and cooperation in place of political and economic compulsion. *See also* POPE PAUL VI, APOSTOLIC LETTER OCTOGESIMA ADVENIENS ("On the 8oth Anniversary of *Rerum Novarum*"), May 14, 1971, # 46. There is a need to establish a greater justice in the sharing of goods, both within national communities and on the international level. In international exchanges there is a need to go beyond relationships based on force, to arrive at agreements reached with the good of all in mind. Relationships based on force have never, in fact, established justice in a true and lasting manner even if at certain times the alteration of positions can often make it possible to find easier conditions for dialogue. The use of force moreover leads to the setting in motion of opposing forces, and from this spring a climate of struggle which opens the way to situations of extreme violence and to abuses. . .. The most important duty in the realm of justice is to allow each country to promote its own development, within the framework of cooperation free from any spirit of domination, whether economic or political. The complexity of the problems raised is certainly great, in the present intertwining of mutual dependences. Thus it is necessary to have the courage to undertake a revision of the relationships between nations, whether it is a question of the international division of production, the structure of exchanges, the control of profits, the monetary system- without forgetting the actions of human solidarity - to question the models of growth of the rich nations and change people's outlooks so that they may realize the prior call of international duty, and to renew international organizations so that they may increase in effectiveness. See POPE PAUL VI, APOSTOLIC LETTER OCTOGESIMA ADVENIENS, # 43.

that place them even beyond the control of individual nations. The guardians of the principle of common good are supposed to be national governments, but the nature of multinational corporations have tended to put some national governments under the whims of these corporations. These corporations pose "the threat of a new and abusive form of economic domination on the social, cultural, and even political level."[954]

5.2.2.3 The Period between the Mid-1970s to the Present

During the Pontificate of Pope John Paul II, the complaint was principally on the trade barriers mounted against the exports of poor countries. The strategy the industrialized countries used in achieving this heinous goal was through the introduction of arms trade, which is instrumental to the waste of poor countries' scarce resources, and at the same time fueling armed conflicts. Therefore, Pope John Paul II vehemently taught that there should be a reform of the international trade system to create room for freer commerce. The Pontiff observed that

> We are thus confronted with a strange phenomenon: while economic aid and development plans meet with the obstacle of insuperable ideological barriers, and with tariff and trade barriers, arms of whatever origin circulate with almost total freedom all over the world.[955]

---

[954] *See id. at 44.* Under the driving force of new systems of production, national frontiers are breaking down, and we can see new economic powers emerging, the multinational enterprise, which by the concentration and flexibility of their means can conduct autonomous strategies which are largely independent of the national political powers and therefore not subject to control from the point of view of the common good. By extending their activities, these private organizations can lead to a new and abusive form of economic domination on the social, cultural and even political level. The excessive concentration of means and powers that Pope Pius XI already condemned on the fortieth anniversary of *Rerum Novarum* is taking on a new and very real image.

[955] POPE JOHN PAUL II, ENCYCLICAL LETTER SOLLICITUDO REI SOCIALIS ("On the Social Concerns of the Church" on the 20th Anniversary of *Populorum Progression*), December 30, 1987, # 24.

What poor countries need is export-oriented strategy and not import-substitution strategy.[956] Pope John Paul II indicated that the reforms needed to include issues such as subsidies, protectionism, and bilateralism.[957] During the Pontificate of John Paul II, the original drive and stability that characterized multilateralism was being attacked by the emergence of bilateral and regional arrangements. This tension heightened with the emergence of Free Trade Agreements (FTAs) in the form of single-market structures.[958] At the heart of the reason for their interest in bilateralism and regionalism is the disappointment expressed by poor and fast-developing countries over the ugly strategy that developed countries use to frustrate the textile and agricultural trade.[959] They believed that this move would end the practice of developed countries to set limits on the quantity and rates of textile and agricultural commercial activities of developing countries.[960]

---

[956] The newly industrializing countries pose perfect examples of how export-oriented strategy can lift economies up progressively. This is what is referred to as "trade-driven economic development." See Donald L. Sparks, "Economic Trends in Africa South of the Sahara, 2001," in *Africa South Of the Sahara 2002,* (31st ed., London, *Europa,* 2001), p. 12.

[957] See POPE JOHN PAUL II, SOLICITUDO REI SOCIALIS, # 42. Bilateralism refers to free trade agreements between two countries, which makes their trade relations freer but maintains barriers against countries that are not party to the agreement. Multilateralism is a trade structure that is open to any willing nation. In multilateralism, once a favor is granted to one of the parties, other parties are automatically entitled to such, all things being equal. This can rightly be interpreted as the principle of non-discrimination, a practice known in international trade law as "most-favored-nation," as will be discussed later. See ROWNTREE, *supra* note 936, at 61.

[958] Examples include the European Economic Community (EEC) and the Free Trade Agreement (FTA) between the United States and Canada. As a single-market, the EEC is, by prior standards, the most ambitious enterprise on the horizon. On one side of the Atlantic also, there emerged the Caribbean Common Market (CARICOM), the Caribbean Basin Initiative (CBI), and the Central American Common Market (CACM). On the other side of the Atlantic, there emerged the Assembly of Region of Europe (ARE), while across the Pacific there emerged the Pacific Basin Forum (PBF) and the Asian-Pacific Organization (APO). Even the Soviet bloc established the Council for Mutual Economic Assistance (COMECON). The United Nations had its regional commissions as well – its Economic Commission for Europe (ECE), its Economic Commission for Africa (ECA), and for the Far East and Asia (ECFEA). There were other similar arrangements between the U.S. and Japan and members of the Association of South-East Asian Nations (ASEAN). See Malachi Martin, *The Keys of this Blood: Pope John Paul II Versus Russia and the West for Control of the New World Order,* New York, Touchstone, 1990, pp. 318-326.

[959] *Id.*

[960] *Id.*

Initiating single-market arrangements sounds plausible, but it does not provide all the solutions needed to establish peace on earth. Therefore, it is unjust for the industrialized countries to mount barriers to the imports of economically disadvantaged countries, so the problem of gaining access to the international market is an issue on which the Church has called for a change of heart. Thus, Pope John Paul II reminds developing countries to take active part in the free market. Abstaining from international trade does not help. Pope John Paul II addressed this problem when he taught that though credit may be given to sectional initiatives, they are nothing compared to the new world order.

> In recent years it was thought that the poorest countries would develop by isolating themselves from the world market and by depending on their own resources. Recent experience has shown that countries that did this have suffered stagnation and recession, while the countries that experienced development were those which succeeded in taking part in the general interrelated economic activities at the international level.[961]

The Catholic Church did not declare single markets as evil but only encouraged the world body (this time the GATT) to modify its rules and their implementation in such a way as to create the sense of mutuality. For instance, in his teaching on free trade, Pope John Paul II addressed the

---

[961] POPE JOHN PAUL II, ENCYCLICAL LETTER CENTESIMUS ANNUS ("On the Hundredth Anniversary of Rerum Novarum"), May 1, 1991, # 33; though the free market is not the only solution to inequalities in the world and the preservation of human dignity, Pope John Paul II stresses its benefits,

> Following the destruction caused by the war, we see in some countries and under certain aspects a positive effort to rebuild a democratic society inspired by social justice, so as to deprive Communism of the revolutionary potential represented by masses of people subjected to exploitation and oppression. In general, such attempts endeavor to preserve free market mechanisms, ensuring, by means of a stable currency and the harmony of social relations, the conditions for steady and healthy economic growth in which people, through their own work, can build a better future for themselves and their families. *See id.* at 19.

issue of "sweat shop objection" to freer trade.[962] The "sweat shop objection" to free trade is scenarios whereby some workers in poor and fast-developing countries are paid wages many times lower than those of industrialized countries. These poor workers are not given any fringe benefits, and they are forced to work long hours in unsafe conditions with no protection from unfair, even brutal treatment.

Their employers make huge gains at the expense of these workers. This unfair labor practice is the way it is because governments of the countries involved either lack the required labor laws, or when they have, they are not fair enough or the laws are not enforced. Therefore, Pope John Paul II indicated that

> There exists, too, a kind of international division of labor, whereby the low-cost products of certain countries that lack labor laws, or which are too weak to apply them are sold in other parts of the world at considerable profit for the countries engaged in this form of production, which knows no frontiers.[963]

The pontiff therefore taught with emphasis on the precarious nature of peace through international trade. International trade plays a crucial role in promoting development.

> It may be that man is destined for work and called to it; in the first place work is for man and not man for work . . . in the final analysis it is always man who is the purpose of the work, whatever work it is that is done by man even if the common scale of values rates it as the merest "service", as the most monotonous even the most alienating work.[964]

962

See ROWNTREE, supra note 936, at 611.

963 POPE JOHN PAUL II, ENCYCLICAL LETTER SOLLICITUDO REI SOCIALIS, # 43.

964 POPE JOHN PAUL II, ENCYCLICAL LETTER LABOREM EXERCENS ("On Human Work"), September 14, 1981. *Laborem Exercens* was presented on the 19th anniversary of Pope Leo XIII's *Rerum Novarum;* both encyclicals discussing the conditions of workers. This is why Pope John Paul II laid some emphasis as follows:

An interesting part of this period is the teaching of the United States Catholic Bishops. In 1986, U.S. bishops published a Pastoral Letter titled *Economic Justice for All: Pastoral Letter on Catholic Social Teaching and the U.S. Economy.* In this pastoral letter, the bishops discussed the relations between the United States and developing countries. They stressed that trade is one of the five ways the U.S. could and should help poor countries. The other four ways the U.S. could help poor countries are increased development assistance, debt forgiveness, increased foreign investment, and food security assurance.

The U.S. bishops acknowledge the indispensable role that trade plays in the economic progress of countries involved. Little wonder that the bishops discussed trade from the perspective of option for the poor. They enjoined that

> An equitable trading system that will help the poor should allocate its benefits fairly and ensure that exports from developing countries receive fair prices reached by agreement among all trading partners. Developing nations have a right to receive a fair price for their raw materials that allows for a reasonable degree of profit.[965]

Though the U.S. Catholic bishops emphasized the benefits of trade as an engine in the rapid economic development of developing countries, they however clarified that the free trade at issue should be "fair trade." The fair trade in question accommodates equitable practices that guarantee fair prices for the exports of poor countries. The vision behind fair trading

---

We are celebrating the ninetieth anniversary of the Encyclical *Rerum Novarum* on the eve of new developments in technological, economic and political conditions, which, according to many experts, will influence the world of work and production no less than the industrial revolution of the last century. There are many factors of a general nature: the widespread introduction of automation into many spheres of production, the increase in the cost of energy and raw materials, the growing realization that the heritage of nature is limited and that it is being intolerably polluted, and the emergence on the political scene of peoples who, after centuries of subjection, are demanding their rightful place among the nations and in international decision-making. These new conditions and demands will require a reordering and adjustment of the structures of the modern economy and of the distribution of work. *See id.* at 19

[965] U.S. Catholic Bishops, Economic Justice for All supra note 60, # 267.

system is one that assures a reasonable degree of profit for both the exporting and importing countries. It must be that the bishops are talking about freer trade and not just free trade, because the latter gives parties freedom to operate, but the former benefits poor countries, as well as removes barriers.

This period under review pays more attention to the conditions of workers. The U.S. Catholic bishops emphasized the link between trade and labor standards, reiterating the issue of Pope John Paul II's "sweat shop objection" to trade. They rejected the exploitative threat to unionized workers, and called for the government and employers to respect the rights of workers, especially in poor countries. This injustice is prevalent in situations where employers of labor in the U.S. ship certain investments overseas because of cheap labor.[966] The bishops have enjoined the government of the U.S. to insist on fair treatment of workers and the respect for their rights even abroad. The U.S. should pay attention, for instance, to

> [T]he extent to which the success in the U.S. market of certain imports is derived from *exploitative labor conditions in the exporting country, conditions that, in some cases, have attracted the investment* in the first place. The United States should do all it can to ensure that the trading system treats the poorest segments of developing countries' societies fairly and does not lead to human rights violations. In particular, the United States should seek effective special measures under the General Agreement on Tariffs and Trade (GATT) to benefit the poorest countries.[967]

Pope Benedict XVI based his teaching on international commercial relations on charity and love. Charity is at the heart of the Church's social doctrine. Integral human development can only be realized when inspired by values of charity and truth. Every responsibility and every commitment spelled out by that doctrine is derived from charity, which, according to the teaching of Jesus, is the synthesis of the entire Law. Charity gives real substance to the personal relationship with God and with one's neighbor;

[966] *Id.* at 269.

[967] *Id.* (emphasis added).

it is the principle not only of micro-relationships (with friends, with family members, or within small groups) but also of macro-relationships (social, economic, and political ones). Charity is at the heart of the Church's social doctrine.[968]

Seeing the obvious inequalities in international relations and the dangers of capitalism that are opposed to mutuality, Pope Benedict XVI called on all countries to embrace the discipline of charity and truth. The Pontiff taught that human and economic development depends on the recognition that humanity is a single family working together in true communion.[969] What is needed is,

> To find innovative ways of implementing the principle of the responsibility to protect and of giving poorer nations an effective voice in shared decision-making. This seems necessary in order to arrive at a political, juridical and economic order that can increase and give direction to international cooperation for the development of all peoples in solidarity. To manage the global economy; to revive economies hit by the crisis; to avoid any deterioration of the present crisis and the greater imbalances that would result; to bring about integral and timely disarmament, food security and peace; to guarantee the protection of

---

[968] POPE BENEDICT XVI, ENCYCLICAL LETTER CARITAS IN VERITATE ("On Integral Human Development in Charity and Truth"), June 29, 2009, # 2; Concerning international relations from the perspective of globalization, Pope Benedict XVI said,

The principle of subsidiarity is particularly well-suited to managing globalization and directing it towards authentic human development. In order not to produce a dangerous universal power of a tyrannical nature, the governance of globalization must be marked by subsidiarity, articulated into several layers and involving different levels that can work together. Globalization certainly requires authority, insofar as it poses the problem of a global common good that needs to be pursued. This authority, however, must be organized in a subsidiary and stratified way, if it is not to infringe upon freedom and if it is to yield effective results in practice.

See id. at 57; *See also* POPE JOHN XXIII, ENCYCLICAL LETTER PACEM INTERRIS ("Peace on Earth"), # 274.

[969]

See id. at 53. Pope Benedict XVI adds that: "The Christian revelation of the unity of the human race presupposes a metaphysical interpretation of the "*humanum*" in which *relationality* is an essential element." *See id.* at 55.

> the environment and to regulate migration: for all this, there is urgent need of a true world political authority....[970]

Concerning human work, Pope Benedict XVI emphasized the importance that the Church attaches to labor unions. The Catholic Church has always encouraged and supported labor unions, especially in this period that such unions should be open to new perspectives which are emerging in the world of work. In his encyclical, *Caritas in Veritate*, Pope Benedict called on labor unions to press for the rights of not just their registered members but also every other worker against the violation of their social rights. By this, labor unions will accommodate all exploited and unrepresented workers who are working under woeful conditions.[971]

Pope Francis teaches that the social concern of the Catholic Church needs some modification in such a way as to involve Christians more. Under him, the teaching of the Church is that Christian conversion demands a review in those areas and aspects of life related to the social order and the pursuit of common good.[972] It is not enough to prepare souls for eternal life, but the Church must also be concerned about every aspect of human life.

---

[970] *See id. at 67.* See also Pope Benedict XVI, *Address to the Members of the General Assembly of the United Nations Organization*, New York, April 18, 2008. This is what Pope John XXIII would consistently refer to as,

> The principles of subsidiarity and solidarity, to seek to establish the common good, and to make a commitment to securing authentic integral human development inspired by the values of charity in truth. Furthermore, such an authority would need to be universally recognized and to be vested with the effective power to ensure security for all, regard for justice, and respect for rights.

See POPE JOHN XXIII, ENCYCLICAL LETTER PACEM IN TERRIS ("Peace on Earth"), # 293; PONTIFICAL COUNCIL FOR JUSTICE AND PEACE, COMPENDIUM OF THE SOCIAL DOCTRINE OF THE CHURCH, # 441; SECOND VATICAN ECUMENICAL COUNCIL, (GAUDIUM ET SPES) (Pastoral Constitution on the Church in the Modern World), # 82.

[971] POPE BENEDICT XVI, ENCYCLICAL LETTER CARITAS IN VERITATE, # 64.

[972] POPE FRANCIS I, APOSTOLIC EXHORTATION EVANGELII GAUDIUM ("On the Proclamation of the Gospel in Today's World"), November 24, 2013, # 182.

> The Church's teachings concerning contingent situations are subject to new and further developments and can be open to discussion, yet we cannot help but be concrete – without presuming to enter into details – lest the great social principles remain mere generalities, which challenge no one. There is a need to draw practical conclusions, so that they "will have greater impact on the complexities of current situations." The Church's pastors, taking into account the contributions of the different sciences, have the right to offer opinions on all that affects people's lives, since the task of evangelization implies and demands the integral promotion of each human being. It is no longer possible to claim that religion should be restricted to the private sphere and that it exists only to prepare souls for heaven.[973]

The position of Pope Francis I makes a lot of sense, in that it is impossible to talk about human dignity, which is the cornerstone of CST, without addressing all aspects of man. We cannot emphasize holiness without addressing all the human questions involved, and one of them, as far as the theme of this book is concerned, is international trade.

> Consequently, no one can demand that religion should be relegated to the inner sanctum of personal life, without influence on societal and national life, without concern for the soundness of civil institutions, without a right to offer an opinion on events affecting society. Who would claim to lock up in a church and silence the message of Saint Francis of Assisi or Blessed Teresa of Calcutta? They themselves would have found this unacceptable.[974]

This is an interesting idea as far as the dynamism required in Catholic social thought is concerned. Authentic faith should consistently involve

---

973 *Id. See also* PONTIFICAL COUNCIL FOR JUSTICE AND PEACE, COMPEDIUM OF CATHOLIC SOCIAL DOCTRINE, # 9.

974 *See* POPE FRANCIS I, ENCYCLICAL LETTER EVANGELII GAUDIUM, # 183.

a deep desire to make the world a better place, to transmit values, and especially to leave the world better than we found it. Human beings must appreciate the world God created and gave to us. There must be love of the human family that dwells on earth. Human beings must appreciate the tragedies and struggles, the hopes and aspirations, as well as the strengths and weaknesses on earth.

The earth is our common home. The central responsibility of politics on earth is the just ordering of society. Based on these facts, Pope Francis eschews any economy of exclusion and inequality.

> How can it be that it is not a news item when an elderly homeless person dies of exposure, but it is news when the stock market loses two points? This is a case of exclusion. Can we continue to stand by when food is thrown away while people are starving? This is a case of inequality. Today everything comes under the laws of competition and the survival of the fittest, where the powerful feed upon the powerless. As a consequence, masses of people find themselves excluded and marginalized: without work, without possibilities, without any means of escape. Human beings are themselves considered consumer goods to be used and then discarded. We have created a "throw away" culture, which is now spreading. It is no longer simply about exploitation and oppression, but something new. Exclusion ultimately has to do with what it means to be a part of the society in which we live; those excluded are no longer society's underside or its fringes or its disenfranchised – they are no longer even a part of it. The excluded are not the "exploited" but the outcast, the "leftovers."[975]

[975] *Id.* at 53. Pope Francis is of the opinion that the world should not continue to watch inequalities and unjust structures that have the potential to disintegrate the world take the center stage. He indicated that inequality among countries engenders violence and insecurity. The present day economic mechanism is characterized by unbridled consumerism and inequality, which prove doubly damaging to the social fabric. "The poor and the poorer peoples are accused of violence, yet without equal opportunities, the different forms of aggression and conflict will find a fertile terrain for growth and eventually explode. When a

The Catholic Church is commissioned by Jesus Christ to raise her moral voice in every aspect of human life. Since this is the case, the Church cannot remain on the sidelines in the struggle for justice.[976] The time has gone when the right ordering of the society from the spiritual and social perspectives was the exclusive preserve of the clergy. Pope Francis calls on Christians, lay faithful, and pastors alike, to make it their primary concern to build a better world. The Church must not only make proposals, but must also work with other Churches doctrinally and pragmatically in her social concerns.[977]

Pope Francis declares that there should be a proper and just management of the earth which he has taught people to understand as our common home. This has a bearing on the understanding that any economic decision in one part of the globe has repercussions everywhere else.[978] The world should always see the demand for wealth distribution, as well as the concern for the poor and human rights, as authentic. This is so because when these concerns are threatened, it dawns on the Church to raise its prophetic voice.[979] It is a moral duty of the Church to speak for the weak and the defenseless when they are exploited.

Worthy of note also is Pope Francis' teaching that the dignity of each human person and the pursuit of the common good are concerns that ought to shape all economic policies.[980]It therefore stands to reason that inequality and exploitation are the roots of social ills. In a revelation on the principles of Catholic social doctrine, Pope Francis teaches that the principle of the common good is indispensable in making the world a better place. He, however, indicates that the common good is not possible without the principles of subsidiarity and solidarity in international relations.[981]

---

society – whether local, national or global – is willing to leave a part of itself on the fringes, no political programs or resources spent on law enforcement or surveillance systems can indefinitely guarantee tranquility." *See id.* at 59.

976 *See* POPE FRANCIS I, APOSTOLIC LETTER EVANGELII GAUDIUM, # 183.

977 *Id.*

978 *See id.* at 206.

979 See POPE FRANCIS I, APOSTOLIC LETTER EVANGELII GAUDIUM, # 218.

980 *Id.* at 203.

981 *Id.* at 240.

At this juncture, it must be pointed out that the Catholic social teaching, as is being taught by the successive popes and the bishops, has consistent subject matter. The issues that have always featured include human dignity (with its concomitant social nature of man, equality of human beings in dignity, inalienable rights which must be respected), the Universal destination of goods, the common good, subsidiarity, solidarity, and option for the poor. Though each pope must present his teaching in his own peculiar style, the above topics have consistently featured in their respective teachings. The popes have rejected injustice, exploitation, inequality and any form of domination. The earth is our common heritage and all hands must be on deck to establish mutual and participatory relations, especially in international commercial relations. One interesting and unique point that Pope Francis raised is to involve everyone in the struggle for justice.

The WTO was established to liberalize international trade in a style that appears to synchronize with the objectives of the Catholic social doctrine. The WTO/GATT system works to help in the realization of the set objectives of international trade. There have been controversies over whether the WTO has lived up to expectations in pursuing its laudable objectives. This discussion will now proceed to outline these objectives. This exercise will throw more light on the degree of effectiveness of the social mission of the Catholic in using its prophetic voice in challenging the WTO to live up to its *raison d'etre.*

5.3 GATT-WTO Principles

The WTO came into existence on 1 January 1995, but its trading system, the General Agreement on Tariffs and Trade (GATT) is 50 years older than the WTO. The GATT has provided the rules for the global trading system since 1 January 1948, when it entered into force after being signed on 30 October 1947. Additional rules over the years are products of the various rounds of negotiations between Members. The WTO and GATT operate harmoniously as one global trading system. Whereas GATT deals with trade in goods, the WTO and its agreements cover trade in services, trade in inventions, creations and designs (*i.e.* intellectual property).[982]

5.3.1 Principles of the GATT-WTO Trading System

Writing down GATT/WTO agreements would be a book length because it is complex. The GATT-WTO agreements are legal texts that cover a wide range of issues such as agriculture, textiles and clothing, banking, telecommunications, government purchases, industrial standards and product safety, food sanitation regulations, intellectual property, and lots more. Because the activities of the GATT-WTO system are lengthy, a certain number of common principles run throughout all the documents. These principles form the foundation of the GATT-WTO multilateral trading system.[983]

5.3.1.1 Non-discrimination Principles

Members of the WTO, like the GATT contracting parties before them, practice international trading without discrimination – or, at least, they are supposed to. The WTO operates within non-discriminatory structures. What this means is that under normal circumstances, a Member cannot discriminate between or among its trading partners with respect to like products. This obligation establishes equality in membership. All Members are treated equally on a most-favored nation (MFN) and national treatment basis: indeed, MFN and national treatment are, taken together, two pillar obligations of GATT, and fall under the rubric of "non-discrimination."[984] GATT Article I:1 states that any advantage, favor, privilege, or immunity

[982] *See* World Trade Organization, "Understanding the WTO," (5th ed.), 2011 available at http://www.wto.org/theWTO last visited February 6, 2014.

[983] *Id.*

[984] The MFN obligation also is a foundation of the General Agreement on Trade in Services (GATS), in Article II, and in the Agreement on Trade Related Aspects of Intellectual Property Rights (TRIPS), Article 4. However, the GATS MFN obligation is conditional, partly for reasons of negotiations on financial services during the Uruguay Round) 1986-1994) and American concerns about free ridership. Accordingly, an Annex to GATS lists MFN exceptions.

granted to any member in respect of like products shall immediately and unconditionally be granted to other Members. For example, an importing country should not apply different tariffs to the same product or producers of the like product of different exporting members; each exporting country should face the lowest (most-favored) tariff on a good applied by the importing country. It is important to state that while MFN has the maxim: "Love your neighbors equally;" the maxim for the National Treatment principle is: "Love your neighbor like yourself." It is better to explore the National Treatment principle further.

5.3.1.2 National Treatment – Treating foreign and domestic producers or businesses equally:

Imported and locally produced goods should be treated equally, especially when foreign goods enter domestic markets. This is applicable to foreign and domestic services, foreign and local trademarks, copyrights, and patents. The goal of this national treatment is to give foreign business commercial counterparts the same treatment as nationals.[985] GATT relies on the term "like product" heavily, and other close terms, to expound its trade liberalizing rules.[986] It is common to nearly all GATT law that certain consequences follow in the use of the term "like products" only if goods resemble one another.

The following GATT provisions are good examples:

1.) The most favored nation (MFN) obligation in GATT Article I:1 depends on an imported item from one country being like that of another country.
2.) The tariff binding obligation in GATT Article II:1, which gives rise to eligibility for a concession agreed upon in trade negotiations,

---

[985] *See* the three major WTO agreements and their provisions in GATT Article 3, Article 17 of GATS, and Article 3 of TRIPS. National treatment only applies once a product, service, or item of intellectual property enters a market. Therefore, charging customs duty on an import is not a violation of national treatment even if locally produced goods are not charged an equivalent tax. See World Trade Organization, "Understanding the WTO," (5th ed. 2011) available at http://www.wto.org/theWTO last visited February 7, 2014.

[986] *See* BHALA, MODERN GATT LAW, 2nd ed., (Vol. 1), *supra* note 96, at 211.

depends on classification of imported merchandise in Schedule of Concessions (which, in turn, is based on the Harmonized System (HS) and its General Rules of Interpretation (GRI). Thus, one of the exceptions in GATT Article II:2 to the tariff binding obligation relies on the concept of "likeness."

3.) The national treatment obligation concerning internal taxation, set out in GATT Article II:1 and III:2, first sentence, depends on an imported item being like a domestic product. The national treatment obligation in GATT Article III:4 depends on an imported item being like a domestic product.

a) The antidumping rules in GATT Article VI:1 presume an imported product that is allegedly dumped is "like" a product destined for domestic consumption or "like" a product in a third country. GATT Article VI:7, which is an exception to the antidumping (AD) rules for agriculture commodity price stabilization schemes, uses the term "like" commodity."

b) GATT Article VII sets out rules about customs valuation, one of which – in GATT VII:1 – is that value be based on the actual value of imported merchandise or of "like" merchandise.

c) GATT Article IX:1 is an MFN obligation for country of origin marking, and applies to "like product" from third countries.

d) The prophylactic rule against quantitative restrictions in GATT Article XI:1 is subject to various exceptions. One of them, in Article XI:2(c), permits import restrictions on agricultural products to enforce, a governmental measure that operates to remove a temporary surplus of the "like domestic product."

e) GATT Article XIII:1 is an MFN obligation for the administration of quantitative restrictions. It requires any permitted restriction to be non-discriminatory with respect to all "like product" from third countries.

f) The subsidy rule in GATT Article XVI:4, which calls for the elimination of export subsidies on non-agricultural products, applies to a subsidy that results in the sale of a good for export at a price lower than the comparable price charged for the "like product" to buyers in the domestic market.

j) The escape clause remedy in GATT Article XIX:1, designed to combat fair foreign competition, requires that there be a "like product" made domestically (or a directly competitive one).[987]

Professor Bhala explains the WTO Agreement as a treaty – the international equivalent of a contract.[988] In an exercise of their sovereignty, and in pursuit of their own respective national interests, WTO Members made a bargain. While they expect to derive certain benefits as WTO Members, they reciprocate by committing themselves to the WTO Agreement. Examples of such commitments are the legal facts statement above. A further discussion of GATT Article III will help to understand national treatment better. Generally, GATT Article III guarantees that WTO Members are bound not to undermine through internal measures their commitments under GATT Article II which provides for protection of negotiated tariff concessions.[989]

The purpose of GATT Article III is two-fold: (1) to avoid protectionism in the application of internal tax, and (2) regulatory measures. More specifically, the purpose of GATT Article III "is to ensure that internal measures 'not to be applied to imported or domestic products so as to afford protection to domestic production.'"[990] This provision is important as it obliges Members of the WTO to provide equality of competitive conditions for imported products in relation to domestic products.[991]

[987] *See id.* at 212.

[988] See BHALA, International Trade Law, supra note 904, at 377.

[989] See *Canada – Import, Distribution and Sale of Certain Alcoholic Drinks by Provincial Marketing Agencies*, B.I.S.D. (39th Supp.) at 27 ¶ 5.30 (1993) (adopted 18 February 1992) [The Appellate Body cited this case stating that although the protection of negotiated tariff concessions is certainly one purpose of Article III, the crux of the matter is that WTO Members should exercise internal measures in way that would not undermine their commitments to the WTO Agreement, especially in treating "like products" (GATT Article III: 1-2 first sentence which applies to like products, and second sentence which applies to directly competitive or substitutable products; GATT Article III:1-2 first and second sentences which apply to fiscal (tax) measures, and GATT Article III:4 which applies to non-fiscal (non-tax) measures.

[990] *See* Section 337 of the United States Tariff Act of 1930, B.I.S.D. (13th Suppl.) at 345 ¶ 5.10 (1990) *quoted in* BHALA, International Trade Law, supra note 890, at 377.

[991] *See United States – Taxes on Petroleum and Certain Imported Substances*, B.I.S.D. (34th Suppl.) at 136 ¶ 5.1.9 (1988) (adopted 17 June 1987); *Japan – Customs Duties, Taxes and Labelling Practices on Imported Wines and Alcoholic Beverages*, B.I.S.D (34th Suppl.) at 83 ¶ 5.5(b) (1988) (adopted 10 November 1987) [where the Appellate Body confirmed the reason

Moreover, it is irrelevant that "the trade effects" of the tax differential between imported and domestic products, as reflected in the volumes of imports, are insignificant or even non-existent.

GATT Article III national treatment obligation is also a general prohibition on the use of internal taxes and other internal regulatory measures so as to afford protection to domestic production.[992] Moreover, it is irrelevant that "the trade effects" of the tax differential between imported and domestic products, as reflected in the volumes of imports, are insignificant or even non-existent.[993] Thus, GATT Article III protects expectations not of any particular trade volume but rather of the equal competitive relationship between imported and domestic products. Members of the WTO are at liberty to pursue their own domestic goals through internal taxation or regulation so long as they do not do so in a way that violates Article III or any of the other commitments they have made in the WTO Agreement.[994]

GATT Article III:1 contains general principles while Article III:2 provides for specific obligations regarding internal taxes and internal charges. Article III:1 articulates a general principle that internal measures should not be applied to afford protection to domestic production. Article III:1 establishes this general principle as a guide to understanding and interpreting the specific obligations contained in Article III:2 and in the other paragraphs of Article III. It also informs the first sentence and second sentence of Article III:2 in different ways.[995]

---

behind GATT Article III indicating that "The intention of the drafters of the Agreement was clearly to treat the imported products in the same way as the like domestic products once they had been cleared through customs."] See *Italian Discrimination Against Imported Agricultural Machinery* B.I.S.D. (7th Suppl.) at 60 ¶ 11 (1959) (adopted 23 October 1958).

992 *See Brazilian Internal Taxes Case*, B.I.S.D. II at 181 ¶ 4 (1952) (adopted 30 June 1949); Panel Report, *United States — Taxes on Petroleum and Certain Imported Substances* (adopted 17 June 1987) BISD 34S/136; *EEC – Regulation on Imports of Parts and Components*, B.I.S.D. (37th Supp.) at 132 ¶ 5.4 (1991) (adopted 16 May 1990); [Appellate Body cited these cases in support of the fact that the sheltering scope of GATT Article III is not limited to products that are the subject of tariff concessions under Article II, but also GATT Article III which is a national treatment obligation also.]

993 *See United States – Taxes on Petroleum and Certain Imported Substances, supra.*

994 *See* BHALA, INTERNATIONAL TRADE LAW, *supra* note 904, at 377.

995 *See id.* at 378.

Article III:1 informs Article III:2, first sentence, by establishing that if imported products are taxed more than like domestic products, then that tax measure is inconsistent with Article III. The words of Article III:2 first sentence require an examination of the conformity of an internal tax measure with Article III by determining (1) whether the taxed imported and domestic products are "like" and, (2) whether the taxes applied to the imported products are in "excess of" those applied to the like domestic products. If the imported and domestic products are "like products," and if the taxes applied to the imported products are "in excess of" those applied to the like domestic products, then the measure is inconsistent with Article III:2, first sentence.[996]

GATT Article III:2 second sentence provides for a separate and distinctive consideration of the protection of a measure in examining its application to a broader category of products that are not "like products." Whether imported and domestic products are "like" is considered on a case-by-case basis. In determining whether the imported and domestic products are "similar products" as the Article stipulates, fairness of such exercise requires a case-by-case approach. In determining whether an internal tax measure is inconsistent with article III:2, second sentence, three pertinent issues are whether:

> the imported products and the domestic products are "directly competitive or substitutable products" which are in competition with each other;
> the directly competitive or substitutable imported and domestic products are "not similarly taxed;" and
> the dissimilar taxation of the directly competitive or substitutable imported and domestic products is applied so as to afford protection to domestic production.[997]

Lastly, GATT Article III:4 deals with national treatment obligation on non-fiscal measures. GATT Article III:4 is a subsidy rule which calls for

---

996 *See id.* at 379; *See also United States – Measures Affecting the Importation, Internal Sale and Use of Tobacco,* B.I.S.D. (41st Supp.vol.1) at 131 (1997) (adopted on 4 October 1994); *Japan – Customs Duties, Taxes and Labelling Practices on Imported Wines and Alcoholic Beverages, supra.*

997 *See* BHALA, INTERNATIONAL TRADE LAW, supra note 904, at 382.

the elimination of export subsidies on non-agricultural products. Article III:4 applies to a subsidy that results in the sale of a good for export at a price lower than the comparable price charged for the "like product" to buyers in the domestic market.[998] Article II:4 does not guarantee any particular volume of trade. Rather, it "obliges Members of the WTO to provide equality of competitive conditions for imported products in relation to domestic products.[999] The Appellate Body Report, *European Communities – Measures Affecting Asbestos and Asbestos-Containing Products,* is an illustrative case on GATT Article III:4 provision.[1000]

In the *EC Asbestos* case, the Appellate Body inferred the meaning of "like product" in Article III:2, first sentence, is narrower than the meaning in Article III:4. That is because the second sentence of Article III:2 plays the role of expanding the national treatment obligation to "directly competitive or substitutable products." Article III:4 has no sentence playing that kind of role. Rather, all the work, as it were, is done by the term "like products." Therefore, it is reasonable to view this term in the context of Article III:4 more broadly than in Article III:2, first sentence, assuming the goal of the interpretative process is to impart strong meaning to the national treatment obligation. Thus, the Appellate Body states this point more succinctly in *EC Asbestos* case: "we conclude that, given the textual difference between Article III:2 and III:4, the 'accordion' of 'likeness' stretches in a different way in Article III:4."[1001]

5.3.1.3 The Principle of Predictability – through the features of stability, binding commitments, and transparency

This refers to the need to ensure foreign companies, investors, and governments that trade barriers will not be raised arbitrarily and that all trade related policies are transparent to foreigners. Predictability is a

[998] *See* BHALA, MODERN GATT LAW, *supra* note 96, at 212.

[999] *See* Appellate Body Report, *European Communities' Asbestos* Case, infra note 986, at para. 97.

[1000] *See* Appellate Body Report, *European Communities – Measures Affecting Asbestos and Asbestos-Containing Products*, WT/DS135/AB/R (adopted March 12, 2001).

[1001] *See Appellate Body Report, European Communities – Measures Affecting Asbestos and Asbestos-Containing Products*, WT/DS135/AB/R, para. 96 (adopted March 12, 2001).

feature that the WTO possesses and this makes the multilateral trading system stable. With stability, businesses have a clearer picture of future opportunities available to them, thereby making planning assuredly possible. When there is stability and predictability, investments flow without mixed feelings; jobs are created and consumers enjoy the fruits of healthy competition in business.[1002]

There is no single GATT-WTO rule on "predictability," but all of them taken as a corpus provide for predictability by creating rule-based system, that is, the multilateral rule of trade law. Among those rules, however, GATT Article X on transparency is particularly noteworthy. GATT Article X provides for measures to guarantee transparency, particularly, publication of trade rules, monitoring and consultation about trade transactions of the Members of WTO for purposes of uniform and impartial administration.[1003] International trade law requires for its effective, practical, day-to-day application transparency.[1004]

Thus, GATT Article X:1 stipulates as follows:

> Laws, regulations, judicial decisions and administrative rulings of general application, made effective by any contracting party, pertaining to the classification or the valuation of products for customs purposes, or to rates of duty, taxes or other charges, or to requirements, restrictions or prohibitions on imports or exports or on the transfer of payments therefore, or affecting their sale, distribution, transportation, insurance, warehousing inspection, exhibition, processing, mixing or other use, shall be published promptly in such a manner as to enable governments and traders to become acquainted with them. Agreements affecting international trade policy which

[1002] *See* The World Trade Organization (WTO) *website,* "Understanding the WTO," available at http://www.wto.org/english/thewto_e/whatis_e/tif_e/devl_e.htm last visited May 7, 2014.

[1003] *See generally,* BHALA, MODERN GATT LAW, *supra* 96 chapter 40.

[1004] *See id.* at 1340. GATT Articles VI:6(c), XI:2, XII:2-4(a)-(c), XIII:3(a)-(c) & XIII:4, XV:8, XVI:1, XVII:4(A)-(c), XVIII, section B, para. 8, 9 & 12(a)-(c), XVIII section C, para. 13, 14, 16 & 18, XVIII, section D, para. 22, XIX:2, XXIV:7(a)&(c), XXVII, XXVIII:1, XXXVII:1, 2(a)-(b) & 5 are provisions that stipulate international trade law transparency requirements for WTO Members. *See* BHALA, MODERN GATT LAW, *supra* 96, at 1341-1343.

> are in force between the government or a governmental agency of any contracting party and the government or governmental agency of any other contracting party shall also be published. The provisions of this paragraph shall not require any contracting party to disclose confidential information which would impede law enforcement or otherwise be contrary to the public interest or would prejudice the legitimate commercial interests of particular enterprises, public or private.

In the WTO system, once countries agree to open their markets for goods or services, they "bind" their commitments. For goods, these bindings amount to ceilings or customs tariff rates. Sometimes some countries tax imports at rates that are lower than the bound rates, a practice that occurs mostly in developing countries. However, in developed countries, bound rates and the rates changed tend to be the same. When a country is said to have changed its bound rates, two things are possible. Either the country must have engaged its trading partners in a prior negotiation for the change or must have arbitrarily effected the change, which is illegal. When any of the two possibilities occurs, the country pays compensation to the affected trading partners. This is a way of assuring predictability and stability in international trading.[1005]

Other ways through which the WTO improves predictability and stability abound. One way is to discourage the use of quotas and other measures used to set limits on the quantities of goods imported. Experience shows that the administration of quotas can lead to more red tape and accusations of unfair practices. Another way is to make the trade rules of countries clear, public, or transparent enough. For this reason, many WTO agreements are made in such a way as to require governments to make their trade policies and practices public within their respective countries, or to notify the WTO compulsorily. Also through WTO's Trade Policy Review Mechanism (TPRM), regular national surveillance of national-level trade policies is assured at multilateral levels.[1006]

[1005] *See* BHALA, MODERN GATT LAW, *supra* note 96, chapter 40.

[1006] *Id.*

5.3.1.4 Engendering Free Trade through Negotiation

The WTO encourages freer trade by lowering barriers to the cross-border flow of goods, services, and intellectual property, and to some degree, foreign direct investment (FDI). Historically and to the present day, barriers (especially in respect of goods) take the form of tariffs or customs duties and measures such as banning of imports or imposition of quotas that restrict quantities of selected imports.[1007] Red tape and exchange rate policies also come into play. Since 1947, when GATT came into existence, there have been nine Rounds of trade negotiations. The Ministerial Conference in Bali, Indonesia Agenda has been in motion since 2103 in preparation for what may be tenth Round of trade negotiation if it succeeds.

Early GATT Rounds focused on lowering tariffs (customs duties) on imported goods. The negotiations in these Rounds, which occurred between the later 1940s until the early 1960s, were so effective that by the mid-1970s, tariff rates of most developed countries, including the United States and those of Europe, on industrial goods had fallen consistently to less than one percent. Later, multilateral trading negotiations, particularly the Tokyo Round, expanded to cover non-tariff barriers on goods, and in the Uruguay Round, to address barriers to trade in services and intellectual property.[1008]

Opening markets can be beneficial. However, opening markets also requires some adjustments. The WTO agreements allow countries to introduce changes gradually through "progressive liberalization." Developing countries are normally given longer time periods to fulfill their obligations based on the Special and Differential Treatment principle.[1009] During the Tokyo Round of negotiations, Members could not agree on

---

[1007] *Id.* The reduction of barriers helps to make the trading system more competitive by discouraging unfair practices such as subsidizing exports and dumping products in foreign markets. Dumping occurs when products are sold in foreign markets at a lower price than in domestic markets and harm is created to industries in the foreign markets. The global trading system should be freer over time with tariff and non-tariff barriers (NTBs) coming down through successive rounds of negotiation. This has been achieved in large measure through the lowering of tariffs on goods, but much room exists to reduce NTBs for goods, and all kinds of barriers to trade in services.

[1008] *Id.*

[1009] *Id.*

the formula for tariff cuts. As a result, Members formed blocs in making their tariff cut offers using different formulae.[1010] However, to achieve the purpose of the Special and Differential Treatment of developing countries, especially least developed countries (LDCs), the Tokyo Round adopted inter alia, established permanently the legal basis for granting preferential trade treatment to LDCs. Also, during the Tokyo Round, LDCs were afforded more flexibility in enacting trade measures designed to meet their economic growth interests.[1011] An *Enabling Clause* was agreed to as the legal basis for the Generalized System of Preferences (GSP) offered by developed countries.[1012] No formula was used for tariff cuts in agricultural products. Rather, the traditional selective product-by-product approach was applied.[1013]

5.3.1.5 Promoting Fair Competition

The WTO is often described as a "free trade" institution, but that characterization is entirely accurate. Sometimes the WTO system accommodates tariffs, and at other times, it allows some other forms of protection, though under occasional circumstances. The character that fits the WTO system is that its system of rules hinges on open, fair, and undistorted competition. For instance, the rules on non-discrimination (MFN and national treatment), dumping (exporting goods at below production cost to gain market share), and subsidies are designed to secure fair trade conditions. These rules establish issues such as what is fair and unfair, methods of government response, and charging additional import duties as compensation for damage caused by unfair trade.[1014]

[1010] *See* BHALA, INTERNATIONAL TRADE LAW, *supra* note 904, at 24-25.

[1011] *Id.* at 26.

[1012] The GSP is a non-reciprocal scheme whereby certain exports from beneficiary developing countries receive duty-free treatment. Until the Tokyo Round, a waiver from GATT obligations like MFN treatment under GATT Article I:1 provided that basis. Technically, the waiver provision contained in Article XXV, did not afford certainty and predictability. The waiver standard is both rigorous and subject to contextual interpretation. Article XXV:5 calls for waiver only under exceptional circumstances. *See* BHALA, INTERNATIONAL TRADE LAW, *supra* 904, at 25-26.

[1013] *See* BHALA, MODERN GATT LAW, *supra* note 96, at 991.

[1014] *Id.*

Other WTO agreements aim to support fair competition, for example, in agriculture, intellectual property, and service-related trading. The agreement on government procurement (normally called a "plurilateral" agreement because it is signed by only a few WTO Member-countries) extends competition rules to purchases by thousands of government entities in many countries. There are tons of other examples, which space would not allow at this stage of this discussion.[1015]

5.3.1.6 Encouraging Development and Economic Reforms

The WTO system contributes immensely to development in Members, especially in developing countries. For instance, developing Members are allowed flexibility in the period they need to take to implement WTO agreements. WTO agreements grant them longer transition periods to adjust to the more unfamiliar and difficult WTO provisions. The extra grace period is particularly so for the poorest, "least-developed" Members. Examples of special treatment of developing countries include asking developed Member-countries to accelerate implementing market access commitments on goods exported by least-developed countries, allowing duty-free and quota-free imports for almost all products from least-developed Members, and increased technical assistance for them. Also, both GATT and WTO agreements provide for special assistance and trade concessions to developing Members. Over three quarters of WTO Members are developing countries and countries with fast developing market economies.[1016]

5.4 GATT-WTO Objectives

Based on the above guiding principles, the WTO Members pledge themselves, individually and collectively to promote national and international actions toward attainment of the following objectives of the WTO:

[1015] *Id.*

[1016] *Id.*

1. To assure a large and steadily growing volume of real income and effective demand, to increase the production, consumption and exchange of goods, and thus to contribute to a balanced and expanding world economy.
2. To foster and assist industrial and general economic development, particularly of those countries that are still in the early stages of industrial development, and to encourage the international flow of capital for productive investment.
3. To further the enjoyment by all countries, on equal terms of access to the markets, products, and productive facilities needed for their economic prosperity and development.
4. To promote on a reciprocal and mutually advantageous basis, the reduction of tariffs and other barriers to trade and the elimination of discriminatory treatment in international commerce.
5. To enable countries, by increasing the opportunities for their trade and economic development, to abstain from measures that would disrupt world commerce, reduce productive employment, or retard economic progress.
6. To facilitate through promotion of mutual understanding, consultation, and cooperation, the solution of problems relating to international trade in the field of employment, economic development, commercial policy, business practices and commodity policy.[1017]

5.5 Status of the Holy See at the WTO

History has it that the founding members of the WTO are the 23 countries represented by their delegates who were signatories to the GATT. These 23 signatories to the GATT are the original "contracting parties" to GATT.[1018] Except for the Union of Soviet Socialist Republics (USSR), which withdrew in the early period of the negotiations, the parties would

[1017] RAJ BHALA, INTERNATIONAL TRADE LAW: INTERDISCIPLINARY THEORY AND PRACTICE (3RD ED. Documents Supplement), Matthew Bender & Co., 2008, pp. 7-8

[1018] Under the GATT Agreement, a "contacting party" was defined not as a "State" or a "nation," but as a government, which applied GATT 1947 under Article XXVI or Article XXXIII or pursuant to Protocol of Provisional Application. See 30 October 1947, *UNTS 55*

have numbered 24.[1019] It was the laudable brevity of the 23 delegates from participating countries that enabled GATT to enter into force on January 1, 1947, as the modern trading system. Those 23 countries automatically became WTO Members on January 1, 1995, along with others who negotiated their accession with existing Members.[1020] Any state or customs territory with full autonomy in the conduct of its trade policies may "accede to" the WTO.[1021]

Apart from the contracting Members, there are other Members who do not have a voting right in the negotiations. They are known as Observers.[1022] The WTO allows the award of Observer status to governments and international governmental organizations.[1023] The permission for government Observer status in the General Council and its subsidiary bodies is for two purposes. First, is to foster acquaintance with the WTO and its activities. Second is to prepare and initiate negotiations for the Observer to accede to the WTO Agreement.

Concerning Observers, the WTO follows a completely split policy with respect to governments, inter-governmental organizations (IGOs) and

---

(1955), 308; *See also* Article XXXII of GATT 1947; MODERN GATT LAW vol. 1, supra note 96, at 5.

[1019] *See* RAJ BHALA, INTERNATIONAL TRADE: INTERDISCIPLINARY THEORY AND PRACTICE, (3rd ed.), Matthew Bender & Co., Inc., 2007, p. 8; *See also* MODERN GATT LAW, supra note 96, at p. 17.

[1020] Every nation applying to join the WTO follows rigorous accession procedures, and the time necessary for completing the accession process varies. If a number of Members are keen to secure market concessions from the applicant, the bargaining and accession processes are more intense and difficult, and hence, lengthy. For this reason, bigger traders tend to take a longer time to join the WTO. For example, it took China, who became a Member in 2001, over 15 years to complete its accession process. As of January 1, the 1995, GATT Agreement had 128 contracting parties that were eligible to become original Members of the WTO due to their status. The WTO Agreement entered into force with 76 Members on January 1, 1995; another 47 original Members accede to the WTO Agreement between the date of its entry into force and the time limit for acceptance according to Article XIV:1 SENTENCE 3 (January 1, 1997). See Article XI: 1; Article XII governs accession procedures. See also BHALA, MODERN GATT LAW, Vol. 1, *supra* note 96, at 7.
See "Handbook on Accession to the WTO," http://www.wto.org/english/thewto_e/acc_e/cbt_course_e/c4s2pl_e.htm last visited February 2, 2014.

[1021] *See* Article 12 of WTO Agreement.

[1022] *See* BHALA, MODERN GATT LAW, *supra* note 96, at 30-32.

[1023] *See* Article V para. 8 of the WTO Agreement

Non-governmental organizations (NGOs).[1024] In addition, different rules for Observer status apply in different organs of the WTO. In principle, each organ is autonomous in its decision to accept governments or NGOs as observers, even though the case of NGOs is an entirely different issue.[1025] Also, unlike the UN, non-state entities with the status of separate customs territories can become full Members of the WTO.[1026]

All three groups mentioned above can be Observers to the Ministerial Conference. Only governments and inter-governmental organizations can be Observers to the General Council and other subordinate bodies. For governments, being Observers first is, in principle their first step on the way to membership at the WTO.[1027] Requests for Observer statuses are addressed to the General Council and must include an expression of intent to initiate negotiations on accession to the WTO Agreement. Observer status, once granted, is limited to a maximum period of five years, within which accession negotiations are expected to begin, though an extension is available.

Observer status in the General Council carries with it certain rights and obligations. Observer governments have access to the main WTO document series. They may request technical assistance from the WTO Secretariat in relation to the operation of the WTO system in general, as well as issues concerning WTO accession.[1028] Observer governments have the right to attend formal meetings of the General Council and its subsidiary bodies, including accession Working Parties, (with the exception of the Committee on Budget, Finance and Administration).[1029] However, as a matter of custom, the General Council holds its informal meetings without Observer governments. Representatives of governments accorded

---

1024 *See* WTO, "International Governmental Organizations granted Observer Status to WTO Bodies," available at http://www.wto.org/english/thewto_e/igo_obs_e.htm last visited March 23, 2014

1025 *See* Daniel L. Bethlehem (ed.), *The Oxford Handbook of International Trade Law,* Oxford University Press, (2009), p. 92.

1026 *See* list of countries negotiating for accession to the WTO available at WTO website www.wto.org/english/thewto_e/acc_e.htm last visited February 7, 2014.

1027 *See* General Council, "Request by the Former Yugoslav Republic of Macedonia for Observer Status in WTO Bodies," in *WT/L/16,* January 20, 1995, Annex 2.

1028 *See* Guidelines, WTO document *WT/L/161,* Annex 2, and para. 9.

1029 See WTO website http://www.wto.org/english/thewto_e/acc_e/acces_e.htm last visited June 24, 2013.

Observer status "may be invited to speak at meetings of the bodies to which they are Observers, normally after Members have spoken. The right to speak does not include the right to make proposals, unless a government is specifically invited to do so, nor to participate in decision-making."[1030]

On the issue of obligation, Observer governments have an obligation to make a financial contribution for the services provided to them of 0.014 percent of the total WTO budget, which is the same as the minimum annual contribution made by the smallest WTO Members.[1031] This figure amounted to about SFr 26,000 for the year 2006 (equivalent of about US $21, 000; € 16, 000).[1032] As will be discussed below, the Holy See was granted Observer status, not based on its economic capacity (the Holy See has no industries as to make investments or contributions like regular Members), but based on its unique nature and mission.[1033] Indeed, the Holy See is not bound to make this contribution.[1034]

With the exception of the Holy See,[1035] these Observer Governments must start negotiations for accession to WTO Agreement within five years of becoming Observers.[1036] In granting Observer status to the Holy See,[1037]

[1030] *See* Guidelines, WTO document *WT/L/161,* Annex 2, and para. 10.

[1031] *See* Guidelines, WTO document *WT/L/161,* Annex 2, and para. 11.

[1032] *Id.*

[1033] *See infra* note 1020.

[1034] *See* WTO Secretariat Budget, "Members' contributions to the WTO budget and the budget of the Appellate Body 2013," http://www.wto.org/english/res_e/booksp_e/anrep_e/anrep13_chap8_e.pdf last visited February 8, 2014. In the account of contributions to the 2013 budget, the Holy See was not listed as a contributor.

[1035] The Holy See became Permanent Observer to the World Trade Organization on July 16, 1997. The Holy See is the only "country" that does not have the obligation to start negotiations for Membership of the WTO. *See* Archbishop Silvano M. Tomasi, "Welcome to the Holy See Mission: Historical Introduction to the Multilateral Activities of the Holy See," [discussing the presence of the Holy See in international diplomatic relations] available at http://holyseemissiongeneva.org/index.php?option=com_content&view=article&id=364 last visited June 2, 2014. *See also* "The Holy See Requests for Observer status in the Ministerial Conference and the General Council," *WT/L/221,* July 2, 1997. The Holy See was granted Observer status based on its uniqueness and universal mission. This is why the requirement in Annex 2 of the Rules of Procedure was waived. See General Council Minutes of Meeting held on July 16, 1997, *WT/GC/M/21,* August 6, 1997, 2. See also Rüdiger Wolfrum, et al., *WTO: Institutions and Dispute Settlement*, Netherlands, Martinus Nijhoff Publihers,(2006), p. 152

[1036] *See* WTO, available at www.wto.org/english/thewto_ejwhatis_ejjorg6_e.htm last visited May 12, 2014.

[1037] The Holy See only applied for Observer status with the WTO two and half years after the creation of the WTO. The WTO came into being on January 1, 1995, while the Holy

the General Council took into account its unique situation and waived the requirement concerning the intention to initiate negotiations for accession, on the understanding that this decision does not constitute a precedent for future decisions on requests for Observer status.[1038] It could also be that the Holy See had no voting right, neither can it join or block consensus at the meetings of the General Council.

At the General Council Meeting on 16 July 1997, the Holy See was granted Observer status as reported by the minutes of the meeting:

> The General Council, on 16 July, granted the Holy See's request for Observer status. In its request, the Holy See said that while it was an independent customs territory, the insignificant size of its trade did not warrant accession to the WTO. Just like the reason for its participation in other international organizations, *the main interest of the Holy See in the WTO is in furtherance of peace, justice, progress and solidarity among nations.* The Holy See thanked members of the General Council, and underlined international trade's role in promoting peace. In welcoming the decision, Mr. Ruggiero said that the Holy See had been playing a useful role in international relations, as shown by its contributions to the United Nations system. He said the WTO shares the Holy See's aim of fostering peace and well-being all over the world.[1039]

Technically, the Holy See could offer suggestions on matters outside of ethics, that is, on purely technical trade matters, but on several occasions, it has chosen not to make its voice heard. A situation like this makes one

---

See became a Permanent Observer on July 16, 1997.

[1038] The General Council has on two occasions deferred consideration of such requests. In one case a Member needed additional time to examine the matter, (see Request from Liberia, WTO document WT/GC/M/57). In the other, the request was withdrawn shortly after its presentation, when an application was made to accede to the WTO. *See* The Lebanese Republic's request for observer status, *WTO documents, WT/L/283* and *WT/GC/M/32,* withdrawn and replaced by request for accession, WTO documents *WT/ACC/LBN/1 and WT/GC/M/40). See also* Holy See, WTO document *WT/GC/M/21.*

[1039] *See* TWN Trade Issues/Rules and WTO, Jun-July 1997, No. 20 available at http://www.twnside.org.sg/trade.htm last visited February 24, 2014 (emphasis added).

also wonder why it took the Holy See about two and a half years after the birth of the WTO to work toward becoming a Permanent Observer at the WTO. Why was the Holy See, whose social mission in international diplomacy centers on social justice, not present in the pre-Uruguay Round, and even during the Uruguay Round? It was during the Uruguay Round, which was launched in September 1986, that the core GATT/WTO Agreements rule of international trade as we have it today were negotiated.

During the Uruguay Round (September 1986-15 April 1994), a bevy of issues that have great impacts on developing and least developed countries featured prominently. Even during the pre-Uruguay Round, discussions were reverberating in every nook and cranny. If the Holy See had assumed Observer status at that time, that it would have enabled it to not only play a vital role in the negotiations but also to help in writing the life-wire of international trade. The Holy See would have well exercised its social mission, commenting and writing the Uruguay Round rules, just like it did with the United Nations.

It could be that the Holy See did not project its mind to the huge issues involved in international trade relations. It could also be that the Holy See wanted to watch first and see which way the tide would go. Whatever deprived the Holy See of its irreplaceable presence at such an all-important gathering could not be regretted enough. Even at that, it still creates many wonders because Popes Leo XIII, John XXIII, Pius XII, Paul VI, and even the *Gaudium et Spes,* as well as Pope John Paul II had all raised their voices against inequalities and exploitation of the poor in international transactions.

Though there cannot be any reason for the Holy See's absence for such a long period of time, compared to the obvious injustice suffered by poor countries, there is another issue that is closely linked to lateness in this matter. Since the Holy See became a Permanent Observer, it has been selective in addressing issues which have come up for negotiation at the WTO. In some cases, the Holy See has voiced its concern vigorously; in other matters, it has just said a little below expectation, yet in many cases the Holy See has remained surprisingly silent. What accounts for Holy See choice not to be as eloquent as it is at the UN is an issue that calls more reflection. Could it be that the Holy See's Permanent Observer status at the UN is technically different from its WTO status? It becomes pertinent to examine the Observer statuses of the Holy See at these two organizations to access the different pitches the Holy See flies in these two entities.

While not required by UN procedure, as a Nonmember State Permanent Observer the Holy See is normally invited to attend UN conferences and participate in these conferences with "all the privileges of a state," including the right to vote.[1040] Because UN conferences operate by consensus, the ability of Nonmember State Permanent Observer to disagree with the majority consensus carries significant power to shape conference outcome.

In contrast to the UN, though the WTO offers the Holy See a somewhat exceptional Permanent Observer status, its decision making is not by consensus as is the case at the UN. The Holy See is the only Observer country that has no obligation to start negotiations for membership as this discussion stated earlier. However, as a Permanent Observer, the Holy See is admitted to Ministerial Conferences, the General Council and subsidiary bodies, but it has no voting right.[1041] On the occasion of these conferences and other moments, the Holy See makes known its point of view in form of an address.[1042] In such address, the Holy See states that the centrality of the human person comes before all the rules and commercial mechanisms; the duty of subsidiarity for States and for international institutions; the responsibility of solidarity toward the less advantaged,[1043] should be given prime consideration. Should the Holy See fold its hands and say its hands are tied? No, rather, the Holy See should reassess its missionary methods and explore more effective ways to approach technical issues at the WTO.

1040 See YASMIN ABDULLAH, "The Holy See at the United Nations Conferences: State or Church?" COLUMBIA LAW REVIEW (1996).

1041 *See* Archbishop Silvano M. Tomasi (Apostolic Nuncio the United Nations), "Welcome to the Holy See Mission: Historical Introduction to the Multilateral Activities of the Holy See," available at http://holyseemissiongeneva.org/ last visited May 9, 2014.

1042 *Id.*

1043 *Id.*

CHAPTER SIX

Critique of the Holy See in International Trade

The Holy See is not a Member of the WTO, but its moral voice sounds loudest because of its neutrality in all matters therein, and its mission is to safeguard and promote the dignity of the human person. Unlike the Members, which are keen to emphasize their commercial self-interest, the Holy See has no import-export interest on a commercially meaningful scale. Its keen interest is to export Catholic Social Justice around the world and see it manifest (*inter alia*) in GATT-WTO law and practice. Manifestly, with no military or economic might, the Holy See is not a super power like the United States, nor a major power like, Canada, the EU, Japan or other industrialized countries of the world. Rather, the moral voice and the universal mission of the Holy See make it a super power from the religious and socio-cultural viewpoint.

In its international presence, the Holy See represents every human being, bearing in mind the God-given dignity of every human person. The Member-countries of the GATT-WTO system do not always respect the dignity of the human person when they negotiate international trade agreements. The GATT-WTO negotiations and agreements affect not only individuals but also the whole world, at least from a commercial point of view. For that reason, the influence of the social mission of the Holy See is indispensable.

This resolute defense of human dignity in the all corners of the earth, and in the WTO, spotlights the unique nature of the Catholic Church,

> No one is excluded from life's hope, from God's love. The Church is sent to reawaken this hope everywhere; especially where it has been suffocated by difficult and oftentimes inhuman living conditions; where hope cannot breathe, it suffocates. We need the fresh air of the Gospel, the breath of the Spirit of the Risen Christ, to be rekindled in people's hearts. The Church is the home where the doors are always open, not only because everyone finds a welcome and is able to breathe in love and hope, but also because we can go out bearing this love and this hope.[1044]

Considering the reason for its international presence and the importance of economic philosophy in the life of every human being, the commercially neutral, yet moral voice of the Holy See is needed in all the operations of the WTO and related agencies. One can excuse the Holy See for its absence at the foundational negotiations of the GATT-WTO system, perhaps because in the immediate aftermath of the Second World War and the rising tensions of the new Cold War, it did not visualize the enormity of the goal that the system set out to pursue. It could also be the Holy See had no visionary experts in trade-related issues within its hierarchy to convince it to raise its much-needed moral voice during the incubatory negotiations of the GATT-WTO system. Or, it could be they had such experts in the field, but did not see any reason to consult them with the thinking that being a Permanent Observer at the UN was enough. But, today, it is inexcusable for the Holy See not to raise its voice when the GATT-WTO system has been found wanting on issues of social justice for decades.

In critiquing the Holy See's relationship with the GATT-WTO system, this discussion examines the unfairness occasioned by certain agreements and workings of the system. In exploring some unfair negotiation of this system, this discussion establishes that, if the Holy See had raised its

---

1044 *See* POPE FRANCIS I, Address to Participants in the Plenary of the Pontifical Council for Promoting the New Evangelization, *Libreria Editrice Vaticana*, October 14, 2013, # 2

prophetic voice, injustice would not have thrived as much as it is thriving in the GATT-WTO system today. Injustice in the system soars high because the Holy See spoke little, or not at all, on GATT-WTO issues that needed the direction of a moral voice, which the Holy See possesses. When the Catholic Church makes her voice heard in the international arena of economic and social discussions, it is in pursuit of its universal mission of proclaiming the Good News to every soul. The Church cannot afford to abandon this *mandatum magnum* given to her by Jesus Christ, the Founder of the Christian faith.

The whole essence of the "great mandate" which Jesus Christ gave to his Church is for the promotion of human dignity. The Catholic Church has never relented in projecting this intangible dignity of the human person.[1045] At the center of her earthly mission, the Church's quest for international order is for the same purpose of safeguarding and promoting the dignity of human beings. Therefore, when the Holy See suggests the establishment of world authority, it is otherwise calling for an international system guided by the principle of subsidiarity to

> implement the principle of the responsibility to protect and to give poorer nations an effective voice in shared decision-making; to enable negotiations to follow a political, juridical and economic order that can increase and give direction to international cooperation for the development of all peoples in solidarity; to manage the global economy; to revive economies hit by crisis; to avoid any deterioration of the present crisis and the greater imbalances that would result; to bring about integral and

[1045] *See* SECOND VATICAN ECUMINCAL COUNCIL, THE PASTORAL CONSTITUTION ON THE CHURCH IN THE MODERN WORLD (Gaudium et Spes), supra note 75, # 63 (affirming, for instance, that the human person is the source, the focus, and the end of all economic and social life); See also PONTICAL COUNCIL FOR JUSTICE AND PEACE, COMPENDIUM OF THE SOCIAL DOCTTRINE OF THE CHURCH, (2004), # 132 (stating that the human person represents the ultimate end of the society, and as such, every activity of the society is ordered to the human person. The reason for this order is because of the transcendental dignity of the human person, which makes the human person unique and unrepeatable), *see id.* at 131; POPE BENEDICT VI, ENCYCLICAL LETTER CARITAS IN VERITATE ("On Charity in Truth"), June 29, 2009, # 25.

> timely disarmament, food security and peace; as well as to guarantee the protection of the environment and to regulate migration.[1046]

In her quest for international ordering of activities to the benefit of human beings, the Church states that she "does not have any technical solutions to offer"[1047] without the concerted efforts of individuals and groups. The Church cannot claim "to interfere effectively in the politics of states"[1048] without a committed support of citizens of such states. The Church has "a mission of truth to accomplish, in every time and circumstance, for a society that is attuned to the human person, to his dignity, and to his vocation."[1049] She can only accomplish such universal mission if more daughters and sons of the society are appreciative of intrinsic dignity of the human person. As part of her universal mission, the Church also calls for an ordered and peaceful coexistence within the human family. In using her prophetic voice, the Church insists on "some universal public authority acceptable to all, endowed with effective power to safeguard for all security, regard for justice, and respect for human rights.[1050]

[1046] Id. at 67; *See also* Pope Benedict XVI, Address to the Members of the General Assembly of the United Nations Organization, New York, 18 April 2008; POPE JOHN XXIII, ENCYCLICAL LETTER PACEM IN TERRIS (Peace on Earth), (1963), # 55; Pontifical Council for Justice and Peace, Compendium of the Social Doctrine of the Church, (2004) # 441.

[1047] SECOND VATICAN ECUMENICAL COUNCIL, GAUDIUM ET SPES (Pastoral Constitution on the Church in the Modern World), December 7, 1965, # 36; POPE PAUL VI, Apostolic Letter *Octogesima Adveniens*, May 14, 1971, # 4; POPE JOHN PAUL II, ENCYCLICLA LTTER CENTESIMUS ANNUS (May 1, 19991), # 43.

[1048] POPE PAUL VI, ENCYCLICAL LETTER POPULORUM PROGRESSIO (On the Development of Peoples) (March 26, 1967) # 13.

[1049] POPE BENEDICT XVI, ENCYCLICAL LETTER CARITAS IN VERITATE (Charity in Truth), (June 29, 2009), # 9, (indicating that the mission of truth is something that the Church can never renounce and that her social doctrine is a particular dimension of this proclamation; it is a service to the truth which sets human beings free).

[1050] PONTIFICAL COUNCIL FOR JUSTICE AND PEACE, GAUDIUM ET SPES (Pastoral Constitution on the Church in the Modern World, *supra* note 75, # 82; POPE JOHN XXIII, ENCYCLICAL LETTER PACEM IN TERRIS, #55; POPE PAUL VI, ENCYCLICAL LETTER POPULORUM PROGRESSIO, #78 (stating that political authority exercised at the level of the international community must be regulated by law, ordered to the common good, and respectful of the principle of subsidiarity).

From the structure of the mission of the Church, therefore, the Holy See gets involved in the affairs of human beings because they constitute the audience for which the Catholic Church engages in a universal mission. For her universal mission, the Catholic Church interferes in international discussions on issues that affect human dignity and influences technical solutions to related problems. The Holy See supports any structures or systems that work toward the promotion and safeguarding of human beings. Conversely, she speaks out in any event or system where the dignity of the human person is violated in any way.

A case in point is the agreement establishing the WTO, which states as follows:

The Parties to this WTO Agreement,

1. Recognize that their relations in the field of trade and economic endeavor should be conducted with a view to raising standards of living, ensuring full employment and a large and steadily growing volume of real income and effective demand, and expanding the production of and trade in goods and services, while allowing for the optimal use of the world's resources in accordance with the objective of sustainable development, seeking both to protect and preserve the environment and to enhance the means for doing so in a manner consistent with their respective needs and concerns at different levels of economic development;
2. Recognize further that there is need for positive efforts designed to ensure that developing countries, and especially the least developed among them, secure a share in the growth in international trade commensurate with the needs of their economic development;
3. Are desirous of the urgent need to contribute to these objectives by entering into reciprocal and mutually advantageous arrangements directed to the substantial reduction of tariffs and other barriers to trade, and to the elimination of discriminatory treatment in international trade relations;
4. Are resolved, therefore, to develop an integrated, more viable and durable multilateral trading system encompassing the General Agreement on Tariffs and Trade, the results of past trade

> liberalization efforts, and all the results of the Uruguay Round of Multilateral Trade Negotiations.[1051]

In granting Observer status to the Holy See, the WTO expressly recognized the unique nature of the Holy See as a sovereign subject of international law and admitted the Holy See's permanent presence without the condition of successfully negotiating its participation as a Member. A communiqué to that effect states categorically that

> Everyone recognizes the close bond that exists between a just economic order, peace, development and social justice. The Holy See, too, has always paid attention to the development of trade relations among states and to the action of international organisms in charge of following and regulating such relationships. Already in 1963, the Holy See accepted the invitation to become a member of the UN Conference for Trade and Development (UNCTAD). Since then, it has uninterruptedly participated in its sessions, following in a parallel manner the evolution of the General Agreement on Tariffs and Trade (GATT), in vigor since 1947. As is known, GATT was not a true and proper international organization, but a permanent secretariat of a series of particular negotiations, in which few countries initially participated, in general the more developed.[1052]

In its debut upon grant of Observer status, the Holy See stated that although "free markets" may be the most efficacious instrument of spreading resources and efficaciously responding to needs, it is impossible to resolve all problems through economic freedom.[1053] Before its elevation

---

1051 See WTO website, Agreement Establishing the World Trade Organization, available at http://www.wto.org/english/docs_e/legal_e/04-wto.pd f last visited December 12, 2014; OR www.wto.org/english/docs_e/legal_e.htm

1052 *See* Vision and Mission, *Volontariato Internazionale per lo Sviluppo (VIS),* "Holy See Approved as Observer to World Trade organization," in *Den Katolske Kirke*, July 17, 1997, available at http://www.katolske.no/nyheter/1997/07/n970718a last visited February 23, 2014.

1053 *Id.*

as a Permanent Observer in July 1997, the Church showed that she would never sound condemnatory of the liberalization of free market per se. Nevertheless, Pope John Paul II asked that free markets be structured in such a way as to respect the primacy of the human person, to which economic systems must be subjected.[1054] In its acceptance speech, the Holy See pledged to "collaborate in building a fair multilateral juridical-economic system for a fuller understanding among peoples, and for social and economic development, especially of the poorest countries."[1055]

In its international presence, therefore, the Holy See pursues intense cooperation in all the world affairs that concern human beings. The acknowledgement of the Holy See's long history of international presence in the GATT-WTO system has a wide range of implications. The Church understands and teaches that certain principles other than just, fair market access ought to be respected for the global trading system to be fully fair to all. One such principle is that trade liberalization should not be enthroned as an end in itself. It is but a means for achieving ultimate objectives such as high and sustainable growth, full employment, and the reduction of poverty. As such, trade policies should be framed with these ends in mind and be evaluated accordingly.[1056] In its intense cooperation with the GATT-WTO system to achieve the noble objectives above, the Holy See has spoken concernedly on issues concerning international trade.

6.1 Multilateral Trade Negotiations– Ministerial Conferences

6.1.1 GATT

Under the first Round of multilateral trade negotiations, the group of 23 countries, also called the original "contracting parties" of GATT, had negotiated tariff reductions. This Round, which came to be known as the

---

1054 *Id. See also* Pope John Paul II, Address to the Pontifical Academy of Social Sciences, April 1997.

1055 *Id.*

1056 *See* World Commission on the Social Dimension of Globalization, A Fair Globalization: Creating Opportunities for All, 2004 available at http://www.ilo.org/public/english/wcsdg/docs/report.pdf last visited October 12, 2014.

Geneva Round, established GATT on January 1, 1948. While adopting the results of the negotiations, this group of 23 had also adopted a set of trade rules to ensure that tariff concessions secured were not frustrated by unfair and restrictive trade measures. Eight rounds of trade negotiations have taken place under GATT.

GATT Trade Ministers meeting at Punta del Este, Uruguay launched the eighth Round of trade negotiations on September 20, 1986. The Punta del Este Declaration, while representing a single political undertaking, was divided into two sections. The first section covered negotiations on trade in goods, and the second initiated negotiations on trade in services. In trade in goods, the Ministers committed themselves to a "standstill" on new trade measures inconsistent with their GATT obligations and to a "rollback" program aimed at phasing out existing inconsistent measures. The Uruguay Round was envisaged to last four years. Negotiations started early in February 1987, on issues such as tariffs, non-tariff measures, tropical products, natural resource-based products, textiles, and clothing. Other issues that also featured were agriculture, subsidies, safeguards, trade-related aspects of intellectual property rights including trade in counterfeit goods, and trade-related investment measures. Some other groups were constituted to review GATT articles, the GATT dispute-settlement procedure, the Tokyo Round agreements, as well as the functioning of the GATT system.

During the Uruguay Round, which was the last Round under GATT, there were seven and a half years of actual negotiations, preceded by four years of negotiations over agenda items. This Round led to the creation of the WTO. With this development, GATT ceased to exist, but all its principles, rules, and agreements formed an integral part of the WTO as GATT 1947 and GATT 1994. At its inception, the WTO consisted of General Agreement on Trade and Tariffs (GATT), General Agreement on Trade in Services (GATS), and Trade-Related Aspects of Intellectual Property Rights (TRIPS).

6.1.2 Unfinished Agenda of GATT

When the Uruguay Round was concluded in December 1993, there was a long list of "unfinished agenda" work that could not be concluded but was a part of the total package. Even today, much of the agenda items remain unfinished. Industrial market access has not improved much for developing and least developed countries; these countries have had no significant gains yet from the phasing out of textile quotas. While non-tariff barriers such as anti-dumping measures increased, domestic support and export subsidies for agricultural products remained high in the rich countries.

Moreover, the Uruguay Round was held responsible for the current deep sense of anguish against the WTO among many of the developing countries. This round had introduced the principles of "single undertaking" and "early harvest." "Single understanding" is a situation whereby a point is accepted when each one agrees. "Early harvest" implies the workability of an agreement upon the completion of negotiations. The implications of the terms "single understanding" and "early harvest" were not quite apparent to many developing countries at the time of launching of the Uruguay Round. The concept of single undertaking appears to have been introduced essentially to make developing countries accept a huge number of obligations (as a high burden of policy adjustments) without many assured benefits.

Also, during the Uruguay Round, the collective bargaining position of the developing countries was severely dented when the LDCs were given a special status and categorization. Many of the current problems confronting the WTO today lie in these issues. Thus, the genesis of the current stalemates or conflicts in the WTO lay in the womb of the Uruguay Round. This is not to say that the Uruguay Round was a failure. The Round recorded gigantic achievements, but practicability today has been a problem. What is on paper is different from what is obtainable in practice, and this is a big problem.

6.1.3 WTO Issues – Ministerial Conferences

After the birth of the WTO in 1995, 9 multilateral trade Ministerial Conferences have already taken place. The topmost decision-making body of the WTO is the Ministerial Conference, which usually meets every two years. It brings together all members of the WTO, all of which are countries or customs unions. The Ministerial Conference can take decisions on all matters under any of the multilateral trade agreements.[1057]

In this respect, the WTO is different from some other international organizations such as the World Bank and International Monetary Fund. In the WTO, power is not delegated to a board of directors or the organization's head. Reaching decisions by consensus through negotiation between and among the Members can be difficult. Its main advantage is that decisions made this way are more acceptable to all members. And despite the difficulty, some remarkable agreements have been reached. But for now, the WTO is a member-driven, consensus-based organization.[1058]

When WTO rules impose disciplines on countries' policies, it is the outcome of negotiations among WTO members. The rules are enforced by the members themselves under agreed procedures that they negotiated, including the possibility of trade sanctions. But those sanctions are imposed by Members, and authorized by the membership. This is quite different from other agencies whose bureaucracies can, for example, influence a country's policy by threatening to withhold credit.[1059]

The Holy See is a Permanent Observer. It ought to have studied the functions of the different bodies that make up the WTO. Such study is important for the Holy See to know where and when to add its spiritual and ethical dimension to debates or negotiations. When the Church knows where the dead bodies are buried, she will better handle them better; otherwise, it would take longer time for her to understand the politics of global trade in the GATT-WTO system.[1060] If the Holy See has been attending Ministerial conferences, it ought to have gained a mastery of the workings of the system. Therefore, it has no excuses not to influence the system more effectively.

1057 *See* UNDERSTANDING THE WTO, "THE ORGANIZATION - Whose WTO is it anyway?" available at http://www.wto.org/english/thewto_e/whatis_e/tif_e/org1_e.htm#ministerial last visited May 12, 2014.

1058 *Id.*

1059 *Id.*

1060 *Id.*

6.1.3.1 Singapore Ministerial Conference – 9-13 December 1996

The inaugural ministerial conference was held in Singapore in 1996 in Singapore (Southeast Asia) in 1996. Its primary purpose was to initiate an international effort among global trading nations to overhaul the structure and mechanisms of the General Agreement on Tariffs and Trade (GATT) while preserving the considerable progress and success achieved by that system since its inception in 1948. Disagreements, largely between developed and developing economies, emerged over four issues initiated by this conference; afterward, these were collectively referred to as the "Singapore issues".

Four main issues which featured in Singapore meeting were transparency in government procurement, trade facilitation (customs issues), trade and investment, and trade and competition. These issues were pushed at the Ministerial Conference by the European Union, Japan, and Korea, and opposed by most of the developing countries. The United States indicated that it could accept some or all of them at various times and preferred to focus on market access. Disagreements between developed and developing economies prevented a resolution of these issues, despite repeated attempts to revisit them. Notably, during the 2003 Ministerial Conference in Cancun, Mexico, no progress was made.

However, some remarkable progress was made in trade facilitation. In July 2004, WTO members formally agreed to launch negotiations. Under the mandate of the so-called "July package", Members were directed to clarify and improve GATT Article V (Freedom of Transit), Article VIII (Fees and Formalities connected with Importation and Exportation), and Article X (Publication and Administration of Trade Regulations). The negotiations also aimed at enhancing technical assistance and capacity building in this area, along with improving effective cooperation between customs and other appropriate authorities on trade facilitation and customs compliance issues.

6.1.3.2 Geneva Switzerland, 2nd Ministerial Conference – 18-20 1998

The second post-WTO Round was the Geneva Round of negotiations held in Geneva, Switzerland, during 1998. In the declaration, the Ministers agreed to establish a preparatory process under the direction of the General Council, to ensure full and faithful implementation of existing agreements, and to prepare for the Third session of the Ministerial Conference. During this conference, differences persisted in the preferences of developed countries.

6.1.3.3 Seattle U.S.A., 3rd Ministerial Conference November 30 – December 4, 1999[1061]

Because of dissent both external and internal, the WTO was forced to cancel its opening ceremonies, and eventually the Ministerial talks collapsed entirely. The inability of the Seattle Ministerial Conference to start the Millennium Round was unprecedented in the history of the postwar global trading system.[1062] Never had trade ministers convened for trade talks and then failed to commence trade discussions.[1063] The failure in Seattle demonstrated the disappointment and disenchantment of many of its Members with the WTO system. It was also a huge blow to the legitimacy of the WTO and called into question its continued viability.

Further, developed and developing countries alike learned that, given proper preparation and solidarity, developing countries now had the ability to flex their collective power to "block any further consensus action in the WTO at any level, signaling a major change in the manner in which the GATT and now the WTO have operated for over fifty years."[1064] In response, the WTO has attempted to be more active in "improving the

---

1061 *See generally*, Hansel T. Phamdl, "Developing Countries and the WTO: The Need for More Mediation in the DSU," 9 Harv. Negot. L. Rev. 331, Spring 2004, p. 2.

1062 *See* JEFFREY J. SCHOTT, THE WTO AFTER SEATTLE, *infra* note 1067, at 5.

1063 *Id.*

1064 David A. Gantz, Failed Efforts to Initiate the "Millennium Round" in Seattle: Lessons for Future Global Trade Negotiations, *17 Ariz. J. Int'l & Comp. L. 349,* 351 (2000).

quality of developing nations' participation,"[1065] especially since the Seattle Ministerial Conference.

The list of WTO detractors in Seattle included anarchists, environmental groups and other non-governmental organizations, labor unions, and even some well-established U.S. industries like steel and electronics. Their combined activities blocked traffic, caused delays, impeded access to venues, and brought enormous media pressure on the WTO and its delegates. More seriously, the conflict quickly escalated such that rioters caused more than $2.5 million in damage from vandalism and looting, while the police responded with batons, pepper spray, and rubber bullets.[1066]

The street theater outside was one thing; the drama within the WTO was another disaster. Compared to the drama outside, the theatre within the Ministerial Meeting may have been as, if not more, tense and divisive. For example, there were serious substantive differences between the United States, the European Union, Japan, and Canada over agricultural subsidies and exemptions for cultural industries.[1067] However, perhaps the most decisive strike against the success of the Seattle Ministerial Conference arose out of the continuing dissatisfaction with the WTO by many of its developing country Members.[1068] In the face of the intense public and media scrutiny focused on the Seattle Ministerial Meeting, representatives of developing countries continually and pointedly "voiced the sense that their concerns and participation were being marginalized, and that those already holding an unequal share of the world's natural and social resources continue to receive an unequal share of the gains from trade."[1069]

Developing countries had both serious procedural and substantive complaints with the WTO. Procedurally, developing countries increasingly

---

[1065] Jeffrey L. Dunoff, The WTO in Transition: Of Constituents, Competence and Coherence, *33 Geo. Wash. Int'l L. Rev.* 979, 981 (2001).

[1066] *See "The WTO Legacy, Seattle Post-Intelligencer"* available at http://seattlepi.nwsource.com/wto/ (last visited September 16, 2013). *See id.*

[1067] *See* Jeffrey J. Schott, "The WTO after Seattle," in Jeffrey J. Schott (ed.), *The WTO After Seattle 3*, 7 (2000); See also HANSEL T. PHAMDL, *supra* note 1061, at 3.

[1068] Diana Tussie & Miguel F. Lengyel, "Developing Countries: Turning Participation into Influence," in Bernard Hoekman *et al.* (eds.,) Development, Trade, and the WTO: A Handbook, 485, 485-86 (2002), pp. 490-491.

[1069] Frank J. Garcia, Trade and Inequality: Economic Justice and the Developing World, *21 Mich. J. Int'l L.* 975, 976-77 (2000).

felt that the WTO was "a developed nations' club" that was effectively controlled by the European Union, the United States, Japan, and the rest of the Organization for Economic Cooperation and Development (OECD).[1070] For instance, it was in Seattle where complaints by developing countries reached their highest pitch about being left out of the "green room" process, in which a select group of countries informally met to decide WTO policies without the presence of full representation.[1071]

Substantively, the developing countries had learned a great deal from their experiences during the previous seven rounds of WTO trade talks. For the most part, developing countries were passive or marginal participants in those discussions, often by choice. It was only in the Uruguay Round that developing countries were truly active in the negotiating process.[1072] In spite of their efforts, there was still a consensus that the Uruguay Round agreements generally favored developed nations and was being implemented in an asymmetric fashion to the detriment of developing countries.[1073] For example, developed countries were pressuring developing countries to target domestic protectionism and abide by Uruguay Round agreements on intellectual property rights and investment measures, even while the developed countries were not honoring their own commitments to phase out trade barriers in agriculture and textiles.[1074]

Developing countries openly displayed their dissatisfaction with the WTO in Seattle. In response to the procedural complaints by developing countries about being excluded from the "green room," U.S. Ambassador Charlene Barshefsky created working groups to give developing countries more participation and input than they had in the previous Singapore Ministerial. The developing countries issued a series of communiqués deeming this attempt at appeasement inadequate, and objected to Ambassador Barshefsky's reservation of the right to use "a 'more exclusive process to achieve an outcome' in the event the working groups were

[1070] James L. Kenworthy,"The Unraveling of the Seattle Conference and the Future of the WTO," *5 Geo. Pub. Pol'y Rev.* 103, 105 (2000)

[1071] JEFFREY L. DUNOFF, THE WTO IN TRANSITION, *supra* note 1065, at 983.

[1072] H.E. Dr. Supachai Panitchpakdi, Keynote Address: The Evolving Multilateral Trade System in the New Millennium, *33 Geo. Wash. Int'l L. Rev.* 419, 429 (2001).

[1073] *See* JEFFREY DUNOFF, THE WTO TENSION, *supra* note 1065, at 14.

[1074] *See* JEFFREY J. SCHOTT, THE WTO AFTER SEATTLE; *supra* note 1067, at 5-6.

unable to reach consensus."[1075] The fact that developing countries insisted on substantial participation and were willing to stall progress until then marked "a sea change from earlier periods."[1076]

With the memory of the events of Seattle still fresh in their minds, the Members of the WTO reassembled on November 14, 2001, for a Fourth Ministerial Conference in Doha, Qatar. This time, the Members could agree to launch a new round of multinational talks, called the "Doha Round." While it is difficult to predict the outcome of the negotiations, there is considerable evidence that the Doha Round was responding directly to many of the concerns raised by developing countries in Seattle.[1077]

6.1.3.4 Doha Qatar, 4th Ministerial Conference 9-14 November 2011[1078] and Doha Round

When the Doha Round was launched, tariff negotiations, which had earlier been customary, were not the primary impulse. Rather, there were

[1075] *See* JEFFREY DUNOFF, *supra* note 1065, at 982.

[1076] *Id.* at 983.

[1077] *See, for example,* Peter M. Gerhart, Slow Transformations: The WTO as a Distributive Organization, *17 Am. U. Int'l L. Rev.* 1045 (2002) (arguing that the Doha Round may mark the WTO's transformation from an organization concerned about the creation of wealth to an organization concerned also about the fair distribution of wealth).

[1078] Inaamul Haque, Doha Development Agenda: Recapturing the Momentum of Multilateralism and Developing Countries, *17 Am. U. Int'l L. Rev.* 1097, 1098 (2002). The WTO Director-General, Mike Moore, proclaimed his belief that "the meeting at Doha will be remembered as a turning-point in the history of the WTO and the trading system and in relations between developed and developing countries within that system." This now seems optimistic, but much of the language emanating from the Doha Ministerial did seem to support Moore's claim. For example, the second paragraph of the Doha Ministerial Declaration reads, "We recognize the need for all our peoples to benefit from the increased opportunities and welfare gains that the multilateral trading system generates. The majority of WTO members are developing countries. We seek to place their needs and interests at the heart of the Work Program adopted in this Declaration." Similarly, the very next paragraph states, "We recognize the particular vulnerability of the least-developed countries and the special structural difficulties they face in the global economy. We are committed to addressing the marginalization of least-developed countries in international trade and to improving their effective participation in the multilateral trading system." *See id.* at 100; See also "World Trade Organization, Doha Ministerial Declaration," Nov. 20, 2001, WT/MIN(01)/DEC/1, at P 2, available at http://www.wto.org/english/thewto_e/minist_e/min01_e/mindecl_e.htm (last visited August 16, 2013) [hereinafter Doha Ministerial Declaration].

two catalysts. At Doha, agriculture-exporting countries, particularly among developing and least developed WTO members, wanted the developed countries, especially the United States, the European Union (EU), and Japan, to eliminate export subsidies for agricultural products. Conversely, developed countries, which tend to be net exporters of services, sought enhanced market access for their service providers, such as commercial and investment banks, insurance companies, architecture and engineering firms, healthcare professionals, and lawyers.[1079]

Many of the Seattle issues, covering the unfinished agenda of Uruguay Round, featured prominently in Doha. This Doha Round was known as the "Development Round" because according to the Ministerial Declaration, it sought to place developing countries' needs and interests at the heart of the Work Program, and it was adopted. In every negotiable issue of the Round, special concessions were granted to developing countries. The Ministerial Declaration stated, "We commit ourselves to the objective of duty-free, quota-free market access for products originating from Least Developed Countries."

The final resolution on Doha issues has still not been achieved, even after more than eight years since its introduction. The reason is lack of a spirit of cooperation on the part of major negotiators on agriculture subsidy and tariff reduction, the two most intractable issues in the Round. Deputy United States Trade Representative (USTR) and United States Ambassador to the WTO, Michael Punke, summarized this collapse as follows:

> "For the first time in the history of multilateral trade negotiations, the major players are not like-minded," Punke declared [at a September 12, 2012 meeting with journalists at the U.S. Mission in Geneva]. "Systematically, we have not absorbed the implications of what that means." Past trade rounds were dominated by the Quad Group – Canada, the European Union, Japan, and the United

[1079] RAJ BHALA, MODERN GATT LAW: A Treatise on the Law and Political Economy of the General Agreement on Tariffs and Trade and Other World Trade Organization Agreements, 2nd ed. Vol. 1, Sweet & Maxwell, 2013, p. 729; *See also* Raj Bhala, Poverty, Islam, and Doha, 36 *The International Lawyer,* 159-196 (2002).

> States – but major developing countries such as Brazil, China, and India played a key role in Doha talks.
> In those earlier rounds, "at the end of the day, the major players came to consensus and then led the rest of the organization towards a broader agreement," Punke noted. "The U.S., the EU, Canada, and Japan were commercial rivals, but they were fundamentally like-minded," he added, noting that the Quad members were all democracies and market economies. "We don't have that situation today. So, what the real question today about moving the trade negotiations forward is: How do we rebuild consensus?"[1080]

The current and future status of the Doha negotiations should be the prime focus of the Holy See's appraisal of the human person in line with the operations of the GATT-WTO system.

In addition to these general principles, the Doha Declaration contained several concessions to developing countries, such as rollbacks of developing country obligations negotiated during the Uruguay Round, while some obligations were extinguished altogether.[1081] Moreover, new interpretations and clarifications on rules and obligations were promulgated that were more in favor of developing countries.[1082]

The specific language in other parts of the Doha Declaration left no doubt that the issues of developing countries were very much on the minds of the WTO and its constituent Members. In addition to the prominent discussion of developing countries in the Declaration preamble, the Doha Declaration explicitly mentions the concerns of developing countries and special and differential treatment with respect to agriculture, services, market access for non-agricultural products, investment, competition policy, government procurement, trade facilitation, rules, environment,

---

[1080] *See* Daniel Pruzin, *Punke Calls for Rebuilding Consensus, Citing Absence of "Like-Minded" Membership*, 29 International Trade Reporter (BNA) 1508 (September 20, 2012) (quoting Deputy USTR and United States Ambassador to the WTO Michael Punke) *quoted in* RAJ BHALA, MODERN GATT LAW, *supra* note 96, at 730.

[1081] PETER M. GERHART, SLOW TRANSFORMATIONS: THE WTO AS A DISTRIBUTIVE ORGANIZATION, supra note 1055, at 1074.

[1082] *Id.*

debt and finance, and technical cooperation and capacity building.[1083] Mention of developing countries is so pervasive throughout the Doha Declaration and Work Program that it appears as though the WTO was overcompensating for its previous passiveness.

6.1.3.5 Cancún Mexico, 5th Ministerial Conference 10-13 September 2003

Immediately following the Doha Round, which was plagued by disagreements, was the Fifth Ministerial Conference in Cancún, Mexico, in September 2003. The aim of the Cancún Conference was to forge agreement on the Doha Round issues. However, attention during the Conference focused on the War on Terror and its expansion. The Cancún Conference collapsed on the grounds of three issues. These controversial issues are as follows:

(1) Several developing countries led by Brazil and India disagreed with the EU over certain Singapore issues, particularly, two of them. These developing countries opposed any negotiations on Foreign Direct Investment (FDI) liberalization and trade and competition policy, possibly because the EU did not want these two issues to feature during the Doha Round.[1084]

(2) The developing countries led by Brazil and India, known as G-22, vehemently opposed the United States' proposal to improve access to their markets for agricultural products without significant cuts in domestic farm subsidies in developed countries and an end to farm export subsidies provided by those countries.[1085]

(3) Negotiations on trade in services were also problematic. Members could not meet deadlines for offers to liberalize services trade. Only a few Member-countries were willing to provide new, commercially meaningful market access. And the Members who pledged to liberalize services trade did little or nothing to increase

[1083] *See* World Trade Organization, Doha Ministerial Declaration, Nov. 20, 2001, WT/MIN(01)/DEC/1, at P 2, available at http://www.wto.org/english/thewto_e/minist_e/min01_e/mindecl_e.htm (last visited February 16, 2013).

[1084] RAJ BHALA, International Trade Law, *supra* note 904, at 66.

[1085] *Id.*

> the scope of their binding.[1086] Moreover, because of the technical complexity of negotiations in services trade, the least developed countries exhibited a lack of the capacity to negotiate effectively. Before the Conference, the EU pressed poor countries to privatize their water and environmental services. The latter saw this pressure as a trap to avoid.[1087]

The Cancún Ministerial Conference collapsed because WTO Members failed to meet a March 31, 2003, deadline for agreement on modalities for agriculture tariff cuts. This problem reduced the likelihood of progress in Cancún. Though the Conference collapsed long before the scheduled end of the Conference in 2003, the developments in Cancún reflected the growing influence of developing countries. Notable in this context has been the emergence of the voice of Africa. The collapse of the talks did not give the African countries any benefits, but the failure of the talks meant that they did not have to make any additional sacrifices. Most G20 members had an indifferent approach to it. The developed Member-countries were perhaps the most disappointed with this outcome.

6.1.3.6 August 2004 Framework Agreement

Because of the fear that the oppositions that were raised during the Doha Round and the Cancún Ministerial Conference that followed, the WTO Director General (Dr. Supachai Panitchpakdi of Thailand) and the Chairman of the WTO General Council (Shotaro Oshima of Japan) issued a first draft for a scheme to continue the Doha Round. This draft was tagged *Framework Agreement,* which highlighted the pivotal role of agricultural issues. It was thereafter transformed to be called *Framework for Establishing Modalities in Agriculture,* to address a good number of issues that affect the human person.

First was the issue of industrial tariffs and other related topics. Industrial tariffs involve agriculture and food processing, which comprise roughly 10 percent of world merchandise trade and less than 4 percent of

[1086] *See* Daniel Pruzin, "Industry Warns of Impact on Services Talks of Failed Attempt on Farm, NAMA Modalities," 23 *INT'L TRADE REP.* (BNA) 1091, 1092 (July 20, 2006).
[1087] *See id.* at 67-68.

the total world Gross Domestic Product (GDP). Experience shows that, naturally, agriculture and food affect every human being daily.[1088]

Second, this draft involved food security. Food sufficiency is a crucial issue for major developing countries and developed countries alike. It was in view of food security that the EU embarked on its Common Agricultural Policy (CAP) after the Second World War. Japan is not left out in this concern for food security. In 2007, a report of the Japanese Ministry of Agriculture, Forestry, and Fisheries (MAFF) disclosed that the abolition of farm tariffs and non-tariff barriers would do more than cause a 2 percent decline in the GDP, and lead to job losses of 3.75 million workers (about 5.5% of the total labor force). The report also said that farm trade liberalization would equally reduce the country's food self-sufficiency from 30 percent to 10 percent. There are other examples.[1089]

Third, another reason the Framework Agreement focused on agricultural issues is because of their inherent complexity and technical detail. Markets for primary and processed commodities are among the most distorted in the global economy. Trade barriers and subsidies are high in this Agreement, and as a matter of fact, more attention is required. In 2001, the trade-weighted average tariff for agricultural products was over three times the average for merchandise trade.[1090]

Fourth, the Doha Round focused primarily on development issues, and was therefore, tagged Doha Developed Agenda. Though most developed countries have a huge GDP, agriculture accounts for only 1.5 to 2 percent of their GDP. In the U.S., for instance, agriculture, surprisingly, accounts for about 1 percent of the GDP, and employs only about 1 percent of the population. For the developed countries, therefore, Doha Round talks on agriculture involved policy issues about managing adjustment costs and multi-functionality. Conversely, the developing and least developed countries' percentage share of agriculture in domestic output is far higher than single digits. Over 70 percent of the poor people in developing countries live in rural areas. Thus, dealing with agriculture

[1088] *See* RAJ BHALA, INTERNATIONAL TRADE LAW, *supra* note 904, at 69.

[1089] *Id.*

[1090] *Id.*

in the *Framework Agreement* directly affects the livelihoods of most of the poor people in most poor countries.[1091]

Thus, for many farmers and related businesses in poor countries, the Doha Round outcomes concerning agriculture could tip the balance between modest hope for prosperity and depressing confinement to poverty. On the other hand, for net food importing countries, the outcomes of the Doha Round on agriculture could raise a long-term concern about food security.[1092] One could understand the tension that erupted before, during, and after the Doha Round negotiations of agriculture and its related issues. The Framework Agreement was a very big issue.

6.1.3.7 Hong Kong, 6th Ministerial Conference– 13–18 December 2005

The sixth WTO Ministerial Conference was held in Hong Kong in 2005. The conference was considered vital if the four-year-old Doha Development Agenda negotiations were to move forward sufficiently to conclude the next Round, which was to be summoned in 2006. In this meeting, Member-countries agreed to phase out all their agricultural export subsidies by the end of 2013 and terminate any cotton export subsidy by the end of 2006. Further concessions for developing countries included an agreement to introduce duty-free and tariff-free market access for goods from the Least Developed Countries, following the 'Everything but Arms' initiative of the European Union but with up to 3 percent of tariff lines exempted. Other major issues were left for further negotiation to be completed by the end of 2010.

Overall, the GATT/WTO has several achievements to its credit. Membership in the WTO has increased steadily. Currently, the 153 Members account for more than 98 per cent of global trade. Tariff barriers have come down significantly, and now there is talk of elimination of tariffs, wherever appropriate, for both developed as well as developing countries. The WTO's dispute settlement system has been found to be useful and effective by most Members. The textiles and clothing trade has

1091 RAJ BHALA, MODERN GATT LAW, Vol. 1, *supra* note 96, at 759.

1092 *See id.* at 760.

been integrated into multilateral trading, a development likely to benefit developing countries.

But a close observer of the world trading order would perhaps fail to see any change in the trading, particularly regarding the competitive practices of nations in the two decades since the launch of the Uruguay Round. Trade frictions are increasing, non-tariff barriers are rampant, bilateralism and regionalism is the order of the day. All these are restricting the free flow of goods and services across the world. Furthermore, the negotiations in the Post-Uruguay Round era have concentrated on the initiatives undertaken by developed countries to achieve success with the unfinished agendas of the Uruguay Round against the efforts undertaken by developing countries and LDCs to remove the unfair imbalances created by the Uruguay Round.

The major developed countries use the WTO aggressively as an effective instrument of globalization. They have so far succeeded in (1) opening the markets of developing countries for their goods and services, and (2) protecting the rights of their intellectual property (*e.g.*, patents and copyrights). They have extracted concessions from the developing countries in all these areas without themselves giving any meaningful concessions to the latter. All this will have a serious adverse impact on the production, trade, and technological development of the developing countries. Indeed, the impact has already been felt in several developing countries in many areas.[1093]

From the foregoing, it does appear that the developed countries have taken advantage of developing countries for many decades. Is it a new Ministerial Meeting or a new Round of trade negotiations that will eliminate the tension in the GATT-WTO system? The question that naturally arises is whether the developing countries will be getting any commensurate concessions from the developed countries for agreeing to start a new round. After all, no developed country ever agrees to any proposal in the GATT/WTO without ensuring that it is to its benefit or without getting at least commensurate concessions from the proponents of

[1093] See Bhagirath Lal Das, *Why the South should oppose new issues and new Rounds in the WTO,* available at Third World Network (TWN) http://www.twnside.org.sg/title/south.htm last visited February 26, 2014.

the proposal. Do developing countries apply similar criteria in deciding on their approach to a new round of negotiations on new issues?[1094]

With the factious competition that erupted in the GATT-WTO system making its functionality most difficult, the door opens for the Holy See to raise its moral voice as a neutral institution though a Permanent Observer. When nothing is done to remedy the situation, it is the human person who suffers the negative impact. The human being has dignity and a transcendent dimension. To safeguard and promote this dignity, an independent moral authority such as the Holy See has a role to play in the GATT-WTO system. The Holy See has executed this interlocutory role in some instances which deserves mention here.

The WTO broke its own rules by not holding a ministerial conference in 2007 since it recorded very low chances of securing a global trade deal. WTO's rules state a conference of ministers from the Member countries should be held once every two years, and the last of such meeting took place in Hong Kong, China, in December 2005. To confirm the ministerial conference was unlikely to hold, the chairmen of the WYO's general council told delegates that the reason was because of the continuing impasse in multilateral trade liberalization talks popularly known as the Doha Round Agenda. The Doha negotiating Round, aimed at tearing down trade barriers, was launched in 2001 but has been mired in deadlock over disputes between developed and developing countries.

The United States and the European Union are under pressure to cut their agricultural subsidies but demand in return that other WTO members, notably developing nations, reduce their tariffs on imported industrial goods. Worse still, the United States has a hard time accepting Brazil, China, and India self-selecting as developing countries to receive the same Special and Differential Treatment as Sri Lanka, Saint Lucia, Swaziland and other developing countries, and even like LDCs. The

---

[1094] See Fatoumata Jawara & Aileen Kwa, Behind the Scenes at the WTO: The Real World of International Negotiations – Lessons of Cancún (updated ed.), London, Zed Books, 2004, p. 118. The developed countries were broadly successful in this endeavor (i.e., the Cancún Ministerial Meeting and the Doha Ministerial Meeting). "In the end it was the developed world, led by the United States and the EU, which appeared to come away with what it wanted. The developing countries achieved a victory in only one area…." *See* International Trade Daily 2001, *quoted in* FATOUMATA JAWARA & AILEEN KWA, BEHIND THE SCENES AT THE WTO, *supra*.

result of this impasse is that the negotiated rules on special and differential treatment are ignored and not given any teeth, to the detriment of the poorest countries. Developing countries feel ignored and disrespected, further contributing to the cultural divide. They are reluctant to enter into negotiations on the new issues while, in their opinion, the "development agenda" and long-standing issues such as fairer rules on agricultural trade remain unaddressed.

6.1.3.8 Geneva Switzerland, 7th Ministerial Conference II – 30 November – 2 December 2009

The WTO General Council, on 26 May 2009, agreed to hold a seventh WTO ministerial conference session in Geneva from 30 November - 3 December 2009. A statement by chairman Ambassador Mario Matus acknowledged that the prime purpose was to remedy a breach of protocol requiring two-yearly "regular" meetings, which had lapsed with the Doha Round failure in 2005, and that the "scaled-down" meeting would not be a negotiating session, but "emphasis will be on transparency and open discussion rather than on small group processes and informal negotiating structures". The general theme for discussion is "The WTO, the Multilateral Trading System and the Current Global Economic Environment."[1095]

LDC-specific issues were underlined as needing attention, including Duty-Free Quota-Free market access, cotton, and the LDC Waiver for Services. The needs of Small and Vulnerable Economies were also emphasized. There was broad agreement that the growing number of bilateral and regional trade agreements is an issue for the multilateral trading system, and that there is a need to ensure that the two approaches to trade opening continue to complement each other. Some support was expressed for the eventual convergence of the two approaches. However, the idea of extending to all Members benefits offered in a regional context was questioned by some.[1096]

[1095] *See* WTO, WTO 7th Ministerial Conference, Geneva Switzerland, 30 November – 2 December 2009, available at http://www.wto.org/english/thewto_e/minist_e/min09_e/min09_e.htm last visited March 2014.

[1096] *See id.*

6.1.3.9 Geneva, Switzerland - 8th Ministerial Conference III – 15-17 December 2011

Trade ministers at the 8th WTO Ministerial Conference in Geneva today, 17 December 2011, adopted a waiver to enable developing and developed-country Members to provide preferential treatment to services and service suppliers of least-developed country (LDC) Members. Of the 153 WTO Members, 31 are LDCs who stand to benefit from preferential treatment designed to promote their trade in those sectors and modes of supply that are of interest to them. Russia, Samoa, and Montenegro made accession concession, and their membership agreement was reached dependent on the ratification of those countries. The consent of Russia`s membership was important, since the country had been the largest major economy outside the organization since the accession of China in 2001.[1097]

6.1.3.10 Bali, Indonesia, 9th Ministerial Conference – 3–6 December 2013

The Ninth World Trade Organization Ministerial Conference was held in Bali, Indonesia. The negotiations were originally scheduled for 3–6 December 2013. However, they had to extend until 7 December for an agreement to be reached. The conference was chaired by the Indonesian Trade Minister Gita Wirjawan. In this conference, 159 members of World Trade Organization agreed to the Bali Package which aims to ease barriers to international trade. Ministerial Conference approved Yemen's membership

[1097] Article XIX:3 of the WTO's General Agreement on Trade in Services (GATS) requires the establishment of modalities for the special treatment for LDCs in the negotiations on trade in services. These modalities were established in September 2003 (TN/S/13). Annex C of the Hong Kong Ministerial Declaration of December 2005 *(WT/MIN(05)/DEC)* also provided guidance in this regard and called upon Members to establish appropriate mechanisms to give effect to the modalities. This waiver, which will last for 15 years from the date of adoption, releases developing and developed-country Members from their legal obligation to provide non-discriminatory treatment to all trading partners (GATS Article II: Most-Favored Nation Treatment), so as to give them legal cover when they give preferential treatment to LDCs. See WTO: "WTO ministers adopt waiver to permit preferential treatment of LDC service suppliers," 2011 *NEWS ITEMS*, 17 December 2011, available at http://www.wto.org/english/news_e/news11_e/serv_17dec11_e.htm last visited October 2, 2013.

of the WTO. Yemen's agreement was also registered, dependent on the country's membership ratification.

The package includes provisions for lowering import tariffs and agricultural subsidies, with the intention of making it easier for developing countries to trade with the developed world in global markets. Developed countries would abolish hard import quotas on agricultural products from the developing world, and instead, would only be allowed to charge tariffs on amount of agricultural imports exceeding specific limits. Another important target is reforming customs bureaucracies and formalities to facilitate trade.

Agreement on Trade Facilitation – reaffirms that the non-discrimination principle of Article V of GATT 1994 remains valid. Agreement will reduce red-tape and streamline customs. It will be legally binding, require some expense and a certain level of technology. LDCs will be supported in building capacities to implement the changes. Although, some critics worry governments may have to prioritize funds for trade facilitation over other important areas such as public health or education.

Development and LDC issues – The Bali Ministerial Conference reached agreement,

(1) on measures Least developed countries (LDCs) and developing countries, including preferential treatment and market access;
(2) on Preferential Rules of Origin for Least-Developed Countries - simplified rules for identifying origin and qualifying for preferential treatment with importing countries;
(3) operationalization of the Waiver Concerning Preferential Treatment to Services and Service Suppliers of Least-Developed Countries - allows preferential treatment to be given to LDCs for 15 years from date of agreement adoption;
(4) on Duty-Free and Quota-Free (DFQF) Market Access for Least-Developed Countries;
(5) on monitoring mechanism on Special and Differential Treatment - consisting of meetings and other methods for monitoring special treatment given to developing countries.[1098]

[1098] WTO, "WTO ministers adopt waiver to permit preferential treatment of LDC service suppliers," 2011 NEWS ITEMS 17, December 2011 available at http://www.wto.org/english/

This was the first global agreement by the WTO Ministerial Conference. Director-General Roberto Azevêdo said: "For the first time in our history, the WTO has truly delivered. We're back in business ... Bali is just the beginning." He also expressed fears of bilateral agreements if the WTO talks failed. The Trade Minister of the host country, Indonesia, Gita Wirjawan, said the agreement was "historic". The United States Chamber of Commerce issued a statement that read: "With this landmark accord on trade facilitation and other issues, the WTO has re-established its credibility as an indispensable forum for trade negotiations."[1099]

6.1.3.11 Nairobi Kenya 10th Ministerial Conference - December 15-19, 2015[1100]

The WTO's 10th Ministerial Conference (MC10) was held in Nairobi, Kenya, from 15 to 19 December 2015 – the first time the multilateral Ministerial conference is held in Africa. [The Ministerial Conference is the topmost body of the WTO under the governance structure set up by the "Marrakesh Agreement Establishing the WTO," and has the authority to take decisions on all matters under any of the Multilateral Trade Agreements.] This Nairobi Ministerial Conference saw the accession of two least developed countries' (Liberia and Afghanistan) to the World Trade Organization (WTO). Ironically, the MC10 was held in Africa at a time when there was growing political divide over the continuation of stalled Doha Development Agenda (DDA) negotiations, as well as the uncertainty over the negotiating function of the WTO. This ugly situation gave impetus to the multiplicity of mega regional trade agreements. This conference also came shortly after similar major international events that occasioned heated augments such as the UN climate talks in Paris and the Sustainable Development Summit in New York - events which were slated

---

news e/news11 e/serv 17dec11 e.htm; *See also* WTO, "'Bali Package' becomes part of the WTO course menu for least-developed countries, "*2014 NEWS ITEMS*, available at https://www.wto.org/english/news e/news14 e/tra 17feb14 e.htm

1099 Al Jazeera news, "WTO deal aims to boost global commerce," 7 December 2013; *See also The New York Times*, "WTO reaches first global trade deal," 7 December 2013

1100 *See*, Tenth WTO Ministerial Conference, Nairobi, Kenya, 15-19 December, 2015 available at https://www.wto.org/english/thewto e/minist e/mc10 e/mc10 e.htm last accessed May 18, 2018.

to use multilateral trade as potential means for advancing sustainability goals. Unfortunately, there was no consensus on the continuation of the Doha Development Agenda negotiations.

All the same, MC10 culminated in the adoption of the "Nairobi Package" - a series of six Ministerial Decisions on agriculture, cotton and issues related to WTO's poorest Member countries (LDCs). The Nairobi package contains a series of six Ministerial Decisions on agriculture, cotton and issues related to least-developed Member countries special circumstances. The centerpiece of the Nairobi Package is a Ministerial Decision on Export Competition including a commitment to eliminate subsidies for farm exports.

The Ministerial decision is that countries currently using export subsidies to support agricultural exports must eliminate those subsidies and governments of those countries are not to revert to trade-distorting export support in future. Under this decision, developed Member Countries committed to remove export subsidies immediately, except for a few agricultural products; developing Member Countries are to do so by 2018.Developing Member Countries are to keep the flexibility to cover marketing and transport costs for agriculture exports until the end of 2023, and the least developed and food-importing countries would enjoy additional time to cut export subsidies. Disciplinary measures such as terms to limit the benefits of financing support to agriculture exports, rules on state enterprises engaging in agriculture trade, and disciplines to ensure that food aid does not negatively affect domestic production, are put in place against Member Countries who may use other forms of subsidies disguised as export policies. On the other hand, developing Member Counties are given longer time to implement these rules.

A decision on a Special Safeguard Mechanism (SSM) for developing countries recognizes that developing countries have the right to temporarily increase tariffs in the face of import surges by using SSM. Members will continue to negotiate the mechanism in dedicated sessions of the Agriculture Committee. Also, a Ministerial Decision on cotton stresses the vital importance of the cotton sector to LDCs. This decision contains three agriculture elements. The first element is on market access whereby the decision was for cotton from LDCs to be given duty-free and quota-free to the markets of developed countries, and to those developing countries declaring that they are able to do so – from January 1, 2016. The domestic support part of the cotton decision acknowledges members' reform in their domestic cotton policies and stresses that more efforts be made concerning it. On export competition for the cotton sector, the decision mandates that developed countries prohibit cotton export subsidies immediately while developing countries do so at a later date.

On Public Stockholding for Food Security, the Ministerial decision commits members to engage constructively in finding a permanent solution to the issue. Under the Bali Ministerial Decision of 2013, developing countries are allowed to continue food stockpile programs, which are otherwise in risk of reaching WTO's domestic subsidy cap, until a permanent solution is found by the 11th Ministerial Conference in 2017.

A huge chunk of the ministerial decisions favor LDCs. First, on Preferential Rules of Origin for LDCs, the Nairobi Ministerial Decision expands on the 2013 Bali Ministerial Decision, which for the first time, set out a set of multilaterally agreed guidelines to help make it easier for LDC exports to qualify for preferential market access. The Nairobi Decision expands this decision by providing more detailed directions on specific issues such as methods for determining when a product qualifies as "made in an LDC," and when inputs from other sources can be combined together into the consideration of issues of origin. The decision calls on preference-granting members to consider allowing the use of non-originating materials up to 75% of the final value of the product. It also calls on preference-granting members to consider simplifying documentary and procedural requirements related to origin. Key beneficiaries are mostly sub-Saharan African Member Countries, which make up the majority of the LDC group who are also proponents of the Nairobi Decision on Preferential Rules of Origin for LDCs.

On the issue of LDCs and Trade in Services, there is a Ministerial Decision on Implementation of Preferential Treatment in Favor of Services and Service Suppliers of LDCs and Increasing LDC Participation in Services Trade. This decision extends for four years the current waiver period under which non-LDC WTO members may grant preferential treatment to LDC services and service suppliers. This waiver which was adopted in December 2011 and which runs for 15 years slated to end in 2026 is now extended to 2030 (with the additional four years). The waiver allows WTO members to deviate from their most-favored nation (MFN) obligation under the General Agreement on Trade in Services (GATS). The decision also instructs the WTO's Trade in Services Council to encourage discussions among members on technical assistance aimed at increasing the capacity of LDCs to participate in services trade.

Another significant outcome of the Nairobi Ministerial Conference was that WTO members representing major exporters of IT products agreeing on December 16, 2015 on the timetable for implementing a landmark deal to eliminate tariffs on 201 information technology products valued at over $1.3 trillion per year. Negotiations on expanded Information Technology Agreement (ITA) were conducted by 53 WTO members, including both developed and developing countries, which account for approximately 90% of world trade in these products. However, all WTO members will benefit from the agreement, as they will all enjoy duty-free market access to the markets of the members eliminating tariffs on these products.

6.1.3.12 Buenos Aires, Argentina, 11th Ministerial Conference, December 10-13, 2017[1101]

Most developing countries, concerned NGOs, and similar organizations mounted tremendous resistance on the conference proceedings to register their disavowal of the way the WTO course. The efforts of Google, Apple, Facebook, and Amazon to convince aggrieved parties about the fact that WTO is on the right track as things stand now were ultimately unsuccessful. WTO members only affirmed existing mandates; there was no new mandate, not even to upgrade the status of discussions. Big business was left empty-handed. At the same time, a positive agenda for change has yet to be agreed.

Less than half of WTO members supported a "Joint Statement on Electronic Commerce" the final day. They plan to hold "exploratory work towards future WTO negotiations," even though there is no mandate from the ministerial conference to take e-commerce further than the

[1101] *See*, Eleventh WTO Ministerial Conference (MC11), December 10-13, 2017 in Buenos Aires, Argentina, available at https://www.wto.org/english/thewto_e/minist_e/mc11_e/mc11_e.htm last accessed May 18, 2018.

"discussions" currently authorized. This represents a repeat of tactics used in the proposed Trade in Services Agreement (TiSA). A self-selected group of countries took it upon themselves to rewrite the WTO's trade in services rules in ways that intrude deeply on nations' right to regulate, and that exclude any development dimension. TiSA had no WTO mandate and was in theory was conducted outside of it, but the secretariat was complicit by facilitating its meetings. The same must not happen with e-commerce.

A majority of countries agreed that their sovereign rights to regulate services in the public interest should not be further limited by the WTO; an attempt by neoliberal proponents to get agreement on new "domestic regulation" disciplines failed. Likewise, most WTO members realize that new negotiations on investment facilitation are unwarranted and decided against a new mandate on this. Other issues like MSMEs and "gender and trade" emerged as Trojan horses to sneak in "new issues" and proponents will likely continue these stealth tactics in the future.

At the same time, Our World is not for Sale (OWINFS)[1102] delegates were deeply disappointed that WTO members again missed a crucial

[1102] In early 2017, trade experts working through the global network, Our World Is Not for Sale (OWINFS), and new digital rights members started developing and sharing substantive analysis of the potential impacts of the "e-commerce" proposals. These revealed that Big Tech's agenda would further its own power while severely limiting developing countries' ability to harness e-commerce for development. These civil society groups held standing room-only events at the WTO Public Forum and published a variety of important papers and research documents (all available at www.ourworldisnotforsale.ne). Just days before the 11th ministerial conference, dozens of members of OWINFS and other civil society organizations (CSOs), received notice that the Argentine government had rescinded their accreditation — already confirmed by the WTO. The international press extensively covered this outrageously repressive move, and OWINFS demanded that all CSOs be allowed to participate, or that the WTO postpone the meeting until an amenable host could be found. Host country governments of some CSOs intervened with the Argentine government, and about half the banned representatives were finally allowed to participate. During the ministerial conference, OWINFS members monitored the negotiations day by day and held twice-daily strategy meetings to share breaking news and create strategies to influence the outcome. They held daily mobilizations in the conference center, bringing their message to the delegates, and conducted extensive media outreach and livestreamed events. They reacted to breaking developments with lightning speed; when an attempt was made to gain support for a liberalization agenda by promoting "gender and trade," they conducted overnight analysis of the true impacts of the proposals, gained the support of hundreds of feminist groups, and warned delegates not to use "gender" as a Trojan horse for neoliberal policies. They constantly advocated for their positions with delegates in Buenos Aires, while their members at home talked to their capital-based decision-makers.

opportunity to address fundamental problems in the global trading system. Despite a mandate to find a permanent solution for public stockholding in agriculture, members failed to remove WTO constraints on countries' ability to feed their hungry populations and improve farmers' livelihoods; on a workable Special Safeguard Mechanism (which would allow countries experiencing import surges to protect domestic farmers); and on disciplining subsidies that distort trade and damage farmers' livelihoods around the world. Likewise, they made no progress on the key issue of WTO constraints to development, having completely ignored the G90 development proposals.

Fortunately, given that there was no concrete ministerial declaration, previous affirmations of the development agenda still stand. It is unfortunate that members were not able to agree to discipline fish subsidies, but given that some members opposed preserving development policy space in fisheries, it is better that members continue consultations in Geneva on this issue.

As the US attempted to bully its way into shaping an outcome in its corporate tech interests, the EU's failure to play a constructive role at the ministerial conference was disappointing, and many right-wing Latin American and Asian countries also went along with the corporate agenda. The African Group, India, the ALBA group of Latin American countries, and others promoting an approach to multilateral trade policy that fosters, rather than constrains, development prospects, saved the day.

A potential paradigm shift toward embracing "plurilateral" agreements emerged from MC11. While the current proliferation of bilateral and mega-regional agreements was going to continue irrespective of the outcome of the Ministerial conference, attempts to gain agreement among "like-minded" countries on e-commerce and other issues within the WTO is a new challenge. This must be carefully watched, as there will be efforts to set a standard among the most neoliberal countries and then to import this into the WTO as a new multilateral obligation. OWINFS members continue to support changes to rules that harm farmers and constrain development in the WTO, and also oppose the expansion of liberalizing trade rules — be they in bilateral, plurilateral, or multilaterally in the WTO.

Summarily, the following Ministerial Decisions were reached during the WTO 11th Ministerial Conference:

Building on the progress made since the 10th Ministerial Conference as reflected in documents TN/RL/W/274/Rev.2, RD/TN/RL/29/Rev.3, Members agree to continue to engage constructively in the fisheries subsidies negotiations, with a view to adopting, by the Ministerial Conference in 2019, an agreement on comprehensive and effective disciplines that prohibit certain forms of fisheries subsidies that contribute to overcapacity and overfishing, and eliminate subsidies that contribute to IUU-fishing recognizing that appropriate and effective special and differential treatment for developing country Members and least developed country Members should be an integral part of these negotiations. Members further agree to re-commit to implementation of existing notification obligations under Article 25.3 of the Agreement on Subsidies and Countervailing Measures thus strengthening transparency with respect to fisheries subsidies.

Members agree to continue the work under the Work Program on Electronic Commerce since our last session, based on the existing mandate as set out in WT/L/274. We will endeavor to reinvigorate our work and instruct the General Council to hold periodic reviews in its sessions of July and December 2018 and July 2019 based on the reports submitted by the relevant WTO bodies and report to the next session of the Ministerial Conference. Members agree to maintain the current practice of not imposing customs duties on electronic transmissions until our next session which we have decided to hold in 2019.

The Ministerial Conference decides as follows: We take note of the work done by the Council for Trade-Related Aspects of Intellectual Property Rights pursuant to our Decision of 19 December 2015 on "TRIPS Non-Violation and Situation Complaints" (WT/L/976), and direct it to continue its examination of the scope and modalities for complaints of the types provided for under subparagraphs 1(b) and 1(c) of Article XXIII of GATT 1994 and make recommendations to our next session in 2019. It is agreed that, in the meantime, Members will not initiate such complaints under the TRIPS Agreement.

The Ministerial Conference decides as follows: We reaffirm our commitment to the Work Program on Small Economies and take note of all the work conducted to date. In particular, we note that document WT/COMTD/SE/W/22/Rev.8 and its previous revisions reflect the work of the Dedicated Session up to the Eleventh Ministerial Conference. We take note of the work carried out since 2015, including that on the challenges and opportunities faced by small economies when linking into global value chains in trade in goods and services, and instruct the CTD to continue its work in Dedicated Session under the overall responsibility of the General Council.

Furthermore, we instruct the Dedicated Session to consider in further detail the various submissions that have been received to date, examine any additional proposals that Members might wish to submit and, where possible, and within its mandate, make recommendations to the General Council on any of these proposals. The General Council shall direct relevant subsidiary bodies to frame responses to the trade-related issues identified by the CTD with a view to making recommendations for action. We instruct the WTO Secretariat to provide relevant information and factual analysis for discussion among Members in the CTD's Dedicated Session, inter alia, in the areas identified in item k of paragraph 2 of the Work Program on Small Economies and, in particular, to continue its work on the challenges small economies experience in their efforts to reduce trade costs, particularly in the area of trade facilitation. The CTD in Dedicated Session shall continue monitoring the progress of the small economy proposals in WTO bodies and in negotiating groups with the aim of providing responses, as soon as possible, to the trade-related issues identified for the fuller integration of SVEs in the multilateral trading system.[1103]

6.2 Illustrative International Trade Law Issues to Which the Catholic Social Doctrine Applies

6.2.1 The Holy See's Ethical Guidelines for International Trade[1104]

Following developments in international trade negotiations and their outcomes, which were factious and tension-ridden, the Holy See

[1103] *See*, Eleventh WTO Ministerial Conference, Buenos Aires, Argentina, 10-13 December, 2017, available at https://www.wto.org/english/thewto_e/minist_e/mc11_e/mc11_e.htm last accessed May 29, 2018.

[1104] *See* Ethical Guidelines for International Trade: Note of the Holy See on the Preparation for the Fifth WTO Ministerial Conference, September 2003, available at http://www.vatican.

enunciated specific guidelines for international trade, as part of its universal contribution to peace in the world. These guidelines are not new, but they are a follow-up to the Church's ageless teaching. Catholic Ethical Guidelines for International Trade was made public in 2003. This strategy still reiterates the Holy See's presence in international life as primarily for promoting the dignity of the person, thereby contributing to the common good of the whole human family. In its teaching on economic relations, especially as it pertains to trade as projected by the GATT-WTO system, the Holy See advocates an equitable system as one of the key factors in development.[1105]

Using its Option for the Poor Principle, discussed above, the Holy See teaches that poor Members of the GATT-WTO system and their peoples deserve as an equitable, rules-based system to participate effectively in global trade. When this structure is available, developing countries can participate in international trade based on "the highest achievable equality of opportunity."[1106] In its reflections on global trade, the Holy See advances the institutional link between trade rules of the GATT-WTO system and human development. The focus of Catholic ethical discernment in the context of global trade is based on the principle of the "inalienable dignity of the human person from which all human rights and every social order

va/roman_curia/secretariat_state/2003/documents/rc_seg-st_20030910_ethics-intern-trade_en.html last visited February 27, 2014. Trade rules, notwithstanding their technical appearance, have a political and social nature, with deep and lasting consequences in the life of humanity. The Holy See does not enter into technical and specialized matters but only provides some ethical guidelines inspired by the fundamental and permanent values of the international community and which ought to guide all its activities, particularly trade.

1105 *See for example*, World Trade Organization, WT/L/221, July 2, 1997.

1106 *See* Ethical Guidelines for International Trade, *infra* note 1100; *See also* Intervention of the Observer of the Holy See to the Fourth Ministerial Conference, Doha, Qatar, November 12, 2001.

spring."[1107] Principally, "the human being must always be an end and not a means, a subject and not an object, not a commodity of trade."[1108]

The Catholic Church is concerned about the level of "national interests" exhibited by WTO developed Members despite all declarations with respect to the development of making targets of the poor Members. The Holy See teaches that such an attitude is detrimental to the realizations of the objectives of the "family of nations," adding that the "family of nations" is characterized by mutual trust, mutual support, and sincere respect. If the family of nations is to remain authentic, as it is known to be, then the wealthy members should not dominate the weak ones. Rather, powerful members of this family should welcome and serve the needs of

---

1107 *See* Pontifical Council for Justice and Peace, Trade, Development and the Fight Against Poverty: Some Reflections on the Occasion of the World Trade Organization "Millennium Round" December 1999, available at http://www.vatican.va/roman_curia/pontifical_councils/justpeace/documents/rc_pc_justpeace_doc_19991118_trade-devel_en.html last visited February 27, 2014. The Holy See mentioned the inclusion of transitional economies like China, India, Brazil, and others in its call for tolerance by developed Members of the GATT-WTO system.

1108 Pope John Paul II, Address to the Plenary Session of the Pontifical Academy of Sciences titled "Globalization: Ethical and Institutional Concerns," April 27, 2001. International trade under the GATT-WTO system can only work for peoples and communities when structured to service human development. Trade should benefit people, not just markets and economies. Economic freedom is only one element of human freedom and the economy is only one dimension of the whole of human activity. *See* POPE JOHN PAUL II, ENCYCLICAL LETTER CENTESIMUS ANNUS, at 39. Economic life cannot be made absolute. Economic activities must be pursued within a broader context of human development, the promotion of human rights and especially, the overarching policies and targets aimed at eliminating poverty. See reflection of the Holy See on the Preparation of the Doha Ministerial Conference, titled "Development Dimensions of the World Trade Organization," *quoted in* ETHICAL GUIDELINES FOR INTERNATIONAL TRADE, *supra* note 1078.

History demonstrates that ensuring some amount of free exchange of goods and services is indispensable for development and peace. However, neither free trade nor any set of rules is fair by themselves. Free trade can only be called such when it conforms to the demands of social justice, and it is fair inasmuch as it allows developed and developing countries to benefit in the same way from the participation in the global trading system and enables them to foster the human development of each and all of its citizens.

the weak ones.[1109] Developed countries should not use weak countries to a selfish end.[1110]

The Holy See has expressed the concern that if the present arrangements in global trade are not transformed, human development plans will be unachievable. The present WTO arrangements in negotiating international commerce are as follows:

> WTO's international legal system is codified to enshrine the results of a series of national concessions on market access. The economic power of each country and its relative negotiating clout has determined the balance between countries' demands and concessions. Such lengthy negotiated agreements are a compromise, and thus not able to respond to all economic needs. Outcomes of such political and economic struggles could not be fully consistent with human development goals, *unless negotiations were guided by a strong commitment for solidarity among countries.*[1111]

In sum, the present GATT-WTO legal framework is not motivated by solidarity, and this problem accounts for why it is fraught with flagrant inconsistencies. First, the present legal GATT-WTO agreements contain limits and exceptions to free trade that are often non-supportive of developing Members. Second, there is no guarantee that free trade is the best trade policy for poor Members. Third, some GATT-WTO rules are so

---

1109 *See* Pope John Paul II, Address to the Fiftieth General Assembly of the United Nations, 14, New York, October 5, 1995. The concept of a "family of nations" calls for an international collective responsibility that promotes development and the universal common good. This implies it is the obligation of richer countries to tackle and remedy the shortcomings and less favorable conditions of poor countries as if these were internal problems of their own. Trade policy must be organized in such a way as not to be harmful to poor countries but as a contributory factor to their sustainable economic development. *See* POPOE JOHN PAUL II, ENCYCLICAL LETTER SOLLICITUDE REI SOCIALIS, nos. 43-45; *See also* JOHN PAUL II, ENCYCLICAL LEETER CENTESIMUS ANNUS, # 52.

1110 See Pope John Paul II, World Day of Peace Message, January 1, 1983.

1111 See ETHICAL GUIDELINES FOR INTERNATIONAL TRADE, *supra* note 1100.

detrimental to the poor countries as to undermine development agenda.[1112] Some GATT-WTO agreements are couched in a way that establishes domestic economic specifications. Most developing country Members accepted the rules guiding such agreements as a "single undertaking." They accepted these agreements hoping to get the net benefits, such as the inclusion of textiles and agriculture in the multilateral scheme to avoid marginalization. However, they are disappointed because rich Members are not ready to reciprocate with concessions that can engender development.[1113]

6.2.2 WTO and Poor Members

The Catholic Church supports international trade under the GATT-WTO arrangement when it places the dignity of human beings and the common good of the "family of nations" at the center of its goals. After assessing the legal framework of the GATT-WTO trade system, the Church expresses her concern about the challenge facing the system. The problem with the GATT-WTO system is that of creating an environment that can give developing countries both economic and political autonomy to achieve development goals. This problem is associated with legitimate concerns regarding labor, social and environmental standards.[1114]

> The integration of the poorer economies into an equitable world trade system is in the interest of all. The enhanced development of the poorer countries is a contribution to global progress, international security and peace. In a globalized economy no one can be insensitive to the situation of those who are lingering on its margins. Inclusiveness is both a moral and an economic value.[1115]

1112 See United Nations Development Program, "Making Global Trade Work for People," New York, 2003, available at http://www.networkideas.org/doc/mar2003/UNDP_Trade.pdf last visited February 27, 2014.

1113 See ETHICAL GUIDELINES FOR INTERNATIONAL TRADE, *supra* note 1100.

1114 *See* ETHICAL GUIDELINES FOR INTERNATIONAL TRADE, *supra* note 1100.

1115 *See* Archbishop Diarmuid Martin, Intervention of the Holy See at the Fourth Ministerial Conference, Doha Qatar, available at http://www.catholicculture.org/culture/library/view.cfm?recnum=4057 last visited January 31, 2014. The WTO cannot exempt itself from

In her dedication toward safeguarding and promoting the interest of the poor (individuals and nations), the Catholic Church has been unrelenting in raising her voice. Though acknowledging significant progress that the Uruguay Round of trade negotiations recorded, the Church still pointed out in 1999 that poverty and marginalization needed to be combated more aggressively. Poverty and marginalization affect poor countries more drastically.[1116] The Holy See pushes for fairer treatment of poor Members, especially the Least Developed Countries' (LDC), whose share of international trade is only half of one per cent, which declined even since 1990. The Church, therefore, requested that further efforts be exerted to ensure that all partners can benefit from open markets and the free flow of goods, services, and capital.

In preaching for fairer accommodation of poor countries, especially LDCs, the Holy See supported the Church's position with Pope John Paul II's teaching that,

> The poor ask for the right to share in enjoying material goods and to make good use of their capacity to work, thus creating a world that is more just and prosperous for all. The advancement of the poor constitutes a great opportunity for the moral, cultural and even economic growth of all humanity.[1117]

The Church's teaching is also buttressed by a message from the former Director General of the WTO, Mr. Mike Moore, on "Global Forum for Poverty Eradication."[1118] In that message, Mr. Moore stated clearly that the aims of trade, development and alleviation of poverty are inextricably linked. He wrote, additionally, that "the objective of trade

---

examining its results in the light of the overarching development targets that the world community has set for the fight against poverty. These development targets are centered on the human person. It is the creative and innovative capacity of people that is the driving force of any modern economy. It is the lives of people, individuals and families that are the victims of an economic downturn.

[1116] *See* ETHICAL GUIDELINES FOR INTERNATIONAL TRADE, *supra* note 1100.

[1117] POPE JOHN PAUL II, ENCYCLICAL LETTER CENTESIMUS ANNUS, # 28.

[1118] See PONTIFICAL COUNCIL FOR JUSTICE AND PEACE, SOME REFLECTIONS ON THE OCCASION OF THE WORLD TRADE ORGANIZATION "MILLENNIUM ROUND, *supra* note 1081.

must be the lifting up of living standards."[1119] Because in today's world trade, development and the fight against poverty are so closely interlinked, it stands to reason that the WTO should endeavor to establish stronger working links with organizations that work towards the establishment of a comprehensive development framework.

Authentic human development, which is the primary motive for which developing countries have joined the multilateral trading system, has not been given a proper definition that will bring about change of mind in the operations of the Members of the GATT-WTO system. Properly defined, development is not restricted to economic growth alone. Authentic human development demands an integral development of the human person. This in turn calls for policies that are prone to capacity building. The Holy See, therefore, teaches that the GATT-WTO system would do well to not overlook human realities, which makes the authentic development of the human person a primary objective.[1120]

Generally, the Church has proposed that the GATT-WTO system engender a structure that allows every Member country, active participation in the operations of the system, by eschewing all forms of discrimination. Deliberations should address deep concerns for the poor Members. The Ministerial Conferences should also contemplate the needs of developing countries and the difficulties they encounter in gaining access to international markets. In raising its voice, the Holy See has always pushed down to particularities in making proposals. In pointing out the shortcomings of the GATT-WTO system in line with poverty and social issues, the Holy See suggests that global trade aim at integral human development.

For the GATT-WTO system to achieve integral human development, the system must take stock country-by-country of poor Members in designing strategies for development. All hands must be on deck to place the standard of living on the major essentials of human existence. While it is the responsibility of a country to identify its own priorities, and recognize local needs according to the particular conditions of its people, their geographical settings, and cultural traditions, it is expected that the

[1119] *Id.*

[1120] See UNITED NATIONS DEVELOPMENT PROGRAM, *supra* note 1086.

multilateral trade rules would do well to also address and respect them.[1121] For example, the GATT-WTO system should foster trade-related issues that are of interest to poor Members for the integral development of their peoples. Market access should be granted to poor countries for products in which they have competitive advantage.[1122]

Concerning the workability of free trade, the Holy See has taught that free trade can only work effectively if parties operate with equality principles. Unfortunately, equality has always eluded the global system. The GATT-WTO system should consider the economic conditions of its unequal Members instead of maintaining a "one-size-fits-all" approach which is unjust. The Holy See therefore proposes that poor Members be granted proportionate and sufficient flexibility regarding implementation of global trade rules.[1123] The central issue in all that the Holy See teaches about equality and justice in international trade is the need for social justice, which is the only strategy that can ensure integral human development for the entire human family.[1124]

The ethical guidelines for international trade, as projected by the Holy See as a Permanent Observer in the GATT-WTO system, do not have many specific teachings on the agreements in international trade,

---

1121 See POPE JOHN PAUL II, ENCYCLICAL LETTER SOLLICITUDO REI SOCIALIS, # 44.

1122 Archbishop Diarmuid Martin, Intervention by the Holy See at the Fourth Ministerial Conference in Doha, Qatar, available at http://www.catholicculture.org/culture/library/view.cfm?recnum=4057 last visited March 2, 2014. Trade liberalization can bring great benefit to poorer countries. Too often, however, this has remained just theoretical, indeed even an ideological affirmation. For the future, the World Trade Organization must take greater stock of exactly how trade liberalization affects the poorer countries in concrete, verifiable terms, on a country-by-country basis. It must help identify the factors that still prevent developing countries from achieving the benefits they desire from participation in the global trading system. It must learn from and apply, as appropriate, the lessons of those countries that have managed to make trade work for development. It must apply policies that help redress the disadvantage that the poorest countries encounter. The Holy See welcomes the moves that have already been taken in this direction. These moves must now be translated into enduring reality. *See id.*

1123 *Id.*

1124 *See* Pope John Paul II, "The Study of Tension between Human Equality and Social Inequalities from the Perspective of the Various Social Sciences," An Address to the Plenary Session of the Pontifical Academy of Social Sciences, November 25, 1994; *see also* Pope John Paul II, Speech to the New Ambassador of the State of Eritrea to the Holy See, December 6, 2001.

especially agreements that are far from helping the poor countries. The general guidelines are helpful but not helpful enough. A situation whereby the Holy See pays more attention to specific agreements in international trade will drive the point home the more. The Holy See will live up to expectations more when it shows interest in the specifics and expands its Gospel message thereupon. However, it may be unfair to say that the Church has not reflected on specific agreements of the GATT-WTO system. It is interesting for other departments of the Vatican bureaucracy to analyze some specifics of the global trade agreements, especially as can be seen in the reflections of the Pontifical Council for Justice and Peace.

6.2.3 Special and Differential Treatment of Developing Countries

There are about 145 provisions spread across the different multilateral agreements bordering on Special and Differential Treatment agreements for developing countries and LDCs. These provisions also stipulate the implementation of this agreement.[1125] Of the 145 provisions, 107 were adopted after the Uruguay Round, and 22 apply to least-developed country Members only. These provisions can be itemized into a six-typology structure as follows:

(i) Provisions aimed at increasing the trade opportunities of developing country Members: Under Special and Differential Treatment agreements, there are twelve provisions aimed at increasing the trade opportunities of developing countries, and one decision.[1126] They are contained in GATT Articles XXXVI-

[1125] *See* WTO Committee on Trade and Development WT/COMTD/W/35 & WT/COMTD/W/66.

[1126] *See* GATT Article XXXIII that provides for Collaboration and the 1980 Sugar Case involving Brazil and the EC (GATT Panel Report, EC – Refunds on Exports of Sugar, B.I.S.D. (27th Supp.) 69-98 (March 1981) (adopted 10 November 1980). In this Case, Brazil petitioned the Panel decrying EC's substantial subsidies of sugar, which consistently exceeded international prices of the product, alleging thereby that EC was "unrestrained" in its "use of massive subsidies." Brazil's case was that the EC "had turned from a net importer into a sizeable net exporter of sugar by displacing more efficient producers, mostly less developed countries, at a time of world over-production." *The Panel ruled that EC had not collaborated*

XXXVIII on Agriculture; Textiles and Clothing; the General Agreements on Trade in Services (GATS); and their Enabling Clause. These provisions consist of actions to be taken by Members in order to increase the trade opportunities available to developing countries.[1127]

(ii) Provisions under which WTO Members should safeguard the interests of developing country Members: consisting of 49 provisions in Part IV of GATT that regulates 13 WTO agreements and two Panel decisions concerning them. Part IV of GATT include; Application of Sanitary and Phytosanitary (SPS)Measures; Textiles and Clothing; Technical Barriers to Trade; Implementation of GATT Article VI; Implementation of GATT Article VII; Import Licensing Procedures; Subsidies and Countervailing Measures; Safeguards; GATS; Trade-Related Aspects of Intellectual Property Rights (TRIPS); the Understanding on Rules and Procedures Governing the Settlement of Disputes; the Decision on Measures Concerning the Possible Negative Effects of the Reform Program on Least-Developed and Net Food-Importing Developing Countries and the Decision on texts relating to Minimum Values and Imports by Sole Agents, Sole Distributors and Sole Concessionaires. These provisions concern either action to be taken by Members, or actions to be avoided by Members, so as to safeguard the interests of developing country Members.[1128]

(iii) Flexibility of commitments, of actions, and use of policy instruments: Thirty provisions across nine different WTO agreements regulate this category of the Special and Different Treatment of developing and least developed Members. They include, GATT Articles XVIII and XXXVI; the Agreement on Agriculture; Technical Barriers to Trade; Trade-Related Investment Measures; Subsidies and Countervailing Measures; GATS; Understanding on Rules and Procedures Governing the

jointly with other contracting parties to further the principles and objectives set forth in GATT Article XXXVI, in conformity with the guidelines given in GATT Article XXXVIII. See also RAJ BHALA, INTERNATIONAL TRADE LAW supra note 890, at 1283-1284.

[1127] *See* WTO Committee on Trade and Development *WT/COMTD/W/35 & WT/COMTD/W/66.*

[1128] *Id.*

Settlement of Disputes; GATT Article XVIII; and the Enabling Clause.

These provisions relate to – actions that developing countries may undertake through exemptions from disciplines otherwise applying to the membership in general; exemptions from commitments developing countries may choose to undertake when compared to Members in general; or a reduced level of commitments developing countries may choose to undertake when compared to Members in general.[1129]

(iv) Transitional time periods: There are 18 agreements and 18 provisions relating to this category of Special and Differential Treatment of developing and least developed countries. They relate to Agriculture; Application of SPS Measures; Technical Barriers to Trade; Trade-Related Investment Measures; Implementation of GATT Article VII; Import Licensing Procedures; Subsidies and Countervailing Measures; and Safeguards. These provisions relate to time bound exemptions from disciplines otherwise generally applicable. The extent to which developing WTO Members have made recourse to transitional time periods varies across the range of agreements.

(v) Technical assistance: There are six agreements and 14 provisions and a Ministerial decision that regulate this category. They include, Application of SPS Measures; Technical Barriers to Trade; Implementation of GATT Article VII; GATS; TRIPS; Understanding on Rules and Procedures Governing the Settlement of Disputes; and the Decision on Net Food-Importing Developing Countries (NFIDCs).[1130]

(vi) Provisions relating to least-developed country Members: There are seven agreements, 22 provisions, and two decisions relating to this subheading. They include, Agriculture; Textiles and Clothing; Technical Barriers to Trade; Trade-Related Investment Measures;

[1129] *Id.*

[1130] *See* WTO Press Release, "Measures Concerning the Possible Negative Effects of the Uruguay Round Agricultural Reform Program on Least-Developed and Net Food-Importing Developing Countries," April 1994, available at http://www.wto.org/english/thewto_e/minist_e/min96_e/netfood.htm last visited February 28, 2014.

> GATS; TRIPS; Understanding on Rules and Procedures Governing the Settlement of Disputes; the Enabling Clause; the Decision on Measures in Favor of Least-Developed Countries; and the Waiver for Preferential Market access for LDCs.[1131]

These provisions, whose applicability is limited exclusively to the LDCs, all fall under one of the above five types of provisions: five fall into the category of provisions aimed at increasing trade opportunities; 11 in the category of provisions under which WTO Members should safeguard the interest of developing Members; one relating to the flexibility of commitments, of actions, and use of policy instruments; three in the category of transition time periods, and two in the category of technical assistance to LDCs.[1132]

The Church has actually proposed that, in making special consideration of poor countries to be more pragmatic, the GATT-WTO system should (1) structure the Special and Differential Treatment in favor of developing countries in such a way as to provide them with technical, legal, and financial assistance; (2) make special and Differential Treatment should go beyond mere preferential tariffs and transition periods; (3) address key elements of economic growth and development, such as knowledge, technological skills, and information; (4) render capacity-building assistance to poor Members in areas such as electronic commerce, environmental policy, competition policy, and financial and telecommunication services; and (5) incorporate new areas such as competition policy, investment, and environmental and workers' rights issues related to trade.[1133]

6.2.4 Intervention of the Holy See on Specific Agreements

6.2.4.1 Agriculture

1131 *See* WTO Committee on Trade and Development WT/COMTD/W/35 & WT/COMTD/W/66

1132 See WORLD TRADE ORGANIZATION COMMITTEE ON TRADE AND DEVELOPMENT, *WT/COMTD/W/77*, October 25, 2000, p. 3.

1133 *See* UNITED NATIONS DEVELOPMENT PROGRAM, supra note

The Holy See sees agriculture as a key sector in the economies of developing countries in such a way as to constitute a major source of livelihood and an "essential dimension of local social cohesion and culture."[1134] Despite insufficient access to resources, infrastructure, credit, information and technology, developing countries are major exporters of a wide range of primary products on the world market. The populations of developing countries depend heavily on some of these export crops. Unfortunately, the buying power of these export crops has declined by almost two thirds in the space of one generation. The reason for the decline in the purchasing power of these export crops originating from developing countries and LDCs is the unfair practices on the part of industrialized countries.

Wealthier countries often maintain strong legal protections in those economic sectors in which the poor countries could have comparative advantage or in which they could be competitive (such as agriculture, textiles, and other labor-intensive industries).[1135] Despite the grant of quota-free and duty-free market access to LDCs, many developed countries still maintain a high level of protection in favor of domestic industries, particularly in agriculture and textiles. Those developed countries often claim the need for additional time to adjust as an excuse. Such unfair practices "constrain poorer countries to share the burden of their own domestic protection through unfavorable trade conditions and dumping measures."[1136]

The trends in primary products' trade, the access to world markets, and diversification of production have a decisive impact on developing countries. These also affect the balance of payments, foreign debt, domestic budget, and the success of savings and investment policies. The Holy See therefore expresses disappointment that

> The international trade system frequently discriminates against the products of the young industries of the

1134 PONTIFICAL COUNCIL FOR JUSTICE AND PEACE, SOME REFLECTIONS ON THE OCCASION OF THE WTO "MILLENIUM ROUND," *supra* note 1091.

1135 *See* HOLY SEE, "Development Dimensions of the World Trade Organization," A Note of the Holy See on the Preparation for the Doha Ministerial Conference, L'Osservatore *Romano,* October 30, 2001.

1136 *Id.*

developing countries and discourages the producers of raw materials.[1137]

The Catholic Church lauds the importance of the Uruguay Round in liberalizing the agricultural sector in global trade. One of the significant consequences of the Uruguay Round was making comprehensive multilateral trade regulation for agriculture. The aim of this laudable global trade regulation was to improve access to markets and to reduce domestic support and export subsidies. The Catholic Church is concerned that the implementation of this trade agreement has not led to the desired result. It has not led to fair and substantial market access for exports of developing Members.

This problem is persistent because liberalization of tropical agricultural products was at a very slow pace and the tariffs were exponentially high. Processed goods like leather, oil seeds, textiles, fibers, and beverages were not any better because tariffs on them were higher. This skyrocketing of tariffs worsened the situation for developing countries. As if escalation of tariff rates were not enough, developed countries introduced other problems. In addition to tariff escalation, antidumping measures and high subsidization of exports in most industrialized countries have together hampered liberalization of agriculture trade even more. These problems have generated a lot of trade distortions on the world market. These unfair practices have jeopardized the chances of small farmers, self-reliance, and local food production in developing countries owing to subsidized food imports.[1138]

[1137] POPE JOHN PAUL II, ENCYCLICAL LETTER SOLLICITUDO REI SOCIALIS, # 43.

[1138] *See* Archbishop Celestino Migliore (Apostolic Nuncio & Permanent Observer of the Holy See to the UN, Statement at the 61st Session of the UN General Assembly (Before the Second Committee, on item 51 (a): Macroeconomic Policy Questions on International Trade and Development, New York, October 17, 2006, p. 2, available at www.holyseemission.org last visited March 2, 2014. In 2006, the Catholic Church, still concerned about the level of inequalities in international trade perpetrated by most developed Members of the WTO who would not want to play by the rules, observed and taught as follows,

The current situation presents inequalities which demand urgent reflection. It has been observed many times that rich countries support their own agricultural sector, which comprises a very small percentage of their populations, with amounts up to $280 billion per year. This amount is ten times greater than the total amount of aid destined annually to

The Holy See's concern is in the right direction. Agriculture is characteristically multifunctional to developed and developing countries alike. Any unfair competition, such as protection of agribusiness industries in the form of subsidization of exports in developed WTO Members, at the expense of poor regions of the world will hurt the latter badly. The situation is even worse for LDCs. For the GATT-WTO system to help reduce inequalities among Members there must be a renewed commitment to control obstacles to market access. The Holy See suggests that agricultural and processed food from developing countries should be granted domestic support in the form of tariffs and export subsidies. Poor Members of the WTO should be granted "bound, duty-free access" as a necessary incentive.[1139]

For the Special and Differential Treatment of the GATT-WTO system to achieve the desired goal for which it was established, agreements relating to it must consider certain realities. In applying the Special and Differential Treatment more effectively, Members, especially developed countries, must consider the varying structural conditions of agribusiness in developed and developing countries. The reason for asking developed countries to put these differences into consideration is to help accelerate reforms in the poor countries. This consideration will also effectuate the commercial integration of these poor countries into global commerce. For practical purposes, some provisions of the Antidumping Agreement[1140] need to be improved.

Africa and is equivalent to the total income of the whole of sub-Saharan Africa. Moreover, a fundamental part of this support is the direct or indirect subsidies for agricultural exports, which end up undermining the agriculture of the poorest countries.

See id.

1139 *See* PONTIFICAL COUNCIL FOR JUSTICE AND PEACE, TRADE, DEVELOPMENT AND THE FIGHT AGAINST POVERTY *supra* note 1103.

1140 Binding tariffs and applying them equally to all trading partners (most-favored-nation treatment, or MFN) are keys to the smooth flow of trade in goods. The WTO agreements uphold the principles, but they also allow exceptions — in some circumstances. Three of these issues are,

Actions taken against dumping (selling at an unfairly low price)
subsidies and special "countervailing" duties to offset the subsidies
Emergency measures to limit imports temporarily, designed to "safeguard" domestic industries.

For effective implementation of differential treatment, the Holy See suggested a revisit to some agreements on imports from developing countries, particularly Article 9.1 on "Antidumping duties less than the margin of dumping."[1141] The Holy See is also concerned about the

---

If a company exports a product at a price lower than the price it normally charges on its own home market, it is said to be "dumping" the product. Is this unfair competition? Opinions differ, but many governments take action against dumping in order to defend their domestic industries. The WTO agreement does not pass judgment. Its focus is on how governments can or cannot react to dumping — it disciplines anti-dumping actions, and it is often called the "Anti-Dumping Agreement."

See UNDERSTANDING THE WTO: THE AGREEMENTS, (Anti-dumping Actions) GATT Agreement on the implementation of Article VI, available at http://www.wto.org/english/thewto_e/whatis_e/tif_e/agrm8_e.htm last visited February 28, 2014. The WTO agreement allows governments to act against dumping where there is genuine ("material") injury to the competing domestic industry. In order to do that, the government has to be able to show that dumping is taking place, calculate the extent of dumping (how much lower the export price is compared to the exporter's home market price), and show that the dumping is causing injury or threatening to do so. GATT (Article 6) allows countries to take action against dumping. The *Anti-Dumping Agreement* clarifies and expands Article 6, and the two operate together. They allow countries to act in a way that would normally break the GATT principles of binding a tariff and not discriminating between trading partners — typically anti-dumping action means charging extra import duty on the particular product from the particular exporting country in order to bring its price closer to the "normal value" or to remove the injury to domestic industry in the importing country. There are many different ways of calculating whether a particular product is being dumped heavily or only lightly. The agreement narrows down the range of possible options. It provides three methods to calculate a product's "normal value." The main one is based on the price in the exporter's domestic market. When this cannot be used, two alternatives are available — the price charged by the exporter in another country, or a calculation based on the combination of the exporter's production costs, other expenses, and normal profit margins. Tthe agreement also specifies how a fair comparison can be made between the export price and what would be a normal price.
See id.
Calculating the extent of dumping on a product is not enough. Anti-dumping measures can only be applied if the dumping is hurting the industry in the importing country. Therefore, a detailed investigation has to be conducted according to specified rules first. The investigation must evaluate all relevant economic factors that have a bearing on the state of the industry in question. If the investigation shows dumping is taking place and domestic industry is being hurt, the exporting company can undertake to raise its price to an agreed level in order to avoid anti-dumping import duty.
Id.

[1141] Article 9.1 of the *Antidumping Agreement* on "Imposition and Collection of Antidumping Duties," states that,

implications of Article 5.8 of the *Antidumping Agreement* on *de minimis* clause.[1142] It is difficult for poor countries, especially the LDCs who do not understand the complex nature of these international regulations, to use their discretion in determining the volume and material injury that may be caused by dumping of products from developed countries. The developed countries may dress dumping in borrowed robes in such a way that developing countries may not figure out what is going on and thereby suffer losses.

The Catholic Church is very constructive in her critique of the Preferential Treatment granted to poor countries in international trade. The Church acknowledges that tariffs reductions that resulted from the Uruguay Round opened new trade opportunities for developing countries, particularly LDCs. At least, trade in non-traditional agricultural products, like fruits and vegetables, favored them. Prior to this development, poor countries from Africa, the Caribbean, and the Pacific had preferential treatment, but that was eroded by trade agreements. A perfect example

---

The decision whether or not to impose an anti-dumping duty in cases where all requirements for the imposition have been fulfilled and the decision whether the amount of the anti-dumping duty to be imposed shall be the full margin of dumping or less are decisions to be made by the authorities of the importing Member. It is desirable that the imposition is permissive in the territory of all Members and that the duty be less than the margin if such lesser duty would be adequate to remove the injury to the domestic industry.
See UNDERSTANDING THE WTO, "Antidumping Actions," http://www.wto.org/english/tratop_e/adp_e/adp_e.htm last visited January 12, 2014.

[1142] Article 5.1 of the Antidumping Agreement states that,
An application under paragraph 1 shall be rejected and an investigation shall be terminated promptly as soon as the authorities concerned are satisfied that there is not sufficient evidence of either dumping or of injury to justify proceeding with the case. There shall be immediate termination in cases where the authorities determine that the margin of dumping is *de minimis,* or that the volume of dumped imports, actual or potential, or the injury is negligible. The margin of dumping shall be considered to be *de minimis* if this margin is less than two per cent, expressed as a percentage of the export price. The volume of dumped imports shall normally be regarded as negligible if the volume of dumped imports from a particular country is found to account for less than three per cent of imports of the like product in the importing Member unless countries which individually account for less than three per cent of the imports of the like product in the importing Member collectively account for more than seven per cent of imports of the like product in the importing Member. *See id.*
There should be some structure to assist the poor countries in figuring out the enormity of unfair practices that developed countries may perpetrate in developing countries that may hinder development and progress.

is the Lomé Convention (trade cooperation). The Lomé Convention Agreement is such that the EU granted many goods exported by ACP countries duty free, while still retaining their tariffs on goods from the EU.[1143] However, the goods involved are traditional agricultural goods. Such trade agreements, therefore, do not increase the chances of developing countries to diversify their trade sustainably. To this end, they cannot compete reasonably with developed countries in non- traditional agricultural productivity.

It becomes necessary to involve the private sector in such a way as to establish a strong international cooperation and contribution. When the private sector is involved more effectively, diversification of agriculture, which was one of the goals of the Food and Agricultural Organization (FAO) Plan of Action, will become realized.[1144] Another concern is the

---

1143 *See* Lomé Convention, Cotonou, June 23, 2000; April 1, 2003; and ACP-EU Council of Ministers in Gaborone, May 2004 to February 23, 2005, available at http://www.eu-oplysningen.dk/euo_en/spsv/all/97/ last visited February 4, 2014. The Lomé Conventions are agreements laying down the framework for cooperation on development policy, economic policy, trade, and industry between the EU and what are known as the ACP countries (countries in Africa, the Caribbean and the Pacific.) Ever since the foundation of the Community, cooperation with ACP countries has formed an important part of EU development policy. Since 1975, the framework for this cooperation has been laid down in a special intergovernmental agreement called the Lomé Convention. This agreement has been renegotiated several times, and the fourth and last in the series (Lomé IV) was signed in 1989, with a life of 10 years. On 23 June 2000, the Lomé Conventions were replaced by a new 20-year partnership agreement between the EU Member States on the one hand, and the ACP countries on the other, which was signed in the capital of Benin, Cotonou – hence, the Cotonou Agreement. The Cotonou Agreement continues the experiences of the Lomé Conventions but also adds some new elements. The objectives of the Cotonou Agreement are to reduce and, in time, eradicate poverty and also to promote sustainable development and the progressive integration of the ACP countries into the global economy. *See id.*

1144 *See* FAO Natural Resources Management and Environmental Department, "Ministerial declaration on agriculture in Small Island Developing States (SIDS)," as part of the approvals made at the Special Ministerial Conference on "The FAO International Plan of Action," March 12, 1999, in Rome, Italy, the available at http://www.fao.org/docrep/006/y5180e/y5180e01.htm last visited February 23, 2014; stating, among other things, that,

".... We have considered the draft Plan of Action on Agriculture in Small Island Developing States, attached to this Declaration, as a basis for further consideration by appropriate bodies of FAO and other relevant bodies of the United Nations system. We will endeavor to:

•address new challenges in the global trading environment; undertake short-term adjustments; and improve competitiveness in agricultural exports;

ineffectiveness of the framework of the United Nations Commission on Trade and Development (UNCTAD) "Common Fund" established in 1979.[1145] The Church regrets that since the UNCTAD Common Fund came into force in 1989, financial resources relating to it have been terribly scarce. For that reason, the Church recommends that the Common Fund be adopted by WTO Member States as a unique opportunity in their negotiations. When adopted by the GATT-WTO system, it would serve to reinforce the commitment to assist in diversifying agricultural trade of developing countries.[1146]

The Holy See also voiced its concern on the impact of agricultural liberalization of LDCs and NFIDCs. The Catholic Church is concerned that the liberalization process in agriculture is likely to have a negative impact on the economies of LDCs and Net-Food-Importing Countries (NFIDCs). The Church observes that the "food import bills of these countries have been increasing…, due to the higher commodity prices (e.g., wheat) caused, partly by a reduction of the volume of subsidized

• move towards more intensified, diversified and sustainable agriculture in order to create an enabling environment for agricultural intensification and diversification; remove production constraints; and improve domestic and export marketing and processing." *Id.*

1145 The United Nations Conference on Trade and Development (UNCTAD) established a COMMON FUND for purposes of financing programs relating to agricultural diversification. This Common Fund, which came into force in 1989 underwent series of modifications. Details of this UNCTAD agreement are available at https://www.icac.org/projects/commonfund/admin/agreement.pdf The reports of the Conference were circulated under the following symbols: first session, TD/IPC/CF/CONF/8; second session, TD /I PC/CF/CONF/ 14 (Part I), and resumed second session TD /I PC/CF/CONF/ 14 (Part I), and resumed second session, TD/IPC/CF/CONF/ 14 (Part II); third session, TD/IPC/CF/CONF/19; fourth session, TD/IPC/CF/CONF/26.

1146 WTO, URUGUAY ROUND AGREEMENT: Decision on Measures in Favor of Least-Developed Countries, available at http://www.wto.org/english/docs_e/legal_e/31-dlldc_e.htm last visited October 4, 2013. Article 2(v) states that

Least-developed countries shall be accorded substantially increased technical assistance in the development, strengthening and diversification of their production and export bases including those of services, as well as, in trade promotion, to enable them to maximize the benefits from liberalized access to markets.

exports."[1147] This growing concern is heightened by instability in food prices and fall in surplus stock available for food aid.[1148]

6.2.4.1.1 Holy See's Proposals Concerning WTO *Agreement on Agriculture*

The major problem with the WTO *Agreement on Agriculture* is the unfair gap between the North and the South. The Church points out that while implementing the Agreement on Agriculture, the developing countries and LDCs opened their markets to the developed countries. Unfortunately, the developed Members did not reciprocate in cutting the huge subsidies that gave their domestic production an upper hand.

> The implementation of the Agreement on Agriculture has resulted in many developing countries opening their domestic local markets for products from industrial countries. Since the production and often the export of these products from the North were frequently highly subsidized, the policy resulted - as proven by the FAO in various studies - in the mass decline and demise of smallholder farms in the countries of the South.[1149]

The Church raises her voice in calling for measures that would help ameliorate the hardship suffered by developing countries in relation to agriculture. The Church is of the view that if small-shareholder farmers in those countries are given greater access to resources, credit, information, and technologies, their agricultural production and livelihoods will increase.

[1147] PONTIFICAL COUNCIL FOR JUSTICE AND PEACE, TRADE, DEVELOPMENT AND THE FIGHT AGAINST POVERTY, *supra* note 1103.

[1148] *See* FAO – Comité des Produits, *Evaluacion de l'incidence du Cycle d'Uruguay sur les marchés agricoles,* November 1998, doc.CCP99/12, P. 14. In 1997-1994, food aid in cereals represented 23% of cereal imports of LDCs against 36% in 1993-1994 and 64% in the mid-1980s. Reduction of food aid in cereal has been even more dramatic for NFIDCs: 22% in the middle of the 1980s; 7.6% in 1993-1994 and 2% in 1997-1998. *See id.*

[1149] *See* Church and Globalization: Ecumenical Dialogue – Reform of the World Trade Order, January 2002, available at https://www.ekd.de/english/1634-1_2002_4.html last visited March 4, 2014.

Concerning food security problems, the Church taught the solution to the problem created in food security is not to be based solely on increasing the food aid dependency of poor countries. Rather, in addition to that strategy, the GATT-WTO system should address the problems facing countries with structural food deficits. There is a popular saying: "Don't give me fish; teach me how to fish." It is not enough to give economic aid to poor countries. It doesn't help much because when that is the case, beneficiaries remain the same. But when they are self-reliant, the objectives of the GATT-WTO system are better achieved. Pope John Paul II addressed this in saying

> As regards food resources ...., it is also important for the populations burdened by the effects of malnutrition and hunger to receive an education that prepares them to provide healthy and sufficient foodstuffs on their own.[1150]

In proffering solutions to the problem of food security, the Catholic Church lauded the Ministerial Conference of the GATT-WTO system on their achievements. The Church expressed her gratitude, especially during the Uruguay Round through the Marrakesh Decision on Measures Concerning the Possible Negative Effects of the Reform on LDCs and NFIDCs. This Decision has helped in monitoring the level of food aid under the Food Aid Convention and in the adoption of guidelines to ensure a sufficient level of food aid in full grant form. While this is a good development, the Church adds that GATT-WTO negotiations should help guarantee the "increase of agricultural productivity and infrastructure, diversification of production and self-reliance in the LDCs and NFIDCs themselves."[1151] The Catholic Church also called for the system to establish coordinating mechanisms that can promote technical and financial assistance for these poor countries.[1152]

[1150] *See* FAO Headquarters, December 5, 1992, # 5 quoted in PONTIFICAL COUNCIL FOR JUSTICE AND PEACE, TRADE, DEVELOPMENT AND THE FIGHT AGAINST POVERTY, *supra* note 1103.

[1151] *Id.*

[1152] *See* WTO – Uruguay Round Agreement, "Decision on Measures Concerning the Possible Negative Effects of the Reform Program on Least-Developed and Net Food-Importing Developing Countries," Article 3(iii) available at http://www.wto.org/english/docs_e/

6.2.4.2 Sanitary and Phytosanitory Measures and Technical Barriers to Trade

The Holy See gives the GATT-WTO high marks for improved trade in agriculture in the Agreement on the Application of Sanitary and Phytosanitary Measures (SPS Agreement) and the Agreement on Technical Barriers to Trade (TBT Agreement). These Agreements relating to international standards and measures are protective of the health and security of agricultural and food products. International standards and measures in these agreements help to check fraudulent practices that would otherwise have dangerous effects on human health and the natural environment.[1153]

The Church points out that the indiscriminate use of anti-tariff measures and trade barriers for health and security purposes are detrimental to poor countries. Those unfair practices can be reduced and the SPS Agreement would be more effectively directed when Members respect transparent and scientific norms. When such unfair practices are brought under control, this facilitates private investments in manufacturing industries in developing countries. Examples of instruments that contain such norms include the *Codex Alimentarius*,[1154] the Plant Protection

---

legal e/35-dag e.htm last visited July 12, 2013. Article 3(iii) of this Agreement states that Ministers agreed.

To adopt guidelines to ensure that an increasing proportion of basic foodstuffs is provided to least-developed and net food-importing developing countries in full grant form and/or on appropriate concessional terms in line with Article IV of the Food Aid Convention 1986. *See Id.*

When this agreement is effectively implemented, LDCs and NFIDCs would be somewhat self-reliant. From all indications, the Church is concerned that this agreement has not been taken seriously, and therefore calls for more commitment.

1153 PONTIFICAL COUNCIL FOR JUSTICE AND PEACE, TRADE, DEVELOPMENT AND THE FIGHT AGAINST POVERTY, *supra* note 1103.

1154 *See* United Nations Food and Agricultural Organization (FAO) and World Health Organization (WHO), *Codex Alimentarius* (International Food Standards), 1963, available at http://www.codexalimentarius.org/ last visited January 12, 2014. The *Codex Alimentarius* Commission, established by FAO and WHO in 1963, develops harmonized international food standards, guidelines, and codes of practice to protect the health of the consumers and ensure fair practices in the food trade. The Commission also promotes coordination of

Convention (IPPC),[1155] or those formulated by the International Office of Epizootics (IOE).[1156]

However, the testing of the quality of food to ensure it meets international standards is not without a price. Implementing the SPS Agreement obviously increases the cost of production for industries in developing countries. Developing countries find it difficult to comply with these international standards since they have difficulties in meeting the cost of special skills and appropriate technologies necessary to comply with such standards. The case is worse for LDCs and NFIDCs.[1157]

---

all food standards work undertaken by international governmental and non-governmental organizations.

[1155] WTO - The WTO and the International Plant Protection Convention (IPPC) available at http://www.wto.org/english/thewto_e/coher_e/wto_ippc_e.htm last visited August 2013. The International Plant Protection Convention (IPPC) is a multilateral treaty for international cooperation in plant protection. The Convention makes provision for the application of measures by governments to protect their plant resources from harmful pests (phytosanitary measures), which may be introduced through international trade. The IPPC is deposited with the Director-General of the FAO and is administered through the IPPC Secretariat located in FAO's Plant Protection Service. The IPPC was first adopted in 1951 and has been amended twice, most recently in 1997. Collaboration between WTO and IPPC concerns the use of international plant protection standards in the context of the SPS Agreement. The WTO's SPS Agreement states that "to harmonize sanitary and phytosanitary measures on as wide a basis as possible, Members shall base their sanitary or phytosanitary measures on international standards, guidelines or recommendations". The Agreement names the IPPC for plant health standards.

See SPS Agreement Introduction, Article 12.3 and Annex A paragraph 3(a).

[1156] FAO - the Office International des Epizooties (OIE), Agreement on the Application of Sanitary and Phytosanitary Measures (SPS) and Agreement on Technical Barriers to Trade (TBT), available at http://www.fao.org/docrep/003/x7354e/x7354e06.htm last visited September 16, 2013. The OIE is an intergovernmental organization created by the International Agreement of 25 January 1924, signed by 28 countries. In May 2006, the OIE totaled 167 Members. The OIE is originally part of the League of Nations and is the worldwide authority for development of animal health and zoonosis standards, guidelines, and recommendations.

[1157] *See* PONTIFICAL COUNCIL FOR JUSTICE AND PEACE, TRADE, DEVELOPMENT AND THE FIGHT AGAINST POVERTY supra note 1103.

6.2.4.2.1 Holy See's Proposals Concerning SPS and TBT Agreements

As a prelude to her proposals concerning the workability of the SPS Measures and TBT Agreement, the Catholic Church reiterates that industrialized Member States of the GATT-WTO system have the duty to provide technical assistance to developing countries. The significance of such technical assistance is to help poor countries meet the requirements of the SPS Agreement.[1158] There is a need for a structure to coordinate this required technical assistance to involve international organizations like the FAO, IFAD, the World Bank, regional development banks, as well as multilateral and bilateral donors. When these international organizations participate, they cooperate with governments and the private sector in developing a national control infrastructure on foodstuffs.[1159]

Instead of ignoring their technical difficulties and lack of skills, Members should encourage developing countries to participate in relevant international organizations relating to setting of standards of the *Codex Alimentarius.* As members of such organizations, developing countries should be inspired to play a more active role through technical empowerment.

[1158] *See* Article 9.1 of the SPS Agreement which states that

Members agree to facilitate the provision of technical assistance to other Members, especially developing country Members, either bilaterally or through the appropriate international organizations. Such assistance may be, *inter alia,* in the areas of processing technologies, research and infrastructure, including in the establishment of national regulatory bodies, and may take the form of advice, credits, donations and grants, including for the purpose of seeking technical expertise, training and equipment to allow such countries to adjust to, and comply with, sanitary or phytosanitary measures necessary to achieve the appropriate level of sanitary or phytosanitary protection in their export markets.

[1159] PONTIFICAL COUNCIL FOR JUSTICE AND PEACE, TRADE, DEVELOPMENT, AND THE FIGHT AGAINST POVERTY supra note 1103; see *also* Pope John Paul II, Address at a Congress on Environment and Health, March 23, 1997, *quoted in* PONTIFICAL COUNCIL FOR JUSTICE AND PEACE, TRADE, DEVELOPMENT AND THE FIGHT AGAINST POVERTY, *supra.* Pope John Paul II said:

The defense of life and the consequent promotion of health, especially among the poorest populations of developing countries, will be at the same time the benchmark and the fundamental criterion of the ecological horizon at a regional and world level.

Pope John Paul II taught that under no condition should implementation of international standards and the IPPC revision process in trade matters, be viewed as more important than human and plant health issues. This teaching came because of the upsurge requirement relating to standards on genetically modified organisms (GMOs). GMO trade is on the increase and has a huge impact on plant, animal, and human health, calling therefore for immediate implementation of the "principle of precaution" and risk assessment contained in the Biodiversity Convention.[1160]

6.2.4.3 Transfer of Technology and Intellectual Property Rights

Though the terms of trade have fast turned into skill-intensive manufacturing and services,[1161] the Holy See believes that technological innovation and knowledge are fast becoming the keys to world trade integration. As a matter of fact, free trade by itself is not able to ensure widespread development. It can only achieve the desired goal in consonance with massive investment in the human capacities of developing countries. Any trade negotiations bereft of long-term political and social goals hinging on development strategies or any trade that does not seek widespread integral human development will obviously fail. The Holy See, therefore,

---

1160 PONTIFICAL COUNCIL FOR JUSTICE AND PEACE, TRADE, DEVELOPMENT AND THE FIGHT AGAINST POVERTY, *supra* note 1103.

1161 *See* the 1996 United Nations Human Development Program Report, in which it was disclosed that,

Generally, the North's manufactured exports to the South have greater skill content than the South's exportS to the North. Even in services the North tends to export skill-intensive products, such as insurance, design and medical care, while the South exports labor-intensive services, such as shipping, tourism and routine data processing. For the above reason, the Catholic Church has defined the significance of the ethical direction of science, technology, and innovation.The international community is entering a critical phase of redefining sustainable development in its three pillars– economic, environmental and social- as an effective way to combat poverty and improve the lives of people worldwide. Investing in education and innovation opens the way toward a future of greater equality and prosperity as they sustain growth, employment and distribution, but with an indispensable condition, that the human person with her dignity, aspirations and fundamental rights be placed at the center of all policies and programs.

See Vatican Radio July 4, 2013 at http://www.news.va/en/news/vatican-representative-calls-for-ethically-respons last visited December 23, 2013.

calls for a robust action on widespread human and technological advance during trade negotiations.[1162]

The progress of a merely economic and technological kind is insufficient. "Development needs to be, above all, true and integral," so as to embrace all the aspirations of the human person who remains its best resource and indispensable protagonist.[1163] The Holy See, therefore, stresses that industrialized Members of the GATT-WTO system have it as a duty in solidarity to transfer appropriate technology to poor Members. Therefore,

> In the field of technology, States, in accord with the duty of solidarity and giving due consideration to the rights of the developers of such technology, have an obligation to ensure a just and equitable transfer of appropriate technology which is favorable to sustaining the development process and protecting the environment.[1164]

Some key Articles of the Agreement on Trade-Related Aspects of Intellectual Property Rights (TRIPS) define issues concerning international transfer of technology.[1165] Article 7 of the TRIPS states that:

[1162] PONTIFICAL COUNCIL FOR JUSTICE AND PEACE, TRADE, DEVELOPMENT AND THE FIGHT AGAINST POVERTY *supra* note 1103.

[1163] See Vatican Radio, "Vatican representative calls for ethically responsible use of technology," July 4, 2013, available at http://www.news.va/en/news/vatican-representative-calls-for-ethically-respons . The Church teaches as follows:
Science, technology and Innovation (STI) are critical dimensions of human knowledge and progress. At the same time, they carry a social mortgage that finds expression in solidarity with poorer individuals and countries and in a lifestyle based on human relations that take precedence over technical mechanisms, as useful as these are. The importance of culture rests on the fact that it speaks of the intelligence of rational beings enabling them to understand and order the world that surrounds them. Besides, knowledge is the result of an incredible amount of observations, analysis and reflections accumulated over centuries and that have become a common patrimony. That is why intellectual property protects an invention for only an agreed period of time after which it becomes public and remains at the service of all. *See id.*

[1164] *See* Memorandum on the Holy See's Position on Environment and Development, in *L'Osservatore Romano* (English ed.), June 10, 1992, no. 23, Point 6.

[1165] *See* for particularly Article 8(2) of TRIPS Agreement; See also Article 66(2) which specifies international transfer of technology to LDCs.

> The protection and enforcement of intellectual property rights should contribute to the promotion of technological innovation and to the transfer and dissemination of technology, to the mutual advantage of producers and users of technological knowledge in a manner akin to social and economic welfare, and to a balance of rights and obligations.[1166]

The greatest problem that the TRIPS Agreement has encountered is its lack of concrete and effective actions. The Holy See stresses the need to reinforce juridical and operational means to promote the transfer of technology and intellectual property rights in terms that are reasonable to developing countries, especially the least advanced ones.[1167] For the GATT-WTO system to realize this goal, poor countries should be assisted to establish the technical and administrative infrastructure necessary to meet the obligations of the TRIPS Agreement.[1168]

It is obvious that there is a huge gap between industrialized countries and developing countries. Transfer of technology to poor countries will not achieve the desired goal without a concomitant transfer of technological skills and capacities. The aim of technology transfer must include a narrowing of the information and technological gap between advanced

---

1166 *See* AGREEMENT ON TRADE-RELATED ASPECTS OF INTELLECTUAL PROPERTY RIGHTS ("TRIPS Agreement"), Article 7 TRIPS Agreement, available at http://www.worldtradelaw.net/uragreements/tripsagreement.pdf last visited February 23, 2014

1167 *See* Vatican Radio, "Vatican representative calls for ethically responsible use of technology," July 4, 2013 available at http://www.news.va/en/news/vatican-representative-calls-for-ethically-respons . In his speech, Archbishop Silvano Tomasi, Holy See's Permanent Observer to the United Nations and other international organizations in Geneva, proposed as follows:

> First, there is a need for an ethically responsible use of technology. Second, in the use and development of Science, technology and innovation (STI) forms of solidarity are required that are truly favorable to the poorest countries. In this way, the promotion of scientific knowledge in developing countries and the transfer of technologies to them becomes a moral component of the common good.

1168 PONTIFICAL COUNCIL FOR JUSTICE AND PEACE, TRADE, DEVELOPMENT AND THE FIGHT AGAINST POVERTY, *supra* note 1103.

nations and developing countries, especially LDCs. Rubens Ricupero, the fifth Secretary-General of UNCTAD, pointed this out in a conference in 1999, when he said

> In the past, technology was essentially embodied in machines. Technology is now embodied in human beings. We now require an incomparably greater effort to teach countries, particularly the least-developed, the small, weak and vulnerable, how to produce and broaden their supply capability in goods and services; how to compete effectively and use modern, electronic means in an increasingly demanding environment; how to take advantage of opportunities provided by the trading system.[1169]

To help reduce the technological gap between developed countries and developing countries, the GATT-WTO system must intensify and promote financial support for a massive program of trade-related technical cooperation. In line with this proposal, the Catholic Church is supportive of the positive initiatives taken in the framework of GATT-WTO technical assistance and coordination with other international institutions like UNCTAD, UNDP, International Trade Center (ITC),[1170] the World Bank, and the Multilateral Investment Fund (MIF). This initiative results in an increase in the WTO's budget and of contributions for trade-related technical assistance. A more complete integration of developing

---

[1169] *See* WTO High Level Symposium on Trade and Development, Geneva, March 17, 1999.

[1170] *See* WTO, World Trade and the International Trade Center, available at http://www.wto.org/english/thewto_e/coher_e/wto_itc_e.htm last visited December 23, 2014; ITC is the joint cooperation agency of UNCTAD and WTO for business aspects of trade development. Originally created by the General Agreement on Tariffs and Trade (GATT) in 1964, ITC has operated since 1968 under the joint aegis of GATT/WTO and the UN, the latter acting through the United Nations Conference on Trade and Development (UNCTAD). It is the focal point in the UN system for technical cooperation with developing countries and economies in transition in trade promotion and export development. While UNCTAD and WTO work principally with governments, ITC works with the business community. In this context, the ITC clarifies the business implications of multilateral trade agreements and assists business in understanding, shaping and benefiting from trade rules. As a subsidiary agency of UNCTAD and the WTO, the ITC is subject to the governing bodies of both.

countries in global trade remains credible and efficacious only when those positive steps are taken. Furthermore, trade can only be significant to poor countries if the percentage of technical cooperation in trade-related activities is reasonably fair enough.[1171]

The Holy See wants the financial support for poor countries to be directed in such a way as to assist those countries in creating legal and infrastructural frameworks that are favorable to investments.[1172] Technical assistance must promote education, technological skills, and research projects that are directed toward empowerment of these poor countries, so much so that they can be self-reliant in the long run.[1173] The use or transfer of technology must respect the principle of the common good.

> Often the development of peoples is considered a matter of financial engineering, the freeing up of markets, the removal of tariffs, investment in production, and institutional reforms — in other words, a purely technical matter. All these factors are of great importance, but we have to ask why technical choices made thus far have yielded rather mixed results. We need to think hard about the cause. Development will never be fully guaranteed through automatic or impersonal forces, whether they derive from the market or from international politics. "Development is impossible without upright men and women, without financiers and politicians whose consciences are finely attuned to the requirements of the common good.[1174]

[1171] *See* PONTIFICAL COUNCIL FOR JUSTICE AND PEACE, TRADE, DEVELOPMENT AND THE FIGHT AGAINST POVERTY, supra note 1103.

[1172] See Vatican Radio, "Vatican representative calls for ethically responsible use of technology," July 4, 2013 available at http://www.news.va/en/news/ [Often, underneath the intricacies of economic, financial, and political interconnections, there remain misunderstandings, hardships, and injustice. The flow of technological know-how increases, but it is those in possession of it who benefit, while the situation on the ground for the peoples who live in its shadow remains unchanged; for them there is little chance of emancipation.].

[1173] *Id.*

[1174] *See* Vatican Radio, "Vatican representative calls for ethically responsible use of technology," July 4, 2013 available at http://www.news.va/en/news/vatican-representative-calls-for-ethically-respons

6.2.4.4 Intellectual Property Rights, Biotechnology, and Farmers' Rights

The Catholic Church has always taught that private property has its significance in its service of the entire human community. Pope John Paul II highlighted this when he said

> All too often, the fruits of scientific progress, rather than being placed at the service of the entire human community, are distributed in such a way that unjust inequalities are actually increased or even rendered permanent.... The Catholic Church has consistently taught that there is a "social mortgage" on all private property, a concept which today must be also applied to "intellectual property" and to "knowledge." The law of profit alone cannot be applied to that which is essential for the fight against hunger, disease and poverty.[1175]

Historically, plant varieties were exempted from the international patent regime in deference to farmers' traditional practices of saving and exchanging seeds. However, after World War II, the situation changed. A certain form of protection was developed, particularly under the International Convention on the Protection of New Varieties of Plants

[1175] Pope John Paul II, Address to the Delegation of the "Jubilee 2000 Debt Campaign," September 23, 1999.

(UPOV),[1176] and most the recently Trade-Related Aspects of Intellectual Property Rights (TRIPS).[1177]

With the advent of the TRIPS Agreement, the complex issue of protection of plant varieties in Article 27.3(b) became topical.[1178] Article 27.3(b) of TRIPS provides for the review of the provisions of patentability of plants and animals other than microorganisms and the protection of plant varieties as of 1999. A vital part of that provision is for Member States to provide for the protection of plant varieties by way of patents or an effective *sui generis* system or some combination of the two. The provision

---

[1176] *See* The International Union for the Protection of New Varieties of Plants UPOV, available at http://www.upov.int/en/publications/tg-rom/index.html . UPOV is an intergovernmental organization with headquarters in Geneva. The acronym UPOV is derived from the French name of the organization, *Union internationale pour la protection des obtentions végétales.* The mission of UPOV is to provide and promote an effective system of plant variety protection, with the aim of encouraging the development of new varieties of plants, for the benefit of society. UPOV was established by the International Convention for the Protection of New Varieties of Plants (the "UPOV Convention"), which was signed in Paris in 1961. The Convention entered into force in 1968. It was revised in Geneva in 1972, 1978, and 1991. The 1991 Act entered into force on April 24, 1998. Reference to the UPOV Convention in this document means the 1991 Act. The purpose of the UPOV Convention is to ensure that the members of the Union acknowledge the achievements of breeders of new varieties of plants by granting to them an intellectual property right on the basis of a set of clearly defined principles. To be eligible for protection, varieties have to be (i) distinct from existing, commonly known varieties, (ii) sufficiently uniform, (iii) stable, and (iv) new in the sense that they must not have been commercialized prior to certain dates established by reference to the date of the application for protection. See also UPOV Publication No. 437(E), July 8, 2011 available at http://www.upov.org/export/sites/upov/en/about/pdf/pub437.pdf last visited July 23, 2013.

[1177] The *raison d'être* of intellectual property protection systems is the promotion of literacy, scientific or artistic production, and inventive activity for the sake of the common good. That protection officially attests the right of the author or inventor to recognition of the ownership of his work and to a degree of economic reward, at the same time as it serves the cultural and material progress of society as a whole. The ultimate cause that intellectual property protection works for is the recognition of the dignity of the human person and his work, in its double dimension, namely as a medium of expression and the growth of the individual personality and as a contribution to the common good. *See id.* See also Article 27, para. 2 of Universal Declaration of Human Rights; Article 15 (1)(c) of International Covenant on Economic, Social and Cultural Rights; POPE JOHN PAUL II, ENCYCLICAL LETTER LABORME EXERCENS nos. 5, 6, 9 and 15

[1178] PONTIFICAL COUNCIL FOR JUSTICE AND PEACE, TRADE, DEVELOPMENT AND THE FIGHT AGAINST POVERTY, *supra* note 1103.

of TRIPS Article 27.3(b) has negative impacts that are critical for millions of farmers in the South.[1179]

In agriculture, farmers play a central role in primarily preserving and enhancing agro-biodiversity through the nurturing of plant and crop varieties specifically suited to diverse local environments. Recently, industrialized countries developed new genetically modified seeds and plant varieties through biotechnological research, in part, with traditional knowledge of local communities and the biodiversity of the South. The Holy See is concerned that the North restricts the flow of this knowledge through legal protection. This unfair practice makes the price of patented seeds higher compared to other seeds. This trend affects other inputs, such as pesticides and fertilizers.[1180]

The Catholic Church has also expressed concern regarding intellectual manifestations of tradition or folklore. Intellectual manifestations of tradition or folklore fall on all fours with the substantial concepts that afford entitlement with what the Catholic Church refers to as "classical"

1179 Id. See TRIPS Agreement, particularly Article 27. Article 27 para. 3(a) authorizes as follows:

Members may also exclude from patentability,
(a) diagnostic, therapeutic, and surgical methods for the treatment of humans or animals;
(b) plants and animals other than micro-organisms, and essentially biological processes for the production of plants or animals other than non-biological and microbiological processes. However, Members shall provide for the protection of plant varieties either by patents or by an effective *sui generis* system or by any combination thereof. The provisions of this subparagraph shall be reviewed four years after the date of entry into force of the WTO Agreement.

1180 *Id.*

protection[1181] of intellectual property.[1182] The Church recognizes that these manifestations constitute a means of constructing and projecting the identity of the members of the community concerned. They also constitute a common asset of that same community, which has grown gradually from small, anonymous contributions of individuals and groups over a great many generations.[1183]

In modern times, particularly since the advent of applied microbiological science, the great social usefulness of biological resources and the end products of their industrial transformation have been indispensable in medical and pharmaceutical fields, as well as in biochemistry. For that reason, there has been a more intensive search for new biological resources and genetic materials all over the world.[1184] This massive search is motivated mainly by the inspiration to develop derivatives that can offer a favorable cost-benefit ratio.[1185]

Industrialized countries have solidified their superiority in invention concepts (novel creations of the human mind and discovery of genetic

---

1181 Classical protection framework for intellectual rights refers to innovative intellectual or artistic activity attributable to a specific natural person or legal entity, definable and registerable by means of a series of technical means (e.g., writing, registration, multimedia dissemination, and so on). "Such legal system is not well suited, however, to the protection of any moral or economic right that may be derived from innovative or creative activities developed or refined throughout history, which are like the social manifestation of the work of several generations and a genius peculiar to the communities, peoples or families." See DOCUMENT SUBMITTED BY THE HOLY SEE ON INTELLECTUAL PROPERTY AND GENETIC RESOURCES, TRADITIONAL KNOWLEDGE AND FOLKLORE FOR THE FIRST SESSION OF GOVERNMENTAL COMMITTEE ON INTELLECTUAL PROPERTY AND GENETIC RESOURCES, TRADITIONAL KNOWLEDGE AND FOLKLORE, April 26, 2001, available at WIPO/GRTKF/IC/1/7, pp. 1-2

1182 World Intellectual Property Organization (WIPO), Intergovernmental Committee on Intellectual Property and Genetic Resources, Traditional Knowledge and Folklore (1st Session), Geneva, April 30 to May 3, 2001, available at *WIPO/GRTKF/IC/1/7.*

1183 *See* POPE JOHN PAUL II, ENCYCLICAL LETTER LABOREM EXERCENS, nos. 3 & 10; United Nations Conference on Environment and Development (UNCED), Convention on Biological Diversity (CBD), Rio de Janeiro, June 1992, para. 11 of Preamble; Articles 4(1); 5(a)-(b); 7(1) of International Labor Organization C169 - Indigenous and Tribal Peoples Convention, 1989 (No.169).

1184 *See* World Intellectual Property Organization (WIPO), "Matters Concerning Intellectual Property and Genetic Resources, Traditional Knowledge and Folklore – An Overview," March 16, 2001, Annex 3, available at *WIPO/GRTKF/IC/1/3.*

1185 *See* HOLY SEE, WIPO DOCUMENT, supra note 1155, at 2.

material existing in nature) by adopting the mechanisms of patent and case law.[1186] This strategic legal development has been expanded to patent genetic components of plants, animals, and human beings that possess biochemical or pharmaceutical properties of usefulness.[1187]

The Church confirms that most of the biological resources that possess great economic and social usefulness have been in territories inhabited by native communities since time immemorial. But these native communities exist within the jurisdiction of countries different from those in which the industrial development of the genetic material takes place and in which patents are obtained. Experience shows that those native communities already have some knowledge and make use of some of the biological properties covered by the patent. Ancestral concern for the soil on the part of indigenous communities generates a right to its use and usufruct. This right extends also to the plants and animals that exist in those territories.[1188]

The biological environment has a close relationship with the culture of the peoples of these communities and constitutes an integral factor of their identity and social cohesion.[1189] In line with the foregoing assertion, the Church declares that it is important to recognize the rights of native populations. These rights originate from the close link between the native populations in the land and its fruits with the biological environment. Because these rights exist, the Church reasons that they be promoted,

---

[1186] *See* WIPO, MATTERS CONCERNING INTELLECTUAL PROPERTY AND GENETIC RESOURCES, supra note 1119, at paragraphs 55-58; See also Directive 98/44/EC of the European Parliament and Council of July 6, 1998 on the legal protection of biotechnological inventions, Articles 3 & 5.

[1187] *Id.*

[1188] *Id.*

[1189] *See* PONTIFICAL COUNCIL FOR JUSTICE AND PEACE, TOWARDS A BETTER DISTRIBUTION OF LAND - The Challenge of Agrarian Reform, November 23, 1997, # 55. The Pontifical Council for Justice and Peace States stresses the close relationship between land and the models of culture, development and spirituality of these populations, means that agrarian reform is a decisive component of the systematic and coordinated plan of action that governments must draw up in order to protect the rights of indigenous populations and guarantee respect for their specific identity. *Id.*

respected, and protected.[1190] Talking about the native populations, the issue of human dignity is quintessential.[1191]

To ensure full respect for personal dignity and freedom of the native populations, any economic exploitation of the biological and genetic resources must be strictly regulated. The native communities where the use and appropriation of genetic resources and knowledge originated have a right to be fully informed on a given project.[1192] The interaction between industries that exploit these resources and the native communities must be defined in such a way as to protect the latter's folklore.[1193] If such economic appropriation is not strictly regulated, folklore creations of local communities might be used as commodities at the expense of the interests and rights of these native communities.[1194] They have a right to

---

[1190] *See id.* at # 11 stating as follows,

In recent decades, various forms of economic activity based on the use of natural resources have steadily expanded into land traditionally occupied by indigenous populations. In most cases, the rights of the indigenous inhabitants have been ignored when the expansion of large-scale agricultural concerns, the establishment of hydroelectric plants and the exploitation of mineral resources and of oil and timber in areas of expanding agricultural frontiers have been decided, planned and implemented. The law is respected while all this is taking place. However, the property rights upheld by the law are in conflict with the right of use of the soil deriving from an occupation and ownership of the land, the origins of which are lost in memory.

See also Pontifical Council for Justice and Peace, *Les peuples autochtones dans l'enseignement de Jean-Paul II*, Vatican City 1993, p. 22.

[1191] *See* ILO C-169, Articles 13-18.

[1192] *See* CHURCH AND GLOBALIZATION, supra note, (indicating that "the provisions of the TRIPS Agreement essentially also result in the selective breeding work of the local population, which constitutes the prerequisites and basis for modern research, is hardly being given any consideration in the form of fair and appropriate benefit or profit sharing arrangements").

[1193] *See* Vatican Radio, "Vatican representative calls for ethically responsible use of technology," available at http://www.news.va/en/news/vatican-representative-calls-for-ethically-respons . Here, the Holy See talks about the concept of culture as including both,

The system of values, norms, preferences and the level of knowledge acquired through the educational system. It follows that culture is a strategic resource for an effective human development, which must include the improvement of human dignity, individual, social, and political freedom, *i.e.* of human rights. Culture in fact is not just an end in itself or the delivery of new products but a way to express interpersonal relations, which constitute the fundamental dimension of human beings. *See id.*

[1194] *See* WIPO, DOCUMENT OF THE HOLY SEE, *supra* note 1155, at # 6 stating that,

The disciplines of intellectual property and labor law have created a network of legal and social institutions whose aim is to defend the rights of individual authors, composers and performers

fair participation in the benefits that may accrue. They also have a right to object to the use of resources derived from their own body.[1195]

The Catholic Church recognizes the link between intellectual property protection and international trade policies. She also participates in the discussion concerning the extension of industrial property to certain scientific discoveries.[1196] These new developments in international intellectual property law call for a wide range of rights and interests, which ought to be respected and protected. The Church did not hesitate to express her concern.

> What is at stake are the rights of the native populations that have developed the traditional knowledge and the expressions of folklore or who occupy the territories from which the genetic material comes, the right of the countries to the resources associated with biological diversity, the right of the inventor or discoverer to remuneration for any intellectual value that he may have added, the possible rights and interests of companies, society's right to or interest in the stimulation of inventive activity and the development of science and the arts, and finally a more general right of all mankind to be assured that the products of scientific progress will serve everyone equally and not only the sectors with the greatest acquisitive potential. The ethical challenge to be met is therefore, that of reconciling the various rights and interests at stake in such a way that the legitimate economic interest does not compromise higher values, such as the social function on inventions

to keep pace with the constant growth of corporate activity in the dissemination of artistic creations, but until now, they have not succeeded in creating sufficient elements with which to protect the rights deriving from folklore creations.

[1195] *See* Articles 4, 5(b) and 10 of the Universal Declaration on the Human Genome and Human Rights, UNESCO, November 12, 1997; *see also* Council of Europe, Convention on Human Rights and Biomedicine, Oviedo, (STE, para. 164), Article 5, Oviedo, April 4, 1997.

[1196] *See* Annex IC of Agreement on Trade-Related Aspects of Intellectual Property Rights (TRIPS) of the Marrakesh Agreement Establishing the WTO, April 15, 1994; Articles 3 & 5 of the European Derivative 98/44/EC; World Intellectual Property Organization (WIPO), "Matters Concerning Intellectual Property and Genetic Resources," supra note 1119, at paragraphs 55 to 66.

> and knowledge and the rights of the peoples with which the knowledge and resources originate.[1197]

The Holy See, as a matter of fact, advocates a unitary vision of law that is structured based on fundamental human rights. Any law relating to intellectual property ownership rights must be cognizant of the value of justice and perpetrate it and reconcile it with human rights.[1198] Enactments relating to intellectual property ought to be made in relation to the higher principle of justice, *i.e.*, the universal destination of goods. Goods of creation are available for all human beings for their subsistence and personal advancement.

The Church also teaches about laws protecting private property to respect the common destiny of all goods, so much so that it must be said that all private property is subject to a social encumbrance. In any event, there is institutional conflict between acquired private property rights overriding community demands; public authorities ought to resolve it with active involvement on the part of individuals and social groups. Private property is not to be understood as an absolute right. It is an instrument with which to achieve effective access to property destined for the whole of humankind. With thought that is true to the Church's teaching, laws must also ensure, at the same time, that all individuals and all families have their essential environment of freedom and just economy in the face of all forms of totalitarianism.[1199]

The Church upholds the classical intellectual property system, which recognized the notion of social encumbrance under its industrial property (patent) heading. In its inclusion of social encumbrance, the classical intellectual property regime defined substantive and time limitations on rights granted. In the case of patents, that system allowed governments discretion about the choice of industrial sectors to be protected. It also gave governments a free determination of the scope of the conditions of patentability, as well as options for opposing patents and compulsory

---

1197 *See* WIPO, DOCUMENT OF THE HOLY SEE, *supra* note 1155, at 7.

1198 *See id.* at 8.

1199 *Id. See also* POPE JOHN PAUL II, ENCYCLICAL LETTER CENTESIMUS ANNUS, nos. 6 & 30; LABOREM EXERCENS, # 14; POPE PAUL VI, ENCYCLICAL LETTER POPULORUM PROGRESSIO, nos. 22 & 23; SECOND VATICAN ECUMENICAL COUNCIL, GAUDIUM ET SPES, nos. 69 & 71.

license regime.[1200] However, under the present legislative strategy of intellectual property, the Church has concerns that the dangers of patent rights are more obvious.

The Church is concerned that the present intellectual property system lumps all industrial and commercial activities in the patent regime together with making uniform all the intellectual property laws. This arrangement carries the risk of totally abandoning the social function in intellectual property and emphasizing only the good of the producer. Patents here protect the rights and interests of the holder regardless of the subject matter that may be affected by the acts of the holder. The social environment where the patent rights may be used is not given equal attention.[1201] From the point of view of economic dynamics, patents constitute a clog on free competition because owners of such rights have discretionary powers to control or charge for acts involving the content of the patent.[1202]

The Holy See has, therefore, vehemently held the position for intellectual property to always serve the common good. The Church also advocates for enactments, case law, and administrative practice to abide by prudent and restrictive rules in terms of scope, to promote and incorporate cases of proven social usefulness. These instruments should respect the rule of law and the notion of social encumbrance. To promote human dignity, there ought to be application of the moderating elements devised by legal science and practice, such as compulsory licensing exclusion of protection for reasons of public policy, and morality in the case of patents or reasonable exceptions to copyright.[1203]

[1200] *See* Pope John Paul II, Message to the Jubilee 2000 Debt Campaign 9September 23, 1999) in *L'Osservatore Romano*, September 25, 1999, p. 5; ENCYCLICAL LETTER CENTESIMUS ANNUS, nos. 31 & 33; Message to the United Nations Special Session on Development (UNSSD), August 25, 1980, nos. 2 & 7 in *L'Osservatore Romano*, August 27, 1980. Obviously, when owners of patents are vested with such enormous powers and discretion, the social environment suffers. The peoples of the local communities are therefore relegated to the background and corporate social responsibility is rendered meaningless.

[1201] *Id.*

[1202] *See* WIPO, DOCUMENT OF THE HOLY SEE, *supra* note, at 9.

[1203] *See* TRIPS Agreement, Article 31 on compulsory licensing; Article 6 and footnote 6 to Article 28 on the exhaustion of rights, Articles 7 & 66.2 on the promotion of development and technology transfer; Article 27.2 on the exclusion of patents on grounds of morality or public policy; and Article 13 on reasonable exceptions to copyright. [What is controversial is the applicability of these important provisions. The Catholic Church declares that when applied and implemented, they will achieve the set objectives. She advocates for new legal

6.2.4.4.1 Holy See's Proposals

After reviewing Article 27.3(b) of the TRIPS Agreement, the Holy See reiterates that the earth is ultimately a common heritage; the fruits of the earth are meant for the benefit of all human beings.[1204] In support of this assertion, the *Second Vatican Council* teaches that

> God intended the earth and all it contains for the use of all men and peoples; so-created goods should flow fairly to all, regulated by justice and accompanied by charity. Whatever forms property may take according to legitimate custom and changing circumstances, this universal destiny of the earth's resources should always be borne in mind.[1205]

TRIPS should strive to close the large gap between industrialized Members and poor Members by providing incentives for innovations that can synchronize with the needs of poor Members. For instance, in the field of agriculture, farmers from poor countries should not be made to pay disproportionate production costs, which normally undermine their livelihood and agricultural operations.[1206]

The other aspect of intellectual property rights the Holy See is concerned about is the aspect that relates to biological resources associated with native communities. Generic and specific exceptions as provided for in Articles 7 and 8 of the TRIPS Agreement do not generate sufficient

---

machinery fully integrated and consistent with the international provisions currently in force. Such legal machinery should impose on Members certain minimum protection requirements for those sectors whose rights and interests are not fully catered for in the system now in force].

1204 *See* INTERVENTION OF THE HEAD OF THE HOLY SEE DELEGATION SPECIAL ENVOY OF HIS HOLINESS POPE BENEDICT XVI TO THE UNITED NATIONS CONFERENCE ON SUSTAINABLE DEVELOPMENT, "Address by His Eminence, Cardinal Odilo Pedro Scherer," Rio de Janeiro - Brazil, JUNE 22, 2012 available at http://www.vatican.va/roman_curia/secretariat_state/2012/documents/rc_seg-st_20120622_rio20_en.html

1205 SECOND VATICAN ECUMENICAL COUNCIL, GAUDIUM ET SPES, supra note 75, # 69.

1206 PONTIFICAL COUNCIL FOR JUSTICE AND PEACE, TRADE, DEVELOPMENT AND THE FIGHT AGAINST POVERTY, *supra* note 1103, at pp. 14-15.

protection of local communities' knowledge. Also, patents are inadequate to guarantee community intellectual rights. As a result, the Catholic Church proposes for the WTO to further consider establishing a more effective *sui generis* system provided for in Article 27.3(b).[1207]

The Church further opines that for the TRIPS Agreement to achieve its general goal, it should promote the sustainable management of biological resources. For sustainable management of biological resources to be achievable, the TRIPS Agreement should recognize the rights of local communities to protect those techniques applied by farmers to enhance biodiversity and improve their plant varieties, as well as ensure equitable sharing of benefits accruing therefrom.[1208] Furthermore, the Church emphasized that a *sui generis* system should be based on non-monopoly rights.[1209] In developing a property rights system for plant

---

[1207] *Id.*

[1208] *See Justitia et Pax*, "A Catholic Statement on Trade Policies and the Interest of Poor People," in *Church and Globalization: Ecumenical Dialogue,* supra, demanding reform of TRIPS as follows,

-Traditional farmers' rights relating to the use of seeds must be included in the TRIPS Agreement.

-Farmers from the South must receive compensation for their selective cultivation work and their traditional knowledge, when corporations develop new varieties on the basis of seeds developed in the South or develop new drugs on the basis of existing biological resources. A system of benefit/profit sharing must be formally accepted by the concerned population before a patent can be issued.

-Article 31b of the TRIPS Agreement must be interpreted as meaning that it allows governments to issue compulsory licenses to produce generic drugs in the case of essential drugs.

-No country must be forced to issue patents on living organisms.

-Public research in the agrarian and pharmaceutical sectors must be extended and provided with greater support within the framework of international development cooperation. Cooperation agreements between the public and private sectors should also be included in this field (public-private partnership).

[1209] *See* PONTIFICAL COUNCIL FOR JUSTICE AND PEACE, TRADE, JUSTICE AND FIGHT AGAINST POVERTY, *supra* note 1103.

varieties, the Church proposed that the WTO pay heed to the resolution of the Convention on Biodiversity.[1210]

The plight of local communities should come first before any commercial targets. For instance, the Holy See teaches that the right of local communities to food security and to healthy and quality nutrition should take priority. To be more pragmatic, TRIPS should provide for substantial financial support for agricultural research, such as in organic agricultural systems. These proposals will be more result-oriented if the WTO grants the request of developing countries for more time to put in place a *sui generis* legislation in response to their local concerns.[1211]

6.2.4.5 Holy See's Proposals on the Agreement on Services

The GATS governs services in international trade. The Holy See raises concern over the obvious imbalance in international trade in services. Developing countries are often placed at the margin as importers and never as exporters of services, particularly in services that have high technological content. Developing countries are only competitive in labor-intensive services. GATS Article XIX envisages further rounds of trade negotiations to achieve greater liberalization in service-related trade. Though the General Agreement on Trade in Services (GATS) provides a glimpse of hope in Article XIX of GATS, much has not been done in that regard. [1212]

The Holy See, therefore, proposes for the GATT-WTO system to adhere to the guidelines offered by Article XIX, particularly paragraph 2, which grants developing countries appropriate flexibility, *i.e.*, special and

[1210] *See* Convention on Biological Diversity, Global Workshop - Key Elements of the Strategic Plan 2011-2020, including Aichi Biodiversity Targets, Brasilia, March 2012, and available at http://www.cbd.int/convention/text/ last visited March 16, 2014. [The Catholic Church is an advocate for local communities to be considered in the management of resources extracted from their immediate environment. The reason behind this advocacy is that these local communities bear the impact of such appropriation of resources and cannot be impoverished without fair compensation.]

[1211] PONTICAL COUNCIL FOR JUSTICE AND PEACE, TRADE, DEVELOPMENT AND THE FIGHT AGAINST POVERTY, *supra* 1103, at p. 15.

[1212] PONTIFICAL COUNCIL FOR JUSTICE AND PEACE, TRADE, DEVELOPMENT AND THE FIGHT AGAINST POVERTY, *supra* note 1103.

differential treatments.[1213] Members should make more commitments on services provided by skilled and semi-skilled workers. Trade negotiations have not achieved the robust achievements expected. In its international interventions, the Holy See calls on governments and employers of labor to respect the guidelines offered by Article XIX, more especially, paragraph 2 thereof.

Furthermore, what the Holy See refers to as "universal service" is of great importance. Universal service includes sectors like financial services, telecommunications, and transport services. These are essential to national economies. Negotiations should consider that this category of services is important to regions economically and geographically removed from trade centers. Multilateral negotiations should make such services accessible to those regions. The GATT-WTO system should promote initiatives to commit private service providers to supply essential services to rural and underdeveloped areas with the necessary infrastructure. For poor and remote regions to participate and benefit from electronic commerce, for instance, they need infrastructure and technology.[1214]

The Catholic Church reiterates that the plurality of cultures and ideas constitutes part of the common heritage of humankind. Local audiovisual products contribute immensely in the circulation and diversification of cultural expression. In audiovisual product markets, therefore, the Holy See appeals for Members to encourage diffusion and preservation of the cultural identities of all peoples. Negotiations should be made to support and protect audiovisual trade with effective international rules.[1215]

The Holy See expresses concern over financial crises that intermittently disrupt commerce and development. The Church therefore calls on the WTO to manage financial services to ensure stability of national financial systems. To ensure this stability, liberalization of trade in financial services ought to be complemented by efficient and prudential regulations and accountability in both private and public sectors. Authorities in developing

---

[1213] *See* WTO, General Agreement on Trade in Services (GATS) Agreement, Article XIX:2 available at http://www.wto.org/english/docs_e/legal_e/26-gats.pdf

[1214] *See* PONTIFICAL COUNCIL FOR JUSTICE AND PEACE, TRADE, DEVELOPMENT AND THE FIGHT AGAINST POVERTY, *supra* note 1103.

[1215] *Id.*

countries should cooperate with their counterparts in other countries in emulating transparent measures.[1216]

6.3 International Trade Law Issues Where the Holy See Either Has Been Silent or Said Little

Because the Holy See has projected itself as a moral voice in the world, much is expected of it from Christians and non-Christians alike. Pope Paul VI earlier taught that the Catholic Church enlightens the world for everyone, with no exception.[1217] It is from this platform that the Church raises an objection to any economy of exclusion and inequality, an economy that debases human dignity and enthrones indifference. The Church believes that "the dignity of the human person and the common good ranks higher than the comfort of those who refuse to renounce their privileges."[1218] The Church singles herself out and raises her moral voice on issues that militate against the full realization of human dignity and the common good.

The original idea about international trade was to benefit people and not just markets and economies. Theoretically, the GATT-WTO system was established as an instrument of hope, but unfortunately, developed Members have not been faithful to the promises and commitments made to the developing Members, especially the LDCs. This unfairness has not only frustrated the poor countries but has also resulted in stalemates that have made negotiations almost impossible. In situations such as these, the world looks up to the Holy See to raise its prophetic voice, as it ought to do naturally. However, whether the Holy See says a little or fails to do so, the need to remind it arises. There are some examples of such scenarios in relation to international trade.

1216 *Id.*

1217 *See* Pope Paul VI, ENCYCLICAL LETTER ECCLESIAM SUAM ("On the Paths of the Church"), August 6, 1964 # 97 9 The Church takes a central position in sharing moral values with everyone, excepting none); See also POPE FRANCIS I, POSTOLIC LETTER EVANGELII GAUDIUM ("On the Joy of the Gospel) November 24, 2013 # 48.

1218 *See* POPE FRANCIS I, APOSTOLIC LETTER EVANGELII GAUDIUM, # 219.

6.3.1 The Ecclesiastica Diplomatica and GATT-WTO System

The primary concerns of the Holy See with respect to international relations involve some basic values. The Holy See's diplomacy has three basic characteristics. First, the Holy See is mindful that the Church is called to promote the moral and ethical aspects of issues everywhere in the world. Second, the Holy See's diplomacy is one of unity. It has no natural boundaries because it is universal and concerns all peoples of the world. Third, it is humanitarian in nature. The diplomacy of the Catholic Church takes sides with the people in respect of the dignity of the human person given to human beings by the Creator.[1219]

Though the Holy See has maintained a diplomatic apostolate since the fourth century,[1220] the Pontifical Ecclesiastical Academy (PEA) was founded in April 1701 under Pope Clement XI. The PEA is the Catholic Church's formal pontifical ecclesiastical diplomatic and human rights training institute.[1221] The bishops propose candidates for the PEA.[1222] Thoughts here would include that the reason for establishing an Academy specifically for training diplomats is for better equipping them with skills

1219 *See* Thomas Aquinas College, Interview with His Excellency, Archbishop Celestino Migliore, Apostolic Nuncio and Permanent Observer of the Holy See to the United Nations, Sparkill, New York, 2006 available at http://www.vaticandiplomacy.org/specialarticles.htm last visited March 12, 2014.

1220 The diplomatic service of the Holy See can be traced back to the First Council of Nicaea when Pope Sylvester I sent legates to represent him during the discussions of the council. The present Academy was created as the Pontifical Academy of Ecclesiastical Nobles in 1701 by Abbot Pietro Garagni, in close collaboration with the Blessed Sebastian Valfrè of the Turin Oratory. *See* La Curia Romana, Storia dell Academia, *infra* note 1195.

1221 *See* La Curia Romana, Storia della Academia - Pontificia Academia Ecclesiastica available at http://www.vatican.va/roman_curia/pontifical_academies/acdeccles/documents/storia_it.htm

1222 Students spend four years at the academy, two years earning a licentiate in canon law (J.C.L.) from a Roman University (such as the Pontifical Gregorian University), then two years earning a doctorate in canon law (J.C.D.). If the students that have been recruited already have a J.C.D., then their time at the PEA is shortened to two years. The courses are usually in diplomatic history, languages, and diplomatic writing and are considered not to be academic but rather focus on the practical skills needed to serve as a diplomat. *See* La Curia Romana, *supra* note 1193; *see also* INTERVIEW WITH ARCHBISHOP CELESTINO MIGLIORE, *supra* note 1159.

to match the dynamics of international diplomacy in a world that changes every day.

A clearer picture of the course content of the PEA training may be helpful. The PEA is the center for the formation of future diplomatic agents of the Holy See. The major requirement is for candidates to be ordained priests first, and therefore possess a degree in theology. According to Archbishop Migliore, PEA academic curriculum consists of two years of specialized studies. The specialized studies are in ecclesiastical diplomacy, international law, monographs on international organizations and on techniques of negotiations. Others are history of ecclesiastical diplomacy, diplomatic styles, courses on great modern cultural and theological strains, and economic and social questions. The students also take courses in information technology. They are expected to possess a working knowledge of any two of the following languages: English, French, Spanish, German, and increasingly, Arabic and the languages of Eastern Europe and Asia.[1223]

Basically, the Holy See's diplomacy course description studies the nature, ends, tasks, organization, specificities, etc., of ecclesiastical diplomacy in the light of the *Motu Proprio Sollicitudo Omnium Ecclesiarum* (1969). It also studies canons 362-367 of the 1983 Code of Canon Law and the United Nations Vienna Convention on Diplomatic Relations (1961). This course is taught in two parts after an introduction.[1224] The PEA is an affiliate of the Pontifical Lateran University, in Rome, Italy.[1225]

While the introduction to this course includes the general rudiments of diplomacy, the first part concentrates on the study of the Vienna Convention on Diplomatic Relations (1961), the mission of Pontifical Representatives accredited to States and governments respecting rules of international rights. It is also dedicated to the study of the criteria of codification, the features of the Convention, and annotations to articles 2-19 of the Vienna Convention. These annotations define dispositions regulating diplomatic relations, terminology, the function of diplomatic mission, the Agreement establishing the mission, as well as receiving

1223 *See* INTERVIEW WITH ARCHBISHOP MIGLIORE, *supra* note 1193.

1224 *See* Ecclesiastica Diplomatica, Ecclesiastical Diplomacy Course Description, Pontifical Lateran University, Rome, Italy available at http://www.vaticandiplomacy.org/accldiplomacycrse.htm last visited March 23, 2104.

1225 *Id.*

state control over the composition and configuration of the mission and precedence.[1226]

The second part of the course studies the *Motu Propio Omnium Ecclesiarum* (1969), which summarizes canons 362-367 of the 1983 Code of Canon Law defining the nature of "the Legates of the Roman Pontiff." It also studies the doctrine and teaching of the Second Vatican Council about ecclesiastical formations of papal legates, emphasizing the inherent right of the Pope to send representatives to secular states. This second aspect further addresses the definition of Papal Representatives, their classification, mission, responsibilities, immunities, and privileges. Special attention is paid to ecclesiastical diplomacy and the humanitarian mission of the Holy See.[1227]

The course content of the Holy See's diplomatic institute covers a wide range of areas but much is still needed. In sustaining its Permanent Observer Mission, the Holy See makes contributions to international debate on current issues such as development, securities, eradication of poverty and inequalities, human rights, etc. In participating in such democratic debate, the Holy See sheds the light of Catholic Social thought on those issues. Being a Permanent Observer, the Holy See is admitted to negotiations on resolutions, declarations, conventions, treaties, *etc.* Therefore, the Holy See contributes to consensus building and in the making of international law through participation in conventions and treaties. Once conventions and treaties are adopted, they form international law. International law does not only contain reciprocal obligations between states, it also deals with the rights of the individual.[1228]

The Holy See also gives its voice to those who have no voice. This is the most challenging but also gratifying aspect of the Holy See's participation in internal affairs. Dioceses, associations, religious congregations, and individuals turn to the Holy See for issues that are humanitarian in nature. Interlocutors give much attention and sometimes operative consideration to the issues the Holy See present thereupon.[1229]

[1226] *Id.*

[1227] *Id.*

[1228] *See* INTERVIEW WITH ARCHBISHOP MIGLIORE, *supra* note 1193.

[1229] *Id.*

Looking at the course content of the Pontifical Ecclesiastical Academy, one wonders whether there is enough room to accommodate details of international law principles that can facilitate the Holy See's expertise to engage in international debate and discussion. Pope Francis rightly points out that "the earth is our common home .... The Church cannot and must not remain on the sidelines in the fight for justice."[1230] Pope Francis I's teaching implies that the diplomats directly involved in representing the Holy See in the four corners of the earth cannot afford to embark on a "crash program" preparation. Training of the Holy See's diplomats ought to be thorough and not just two years of training at the Pontifical Ecclesiastical Academy. Considering how vast international law is and the wide range of international issues, the two-year training at the PEA is inadequate. Moreover, academic training can only empower a person with principles and not concrete experiences.

It is true that one can also gain experience through internship and participation in international conferences and diplomatic interactions, but having the principles prior to those experiences enriches one's skills. An example is the vastness of the GATT-WTO system. There are many categories of WTO Agreements and Annexes, so much so that being present at Ministerial conferences or other WTO meetings cannot cure the lack of education about the system. Understanding the deliberations and the manner with which Members apply concessions as instruments of international commercial transaction is an important tool. Being present as a Permanent Observer without understanding the historical background and politics influencing why countries react the way they do will make an observer impotent in intervening.

6.3.2 Duration it took for the Holy See to intervene in the GATT-WTO Issues

As this book argued above, it is baffling why the Holy See could not say much right from the beginning of the GATT system in 1947, and even paid lip service until 1997, when it eventually joined the WTO as

[1230] POPE FRANCIS I, APOSTOLIC LETTER EVANGELII GAUDIUM (The Joy of the Gospel), November 24, 2013, # 183.

a Permanent Observer. In Igbo tradition in Nigeria, Africa, it is said, "Whoever is absent during the burial of a corpse starts to search for it from the wrong side." The world has been searching for the ill-fated Malaysian Flight 370 that disappeared with 239 passengers on board on March 8, 2014. Irrespective of the sophisticated technology applied, the search has been on for 55 days, yet the world has no clue as to the whereabouts of the airplane and those on board. The Holy See was not present when the GATT-WTO system metamorphosed into its present structure. In the light of its regrettable absence from the onset, the Holy See sounds like one talking about dead bodies without knowing where they are buried.

Often, a late-comer is normally fed with second-hand information that lacks originality, information that is based on the opinion of the giver and, therefore, opinionated and lacking certainty. Being late, the Holy See could have been informed by parties with vested interest. Looking at the aims and objectives of the GATT-WTO system, the Holy See could also face some confusion. The objectives of the system being one thing and what is in practice being a different thing altogether may cause the Holy See to elongate the Church's apprenticeship. When the Church spends many more years studying the system, it takes a longer time to make a much-expected impact. The result will be the continued stalemate at the WTO deliberations without much impact of the Church's moral influence. Even if this argument sounds a mere speculation, one wonders why the Church, after all these years, has either said nothing or very little on certain issues in the GATT-WTO system.

6.3.3 Injustice in Concession Requirement

Developing countries are known to be cooperative in giving concessions to the developed countries without getting any commensurate concessions from the latter. Developing countries agree to such measures as required by the GATT-WTO system in the spirit of cooperation, for example, in the areas of textiles, leather, jute, etc., in which the developed countries needed the poor countries to support an adjustment process as a way of supporting the former. Often, Ministerial conferences and trade negotiations end up in stalemate because Members are not able to make concessions that are reciprocal and acceptable.

Ordinarily, in trade negotiations the terms "concession" and "compensation," are contemplated. These terms derive from a protectionist approach to trade negotiations. "Concession refers to an initial reduction in a tariff or non-tariff barrier of one country and the reciprocal reduction from another country is "compensation."[1231] This is what is seen in a multilateral trade "Round," a term which conjures up the image of boxing where each boxer fights to win.[1232] This struggle is all about presumes a general parity among Members of the WTO in terms of their economic incentives, legal positions, and bargaining capabilities.[1233] However, the reality is that not all WTO Members are alike. A case in point is the special and differential treatment of developing countries and LDCs. Professor Bhala was right when he wrote that, in tariff negotiations, some WTO Members have idiosyncratic needs.[1234] Paragraph 1 of GATT Article XXVIII *bis* deviates from helping to realize the special needs of less privileged Members. This paragraph stresses the importance of negotiations on a reciprocal and mutually advantageous basis. Therefore, it compromises the needs of poor Members by making reciprocity the invariable principle.[1235] Moreover, it is a way of making demands on Members that unequal equally.

GATT Article XXVIII:3 needs a special attention in this discussion because it deviates from the above provision that makes reciprocity the invariable principle of trade negotiations. It provides as follows,

> Negotiations *shall* be conducted on a basis which affords adequate opportunity to *take into account* ...the needs of less-developed countries for a more flexible use *of tariff protection to assist their economic development* and the

[1231] *See* BHALA, TRADE, DEVELOPMENT AND SOCIAL JUSTICE, supra note 56, at 331.

[1232] *Id.*

[1233] *See id.* at 334.

[1234] *Id.*

[1235] GATT Article XXVIII:1 *bis* states that tariffs often constitute "serious obstacles to trade." It also prescribes that trade negotiations to reduce tariffs substantially are "of great importance to the expansion of international trade." GATT Article XXVIII:1 concludes by authorizing contracting parties to sponsor tariff negotiations from time to time. GATT Article XXVIII:2 offers methodologies as to help reduce tariffs and emphasized the importance of contracting parties' participating in earnest. *See id.*

special needs of these countries to maintain *tariffs for revenue purposes.1236*

The use of "shall" rather than "should" or "ought," transforms the provision into a mandate, thereby taking it out of mere exhortation.[1237] This interpretation is so sound that Professor Bhala suggested that Article XXVIII:3(b) *bis* be put in the Almsgiving rule.

> Almsgiving category is sufficiently broad to include transfer of financial capital, human capital, or technology that might not be open or direct. It is important that the Almsgiving category does not omit rules with potential to help Third World countries. Rules containing tariff protection, and tariff revenues, are examples, and from its language, GATT Article XXVIII:3(b) *bis* covers both. To put it bluntly, writing a check for, say, $100 million and handing it over to a poor country is a form of giving alms. So, too, is allowing the poor country to garner $100 million in customs duties on imported merchandise.[1238]

Professor Bhala's position is worthy of further reflection. Come to think of it, GATT Article XXVIII:3(b) *bis* requires negotiations on tariff negotiations to consider the special needs of less developed countries in two respects. First, many such countries use tariffs as an instrument by which to protect infant industries. They also use tariff walls to help ailing industries; often state-owned enterprises revive to meet global competition – or at least, contract in an orderly fashion. Second, many less developed countries suffer from dreadfully inefficient (and corrupt) income tax collection systems. They rely on tariff collections as a principal source

---

[1236] GATT Article XXVIII:3(b) *bis* (emphasis added) *quoted in* BHALA, TADE, DEVELOPMENT AND SOCIAL JUSTICE, *supra* note 56, at 338. A committee report issued during the Dillon Round noted the special needs of less developed countries, and referenced this provision. See *Second Report of Committee I, B.I.S.D. (8th Supp.) 103, ¶ 13 at 110* (1960) (adopted on 19 November 1959).

[1237] *See* BHALA, TRADE, DEVELOPMENT AND SOCIAL JUSTICE, supra note 56, at 338.

[1238] *See id.* at 339.

of government funding. Applying and collecting duties at the border on imports is far easier for them than accurately assessing income tax liability within their borders, and thereafter either collecting income taxes owed, or administering a withholding system.[1239]

GATT Article XXVIII:3(b) *bis* provision insists developed countries not force large, rapid cuts in tariffs that would topple over the protective wall needed by certain industries in these countries. No matter what the argument may be, the obvious fact is the existence of the GATT Article XXVIII:3(b) *bis* provision. This provision grants aid to the domestic industries receiving the protection by shielding them (at least partly) from import competition. It demands rich countries not to call large tariff reduction commitments that would constrict or cut-off the revenue stream needed by less developed countries. Therefore, special and differential treatment exists to help keep money in the coffers of the treasuries of less developed countries.[1240]

That said, GATT Article XXVIII:3(b) *bis* buttresses the Almsgiving Rule which obligates developed countries to consider the special needs of less developed countries. However, GATT Article XXVIII:3(b) *bis* does not amount to an instruction not to apply the reciprocity principle in tariff negotiations to developing countries. GATT Article XXXVI:8 could be interpreted to offer an overall balance. Developed countries could take into account the needs of impoverished countries by, for example, not insisting on a reduction tariffs in key sectors of a developing country's economy, or agreeing to a lengthy phase-out period for tariffs.[1241]

The above interpretation is reinforced by juxtaposing GATT Article XXVIII:3 *bis* with Article XXXVI:8. Professor Bhala argues that if GATT Article XXVIII:3 bis were an exception from the reciprocity principle in tariff negotiations for less developed countries, then GATT Article XXXVI:8 would be nearly superfluous. GATT Article XXXVI:8 provides that "the developed country contracting parties do not expect reciprocity for commitments made by them in trade negotiations to reduce or

[1239] *Id.*

[1240] *Id.*

[1241] *See id.* at 340.

remove tariffs and other barriers to the trade of less developed contracting parties."[1242]

From the nature of the provision of GATT Article XXXVI:8, one can see that GATT Article XXVIII:3 *bis* does not go so far as to exempt less developed country WTO Members from the reciprocity principle.[1243] GATT Article XXXVI:8 provides for that exemption and even goes further to cover both tariff and non-tariff barrier reduction negotiations. Put into the perspective of the theological framework, GATT Article XXVIII:3 bis is an Almsgiving Rule. However, GATT Article XXXVI:8 provides for that reciprocity exemption, a moral one though.[1244] It provides that a poor country, given the structure and condition of its economy, should not be required to pay for a concession offered by a rich country on exports from the poor country.[1245] Put more bluntly, a poor country should not be

[1242] *See* GATT Article XXXVI:8.

[1243] It might be helpful to itemize the seven "principles and objectives for less developed WTO Members stipulated in GATT Article XXXVI. They are,

Living standards (Paragraphs 1(a), 1(c), and 1(d): Living standards should be raised, and the disparity in them between rich and poor countries should be narrowed.

Export market access (Paragraphs 1(b), 3, and 4): Market conditions should be more favorable and acceptable with respect to access for primary product exports from less developed countries, and more generously should help these countries increase their share in world trade, so they can implement their development plans.

Export prices (Paragraph 1(b), 2, and 4): Market conditions should be stabilized and improved with respect to primary product prices, so that the value of primary product exports from less developed countries rises to equitable levels that provide these countries with funds for development.

Export diversification (Paragraphs 3 and 5): Market conditions for processed and manufactured products should be increased so as to help less developed countries avoid excessive dependence on the exports of primary products, and thereby to diversify their sources of export revenues.

Joint and collaborative action (Paragraph 1(d), 6, and 7): The world's trading nations should undertake joint action, and action in cooperation with international lending agencies and United Nations organs, to further the development objectives of poor countries.

Rule of law (Paragraph 1(e): A multilateral legal framework should govern trade relations between rich and poor countries, and should enhance economic and social development through trade.

Preferences (Paragraph 1(f) and 8): Developed countries should enable developing countries to undertake special measures to promote their trade and development objectives, and developed countries should not expect reciprocal benefits when offering concessions on tariff or non-tariff barriers to developing countries.

[1244] BHALA, TRADE, DEVELOPMENT AND SOCIAL JUSTICE, *supra 57* at 341.

[1245] *See* RAJ BHALA & KEVIN KENNEDY sections 1-3(b) at 80 (1998, with1999 SUPPLEMENT), *quoted in* BHALA, TRADE, DEVELOPMENT AND SOCIAL

asked for reciprocal concessions, and should be allowed to free-ride on the adherence by other countries to the MFN obligation.

GATT Article XXXVI:8 is a quintessential example of Almsgiving Rule and it explains the issue of reciprocity clearer for purposes of the exemption of the principle for less developed countries. The provision states

> Do not expect reciprocity means, in accordance with the objectives set forth in this Article, that the less-developed contracting parties should not be expected, in the course of trade negotiations, to make contributions which are inconsistent with their individual development, financial and trade needs, taking into consideration past trade developments.[1246]

The language of GATT Article XXVIII:3(b) *bis* is susceptible to abuse by developed countries. It is possible that developed countries may place emphasis on the phrase "take into account."[1247] To put this provision in the Almsgiving category is not enough. Implementing it is more pragmatic. The nature of Catholic Social Justice Theory calls for more action on the part of the Church in her universal mission. While credit is given to great thinkers like Professor Bhala, the Holy See should take reasoning further by making it part of its missionary strategy. The Holy See can also utilize great brains it has in the Catholic Church as consultants or advisers. Perhaps, the Holy See has not thought about interpreting GATT Article XXVIII:3(b) *bis* and GATT Article XXXVI:8 the way Professor Bhala has analyzed them. Like, Pope Saint John XXIII did, the Catholic Church should try not to concentrate the methodology and strategies of her universal mission solely on the hierarchy alone. The Holy See would do better if it reaches out to other daughters and sons of the Catholic Church and utilize the wealth of knowledge they possess. Two good heads are better than one.

JUSTICE, *supra* note 57, at 341

[1246] *See* GATT Article XXXVI, paragraph 8.

[1247] BHALA, TRADE, DEVELOPMENT AND SOCIAL JUSTICE, *supra* note 56, at 341.

6.3.4 Developing Countries and the WTO Dispute Settlement Mechanism

The central objective of the Dispute Settlement Understanding (DSU) is for the Members concerned to settle a dispute between them in a manner that is consistent with the WTO Agreement.[1248] Accordingly, bilateral consultations between the parties are the first stage of formal dispute settlement.[1249] Bilateral consultations give the parties an opportunity to discuss the matter and to find a satisfactory solution without resorting to litigation.[1250] Only after such mandatory consultations have failed to produce a satisfactory solution within 60 days may the complainant request adjudication by a panel.[1251] Even when consultations have failed to resolve any dispute, it always remains possible for the parties to find a mutually agreed-upon solution at any later stage of the proceedings.

Based on DSU's right to bilateral consultation, the WTO claims that all Members are on equal footing and that even poor countries are on a more equal footing than the industrialized ones.[1252] However, developing Members wanting to avail themselves of the benefits of the dispute settlement system face considerable burdens. For example, developing countries, especially the smaller ones, often do not have enough specialized human resources who are experts in the intricacies of the substance of WTO law or the dispute settlement procedure. The growing body of jurisprudence developed by panels and the Appellate Body makes it increasingly difficult for trade officials of poor Members to master both the substance and the procedural aspects of WTO law, including the latest developments.[1253]

Though the new dispute settlement process has brought about a certain degree of improvement over the past, some recent trends have been averse

---

1248 *See* DSU Article 3.7, available at http://www.wto.org/english/tratop_e/dispu_e/dsu_e.htm last visited March 23, 2014.

1249 *See* DSU Article 4.

1250 *See* DSU Article 4.5.

1251 *See* DSU Article 4.7.

1252 *See* WTO, "Developing country Members in dispute settlement — theory and practice," available at http://www.wto.org/english/tratop_e/dispu_e/disp_settlement_cbt_e/c11s1p1_e.htm last visited March 2, 2014.

1253 *Id.*

to the interests of developing countries.[1254] The powerful Members of the GATT-WTO system influence judicial lawmaking through the selection of members of the Appellate Body. In practice, the European Commission and the United States have special privileges that empower them to veto the selection of candidates for the Body.[1255] The Panels and Appellate Body have often adopted interpretations which constrain the rights of developing countries and enhance their obligations. Four cases can illustrate this point better.

(i) In the Venezuela gasoline case,[1256] the Appellate Body expanded the discretion of a country in taking trade-restrictive measures for the conservation of non-renewable natural resources. The Appellate Body said the discretion of a country in this matter is not limited by the test of necessity. Rather, it is adequate if there is a nexus between the particular trade-restrictive measure and the protection of a non-renewable natural resource.

(ii) In the Indian Woolen shirts case,[1257] the Appellate Body said that the onus of justifying the trade restraint in the textiles does not lie on the country applying the restrictive measures; rather it is the complaining country which has to demonstrate that the conditions prescribed for the restraint have not been fulfilled

(iii) In the Indonesia car case,[1258] the Panel denied developing countries the flexibility, allowed in the Agreement on Subsidies, to give subsidies for the use of domestic products in preference to an

---

1254 *See generally,* Bhagirath Lal Das, "Strengthening Developing Countries in the WTO (Trade and Development Series No. 8)," Third World Network (TWN).

1255 *See* Raghavan Chakravarthi, "WTO establishes Appellate Body," November 30, 1995 available at http://www.sunshine.org/trade/process/followup/1995/index.htm last visited March 23, 2014.

1256 United States - Standards for Reformulated and Conventional Gasoline, WT/DS2/AB/R available at http://www.worldtradelaw.net/reports/wtoab/us-gasoline(ab).pdf last visited March 12, 2014.

1257 United States – Measure affecting Imports of Woven Wool Shirts and Blouses from India, WTDS33/R 1997 available at http://www.wto.org/english/tratop_e/dispu_e/33r.pdf last visited April 1, 2014.

1258 *See* Indonesia — Certain Measures Affecting the Automobile Industry, WT/DS54/R, WT/DS55/R, WT/DS59/R, WT/DS64/R available at http://www.meti.go.jp/english/report/downloadfiles/gCT9917e.pdf

imported product. The Panel took the stand that such a measure would violate the Agreement on Trade-Related Investment Measures (TRIMs).

(iv) In the many interpretations on the recent *Shrimp-Turtle and United States* case,[1259] the Appellate Body has given at least four interpretations that have adverse implications for developing countries. (a) The Appellate Body established the primacy of the conservation of the environment over the free flow of goods under the normal GATT rules. This has the implication of diluting the disciplines on the general exceptions provided for in GATT Article XX.[1260]

The Holy See has addressed the shortcomings of developing countries regarding the DSU process,[1261] but only minimally, without the persistent tone it deserves. The Doha Ministerial Declaration's mission was to infuse developing countries' concerns into virtually every facet of WTO activity, particularly in the latter's section on dispute settlement.[1262] Because prior to the Doha Round, developing countries were absent in the WTO section on dispute settlement, the Doha Ministerial Declaration agreed to create an avenue for negotiations involving developing countries. Such negotiations

---

[1259] *See* the *U.S. – Shrimp-Turtle and United States – Import Prohibition of Certain Shrimp and Shrimp Products, Recourse to Article XX: 5 by Malaysia* (2001). The decision here enabled the United States to maintain measures banning the importation of Shrimp from certain countries that do not require the use of turtle-excluder devices in shrimp-net fishing.

[1260] *See* GATT Articles XX: (a) & (b) on the General exceptions which are not counted as measures that would be arbitrary or unjustifiable discrimination between countries, available at http://www.wto.org/english/docs_e/legal_e/gatt47_02_e.htm last visited March 23, 2014.

[1261] *See* PONTIFICAL COUNCIL FOR JUSTICE AND PEACE, TRADE DEVELOPMENT AND THE FIGHT AGAINST POVERTY, *supra* note 1103.

[1262] DSU Article 4.10 states that, "during consultations Members should give special attention to the particular problems and interests of developing country Members." [The word "should" in this provision only urges and advises members to give special attention to the particular problems and interests of developing countries and is therefore not a mandatory provision. The provision is more declaratory than operative and does not provide any operative content. It does not state exactly who gets what assistance from whom. As a result, it does not create an enforceable obligation on the part of the members.] See V. Delich, "Developing Countries and the WTO Dispute Settlement System," in Bernard Hoekman *et al.* eds., *Development, Trade and the WTO: A Handbook*, 62 (2002), pp. 71, 72-73; *See also* A. Alavi, "African Countries in the WTO's Dispute Settlement Mechanism" *25 Development Policy Review* (2007), pp. 25-42.

were aimed at improvements and clarifications of the DSU.[1263] The mission of the Holy See being centered on speaking for the poor, it should not relent on raising this issue continuously until it is implemented.

The above point may look plausible because the omission of developing countries in the original DSU is an index that is not surprising after all. Dispute settlement is supposed to be a neutral, objective, and fair process of strict legal interpretation, where favoritism, even for the weak, should not be allowed. The Doha Ministerial Declaration is not binding but hortatory in WTO Members. It is supposed to be the Holy See that should use its teaching on charity and mercifulness as discussed above to appeal to developed countries. Without that push, it is difficult to get the latter to change their minds from using the DSU as it is, to victimize developing countries.[1264]

6.3.5 Regional Trade Agreements (RTAs)

The multilateral trading system tolerates, GATT Article XXIV and GATS Article V, regional trade agreements (RTAs).[1265] Regional trade agreements represent an important exception to the WTO's principle of nondiscrimination. The 2003 World Trade Report states

> RTAs can complement the multilateral trading system, help to build and strengthen it. But by their very nature RTAs are discriminatory; they are a departure from the MFN principle, a cornerstone of the multilateral trading system. Their effects on global trade liberalization and economic

[1263] *See* Paragraph 30 of Doha Ministerial Declaration, WT/MIN(01)/DEC/1, November 20, 2001

[1264] *See* Robert E. Hudec, Developing Countries in the GATT Legal System.

[1265] *See* GATT Article XXIV (stating that WTO Members have the right to join RTAs or Customs Union. *See also* Appellate Body Report on *Turkey - Textiles (WT/DS58)*, para. 58. Presently, Article XXIV and WTO jurisprudence clearly establish that it is for the parties to the RTA to prove that the concerned free-trade area or customs union is compatible with Article XXIV of GATT (and/or Article IV of GATS).

> growth are not clear given that the regional economic impact of RTAs is *ex ante* inherently ambiguous.[1266]

This upsurge of regional trade agreements got further fuelled by the failure of the Seattle and the Cancún Ministerial Conference of WTO.[1267] Failures of the Seattle and Cancun Ministerial Conferences highlighted inherent problems of the multilateral trading system and pushed many countries to divert their negotiating energies into regional trade agreements. Regional Trade Agreements (RTAs) are defined as groupings of countries that are formed with the objective of reducing barriers to trade between members. But contrary to what the name suggests, these agreements or unions have also been concluded between countries not necessarily belonging to the same geographical region.[1268]

The Holy See has condemned the proliferation of regional trade arrangements. The Holy See's condemnation of trade regionalism stems from a move away from multilateral trade agreements traditionally drawn up at the WTO, which is muddled up in secrecy and not beneficial to all countries.

> Currently there is a clear tendency to further enlarge these RTAs to form mega-regional trade agreements such as the Transatlantic Trade and Investment Partnership, or the Trans-Pacific Partnership. Certainly, the enlargement of regional trade agreements is a step toward further trade liberalization but we have to bear in mind that these agreements inevitably threaten the desirability to reach an agreement on a truly multilateral basis. In fact, by entering a regional trade agreement a country reduces the

[1266] *See* WORLD TRADE REPORT (WTR) 2003, p. 27 available at http://www.wto.org/english/res_e/booksp_e/anrep_e/world_trade_report_2003_e.pdf

[1267] *See* The WTO Legacy, Seattle Post-Intelligencer, available at http://seattleepi.nwsource.com/wto/ last visited June 12, 2013. Riots were because people disapproved of growing inequalities and injustice in the GATT-WTO system.

[1268] *See* "Unlocking the benefits of world trade" *The Economist,* Oct 30, 2003

> incentives to extend its efforts on trade liberalization at a multilateral level.[1269]

The Holy See's reason for not encouraging the proliferation of RTAs, particularly mega-RTAs, is because

> We know that only the multilateral system is a clear, equitable system that provides effective guarantees for small and poor countries, which tend to be penalized in a Regional Trade Agreement where it is asymmetric. Among the most damaging concessions developing countries make in regional and bilateral agreements, are those enhancing the monopolies on life-saving medicines, which reduce access and affordability, and those that provide excessive legal rights to foreign investors, limiting the policy space for nations to promote sustainable and inclusive development.[1270]

What the Holy See says about regional trade is important though it might not have had any direct effect at the Bali Ministerial Conference. It is a continuation of the Catholic Church's passionate defense of the world's poor and a show of her missionary advocacy in such a way as to show its readiness to speak the truth, even to the most powerful nations of the world. By calling for a stop to the proliferation of RTAs and mega-RTAs, the Holy See reassures the less-fortunate in the world that it can resist most unjust and unjustifiable aspects of regionalism through its projection of the Gospel principles at all levels.

1269 *See* Statement by H.E. Archbishop Silvano M. Tomasi, Apostolic Nuncio, Permanent Observer of the Holy See to the United Nations and Other International Organizations in Geneva at the 9th Session of the Ministerial Conference of the World Trade Organization, Bali, Indonesia, December 3-6, 2013, # 10.

1270 *Id. See also,* e.g., "All costs, no benefits: How TRIPS-plus intellectual property rules in the US-Jordan FTA affect access to medicines," Oxfam Briefing Paper No. 102, March 21, 2007, available at http://www.oxfam.org/sites/www.oxfam.org/files/all%20costs,%20no%20benefits.pdf; UNCTAD, "Towards a New Generation of International Investment Policies: UNCTAD's Fresh Approach to Multilateral Investment Policy-Making," IIA Issues Note No. 5, July 2013, e http://unctad.org/en/PublicationsLibrary/webdiaepcb2013d6_en.pdf

The Holy See's defense of the dignity of the human person is worthy of emulation, but still, considering the effectiveness of such a strategy as it mounts from time to time, it needs to do more. Nobody expects the Holy See to comment on all unjust structures in the international arena. When the Holy See raises its moral voice, it is expected to be more persistent. The mission of the Holy See can never go on sabbatical even if everybody accepts and implements the Gospel message. Because the Holy See has a privileged position in the world to be a watch-dog on international issues, all eyes are on the Holy See to speak out against any event that can increase discrimination and weaken global economic agenda.

The Holy See may not be expected to raise its voice only verbally or in writing. It may be more pragmatic than that. During a penitential service for instance, on March 28, 2014, just before Pope Francis I heard confessions in St. Peter's Basilica, he knelt at a confessional before a priest, publicly making his own confession of sins.[1271] Though the Pope's action is a break in tradition, its practical significance is highly commendable. By doing this, the Pope does not need to sermonize on the indispensability of the sacrament of Penance. Cardinal Renato Raffaele Martinos of the *Dignitatis Humanae Institute* says that Pope Francis' uniqueness and magnetism is seen in his ability to instruct with his words but effectively teach through his actions.[1272]

His action is more effective than preaching on the importance of confessions for hours at the pulpit. This evangelizing strategy has resilient qualities that are worthy of emulation in all the four corners of the earth, differences notwithstanding. The Church can alternate her prophetic strategy with more practical techniques like Pope Francis I has done. In the same manner, the Holy See can avoid intra-practices that are like the shortcomings of the GATT-WTO system.

Imagine what will happen, if the Holy See addresses the issue of inequalities and the use of power in its dealings. It is only by eschewing all forms of injustice and inequalities from within that the Holy See can

---

1271 *See* The Sacred Page, "Pope Francis goes to confession," March 28, 2014 available at http://www.thesacredpage.com/2014/03/picture-pope-francis-goes-to-confession.html last visited March 29, 2014 (an unprecedented footage, because no Pope has ever gone to confession in public before Francis I).

1272 *See L'Osservatore Romano*, English Edition, December 13, 2013, p. 7.

make more serious impacts on the world. Where the Catholic Church has a skeleton in the cupboard, it cannot expect to influence the world as much as it would have if it were otherwise. For instance, factors that throw things out of whack are collusion and corruption, *i.e.*, the lack of good faith and fair dealing. Once the Church sets a good example of itself in those areas, she will be best prepared to use them as veritable strategies.[1273]

Furthermore, a pertinent question needs to be reiterated at this juncture. Before the Holy See makes decisive pronouncements on the international scene as part of its evangelizing methodology, it needs to avail itself of the counsel of experts in a particular field concerned. It is not enough to sermonize on the need to put a stop to proliferation of RTAs without addressing the root causes of such proliferation. Also, an assessment of the other side of the coin in every argument is often very helpful. It will be good for the Holy See to know that it is impossible to eliminate regional trade agreements. They have come to stay, and country members of these regional arrangements have gone too far with their commitments. Some functions are, in principle, better carried out at a regional or sub-regional level.

If RTAs are assessed merely as tariff-reducing exercises, one may say that such exercises can divert trade and can only be viewed as second best. But when we reflect on the fact that the WTO alone has not and cannot eliminate all trade barriers, the possible realistic alternative is obviously second best. Also, experience has it that trade liberalization at the WTO is only partial. The implication is that any other arrangement to achieve more trade liberalization is acceptable.

It is not true that the only objective behind the proliferation of trade regionalism is tariff-related. Many of the regional agreements cover far more than tariffs. They implement rules and regulatory frameworks that not all countries are willing to sign. Global trade may be optimally beneficial, but circumstances have made many countries shy away from what may be referred to as "global federal government." The growing

---

1273 Pope Francis I says there are two images of the Church: a Church which evangelizes and goes out of herself by hearing the word of God with reverence and proclaiming it with faith; and the worldly Church living within herself, of herself, for herself. Jesus knocks from within the Church so that we can let him out for people to be saved. See *Inside the Vatican*, March 29014, p. 28.

inequalities and the inability of developed nations and developing countries to conclude the Doha Development Round (DDR) and launch a new series of plurilateral agreements governed by a new protocol of understanding is a big problem.[1274]

The Catholic Church should instead invest more efforts into investigating the core reasons why there is proliferation of regional trade arrangements instead of calling for their elimination. The stagnation of the DDR, which has a worthy objective though not perfect, is a case in point. The diversity characteristic of WTO Membership is an import issue and, as a result, no one size can fit all. Some members legitimately reject new rules and obligations that would constrain their policy space. For others, new rules are costly in terms of opportunities foregone. However, there are strong reasons to believe that additional rules could aid in the integration required for fully exploiting the potential of the global economy.[1275] When Members are not able to realize their set objectives, they defect to other arrangements to accomplish that purpose. One cannot stop child-abuse by telling a child to stop crying without first addressing the source of the abuse.

Trade regionalism might be an opportunity to tighten the disciplines permitting FTAs, which has not been optimally realized in the GATT-WTO system. Regional trade arrangements are critiqued for trade diversion that is alleged to hamper full free trade. That argument begs the question because it is of no effect to talk about the consequences of an action, or lack of action, without referring to the cause of an action. Major industrialized countries have a vested interest in the negotiations of multilateral agreements, and developing countries do not have equal opportunities. This is a selfish attitude which affects enforcement of GATT-WTO agreements.

However, the Holy See is right in critiquing the Trans-Pacific Partnership (TPP)[1276] and the Transatlantic Trade and Investment

---

[1274] *See Robert Z. Lawrence, "Competing with Regionalism by Revitalizing the WTO," in Ricardo Meléndez-Ortiz et al, The Future and the WTO: Confronting the Challenges, ICTSD Program on Global Policy and Institutions, July 2012.*

[1275] *Id.*

[1276] *See The New American, "How Free Trade Agenda is Knocking Down America," September 2, 2013 available at* http://www.thenewamerican.com/files/TNA2917.pdf *last visited April*

Partnership (TTIP),[1277] because such arrangements that further expand the regional trade agreements are not in the interest of a just global economy. When that level of agreement is established, it threatens the desirability of countries to engage in multilateral agreements. TPP and TTIP are strategies that developed countries are using to extend their diplomacy and mundane economics so that they can still set a pace for, and dominate developing countries. The initiators of such trade arrangements hide under the canopy of the argument that the DDR is locked in a closet, while the alternative is to embark on such mega-regional trade agreements. They have a hidden agenda and this is selfish.[1278]

It will be wiser for the Holy See to also reach out to these new trade agreements and study their *modus operandi* to know the best strategy to adopt in inculcating social justice in the system. With the vested interest of the powers behind TPP and TTIP, it is almost impossible to stop them. Their strategies are packed in such a way as to convince the victims of the attractiveness of such trade arrangements, and it is difficult to otherwise convince the countries that entered such agreements. The goal of the social mission of the Catholic Church is to safeguard and promote the dignity of the human person by making any policy or program that concerns him/her pass through the crucible of the Gospel message. This test can only work effectively when the Holy See gets more involved in any system that affects the dignity of the human person, and not by attacking it from outside, or paying lip service to such a system.

6.3.6 Market Access for LDCs

While the Ricardian concept of comparative advantage and free trade are espoused as a principle of the free market system that provides opportunities for all to benefit from globalization, developed countries

---

3, 2014 (The TPP involves a free trade agreement between the United States and 11 Pacific Rim nations, including Japan).

1277 *Id. The TTIP involves a free trade agreement between the United States and the European Union (EU).*

1278 *See* Gary Hufbauer & Julia Muir, "The Trans-Pacific Partnership," in RICARDO & MELÉNDEZ-ORTIZ, supra note 1188 at 47-52.

have not entirely embraced this paradigm in their own trade policies.[1279] This inconsistency could be seen in several examples of the Uruguay Round Agreements.[1280] The Agriculture Agreement reflected the double standards of developed countries, which called for developing countries to open their markets, while maintaining huge subsidies and high tariffs that depressed global prices, undermining the development potential of developing countries (*e.g.*, cotton, textiles, and clothing).[1281] In the area of industrial products, developed countries retained high tariffs, tariff escalation, and tariff peaks for labor-intensive products, precisely in the areas in which most developing countries had a comparative advantage.[1282]

At the WTO's Fourth Ministerial Conference held in Doha, Qatar, in November 2001, ministers recognized the central role that international trade can play in the promotion of economic development. Ministers acknowledged that most WTO Members are developing countries, and as a result, they agreed to continue making positive efforts to ensure

---

[1279] *For e.g.*, in the Trade-related Investment Measures (TRIMs) Agreement, developing countries were pushed to reduce their right to policy intervention to support their economic development, whereas developed countries utilized similar instruments in their own economic development strategies in the past – thus they were "kicking the ladder behind them." Similarly, the Trade-Related Aspects of Intellectual Property Rights (TRIPs) Agreement reflected a lack of attention to balance the potential benefits of increased research with the high costs of reduced competition and monopoly power granted to pharmaceutical countries by patent rights. While there has been a growing recognition that the increased flow of goods across borders does require regulation to protect human health, physical safety, and the environment, there has been wide criticism of the unilateral imposition of these standards on the global trading system, which often reflects the norms and interests of the larger developed countries who initiate them. In addition, Mutual Recognition Agreements (MRA) on standards have been negotiated between a few developed countries, facilitating trade between them and thus increasing the barriers to entry for developing country exports. *See* Faizel Ismail, "Mainstreaming Development in the World Trade Organization," *Journal of World Trade* 39 (1), 2005, pp.15-16; *See generally also,* Faizel Ismail, "On the Road to Cancun: A Development Perspective on EU Trade Policies and Implications for Central and East European Countries," *Journal of World Investment* (August 2003); Ha-Joon Chang, *Kicking Away the Ladder: Development Strategy in Historical Perspective*, London, Anthem Press (2002); Faizel Ismail, The Doha Declaration on TRIPs and Public Health and the Negotiations in the WTO on Paragraph 6," *Journal of World Intellectual Property* (May 2003).

[1280]

[1281] *See* John N. Barton, Judith L. Goldsten, et al., The Evolution of the Trade Regime, Princeton University Press, 2006, pp. 93-94

[1282] *See* Faizel Ismail, "Mainstreaming Development in the World Trade Organization," *Journal of World Trade* 39 (1), 2005, p. 15.

that developing countries, and in particular LDCs, secure a share in the growth of world trade commensurate with their development needs. Thus, in launching the Doha Development Agenda (DDA) talks, they placed developing countries' needs and interests at the heart of the negotiations.[1283]

Furthermore, specific efforts are being made in the negotiations to address the needs of the LDCs, as well as those of "small and vulnerable economies".[1284] The official indicators toward progress of achieving the goals of increased market access in meeting the needs of developing and least-developed countries, is what is referred to as "Duty Free Quota Free Market Access" (DFQFMA). This includes (1) increased duty-free access for developing countries; (2) tariff reduction (especially on agricultural products, textiles and clothing); and (3) the reduction of trade-distorting subsidies from developed countries. These elements are part of the WTO agreements and are subject to negotiations.

Regrettably, the American negotiating position is it will implement DFQF market access for LDCs only as part of a Doha Round agreement.[1285] The African Growth and Opportunity Act (AGOA) provides duty-free (but not quota-free) market access for 98 percent of tariff lines for less developed beneficiaries, not all of whom are LDCs.[1286]The Doha Development Round (DDR) goal has stagnated for many years now. The Holy See has not been consistent in pointing out and appealing to Members, especially the rich and fast-developing ones, to avoid such argument that they wouldn't implement any of the DDR agreements unless all the agreements are taken together. The Holy See has not utilized

---

1283 *See* WORLD TRADE ORGANIZATION, "Millennium Development Goals – Doha Development Agenda" available at http://www.wto.org/english/thewto_e/coher_e/mdg_e/dda_e.htm last visited March 30, 2014.

1284 *Id.*

1285 *See generally*, ELLIOTT K.A., OPENING MARKETS FOR POOR COUNTRIES: ARE WE THERE YET?, Center for Global Development Working Paper 184, 2009; BOUET A., et al., THE COSTS AND BENEFITS OF DUTY-FREE, QUOTA-FREE MARKET ACCESS FOR POOR COUNTRIES: WHO AND WHAT MATTERS, Center for Global Development Working Paper 206 (2010).

1286 *See* for details, International Trade Administration, African Growth and Opportunity Act (AGOA) available at http://trade.gov/agoa/ last visited April 2, 2014. The African Growth and Opportunity Act (AGOA) was signed into law on May 18, 2000, as Title 1 of The Trade and Development Act of 2000. The Act offers tangible incentives for African countries to continue their efforts to open their economies and build free markets.

its long history of effective diplomacy to unearth where the dead bodies are buried and to therefore persuade the United States[1287] and Africa to emulate the examples of other developed Members in implementing the DFQF agenda, which will be beneficial to LDCs.

6.3.7 GATT Article XXI – The Security Exception

Apart from undermining social justice, the environment, jobs, and food safety through its power over governments, the WTO also bolsters military spending, weapons production, and the international weapons trade. This problem is based on the premise that the only legitimate role for governments is to ensure order within their borders. For that reason, the WTO undermines social and environmental policies. It protects the war industry through a "security exception" in GATT Article XXI. Therefore, the GATT Article XXI security exception allows governments' free rein over actions taken in the name of national security. This implies that a country cannot be stopped from taking any action it considers necessary to protect its essential security interests. GATT Article XXI permits:

> Actions relating to the traffic in arms, ammunition and implements of war and such traffic in other goods and materials as is carried on directly for the purpose of supplying a military establishment or taken in time of war or other emergency in international relations.[1288]

[1287] *See* for e.g., Joseph Stiglitz, *The Roaring Nieties,* New York, W.W. Norton (2003)

[1288] *See* GATT Article XXI: Security Exceptions, which provides that
Nothing in this Agreement shall be construed,
(a) to require any contracting party to furnish any information the disclosure of which it considers.
contrary to its essential security interests; or
(b) to prevent any contracting party from taking any action which it considers necessary for the protection of its essential security interests;
(i) relating to fissionable materials or the materials from which they are derived;
(ii) relating to the traffic in arms, ammunition and implements of war and to such traffic in other
goods and materials as is carried on directly or indirectly for supplying a military establishment;
(iii) taken in time of war or other emergency in international relations; or

GATT Article XXI is the most powerful exception in the WTO because governments define for themselves their "essential security interests" and protect what they want by couching it in terms of that exception. That implies that the war industry is shielded from WTO challenges, thereby stimulating military spending and militarizing the economy. It looks exciting that because of this GATT XXI exception, governments can promote jobs, new emerging industries, or high-tech manufacturing through military spending. However, in the long run, world peace and human lives and property are jeopardized. The danger is that through this exception, any government can continue to subsidize military corporations.[1289]

The Holy See has vehemently critiqued the proliferation of weapons of mass destruction in the world. Promoting the dignity of the individual is the Church's main concern in her social teaching. The realm of economics is so complicated that one must approach it with some caution. Economics is no longer based on necessity and utility or what the people want. Rather, nowadays, economics is based on the fancies, the moods, the mechanical tricks, absent-mindedness, and the other weaker side of the human being.[1290] Because every economic decision has a moral consequence, the Holy See should study reasons behind every economic theory or law that

(c) to prevent any contracting party from taking any action in pursuance of its obligations under the United Nations Charter for the maintenance of international peace and security. *See* Understanding WTO available at http://www.wto.org/english/res_e/booksp_e/gatt_ai_e/art21_e.pdf

[1289] *See* the *Bombardier Aerospace Case*, WT/DS70/R, April 14, 1999; WT/DS222/R, January 28, 2002; *See also* Charles Goldsmith & Christopher J. Chipello, "Canada, Brazil Lose WTO Plane Cases" *Wall Street Journal*, Brussels, March 15, 1999, p. 5 [In 1999, a WTO dispute Panel ruled against Canada, and its Technology Partnerships were accused of subsidizing the aerospace and defense industry. The program was used by Bombardier Aerospace to build and export regional passenger jets. The WTO Panel ruled that the non-military subsidies were unfair. For that reason, the Canadian government redesigned the program to be WTO-friendly. As such, the Canadian Department of National Defense announced a $30 million annual subsidy program for weapons corporations to develop new weapons. This wouldn't be challenged at the WTO because it falls within the GATTS national security exception provision (GATT Article XXI). It could then be used to fund Bombardier's military production]. See Canadian Press, "$30 million for defense contractors," October 18, 1999.

[1290] *See* Dale Ahlquist, "The Trouble with Catholic Social Teaching," *patheos*, October 23, 2012 available at http://www.patheos.com/blogs/markshea/2012/10/dale-ahlquist-on-the-trouble-with-catholic-social-teaching.html last visited March 31, 2014.

affects the human person in any way. For instance, it is not making profit that is the concern in the GATT Article XXI national security exception. What raises concern is its negative impact on the life and freedom of the individual.

The expectation, therefore, is for the Holy See to invest its missionary strategies in such a way as to influence change to such an exception, but unfortunately it has not done so as effectively as it ought to. The Holy See is not a global legislator, but events and its mission in the world have put it in such a position as to influence certain legislation as may militate against the full realization of human dignity. The Catholic Church teaches that humanitarian intervention is so obligatory that it is not only a national responsibility but also a duty of nations and the international community.[1291] This implies that the Church is bound to raise her moral voice any time such a venture is treated with any form of indifference, and this includes mapping out strategies to influence laws to fall in line with that teaching. The commitment of the Holy See is to "dialogue with the world," and to speak in such a way as to make it clear that "the Church is seeking with it the truth and the just solution of the difficult problems of human life."[1292]

With her heuristic method, the Church finds out the truth mostly on her own, especially as she goes about her mission on earth. The Church's proposals to modernity should be through "the power of arguments," rather than by "moralization or exhortation."[1293] Therefore, the mission of the Christian faith is to liberate, in the most profound sense of human freedom.[1294] *Gaudium et Spes* demonstrates that when it teaches that

> What the world aspired to and what the world suffered were the joy and hope, the grief and anguish of the followers of Christ as well.... The Church lives in the world and for the world because nothing that is genuinely human fails to find an echo in Christian hearts.[1295]

[1291] *See* GEORGE WEIGEL, supra note 74, at p. 665.

[1292] *Id.* at p. 167.

[1293] *See Acta Synodalia* II-5, pp. 298-300 *quoted in* WEIGEL, supra note 74, at 167.

[1294] *See id.* at 169.

[1295] *See* THE SECOND VATICAN ECUMENICAL COUNCIL, GAUDIUM ET SPES, # 1

The Catholic Church is to be understood from the perspective of the sheep metaphor. The Church is made up of shepherds living with the smell of sheep. Whatever it takes to identify with the sheep and to better guide them into fulfillment is the responsibility of the Church.

6.3.8 Labor Standards

The Church has taught consistently concerning the protection of workers, especially as is evident in the social encyclical letters of Popes and reflections of some major groups and individuals. The Holy See has reiterated that labor standards constitute crucial subject matter in different international, regional, and national fora. It has, therefore, called for the adoption and adherence to the principles established by the 1999 ILO Convention.[1296] This call qualifies as a general appeal to the world trade body without going into details. However, it would have been more effective to reiterate the teachings of the Popes on human labor from time to time, without taking for granted that the public is willing to search for the Catholic Social encyclicals.

There are many stakeholders who do not want to hear any sermonizing on what the moral code requires of them in trade-related matters. Take, for instance, China; Chinese workers are denied the right to form independent unions, are often paid less than the minimum wage, and are denied overtime pay. And China's network of prison camps would be available to conveniently supply slave labor to produce export goods. China does this, not because there are no laws, but because many laws are not effectively enforced.

The president of the United Steelworkers in the U.S., Leo Gerard, observed that,

> The fact of the matter is you can't fix NAFTA by putting in environmental rights and labor rights and pretending that will fix it. In fact, Canada's environmental and labor

[1296] See PONTIFICAL COUNCIL FOR JUSTICE AND PEACE, TRADE, DEVELOPMENT AND THE FIGHT AGAINST POVERTY, supra note 1103.

> standards are higher than America's. Mexico's are also higher, but they are not enforced.[1297]

There is another problem with labor standards as they relate to international trade. It is not enough to talk about labor standards every day at the WTO. It is problematic to use trade as leverage to raise foreign labor standards. Some nations have lower standards compared to what is obtainable in the United States and other industrialized countries. It would amount to telling these countries that they don't have the right to set their own labor laws. In some developing countries like India and Nigeria, trade unionism is legal. In others, unionism is illegal. These instances have not made wages any better.[1298]

6.3.9 Patent Injustice – World Trade Rules that Threaten the Health of Poor People

The nature of the WTO's agreement on intellectual property rights and their implementation makes the cost of vital medicines high for poor people. The ever-increasing gap between industrialized countries and poor countries is a serious cause of worries in different quarters. Public health in industrialized countries is being transformed day by day with breathtaking medical advances.[1299] Major breakthroughs in the detection and treatment of disease are increasing life-expectancy and reducing vulnerability to sickness.[1300] On the other side of the divide, the story is different. The vast majority of countries are poor, and millions of people suffer protracted

---

[1297] *See* Ian Fletcher, *Free Trade Doesn't Work: What Should Replace it and Why?* Sheffield, Coalition for a Prosperous America, 2011, p. 85.

[1298] *Id.*

[1299] Judy Rein, "International Governance through Trade Agreements: Patent Protection for Essential Medicines," *21 Nw. J. Int'l L. & Bus. 379, 379* (2001) ("Significant public and private investment, particularly in the United States, converted this killer into a manageable chronic disorder for many in the developed world."); James Thuo Gathii, "Construing Intellectual Property Rights and Competition Policy Consistently with Facilitating Access to Affordable AIDS Drugs to Low-End Consumers," 53 *Fla. L. Rev.* 727, 733-34 (2001) (stating that "drug treatment has quadrupled the median survival time for Americans diagnosed with AIDS from one to four years" and decreased mortality rates by seventy-five percent).

[1300] *See* Oxfam Great Britain, "Patent Injustice: How world trade rules threaten the health of poor people," February 1, 2001, p. 3, available at http://policy-practice.oxfam.

bouts of sickness and disability with devastating impacts on levels of poverty and vulnerability.[1301]

The health gap between rich and poor countries is reinforcing wider inequalities in income and opportunity and undermining efforts to meet internationally-agreed human development targets. Much of the premature death and disability could be avoided and the health gap closed if poor people had access to affordable medicines. To worsen the matter, those most in need are least able to afford treatment.[1302] The reason is not far-fetched. In developing countries, household poverty, inadequate public spending, and weak public health infrastructures combine to place effective treatment beyond the means of the poor. Conversely, it will be a problem of short-sightedness to think that the problem concerns poor countries alone. Experience has shown that infectious diseases do not respect national borders, and poverty in poor countries might generate anger, which may in turn affect rich countries drastically.[1303]

The Holy See has made frantic efforts to point out this injustice to the global body on the general level. And it is important to acknowledge the great impact the Church has made on the international arena generally and the GATT-WTO system. However, it must also be stated that the Holy See approaches the problem from the general point of view, without getting down to the nitty-gritty of the problem. Without making insinuations that the Holy See tickles the ears of the superpowers in the GATT-WTO system, the Holy See appears to be approaching international issues a little too diplomatically, so as not to offend key actors. With the exalted position of the Catholic Church in the world, Christians and non-Christian alike expect the Church to be more prophetic at the WTO.

According to Article 27 of TRIPS, all Members are required to provide exclusive marketing rights to holders of patents on pharmaceutical products for a period not less than twenty years. This provision restricts the right of governments to allow the production, marketing, and importation of cheap copies of patented medicines (otherwise known as generic drugs). Such

---

org.uk/publications/patent-injustice-how-world-trade-rules-threaten-the-health-of-poor-people-114044 last visited March 21, 2014.

1301 *Id.*

1302 *Id.*

1303 *Id.*

WTO rules restrict competition, increase prices, and further reduce the already limited access of poor people to vital medicines.[1304] By impeding developing countries in their efforts to make or obtain cheap medicines for HIV/AIDS and other critical needs, for instance, TRIPS increases the costs of medicines and limits access to them.[1305]

[1304] *See* TRIPS Agreement, particularly Article 27. Article 27 para. 3(a) authorizes as follows, Members may also exclude from patentability:
(a) diagnostic, therapeutic and surgical methods for the treatment of humans or animals;
(b) Plants and animals other than micro-organisms, and essentially biological processes to produce plants or animals other than non-biological and microbiological processes. However, Members shall provide for the protection of plant varieties either by patents or by an effective *sui generis* system or by any combination thereof. The provisions of this subparagraph shall be reviewed four years after the date of entry into force of the WTO Agreement.
This provision gives governments too much discretion. There is no definitive clause to make the removal of patentability compulsory. This provision is a departure from the focus of GATT on non-discrimination between domestic and foreign producers and among different foreign producers. Therefore, TRIPS protections are not about free trade; rather they are restrictions on trade and protections of monopoly justified in theory by their aim of fostering innovation. In practice, however, they often end up merely protecting the rights of the powerful to extract more wealth from poor countries. A case in point is the Pharmaceutical Research and Manufacturers of America (PhRMA), one of the world's most politically influential and well-financed industrial lobbies. PhRMA backs its claim to patent rights with threats of trade sanctions against any non-complying country. PhRMA's power comes from the enormous influence it has over the office of the United States Trade Representative (USTR) and Section 301 of the U.S. national trade legislation. *See* OXFAM GREAT BRITAIN, *supra* note 1274, at 4.

[1305] *See* MAILBOXES AND THE 1998 INDIA PATENT PROTECTION CASE, in which the United States argued successfully before the WTO Panel that India's *Patent Act* provides for drugs, pharmaceuticals, and agricultural chemicals not to be patentable in contravention of TRIPS Articles 63:2. The Appellate Body upheld Articles 70:8 and 70:9 findings of the Panel. See also RAJ BHALA, INTERNATIONAL TRADE LAW, *supra* note 904, at 1625-1636; *See also* Kara M. Bombach, Note, and "Can South Africa Fight AIDS? Reconciling the South African Medicines and Related Substances Act with the TRIPS Agreement," *19 B.U. Int'l L.J. 273, 288* (2001) ("Some critics argue that, because TRIPS provides for worldwide patent protection, drugs become more expensive in developing countries."); Andrew Pollack, "Defensive Drug Industry: Fueling Clash Over Patents," *N.Y. Times,* April 20, 2001, at A6 ("Drug patents are under attack, blamed for high AIDS drug prices that deny life-saving therapy to millions of people in developing countries."); Pharmaceutical Research and Manufacturers of America (PhRMA), Health Care in the Developing World: The Global Challenge of AIDS, at http://world.phrma.org/global.challenge.aids.html (last visited March. 5, 2014); *see also* Agreement on Trade-Related Aspects of Intellectual Property Rights, Including Trade in Counterfeit Goods, Apr. 15, 1994, Marrakesh Agreement Establishing the World Trade Organization, Annex IC, Legal Instruments-Results of the Uruguay Round *vol.*

The application of these rules relating to patent rights causes serious problems in the treatment of certain deadly sicknesses. For instance, patent rights have caused a lot of setbacks in the treatment of HIV/AIDS, childhood pneumonia, and other deadly diseases.[1306] Developing countries and human rights activists claim that these prohibitively expensive drug prices are the result of strong patent protection, which governments must provide under the TRIPS Agreement.[1307] While TRIPS is mostly favorable to the rich industrialized world and its multinational corporations,[1308] it provides some flexibility for states to address their public health needs by allowing several public interest exceptions to patent protection.[1309]

31, 33 I.L.M. 81 (1994); TRIPS provides an international framework of intellectual property obligations that is binding on World Trade Organization (WTO) member states.

1306 *See* UNICEF *et al., Sources and Prices of Selected Drugs and Diagnostics for People Living with HIV/AIDS* 5 (2001), available at http://www.unaids.org/acc-access/access-drugs/Sources05Ol.doc [hereinafter Sources & Prices]; *See* Judy Rein, supra note 1273, at 379. In sub-Saharan Africa, where approximately seventy-five percent of people live on less than two dollars a day; Joint United Nations Program on HIV/AIDS & WHO, AIDS Epidemic Update at 2, 3, U.N. Doc. UNAIDS/01.74E, WHO/CDS/CSR/NCS/2001.2 (2001), available at http://www.unaids.org/worldaids day/2001/Epiupdate200l/EPIupdate200 len.pdf, at 7, only an estimated 10,000-25,000 Africans are receiving anti-retroviral treatment, Sources & Prices. *Id.* at 5. *See also* Barton Gellman, "An Unequal Calculus of Life and Death: As Millions Perished in Pandemic, Firms Debated Access to Drugs," *Wash. Post*, Dec. 27, 2000, at Al (stating that only "one-tenth of 1 percent" of infected Africans receive HIV/AIDS drug therapy).

1307 *See* Kara M. Bombach, "Can South Africa Fight AIDS? Reconciling the South African Medicines and Related Substances Act with the TRIPS Agreement," *19B.U. Int'l L.J. 273,* 288 (2001) ("Some critics argue that, because TRIPS provides for worldwide patent protection, drugs become more expensive in developing countries."); Andrew Pollack, "Defensive Drug Industry: Fueling Clash Over Patents," *N.Y. Times,* April 20, 2001, at A6 ("Drug patents are under attack, blamed for high AIDS drug prices that deny life-saving therapy to millions of people in developing countries."); Pharmaceutical Research and Manufacturers of America (PhRMA), Health Care in the Developing World: The Global Challenge of AIDS, at http://world.phrma.org/global.challenge.aids.html (last visited March 5, 2014).

1308 James Thuo Gathii, "Construing Intellectual Property Rights and Competition Policy Consistently with Facilitating Access to Affordable AIDS Drugs to Low-End Consumers," *53 Fla. L. Rev. 761* (2001).

1309 *See id.* at 759-70 (discussing the public interest logic of TRIPS); Judy Rein, "International Governance Through Trade Agreements: Patent Protection for Essential Medicines," *21 Nw. J. Int'l L. & Bus. 387,* (2001) at 387 (discussing TRIPS and the North American Free Trade Agreement and noting that "the intellectual property provisions of the trade agreements leave substantial room for countries to exercise regulatory control over pharmaceutical pricing").

Using controversial practices such as compulsory licensing and parallel importing, drug prices in developing countries could feasibly be reduced by ninety percent.[1310] Most developing countries cashed in on this flexibility to make AIDS drugs accessible to their citizens by adopting laws that would reduce the prices of HIV/AIDS drugs. For instance, in 1997, the South African Parliament proposed an amendment to its existing Medicines and Related Substances Control Act ("Medicines Act Amendment") to allow the government to take measures to ensure wider access to essential drugs.[1311] The multinational drug companies, in tandem with the U.S. government, however, opposed such legislation aggressively, characterizing it as an infringement on their intellectual property rights by allowing practices such as parallel importing and compulsory licensing.[1312]

6.3.10 Textiles and Clothing

The Holy See has said a little about the textiles and clothing trade. It has merely called on developed countries importing textiles and clothing

[1310] Joint Press Release, Mèdecins Sans Frontières *et al.,* Generic AIDS Drugs Offer New Lease on Life to South Africans; Importation of Generics Cuts Price in Half (Jan. 29, 2002) ("Our project shows that antiretroviral therapy is feasible in a resource-poor setting."), at http://www.msf.org/countries/page.cfm last visited March 23, 2014.

[1311] Naomi A. Bass, "Implications of the TRIPS Agreement for Developing Countries: Pharmaceutical Patent Laws in Brazil and South Africa in the 21st Century," *34 Geo. Wash. Int'l L. Rev. 191, 210* (2002).

[1312] See Susan K. Sell, TRIPS and the Access to Medicines Campaign, *20 Wis. Int'l L.J. 481, 500-02* (2002) (describing U.S. pressure on South Africa and Thailand, on behalf of the drug industry, to prevent the implementation of laws to make HIV/AIDS drugs cheaper); Bess-Carolina Dolmo, "Examining Global Access to Essential Pharmaceuticals in the Face of Patent Protection Rights: The South African Example," *7 Buff. Hum. Rts. L. Rev. 137, 151* (2001) (discussing responses of U.S. interests to South Africa's law); Submission of PhRMA for the "Special 301" Report on Intellectual Property Barriers (Pharmaceutical Research and Manufacturers of America 2002) (requesting that the United States take action against countries such as South Africa and Brazil), http://www.phrma.org/international/special301 (last visited January 9, 2014); see also Barbara Larkin, U.S. Department of State, U.S. Government Efforts to Negotiate the Repeal, Termination or Withdrawal of Article 15(c) of the South African Medicines and Related Substances Act of 1965 (Feb. 5, 1999) (detailing U.S. government's actions to "defend the legitimate interests and rights of U.S. pharmaceutical firms" in South Africa), http://www.cptech.org/ip/health/sa/stdept-feb51999.html last visited March 5, 2014.

to remove restrictions on such products from developing countries.[1313] There were multiple and complex barriers to trade in textiles and clothing prior to the Uruguay Round.[1314] These barriers were major concerns to the WTO Members, especially the developing countries. Before the Uruguay Round, countries exporting textiles and clothing were obliged, through the Multi-Fiber Agreement (MFA) of 1961 and its four successors,[1315] to limit their exports to specific quotas, above which high tariffs were applied.[1316] The Uruguay Round Agreement on Textiles and Clothing provides for

---

1313 *See* PONTIFICAL COUNCIL FOR JUSTICE AND PEACE, TRADE, DEVELOPMENT AND THE FIGHT AGAINST POVERTY, *supra* note 1103.

1314 *See* WTO, Textiles: Agreement, available at http://www.wto.org/english/tratop_e/texti_e/texintro_e.htm

Before the Agreement took effect, a large portion of textiles and clothing exports from developing countries to the industrial countries was subject to quotas under a special regime outside normal GATT rules. Under the Agreement, WTO Members have committed themselves to remove the quotas by 1 January 2005, by integrating the sector fully into GATT rules. *See id.*

1315 *See* WTO 1995, Articles 2-8 and Annex of Agreement on Textiles and Clothing (ATC), available at http://www.wto.org/english/tratop_e/texti_e/texintro_e.htm last visited March 12, 2014.

1316 *See* JOHN H. BARTON *et al.*, THE EVOULTION OF TRADE REGIME, supra note, at 99-100 [indicating that the trends in the control of the textile and clothing industry up until it came to Agreement on Textile and Clothing (ATC). Attempt at separating the textile trade rules from those for other manufacturing products began in the 1950s with the introduction of "voluntary export restraints (VERs) initially by Japan at accession to the GATT in 1955, and by Hong Kong, India, and Pakistan in 1956. First attempt to regulate textile trade in the postwar period dates back to the lead-up to the Kennedy Round. As a result, a Short-Term Agreement on Cotton Textiles was negotiated in 1961 allowing developed countries to control import of cotton textiles from countries such as Japan deemed to be actual or potential sources of market disruption. This was replaced by a Long-Term Arrangement Regarding International Trade in Cotton Textiles (LTA) in 1962, and renewed in 1967 and 1970. That was a departure from the normal GATT practices. In 1974, the Multi-Fiber Arrangement (MFA) replaced the LTA, as a way of gaining the support of the U.S. textile industry for a broader trade Round, extending the coverage of the new Agreement to all textiles and clothing, of wool, cotton, or synthetic fibers. A 6% quota growth was allowed and provision was made for small and new suppliers. A Textile Surveillance Board was also created to monitor the arrangement. The MFA was renewed in 1977, 1981, and 1986. The Agreement on Textiles and Clothing (ATC) that emerged from the Uruguay Round replaced the MAFA.]

the phasing out of the MFA quotas and tariff reduction over a 10-year period.[1317]

Industrial development in textiles and clothing for most poor countries is one of the most important weapons to fight poverty and underdevelopment. In fact, textiles represent a major share of OECD imports from developing countries (more than 45 percent in the 1980s).[1318] About 90% of the workers in garment factories in most poor countries are women. Through their work in garment factories, women provide the family's main source of income.[1319]

Unfortunately, developing countries have suffered the impact of the non-compliance of major developed countries to the provisions of the MFA Agreement. The textiles and clothing industry is one of the few sectors of light manufacturing in which poor countries could develop their export capacity. The major industrialized countries, particularly the United States and the EU, are aware of the potential for expansion from the developing countries. Politicians in these economically advanced countries mounted pressures to maintain trade barriers on that industry.

> The chief potential beneficiaries of the Agreement, developing countries, have cited the ATC Agreement as one of a number of examples of their limited satisfaction with the operation of the WTO. Though the obligations of developing countries have increased, many have yet to see concrete benefits from the agreement. While they could potentially gain from the ATC, such benefits are uncertain given the dominant competitive position that China holds in textile trade. The developing world fears

[1317] *See* WTO, "Textiles: Agreement - The Agreement on Textiles and Clothing; Textiles Monitoring Body," (TMB), available at http://www.wto.org/english/tratop_e/texti_e/texintro_e.htm [Since 1 January 1995, international textiles and clothing trade has been going through fundamental change under the 10-year transitional program of the WTO's Agreement on Textiles and Clothing (ATC). Before the Agreement took effect, a large portion of textiles and clothing exports from developing countries to the industrial countries was subject to quotas under a special regime outside normal GATT rules.]

[1318] *See* JOHN H. BARTON *et al.*, THE EVOLUTION OF TRADE REGIME, *supra* note 1277, at 100.

[1319] *See* PONTIFICAL COUNCIL FOR JUSTICE AND PEACE, TRADE, DEVELOPMENT, AND THE FIGHT AGAINST POVERTY, *supra* note 1103.

> that the United States (and possibly the EU and Japan) may not be able to deliver the large dose of liberalization that began at the end 2004 in the face of domestic pressure from textile firms and unions.[1320]

Events show that developed countries, particularly the U.S., the EU, and Japan, have not stopped restricting exports from poor countries. Developed countries have not relented in protecting their domestic industries against competition from the developing countries' exports. This would obviously defeat the whole essence of the regulation of the textile and clothing trade and choke the poor countries, which depend on that industry for their economic growth. Considering the social mission of the Holy See to defend the dignity of the human person and communities based on the principle of the Option for the Poor, it is not enough to urge the developed countries to remove restrictions on such products. The Church can do more. Making a general statement like that may not be as effective as initiating diplomatic dialogue with the defaulting countries and appealing to them, using the principles of charity, mercifulness, and almsgiving discussed above.

The Holy See should strengthen the notion of theology in action in all its diplomatic activities. Propagating theological virtues in the international arena would sound like preaching to the choir unless the Church embarks on a deeper investigation of the history and the reason behind why developed countries react the way they do. The Church cannot be effective by merely preaching from the pulpit. She should reach out more to experience the feelings of peoples and nations. The Church should get all her adherents more committed to moderating the worldly inclinations with the Gospel principles. In that way, a Christian who participates in negotiations in any part of the world will respect Christian principles. Again, it is good for evangelizers to respect the sheep metaphor.[1321]

1320 *See* John H. Barton, Judith L. Goldstein, et al., The Evolution of the Trade Regime: Politics, Law, and Economics of the GATT and WTO, Princeton University Press, 2006, p. 101

1321 *See Inside the Vatican*, March 2014, p. 28.

6.3.11 Corruption in Developing Countries

The foregoing argument of this dissertation sounds like suggesting that developing countries and LDCs can do no wrong. But that is not true. This dissertation is concerned with analyzing Catholic Social Justice Theory and with situating its irreplaceability in international affairs. In recounting some of the achievements of CST in the international affairs, this dissertation does not impose all blames of underdevelopment of poor countries on industrialized countries alone. There is no reason to exonerate poor countries from unfair practices occasioned by their undemocratic internal politics. In fact, most developing countries and LDCs to a large extent contribute to their own woes. The most recurrent malaise that makes their development redundant is the problem of corruption.

A report of Global Financial Integrity titled *Illicit Financial Flows from Developing Countries: 2002-2011,1322* says, "across the world, countries that are in the direst need of funding and investment are losing hundreds of billions of dollars every year to illicit outflows of capital, according to a recent report – and sub-Saharan Africa, the most poverty-stricken region on earth, is losing the most as a percentage of GDP."[1323] The report further said that

> The world's developing countries lost a total of $946.7 billion to corruption, trade misinvoicing and tax evasion in 2011, according to the research. And to make matters worse, the amount that gets spirited away is growing larger with each passing year. Money lost to corruption in developing nations was 13.7 percent greater in 2011 than was lost the year before; illicit outflows totaled $832.4 billion in 2010. The total figures are staggering:

[1322] *See* Dev Kar & Brian LeBlanc, "Illicit Financial Flows from Developing Countries: 2002-2011," Global Financial Integrity, December 2013 available at http://iff.gfintegrity.org/iff2013/Illicit_Financial_Flows_from_Developing_Countries_2002-2011-LowRes.pdf

[1323] *See also,* Jacey Fortin, "Trillion Dollar Theft: In Developing Countries, Staggering Losses Due To Corruption Exceed Incoming Aid, Says Report," *International Business news,* Sunday, April 06, 2014.

> between 2002 and 2011, developing countries lost about $5.9 trillion to illicit outflows.[1324]

The resource curse (Dutch disease) lingers when politicians are inexperienced in policies that could help diversify exports. But this problem of depending on one or very few exports gets worse when the government is corrupt in the management of the economy. Some of the industrialized and wealthy Members of the WTO have been incriminated in shameful corrupt practices that have enveloped most developing countries. In the United States, it came to light in 2004 that Riggs Bank, in Washington, D.C., was holding huge deposits from the president of Equatorial Guinea and writing him cringingly effusive letters of encouragement. In the year 2000, it was revealed that the family of Sani Abacha, a former military dictator of Nigeria, had made massive deposits in London. Switzerland was also implicated in the gross misconduct, and remained uncooperative until shamed into releasing the billions of dollars in its banks belonging to Nigeria.[1325]

While it is highly commendable for the Holy See to promote the cause of the poor nations of the World at the United Nations, the WTO, and other international organizations, it is equally important for it to examine and extend its social mission to these poor countries. The Catholic Church should consistently reiterate that heaven helps those who help themselves. It is true that the Holy See cannot address every bugging issue, but once any issue affects the full realization of the dignity of the human person, it becomes incumbent on the Church to raise her moral voice. It must be stressed without qualification that exploitation is bad in all its ramifications, whether perpetrated by industrialized countries or individualized, no matter where they may be.

[1324] *Id.*

[1325] *See* Paul Collier, *The Bottom Billion: Why the Poorest Countries are Failing and what can be done about it,* Oxford University Press, 2007, pp. 135-136.

CHAPTER SEVEN

Closing Reflections

At this juncture, this discussion recaps of the components of its central topic, namely, the *Holy See, Catholic Social Justice, International Trade Law, and the Social Mission of the Catholic Church as projected in the GATT-WTO system.* It is also proper here to revisit the thesis posited in the introductory section. The account of the Holy See's participation in international affairs is fascinating. That the Holy See seeks to influence the GATT-WTO system through application of social justice as a Permanent Observer is compelling. At least there is a watchdog that takes a stance less driven by commercial self-interest than by the primacy of morality, promoting the dignity of the human person and the common good, thereby raising a voice for the less fortunate.

The priorities and principles of the Holy See for its bilateral relations are to:

- Give priority to the human person, to his dignity and rights;
- Promote and, if necessary, defend justice and peace;
- Promote international development;
- Help to establish an international order that is founded on justice and rights;
- Ensure the equality of nations and support all institutions that foster democracy as the basis of political and social life;
- Promote conflict prevention and resolution;
- Combat human trafficking and protect victims of forced labor;

- Promote inter-religious dialogue and dialogue on environmental issues;
- Reject war and give priority to negotiation and the use of juridical instruments.

At the multilateral level, the Holy See seeks a gradual decrease in military expenditure; effective disarmament; respect for cultures and religious traditions; solidarity with the poorer countries, helping them to be the architects of their own development; and defense of life and family.[1326] This is just one out of the many anomalies that the Holy See seeks to address always. The practice of regularized exchange of goods and services between and among nation-states for mutual advantage under an orchestrated system of rules as is the case in the GATT/WTO system, ought to generate moral duties – duties that exist between and among parties to the system. These duties, duties arising from participation in international trade, are duties not to do any harm, duties to provide basic goods, and duties to distribute certain benefits and burdens fairly and equitably. These duties are inherent in the aims and objectives for which the GATT/WTO system was established. These are "international relative gains which require that the gains of international trade are to be distributed equally unless unequal gains flow … to poor countries."[1327] Therefore, the Church pursuit of common good from the perspective of moral values is legit.

Other supportive authorities abound. Justice among people and for all the world's peoples is the fundamental rationale for establishing the United Nations Organization (U.N.O). In the Preamble to the UN Charter, the commitment to justice for people is expressed as a reaffirmation of the faith in fundamental human rights, in the dignity and worth of the human person, and in the equal rights of men and women.[1328] What is

1326 *See* VATICAN CITY STATE available at http://www.vaticanstate.va/content/vaticanstate/en.html ; THE PERMANENT OBSERVER MISSION OF THE HOLY SEE TO THE UNITED NATIONS (NY) available at http://www.holyseemission.org/events/index.aspx?y=2013 ; HOLY SEE WEBSITE http://www.vatican.va

1327 James Aaron, *Fairness in Practice: A Social Contract for a Global Economy*, Oxford University Press, 2012, p.18 [emphasis added].

1328 *See* Charter of the United Nations available at http://www.un.org/en/sections/un-charter/un-charter-full-text/

required is the promotion of social progress and better standards of life in larger freedom and of the economic and social advancement of all peoples. This has close connection with Article 1 of the Charter, which is "to achieve international cooperation in solving international problems of an economic social, cultural or humanitarian character, and in promoting and encouraging respect for human rights and for fundamental freedoms for all without distinction as to race, sex, language or religion."[1329] From the foregoing, it stands to reason that justice derives from equality of rights for all peoples and the possibility for all human beings, without discrimination, to benefit from the economic and social progress disseminated and secured through international cooperation.

Industrialized nations worked hard to neutralize the role of the United Nations and its specialized agencies as forums for debate and for important decisions regarding the functioning of the world economy. These affluent countries succeeded in the mid-1970s up until now when they adopted the better-controlled brain-child, the Bretton Woods institutions which have strengthened the stronghold on global economic development. Developing countries mounted efforts in futility to lessen the selfish interests of the richest nations in that regard. Nationalization and expropriation which were tools adopted by developing nations to control the excesses of transnational corporations have also disappeared courtesy of pressures from wealthy nations. The only hope of these poor nations is the GATT/WTO system. Through the GATT/WTO system, these nations pursue arrangements and agreements to promote their exports and gain access to the markets of affluent countries.

Justice is sought through efforts to ensure the elimination of the measures and practices (such as domestic agricultural subsidies) that allow some countries (least developed and developing Member Countries) to maintain an unfair advantage over others. If the guiding principle of the world market economy is competition on an open and even playing field, obstacles to fair competition should be removed for the least/less privileged members. The United Nations Millennium Declaration Goal lays credence to the above argument. Section III of the Declaration focuses on development and poverty eradication. The right to development is

---

[1329] *Id.* [This purpose is reiterated in Article 13 as one of the functions of the UN General Assembly, and in Articles 60 and 62 about the role of the Economic and Social Council]

for everyone and the entire human race. This is aimed at fighting abject and dehumanizing conditions endured by billions of men, women and children.[1330] Unfortunately, there is no mention of distribution of income and wealth among countries of the world, neither is there any mention of the various gaps that separate developed and developing countries. However, the UN mentions in its Millennium Development Goals that development will depend first on "good governance within each country" but also on "good governance at the international level and on transparency in the financial, monetary and trading systems."[1331] In all these goals, the Holy See is the only power in the world that is neutral enough to pursue these noble goals for the less privileged countries of the world.

Looking at Catholic Social Justice Theory, one sees a continuous reenactment of Jesus' mission on earth. Jesus did not come as a blue-eyed right-winger, a guilt-ridden liberal, or a compromising centrist. He came into the world among dispossessed and hopeless humans. He didn't just come among them; He came to announce an entirely new way of thinking and living. He didn't come to establish a welfare program; His coming rather calls for a change of heart, a revolution of spirit, a transformation of our consciousness, a departure from the status *quo ante.* The way of Christianity goes beyond the familiar options of abandoning the poor, controlling the poor, or even helping the poor from places of isolation and comfort. Christianity leads us to a new relationship with one another, a deep reconnection, and a restoration of the shattered covenant.[1332] The Holy See sets out to dwell on those principles.

An Australian aboriginal woman once said, "If you are coming to help me, you are wasting your time. But if you have come because your liberation is bound up with mine, then let us work together."[1333] This book has argued that the Church's preference for the poor is not to be understood as the Church taking sides in a class struggle. It is not a preference of one group or individual as opposed to others. The "poor" in question must be understood not only as those oppressed by a combination

---

[1330] See UN Millennium Development Goals, 2015, available at http://www.un.org/millenniumgoals/

[1331] *Id.*

[1332] *See* Jim Wallis, *The Soul of Politics: Beyond Religious Right and Secular Left*, New York, Maryknoll, 1995, p. 181.

[1333] *See id. at* 181.

of poverty, powerlessness, and exclusion from the community but also more on common features of vulnerability and lack of power. They are often alone and have no protector or advocate. That is why Pope John Paul II said, "Promises made to the poor should be particularly binding, and the failure to keep commitments . . . to the poor is a serious moral question."[1334] This situation is manifest in biases operative in almost every aspect of life in the society.[1335]

The Church is aware that the situation of such people is tied to issues of power and participation in society, profoundly assaulting human dignity. Thomas E. Clark explains this better:

> Human dignity is most tragically affronted, not by material deprivation as such, but by every projection of contempt onto individuals and especially onto groups, on whatever basis. Oppression in its most dehumanizing form happens when a dominant culture says to whatever group it has chosen for scapegoating, you are of lesser worth – of no worth. The economic pastoral, despite its focus on economic oppression, moves toward this understanding of poverty, I believe, when it makes participation, not provision of material goods, the key to justice for the poor. "The ultimate injustice is for a person or group to be actively treated or passively abandoned as if they were nonmembers of the human race. To treat people this way is effectively to say that they simply do not count as human beings. This can take many forms, all of which can be described as varieties of marginalization or exclusion from social life.[1336]

The social mission of the Church emphasizes the dignity of the human person to show that nature has blessed every human being with equal dignity. Any arrangement or policy that does not respect this principle is

---

1334 *See* Pope John Paul II, Message for the World Day of Peace, 2003.

1335 *See* FRED KRAMMER, DOING FAITHJUSTICE, *supra* note 727, at 148-9.

1336 *See* Thomas E. Clarke, "Option for the Poor: A Reflection," in *America,* Vol. 158, No. 4, January 30, 1998, p. 96.

deemed as abnegation. For that reason, every project, idea, or system must be evaluated by whether it moves people toward greater connection with one another. The Church's social mission is unending because society has forgotten the promotion of human dignity that should be the hub of every decision that affects human beings in any way. The Church embarks on her social mission to every corner of the earth because our social attitudes and economic structures have been directed in such a way as to disregard that dignity. Any time the dignity of the human person is violated in any way, deliberate or not, it is difficult to remedy it by using the same principles that legally harmed it. For that reason, the Holy See should appeal to principles such as mercifulness, charity, compassion, mortification, almsgiving, and the like in her Social Justice Theory. Although these principles are not contemplated in the law but they can be implied.

Very often, Catholic Social Theory is critiqued for not respecting socio-political and economic systems that are necessary for progress in the economies of the world. That sounds plausible, but it is not a strong argument. A deeper reflection on that point discloses the obvious weakness of such an assertion. The universal law teaches that an actor has a duty to ensure that other actors are not treated merely to some end. In other words, every actor is required to refrain from acts that may treat others to an end. For example, universal law would expect countries that are parties to Free Trade Agreements to eliminate any exploitative clauses in international trade agreements. Moreover, looking at what is going on in the GATT-WTO system, there is the need for a revisit to that universal principle.

The absence of that universal principle causes Members of the WTO to fall to the temptation of protectionism that promises to deliver some illusory short-run benefits while preventing more conspicuous long-term gains. Lack of consideration for the plight of the less-fortunate in the world increases the dichotomy between the rich and the poor in a way that the poor are confronted with a strong increase in inequality in all countries. In international trade, this lack is detrimental to the liberalization of trade. The situation is such that during commercial negotiations between countries of the world, whether in multilateral trade or bilateral trade, the industrialized parties often do not play by the rules.

The world sings the same tune, and there is an urgent need for a voice that is different, not only a different voice but also a voice that takes a neutral perspective. When the world tries to solve its problem, it doesn't go far enough in finding a solution because of the direct and selfish involvement of individuals and nations. While individuals, groups and nations export goods and services for solutions to their problems, the Catholic Church exports the Gospel message of Christ for the good of every individual, groups and nations. The Catholic Church has a peculiar voice, a voice that proposes a clear resolution, a voice that champions human dignity with the aim of enhancing a win-win resolution. The Church calls for countries to respect the dignity of individuals in directing FTA negotiations at every level of negotiation.

In its presence in international affairs, especially in international trade, the Holy See uses theological concepts to formulate its concept of social justice and proposals for legal change. This mentality explains the omnipresence of Christian theological principles in many areas of public policy. It is interesting how the Catholic Church applies her theological principles to international trade law, using them to influence international decisions and commercial transactions. It is also amazing to see how committed the Church has proved herself as an institution established by Christ to continue his universal mission on earth. The reason for the Holy See's projection of theological virtues explains its belief that justice is a fully constitutive dimension of the Gospel. For that reason, the Church cooperates with every legitimate means in reducing the negative effects of globalization, such as the domination of the powerful over the weak, especially in the economic sphere.

In the light of the application of theological principles in its social justice theory, this dissertation tried to explain certain terms that featured consistently in this discussion. The discussion also traced the history of the Holy See's involvement in international affairs, concluding that the long history of the Church's presence in the international arena and her achievements give credence to her suitability to intervene in the GATT-WTO system. The Literature review exercise above speaks volumes about the indispensability of the Social Justice theory of the Catholic Church. This peculiarity is a product of the Holy See's neutrality and dogged ability to broker peace in the world and among nations. Anyone can look at the relentless efforts of the Holy See, even in the face of criticisms levelled against it in the world, as a sign of its commitment in the world.

The discussion about the Judeo-Christian principles characteristic of the Holy See's mission on earth is very interesting. The Holy See pursues no interest of its own except the common good and the promotion of human dignity. In that way, the Church is the advocate for every individual and every group, irrespective of their religious, cultural, or political affiliation. In doing that, the Holy See marks the universal character of its mission on earth. In recounting the achievements of the Holy See as a Permanent Observer to the U.N., the GATT-WTO system, and other international organizations, this discussion highlights the uniqueness of the Holy See in the world. That is a way of giving kudos and making it work.

In analyzing Papal encyclicals and other authoritative documents of the Magisterium, as well as the establishment of nunciatures and diplomatic missions all over the world, this discussion outlines the unique strategies the Holy See has employed in its long history of involvement in world affairs. The Holy See tries to train its representatives in the world. The establishment of nunciatures and diplomatic missions in many countries of the world is a powerful strategy that can enhance its mission and make it result-oriented. Such methodology makes its presence felt in every corner of the earth. The nunciatures and diplomatic missions are signposts pointing out to human beings and nations of the world the direction human and social actions must take so that they conform to the universal and immutable principles of faith and morals. Clearly, the mission divinely assigned to the Holy See is the defense of the eternal values of morals and of religion as they relate to all aspects of private and public life.

Therefore, the fundamental issue of the Holy See's intervention in international trade law is to regulate every evolving social life according to the dictates of universal and moral principles. The attainment of physical, intellectual, and even moral perfection is not to impede the achievement of spiritual and supernatural aspirations. Put another way without sounding repetitive, the participation of the Holy See in international activity is primarily for the person, thereby contributing to the common good of the whole human family. In the field of economic relations, and specifically as pertains to international trade law, the Holy See advocates an equitable system as one of the key factors in development. The Holy See's involvement in the GATT-WTO system as a Permanent Observer is because the objective the system set out to achieve is the implementation of a legal framework of international trade law in which there would be no room for unfair unilateral commercial actions.[1337]

Developing countries and their peoples are in dire need of an equitable, rule-based system in which they can participate in global trade based on the highest achievable equality of opportunity. The Holy See does not go into technical and specialized matters. It only proposes some ethical guidelines in furtherance of its theological principles and as part of its missionary methodology. The Church ought to be effective in her proposals in the GATT-WTO system because it gets the opportunity to address the individuals and agencies that are directly concerned with making the major decisions in the system.

At this juncture, having explored the details of the Church's involvement in world affairs from the GATT-WTO perspective, it makes sense to revisit some questions posited earlier. How successful is the Catholic Church as a Permanent Observer at the WTO? Is the Church promoting the common good and the dignity of the human person in international trade as effectively as she should? Is the Holy See effectively influencing the GATT-WTO system with its Social Justice Theory? These questions cannot be effectively addressed by answering "yes" or "no." Therefore, for a better understanding and for a better assessment of the thesis of this discussion, these questions are best taken separately.

Events have shown that the Catholic Church has made commendable strides in promoting the common good and the dignity of the human person. Her unflinching support of policies and programs that promote the common good and the dignity of the human person lend credence to that assertion. The Holy See presents its moral authority and its ethical principles in furtherance of its mission in the world. Being a Permanent Observer, the Holy See uses its right to speak to the WTO to play its uniquely "prophetic" role in the biblical sense of the term. It is an opportunity for the Church to proclaim to the whole world the dignity of the human person; the equality of all nations; to proclaim that all nations are equally solidary; all nations constitute a "family of nations" called together to promote international common good. By raising its moral voice, the Church endeavors to create a climate of greater trust among

[1337] *See* World Trade Organization, WT/L/221, July 2, 1997.

nations. Therefore, in answer to the first question above, the Church is influencing the dynamics of international trade law through her consistent promotion of the common good and the dignity of the human person.

Though the answer is "yes" to the second question concerning whether as a Permanent Observer to the WTO, the Holy See is effectively influencing the system with its Social Justice Theory; this discussion believes the Church could still do more. The Holy See has recorded a great number of achievements in the GATT-WTO system, but the growing inequalities among WTO Members and the stalemate that has been characteristic of negotiations since 2001 call for the Church to do more. It is true that the Church cannot do it alone, but in her prophetic role, the Church cannot rest on her oars. We have not arrived at the Promised Land in achieving justice and peace in the GATT-WTO system. Therefore, to the third question of whether the Holy See can do more to influence the WTO rules to foster equity and fairness and thereby help in solving inequalities, this dissertation answers "yes." More so, to that effect, there are a couple of suggestions as to what the Church can do regarding further expectations on her.

Religious values and principles are not a blueprint for policy. The teaching of the Church represents both a lens through which to see the world and a motivational force to transform it. It is the light to see the road ahead rather than the road map. The Church can only achieve that change by paying attention to the global and local society to avoid narrowness and banality. The Church needs to embrace local realities more because it helps her to keep her feet on the ground.

The Holy See ought to address the hierarchical culture in all its operations. Catholic Social Teaching (CST) is hierarchically directed. The authority of CST is authoritatively drawn from the Church Magisterium, namely, Papal Encyclicals, Papal Exhortations and the like. It is such because of the seriousness of Papal Infallibility; when one approaches the social teaching of the Church, one finds that it agrees with practically everything, but once its texts have been studied, practically nothing stays in the mind. This is true of public opinion when a social encyclical comes out; opinions are aroused, positions taken. However, it does not take long for the document to be consigned to oblivion, except for one or two paragraphs, and these continue to be its only links with the mind. The fact is that the encyclicals and social documents are often identified with a certain number of inspirational nuclei.

The Compendium of the Social Doctrine of the Church is recommended to Christians as the most suitable tool for the study and understanding of CST. Often people see those documents as the exclusive preserve of the authorities of the Church, which diminishes the sense of duty on the part of the Catholic faithful. The inherent danger in this approach is for Catholic adherents to see this approach as a way the Church wants them to take note of principles contained in those documents. There is no concrete incentive for them to make such principles a lens to assess whatever happens in the world or their immediate environment.

Pope Francis I taught in his Apostolic Letter *Evangelii Gaudium* that neither the Pope nor the Church has a monopoly on the interpretation of social realities or the proposal of solutions to contemporary problems. The Pope or the Church cannot single-handedly utter a unified message or solution that has universal validity, and as a result, Christian communities should analyze with objectivity the situation proper to their own localities or countries.[1338] This implies that CST is the concern of every Christian, any time any day. To achieve this objective, the Church should adopt strategies to make missionaries take this more seriously. Actions should speak louder than words. The Church should make her CST a central part of her teaching at every level. It should not be left for the authorities alone. The encyclicals should empower the clergy and laity alike to produce works on social justice.

There is a division among bishops and other missionaries on the CST. Some bishops and other members of the clergy tend to be conservative personalities, defenders of the status quo, indifferent or hostile to modern CST, while others (very few) address new social teachings of the Church. The question is whether the Catholic Church applies its own social teaching in either its internal organization or its social counsel. If CST has this problem whereby missionaries pick and choose, then it will fail to achieve its main goals of projecting the dignity of human beings and the common good. When you come to a diocese, for instance, and few priests talk tacitly about CST and its applicability in the daily lives of Christians,

[1338] *See* POPE FRANCIS I, ENCYCLICAL LETTER EVANGELII GAUDIUM, # 184.

the efforts of the Holy See in presenting CST principles in the GATT-WTO system becomes ineffective.

A more practical example can be taken from the pitiable situation in Latin America. In Latin America, inequality and great pockets of misery have continued to rise irrespective of the enormous natural resources available in that region. These woes are worsened by corporate malpractices of multinational companies and ineptitude of the governments in that region. The faith communities have a special responsibility to fight public apathy, appeal to people's consciences, and promote public policy for the common good. Unfortunately, the leaders of these faith communities are not united.

> Some bishops have marched against mining companies that were poisoning people's water supplies. Others have been photographed in the tabloids hobnobbing with the mine owners. Fine, the Church is part of the establishment; but some religious leaders are prisoners of their upbringing and others are able to slip free of that noose and relate to other classes, including the poor. You don't need to put an ideological label on their foreheads. People recognize who they are.[1339]

The Holy See should explore the issues of the individual ideologies of the members of the hierarchy more tenaciously to avoid opinions and inclinations that are opposed to the CST. Keeping issues of identity under control and sharpening its social message will help the Church collaborate with a larger set of actors.[1340] The missionary landscape of the Holy See should reflect more on the ideas of the different schools of thought concerning the social mission of the Catholic Church in the world. Though Jesus Christ never discriminated against any person or group, he, stood for the downtrodden, the less-privileged, and other classes of poor people. Whatever the inclination of any member of the Church's hierarchy may be, it should be subservient to the mission of Christ. Opinion is not to

[1339] *See* Robert Calderisi, *Earthly Mission: The Catholic Church and World Development*, Yale University Press, 2013, p. 237.

[1340] *Id.*

take precedence over the overarching missionary philosophy of the founder of the Catholic faith, Christ himself.

The Catholic Church should embark on synods at all levels involving the clergy and the laity to address the urgency of the principles of CST and the modalities for inculcating those principles to dispose people to assimilate them. It is only when there is intra-tolerance of the CST that Christians will be able to project these principles to others. Furthermore, the laity ought to be involved more in this process. The Catholic Church should devise a means of making families, at least Catholic families to make CST a household event in such a way as to enhance interest in it.

Also, CST has been the province of the patriarchal Church where only men write the documents and sit in decision-making capacity in the deliberative bodies of the Church. Women should be encouraged to make inputs, even more. Most documents of the Church's Magisterium on social justice are always footnoting the Fathers of the Church with no mention of the Mothers of the Church, except mention of the Virgin Mary and some saints, including writings of female saints. Women can make significant contributions to the Church's thinking on charity and social justice. Some of the great thinkers in the world are women, and the Church should believe that such women are also her members. They should be encouraged more to survey the opportunities of not only studying but also making meaningful contributions in the field of CST. This is exactly why a synod on CST is much needed not just for clergy and laity but also a laity that involves both men and women equally.

In 1994, the National Conference of U.S. Bishops admitted the existence of sexism within the Catholic Church. The bishops voted overwhelmingly to encourage women to seek positions of leadership within the Church. Since that event, eighty-five percent of all parish ministry positions in dioceses of the United States are open to non-clergy according to a study available to the U.S. bishops.[1341] It is obvious that there are many women agitating for greater say in religious matters. Apparently, without going into the controversial issue of women ordination, it is important

[1341] *See* Holly Selby, "U.S. bishops admit sexism within the Catholic Church," in THE BALTIMORE SUN available at http://articles.baltimoresun.com/1994-11-17/news/1994321003_1_sexism-church-hierarchy-roman-catholic-church last visited May 9, 2014.

that the Church use gender-neutral language and explore new ways for women to participate in leadership. The Church should explore new ways of emphasizing equality of men and women to synchronize with her universal mission concerning the dignity of human beings. However, that is not all. There is more to that.

People have suggested that in exploring new ways for women to participate in leadership in the Church, they should be encouraged to enter studies such as Canon law and Theology to enhance their authority in the Church. They have also been asking for equal rights of women to move into high-ranking positions such as diocesan chancellors, canon lawyers or marriage tribunal members. These jobs have been traditionally, but not legally restricted to priests and men.[1342] However, following the thrust of this dissertation, it is not all about taking up leadership positions and securing high-ranking positions. It should be centered more on getting women to assimilate Catholic Social Justice Theory so that they can represent the Church in all walks of life. Engendering equality of women and men would promote equal dignity of the human person and the common good at every moment. Emphasis should be placed on new ways of exploring options that would highlight equality of women and men so as to enable women to participate more effectively in CST. All hands must be on deck to involve women in the universal mission of the Catholic Church so that they can use more of their charisma in promoting human dignity and the common good.

The popes have sought to formulate moral directives and have stayed away from purely technical aspects. They have spoken for a worldwide audience, confining themselves to general directives. They carefully avoid the extreme positions of outright individualism or outright collectivism. Their basic assumptions are that the human person is necessarily a social being; every person has a dignity that raises him above all creation; human rights are inherent, inalienable, and linked to corresponding duties; and the primary objective of a social order is justice. Social justice is to be achieved based on reform of morals; self-help through organization; wider ownership of productive property; sound social legislation; and organization of international economic life. Sometimes these papal

---

[1342] *Id.*

teachings are structured in a language that appears a bit beyond the scope of the average Christian.

The Holy See should endeavor to adopt a simpler language that would be more easily comprehensible to every reader. Pope Francis I used the sheep metaphor when he said that shepherds ought to live with the smell of sheep. There arises the need for more grass root evangelization processes that involve the sheep in all its ramifications. The Catholic Church is for both the sheep and the shepherds. The total commitment of the lay faithful will solidify a common front for the propagation of CST.

Church teaching has always presumed that all human activity should occur in accord with moral norms. In the extension of moral theology to include a vigorous social ethic for institutional life in the modern world, the application of this persevering conviction to economic policy has led more conservative economic critics to assert that stressing moral standards too strictly in the economic realm will endanger the economic productivity that the moralists take for granted. That is only a thought, while the reality is another issue. But it is important to stress that CST is only partially capable of providing the comprehensive social theory it seeks to develop from theological principles and natural law.

The Catholic Church should dispose Christians from all walks of life to participate actively in her quest to address political and socio-economic problems. Their meaningful suggestions could contribute to the dynamics of CST. The Lay faithful have a lot of resources to bring to the missionary mandate of the Church. They should not be relegated to the observer status that has characterized their membership of the Church for centuries now. The Catholic Church does not have experts among her hierarchy who can lay claim to being *Scit Omnia* and experts in all walks of life. Their approach to issues should not create such an impression either.

The number of Catholics who feel morally obliged to carry the teaching of the encyclicals and the CST into practice in their economic relations is small and disappointing. How many Catholic employers honestly strive to apply that teaching in the wages that they pay or in their attitude toward labor unions? "Good" Catholics, "prominent" Catholics, "pillars of the Church" still disregard the papal injunctions on these matters. How many Catholic employees consider adequately their duties to their employers, as taught in the encyclicals? Finally, I would raise some important questions.

Do Catholic institutions strive to apply the teachings of the CST or the Church's Magisterium on wages and labor unions in their relations with their employees? What is the attitude of the average Catholic Christian toward CST principles? Since international trade affects the daily lives of human beings, how is the Church approaching grassroots strategies to educate everybody concerning the signs of the present period?

Worthy of mention here is the formation of Holy See diplomats. This discussion has analyzed the duration of training of diplomats who represent the Catholic Church in the nunciatures and other diplomatic missions. When future diplomats spend barely two years studying international law, diplomacy, and other aspects of international transactions, it does not sound like enough time. Come to think about it, priests who spend barely two years at the Pontifical Ecclesiastical Academy cannot be well equipped to embark on such highly technical diplomatic engagements in the world. Considering the complexity of international law and life, it would sound like a crash program. It would also look bizarre for future diplomats of the Holy See to embark on an ecclesiastical diplomacy course because that is only the tip of the iceberg.

The Church should make the period of study at the Diplomatic Academy longer to enable the students to cover other necessary areas of international law and international life, to gain the wealth of experience necessary for a more result-oriented diplomacy. Over the years, the Holy See has recorded many achievements in international affairs, but that is not a barometer for measuring the effectiveness of a two-year course. The Church should incorporate CST as part of the diplomatic training. The Church should equally extend the teaching of CST to all Catholic institutions with emphasis on its centrality of the Church's presence in the world.

Closely linked to the formation of diplomats is the need for the Catholic Church to also initiate the training of other members of the hierarchy in such a way as to embrace the Catholic Social Doctrine without individual opinions. It is not enough to train only future Church diplomats at the diplomatic school in Rome. Leaders of the Church at all levels of the hierarchy should be informed about the Church's missionary vision, at least from the perspective of the CST. Most bishops and priests are so indifferent to CST that in their respective jurisdictions, little or nothing is said about social justice as taught by the Catholic Church. It is a contradiction for a Catholic bishop or priest to be uncatholic, or to be a Catholic his own way. There is no room for individualism in the Catholic Church.

The Catholic Church should start thinking about training episcopal candidates in such a way as to hold tenaciously to CST principles and influence the flock to do the same. It is not enough to appoint somebody who was into business, or who worked in a certain industry to be a bishop, or even a priest, without first disabusing his mind of any bias or misconceptions that are deep-seated in him. There is a need for the Church to establish a leadership institute in line with her missionary philosophy to inculcate in Church leaders the necessary concepts they ought to have. While Church diplomats evangelize on the national, regional, and international levels, bishops and priests with the lay faithful should embrace the principles of the CST and sustain the work of the diplomats. There ought to be a mechanism in place for the local clergy to follow up the diplomatic efforts of the Holy See.

Finally, attention should be drawn to the Church's emphasis on justice as the reason behind the pursuit of the Church's mission as it concerns the human person. The world may not understand that logic even though it is sound logic. More emphasis should be placed on charity and other virtues, such as mercifulness, almsgiving, mortification, generosity, and the like. Appeals to justice cannot be as effective as appeals to such virtues.

CONCLUSION

It is a common knowledge that income-related inequalities, notably in the ownership of capital and other assets, in access to a variety of services and benefits, and in the personal security that money can buy is growing. There is also greater inequality in the distribution of opportunities for remunerated employment, with worsening unemployment and underemployment in various parts of the world affecting a disproportionate number of people at the lower end of the socio-economic scale. There has also been growing inequality gap between the richest and poorest countries, measured in terms of national per capita income. This accounts for the reason why extreme poverty experienced by those whose income is barely sufficient for survival, remains widespread. Indigence levels have risen in most affluent countries, in countries once part of the Soviet bloc and in various parts of Africa, but have remained stable in Latin America and have declined in Asia.[1343]

The question should be whether the aims and objectives for which the GATT/WTO was established have been realized. The answer is NO. Also, the pursuit of international cooperation for development through the United Nations has not been realized because the exercise is characterized by enormous difficulties and controversies. It baffles me why not many people of nations are interested in pursuing the objectives of the non-aligned movement. The non-aligned movement was, as its name suggests, a political effort to avoid poor underdeveloped nations' dependence on either of the superpowers of the time in history. It proposed ideas and strategies

[1343] *See generally,* International Forum for Social Development: Social Justice in an Open World – The Role of the United Nations, United Nations Publication, no. 06.IV.2, New York, 2006

for establishing effective relations with superpowers, for defining global position and status of formerly colonized countries, and for combating neo-colonialism. Even though the non-aligned movement did not furnish any new theory for economic growth or a new vision for social progress, industrialized nations have never put that into consideration during negotiations at the WTO.

The Holy See has made substantial strides in addressing the myriad problems that plague the human person in the world. Catholic Social Justice Theory has unique characteristics that should display the indispensability of the Church's moral voice in world affairs. CST is only partially capable of providing the comprehensive social theory it seeks to develop. CST is strong in morals but less useful in practical economic applications. Catholic Social Justice Theory applies well to the need of society from a moral yardstick. The Catholic Church has served as an ethical standard for centuries in almost every social arena, save economics. The process of interpreting theology into economic policy needs more patch-ups to win the ear of mainstream economic thought. Therefore, the Church needs to double her efforts in reassessing the dynamics of her CST.

International trade negotiations and outcomes need Catholic Social Justice Theory as an umpire. Obviously, the Catholic Church has made some meaningful contributions as a Permanent Observer in the GATT-WTO system as variously stated above. However, looking at the stalemate situation at the WTO since the Doha Round and the growing inequalities and inequities among nations in pursuit of wealth and power, the Church needs to adjust her methodology and missionary techniques to be a more effective advocate for implementing that Theory in the real world of the multilateral trading system. The Church needs to utilize all her daughters and sons and not restrict missionary operations as an exclusive preserve of the hierarchy or a select few. Serving as eloquent and pragmatic umpire in the world is not a choice, rather, it is at the center of the Church's missionary mandate.

BIBLIOGRAPHY

Books and Book Chapters

Eric Fratini, THE ENTITY: FIVE CENTURIES OF VATCAN ESPIONAGE (St. Martin's Press) (2008)

Avro Manhattan, THE VATICAN IN WORLD POLITICS (Gaer Associates) (1949)

Barry Eichengreen, *The Political Economy of the Smoot-Hawley,* in RESEARCH IN ECONOMIC HISTORY (1989)

Douglas Irwin A., *From Smoot-Hawley to Reciprocal Trade Agreements: Changing the Course of U.S. Trade Policy in the 1930s,* in Michael Bordo D., *et al* (eds.), THE DEFIING MOMENT: THE GRAET DEPRESSION AND THE AMERICAN ECONOMY IN THE TWENTIETH CENTURY, University of Chicago Press (1998)

Charlae Kindleberger P., THE WORLD IN DEPRESSION, 1929-1939, (University of California Press) (1973)

Peter Temin, LESSONS FROM THE DEPRESSION: THE LIONEL ROBBINS LECTURES FOR 1989, (MIT Press) (1989)

Fatoumata Jawara & Aileen Kwa, BEHIND THE SCENES AT THE WTO: THE REAL WORLD OF INTERNATIONAL TRADE NEGOTIATIONS – THE LESSONS OF CANCÚN, Zeb Books Ltd, (updated ed. 2004)

James Crawford, THE CREATION OF STATES IN INTERNATIONAL LAW, Oxford Press (2nd ed. 2006)

________BROWNLIE'S PRINCIPLES OF PUBLIC INTERNATIONAL LAW (2013)

Roman A. Melnyk, THE VATICAN DIPLOMACY AT THE UNITED NATIONS: A HISTORY OF CATHOLIC GLOBAL ENGAGEMENT, Edwin Mellen Press (2009)

Edward J. Gratsch, THE HOLY SEE AND THE UNITED NATIONS 1945-1995 (1997)

John Rawls, A THEORY OF JUSTICE (1990)

John Hunsaker & Brenda Hanzl, UNDERSTANDING SOCIAL JUSTICE PHILANTHROPY, National Committee for Responsive Philanthropy (2003)

Walker & Walker, *Social Inclusion, Anti-Racism and Democratic Citizenship*, in Anver Saloojee (ed.), THE LAIDLAW FOUNDATION (2003)

Ray Deaux & Mark Snyder (eds.), THE OXFORD HANDBOOK ON PERSONALITY AND SOCIAL PSYCHOLOGY 92012)

Thomas Patrick Burke, THE CONCEPT OF JUSTICE: IS SOCIAL JUSTICE JUST? (2013)

Loretta Capeheart & Dragan Milovanovic, SOCIAL JSUTICE: THEORIES, ISSUES, AND MOVEMENTS (2007)

David Miller, PRINCIPLES OF SOCIAL JUSTICE (2001)

Brian Barry, WHY SOCIAL JUSTICE MATTERS (2005)

Maurianne Adams, *et al* (eds.), TEACHINGS FOR DIVERSITY AND SOCIAL JUSTICE (2010)

Bellah Robert et al, HABITS OF THE HEART: INDIVIDUALISM AND COMMITMENT IN AMERICAN LIFE, University of California Press (1996)

Paul Tillich, THE COURAGE TO BE, Yale University Press (1952)

Alisdair Macintyre, AFTER VIRTUE: A STUDY IN MORAL THEORY, (2nd ed.), University of Notre Dame Press (1984)

D.D Raphael, PROBLEMS OF POLITICAL PHILOSOPHY, Macmillan Press (1979)

PAUL Ricoeur, ONESELF AS ANOTHER (translated. by Kathleen Blamey, University of Chicago Press) (1992)

O.P. Gauba, DIMENSIONS OF SOCIAL JUSTICE, (National Publishing House) (1983)

K. Allan, THE SOCIAL LENS: AN INVITATION TO SOCIAL AND SOCIOLOGICAL THEORY (Pine Forge Press) (2007)

Daniel Groody G., GLOBALIZATION, SPIRITUALITY, AND JUSTICE, (Marknoll) (2008)

Bennett Harold V., INJUSTICE MADE LEGAL: DEUTERONOMIC LAW AND THE PLIGHT OF WIDOWS, STRANGERS, AND ORPHANS IN ANCIENT ISRAEL, (Eerdmans) (2002)

David Bohr, CATHOLIC MORAL TRADITION, (Our Sunday Visitor) (1999)

Raj Bhala, TRADE, DEVELOPMENT, AND SOCIAL JUSTICE (Carolina Academic Press) (2003)

_______INTERNATIONAL TRADE LAW: INTERDISCIPLINARY THEORY AND PRACTICE, (Mathew Bender & Co.) (2008)

_______MODERN GATT LAW: A TREATISE ON THE LAW AND POLITICAL ECONOMY OF THE GENERAL AGREEMENT ON TARIFFS AND TRADE AND OTHER WORLD TRADE ORGANIZATION AGREEMENTS vols. 1 & 2 9Sweet & Maxwell) (2013)

_______DICTIONARY OF INTERNATIONAL TRADE LAW 92nd ed.) (Mathew Bender & Co.) (2012)

_______INTERNATIONAL TRADE LAW: INTERDISCIPLINARY THEORY AND PRACTICE (DOCUMENTS SUPPLEMENT) (3rd ed.) (LexisNexis) (2008)

Charles Rodgers, AN INTRODUCTION TO CATHOLIC SOCIAL TEACHING, (Ignatius Press) (2000)

Richard P. Mcbrien, CATHOLICISM, (HarperOne) (1994)

George Weigel, THE WITNESS TO HOPE: THE BIOGRAPHY OF POPE JOHN II (1920-2005), (1st ed.) (Harper Perennial) (1999)

Martin Malachi, THE KEYS OF THIS BLOOD: POPE JOHN PAUL II VERSUS RUSSIA AND THE WEST FOR CONTROL OF THE NEW WORLD ORDER, (Touchstone) (1990)

Frank Garcia J., TRADE, INEQUALITY, AND JUSTICE: TOWARD LIBERAL THEORY OF JUST TRADE, (Translational Publisher Inc.) (2003)

_______GLOBAL JUSTICE AND INTERNATIONAL ECONOMIC LAW: OPPORTUNITIES AND PROSPECTS (2012)

_______GLOBAL JUSTICE AND INTERNATIONAL ECONOMIC LAW: THREE TAKES (2013)

Bernard M. Hoekman & Mavroidis Petros, WORLD TRADE ORGANIZATION: LAW, ECONOMICS, AND POLITICS (2007)

Bernard M. Hoekman & Michael K. Kostecki, THE POLITICAL ECONOMY OF THE WORLD TRADING SYSTEM (2008)

John Jackson J., SOVEREIGNTY: THE WTO AND CHANGING FUNDAMENTALS OF INTERNATIONAL LAW (2006)

_______THE JURISPRUDENCE OF GATT AND THE WTO: INSIGHTS ON TREATY LAW AND ECONOMIC RELATIONS (2000)

Christian Joerges & Ernst-Ulrich Petersmann (eds.), CONSTITUTIONALISM, MULTILEVEL TRADE GOVERNANCE AND SOCIAL REGULATION (2006)

Ernst-Ulrich Petersmann, INTERNATIONAL ECONOMIC LAW IN THE 21ST CENTURY (2012)

Markus Gethring W., *et al,* WORLD TRADE LAW IN PRACTICE (2006)

John Barton H., *et al,* THE EVOLUTION OF THE TRADE REGIME – POLITICS, LAW, AND ECONOMICS OF THE GATT AND THE WTO (2006)

Deborah Cass Z., CONSTITUTIONALIZATION OF THE WORLD TRADE ORGANIZATION: LEGITIMACY, DEMOCRACY, AND COMMUNITY IN THE INTERNATIONAL TRADING SYSTEM (2005)

Peet Richard, UNHOLY TRINITY: THE IMF, WORLD BANK AND WTO (SIRD) (2003)

Davey William, *A Very Brief History of the GATT/WTO System,* in Andrew GuzmanT. & Joost Pauwelyn H.B., (eds.), INTERNATIONAL TRADE LAW, (2003)

Daniel L. Benthlehem (ed.), THE OXFORD HANDBOOK OF INTERNATIONAL TRADE LAW (2009)

G.P. Murdock, SOCIAL STRUCTURES, Macmillan Press (1994)

William N. Stephens, THE FAMILY IN CROEE-CULTURE PERSPECTIVE, (Holt, Reinhart & Winston) (1963)

Hyginus Eugene Cardinale, THE HOLY SEE AND THE INTERNATIONAL ORDER, (1976)

Robert F. Illing, AMERICA AND THE VATICAN: TRADING INFORMATION AFTER WWII 92011)

Cyrus Shahrad, SECRETS OF THE VATICAN (2007)

Robert John Araujo & John A. Lucal, PAPAL DIPLOMACY AND THE QUEST FOR PEACE: THE VATICAN AND INTERNATIONAL ORGANIZATIONS FRO THE EARLY YEARS TO THE LEAGUE OF NATIONS (2004)

Bernard J. O'Connor, PAPAL DIPLOMACY: JOHN PAUL II AND THE CULTURE OF PEACE (2005)

Jorri C. Duursma, FRAGMENTATION AND THE INTERNATIONAL RELATIONS OF MICRO-STATES: SELF-DETERMINATION AND STATEHOOD (1996)

Michael Collins, THE VATICAN (2011)

Bart McDowell, INSIDE THE VATICAN (2005)

Reese J. Thomas, INSIDE THE VATICAN: THE POLITICS AND ORGANIZATION OF THE CATHOLIC CHURCH (1998)

Francis X. Blouin Jr., (ed.), VATICAN ARCHIVES: AN INVENTORY AND GUIDE TO HISTORICAL DOCUMENTS OF THE HOLY SEE (1998)

Vincent Viaene (ed.), THE PAPCY AND THE NEW WORLD ORDER: VATICAN DIPLOMACY, CATHOLIC OPINION AND INTERNATIONAL POLITICSO XIII (2005)

Robert Calderisi, EARTHLY MISSION: THE CATHOLIC CHURCH AND WORLD DEVELOPMENT (2013)

Michael Fahye, The Mission of the Church: To Divinize or to Humanize? PROCEEDINGS CTSA (1976)

Jeffrey K. Hadden, THE GATHERING STORM IN THE CHURCHES 91969)

John A. Coleman, *American Catholicism and Strategic Social Theology*, in Irene Woodward (ed.), THE CATHOLIC CHURCH: THE UNITED STATES EXPERIENCE (1978)

James M. Gustafson, THE CHURCH AS A MORAL DECISION MAKER (1962)

Richard W. Grant, THE HOLY SEE IN INTERNATIONAL RELATIONS (1986)

Triggs d. Gllian, INTERNATIONL LAW: CONTEMPORARY PRINCIPLES AND PRACTICES (2006)

Ian Brownlie, PRINCIPLES OF PUBLIC INTERNATIONAL LAW 92003)

________Rebirth of Statehood, in Malcolm D. Evans, ASPECTS OF STATEHOOD AND INSTITUTIONALISM IN CONTEMPORARY EUROPE (1996)

Dom B.C. Butler, THE THEOLOGY OF VATICAN II (Darton, Longman & Todd) (1967)

Charles Curran, CATHOLIC SOCIAL TEACHING 1891-PRESENT: A HISTORICAL, THEOLOGICAL, AND ETHICAL ANALYSIS (2002)

Kenneth R. Himes, CHRISTIANITY AND THE POLITICAL ORDER: CONFLICT, COOPTATION AND COOPERATION (2013)

________MODERN CATHOLIC SOCIAL TEACHING: COMMENTARIES AND INTERPRETATIONS (2005)

________RESPONSES TO 101 QUESTIONS ON CATHOLIC SOCIAL TEACHING (2002)

Edward P. Deberri, et al, CATHOLIC SOCIAL TEACHING: OUR BEST KEPT SECRET (2003)

Micahel Pennock, CATHOLIC SOCIAL TEACHING: LEARNING AND LIVING JUSTICE (2007)

Thomas Massaro, LIVING JUSTICE: CATHOLIC SOCIAL TEACHING IN ACTION (2011)

________CATHOLIC SOCIAL TEACHING AND UNITED STATES WELFARE REFORM (19980

Philip Land, CATHOLIC SOCIAL TEACHING AS I HAVE LIVED, LOATHED AND LOVED IT (1995)

Marvin L. Kier, CATHOLIC SOCIAL TEACHINGS AND MOVEMENTS (2001)

Perry Roets, CATHOLIC SOCIAL TEACHINGS: A BRIEF SOCIAL CATECHISM (1999)

Jerry Windley-Daoust, LIVING JUSTICE AND PEACE: CATHOLIC SOCIAL TEACHING IN PRACTICE (2008)

Mary Jo Bane & Lawrence M. Mead, LIFTING UP THE POOR: A DIAOGUE ON RELIGION, POVERTY & WELFARE REFORM (2003)

David O'Brien & Thomas Shannon, CATHOLIC SOCIAL THOUGHT: THE DOCUMENTARY HERITAGE (2010)

Daniel K. Finn (ed.), THE TRUE WEALTH OF NATIONS: CATHOLIC SOCIAL THOUGHT AND ECONOMIC LIFE (2010)

________THE MORAL ECONOMY OF MARKETS: ASSESSING CLAIMS ABOUT MARKET AND JUSTICE (2006)

________THE MORAL DYNAMICS OF ECONOMIC LIFE (2012)

Rupert J. Ederer, ECONOMICS AS IF GOD MATTERS: MORE THAN A CENTURY OF PAPAL TEACHING (2011)

Thomas E. Woods, THE CHURCH AND THE MARKET: A CATHOLIC DEFENSE OF THE FREE ECONOMY (2005)

Roland Tracey, BENEDICT XVI: A GUIDE FOR THE PERPLEXED (T & T Clark) (2010)

Eric A. Posner & Alan O. Sykes, ECONOMIC FOUNDATIONS OF INTERNATIONAL LAW (2013)

Kelsey Timmerman, WHERE AM I WEARING: A GLOBAL TOUR TO THE COUNTRIES, FACTORIES, AND PEOPLE THAT MAKE OUR CLOTHES (2012)

Sue Arrowsmith & Robert D. Anderson, THE WTO REGIME ON GOVERNMENT PROCUREMENT: CHALLENGE AND REFORM (2011)

Rorden Wilkinson & James Scott, TRADE, POVERTY, DEVELOPMENT: GETTING BEYOND THE WTO's DOHA DEADLOCK (2013)

James Harrison, THE HUMAN RIGHTS IMPACT OF THE WORLD TRADE ORGANIZATION (2007)

Donatella Alessandrini, DEVELOPING COUNTRIES AND THE MULTILATERAL TRADE REGIME: THE FAILURE AND PROMISE OF THE WTO's DEVELOPMENT MISSION (2010)

A.K. Koul, GUIDE TO THE WTO AND GATT: ECONOMICS, LAW AND POLITICS (2006)

David A. Gantz, LIBERALIZING INTERNATIONAL TRADE AFTER DOHA: MULTILATERAL, PLURILATERAL, REGIONAL, AND UNILATERAL INITIATIVES (2013)

Federico Ortino & Ernst-Ulrich Petersmann (eds.), THE WTO DISPUTE SETTLEMENT SYSTEM 1995-2003 Vol. 18, (2004)

Gregory Shaffer & Ricardo Melendez-Ortiz (eds.), DISPUTE SETTLEMENT AT THE WTO: THE DEVELOPING COUNTRY EXPERIENCE (2012)

Ross Becroft, THE STANDARD OF REVIEW IN WTO DISPUTE SETTLEMENT: CRITIQUE AND DEVELOPMENT (2012)

Kamal Malhotra, MAKING GLOBAL TRADE WORK FOR PEOPLE (2003)

Melaku Geboye Desta, THE LAW OF INTERNATIONAL TRADE IN AGRICULTURAL PRODUCTS: FROM GATT 1947 TO THE WTO AGREEMENT ON AGRICULTURE (2002)

Chi Carmody, *et al*, GLOBAL JUSTICE AND INTERNATIONAL ECONOMIC LAW: OPPORTUNITIES AND PROSPECTS, ASI Studies in International Legal Theory (2012)

John F. Pollard, THE VATICAN AND ITALIAN FASCISM 1929-1932: A STUDY IN CONFLICT (2005)

Josef Lecler S.J., THE WTO SOVEREIGNTIES: A STUDY OF THE RELATIONSHIP BETWEEN THE CHURCH AND THE STATE (1952)

John Eppstein, THE CATHOLIC TRADITION OF THE LAW OF NATIONS 418-26 (1935)

Lassa Francis L. Oppenheim, INTERNATIONAL LAW: A TREATISE (1955)

Robert A. Graham, THE RISE OF THE DOUBLE DIPLOMATIC CORPS IN ROME: A STUDY IN INTERNATIONAL PRACTICE 1870-1875 (1952)

Sidney Z. Ehler & John B. Morrali (trans. and eds.), CHURCH AND STATES THROUGH THE CENTURIES: A COLLECTION OF HISTORIC DOCUMENTS WITH COMMENTARIES (1954)

Rebecca Wallace, INTERNATIONAL LAW 2nd ed., (1992)

Christian Nwachukwu Okeke, CONTROVERSIAL SUBJECTS OF INTERNATIONAL LAW (1974)

Francis Sweeney (ed.), THE VATICAN AND WORLD PEACE, (Colin Smythe) (1970)

Peter Habblethwaite, THE YAER OF THREE POPES, (Collins) (1978)

Melquiades J. Gamboa, ELEMENTS OF DIPLOMATIC AND CONSULAR PRACTICE: A GLOSSARY, (Central Law Book Pub.) (1966)

Brian J. Benstad, CHURCH, STATE, AND SOCIETY: AN INTRODUCTION TO CATHOLIC SOCIAL DOCTRINE (2011)

Jost A. C. Kay & H. Thorisodottir (eds.), SOCIAL AND PSYCHOLOGICAL BASES OF IDEOLOGY AND SYSTEM JUSTIFICATION (2009)

John O'Connor, THE ESSENTIAL CATHOLIC HANDBOOK: A SUMMARY OF BELIEFS, PRACTICES, AND PRAYERS, (1997)

Donal Dorr, OPTION FOR THE POOR: A HUNDRED YEARS OF VATICAN SOCIAL TEACHING (1983)

Fred Kammer S.J., DOINF FAITHJUSTICE: AN INTRODUCTION TO CATHOLIC SOCIAL THOUGHT (2004)

Jeremy Bentham, INTRODUCTION TO THE PRINCIPLES OF MORALS AND LEGISLATION (1948)

Terence Ball & Richard Dagger, POLITICAL IDEOLOGIES AND THE DEMOCRATIC IDEAL (6th ed., (2006)

Karol Wojtyla, LOVE AND RESPONSIBILITY (trans. by H.T. Willetts) (1993)

John Stuart Mill, UTILITARIANISM, (1966)

Karen Lebacqz, SIX THEORIES OF JUSTICE: PERSPECTIVES FROM PHILOSOPHICAL AND THEOLOGICAL ETHICS (1986)

Mario Falco, THE LEGAL POSITION OF THE HOLY SEE BEFORE AND AFTER THE LATERAN AGREEMENTS (1935)

Johanness Wilhelmus Schneider, TREATY-MAKING POWER OF INTERNATIONAL ORGANIZATIONS (1959)

André Dupuy, WORDS THAT MATTER: THE HOLY SEE IN MULTILATERAL DIPLOMACY, AN ANTHOLOGY (1970-2000) (2003)

Douglas Irwin, FREE TRADE UNDER FIRE (2002)

Paul Collier, THE BOTTOM BILLION: WHY POOREST COUNTRIES ARE FAILING AND WHAT CAN BE DONE ABOUT IT (2007)

Ian Fletcher, FREE TRADE DOESN'T WORK: WHAT SHOULD REPLACE IT AND WHY (2011)

Matthew Clayton & Andrew Williams (ed.), SOCIAL JUSTICE (2011)

Jim Wallis, THE SOUL OF POLITICS: BEYOND RELIGIOUS RIGHT AND SECULAR LEFT (1995)

Jerry Mander & Edward Goldsmith (eds.), THE CASE AGAINST THE GLOBAL ECONOMY AND FOR A TURN TOWARD THE LOCAL (1996)

Encyclopedias and Dictionaries

Encyclopedia Britannica Online, available at http://www.britannica.com

D.P. Simpson, CASSELL'S LATIN DICTIONARY (5th Ed. 1968)

New Catholic Encyclopedia (2nd ed., Vol. 7) (2003)

Henry Campbell Black, et al., BLACK'S LAW DICTIONARY 1891-1991, (Centennial ed.) (1992)

MERRIAM-WEBSTER'S COLLEGIATE DICTIONARY (11th ed., 2011)

Bart Drubbel (ed.), THE 21ST CENTURY WEBSTER'S INTERNATIONAL ENCYCLOPEDIA (2003)

READER'S DIGEST ILLUSTRATED ENCYCLOPEDIC DICTIONARY Vol. A-K (1987)

Rudolf Bernhardt (ed.), ENCYCLOPEDIA OF PUBLIC INTERNATIONAL LAW Vol. 4, Q-Z (2000)

THE OXFORD ENGLISH DICTIONARY (2nd ed. 2001)

J.N.D. KELLY, OXFORD DICTIONARY OF POPES 44 (1986)

Mary Hawkesworth & Maurice Kogan (ed.), ENCYCLOPEDIA OF GOVERNMENT AND POLITICS, Vol. 2 (1992)

James R. Fox, DICTIONARY OF INTERNATIONAL AND COMPARATIVE LAW (1992)

Jon Hendricks, "Dependency Theory," ENCYCLOPEDIA OF SOCIOLOGY (2nd ed.) (2000).

Documents of Church Magisterium

THE SECOND VATICAN ECUMENICAN COUNCIL, GAUDIUM ET SPES (The Pastoral Constitution on the Church in the Modern World) December 7, 1965

CATECHISM OF THE CATHOLIC CHURCH (1994)

CODE OF CANON LAW (1983)

Pope Pius IX, ENCYCLICAL LETTER *Notis et Nobiscum* (On the Church in the Pontifical States) (1849)

________Respicientes (Protesting the Taking of the Pontifical States) (1870)

Pope Leo XIII, ENCYCLICAL LETTER *Rerum Novarum* (On the Condition of Labor) (1891)

________Immortale Dei (Encyclical Letter on the Christian Constitution of States) (1885).

________ENCYCLICAL LETTER Libertas Praestantissimum (On the Nature of Human Liberty) (1888).

Pope Pius XI, ENCYCLICAL LETTER Quadragesimo Anno (After Forty Years) (1931)

________ENCYCLICAL LETTER Divini Redemptoris (On Atheistic Communism) (1937)

Pope Pius XII, ENCYCLICAL LETTER *Sertum Laetitia* (On the Hundred and Fiftieth Anniversary of the Establishment of the Hierarchy in the United States) (1939)

________ENCYCLICAL LETTER *Summi Pontificatus* (On the Unity of Human Society) (1939)

________ENCYCLICAL LETTER *Evangelii Praecones* (On Promotion of Catholic Missions) (1951)

________Christmas Radio Broadcast Message (1952)

________Christmas Radio Broadcast Message (1944)

________Radio Message for the Fiftieth Anniversary of *Rerum Novarum* (1941)

Pope John Paul II, ENCYCLICAL LETTER *Centesimus Annus* (Hundredth Year of *Rerum Novarum)* (1991)

________ENCYCLICAL LETTER *Sollicitudo Rei Socialis* (On the Social Order) (1987)

________ENCYCLICAL LETTER *Redemptoris Missio* (On the Mission of the Redeemer) (1990).
________POST-SYNODAL APOSTOLIC EXHORTATION *Christifideles Laici* 4o, *AAS* 81 (1989).
________ENCYCLICAL LETTER *Laborem Exercens* (On Human Work) (1981).
________ENCYCLICAL LETTER *Redemptor Hominis* (On the Redeemer of Man). (1979)
________ENCYCLICAL LETTER *Fides et Ratio* (Faith and Reason) (1998)
________ENCYCLICAL LETTER *Veritate Splendor* (On the Splendor of Truth) (1993).
________ENCYCLICAL LETTER Evangelium Vitae (On the Gospel of Life) (1995)
________Opening Speech to the Second Vatican Council, October 11, 1962
________POST-SYNODAL APOSTOLIC EXHORTATION *Ecclesia in America* (The Church in America) (1999)
________APOSTOLIC EXHORTATION *Reconciliatio et Paenitentia* (On Reconciliation and Penance in the Mission of the Church Today) (1985)
________Address to the World Council of Churches June 25, 1984
________World Day of Peace Message (1981)
________Dignity of the Human Person Founded on Justice and Peace: Address to the 34th Plenary Session of the United Nations General Assembly 9th Plenary Meeting (1979)
________Address to thc Plenary Session of the Pontifical Academy of Sciences on "Globalization: Ethical and Institutional Concerns, April 27, 2001
________ "The Study of Tension Between Human Equality and Social Inequalities from the Perspective of the Various Social Sciences," An address to the Plenary Session of the Pontifical Academy of Social Sciences, November 25, 1994
Pope Paul VI, ENCYCLICAL LETTER *Ecclesiam Suam* (On the Paths of the
Church) (1964)

________ENCYCLICAL LETTER *Populorum Progressio* (On the Development of Peoples) (1967)

________APOSTOLIC LETTER *Sollicitudo Omnium Ecclesiarum* (The Care of the Churches – On the Duties of Papal Representatives) (1969)

________ENCYCLICAL LETTER *Octogessima Adveniens* (A Call to Action – On the Eightieth Anniversary of *Rerum Novarum*) (1971)

________APOSTOLIC EXHORTATION Evangelii Nuntiandi (On Evangelization in the World) (1975)

________Message to the International Conference on Human Rights (1968)

________Appeal for Peace: Address to the 20th Session of the United Nations General Assembly (1965)

Pope John XXIII, ENCYCLICAL LETTER Mater et Magistra (On the Church as Mother and Teacher – Christianity and Social Progress) (1961)

________ENCYCLICAL LETTER Pacem in Terris (On Peace on Earth) (1963)

Pope Benedict XVI, ENCYCLICAL LETTER *Deus Caritas Est* (God is Love) (2005)

________ENCYCLICAL LETTER *Caritas in Veritate* (Love in Truth) (2009)

________Address to the Members of the General Assembly of the United Nations Organization (2008)

Pope Francis I, APOSTOLIC EXHORTATION *Evangelii Gaudium* (Proclamation of the Gospel in Today's World) (2013)

________Address on World Mission Day (2013)

________Address to the Pontifical Ecclesiastical Academy, June 6, 2013

________Address to Participants in the Plenary of the Pontifical Council for Promoting the New Evangelization, October 14, 2013

Pontifical Council for Justice and Peace, COMPENDIUM OF THE CATHOLIC SOCIAL DOCTRINE (2004)

CONGREGATION FOR THE DOCTRINE OF THE FAITH, *Libertatis Conscietia* (Instruction on Christian Freedom and Liberation) (1986)

Pope Benedict XVI, Address to the General Assembly of the United Nations, April 18, 2008 *UN/GA58/314* (2008)

Archbishop Jean-Louis Tauran, Lecture on THE PRESENCE OF THE HOLY SEE IN INTERNATIONAL ORGANIZATIONS, April 22, 2002

Cardinal Giovanni Lajolo, LECTURE ON PAPAL DIPLOMACY, November 7, 2008

United States Conference of Catholic Bishops, ECONOMIC JUSTICE FOR ALL: PASTORAL LETTER ON CATHOLIC SOCIAL TEACHING AND THE U.S ECONOMY (1986)

Lombardi Editorial, The Family of Nation on the Vatican Radio, The Voice of the Pope and the Church in Dialogue with the World, September 30, 2011

Archbishop Dominique Mamberti, Holy See on Main Challenges Facing the Family of Nations, An Address, October 8, 2011

John P. Beal *et al.,* (eds.), NEW COMMENTARY OF THE CODE OF CANON LAW (2000)

The Second Vatican Ecumenical Council, THE DOGMATIC CONSTITUTION ON THE CHURCH (*Lumen Gentium*) November 21, 1964

Robert A. Sirico & Maciej Zięba, O.P. (eds.), *The Social Agenda: A Collection of Magisterial Texts,* PONTIFICAL COUNCIL FOR JUSTICE AND PEACE (2000)

CONGREGATION FOR CATHOLIC EDUCATION, *Guidelines for the Study and Teaching of the Church's Social Doctrine in the Formation of Priests* (1988)

IUSTITIA ET PAX PONTIFICAL COMMISSION, At the Service of the Human Community: *An Ethical Approach to the International Debt Question* (1986)

Angelo Cardinal Sodano, Addressing the Future: The Holy See's Presence in International Affairs, SETON HALL JOURNAL OF DIPLOMACY AND INTERNATIONAL RELATIONS, Winter/Spring 2001

Archbishop Silvano M. Tomasi, Address to the 9th Session of the WTO Ministerial Conference, Bali, Indonesia, December 3-6, 2013

Journals Articles, and Newspapers

Faizel Ismail, Mainstreaming Development in the World Trade Organization, JOURNAL OF WORLD TRADE, 39(1) 92005)

Raymond L. Flinn, *Letter from the Vatican: Common Objectives for Peace,* SAIS REVIEW, Vol. 16, No. 2 Summer-Fall (1996)

Gordon Ireland, The State of the City of the Vatican, 27 AVE MARIA JOURNAL OF INTERNATIONAL LAW 272, 272 (1933)

Yasmin Abdullah, *The Holy See at the United Nations Conferences: State of Church?* 96 COLUM. L. REV. 1835, 1843 (1996)

Jean Leon Boucher, *The Development and Operational Issues of Social Justice Programs at State Universities in the United States of America,* JOURNAL FOR CRITICAL EDUCATION POLICY STUDIES (JCEPS*)* Vol. 8 Issue 2 (2010)

Frank J. Garcia, *Trade and Inequality: Economic Justice and the Developing World,* 21 MICHIGAN JOURNAL OF INTERNATIONAL LAW REVIEW 975 (2000)

Frank J. Garcia, *Building a Just Trade Order for a New Millennium,* 33 THE GEORGE WASHINGTON INTERNATIONAL LAW REVIEW (2001)

Soru Roberto, *Pope on Latin Trip, Attacks Pinochet Regime,* NEW YORK TIMES, April 1, 1987.

Cephas Lumina, *Free Trade or Just Trade? The World Trade Organization, Human Rights and Development* (part 1), 14 LAW, DEMOCRACY & DEVELOPMENT (2010) available at www.ajol.info/index.php/1dd/article/viewFile/68289/56371

John F. Pollard, *Eighty Years of Deadlock,* THE TIMES February 10, 1929 available at http://webspace.webring.com/people/qs/sabathage/times1.html

Robert J. Araujo, *The Holy See: International Person and Sovereign*, AVE MARIA INTERNATIONAL LAW JOURNAL, Inaugural Issue, Vol. 1, 2011

Francis X. Murphy, *Vatican Politics: The Metapolitique of the Papacy,* 19 CASE W. RES. J. INT'L L. 375 (1987).

Philip Hughes, *The International Action of the Papacy – Introductory: Before the Reformation,* THE TABLET (November 2, 1940).

Walter Ullman, *The Development of the Medieval Idea of Sovereignty,* ENG. HIST. REV., Jan 1, 1949, no. CCL.

John Keating Cartwright, *Contributions of the Papacy to International Peace,* 8 CATH. HIST. REV., 160 (1928)

Edward G. Bourn, *The Demarcation Line of Alexander VI: An Episode of the Period of Discoveries,* 1 YALE REVIEW 35, 55 (1892)

F. Matthews-Giba, O.F.M., *Religious Dimensions of Mediation,* 27 FORDHAM URB. L.J. 1695 (2000)

Josef Kunz, *The Status of the Holy See in International Law,* 46 AVE MARIA J. INT'L L. 308, 311 (1952)

L.J.S. Wood, Vatican Politics and Policies, 128 ATLANTIC MONTHLY 398, 404 (1921)

Maria L. Hecker, Constitutional Issues Raised by Diplomatic Relations between the United States and the Holy See, 15 HASTINGS CONSTITUTIONAL LAW QUARTERLY 101, 103 (1987)

Patrick Henry, 'And I Don't Care What it is:' The Tradition-History of Civil Religious Proof-Text, JOURNAL OF THE AMERICAN ACADEMY OF RELIGION 49(1) (March 1981)

Di Giovann Lajolo, *Diplomazia Vaticana: Uno Strumento docile e fedele al papa,* 30 GIORNI, (March 2006)

H.F. Cumbo, *The Holy See and International Law,* 2 INTERNATIONAL LAW QUARTERLY 603 (1948)

ILC Yearbook, 1956/II, 107 & 108

S. Z. Ehler, The Recent Concordats, 104 HISTORICAL REVIEW (1961)

CIA World Factbook, http://www.cia.org/library/publications/the-world-factbook (The Holy See)

David Roche, *There is No Clash of Civilizations,* WALL STREET JOURNAL, Europe, November 29, 2001

Thomas Mountain, The Pirates of Puntland: A Tale of Somali Pirates, Ethiopia and the U.S.A., COUNTERPUNCH, August 27-29, 2010

Mark Silk, *Notes on the Judeo-Christian Tradition in America,* AMERICAN QUARTERLY, 36(1) (1984)

Dennis Prager, The Case for Judeo-Christian Values: Parts I-IV, (2005) available at http://www.theroadtoemmaus.org/RdLb/3IJdXn/Jd/PragerJdXnValus.htm

Ban Ki-moon (UN Secretary-General), *Message for the World Day of Social Justice,* February 20, 2011 http://www.cost.eu/media/newsroom/social-justice

Dan Froomklin, 'New Social Justice Index Places U.S. Near Bottom,' THE HUFFINGTON POST (2011)

Daniel M. Cowdin, "JOHN PAUL II and Environmental Concern: Problems and Possibilities," LIVING LIGHT 28 (1991)

Raj Bhala, *Philosophical, Religious, and Legalistic Perspectives on Equal Human Dignity and U.S. Free Trade Agreements,* ANUARIO ANDINO DE DERECHOS INTELECTUALES, AÑO VIII-N (2012)

Fernando R. Tesón, *The Kantian Theory of International Law,* 92 COLUMBIA LAW REVIEW 53 (1992)

Heiner Bielefafeldt, Autonomy and Republicanism: Immanuel Kant's Philosophy of Freedom, 25 POLITICAL THEORY 524, 525 (1997)

Oscar Schachter, Human Dignity as a Normative Concept, 77 AVE MARIA JOURNAL OF INTERNATIONAL LAW 848, 849 (1983)

Pope John Paul II, Address to the Fiftieth General Assembly of the United Nations, 13 L'OSSERVATORE ROMANO, English ed., 11 October 1995

Pope Paul VI, Message to the International Conference on Human Rights, L'OSSERVATORE ROMANO, April 15, 1968

D.Q. McInerny, The Social Thought of Jacques Maritain, THE CATHOLIC SOCIAL SCIENCE REVIEW 12 (2007)

Henry Volken, S.J., *Preferential Option for the Poor,* PROMOTIO JUSTITIAE, No. 29 (1984)

Jean-Yves Calvez, S.J., The Preferential Option for the Poor: Where Does it Come for Us? STUDIES IN THE SPIRITUALITY OF JESUITS, Vol. 21 (1984)

Robert John Araujo, *International Personality of Intergovernmental Organizations: Do Their Capacities Really Depend Upon Their Constitutions?* 4 INDIANA JOURNAL OF INTERNATIONAL LAW 42, 61 (1964)

Tiyanjana Maluwa, *The Holy See and the Concept of International Legal Personality: Some Reflections,* 19 COMPARATIVE & INTERNATIONAL LAW JOURNAL OF SOUTH AFRICA 1 (1986)

_______*The Treaty-Making Capacity of the Holy See in Theory and Practice: A Study of the Jus Tractum of a Non-State Entity,* COMPARATIVE & INTERNATIONAL LAW JOURNAL OF SOUTH AFRICA 20 No. 2 (1987)

Gaetano Arangio-Ruiz, *On the Nature of the International Personality of the Holy See,* 29 REVUE BELGE DE DROIT INTERNACIONAL (R.B.D.I.) 354 (1996)

Oliver James Lissitzyn, *Territorial Entities Other than Independent States in the Law of Treaties,* 125 HAGUE RECUEIL 1 (1965)

Roland Minnerath, *The Position of the Catholic Church Regarding Concordats from a Doctrinal and Pragmatic Perspective,* CATHOLIC UNIVERSITY LAW REVIEW 467 (1998)

Raymond L. Buell, *France and the Vatican,* 36 POLITICAL SCIENCE QUARTERLY, 30 (1921)

Felix Abbe Klein, *Breaking and Renewing Diplomatic Relations between France and the Holy See,* 112 THE CATHOLIC WORLD 577 (1921)

Editorial Comment, The Papacy in International Law, AVE MARIA JOURNAL OF INTERNATIONAL LAW 864 (1914)

Emeka Xris Obiezu, O.S.A., *The Holy See in the United Nations: An Assessment and Critique,* NTR Vol. 26 No. 1, September 2013

Arthur Jones, *Catholics Were there at the Start,* NATIONAL CATHOLIC REPORTER, October 1, 1999

Christopher J. Chipello, "Canada, Brazil Lose WTO Plane Cases," WALL STREET JOURNAL, March 15, 1999

Stephen Rowntree, *The Ethics of Trade Policy in Catholic Political Economy,* THEOLOGICAL STUDIES, 65 (2004).

Hansel T. Phamdl, *Developing Countries and the WTO: The Need for More Mediation in the DSU,* 9 HARVARD NEGOTIATION LAW REVIEW 331 (2004)

David A. Gantz, Failed Efforts to Initiate the Millennium Round in Seattle: Lessons for Future Global Trade Negotiations, 17 ARIZONA JOURNAL OF INTERNATIONAL & COMPARATIVE LAW 349, 351 (2000)

Jeffrey L. Dunoff, The WTO in Transition: Of Constituents, Competence and Coherence, 33 GEOGE WASHINGTON INTERNATIONAL LAW REVIEW, 979, 981 (2001)

Kara M. Bombach, Can South Africa Fight AIDS? Reconciling the South African Medicines and Related Substances Act with the TRIPS Agreement, BOSTON UNIVERSITY INTERNATIONAL LAW JOURNAL 273, 288 (2001)

James Thuo Gathii, Constructing Intellectual Property Rights and Competition Policy Consistently with Facilitating Access to Affordable AIDS Drugs to Low-End Consumers, 53 FLORIDA LAW REVIEW 761 (2001)

Naomi A. Bass, Implications of the TRIPS Agreement for Developing Countries: Pharmaceutical Patent Laws in Brazil and South Africa in the 21st Century, 34 GEORGE WASHINGTON INTERNATIONAL LAW REVIEW, 191, 210 (2002)

Sussan K. Sell, TRIPS and the Access to Medicines Campaign, 20 WISCONSIN INTERNATIONAL LAW JOURNAL, 481, 500-02 (2002)

Bess-Carolina Dolmo, Examining Global Access to Essential Pharmaceuticals in the Face of Patent Protection Rights: The South African Example, 7 BUFFALO HUMAN RIGHTS LAW REVIEW 137,151 (2001)

Case law

Ponce v. Roman Catholic Apostolic Church, 210 US 296, 318 (1907)

Interights on behalf of Sofia Yakubu Husaini, et al v. Nigeria, African Commission on Human Rights, and Peoples' Rights Commission, No. 269/2003 (2005)

Marsh, Nebraska State Treasurer, et al v. Chambers, 463 U.S. 783 (1983)

Simpson v. Chesterfield County Board of Supervisors, 404 F.3d 276 (4th Cir. 2005)

United States – Standards for Reformulated and Conventional Gasoline, WT/DS2/AB/R

United States – Measure Affecting Imports of Woven Wool Shirts and Blouses from India WTDS33/R (1997)

United States – Shrimp-Turtle and United States-Import Prohibition of Certain Shrimp and Shrim Products, Recourse to Article XX:5 by Malaysia (2001)
Indonesia – Certain Measures Affecting the Automobile Industry, WT/DS54/R, WT/DS55/R, WT/DS59/R, WT/DS64/R
Appellate Body Report on Turkey – Textiles (WT/DS58)
Bombardia Aerospace Case, WT/DS70/R April 14, 1999, *WT/DS222/R,* January 28, 2002
Mailboxes and the 1998 India Patent Protection Case

Official Reports and Documents

United Nations Universal Declaration of Human Rights (UDHR) (1948)
International Convention on Economic, Social, and Cultural Rights (ICESCR) (1966)
United Nations, SELECTED LEGAL OPINIONS OF THE SECRETARIAT OF THE UNITED NATIONS AND RELATED INTER-GOVERNMENTAL ORGANIZATIONS, *UN.Doc.ST/LEG/8* (1962)
UN-GENERAL ASSEMBLY RESOLUTION 2102(XX), December 20, 1965
UN-GENERAL ASSEMBLY RESOLUTION 2205(XXI), December 17, 1966
United States Department of State, COMMERCIAL POLICY SERIES No. 71 (Publication No. 1660) (1994)
United Nations Juridical Year Book 164, 167, *U.N. Doc.ST/LEG/SER.C/13* (1975)
GATT *Final Act,* Geneva, 55 U.N.T.S. 194 (1947)
Gaetano Arangio-Ruiz, *The Nature of the International Personality of the Holy See,* REVUE BELGE DE DROIT INTERNATIONAL, (1996)
United Nations Proclamation on the International Year of Families (1994)
The Singapore Commonwealth Declaration (1971)
United Nations, TREATY SERIES, UNITED NATIONS PUBLICATIONS (1964)

RESTATEMENT (THIRD) OF THE FOREIGN RELATIONS LAW OF THE UNITED STATES [sections] 201 (1986)
MONTEVIDEO CONVENTION ON THE RIGHT AND DUTIES OF STATES (1933)
UNDERSTANDING THE WORLD TRADE ORGANIZATION available at http://www.wto.org
United Nations Treaty Series Online Collection (UNTS), available at http://treaties.un.org/Pages/UNTSOnline.aspx?id=1
United States Tariff Act, *9 USC Chapter 4 – TARIFF ACT OF 1930*
UN General Assembly, 58th Session, 92nd Plenary Meeting, *A/58/pv.92,* July 16, 2004
WTO Document, Guidelines *WT/L/161* Annex 2, paragraphs 10 & 11
WTO Ministerial Conference and THE General Council *WT/L/221* July 2, 1997
WTO General Council Minutes of Meeting July 16, 1997, *WT/GC/M/21* August 6, 1997
WTO Documents *WT/L/283, WT/GCM/32, WT/ACC/LBN/1, WT/GC/M/40 and WT/GC/M/21*
World Commission on the Social Dimension of Globalization, A Fair Globalization: Creating Opportunities for All (2004)
WTO Committee on Trade and Development *WT/COMTD/W/35 & WT/COMTD/W/66*
The Codex Alimenatrius Commission, *Codex Alimentarius* (International Food Standard) (1963) http://www.codexalimentarius.org/
WIPO, Matters Concerning Intellectual Property and Genetic Resourcs, Traditional Knowledge and Folklore, *WIPO/GRTKF/IC/1/3* (2001)